Comparative Criminal Justice Systems

Comparative Criminal Justice Systems

FIFTH EDITION

HARRY R. DAMMER
University of Scranton

JAY S. ALBANESE
Virginia Commonwealth University

WADSWORTH
CENGAGE Learning

Australia • Brazil • Japan • Korea • Mexico • Singapore • Spain • United Kingdom • United States

***Comparative Criminal Justice Systems,* Fifth Edition**

Harry R. Dammer and Jay S. Albanese

Editor-in-Chief: Linda Ganster

Executive Editor: Carolyn Henderson-Meier

Assistant Editorial: Casey Lozier

Associate Media Editor: Andy Yap

Executive Brand Manager: Melissa Larmon

Senior Market Development Manager: Michelle Williams

Manufacturing Planner: Judy Inouye

Rights Acquisitions Specialist: Thomas McDonough

Design, Production Services, and Composition: PreMediaGlobal

Text Researcher: Q2A/Bill Smith

Cover Image: ICC Building and Mandela's Cell/ © Harry R. Dammer, Ph.D.

Library of Congress Control Number: 2012952065

ISBN-13: 978-1-285-06786-5
ISBN-10: 1-285-06786-X

Wadsworth
20 Davis Drive
Belmont, CA 94002-3098
USA

Cengage Learning is a leading provider of customized learning solutions with office locations around the globe, including Singapore, the United Kingdom, Australia, Mexico, Brazil, and Japan. Locate your local office at **www.cengage.com/global.**

Cengage Learning products are represented in Canada by Nelson Education, Ltd.

To learn more about Wadsworth, visit **www.cengage.com/Wadsworth.**

Purchase any of our products at your local college store or at our preferred online store **www.cengagebrain.com.**

Printed in the United States of America
1 2 3 4 5 6 7 16 15 14 13 12

This edition of the book is dedicated to a very special person who for decades, through her selfless dedication to students and researchers in criminal justice, has made our lives more interesting and far more pleasant—thank you, Phyllis Schultze of the Don M. Gottfredson Library at Rutgers University School of Criminal Justice.

Harry and Jay

Brief Contents

Brief Contents

Contents

Comparative Criminal Justice at the Movies

Critical Thinking Exercises

Preface

Writing a textbook on comparative criminal justice is a daunting task. The world is a diverse and complex setting for both crime and justice in their many forms. The serial treatment of criminal justice systems gives little basis for comparison, while criminal justice process-oriented comparisons can prove too abstract for the student without international legal experience. Therefore, an effort is made here to effect a compromise between these approaches: the book is organized according to criminal justice process with a strong emphasis on comparisons among countries, but the focus is centered on six model countries, each exemplifying a distinct family of law or justice system arrangement that affects the criminal process. The use of the model countries brings the material to a concrete, national level. The model countries chosen are England, exemplifying a Common Law system; France, exemplifying a unitary Civil Law system; Germany, exemplifying a federal Civil Law system; the People's Republic of China, exemplifying a Socialist Law system; Saudi Arabia, exemplifying a Sacred Law system; and finally Japan, exemplifying a hybrid system made up of elements of various others but distinctive in its own right. The United States is used as a comparison throughout.

While the choices made in the formulation and selection of comparative justice material are sometimes difficult, this book and its contents are essential topics for any serious student of criminal justice. The call for the study of international crime data, the adjudication of war criminals, and the attempt to coordinate law enforcement globally are just three stark examples of the need for further understanding of transnational crime and justice issues. With rapid changes in global communication, travel, and commerce, the problems of international and comparative criminal justice are sure to increase in scope and intensity throughout the twenty-first century.

Ideally, the student in a course on comparative criminal justice has taken at least an introductory criminal justice course and perhaps an introductory government course. However, for those who have not, the book tries to introduce all criminal justice topics in clear and simple language. This book was written and updated to meet the needs of students in upper-level courses in their final years of undergraduate studies but has also been used for graduate students. The style of writing is meant to be accessible to all levels of students, and the book contains a large number of examples, cases, and other pedagogical materials that bring the subject to life for all students.

After a general introduction that includes a discussion of the importance of comparative study and an exposition of comparative crime data, the book introduces not only each family of law in some detail but also each model country and its unique characteristics. This sets the stage for comparisons of the three main aspects of the criminal justice system: police, courts, and corrections among these countries. The approach incorporates historical, political, economic, and social factors that are central to understanding different countries and their legal systems.

In addition to its comparisons of countries in terms of their crime and justice situations, the book also addresses pressing issues of criminal justice that provide a challenge to policy makers and justice officials worldwide. These issues are supranational courts, terrorism, international organized crime and human trafficking, and the treatment of juveniles.

NEW UPDATES TO THIS EDITION

The fifth edition of this book includes many changes, revisions, and updates, including:

- New chapter opening case study vignettes (every chapter).
- New chapter learning objectives (every chapter).
- Movie boxes in every chapter ("Comparative Criminal Justice at the Movies") summarizing recent movies dealing with comparative criminal justice issues and asking students to apply material from the text.
- A critical thinking exercise box in every chapter, based on news of crime and criminal justice in comparative context and asking students to apply material from the text.
- A separate chapter (the only book of its kind to include one) on international crime trends, including new data on crime victimization in 30 countries and 33 world cities, and homicides in 54 countries.
- The addition and updating of numerous tables that summarize information contained in the text.
- Separate sections about the correlates of crime, policing, hybrid courts, and the incarceration of supranational criminals.

Detailed Changes

Chapter 1

- Addition of learning objectives at beginning of chapter
- New chapter vignette used at opening of chapter
- Explanation of differences between international and transnational crimes
- New table, text, and figure specifying and defining major categories of transnational crimes and their context
- Critical thinking explained and used as basis for critical thinking exercise in chapter

Chapter 2

- New chapter opening on human trafficking
- Both human trafficking and cybercrime described (with fuller detail in Chapter 11)
- Comparative data on crime victimization in 30 countries and 33 world cities, as well as statistics on homicides in 54 countries
- Causes and correlates of crime around the world receive expanded treatment
- New chapter learning objectives

Chapter 3

- New chapter opening vignette on the trial involving international crimes
- New section on shared notions of justice around the world
- New table on the Nine Core International Human Rights Instruments
- Updated tables summarizing the four families of law
- New learning objectives

Chapter 4

- New demographic variables added to Table 4.1 for each model country.
- Updated crime data in model countries
- Updated and new pedagogical elements (learning objectives)
- New chapter opening vignette
- Revised discussion of crime trends and issues in each model country

Chapter 5

- New chapter opening scenario and learning objectives
- Entirely new section about police corruption including a new table describing forms of police corruption
- Updates of "issues of concern" section for police in model countries, including issue of policing the 2012 Summer Olympics
- New agencies added to international law enforcement section
- Updated section on police and diversity
- Updated section on police and privatization

Chapter 6

- New pedagogical learning objectives and opening vignette
- New table on legal accessibility in model and selected countries
- Modified table with comparison of criminal procedure rules in the International Criminal Court, the International Criminal Tribunal for the Former Yugoslavia (ICTY), and the Special Tribunal for Lebanon

- Updates in procedural section of each legal tradition, including new embedded direct web links to criminal procedure laws in each of our model countries
- Table comparing criminal procedure in model countries
- Table comparing constitutional review in model countries

Chapter 7

- Updates on current number and changes in courts in all model countries
- New material on the effectiveness and public opinion surrounding the saiban-in mixed courts in Japan
- New information about the impact of the Constitutional Reform Act in England
- Updates on reforms in constitutional council in France
- Updates on judicial mediation in China
- Full revision of supranational courts section
- Updated numbers of court cases in each supranational court
- New box listing all supranational courts and dates of establishment
- Update of U.S. policy toward Rome Statute and International Criminal Court
- Comparison of tribunals of Nuremburg and Tokyo, the International Criminal Tribunal for the Former Yugoslavia (ICTY), and the International Criminal Tribunal for Rwanda (ICTR)
- Additional section explaining the different internationalized courts present in the world today
- New section on the challenges facing supranational courts
- New courtroom diagram of Nuremburg Trial
- New opening vignettes and new learning objectives

Chapter 8

- New chapter opening vignettes and pedagogical learning objectives
- Fully updated sections on international imprisonment and death penalty
- New information about use and future of death penalty in China
- New information about the incarceration of woman and minorities around the world
- Updated examples of sentences given around the world
- Updated data on world imprisonment rates and use of the death penalty
- Tables about purposes of criminal sanctions in model countries

Chapter 9

- New pedagogical learning objectives and opening vignette
- Updated all international prison data

- Updated information and statistics on and model country use of incarceration
- New international examples of prison crowding, prison conditions, and prisoner rights
- Updated section on incarceration of supranational criminals

Chapter 10

- New pedagogical learning objectives
- New chapter opening vignette about terrorism based on the killing of Osama bin Laden in 2011
- Entirely new information about the evolving form of "new terrorism"
- Updated information about the prevalence of domestic and international terrorism
- Examples of terrorist acts throughout chapter and figure on international terrorist acts

Chapter 11

- New chapter opening case study vignette and learning objectives
- New section of human trafficking
- New section on cybercrime
- Four new tables on human trafficking and cybercrime issues
- Updated table on measuring corruption

Chapter 12

- New chapter opening case study vignette and learning objectives
- Two updated tables on juvenile arrests and imprisonment
- Updated narrative on juvenile justice around the world
- Summary of the four major United Nations instruments to develop international standards relating to juvenile delinquency
- New critical thinking exercise on *Life without Parole for Juvenile Offenders*

ANCILLARIES

A number of supplements are provided by Cengage Learning to help instructors use *Comparative Criminal Justice Systems* in their courses. Supplements are available to qualified adopters. Please consult your local sales representative for details.

- **Instructor's Manual with Test Bank.** The manual includes learning objectives, key terms, a detailed chapter outline, a chapter summary, discussion topics, student activities, media tools, and a newly expanded test bank.

The learning objectives are correlated with the discussion topics, student activities, and media tools. Each chapter's test bank contains questions in multiple-choice, true-false, completion, and essay formats as well as new scenario-based questions with a full answer key. The test bank is coded to the learning objectives that appear in the main text and includes the page numbers in the main text where the answers can be found. The manual is available for download on the password-protected website and can also be obtained by e-mailing your local Cengage Learning representative.

- **PowerPoint Slides.** These handy Microsoft PowerPoint slides, which outline the chapters of the main text in a classroom-ready presentation, will help you in making your lectures engaging and in reaching your visually oriented students. The presentations are available for download on the password-protected website and can also be obtained by e-mailing your local Cengage Learning representative.

ACKNOWLEDGMENTS

The writing of the fifth edition was greatly assisted by numerous people who merit special recognition. I would like to thank my wife, Eileen Sulzbach-Dammer, for her patience through another book revision process. And a special thanks to my conscientious and competent student assistants, Adrianna Hughes and Cheryl O'Donnell. (HD)

Thanks to Leslie King for her understanding of the many complex issues expressed in this book, and to Thomas and Kelsey for recognizing the importance of both movies and critical thinking in reaching today's student audience. My students at Virginia Commonwealth University provided a sounding board for a number of the ideas and the presentation of information in this book. (JA)

Acknowledgment is also due to our editor at Wadsworth-Cengage, Carolyn Henderson Meier, for her patience with the authors during the writing process. Also, Kailash Rawat was very helpful and efficient during the editing and production process. Finally, the valuable contributions of the external reviewers who provided advice for the fifth edition are greatly appreciated.

Finally, the following reviewers provided valuable insight and criticism. We would like to thank:

Martha Earwood, University of Alabama at Birmingham

Arthur Hayden, Kentucky State University

Mikaila Arthur, Rhode Island College

John O'Neill, Stevenson University

Melanie-Angela Neuilly, Washington State University

Richard Pacelle, Georgia Southern University

Larry Salinger, Arkansas State University

James Jengeleski, Argosy University

Mary G. Wilson, Kent State University Trumbull

Allan Barnes, University of Alaska Anchorage
Connie Singh, Simon Fraser University
Enrique Arias, John Jay College
James Luongo, St. John's University
Caryl Segal, University of TX Arlington
Carol Trent, University of South Florida
Charles Deisler, University of Central Florida
Henry Beattie, SUNY Orange
Karin Orr, Merrimack college
Hyesun Kim, Worcester State University

1  Introduction

Key Terms and Concepts

comparative criminal justice
comparative criminology
criminal justice system
international crimes
transnational crimes
critical thinking
ethnocentrism
globalization
independent state

Chapter 1 Learning Objectives

Distinguish international criminal justice from comparative criminal justice.

Describe the value of comparing systems and issues of criminal justice.

Discuss globalization and its effects on crime and criminal justice.

Explore how countries have adopted methods from others to change how they practice criminal justice.

Describe the purpose of the historical-political approach.

As both crime and justice become more global in scope, comparative criminal justice has become a central part of a complete understanding of the crime and justice situation today. Consider the case of Harout Sarafian and David Fagerness in Hollywood, California. Police authorities in the United States discovered an online "Lost Boy" bulletin board after being provided with information from Eurojust, the judicial cooperation arm of the European Union. Eurojust had obtained the information from Italian and Norwegian authorities, who had learned that a man in Hollywood was communicating online with someone in Italy about child pornography and how to engage in child sex tourism in Romania. Acting on this information, the FBI executed search warrants that led to the discovery of the Lost Boy network, which had 25 members in the United States, Belgium, Brazil, Canada, France, Germany, New Zealand, and the United Kingdom.

The creation and distribution of child pornography is a crime in most countries, but the nature of a crime like this makes an effective response extremely complicated. How should differences among national laws be handled? What is the protocol for police investigation and the sharing of information? In what nation(s) should the suspects be adjudicated? What is an appropriate punishment for participation in this type of criminal network? These are all important questions, so the significance of international agreements, effective communication among criminal justice agencies around the world, and a coordinated response is apparent. All these questions are the subject matter of comparative criminal justice.

This book answers these questions and describes the different criminal justice systems of countries outside the United States. It explores basic philosophies of law and justice; the organization of law enforcement; adjudication alternatives; methods of rehabilitation and punishment of convicted offenders; and the particular issues of transnational organized crime, juvenile justice, and terrorism. International and comparative processes will be compared to those in the United States, offering the reader context in evaluating different approaches to crime, law, and justice around the world.

DEFINING TERMS

It is important to be clear about the central terminology of comparative criminal justice. **Comparative criminal justice** investigates and evaluates a national system of justice in terms of other countries, cultures, or institutions. The key root word is *compare*, and comparative criminal justice offers a systematic method to examine the strengths and weaknesses of different approaches to crime, law, and justice around the world.

The term **comparative criminology** is the study of the causes and correlates of crime in two or more cultures. In comparative criminology, we try to explain why crime occurs in different forms and at different levels in one country versus another (Winslow and Zhang, 2008). Although a major focus of this book is on the criminal justice systems and their operations across countries, we will discuss reasons that some crime rates are high or low in different countries in Chapters 2, 10, 11, and 12.

Criminal justice system is the term used to explain and understand all of the agencies whose goal is to control crime. It consists of police, courts, and corrections agencies, which act to enforce the law, adjudicate suspects, and deal with convicted offenders.

International crimes have been described as "crimes against the peace and security of mankind" (Adler, Mueller, and Laufer, 2009). International crimes are based on international agreements between countries or on legal precedents developed through history, and include offenses such as such as genocide, torture, and enslavement of populations.

These are among the acts identified by consensus among nations as being illegal everywhere. The list of international crimes has grown over the years as nations have come to share common concern about various behaviors, so some national and transnational crimes have become international crimes as world nations reach consensus on unacceptable forms of conduct. For example, the former president of Liberia, Charles Taylor, was found guilty of aiding and abetting crimes including murder, rape, sexual slavery, and mutilations committed by rebel forces against the civilian population during Sierra Leone's civil war. The 11-year conflict killed more than 50,000 people (McDougall, 2012). Taylor's trial was held at the International Criminal Court in the Netherlands, which was founded in 2002 to adjudicate international crimes. The International Criminal Court (discussed in Chapter 7) was developed to ensure that even powerful national leaders who abuse their power can be held to account for the commission of international crimes.

Transnational crimes are offenses whose inception, acts, and impact involve more than one country. These crimes usually involve the provision of illicit goods or illicit services, or the infiltration of business or government. Table 1.1 summarizes the most common transnational crimes and brief definitions. All of the offenses in Table 1.1 are transnational crimes when they occur across national borders, according to the definition above.

Most contemporary examples of transnational crime can be placed in one of the categories in Table 1.1. For example, sea piracy is a modern form of racketeering and extortion, theft of cultural objects is a form of trafficking in stolen property, and theft of intellectual property such as DVDs and software codes is usually a combination of counterfeiting and fraud. Transnational crimes are occurring with increasing frequency as opportunities expand for the global movement of people, products, technology, and communications. For example, authorities in Mexico have seized nearly 100,000 guns used in criminal enterprises from

TABLE 1.1 A Typology of Transnational Crimes

Transnational Crime	Type of Conduct	Brief Definition
Drug trafficking	Provision of illicit goods	The manufacture or distribution of controlled substances
Trafficking in stolen property	Provision of illicit goods	The sale, distribution, or large-scale possession of property obtained in violation of the law
Counterfeiting	Provision of illicit goods	Forged or faked documents or products intended to deceive the purchaser
Human trafficking	Provision of illicit services	Recruitment, transportation, or harboring of persons for the purpose of exploitation, such as prostitution and forced labor
Cybercrime and fraud	Provision of illicit services	Obtaining property through deception of the owner, often accomplished using computers and the Internet
Commercialized vices (sex and gambling)	Provision of illicit services	Systematic provision of sexual or gambling services in violation of applicable laws
Extortion and racketeering	Infiltration of business or government	Obtaining the property of another or unfair competitive advantage because of threats of future physical injury, property damage, or exposure to criminal charges, as part of an ongoing criminal enterprise
Money laundering	Infiltration of business or government	Disguising funds obtained from illegal activity, using banks or businesses, to make it appear as lawful income
Corruption	Infiltration of business or government	The misuse of power or position for unlawful gain or advantage

2007 to 2011. After they provided information about these guns to the U.S. Bureau of Alcohol, Tobacco, Firearms, and Explosives (ATF), it was determined that 68 percent of these guns originated in the United States and were smuggled or otherwise illegally brought into Mexico and used primarily in drug trafficking enterprises (Yost, 2012). In another case, charges were brought against a group that imported 37,000 bottles of counterfeit perfume into the United States from China, packaging it and selling it falsely as well-known brands (U.S. Department of Justice, 2011). In both these cases, the cross-national nature of the criminal schemes is apparent, and, as Table 1.1 indicates, these are both examples of the transnational provision of illicit goods.

There may be some overlap between transnational and international crimes, because a few crimes can sometimes be placed in both categories (such as international drug trafficking), but they are not the same. Transnational crimes always involve at least two countries, whereas some international crimes can occur within the boundaries of only one country, as with genocide or apartheid. The term *transnational crime* will be used consistently throughout this book to describe the illegal activities that occur across international boundaries.

THE ORIGINS AND GROWTH OF COMPARATIVE CRIMINAL JUSTICE

The origins of the comparative method in areas other than criminal justice can be traced back to ancient times. However, comparative criminal justice is a relatively new field of inquiry that applies the comparative methodologies used in law and political science to the social sciences of sociology, criminology, and criminal justice. Its origins can be traced back to the 1700s, the "Age of Enlightenment," and to a man who is considered by some to be the first criminologist—Cesare Beccaria (1738–1794). In 1764, Beccaria's essay on crime and punishment called for changes in Western European criminal justice, including the abolition of the death penalty, torture, and secret trials (Sherman, 2003; Hagan, 2007). Soon thereafter, others such as Jeremy Bentham (1748–1832), Adolph Quetelet (1796–1874), Alexis de Tocqueville (1805–1859), and Emile Durkheim (1858–1917) conducted cross-national studies of crime.

During the mid-1800s, criminal justice professionals began the search to learn more about cross-national crime. The General Statistical Congress was held in Brussels in 1853, the International Congress on the Prevention and Repression of Crime was held in London in 1872, and the First International Police Congress was held in Monaco in 1914. These meetings were the first large-scale attempts to collect data on international crime and to deal with issues related to crime and justice on an international scale. Because of the larger world problems in the first half of the twentieth century, including two world wars, there was little interest in comparative crime, and justice research was limited to individual countries looking inward to their specific crime problems. That changed in the late 1960s, when the United Nations developed the first Crime Prevention and Criminal Justice Branch under the direction of Gerhard O. W. Mueller.

Since that time there has been a steady and renewed interest in international crime and justice issues. Many criminologists, governmental agencies, and international organizations have come to see the value in the study and dissemination of information on issues of international and comparative criminal justice. Various forms of statistical data have been compiled by the International Criminal Police Organization (Interpol) and the World Health Organization (WHO), and through the International Crime Victim Surveys (ICVS). The United Nations has created a large group of criminal justice information providers, including the Dag Hammarskjold Library in New York City and the website of the United Nations Office on Drugs and Crime (UNODC).

The National Institute of Justice (NIJ) is the research, development, and evaluation agency of the U.S. Department of Justice. Recognizing the need to better identify and describe crime and support those who fight crime, NIJ decided to develop an International Center in 1998. The International Center's mission is to stimulate and facilitate research and evaluation on transnational crime and justice issues and to disseminate the knowledge gained throughout the national and international criminal justice communities. Since its inception, the International Center has worked with the United Nations and its various institutes to mount a variety of studies on topics like transnational organized crime, corruption, and human trafficking (Finckenauer, 2000; Albanese, 2007).

In recent years, academics have had considerable interest in comparative crime and justice. In the United States, prominent American scholars have called for "globalizing" criminal justice curricula (Adler, 1996) and for "internationalizing" criminology and criminal justice study (Friday, 1996). Comparative criminal justice courses in colleges and universities have flourished in recent years (Peak, 1991; Cordner et al., 2000; Dammer and Reichel, 2007). The John Jay College of Criminal Justice in New York City developed what is the first full-fledged bachelor's degree in international criminal justice (Natarajan, 2002). Various forms of written and electronic material on the subject have now been published, with thousands more cross-national studies as compared to a mere decade ago (Adler, 1995; Howard et al., 2000; Natarajan, 2012).

WHY COMPARE SYSTEMS OF AND ISSUES IN CRIMINAL JUSTICE?

There are many reasons to study and compare issues in and systems of criminal justice. From a broader perspective, everything we perceive is based on comparison. As political scientist Karl Deutsch put it:

> We call an event unique if it is similar in very few aspects or dimensions, and different in very, very many from others. Without attempting comparison, how could we know that something was unique? If something were truly unique in any aspect, how could we discuss it? We should have no words for it. We could only talk about it in negatives, calling it ineffable, unmeasurable and so on, and then we would be very close to magic or religion and well away from science. (1996, p. 31)

Therefore, comparisons lie at the foundation of all our thinking, because it is only through comparison that we can assess the relative utility of laws, policies, programs, and alternative actions of all types.

Comparison is also a key element in critical thinking. **Critical thinking** is purposeful mental activity which permits us to examine the relative strength of evidence, arguments, and alternative courses of conduct. In many ways, the ability to think critically helps us to solve daily problems and even make important life choices. There are many ways to engage in critical thinking. One way is to follow a simple three-step process. First, we determine what we know about an issue and ask ourselves why we think that way. For example, maybe we feel that the death penalty is a legitimate way to punish offenders because we believe that it is less costly than life imprisonment. Second, we seek out the opposite side of the story. In the case of the death penalty, we may learn about the volume of research indicating the actual cost of life imprisonment compared to the death penalty. Finally, we objectively weigh the evidence, compare the diverging opinions, and then make a decision based on the available evidence.

For the purposes of this book, there are three practical reasons we should compare systems of and issues in criminal justice: (1) to benefit from the experience of others, (2) to broaden our understanding of different cultures and approaches to problems, and (3) to help us deal with the many transnational crime problems that plague our world today.

To Benefit from the Experience of Others

"The reason for comparing is to learn from the experience of others and, conversely, that he who knows only one country knows none." This profound statement by George Sartori was made to illustrate the importance of international comparative study in the field of political science (1996, p. 20). But his remarks are equally relevant to criminal justice study. Comparative work in criminal justice is an excellent vehicle for learning more about how others practice criminal justice. When we can learn about the criminal justice processes of other countries, we are then able to develop hypotheses that will help us begin to solve our own problems related to crime and justice (Burnham, 1998; Zimring, 2006).

In all areas of the criminal justice system—police, courts, and corrections—there are many examples of how nations have adopted others' methods of criminal justice implementation. For example, people wonder why Japan has a much lower crime rate than the United States or, indeed, most other Western nations. The Japanese themselves give some of the credit for their low crime rates to their police methods—most notably, community policing. Many countries have become interested in adopting Japanese police practices, including the use of kobans (small local police stations). Many U.S. cities, including Atlantic City, Detroit, and Houston, have modified the Japanese methods and use them in their local police operations.

Many countries have also adopted rules of criminal procedure that were pioneered by others. In fact, some criminal procedure rules, such as the right to counsel at an early stage of the criminal process, are becoming nearly universal in systems of justice around the world. And many countries have even adopted entire legal codes from the codes of others. The Napoleonic Code of civil law, developed in France in the early nineteenth century, was one such export, as was the French penal code, also developed under Napoleon. Another export in the late nineteenth century was the German Civil Code. These codes have had an enormous influence on the development of legal systems and criminal justice systems throughout the world (Merryman, 1985).

Corrections strategies also tend to spill over borders. For example, the idea of day fines, which was first developed in Scandinavian countries, has been adopted by Germany and, more recently, by Great Britain and the United States. And New Zealand, Belgium, Australia, Canada, and the United States all have implemented different kinds of restorative justice programs. Restorative justice is an idea that was cultivated by many victims'-rights advocates in the United States, but it has its roots in the justice practices of many indigenous cultures.

There are many other examples of countries borrowing or adapting criminal justice practices from the United States. In the nineteenth century, many European countries, especially France, copied American methods of incarceration—specifically, the Auburn system and the Pennsylvania system. More recently, former communist countries in Eastern Europe have called upon the FBI to help train them in the fight against corruption and organized crime (King and Ray, 2000). Many countries have also improved their ability to collect and disseminate crime statistics using the U.S. models of the Uniform Crime Reports (UCR) and National Crime Victimization Surveys (NCVS).

However, specific practices should be adopted only after serious thought and evaluation. Criminal justice system reformers are aware that it is naive to try to import institutions that are bound to local cultural values without modifying them to conform to the new context. For example, it would be shortsighted for U.S. policymakers to think that we could easily implement a strict corporal punishment system like that found in Islamic societies, given the significant differences in the diversity of the population and the process by which laws are made.

To Broaden Our Understanding of the World

A second reason for studying the administration of justice in other countries is to broaden our understanding of other countries and cultures. If we fail to broaden our understanding of other countries we are more likely to fall prey to the problem of **ethnocentrism**—the belief that one's own country or culture does things "right" and all other practices are "wrong" or "foreign." Ethnocentrism is a common phenomenon, as people often think their country, culture, or religion is better than all others. In terms of crime and criminal justice, ethnocentrism is a problem because it can lead to crime within and across borders as well as discrimination, oppression, or violent ethnic-based conflicts.

Americans are frequently astonished to hear about practices related to crime and punishment in other systems. Why does one country, Saudi Arabia, cut off a hand or a foot or stone a person to death as punishment for certain criminal acts? Why is lengthy pretrial detention without bail condoned in some countries, such as France, as a way to ensure greater justice? Why does Japan have so few lawyers compared to most countries, especially the United States? The fact is that a nation's way of administering justice often reflects deep-seated cultural, religious, economic, political, and historical realities. Learning about the reasons for these different practices can give us insight into the values, traditions, and cultures of other systems. Such broadening of perspective helps us see our own system in more objective terms.

To Deal More Effectively with Transnational Crime Problems

A third good reason to study criminal justice from a comparative perspective is the increasing need to address transnational and international crime problems. These problems have become imperative because the multicultural world we now live in has entered the stage of globalization. **Globalization** is the term used to describe how the world has become interdependent in terms of the events and actions of people and governments around the world. In short, globalization embodies the idea that the world is "getting smaller." Globalization has occurred as a result of a number of cultural and technological changes in the twentieth century (Adler & Mueller, 1996; Albanese, 2011).

Tremendous innovations in communications, ease of worldwide travel, and growth in technology—especially the Internet—have served to fuel the move to globalization. Numerous worldwide events, such as the end of the Cold War and the subsequent demise of the former Soviet Union, the changing of China to a market economy, and the creation of free-trade blocs such as the European Union and the North American Free Trade Agreement (NAFTA), have also fueled the globalization process. One of the results of globalization, however, is the rise in international and transnational crime.

A recent trend in criminal justice is to look at the impact of globalization on crime (Bossard, 2003; Nelken, 2010). This approach supports the view that crime transcends national boundaries; for example, ease of travel by air has enabled criminals to do their work in other countries or easily escape to a safe haven. As air and sea trade have increased, so has the smuggling of illegal goods such as drugs and guns. Strong evidence suggests that some individuals have even engaged in the illegal smuggling of human organs to wealthy persons in other countries who need medical assistance. In countries that are in economic or political turmoil, many persons attempt to flee, causing problems such as international criminal activity, refugee flows, the spread of contagious disease, and nuclear weapons and drug trafficking (Cusimano, 2000, p. 4; Sherman and Margolin, 2011; Varese, 2012).

Figure 1.1 illustrates how transnational crime is strongly connected to larger social, economic, and government influences. The figure illustrates how transnational crime is a form of illicit enterprise, involving a network of individuals who look to make a profit from an available opportunity (involving illicit goods, illicit services, or the infiltration of business or government). Regardless of the criminal opportunity chosen, the network of individuals needs a supply to exploit (e.g., drugs, stolen property, desperate migrants), as well as a steady demand of consumers to purchase the illicit good or service. This profitable activity is pressured further by government agencies (e.g., police and business regulators) and competitors (e.g., other organized crime networks). In order to adapt to this pressure, and thereby survive and continue to make a profit, illicit methods are used to deal with these pressures by infiltrating legitimate or government agencies, using extortion, corruption, and money laundering. The result is that the

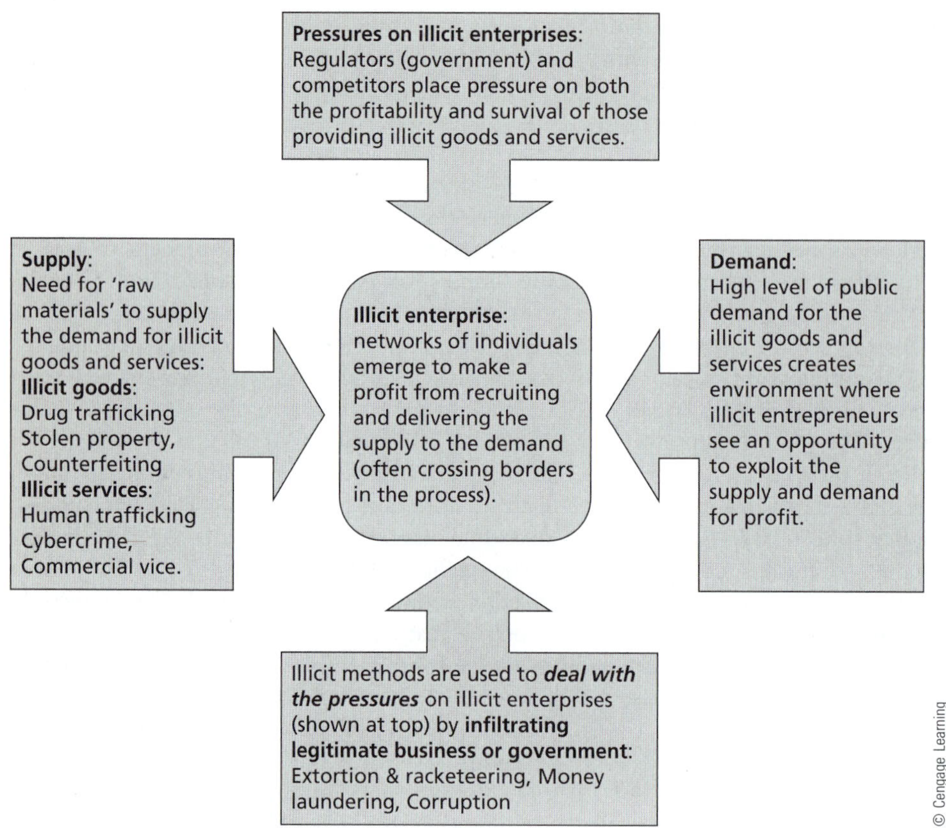

FIGURE 1.1 The Organization of Transnational Crimes

perpetrators of transnational crimes must be both entrepreneurial and organized, and they must be responsive to the pressures of supply, demand, regulators, and competitors in order to survive and make a profit (Albanese, 2011).

Technological growth also has contributed directly to the vast increase in the types and volume of transnational crime, with computers and telecommunications playing a key role. "The very networks that legitimate businesses use to move goods so cheaply are the same networks that criminals use to move illicit goods so easily" (Winer, 1997, p. 41; Naim, 2006). So technology, like all advances, can be used for good or bad.

Sensitivity to the values of and problems faced by other countries also helps in resolving conflicts or overcoming barriers to cooperation across borders. And if the recent past has taught us anything, the key to solving the problems of transnational crime and criminal justice is global cooperation. We now know that in order to effectively deal with terrorist groups like al-Qaida, we must work internationally to eliminate their worldwide financial and communication networks. To address drug trafficking into the southern regions of the United States, we must work effectively with Mexican law enforcement agencies, a task that is made more difficult by the corruption at various levels of government and at the border (Casey, 2010).

If we wish to serve justice well, whether it be for crimes committed within our borders or in another region of the world, international cooperation is an essential ingredient. Without international cooperation we cannot find, extradite, or serve justice on those who violate laws and cause pain, suffering, and loss throughout the world.

THE HISTORICAL-POLITICAL APPROACH

The general approach taken in this book can be characterized as historical and political. Individual national arrangements for the administration of justice develop over the course of centuries in response to local needs, efforts by individual leaders, and historical events. For example, if we wish to learn more about the reasons for the current violent crime rate within a country, it is imperative to understand the historical forces behind violent crime development in that country (Neapolitan, 1999). Therefore, this book contains relevant historical information that bears upon the systems of justice we are examining.

The political context of systems of justice is also important because criminal justice agencies are governmental institutions, and they reflect political decisions about law and the administration of justice. In the United States, for example, it would be difficult to understand the development of criminal procedure over the years if we did not have a good understanding of the role of the U.S. Supreme Court in American government. In this book, then, criminal justice arrangements are examined in a historical context with attention to the political developments that affect the process.

Social and economic forces are also extremely important in shaping attitudes and developments related to administration of justice, and they are often tied to historical and political events. Understanding the power of drug trafficking gangs in Latin America, drug use patterns in developed countries, and ongoing conflicts in African countries must account for social and economic forces in those societies. These influences will be noted where relevant in our discussion.

MODEL SYSTEMS

This book will describe and compare six model systems of justice as manifested in six different nations. There are 192 independent states in the world. **Independent state** refers to people who are politically organized into a sovereign state with a definite territory. A *sovereign state* is an internationally recognized unit of political authority. In addition, there are 76 "dependencies" or "areas of special sovereignty" that are associated in some way with an independent state. Examples are Puerto Rico and American Samoa, which are dependencies of the United States, and Bermuda and the Cayman Islands, which are politically tied to the United Kingdom.

To make matters more complex, there are even more "nations" than independent sovereign states. Nations can be any group with a common cultural, ethnic, racial, or religious identity, such as the different Native American groups present in North America (Cusimano, 2000). Each sovereign state or nation has its own unique system of law and justice. The student of comparative criminal justice cannot learn all the facts about all these systems in depth. In fact, such information gathering does not necessarily result in better understanding of the nature of crime and justice in any particular system. But by describing in some detail the particular arrangements in representative or model systems, we can keep the discussion in better focus than would otherwise be possible.

Our model systems are found in the countries of England, France, Germany, China, Japan, and Saudi Arabia. These systems are "models" in the sense that they closely reflect the workings of particular historical families of law within various political frameworks. From this point on, we will use the terms *model countries* and *model systems* interchangeably. Chapter 3 will introduce these systems and their respective families of law. The choice of these six model countries does not imply that they are superior in any way to other countries that may have a similar legal background. Information about a number of other countries would have been equally informative for comparative purposes, but that would result in a much longer book. The six model countries were chosen because of their long history, their stability, and their representation of different legal traditions. Notable in exclusion are developing countries in Africa and the emerging democracies of Eastern Europe, but turbulent political situations in many of these countries, coupled with the dearth of material available in English, makes their inclusion premature. It is our hope that, after reading this book, you will be inspired to study other systems in different countries to apply what you have learned here.

BASIC VALUES IN THE CRIMINAL JUSTICE SYSTEM

The values of any system of justice may be classified as professed values and underlying values. *Professed values* are those that are proclaimed as values by the participants in the system. For example, equal justice under law—the ideal that all individuals, regardless of social status or background, should be treated equally and according to an existing rule—is a professed value of most established systems of justice. In the British and American systems of justice, another professed value is that the government has an obligation to prove an individual's guilt without any requirement that the individual cooperate with the prosecution. This value lies at the heart of the adversary process.

Underlying values are those that are not openly proclaimed but that nevertheless govern actions within the criminal justice system. Efficiency, or expeditious handling of cases, is one such value that may conflict with the value of equal justice under law. Tolerance or intolerance of certain kinds of substance abuse, or prejudice against certain groups of individuals, are examples of underlying values in the criminal justice process. For example, in the Chinese criminal justice system, there are numerous situations in which individuals have certain rights that may protect them from governmental intrusion and abuse—a professed value. According to the underlying values of Chinese society, however, societal needs are more important than individual rights, so individual rights may become secondary during a legal proceeding.

Underlying values are harder to understand and distinguish than professed values, and they require lengthier and more intense study. This presents a problem for students of comparative justice, as such values and the practices they engender are easy to miss in a superficial description of a justice system. Although examples of research in comparative criminal justice that focuses on underlying values are limited (Berman, 1963; Rosch, 1987; Abramson, 2003; Klenowski, 2009), it is important that we appreciate their significance within the context of a justice system. The student of comparative criminal justice must acquire knowledge of professed values while also understanding which underlying values are present. These values will be highlighted in this book as we discuss particular practices in criminal justice systems.

POLITICAL CULTURE VERSUS POLITICIZED JUSTICE

Administration of justice is a governmental function, and therefore reflects the political culture of a nation. When we speak of *culture*, we are talking about deep-seated patterns of behavior and thought that have developed over the course of a society's history. A nation such as Germany, with a political culture that emphasizes legalism, or close adherence to rules, is bound to reflect that concern in its justice system. A nation with a political culture that values community welfare over individual rights, as does Japan's, will reflect those values in its justice system. In the Chinese legal system, independence of the judiciary is not valued to the extent that it is in the United States. This is because the political culture in China emphasizes the needs of the collective (the entire society) and discourages independent action by citizens. In the United States, by contrast, the fear of centralized power that dominated the discussion at the Constitutional Convention in 1787 was reflected in a federal judiciary whose insulation from political influence was supposed to be guaranteed by a life term. Revolutionary or postrevolutionary societies and settled societies will have different approaches to justice.

The fact that administration of justice in a given country reflects that country's political culture does not mean that justice is politicized. *Politicized justice* involves perverting the judicial or criminal justice process to achieve particular political ends, usually to punish enemies of the regime in power or to deter others from joining those enemies. Politicization of justice occurs in all countries on occasion and in some countries on a regular basis. Politicized justice may also involve an attempt to get publicity for causes that are supported by a regime's opponents. The trials of Stalin's opponents in the Soviet Union of the 1930s and of the Chicago Seven in the United States of the 1960s have been cited as examples of politicized justice (Danelski, 1971; Juviler, 1976). More recently, we can look to the treatment of those persons involved in the 1989 Tiananmen Square incident in China, where over 800 persons died from Red Army bullets and countless others were incarcerated without trial in another example of politicized justice. Although politicized justice is hard to demarcate with precision (because it is usually mixed with real violations of conventional law), it is an object of concern throughout the world.

THE PLAN OF THIS BOOK

We will consider each stage of the criminal justice process, from arrest through punishment, as it exists in the model countries chosen. We will also look at crime rates, legal cultures, trial processes, sentencing philosophies, and penal systems. Because of the tremendous variety of criminal justice practices and institutions, it would be confusing (or even impossible) to discuss all of them. Fortunately, major systems can be classified according to historically based families of law. These families of law, also called legal traditions or legal systems, are four in number: Common Law, Civil Law, Socialist Law, and Sacred Law. All modern legal systems are based at least partially on one or another of these historical legal arrangements. We will describe these families of law before we examine criminal justice processes, and we will group countries according to their major orientation toward one or another family. This approach will simplify the task of considering all systems, making clear major similarities and differences around the world.

To further add to the coherence of comparative criminal justice, we will describe in summary form the rules and practices in the six model countries: England, Germany, France, China, Japan, and Saudi Arabia. These countries were chosen because they represent different governmental and legal structures, as well as different cultural traditions that affect the criminal justice process.

England has a unitary centralized government and historically has been the prototype of a Common Law system. France, also with a unitary centralized government, is a model of a Civil Law system and, indeed, was the leading nation in developing the modern Civil Law tradition. Germany, a federal nation with both state and national levels of government, has implemented its own version of Civil Law since the latter part of the nineteenth century. China, the most populous country in the world, is one of the few that still uses the Socialist legal system. And although Socialist systems actually practice a variant of Civil Law, they have enough distinctive characteristics to warrant classification as a separate family. Japan has a truly hybrid system. At various times in its history, Japan has adopted Chinese, French, German, and American law, all of which continue to influence and inform Japanese law and justice. The product, however, is distinctly Japanese and is attuned to the particular culture and social needs of the Japanese people. Finally, Saudi Arabia adheres to the Sacred Law tradition with a justice system based on principles of Islamic law as outlined in the Koran. This fact makes its justice system distinct from those of the other model nations, which have secular legal systems. Because of the familiarity of the American system to most readers, the U.S. system will be referred to frequently in this book to provide points of contrast with other systems.

SUMMARY

This chapter describes many of the reasons for studying comparative crime and justice. It explains how comparing across national borders helps us to learn how other nations approach crime and justice, increases our understanding of other cultures, and provides a basis for dealing with the increasing global crime problem. Although a relatively new field of study, comparative criminal justice has grown considerably in recent years and will continue to do so in a globalized world. We review how professed and underlying values are practiced by various governments and affect crime and criminal justice. The historical-political approach is employed to explain and understand the context for differences in criminal justice around the world. We will augment our understanding of criminal justice practice around the world using six model systems representing different families of law and diverse cultural values and traditions.

Comparative Criminal Justice at the Movies

Movies seek to entertain and inform the audience about a story, incident, or person. Many good movies also hit upon important substantive themes relevant to understanding crime and justice in comparative perspective. Read the movie summary below (and watch the movie if you haven't already) and answer the questions below to make the subject matter connections to comparative criminal justice.

Hotel Rwanda (2005)
Terry George, Director

Genocide occurred in Rwanda during a period of 100 days in 1994, and the world did not take notice. An estimated 1 million members of the Tutsi tribe were massacred by members of the Hutu tribe in a tragic case of ethnic rivalry and hatred. The movie *Hotel Rwanda* tells the story of a hotel manager who saved the lives of 1,200 people during the genocide. The manager, Paul (Don Cheadle), is a Hutu who is married to a Tutsi, bringing the tension to the personal level.

Rwanda had previously been ruled by Belgium, and during that period the Tutsis ruled and the Hutus were oppressed and many were killed. The Hutus are now in control, and the genocide consisted of armed troops searching for and slaughtering Tutsis. The movie shows how the United Nations and the international community ignored the impending massacre and failed to intervene while it was occurring. A colonel (Nick Nolte) represents the UN as a peacekeeper, and he is portrayed in the film reporting the situation to his superiors and being ignored. Paul also informs his corporate headquarters of what is going on, but his hotel location is not a priority for them. These two men then act on their own to save as many lives as possible.

Rather than being a film about a million deaths, it is a film about how two people responded to tragedy when no one else did. It shows how they used finesse and guile to take on genocide and managed to save many lives in the process, even though the situation was an impossible one. *Hotel Rwanda* raises important questions about human strength and weakness in the face of persecution.

Questions

1. Does this movie describe transnational or international crimes?
2. How could such a large massacre happen without outside intervention? Do you think it could happen again?

Critical Thinking Exercise

Critical thinking requires the ability to evaluate viewpoints, facts, and behaviors objectively to assess information and methods of argumentation in order to establish the merit of an action, law, policy, or procedure. Please evaluate this scenario objectively, applying your knowledge of comparative criminal justice to the facts of the case presented, and answer the questions that follow it.

Honor Killing

Three teenage girls in Pakistan, ages 16–18, were kidnapped, taken to a remote area, shot, and then buried while still breathing in a case of "honor killing" at which local officials officiated. Under tribal tradition, marriages are carefully arranged by elders. Marrying without permission is considered an insult to the honor of the tribe. Honor killings are done to serve as a warning to others. One Pakistani legislator said, "These are centuries-old traditions and I will continue to defend them. Only those who indulge in immoral acts should be afraid." According to a report by Human Rights Watch, a nongovernmental organization (NGO), there have been 4,100 honor killings in Pakistan since 2001, with others occurring in other Muslim countries. (Honor killing is not advocated under Islamic religious tradition, but it has a long tribal tradition in some countries and is not dealt with harshly, according to in-country observers.)

Questions

1. Is this case an international or a transnational crime, and why?
2. Given the very serious nature of the conduct and the lack of an urgent response within the countries where it occurs, what should be the response and approach to prevent continuing honor killings?

SOURCES: Safed Shah, "Tribal Traditions and Three Girls' Gruesome Demise," *The Globe and Mail* (Canada), September 1, 2008, p. A8; Jeff Jacoby, "Honor Killing Comes to the U.S.," *The Boston Globe*, August 10, 2008; see also Phyllis Chesler, "Worldwide Trends in Honor Killings, *Middle East Quarterly*, vol. 17 (Spring 2010), pp. 3-11.

DISCUSSION QUESTIONS

1. How do international and transnational crime differ?
2. Why should we study comparative criminal justice?
3. Using newspapers, magazines, or the Internet, find one example of how a country has borrowed an idea or way of doing criminal justice.
4. What are some of the underlying values that are present in the U.S. criminal justice system?
5. What are the advantages of using a historical-political approach to the study of comparative justice systems?

FOR FURTHER READING

Maier-Katkin, D., D. P. Mears, and T. J. Bernard. (2009). Towards a Criminology of Crimes against Humanity. *Theoretical Criminology*, vol. 13, pp. 227-255.

Hagan, J., and W. Rymond-Richmond. (2008). *Darfur and the Crime of Genocide*. Cambridge University Press.

Nelken, D. (2010). *Comparative Criminal Justice: Making Sense of Difference*. Sage Publications.

Ragin, C. C. (1989). *The Comparative Method: Moving beyond Qualitative and Quantitative Strategies*. University of California Press.

Winterdyk, J. A., and L. Cao. (2005). *Lessons from International/Comparative Criminology/Criminal Justice.* deSitter Publications.

Zimring, F. E. (2006). The Necessity and Value of Transnational Comparative Study: Some Preaching from a Recent Convert. *Criminology & Public Policy*, vol. 5, pp. 615-622.

WEB PAGES FOR CHAPTER

Go to http://www.ojp.usdoj.gov/nij/international/ to visit the International Center of the National Institute of Justice within the U.S. Department of Justice.

See http://www.cia.gov/library/publications/the-world-factbook/index.html to visit the CIA World Factbook, which provides socio-demographic, political, and criminal justice information about 268 geographic entities.

Go to http://www.unodc.org/ to visit the web page of the United Nations Office on Drugs and Crime and view its scope of work.

2

Measuring and Comparing Crime in and across Nations

Key Terms and Concepts

dark figure

developed country

developing country

International Crime Victim Surveys (ICVS)

Interpol

National Crime Victimization Survey (NCVS)

risk of crime

self-report surveys

Uniform Crime Reports (UCR)

United Nations Surveys of Crime and Trends and Operation of Criminal Justice Systems (CTS)

Chapter 2 Learning Objectives

Discuss why we should measure and compare crime statistics in other countries.

Explore some reasons for the high rate of violent crime in the United States.

Identify the primary sources of international crime statistics.

Analyze the three major limitations of international crime statistics.

Describe how to best compare international crime statistics.

Amador Cortes-Meza was the ringleader of an organization that brought 10 victims (including four juveniles) to the United States and forced them into prostitution. Nine of the victims testified at trial that Amador, his brother, and a nephew tricked and deceived young women in Mexico into coming to the United States. The case was investigated by U.S. Immigration and Customs Enforcement's Homeland Security Investigations in Atlanta, which found that Amador and his family members would pretend to be romantically interested in the young girls, many of whom were from rural areas and some of whom did not have much education. The suspects would promise the victims that they would have a life together and then tell the women they needed to travel to the United States to make money working in restaurants or cleaning homes.

Amador obtained false identification for the victims and made arrangements to smuggle them into the United States. The victims were held in homes near Atlanta, and the suspects took turns monitoring the victims. Drivers transported the victims to clients' residences, where the victims were required to engage in commercial sex—sometimes up to 20 times a night. The victims testified that when they refused to engage in prostitution, Amador or his codefendants would beat them and threaten them and their families back in Mexico with physical harm. The co-conspirators and the drivers split the proceeds of the prostitution.

Ultimately, five suspects pleaded guilty. They each received sentences ranging from 10 to 20 years in prison, except for Amador, who received a 40-year prison term. The U.S. Attorney remarked, "No one wants to believe that there are people who will enslave other human beings and require them to commit innumerable commercial sex acts. Yet this intolerable crime is happening right in our own neighborhoods in metropolitan Atlanta" (Irving, 2011; U.S. Department of Justice, 2011a). This case is an example of a human trafficking enterprise whereby an illicit service was provided by recruiting, transporting, and exploiting victims for their forced labor (see Table 1.1 in the previous chapter).

Unfortunately, there is no national or international count of any of the nine transnational crimes listed in Chapter 1, including human trafficking. These crimes occur across borders, most are undetected, and many have only recently been defined as transnational crimes, so global awareness and response is still in its early stages. Human trafficking and related forms of transnational organized crime are discussed further in Chapter 11, but it should be noted that, like other forms of transnational crimes (e.g., cybercrime, racketeering, counterfeiting, corruption, and all those listed in Table 1.1), it is a compound crime. A compound crime includes the lesser crimes, such as theft, assault, robbery, and sometimes rape, as a consequence of larger criminal conspiracies. Although reliable counts of transnational crimes do not exist, there are counts of the lesser crimes because concern about these offenses has existed for many more years. It is hoped that more attention to generating reliable counts of transnational crimes in the future will enable all countries to assess progress in preventing them.

It is estimated that crime generates $2.1 trillion in annual global proceeds, according to the United Nations Office on Drugs and Crime and the World Bank. This represents 3.6 percent of the world's gross domestic product, which is the size of one of the world's top 20 national economies (Reuters, 2012). Crime is increasingly international, transnational, and worldwide in scope. On one level, we have made considerable progress with the collection of crime statistics for individual nations. Yet even with this growing knowledge, we still do not have precise knowledge of the true extent of transnational crime.

It is very difficult to account for the frequency of transnational crimes for at least three reasons. First, they are often difficult to detect due to their secretive and multi-jurisdictional nature. In order to detect arms trafficking, for example, information is required about activities committed by the buyer, seller, and manufacturer of the illegal arms for sale, which poses tremendous problems of detection and determining location. Second, transnational crimes by definition are committed across legal jurisdictions. This makes it difficult to determine government responsibility for detection, law enforcement, and prosecution. Whose problem is it: that of the source country, transit phase, or destination location? Finally, these crimes often extend over a period of time, with detection often occurring long after the crime is committed. By then, evidence is often difficult to find and suspects have absconded. At present, there is no universal method of counting the plethora of transnational crimes, although some promising methods are underway.

We know that crime is universal—there is no country without crime. French sociologist Emile Durkheim observed more than a century ago that "Crime is present not only in the majority of societies … but in all societies of all types. There is no society that is not confronted with the problem of criminality" (Durkheim, 1895, pp. 65–66; Newman, 1999). Nevertheless, crime rates vary considerably both within and among countries. Although crime may be less of a problem in Iceland, for example, than it is in Colombia or even the United States, the problem is present everywhere. We can also say that because of globalization, there are more kinds of crimes of international concern than was the case 25 years ago. Whereas drug trafficking and money laundering were the primary issues of transnational concern in years past, other crime issues such as corruption, trafficking of human beings, terrorism, weapons trafficking, and cybercrime have since emerged as leading problems of transnational crime.

WHY MEASURE AND COMPARE CRIME DATA?

Crime is a worldwide problem that directly or indirectly touches every one of us in multiple ways: as victims, in paying higher prices for products and services, and in living with the consequences of fear and corruption. The primary reason to understand and compare crime data is to determine risk. **Risk of crime** evaluates the probability that certain crimes will occur and their potential harm. How great is the risk that we will be victimized? How should we adjust our behavior to account for known instances of crime? Can we better anticipate the circumstances around which crime occurs?

In a global context, the questions to be answered become even more important to our security. What is the risk of crime in a certain country? How safe is one country versus another? How does the crime rate in the United States compare with rates in other countries? What offenses produce the most harm to the most people? The answers to these questions directly influence our fear and our behavior as citizens, and the policies and actions of individual countries and the world community of nations.

Crime statistics summarize experience, so we can judge more effectively whether we live in a safe place, what crimes we should be most concerned about, what locations we should avoid, and what behaviors we should change to reduce our chances of being a victim of crime.

Learning more about crime data is important in the same way that gaining more knowledge about medicine, poverty, or the environment is important in evaluating personal and societal conditions. Acquisition of this knowledge can improve the quality of life for citizens and help government leaders make rational decisions about ways to allocate our valuable resources. In a larger sense, measured knowledge of social conditions such as crime is essential to the health of any democracy (American Sociological Association, 1999).

Measuring crime and comparing crime data in other countries serve at least two larger purposes as well. First, collecting data about crime allows us to determine the kinds and extent of crimes reported in any one country and, more importantly, to distinguish long-term patterns from year-to-year trends. This is in contrast to the practice of looking at crime data for one period of time, as in a snapshot, and then making limited observations and drawing limited conclusions about the data, because we do not know whether we are in the middle of an unrecognized trend up or down.

An example illustrates the importance of observing data over a period of time. Suppose there have been 1,000 car thefts in a country during the year, with a rate of 5 thefts per 100,000 persons. This figure by itself means little; it may or may not be cause for alarm. However, if we can show that the rate of car thefts increased 10 percent from last year, and 20 percent over the last three years, then we can consider the problem to be increasing in seriousness and worthy of further consideration. Therefore, knowledge of trends over time is an essential purpose of gathering crime statistics.

Understanding crime trends is important both domestically and internationally. Evidence indicates that increased crime risk to citizens often prompts public officials to respond to address specific crime problems. For example, if the United States determines that the main entry point of illegal drugs is through its southern border, officials may wish to devote more effort to improving relations with Mexican criminal justice officials and spend more money on border patrols, immigration control, and impacting drug use trends. Therefore, perceived risk and social action are closely tied to each other.

Second, measuring crime and comparing crime data provide clues as to why some nations are more successful than others in controlling crime rates. In this way, we can learn from the experiences of other countries. Suppose we review the criminal justice system of a country and find that a lower crime rate is associated with specific policies relating to families, drugs, alcohol, or crime prevention. We may then study these policies and see whether they can be adapted to our own situation. For example, an assessment of various drug treatment programs in the prisons of five different countries found that programs containing both individual and group counseling, coupled with follow-up aftercare, had a significant impact on substance abuse. Given the large number of inmates who were using drugs at the time of their offense, these cross-national results suggest that substance abuse treatment within corrections is worth the investment (Reyes, 2009). This kind of comparative information can inform the crime prevention and criminal justice responses in many countries.

THE HISTORICAL BACKGROUND OF INTERNATIONAL CRIME DATA

The first attempt to collect data on crime at the international level occurred in 1853 at the General Statistical Congress in Brussels. Soon thereafter, in 1872, another attempt was made at the International Congress on the Prevention and Repression of Crime in London. The major issue discussed at both of these meetings was how to define certain crimes, for the comparability of definitions clearly was to be a major stumbling block in the collection of crime data. The problem of definitions remained an issue in 1946 at the conference of the International Penal and Penitentiary Foundation (IPPF), which soon handed over most of its functions to the newly formed United Nations (UN) organization.

In the early years of the UN, attempts were made to develop a mechanism for collecting criminal data at the international level. The Economic and Social Council of the UN passed several resolutions from 1948 to 1951, but they met with little success. Only one cross-national crime survey was conducted over the period 1937–1946 (Burnham, 1997). Between the 1940s and the early 1970s, crime data collection was limited to the

International Criminal Police Organization (ICPO), more commonly called **Interpol**, which tried to collect data from as many of its member nations as cared to report them. Interpol has since discontinued this statistical effort, in favor of providing information for investigative support to police agencies worldwide.

In 1970, a breakthrough occurred when the UN General Assembly resolved through its Crime Prevention and Criminal Justice branch to develop a survey that would collect information from member countries about crime rates and the operations of criminal justice systems. The first survey, covering the years 1970–1975, appeared in 1977 with 64 nations reporting (Fields & Moore, 1996, p. 17). The UN carried out the tenth UN survey in 2008 with 86 nations responding. The survey is administered by the United Nations Office on Drugs and Crime and is now called the **United Nations Surveys of Crime and Trends and Operation of Criminal Justice Systems (CTS)**. The CTS questionnaire consists of four parts dealing primarily with statistical information about the main components of the criminal justice system (police, prosecution, courts, and prisons) and an Annex. The Annex was developed for countries in Europe and requested supplementary information on police-recorded crime statistics relating to homicide and thefts of motor vehicles. Therefore, the CTS focuses more on information about criminal justice systems than on the measurement of crime.

THE DIFFERENT KINDS OF CRIME DATA

There are three major ways to count crime because there are often three perspectives on each criminal incident: those of the offender, of the victim, and of the police. Clearly, an offender and victim are involved in every crime, and many times the police are called to respond, providing a third way to count criminal incidents. This section summarizes major crime-counting efforts under each of these perspectives.

The Police Perspective

Because crime statistics are gathered by governments, it is not surprising that there has been much world experience with counting crime through reports to the police. In the United States, these police reports are called the **Uniform Crime Reports (UCR)**, and are collected by each police agency in the United States and compiled by the Federal Bureau of Investigation annually. The UCR program has been under way since 1930, so it has the benefit of assessing trends over time, but the count of crime it provides has serious flaws, which affect its accuracy. Most serious is that the UCR, like all police counts, counts only those crimes reported to the police—crimes that do not come to the attention of police are missed. It has been found that less than half of all crimes are reported to police, so a great deal of crime is overlooked when using police statistics to count crime. Second, the UCR program is voluntary, so not all police departments report crime data every year—and some departments have not been diligent in counting crimes in their jurisdiction, resulting in further undercounts (State Police, 2004; Lynch & Jarvis, 2008; Maki, 2012). Third, the UCR program gathers information on a limited range of offenses: criminal homicide, forcible rape, robbery, aggravated assault, burglary, larceny, motor vehicle theft, and arson. As we have noted, none of the major transnational crimes are included as listed in Chapter 1. Fourth, the UCR program counts arrests for 29 other generally less serious offenses, but arrests occur even less often than do reports of crimes to police, so they cannot be used to count criminal incidents accurately.

In recent years, the National Incident-Based Reporting System (NIBRS) has been developed to broaden the extent and depth of crime data gathered by police agencies. The NIBRS collects data on every incident and arrest within 22 offense categories made up of 46 specific crimes. For each of the offenses coming to the attention of law enforcement, specified types of facts about each crime are reported. The FBI has certified 31 state UCR programs for NIBRS participation so far, but the data from those agencies represent 25 percent of the U.S. population and 25 percent of the crime statistics collected by the UCR Program (FBI, 2010). Therefore, the potential of the NIBRS program as a national data source has not yet been realized. It is important to recognize that the limits of police-based crime statistics are shared by police agencies around the world.

The Victim Perspective

Significant efforts have been made in recent years to develop systematic crime data by interviewing citizens to learn about the nature and extent of their crime victimization (whether or not they were reported to police). In order to know who has been the victim of a crime, a representative sample of the population (from 76,000 households including more than 135,000 persons) is selected, and participants are asked questions about their experience with crime in recent months. The **National Crime Victimization Survey (NCVS)** was developed in the United States during the 1970s, and it is now an annual survey covering six crimes: rape, robbery, assault, larceny, burglary, and motor vehicle theft (U.S. Bureau of Justice Statistics, 2010). NCVS has found that the total number of crimes committed in the United States is at least double the number reported to the police in the UCR.

The NCVS improves our knowledge of the true extent of crime by reducing the **dark figure** of crime; that is, the amount of crime occurring which is unknown to police or the general public. In addition to improving our knowledge about crimes committed, the NCVS also enhances our knowledge about criminal behavior and the consequences of crime on victims. In this way, we can use the NCVS to build explanations of the circumstances of crime and crime prevention approaches.

While the Uniform Crime Reports collect a little information about all crimes known to police, victimization surveys collect exhaustive information about a smaller number of crimes from a representative sample of the population, whether or not the victimization was reported. There is fairly close correspondence between the crime definitions used by the UCR and NCVS, so it is possible to assess national crime information from two points of view: those of the victims and the police. The NCVS finds that, overall, approximately 50 percent of violent crimes (rape, robbery, assault) and 40 percent of property crimes (burglary, larceny, motor vehicle theft) are reported to police. Therefore, victimization surveys reveal that there is between two to three times more crime occurring than is reported in police statistics.

The Offender Perspective

A third way to count crime is from the perspective of the offender. This perspective is gathered from **self-report surveys**, in which people are asked to report their own delinquent and criminal acts in an anonymous questionnaire or confidential interview. Self-reporting is helpful because it is able to compare information about known offenders with those who have not been caught. Self-reports also provide information about "victimless crimes," in which the offender and victim are the same person (e.g., drug use) or engage in conduct consensually (e.g., prostitution).

Most self-reports are surveys of smaller samples of youth and, less often, adults. A national survey in the United States had findings consistent with those of other self-report surveys: Virtually all persons break the law at one time or another, although only 10 to 20 percent are caught and arrested, and few commit serious crimes or do so frequently (Piquero, Brezina, & Turner, 2005). However, self-report surveys are used mostly with young persons and rarely in national samples, so self-report surveys have limited utility in understanding the overall crime rate and are much less likely to be used in cross-national comparisons due to their limited size and duration.

An exception is the International Self-Report Delinquency (ISRD) study, which has used a standard instrument to compare juvenile rates of crime in 12 European locations and the United States. The results showed that between 80 and 90 percent of juveniles had committed either one or a combination of property, violent, and drug crimes (Junger-Tas, Terlouw, & Klein, 1994). A second international administration of this instrument gathered self-reported information from 70,000 12- to 15-year-old youths in 28 countries with similar results. Although the self-report methodology has not been applied on such a large scale in an international context until recently, this method has documented that the vast majority of juveniles violate the law but that most do not go on to become adult criminals (Howard et al., 2000; Junger-Tas et al., 2010).

INTERNATIONAL CRIME DATA

Given the three possible perspectives on counting crime, it is important to determine their availability on an international level for cross-national comparisons. Many industrialized countries have some kind of crime reporting system published from the reports to police agencies. There is no standardization among countries, however, in how crimes are recorded because of the many differences in criminal codes and in the precise definitions of various crimes. As a result, the reporting and publication of crimes reported to the police remains largely an exercise for individual nations, with too many differences to compare across national boundaries.

The United Nations has been interested in comparable crime data since its establishment as an organization after World War II. Its surveys are the most comprehensive, but the response rates from member states is often less than 50 percent, and developing countries are underrepresented. A **developing country** is one with a low level of material and social development, measured by such indicators as income per person, life expectancy, and literacy rates. A majority of the world's nations are developing countries. Conversely, **developed countries** are those with a high level of development, measured by the factors above, plus other indicators such as gross domestic product and industrialization.

Interpol's efforts to gather police statistics biennially began in 1950, but the results have not been published in recent years. Interpol even removed all crime statistics from its public website in 2006 because the statistics reported to them did not correlate well with crime data generated from the UN or the Council of Europe, leading to questions of reliability and validity in the reporting from member nations (Killias & Aebi, 2000; Van Dijk, 2008, p. 16;). It is also a problem of all international crime statistics that countries are sometimes embarrassed by the results and do not report them comprehensively for reasons involving political criticism. There are examples in many countries of crime statistics being used within countries to attack the political party in power or to deny the validity of the data themselves. In many ways it is a shame that greater effort is not devoted to better international crime data in the same way that international efforts have been established to measure economic activity, diseases, infant mortality, literacy, employment, and agriculture across nations via the International Monetary Fund, World Bank, World Health Organization, United Nations Development Program, and International Labor Organization.

The best available sources of international crime data are international victimization surveys. Victimization surveys have the advantage of avoiding government-controlled data collection or screening (through the police or the political process), and these surveys use standard crime definitions to avoid the differences in definitions among the world's criminal codes. The results are based on interviews with a sample of the population, rather than relying only on offenses that come to the attention of police. Although the initial modern crime victimization survey was conducted in the United States in 1965, the first national study was carried out in Finland in 1970. Soon thereafter, international studies were undertaken in Denmark, Sweden, Norway, and the United Kingdom (Jousten, 1994).

The first major comparative victimization survey was developed and carried out in 1988 by three European criminologists, Jan van Dijk, Pat Mahew, and Martin Killias. The second was conducted in

1992–1994, the third in 1996–1997, and the fourth in 2000. These surveys, now formally called the **International Crime Victim Surveys (ICVS)**, are conducted through the coordinated efforts of the Ministry of Justice of the Netherlands and the United Nations Interregional Crime and Justice Research Institute, located in Italy. The ICVS is now the most extensive standardized survey of victims in the world (Nieuwbeerta, 2002). The primary collection tool used in the ICVS is computer-assisted telephone interviewing, which randomly selects and calls a sample of 800 to 2,000 individuals in each country. In some countries, smaller samples are used because of logistical difficulties, and where telephone ownership is limited, in-person interviews are conducted.

The ICVS surveys ask representative samples of individuals from households about 10 specific offenses they have may have experienced, and their perceptions and attitudes, over the year leading up to the survey. The ICVS is interested in incidents both reported and not reported to the police, and the reasons why people do or do not choose to notify the police. It provides a count of how many people are affected by crime. Those who mention an incident of any particular type are asked some additional questions about what happened (Van Dijk, 1997, p. 15). Respondents are also asked a series of questions concerning their attitudes toward police performance, actions taken to protect against victimization, how safe they feel at home, how safe they feel in the streets, their levels of home security, and attitudes toward punishment.

Data from several administrations of the ICVS are available from 30 countries, including a majority of developed nations. In addition, separate data from 33 major cities are included to add greater representation from developing countries for which nationwide data is not available. Two large tables are presented here to display the levels of crimes uncovered by the ICVS by country and by major city. The numbers reflect the percentage of those aged 16 and over who experienced a specific crime at least once over the course of a year. The numbers do not reflect the number of times that people were victimized during the year, so they do not count total crimes per population (incidence rates), but the ranking of countries by prevalance rates has been found to be similar to rankings by incidence rates (crimes per 100,000) (Van Kesteren, Mayhew, & Nieuwbeerta, 2000). In addition, these figures are estimates generated from a representative sample of interviews in each location. These estimates are precise within statistical confidence limits of between 0.5 to 1.5 percent, meaning that a victimization rate of 5.0 percent indicates that there is a 90 percent certainty that the true crime rate lies between 4.2 and 5.8 percent.

Table 2.1 summarizes the percentage of people victimized one or more times by any of the 10 crimes included in the ICVS. The table includes six of these crimes, with the others being theft from a car, motorcycle theft, bicycle theft, and attempted burglary. Nearly 16 percent (15.7) of the adult population of the 30 participating countries were the victim of at least one crime over the course of a year. Countries with overall victimization rates that are statistically higher than average include Ireland, England and Wales, New Zealand, Iceland, Northern Ireland, Estonia, the Netherlands, Denmark, Mexico, Switzerland, and Belgium. Countries with rates near the average include the United States, Canada, Australia, and Sweden. The countries with the highest victimization rates are a mix of developed and developing countries, which suggests that poverty is not a major contributor to crime rates. Countries with the lowest levels of victimization include Spain, Japan, Hungary, Portugal, Austria, France, Greece, and Italy, which are also heterogeneous in composition and culture.

The last three rows of Table 2.1 illustrate victimization trends over time. It can be seen that there has been a general downward trend in victimization rates across all crime categories. Therefore, the widely reported experience of crime declines in the United States and Europe are mirrored in many other countries as well. Indeed, the availability of these crime data across countries permits some assessment of national crime control policies. For example, the general downward trend in crime beginning in the 1990s was roughly the same across countries. The findings from a study of 26 countries,

TABLE 2.1 One-Year Victimization Rates in Participating Countries (Percentages)

Country	Overall Rate for 10 Crimes*	Car Theft	Burglary	Robbery	Theft of Personal Property	Sex Offenses against Women	Other Assaults
Australia	16.3	1.1	2.5	0.9	3.6	4.0	3.4
Austria	11.6	0.1	0.9	0.4	3.4	2.2	1.9
Belgium	17.7	0.5	1.8	1.2	3.4	0.9	3.6
Bulgaria	14.1	1.2	2.5	0.9	3.4	0.2	1.7
Canada	17.2	0.8	2.0	0.8	4.0	2.3	3.0
Denmark	18.8	1.3	2.7	0.9	3.3	1.9	3.3
England and Wales	21.8	1.8	3.5	1.4	6.3	1.9	5.8
Estonia	20.2	0.5	2.5	1.6	5.6	1.1	2.7
Finland	12.7	0.4	0.8	0.3	2.3	1.4	2.2
France	12.0	0.6	1.6	0.8	3.3	0.4	2.1
Germany	13.1	0.2	0.9	0.4	3.0	2.4	2.7
Greece	12.3	0.3	1.8	1.4	5.3	1.7	2.4
Hungary	10.0	0.2	1.7	0.9	3.0	0.1	1.2
Iceland	21.2	1.0	1.6	0.8	6.9	3.0	5.9
Ireland	21.9	1.2	2.3	2.2	7.2	3.8	4.9
Italy	12.6	1.0	2.1	0.3	2.4	0.7	0.8
Japan	9.9	0.1	0.9	0.2	0.3	1.3	0.6
Luxembourg	12.7	0.6	1.7	0.7	2.9	0.6	2.3
Mexico	18.7	0.9	3.0	3.0	4.3	1.5	2.2
Netherlands	19.7	1.0	1.3	0.5	3.7	1.9	4.3
New Zealand	21.5	1.8	3.2	1.1	4.1	2.5	4.9
Northern Ireland	20.4	1.4	1.4	1.1	5.1	3.0	6.8
Norway	15.8	0.7	1.2	0.8	4.8	2.5	2.9
Poland	15.0	0.7	1.4	1.3	3.5	1.3	3.0
Portugal	10.4	1.5	1.4	1.0	1.6	0.5	0.9
Scotland	13.3	0.3	1.5	0.9	2.9	1.5	3.8
Spain	9.1	10.0	0.8	1.3	2.1	0.3	1.6
Sweden	16.1	0.5	0.7	1.1	2.4	3.3	3.5
Switzerland	18.1	0.2	1.6	0.8	5.9	2.9	2.5
United Kingdom	21.0	1.8	3.3	1.3	5.7	1.9	5.4
USA	17.5	1.1	2.5	0.6	4.8	3.6	4.3
1995 average	20.3	1.3	2.0	1.1	4.6	2.3	4.0
2000 average	18.4	1.0	2.0	1.0	4.1	2.0	3.8
2005 average	**15.7**	**0.8**	**1.8**	**1.0**	**3.8**	**1.7**	**3.0**

*The other crimes not included in this table are theft from a car, motorcycle theft, bicycle theft, and attempted burglary.

SOURCE: ICVS and EU International Crime Surveys, 2005. Jan Van Dijk, John van Kesteren, and Paul Smit. (2007). *Criminal Victimization in International Perspective*. The Hague: Bibliotheek WODC.

using ICVS data, provided little support for country-specific explanations for the crime drop. That is to say, if severe punishment played an important role in the crime declines, countries that implemented more imprisonment and intensive policing prior to and during the period of the crime drop (such as the USA and the UK) would have had a sharper crime reduction than the countries that did not change their emphasis on crime control during the same period. But that did not occur; the crime drop occurred everywhere. The findings of the study suggest that the explanation for the crime drop may lie in factors that changed more universally, such as improved antitheft measures in automobiles (Tseloni et al., 2010).

Table 2.2 summarizes the results of victimization surveys carried out in 33 major cities around the world. This group is very diverse, comprising cities in both developed and developing countries, some of which have not yet participated in national-level victimization surveys. It can be seen that the average victimization rate in these cities is 21.5 percent, higher than the 15.7 percent average rate in national surveys (depicted in Table 2.1). In nearly every country, victimization rates are 25 to 33 percent higher in these large cities than in the nations as a whole. The rate of victimization in these major cities is higher in developing countries (28.4 percent) than it is in developed countries (19.9 percent). The five cities with the lowest victimization rates are Hong Kong, Lisbon, Budapest, Athens, and Madrid.

Table 2.1 shows that 0.8 percent of citizens had a car stolen during the previous year (on average). In major world cities the victimization rate is higher, at 1.3 percent (1.1 percent in developed countries and 1.8 percent in developing countries). In many countries car theft rates have dropped by half over the last 10 years, despite the fact that car ownership has increased. This declining rate is likely due to growing use of antitheft devices in cars, such as automatic locks, alarms, and electronic ignition systems. Interestingly, the likelihood of theft from or out of a car is much more common than that of

TABLE 2.2 One-Year Victimization Rates in 33 Major World Cities (Percentages)

City/Country	Overall Rate for 10 Crimes*	Car Theft	Burglary	Robbery	Theft of Personal Property	Sex Offenses against Women	Other Assaults
Amsterdam (Netherlands)	27.0	0.7	2.1	1.1	4.4	3.2	5.9
Athens (Greece)	13.5	0.7	1.7	0.7	3.5	1.1	2.4
Belfast (North Ireland)	26.1	1.9	2.9	2.5	5.9	2.0	9.2
Berlin (Germany)	19.3	0.4	1.1	1.2	5.2	2.5	4.1
Brussels (Belgium)	20.2	0.9	3.1	2.5	6.0	0.2	2.6
Budapest (Hungary)	12.6	0.4	1.2	1.1	5.5	0.3	1.6
Buenos Aires (Argentina)	31.2	2.1	2.0	10.0	6.6	2.1	3.2
Copenhagen (Denmark)	22.9	1.0	2.6	1.2	4.6	3.8	3.6
Dublin (Ireland)	25.7	3.0	2.6	1.8	6.8	0.8	3.9
Edinburgh (Scotland)	16.6	0.4	1.4	1.2	4.6	1.2	4.6

TABLE 2.2 (continued)

City/Country	Overall Rate for 10 Crimes*	Car Theft	Burglary	Robbery	Theft of Personal Property	Sex Offenses against Women	Other Assaults
Johannesburg (South Africa)	23.5	2.6	5.4	5.5	6.9	1.7	11.2
Helinski (Finland)	20.5	1.7	4.4	1.4	3.0	4.3	4.5
Hong Kong (China)	7.8	0.0	0.6	0.4	3.6	1.2	1.2
Istanbul (Turkey)	17.9	0.9	4.6	0.9	3.2	2.5	0.6
Lima (Peru)	N/A	0.3	6.8	7.4	12.3	4.7	N/A
Lisbon (Portugal)	9.7	2.0	0.7	1.9	2.4	0.4	1.3
London (England)	32.0	1.3	4.5	2.6	10.2	3.0	8.6
Madrid (Spain)	13.7	1.8	1.1	1.5	4.4	0.7	2.9
Maputo (Mozambique)	37.7	1.9	12.6	7.6	9.9	2.6	6.2
New York (USA)	23.3	1.6	1.9	2.3	7.7	3.5	5.1
Oslo (Norway)	21.5	1.0	1.9	1.0	7.5	2.3	4.1
Paris (France)	17.8	0.2	1.9	1.2	4.8	0.5	3.1
Phnom Penh (Cambodia)	41.3	0.2	15.8	1.8	12.8	1.4	6.8
Reykjavik (Iceland)	26.4	1.0	2.2	0.7	8.2	2.6	7.0
Rio de Janeiro (Brazil)	15.0	1.7	1.0	5.1	2.5	1.3	1.5
Rome (Italy)	16.6	3.4	1.5	0.7	3.2	0.9	1.2
Sao Paulo (Brazil)	21.7	4.2	1.5	5.4	2.0	1.3	2.6
Stockholm (Sweden)	22.5	1.8	2.1	0.7	4.0	0.8	3.2
Sydney (Australia)	15.9	0.7	2.2	1.1	3.7	n/a	2.8
Tallinn (Estonia)	29.3	0.6	3.7	2.8	9.6	1.4	3.7
Vienna (Austria)	17.2	0.4	2.8	0.8	5.7	1.3	2.5
Warsaw (Poland)	21.9	1.6	2.4	2.8	5.3	2.3	2.6
Zurich (Switzerland)	20.1	0.2	2.7	1.7	7.7	3.1	3.5
2005 Average	21.5	1.3	3.2	2.4	5.9	1.9	4.0

*The other crimes not included in this table are theft from a car, motorcycle theft, bicycle theft, and attempted burglary.

SOURCE: ICVS and EU International Crime Surveys, 2005. Jan Van Dijk, John van Kesteren, and Paul Smit. (2007). *Criminal Victimization in International Perspective.* The Hague: Bibliotheek WODC.

the car itself being stolen. The victimization rate for theft from a car was 3.6 percent (not shown in the tables) versus 0.8 for car theft, although the rates are falling in recent years for both types of theft.

Motorcycles were found to be stolen much more often than cars, and such thefts are generally highest in countries with the highest rates of motorcycle ownership, such as Italy (33 percent of adult citizens own a motorcycle), Greece (32 percent), Japan (29 percent), and Sweden (25 percent). Finland, Austria, the Netherlands, and Germany also have motorcycle ownership rates of more than 20 percent. Bicycles are an important means of transportation in many countries, and they have a theft rate of 2.9 percent for countries and 3.3 percent for major world cities (data not shown in the tables). The highest rates of bicycle theft exist in the Netherlands, Denmark, Finland, Japan, and Sweden (5 percent or higher), while the lowest rates occur in Portugal, Spain, France, Bulgaria, Australia, and New Zealand (under 1.5 percent). As you might expect, the rate of bicycle theft is much larger than rates of motorcycle or car theft.

Residential burglary occurs in 1.8 percent of households on average in the 30 countries surveyed. Burglary rates in major cities were generally higher, averaging 3.2 percent. The highest rates of residential burglary are found in England and Wales, New Zealand, Mexico, Denmark, Bulgaria, Australia, Estonia, and the United States (all with rates of 2.5 percent or higher). The lowest burglary rates were found in Sweden, Spain, Finland, Japan, Austria, and Germany (all below 1 percent). In major cities in developing countries, burglaries occur significantly more often than in developed countries (6.4 percent versus 2.3 percent). The general decline in average national burglary victimization rates is likely associated with increasing security awareness on the part of residents, growing use of alarms, and more residents working in or near the home.

Another type of crime covered by the ICVS is theft of personal property that includes no personal confrontation, threat, or force. Examples include theft of wallets, purses, clothing, equipment, or accessories. Pickpocketing accounted for a third of these cases. Rates of theft of personal property are mixed, although national averages are generally declining. Ireland, Iceland, England and Wales, Switzerland, Estonia, Greece, and Northern Ireland have the highest rate of thefts (greater than 5 percent). London, Tallinn, Reykjavik, New York, Zurich, and Oslo are the cities with the highest victimization rates for personal theft.

Robbery includes theft by force or threat, and attempts to do so, using personal confrontation. Like other offenses, robbery victimization is higher in major cities (2.4 percent) than at the national level (1 percent). Robbery rates in developing countries are significantly higher (6.1 percent). National trends indicate that rates are decreasing in most countries. Interestingly, about 60 percent of robberies involved more than one offender, and a weapon was present in 28 percent of cases at the national level but in 39 percent in major cities. Cities with the highest proportion of robberies at gunpoint are Phnom Penh (66 percent), Rio de Janeiro (56 percent), Sao Paulo (51 percent), Johannesburg (47 percent), and New York (27 percent).

Sex-related offenses are measured in the ICVS by asking about victimization in a broad way, "People sometimes grab, touch, or assault others for sexual reasons in a really offensive way (inside or outside the home)." Therefore, responses include offenses far less serious than the crime of rape, although rapes would also be included. Measuring these incidents is very difficult because of differences in acceptable sexual behavior among countries and the somewhat greater likelihood of nonreporting of these offenses to interviewers, despite the anonymous nature of the telephone interview. An average of 1.7 percent of women reported a sexual victimization, a rate that has been dropping across nations. Sexual offenses occur somewhat more often in major world cities (1.9 percent).

When sexual offenses are divided into two groups—sexual assault (rapes, attempts, indecent assault) and less serious cases of offensive sex-related behavior—sexual assaults occur at a rate of 0.6 percent on average and at only slightly higher rates in major cities (0.7 percent). Cities in developing countries, however, have higher rates of sexual assault (1.2 percent average), although the cities of New York, Copenhagen, and Helsinki also have rates of 1.0 percent and above. Taking all sexual offenses together, victims knew the offender in about half the cases. In cases where the victim knew the offender's name, it was a colleague or boss (17 percent), an ex-intimate partner (11 percent), current intimate partner (8 percent), or close friend (16 percent). The vast majority of sex offenses involved one offender (78 percent), and the use of weapons was uncommon (8 percent of cases).

The last category of crime covered by the ICVS involves assaults. The question asks whether the person was "personally attacked or threatened by someone in a way that really frightened you (inside or outside the home)." On average, there was a 3.0 percent victimization rate for assaults across nations, a figure that has been declining in recent years. Higher than average rates were reported in Northern Ireland, Iceland, England and Wales, Ireland, the Netherlands, New Zealand, and the United States. The lowest rates of assault victimization were in Italy, Portugal, Hungary, and Spain (below 2 percent).

The characteristics of assaults showed that victims knew the offender in about half the incidents, and that weapons were used in 17 percent of cases. Mexico (16 percent), the United States (6 percent), and Northern Ireland (6 percent) had the highest percentages of gun-related attacks. In major world cities, 22.6 percent of assaults involved a weapon of some kind. Cities with the highest rates of attacks with guns include Rio de Janeiro (39 percent), Sao Paulo (35 percent), Phnom Penh (13 percent), Johannesburg (13 percent), Istanbul (10 percent), New York (10 percent), Brussels (10 percent), Maputo (7 percent), and Belfast (6 percent). The ICVS also asked about household gun ownership. Handgun ownership ranged from 0 percent in Japan to 6 percent in Lima, 6.8 percent in Argentina, and 17.6 percent in the USA. The average gun ownership rate in Europe is 3.2 percent.

In sum, international victimization surveys provide the best available information about crime rates internationally because they include crimes both reported and unreported to police, and because they use a standardized questionnaire with uniform definitions of offenses. Approximately half of all crimes are found to be reported to the police, with higher reporting rates in developed countries and lower reporting rates in developing countries. Nevertheless, the ICVS surveys only residences, so crimes against commercial establishments are not counted. Individuals may also underreport some victimization because they involve people close to the victim, a particular problem with victims of sex crimes (Zvekic & Alvazzi del Frate, 1995). For these reasons, the ICVS likely underreports to some extent the true extent of the crimes it measures. In research conducted by G. O. W. Mueller, a former chief of the UN Crime Prevention Branch, it was found that countries fail to keep accurate crime statistics for a number of reasons. Mueller found that, although all countries do collect some form of crime data, many do not participate in the international crime surveys. Among the reasons are the following:

- Countries are so small that administrative staffs may not be able to handle the requests.
- Some countries are too involved in civil war to keep track of crime problems.
- "New" emerging countries have not developed a system of collection and dissemination of crime data.
- Some countries lack the technical resources and knowledge necessary to report crime data.
- Some countries have the resources but still refuse because they are concerned that crime data will negatively affect the nation's world standing or tourist trade. (Mueller, 1997)

A more complicated problem in comparing crime rates across nations is that of nonstandardized definitions of crime among countries. This problem has plagued comparative researchers for many years (see Ancel, 1952; Wolfgang, 1967). At the root of the problem of nonstandardized definitions is the issue of determining what is a *crime* versus what is *legal.* All nations agree that major predatory actions such as murder, robbery, and burglary should be illegal. When it comes to certain other actions, however, we may find that what is criminal in one country is acceptable behavior in another. Here are a few examples:

- Prostitution, largely illegal in the United States, is sanctioned and licensed in Japan and parts of Germany.
- Gambling, largely illegal in the United States, is legal in many other countries, including Japan, Germany, and France.
- Drinking alcoholic beverages, legal in most countries, is illegal in certain Muslim societies, including Iran and Saudi Arabia.
- Cases that would constitute minor traffic offenses in the United States are often classified as "professional negligence" in Japan on the theory that a driver's license constitutes a kind of professional certification.
- Sexual acts such as those of adultery, fornication, and homosexuality, which are not usually handled as criminal cases in Western countries, may result in very grave sanctions, including death, in fundamentalist Muslim countries such as Iran and Saudi Arabia.

What a country decides is illegal tells us something about that nation's social, economic, and political situation. For example, the need for a sober and reasonably docile working class in the early stages of the Industrial Revolution led to criminalization of acts such as vagrancy, loitering, drunkenness, and brawling. Religion-based governments tend to criminalize acts that dishonor the religion or violate its moral code. Socialist governments criminalize incursions against property belonging to the state (e.g., educational, government, or military buildings). Nations that, for economic reasons, wish to segregate people along racial or ethnic lines pass laws against miscegenation or other kinds of social contact between groups. In each case, actions that are perfectly legal in one country are defined as crimes in another.

HOMICIDE RATES

Homicide rates are of particular interest, not only because homicide is the ultimate offense against an individual and the social order but also because statistics on homicide rates should be more reliable than those for other crimes because of the presence of a human body in nearly every case. Of course, some homicides are masked as accidents and suicides, and there are cases in which individuals disappear and we can only guess whether or not they have been murdered. In general, however, the reality of a dead body forces the state to make a determination as to the cause of the individual's demise.

Despite the presence of a dead person under suspicious circumstances, counts of homicides within and among countries are not always consistent. Police agencies, public health agencies, and various other government agencies count deaths, but they do not always reach the same totals nor the same conclusions about the cause of death (Gabor et al., 2008; Karch & Logan, 2008). For example, a person hospitalized due to an assault can develop an infection and die. Although this is can be considered a criminal homicide in many nations (i.e., the assault caused the infection, which caused the death), not all nations or health statistics agencies would count this as a criminal homicide. Many jurisdictions would simply count this as a hospital death due to infection, because there is no ability to track the original cause of the hospitalization.

Developing nations often do not have the government resources to count deaths systematically or to classify them carefully. This probably causes some of the larger variation in homicide rates displayed in Table 2.3, because it is unlikely that actual homicide rates vary dramatically over short periods of time within a country, absent major civil conflict.

Table 2.3 presents homicide rates (per 100,000 population) for 54 nations around the world. Nations were chosen based on the availability of data over multiple years, using UN crime surveys, Geneva Declaration reports, and individual country reports. It can be seen that developing countries often have higher homicide rates than developed

TABLE 2.3 Homicide Rates in 54 Countries (Rate per 100,000 Population)

Country	2000	2008	Country	2000	2008
Honduras	50	58	Portugal	2.5	2.5
Venezuela	33	52	Armenia	3.3	2.5
El Salvador	37	49	Switzerland	2.6	2.3
Jamaica	34	49	Finland	2.9	2.2
Guatemala	26	45	Scotland	2.0	2.1
Trinidad and	10	42	New Zealand	1.2	2.0
Tobago			Canada	1.6	1.8
South Africa	50	37	Hungary	2.0	1.6
Colombia	63	36	Chile	1.9	1.6
Belize	16	31	France	1.8	1.6
Brazil	27	26	Belgium	2.8	1.5
Dominican Republic	13	24	England and Wales	1.6	1.4
Russia	28	17	Czech Republic	1.7	1.3
Panama	10	13	Australia	1.6	1.2
Nicaragua	9	12	Spain	1.3	1.2
Mexico	14	10	Italy	1.3	1.1
Kyrgyzstan	8.4	8.5	Iceland	1.8	1.0
Lithuania	1	8.1	Saudi Arabia	0.5	0.9
Costa Rica	6.3	7.7	Sweden	1.1	0.9
Belarus	10	7.5	Germany	1.2	0.9
Georgia	4.8	7.3	Denmark	1.1	0.9
Latvia	1	6.5	Austria	0.9	0.7
USA	5.6	5.4	Norway	1.1	0.7
Argentina	7.2	5.3	Morocco	0.4	0.5
Moldova	8.1	4.8	Hong Kong	0.6	0.5
Mauritius	2.2	4.0	Japan	0.5	0.4
Philippines	7.6	3.8	Singapore	0.9	0.4
Romania	2.5	2.5			

countries, although there are some exceptions. The world average homicide rate is approximately 7.5 per 100,000 population. The three regions with the highest homicide rates are Southern Africa, Central America, and South America. Western and Central Europe, East Asia, and Southeastern Europe are the three regions with the lowest rates of homicide.

Approximately 60 percent of all homicides are committed with firearms, ranging from a low of 19 percent in Western and Central Europe to a high of 77 percent in Central America (Geneva Declaration Secretariat, 2011). The data show that in recent years there has been a general decline in homicide rates in most countries, which corresponds to the decline in crime rates across many countries. The availability of homicide data across countries and over time is crucial to permit assessment of changing national policies and socioeconomic conditions within countries to evaluate potential explanations for homicide trends (McPhedran, Baker, & Singh, 2011).

Crime Rates in Model Countries

If we want to study and compare the crime rates in our model countries of France, Germany, Japan, Saudi Arabia, England, and China, it can be seen that the lowest homicide rates are in Japan, Saudi Arabia, and Germany. France and the United States have higher homicide rates. China does not have homicide rates published regularly over time, although Hong Kong reports very low rates of homicide.

The International Crime Victimization Surveys show that for the 10 crimes surveyed the United States has the highest overall rates, followed by England and Wales, Germany, and France. Neither China nor Saudi Arabia participates in the ICVS, although Hong Kong has generally low crime rates. Japan has the lowest overall crime rates, much lower than the other model countries or the United States.

THE EXCEPTIONS: COUNTRIES WITH LOW CRIME

We look with fascination at those societies that seem to have "beaten the odds" with respect to increased industrialization and accompanying increased crime. Switzerland, landlocked, mountainous, and located in the heart of Europe, has remained aloof from foreign entanglements and has been a pacifist society for centuries in the midst of multiple European wars. Japan, by contrast, is an island nation, expansive and dynamic, with a history of warlike and imperialistic behavior prior to its defeat in World War II. With a population of 7.3 million, Switzerland is a rather small nation; in fact, after Luxembourg, Denmark, and Norway, it has the smallest population in Western Europe. Japan's population is 127 million, about 40 percent of the population of the United States. Much of Japan's land mass is mountainous and uninhabitable, so most of its people are crowded into coastal cities on Japan's two major islands, Honshu and Kyushu.

The fact that Japan is so often included in comparisons among Western countries reflects the fact that the degree of wealth accumulation, industrialization, and modernization that has occurred in that country makes it appear to be part of the Western world. In fact, however, Japanese industrial might masks the fact that Japanese culture is both highly peculiar to that society and different from Western culture in many ways. For instance, Japanese culture stresses group norms, the suppression of individualism, suspicion of outsiders, harmony, and conflict avoidance. Japan practices a kind of modified capitalism in which the government is highly involved in industrial development and social welfare. Another related perspective is that in Japan there is an emphasis on informal local-based group formation (such as within schools or workplaces) along with a strong emphasis on security and rules within those settings. These elements produce a high level of self-control and consequently a built-in crime-control mechanism. This is in contrast to countries in the Western world such as the United States that emphasize that individual freedoms are superior to the group and where rules are more limited and permissive. The result is a weakening of crime prevention in Western-type nations and the emphasis on punishment rather than prevention (Komiya, 1999; Falsafi, 2010).

Another explanation for the disparity in crime rates between Japan and the United States is the abundant heterogeneity and multiculturalism of United States. These factors have assuredly contributed to the growth of the large American cities where much crime often occurs. Although this may be true, it hardly explains the fact that crime rates actually declined during the years of rapid urbanization and industrialization in Japan, whereas they have gone in the opposite direction in the United States.

Although there may be some validity to different theories as to why Japan has a low crime rate, no clear explanation for the phenomenon exists. It is worth noting that in each neighborhood in Japan, police officers organize both crime prevention and traffic safety associations. These crime prevention associations meet regularly with police, discuss strategies, and organize yearly festivals or other celebrations. The close surveillance over the Japanese population by the police may have some effect on the crime rate. There is wide discretion to avoid arrests in local cases, because local police officers often know all the citizens and can seek different ways to handle criminal situations. Certainly, close surveillance is a factor in the high apprehension rate of offenders in Japan, a rate far surpassing that of Western nations (Bayley, 1991).

Low crime rates in Japan cannot be attributed to high punitiveness in the criminal justice system, however. The incarceration rate is well below that of the United States, and prison sentences are generally short in comparison with those in Western nations. In fact, prison is seen as so much of a last resort in Japanese corrections that only hard-core criminals are sent there. Prison life itself is highly regimented and work oriented in Japan.

Another model country, Saudi Arabia, also has a comparatively low crime rate. It does not participate in the ICVS. Saudi Arabia is not a highly developed country in some ways and is certainly not highly urbanized, despite its great wealth per capita. Also, a sizable portion of the population continues to be nomadic Bedouins, who are unlikely to resort to a formal legal system to settle their disputes and resolve their crime problems.

The Saudis themselves offer two explanations for their low crime rate. The first is that the harsh corporal punishments they employ, which are based on a philosophy of retribution, serve as effective deterrents to crime. The second, and contradictory, explanation is that Saudis commit fewer crimes not for fear of punishment but because of their devotion to the Qur'an (Koran) and its teachings. According to the proponents of this argument, since the criminal law and the punishments for breaking that law are contained in the holy book and merely administered by the government, it is widespread religious belief and practice that inhibits lawbreaking.

One scholar claims that Saudi Arabia was a hotbed of banditry until the fundamentalist regime of King Abdul Assiz created the modern Saudi state in 1932 and the people became more law-abiding (Badr-el-din, 1985). This scholar thus concludes that it was the religious nature of the state that made the difference.

The puzzle remains: Why is it that some societies have been able to maintain low crime rates while succeeding as developed societies and economies? A closer look is needed, not only at crime data but at the variations in the social fabric and criminal justice response of various countries, to see what criminogenic and crime-control forces are at work (see box "Reasons for Crime").

HOW DOES THE UNITED STATES MEASURE UP?

A review of international crime data clearly reveals that the United States has a high level of crime. But that is only part of the story. When we compare the United States to other countries, we see that the American crime problem is really one of violent crime—robbery and murder in particular. The murder rate in the United States is much higher than that of other countries with similar developed societies and economies.

Even though the United States may be safer than some countries in a number of crime categories, crime is still undeniably a major social problem. Why does the United States have such a high rate of violent crime? Among the reasons that have been mentioned are the significant economic disparity between rich and poor, the heterogeneity of the population, the widespread urban areas, and even the extensive images of violence in the media. Many observers claim that the increase in crime is the result of a general disrespect for authority beginning in the 1960s. Others state that the strong influence of drugs, more specifically the increase in the use of crack and cocaine in the 1980s, fueled violent crime rates. Others focus on socioeconomic factors or deterrence (see Bellis et al., 2011; Zimring, 2001).

Some scholars have tried to understand the problem by looking at the historical factors associated with violence. They claim that the United States has historically been a violent nation, with Indian wars, race riots, frontier feuds, and vigilantism as savage norms at various periods of our history (Brown, 1979). Agrarian uprisings and labor conflicts have added to this background of violence. Reed (1974) described violence as one of the distinguishing characteristics of the American South. In addition, assassinations and multiple homicides are not unusual occurrences, at least since the Civil War. By contrast, European nations, with their older civilizations and more homogeneous populations, may have evolved beyond the stage of easy recourse to violence as a way to settle disputes or as a norm in the socialization of young boys.

Easy access to guns is another factor that may contribute to the high homicide rates in the United States. Homicides are most often committed with guns, especially handguns, which is in sharp contrast to most other developed countries, where ownership of guns is strictly regulated (Brandl & Stroshine, 2011). Nevertheless, the presence of motivated offenders, most common in developing countries, also appears to contribute to levels of serious crimes (DeLisi & Conis, 2011). It is difficult to separate the relative importance of different factors in influencing crime rates within countries, as well as across countries, because even a large number of factors explain only a very small proportion of crime (see boxed insert).

Our discussion of the causes of crime is only a brief summary, because thousands of articles and books have been written on the subject of the causes and correlates of crime. In the attempt to make sense of the reasons behind criminal behavior, one fact remains: In most countries today, crime is perceived to be a serious problem that defies an easy solution.

Reasons for Crime: Correlates and Causes

The struggle to understand the causes and circumstances of crime continues through research, policy, and prevention efforts because of the seriousness of the problem and the harm it produces. Causal explanations of crime are varied, and no single explanation accounts for all crime, but these explanations can be grouped into four general types. Summarized in Table 2.4, these four approaches to explaining criminal behavior include classical, positivist, ethical, and structural explanations.

Positivist

The positivist perspective in criminology corresponds with the rise of social science and the scientific method in the late 1800s. Positivism looks to internal or external influences as the cause of criminal behavior. Numerous efforts to explain crime have been attempted, employing some combination of psychological, social, economic, and biological factors, although most rely on social factors (Akers & Sellers, 2008; Williams & McShane, 2009). All these theories have in common the assumption that changes in these conditions will reduce or prevent criminal behavior.

There are many factors that may "push" a person toward a crime, but these factors do not determine that decision. Therefore, positivistic explanations point to conditions that make crime an easy choice, but they do not explain why or how that choice is made, rather than other choices that would not involve committing a crime.

A different type of positivistic approach focuses on "criminal settings" (environments conducive to criminal activity) rather than on the motivations of individuals or groups of people. These rational-choice theories attempt to explain why offenders commit crimes in some situations and not in others by examining how circumstances affect criminal thinking (Cornish & Clarke, 1986). A popular explanation of this type is routine activities theory, described by Marcus Felson. He observed that three things must occur simultaneously for a criminal event to occur: a motivated offender, a suitable target, and the absence of a

TABLE 2.4 Four Approaches to Criminal Behavior

Approach to Crime Causation	Primary Cause of Crime	Prescribed Remedy
Positivist	Internal or external factors (i.e., social, economic, psychological, or biological influences)	Rehabilitation or reform by changing these internal or external conditions, or changing a person's reaction to them.
Classical	Free-will decision guided by hedonistic tendency to maximize pleasure and minimize pain.	Deterrence through threat of apprehension and punishment.
Structural	Political and economic conditions promote a culture of competitive individualism in which individual gain becomes more important than the social good.	More equitable distribution of power and wealth in society, so that all individuals have a greater stake in a better society.
Ethical	Free-will decision is guided by ethical principles in which an individual fails to appreciate an act's wrongfulness and lacks empathy for the victim.	Education and reinforcement in ethical decision making from an early age; reduction of external factors that promote unethical decisions.

capable guardian to intervene (Felson, 2010). According to this view, routine activities of everyday life bring potential offenders and victims together. Changes in society that have led people to work and play farther from home, fewer children to have continuous supervision, and more homes to be empty during the day, along with related social trends, lead to changes in crime rates in neighborhoods and cities because motivated offenders, suitable targets, and absence of guardians are occurring together more often. Therefore, crime control becomes a matter of educating potential victims about being targets and avoiding situations without guardians. This explanation does not deal with the important issue of how motivated offenders develop in the first place, but it states that individuals with low self-control exist and will exploit suitable targets if those targets are not well protected.

Classical

In many ways, the classical perspective is the converse of positivism. Rather than focusing on influential factors that contribute to crime, classicists see crime as the result of a free-will decision to choose it. This free-will decision is guided by the pain-pleasure principle: that is, people always will act in a way that maximizes pleasure and minimizes pain. Classicists believe that people are hedonistic and will naturally seek pleasure at every opportunity and avoid pain. The way to prevent crime, in this view, is through deterrence. Criminal behavior is prevented, therefore, when the pain associated with criminal conduct (i.e., the likelihood of apprehension and punishment) is greater than the pleasure derived from the crime (usually economic gain).

Michael Gottfredson and Travis Hirschi offer a classical explanation that they intend to explain "all crime." They believe that crime results from "the tendency of individuals to pursue short-term gratification in the most direct way with little consideration for the long-term consequences of their acts." This tendency is associated with impulsiveness, aggression, and lack of empathy. They base this theory on the classical assumption that "human behavior is motivated by the self-interested pursuit of pleasure and avoidance of pain" (Hirschi & Gottfredson, 1990, p. 90). Following the classical view, the only effective way to prevent criminal behavior is through the threat of apprehension and punishment that will outweigh (at least in the mind of the offender) the pleasure derived from the criminal conduct.

The problem with the general theory of crime, and with the classical viewpoint in general, is an overemphasis on the impact of penalties for crime prevention. First, deterrence is not very effective in criminal justice because the odds of apprehension are quite low and uncertain. Second, the hedonism, or tendencies toward short-term gratification, must come from somewhere. If they are innate, what prevents the

continued on following page

continued from previous page

majority of us from engaging in a life of crime? If only some of us have these tendencies, where do they come from? Classical explanations have difficulty with these questions.

Structural

The structural perspective focuses less on individual behavior and more on how acts come to be defined as criminal. Social, economic, and political circumstances cause certain behaviors to be defined as criminal, resulting in a great deal of "marginal" criminal behavior, such as gambling, prostitution, and vagrancy. Structuralists argue that we create some of our own organized crime problems by prohibiting gambling unless the state is running the game, or disallowing prostitution unless it is sanctioned by the state. These inconsistencies are viewed by structuralists as a mechanism by which we create illicit markets and then prosecute people for catering to the demand that the state has manufactured (Reiman, 2007).

On the one hand, the structural view can illuminate the inconsistencies in our laws regulating gambling, sex, and other consensual "vices." On the other hand, it offers little help in understanding the behavior of specific individuals who choose to violate the law.

Ethical

The ethical perspective sees crime as a moral failure in decision making. In this view, crime occurs when a person makes a criminal choice because of the failure to appreciate the act's wrongfulness and its impact on the victim. The ethical explanation of criminal conduct recognizes that external factors play a role in influencing some people to engage in crime, but these factors do not cause the crime by themselves, as positivists suggest. In a similar way, the ethical perspective sees a freely willed decision that lies at the base of virtually all criminal behavior, but there is no hedonistic tendency to engage in crime controlled only by the risk of apprehension, as the classicists suggest.

Instead, crime occurs when criminal acts bring pleasure rather than guilt or shame, according to the ethical perspective on crime. Ethicists argue that people are often incapable of thinking through decisions in ethical terms because ethical principles and decision making are rarely part of the educational process and are often not modeled or taught by parents, the educational system, or the larger society. Lacking education and experience with ethical decisions, people often do what comes naturally: They make decisions based on their own self-interest, and they fail to understand or appreciate the legitimate interests of others or of the community at large (Albanese, 2012).

Religious explanations are based on the ethical perspective, arguing that lack of religious values and failure to live a religious lifestyle lead to a proliferation of crime in society. This idea is generally shared in countries that have a "sacred base." That is, they utilize some sacred text (e.g., the Bible, the Talmud, or the Qu'ran) as a basis for law and social control. Countries with a strong sacred and religious base have generally experienced lower crime rates than other countries. The most obvious examples can be found in the Islamic nations of Iran and Saudi Arabia. In these countries, sacred (religious) and secular (nonreligious) laws are not developed or practiced in isolation from each other. Other countries in which sacred or religious principles are deeply ingrained in societal structures include Israel, where Judaism is practiced; India, where the majority of persons practice some form of Hinduism; and Japan, where Buddhism and Confucian thought form a spiritual foundation.

Whether religion does, in fact, reduce crime in a society is not scientifically established. Some have argued that it is questionable to imply that an increase in a person's religiousness will cause a decrease in criminal behavior or delinquency (Sutherland & Cressey, 1974). Yet some research has indicated that religion decreases victimless criminality such as marijuana usage and that in "moral communities" (places where religion is paramount with community members) crime can be reduced (Cochran, 1987; Stark, Kent, & Doyle, 1982).

Quantitative and Qualitative Factors

Other researchers have grouped large numbers of factors to determine the influence on crime rates of such multifaceted concepts as "modernization" or "industrialization" (Howard et al., 2000; Uludag et al., 2009). Criminologist Freda Adler identified 10 "nations not obsessed by crime," including low-crime countries in Western Europe, Latin America, the Middle East, and Asia. Saudi Arabia and Japan, two of our model countries, are included in her list of low-crime societies. Adler examined the influence of 47 different variables on crime rates, from population and per-capita income to education level and divorce rates. She found no strong association between any of these factors and crime rates. She then looked in detail at qualitative factors present in each of the 10 low crime countries and found that "all 10 countries appear to have developed some form of strong social control, outside and apart from the criminal justice system ... [which]

transmit[s] and maintain[s] values by providing for a sharing of norms and by ensuring cohesiveness" (Adler, 1983, p. 130). The 10 countries displayed some combination of historically strong family systems, cohesive local communities, and strong religious institutions, which provide ongoing reinforcement for shared norms and values that contribute to low crime rates. This study is interesting because it recognizes that the failure to develop a better understanding of the causes and prevention of crime may require examination of qualitative factors not yet completely understood or measured effectively.

SUMMARY

We measure crime and compare crime data across nations to determine the types and extent of crime, to identify long-term trends, and to learn why some countries are more successful than others in controlling crime. International crime data collection dates back to the mid-nineteenth century, although there are no comprehensive international crime statistics. Modern sources of international crime data rely largely on the International Crime Victimization Surveys, which have had some remarkable findings:

1. Crime rates have generally been declining in recent years, especially in developed nations.
2. Given the known circumstances of some crimes, more attention should be given to increasing the difficulty of carrying out these crimes (e.g., theft and burglary), which requires crime prevention measures.
3. In crime measurement, more attention needs to be given to serious nonconventional crimes such as organized crime, human trafficking, and corruption.
4. Performance of police in victim satisfaction and in improving victim's perceptions of crime reporting and crime prevention requires greater attention.

Studying variation in crime rates around the world can help us to understand the underlying social factors associated with crime rates and to find ways to mitigate the problem of crime.

Comparative Criminal Justice at the Movies

Movies seek to entertain and inform the audience about a story, incident, or person. Many good movies also hit upon important substantive themes relevant to understanding crime and justice in comparative perspective. Read the movie summary below (and watch the movie if you haven't already) and answer the questions below to make the subject matter connections to comparative criminal justice.

Taken (2008)
Pierre Morel, Director

Human trafficking is considered one of the most serious forms of crime because it often involves kidnapping or coerced enslavement and sexual assault of the victim. Bryan Mills (Liam Neeson) is a retired U.S. government agent who retired to California to be near his teenage daughter Kim (Maggie Grace), who now lives with her mother and wealthy stepfather. Kim convinces her father to allow her to travel to Paris with her friend Amanda. The girls arrive in Paris and let it slip to a stranger that they are alone in France. Based on this information, an Albanian gang of human traffickers kidnap the girls for the purpose of selling them as enslaved prostitutes. Kim has only seconds to call her father and give him some basic information about the attackers.

continued on following page

continued from previous page

The remainder of the film follows Bryan Mills as he searches all over Paris to find his daughter and obtain her release from her captors. Mills' investigative work is remarkable as he quickly pieces together the background and location of the kidnappers using small threads of information. During this process he attempts to obtain information from a French intelligence officer, only to discover later that the officer is protecting the traffickers in an apparent bribery scheme.

After several incredible fight scenes (and escapes), Mills kills a number of traffickers in his search to locate his daughter. He manages to locate her just as she is being taken away in a yacht to be trafficked out of the country.

Questions

1. What crimes discussed in Chapter 2 occur in this movie? Can you describe their elements?
2. Why do you believe that corruption is often found in cases like these to "protect" criminal enterprises like this one from discovery?
3. Why do you believe that human trafficking (discussed further in Chapter 11) is not included in the ICVS, and that no systematic international count of these incidents yet exists?

Critical Thinking Exercise

Critical thinking requires the ability to evaluate viewpoints, facts, and behaviors objectively to assess information and methods of argumentation in order to establish the merit of an action, law, policy or procedure. Please evaluate this scenario objectively, applying your knowledge of comparative criminal justice to the facts of the case presented, and answer the questions that follow it.

Wales Has "Third-Highest Rate of Violent Crime in the World"?

Wales has the third-highest rate of recorded violent crime in the world, according to shocking new figures in a report compiled by a Welsh Assembly Government statistician. Only England and Northern Ireland have recorded higher levels of violent crime, the report says, with alcohol-fuelled fights in Welsh towns and cities helping propel the nation to the top of a list of 39 countries. The only other three countries that recorded more than 1,000 incidents are Austria, New Zealand, and Sweden. Experts said the figures highlight the level of nighttime violence in Wales, but they warned that the figures must be treated with caution because the figures could also be explained by extensive CCTV coverage and enhanced policing at night.

Professor Jonathan Shepherd, director of the Violence Research Group at Cardiff University, said the statistics did not mean Wales was significantly more dangerous than Latvia, which is at the lower end of the table. "The police data for violent crime as a broad category is more a measure of police activity. But it is still safe to say that there is a problem with violence in Wales."

The international crime comparison figures also revealed the murder rate in Wales was just over 10 per 100,000 people, slightly below England, and half the level in Scotland. Lithuania topped the table with nearly 90 murders per 100,000 people. Serious crimes most commonly associated with larger cities, like robbery and burglary, were also more common in England —Wales was 26th out of 41 countries for robbery. Wales had 256 police officers per 100,000 people and was placed 27th out of 41 countries by that measure. Shadow Welsh Secretary Cheryl Gillan said the figures "highlight in stark terms just how far behind many countries Wales has fallen when it comes to reducing many crimes. Behind these figures are individual tales of lives affected and victims left injured. [The] Labour [Party] has failed to get a grip on crime and its causes in Wales and across the UK."

Questions

1. The article's headline is misleading. Why?
2. What did the report being discussed in the article actually compare?
3. The article discusses the level of police activity. Why is that relevant?
4. How would you describe the crime situation in Wales given the data presented in the article?

SOURCE: David James, "Wales Has 'Third Highest Rate of Violent Crime in the World'; Shock at Survey into Recorded Incidents Tally," *The Western Mail*, September 9, 2008, p. 12.

DISCUSSION QUESTIONS

1. Which international crime data do you believe provide the most helpful information? Explain.
2. To what extent can we rely on crime data from other nations? How can we evaluate such data?
3. What factors might contribute to the very low crime rates in Japan? To the relatively higher rates in the United States?
4. Study the tables in the chapter that provide crime data for selected countries and find some with high or low crime rates. Why might there be such a disparity between certain countries?

FOR FURTHER READING

Geneva Declaration Secretariat. (2011). *The Global Burden of Armed Violence.* www.genervadeclaration.org.

Howard, G., G. Newman, and W. A. Pridemore. (2000). "Theory, Method, and Data in Comparative Criminology." In *Measures and Analysis of Crime and Justice* (vol. 4). U.S. Department of Justice, Office of Justice Programs.

Uludag, S., M. Colvin, D. Hussey, and A. L. Eng. (2009). "Democracy, Inequality, Modernization, and Internal Variations in Personal Crime Victimization." *International Criminal Law Review*, vol. 19, 265–286.

Van Dijk, J. (2008). *The World of Crime.* Los Angeles: Sage Publications.

WEB PAGES FOR CHAPTER

http://bjs.ojp.usdoj.gov/ is the website of the U.S. Bureau of Justice Statistics International Justice Statistics. It includes links to international crime data sources.

http://www.unicri.it/wwd/analysis/icvs/publications.php is a summary of major publications and analyses based on the International Crime Victim Surveys.

http://www.genevadeclaration.org/fileadmin/docs/Global-Burden-of-Armed-Violence-full-report.pdf is the report of the Geneva Declaration, which provides a thorough analysis of homicide and violence in countries around the world.

3  Families of Law

Key Terms and Concepts

Canon Law
civil law
Civil Law
commercial law
Common Law
Corpus Juris Civilis
criminal law
habeas corpus
Hudud crime
hybrid legal tradition
indigenous laws
international human rights movement
Islamic law
judicial independence
ombudsman
private law
procurator
public law
Sacred Law
secular law
Shari'a law
Socialist Law
stare decisis
tazirat crime
writ of mandamus

Chapter 3 Learning Objectives

Identify the reasons for international agreements on crime-related matters after World War II.

Examine distinguishing characteristics of each legal family of law.

Understand the various types of laws.

Describe the differences between Civil Law and Socialist Law.

Explain the key aspects of Islamic law.

Thomas Lubanga Dyilo was founder of a rebel group inside the Democratic Republic of the Congo (DRC) in Africa. The rebel group was called the Union of Congolese Patriots (UPC), and Thomas Lubanga Dyilo was president of the UPC and established its military wing, the Patriotic Force for the Liberation of the Congo (FPLC). Under his leadership, the UPC became one of the main actors in the Ituri conflict between the Hema and Lendu ethnic groups. It seized control of the gold-rich Ituri region in 2002 and demanded that the Congolese government recognise Ituri as an autonomous province. The UPC allegedly killed 800 civilians on the basis of their ethnicity and is reported to have destroyed 26 villages in one area, killing at least 350 people and forcing 60,000 to flee their homes. Human rights organizations claimed that Lubanga Dylio had 3,000 child soldiers between the ages of 8 and 15 fighting for him. He reportedly ordered every family in the area under his control to help the war effort by donating something: money, a cow, or a child to join his militia.

Lubanga Dylio was arrested in 2005 in connection with the killing of nine Bangladeshi United Nations peacekeepers in Ituri. In 2006, Lubanga became the first person arrested under a warrant issued by the International Criminal Court for the war crime of "conscripting and enlisting children under the age of fifteen years and using them to participate actively in hostilities." His trial began in 2009, and he was found guilty in 2012. He faces a maximum sentence of life imprisonment (Lubanga Trial, 2012).

SHARED NOTIONS OF JUSTICE

Lubango Dylo was found guilty before a three-judge panel. The judges were from the countries of the United Kingdom, Bolivia, and Costa Rica. The International Criminal Court stepped in when it appeared that, given ongoing conflicts, no government in the region was capable of bringing the suspected war criminal to justice (van Laar, 2011). This case is a remarkable achievement in human history, because countries of very different legal traditions came together around shared notions of justice to ensure that war crimes did not escape accountability.

The International Criminal Court (discussed further in Chapter 7) emerged as part of the **international human rights movement,** which arose after World War II when the nations of the world wanted to prevent incidents like the Holocaust from occurring again. The United Nations was established as a mechanism to channel global human rights and citizen protection efforts during that period, and it adopted of the Universal Declaration of Human Rights (UDHR) in 1948. For the first time in history, the Declaration spelled out basic civil, political, economic, social, and cultural rights that all human beings should enjoy, regardless of the country in which they live. The UDHR, the International Covenant on Civil and Political Rights and its two protocols, and the International Covenant on Economic, Social and Cultural Rights form the so-called International Bill of Human Rights.

A number of enforceable treaties and international conventions have been adopted since 1945, becoming part of international law. When nations ratify these agreements, they assume the obligations to protect the specific human rights by taking specific actions. Most individual nations also have constitutions and laws to protect basic human rights, and the binding international agreements are designed to recognize that these rights are observed everywhere humans exist and are not revoked at the whim of a particular government or leader.

During the last 50 years, more widely shared notions of justice have emerged as countries have communicated through the United Nations and other regional and international organizations about issues of common concern. Specific problems of the status and treatment of women, children, migrants, and the disabled; racial and ethnic discrimination; use of torture; capital punishment; and the civil rights of all citizens are shared concerns about which most countries of the world have reached agreement. There are nine core international human rights instruments (conventions, treaties, and protocols), which were negotiated by the world's nations to spell out these rights and obligations. These instruments are summarized in Table 3.1.

These international agreements were the result of discussion and negotiations among countries from all over the world with different histories, customs, and legal traditions. It is a positive sign that consensus has grown dramatically over the last

TABLE 3.1 The Nine Core International Human Rights Instruments (treaties, conventions, protocols)

There are nine core international human rights instruments. Each of these treaties, conventions, and protocols has established a committee of experts to monitor implementation of its provisions by state parties. Some of these agreements are supplemented by optional protocols dealing with specific related concerns.

International Human Rights Instrument	Abbreviation	Date enacted
International Convention on the Elimination of All Forms of Racial Discrimination	ICERD	21 Dec 1965
International Covenant on Civil and Political Rights	ICCPR	16 Dec 1966
International Covenant on Economic, Social and Cultural Rights	ICESCR	16 Dec 1966
Convention on the Elimination of All Forms of Discrimination against Women	CEDAW	18 Dec 1979
Convention against Torture and Other Cruel, Inhuman or Degrading Treatment or Punishment	CAT	10 Dec 1984
Convention on the Rights of the Child	CRC	20 Nov 1989
International Convention on the Protection of the Rights of All Migrant Workers and Members of Their Families	ICRMW	18 Dec 1990
International Convention for the Protection of All Persons from Enforced Disappearance	CPED	20 Dec 2006
Convention on the Rights of Persons with Disabilities	CRPD	13 Dec 2006
Optional Protocol of the Covenant on Economic, Social and Cultural Rights	ICESCR-OP	10 Dec 2008
Optional Protocol to the International Covenant on Civil and Political Rights	ICCPR-OP1	16 Dec 1966
Second Optional Protocol to the International Covenant on Civil and Political Rights, aimed at the abolition of the death penalty	ICCPR-OP2	15 Dec 1989
Optional Protocol to the Convention on the Elimination of All Forms of Discrimination against Women	OP-CEDAW	10 Dec 1999
Optional protocol to the Convention on the Rights of the Child, on the involvement of children in armed conflict	OP-CRC-AC	25 May 2000
Optional protocol to the Convention on the Rights of the Child, on the sale of children, child prostitution, and child pornography	OP-CRC-SC	25 May 2000
Optional Protocol to the Convention against Torture and Other Cruel, Inhuman or Degrading Treatment or Punishment	OP-CAT	18 Dec 2002
Optional Protocol to the Convention on the Rights of Persons with Disabilities	OP-CRPD	12 Dec 2006

half-century, but it is important to recognize the historical basis for the different legal traditions in place around the world. These legal traditions, or families of law, continue to guide the operation of the police, courts, and corrections within individual countries. International bodies, like the International Criminal Court, attempt to merge the best parts of each of three legal traditions to adjudicate international crimes (Findlay and Henham, 2012; Jackson and Summers, 2012; Schiff , 2012).

HISTORICAL ORIGINS OF LEGAL TRADITIONS

According to the biblical Book of Exodus, Moses went up to Mount Sinai, where God gave him a tablet of stone listing ten rules. These rules, called the Ten Commandments, are familiar to most of us; they include "Thou shalt not murder," "Thou shalt not steal," and "Thou shalt not commit adultery." The Ten Commandments formed the basis of a code of ethics and, in some cases, a body of laws that has guided Western civilization for several thousand years. They are written rules that tell people what is and is not illegal and unethical behavior in the eyes of God. These rules also tell people what behavior will be punished by the state, in the many instances where governments have adopted religious traditions as part of their law.

Another prominent Jewish leader in ancient times, the wise King Solomon, made it his practice to settle disputes among his subjects by having them appear and present their cases to him in person. According to the famous biblical story, two women claiming the same baby appeared before Solomon so that he could decide which of them was the real mother. Solomon ordered his guards to cut the baby in half and give each woman half. One woman immediately spoke up and said that she would relinquish her claim to the baby rather than have the child killed. Solomon awarded the baby to this woman, pronouncing that the true mother would be more concerned with the baby's welfare than with her personal claim. The bible presents this story to exemplify the wisdom of Solomon. In contrast to the Ten Commandments of Moses, which represent rules of conduct for people to follow, the story of Solomon and the baby reflects a different kind of rule making, one based on responding to cases as they arise.

All legal systems of modern nation-states combine the kinds of rule making that are typified in the stories of Moses and Solomon. In other words, all modern legal systems combine written laws that place limits on behavior (code-based systems), together with rules developed from decisions handed down in particular cases (case-based systems).

There is a difference in emphasis and historical traditions in code-based systems and case-based systems, which will be noted as we refer to the different legal systems of the world as "legal families" or "legal traditions." Although used interchangeably, these terms technically do not have the same meaning. *Legal system* is the term used to refer to the agencies, procedures, and rules that make up how a country makes laws, enforces laws, and dispenses justice. *Legal families* or *legal traditions* are broader terms used to understand the legal system and the cultural and historical foundations of that system (Merryman, 1985; Glen, 2000). These terms allow us to place specific systems within a family or tradition and make general statements about the law and process of justice in a country.

Unfortunately, any classification scheme conceals individual differences. Because each nation in the world has its own distinct family or tradition, and none rely solely on the elements of a single tradition, it is possible to claim that there are really no clear-cut or "pure" Common Law, Civil Law, Socialist Law, or Sacred Law legal traditions present in the world today. For example, a country may incorporate elements of the Civil Law with Common Law or Civil Law with Socialist Law. The most typical form of borrowing is to combine some aspects of the Common Law and Civil Law systems. Because many countries borrow from others, we could add a fifth legal tradition to our classification scheme and say that all countries have a **hybrid legal tradition,** or one that combines different aspects of more than one legal tradition.

Technically, the hybrid legal tradition is the most common of the legal traditions because most countries borrow some aspects of criminal justice from other countries or from multiple religious traditions. For our purposes, however, we restrict using the term *hybrid legal tradition* only to countries that have not historically or politically developed one clear or primary legal tradition. For example, the legal traditions of many former colonized nations in Africa and elsewhere can be easily called hybrids because they do not fall into one of the more common legal families. Among the countries whose traditions are considered hybrids of this sort are Japan, Egypt, Indonesia, Myanmar, the Philippines, Scotland, and South Africa. Japan may offer the best example of this hybrid form. The Japanese began to inculcate Roman Civil Law into their legal tradition in the late 1800s, were strongly influenced by German law in the early 1900s, and added elements of Common Law after World War II. Less obvious are the other hybrid combinations in countries such as China and India that combine the ancient sacred traditions of Confucianism and Hinduism, respectively, into their current legal traditions.

In subsequent chapters, we will discuss the development of a hybrid legal tradition in Japan in more detail. In this chapter, however, and throughout the book, we will concentrate on four major traditions or families: Civil Law, Common Law, Socialist Law, and Sacred Law. We have chosen to describe the legal families in this common form although we acknowledge that others are present in the literature (e.g., Glen, 2000). Table 3.2 lists several nations within the four main legal families.

ROOTS OF ANCIENT LEGAL TRADITIONS

This chapter cannot include all the different kinds of legal traditions in history, or even all those practiced in the world today. Many legal traditions that were used for centuries or that exist today in a few places will be mentioned briefly. We refer to some legal traditions as *ancient* because they originated centuries ago and are now extinct. *Lesser employed* describes legal traditions that are currently used somewhere in the world but are specific to only one or a limited number of countries and geographic regions.

Many ancient and now extinct legal families have been recorded in history. According to John Henry Wilmore, who conducted the most comprehensive study of the evolution of the different legal families, there have been 16 major forms of legal systems in the world; Table 3.3 lists these ancient and historical legal systems. Four of these ancient systems—Egyptian, Mesopotamian, Chinese, and Hebrew—are discussed here because they helped to form much of the foundation for our modern legal families.

The oldest known formal legal system was the Egyptian system, which is believed to date back as far as 4000 B.C. Egyptian rulers developed an extensive system for handling legal procedures that included codes to direct citizen behaviors and a judicial system to handle disputes (Wilmore, 1936). Around the same time, the Mesopotamian system emerged in the Near East; it lasted until the first century B.C.. The Mesopotamian system is best known for the development of the Code of

TABLE 3.2 Examples of Countries Representing the Four Major Families of Law

Family of Law	Representative Countries
Civil Law legal tradition	Belgium, Chile, France, Germany, Italy, Luxembourg, Portugal, Spain
Common Law legal tradition	Australia, Canada, England, India, New Zealand, United States
Socialist Law legal tradition	China, Cuba, North Korea, Vietnam
Sacred Law legal tradition	Iran, Malaysia, Nigeria, Pakistan, Saudi Arabia, Sudan

TABLE 3.3 Ancient Legal Systems in History

Egyptian
Mesopotamian
Chinese
Hindu
Hebrew
Greek
Roman
Maritime
Japanese
Mohammedan
Celtic
Germanic
Slavic
Ecclesiastical
Romanesque
Anglican

Hammurabi, king of Babylon. Hammurabi's code sought to prevent the strong from oppressing the weak. The code contained 282 laws covering such matters as property rights, renting, and medical treatment. The most famous passage in the code was the law stating "an eye for an eye, a tooth for a tooth," which was later included in the Old Testament (Grove, 1997).

Some 1,500 years after the Egyptian legal system began, the Chinese developed their own legal system, much of it rooted in the philosophy of a man popularly known as Confucius (c. 551–479 B.C.). Confucianism is, in fact, more of a moral system that stresses the development of individual moral virtue (through duties owed to family members and friends) as an alternative to the coercive power of the state in producing good behavior. It has influenced Chinese governmental and educational practices, and individual attitudes toward correct personal behavior and duty to society.

Hebrew law, also called Talmudic law, is rooted in the word of God as revealed to Moses. Developed around 1200 B.C. as a result of the birth of Judaism around 2000 B.C., Hebrew law is found in the first five books of the Hebrew Torah (constituting the Christian Pentateuch—Genesis, Exodus, Leviticus, Numbers, and Deuteronomy). Hebrew law includes the Torah and the Talmud, a guide to both civil and religious laws, as well as other writings. Judaism began before the time of Christ with Moses's receiving the two tablets of stone and the subsequent recording of the first five books of the Bible.

Indigenous Law

In addition to religious laws practiced in religious communities, many forms of indigenous law are observed throughout the world. **Indigenous laws** are native laws of persons who originate from or live in a particular area. Although the term *indigenous* is the most common term used when describing persons or laws that originate from a certain area, other common terms used to describe them are *native, aboriginal*, or the more recently adapted term *chthonic.* The latter term, rooted in the Greek word *kthonos*, or earth, describes people who live ecological lives and live in close harmony with the earth (Goldsmith, 1992).

Approximately 200 million persons, about 4 percent of the world's population, are included in the 3,000 indigenous nations present in the world today (Rosen, 1992; Lauderdale, 1997). There are literally thousands of indigenous laws that have influenced legal systems throughout the world. In some isolated areas, indigenous laws have contributed to the formation of small, private legal societies. Just as we speak of Common (U.S.), Socialist (Chinese), or Sacred-Islamic (Saudi Arabian) law, anthropologists speak about Tongan, Tiv, or Zapotec law in the South Pacific islands, African bush, and Mexican mountains, respectively. In each of these societies, the definition of what is a crime and how to settle disputes and punish criminals varies considerably (Lubman, 1983).

In the United States, indigenous law is practiced by Native Americans on reservations. One example is the Navajo nation, which calls for traditional justice to be swift, direct, and personal and emphasizes restoration of harmony and reacceptance into the community rather than punishment and ostracism (Armstrong, Guilfoyle, & Melton, 1996). Similarly, indigenous laws are practiced by the aboriginal populations of Australia, New Zealand, and Asia; throughout the Americas; and in many regions of Africa. In Nigeria, the most serious crimes are tried in federal courts that are run according to the British-imposed English Common Law. However, all other offenses are still heard by tribal (indigenous) courts of justice based on native laws and customs. In southern Nigeria these laws are unwritten, whereas in the northern regions they are available in written form (Ebbe, 1996).

PUBLIC, PRIVATE, CIVIL, AND CRIMINAL LAW

Before proceeding with the discussion of the main legal families in the world today, a few terms that will be used with some frequency from now on need to be explained. These are *public law*, *private law*, *civil law*, and *criminal law*.

Public law is law developed by modern states in their legislatures or through their regulatory processes. It deals largely with the relations between governments and citizens. It includes constitutional law, criminal law, tax law, environmental law, and the myriad other laws that bodies like Congress pass each year. Most statutory law today is public law, designed to regulate the relationship between citizens and agencies of the government.

Private law, by contrast, is the law that regulates behavior between individuals that involves no large public interest. It involves contracts, torts, inheritances, wills, marriage and family matters, and private property matters. Although private law is promulgated and enforced through the state either in codes or in case law, it tends to evolve slowly and in general does not have the political dimensions or implications of public law because it involves disputes between private parties.

Another term for private law is **civil law**, especially in Anglo-Saxon legal systems. It is distinguished from criminal law because, at least in modern times, **criminal law** is defined as an offense against the state rather than as a dispute between individuals. In all criminal cases, whether major or minor, the state—not the victim—is technically the aggrieved party, and it is the state that has the obligation to see that justice is done. So a theft or robbery involves an individual victim, but these offenses are crimes because they pose a threat to the social order and are therefore part of the criminal law. They represent more than private disputes between individuals. In this way, the state fulfills its obligation to maintain the public order and to minimize episodes of private vengeance. Because of the potentially severe consequences for an accused person convicted of a crime (denial of liberty), standards of proof and details of procedure in criminal cases are usually more stringent than in civil cases, where only monetary compensation is usually at stake.

The distinction between civil law and criminal law, which exists in all modern systems of law, creates a certain amount of confusion when one is talking about families of law. The confusion arises because one major family of law is known as the Civil Law family. Although there are some historical reasons this family of law has the same name as the branch of law that is distinguished from criminal law, the term *Civil Law family* is used to denote the entire legal culture of a nation that uses that tradition, not just the noncriminal aspects of that nation's law. These terms may seem confusing at present, but their meaning will become clearer as we consider issues like criminal procedure in Civil Law systems.

The Civil Law family is sometimes called the Continental, Romano-Germanic, or Roman Law because its origins are in the old Roman Code of Justinian and the laws of the Germanic tribes, such as the Franks and the Bavarians, that bordered the Roman Empire in central Europe and eventually conquered most of Europe (Ehrmann, 1976; David & Brierly, 1978). Although the terms other than Civil Law avoid the problems of confusion between the Civil Law family and civil law in general, they present another problem, because most texts and histories continue to use the term Civil

Law to distinguish that family of legal systems from the other major families. To make the matter less complicated in this book, we will capitalize *Civil Law* when it denotes the family of law and lower-case *civil law* when it refers to noncriminal law.

Historically, the Civil Law, Common Law, and Sacred Law developed over the course of centuries, whereas Socialist Law was a twentieth-century phenomenon. As a result, the Civil Law and Common Law have changed quite radically over time, whereas Socialist Law did not undergo major transformations until recently. With the collapse of communist governments in Eastern Europe and the Soviet Union, and the efforts to modernize the economy in China, major changes are occurring in Socialist Law in the twenty-first century.

Similarly, Sacred Law, largely practiced as Islamic law, is based on the Qur'an, the holy book of Islam, but it has also been extended by the commentaries of major schools of Islamic scholars. In the remainder of this chapter, we will examine how these major legal systems arrived at their current place in history.

THE CIVIL LAW

The Civil Law tradition is the most pervasive legal tradition in the world. It is found throughout Western Europe, in Latin America, and in parts of Africa and the Far East. Indeed, it was historically the basis of law in socialist countries, and Socialist Law, although classified separately, has many elements of the Civil Law. As noted earlier, the Civil Law is sometimes called Romano-Germanic, Roman, or Continental law because of its historical roots.

The **Civil Law** is code-based law. A centerpiece of the Civil Law tradition is codification, or the absolute primacy of written codes of law (Friedrichs, 2001). Civil Law is like the Ten Commandments of Moses, which were published so that all people could know and follow them. Four major codifications of law, each building on the previous one, are involved in the history of the Civil Law. These are the Roman Law of the emperor Justinian, the Canon Law of the medieval Catholic Church, the Napoleonic Code of early nineteenth-century France, and the German Law of the People (*Bürgerliches Gesetzbuch*), which was compiled under Otto von Bismarck after the German Empire was established in 1870. In each case, the legal code derived from earlier laws, customs, and informal regulations (Ehrmann, 1976; David & Brierly, 1978; Glendon, Gordon, & Osakwe, 1985; Merryman, 1985).

Writing a set of laws is not as simple as it may sound. As in writing constitutions, the framers must be concise, must cover all contingencies, and must not depart radically from accepted custom. The laws must be at once general enough to allow for particular cases to fit into the scope of legal rules, and also specific enough to provide adequate guidance for those whose job it is to administer the law. The different incarnations of the Civil Law met these requirements with varying degrees of success.

Roman Law

In the sixth century A.D., the Byzantine emperor Justinian arranged for the compilation and codification of the law then in force in the Roman world. The result was the **Corpus Juris Civilis**, also known as the Institutes of Justinian. Included in this code were laws pertaining to family, property, torts, and contracts.

Justinian's goal was to simplify the massive amounts of legal materials, understood only by legal counselors and often contradictory or unclear, that made up the laws of the empire. After the code was compiled, Justinian ordered that all previous works of legal commentary and all previous law be disregarded. He also forbade commentary on his own code by legal scholars. (Obviously, lawyers who obfuscated the law and made themselves indispensable through their specialized knowledge of different branches of the law were a problem in Justinian's time as well as our own.) Although learned commentaries by legal scholars are very important in Civil Law countries today, the judicial tradition of referring to the law itself rather than to precedents established in prior cases remains an essential part of the Civil Law tradition and an important feature that distinguishes it from the Common Law.

The Institutes of Justinian, although gradually modified through contact with local legal traditions, especially Germanic tribal law, remained enormously influential. In fact, it became both the basis of legal study in medieval universities and the backbone of some national legal systems during the period of the development of nation-states in the sixteenth and seventeenth centuries. Even today, law students in countries that use the Civil Law must take a course in the Corpus Juris Civilis, or Roman law.

Canon and Commercial Law

Although Roman law remained a source of law throughout Europe for many centuries, the Roman Catholic Church developed its own law, **Canon Law**, which dealt with church and spiritual matters. Canon Law goes back to the fourth century, claiming its roots in divine law as decreed by the Pope and other church authorities and administered by ecclesiastical, or church, courts. Church officials, usually priests with training in Canon Law, preside over these courts. Canon Law includes provisions regulating family life and morals, as well as rules for church governance. Over the years it has been influential on Western laws related to marriage, inheritance, property, contracts, crimes of torts, and judicial procedure (Berman, 1983). Today, Canon Law is still used to govern matters within the Catholic Church; one of the most common usages of the law is the granting of marriage annulments (Friedrichs, 2001).

It is hard for us today to realize that two systems of law, claiming authority over different matters and running separate court systems, could have coexisted in medieval Europe. In truth, however, this is no stranger than the dual court systems (state and federal) and the sometimes overlapping state and federal laws that exist in the United States. Although there were jurisdictional disputes in specific cases, and the church tended to assume simultaneous jurisdiction in some matters regarding family relations, this dual court system seems to have worked quite well overall.

As trade and commerce among nations became more complex, an important new body of law, commercial law, developed in Europe during the Middle Ages. **Commercial law** is a body of legislation that deals with the exchange of goods between cities or nations. This law developed initially in the large merchant cities of Italy, but it was soon adopted by other countries and became, like Roman and Canon Law, a kind of internationally accepted law in Europe.

With the rise of nation-states, the Protestant Reformation, and the seemingly endless wars that wracked Europe in early modern times, much of the commercial law fell into disuse or was practiced only partially, in conjunction with local customary law. Various rulers made more or less successful efforts to codify the laws of their countries. It was not until the early nineteenth century, however, that a legal code rivaling that of Justinian in terms of influence and comprehensiveness was drawn up. This was the famous French Civil Code of 1804, or Napoleonic Code, named after the French emperor Napoleon, who ordered its development.

The Napoleonic Code

The revolution of 1789 was a major turning point in French history. The revolutionaries abolished the hereditary monarchy, executed King Louis XVI and Queen Marie Antoinette, and proclaimed a republic based on the principles of liberty, equality, and fraternity. A period of turmoil and confusion ensued that featured several attempts toward republican government during the 1790s. Napoleon Bonaparte, a Corsican by birth, gradually rose to power due to his military and administrative genius, his ambition, and his ability to take advantage of the deteriorating political situation in France. Eventually, Napoleon made himself the first emperor of France and enacted a series of governmental reforms that significantly changed the administrative and legal structures of that country. After numerous military adventures, Napoleon's career ended at the famous Battle of Waterloo in 1815. His governmental reforms, however, including the civil code, the administrative court structures, and the local governmental structures of France, have survived.

The case of Napoleon and the civil code exemplifies what often happens when a postrevolutionary or post-conquest government takes over in a country. One of the best ways to discredit previous governments, and to consolidate the power of the new government, is to throw out the old laws and create new ones. Legal and judicial personnel, those with a major stake in the prevailing system, are usually purged at the same time. As we will see, this is what happened in England at the time of the development of the Common Law. It is also what happened in the twentieth century in communist countries such as the former Soviet Union, China, and Cuba. Often, these radical changes eventually accommodate themselves to existing traditional practices and rules.

The Napoleonic Code was drawn up by legal experts and went into effect in 1804. These experts brought together in one code much of the law that was practiced in various parts of France—some based on Canon Law, some on Roman law, some on commercial law, and some on the feudal practices in existence before the revolution. But the code-makers went much further, also incorporating into this code many of the new ideas about private property and relations between people fueled by the Enlightenment. Therefore, this code was the first set of truly modern laws.

The Napoleonic Code consisted of 2,281 rules, or articles, covering a variety of subjects: persons (including marriage, divorce, and family law), property, torts, and contracts (Schwartz, 1956). This body of law was to supersede all law that had been in use in France prior to the Revolution. Since part of its objective was to create a body of law that would not depend on interpretation by lawyers, the code-makers aimed to create law that was simple, easy to understand, nontechnical, and accessible to the masses. In this they generally succeeded, and the Napoleonic Code has come down to us as a paradigm of a spare, well-written, well-conceived, and comprehensive code that somehow typifies the vaunted French spirit of rationalism. As Merryman observes:

> The French Civil Code of 1804 was envisioned as a kind of popular book that could be put on the shelf next to the family Bible. It would be a handbook for the citizen, clearly organized and stated in straightforward language, that would allow citizens to determine their legal rights and obligations by themselves. (1985, p. 28)

Of course, women today would find many of the provisions of the French Civil Law to be unacceptable. Husbands were given authority over their wives, who owed them obedience. Wives could not sell or buy property, or even receive free property, without their husband's permission. Husbands had control over community property and could administer any property a wife brought to a marriage (Tunc, 1956, p. 36).

Napoleon's influence on the criminal law was even more extensive than on the civil law. He fostered the Code Penale of 1810, a truly harsh criminal law. Napoleon had little sympathy for lawbreakers and believed in the deterrent effect of severe penalties. Postrevolutionary France was going through a period of lawlessness and high crime rates, and the French people were inclined to support a stern criminal code (Wright, 1983, p. 53). Throughout the nineteenth century, the Napoleonic Code exerted a major influence on other countries that sought to codify their laws.

The earliest countries to adopt the French code were those that were conquered by Napoleon: Belgium, the Netherlands, Poland, and part of Germany. France also exported its codes to its colonies in Africa and the Near and Far East, and even to its former colonies in North America, including Quebec (in Canada) and the State of Louisiana (in the United States). Louisiana, because of its direct influence from a French legal heritage, retained many elements from the Napoleonic Code, including elements of contract law and marital property law. Over time, however, Louisiana law has been revised to conform with the principles of the Common Law tradition (Friedrichs, 2001).

The German Civil Code

Almost a century passed between the time that the Napoleonic Code went into effect and the time that Germany developed its own civil code. Whereas the French code was a model of simplicity, the German code was long, academic, and complex. In addition, the French code had been drawn up in the course of a few years, but it took 20 years to put together the German code. Although both the German and French codes represented attempts to pull together and control new nations, the unification of Germany took place in 1871, but the code did not actually go into effect until 1900. The German code was the end result of a massive scholarly effort to study previous law, develop a philosophy of law, and provide a rational basis for legal development. Much local (indigenous) law was incorporated into the German code. It shared with the French, however, roots in Roman law and post-feudal ideas about property and personal rights (Glendon, Gordon, & Osakwe, 1985).

The Importance of the French and German Civil Codes

Both the French and the German codes have been enormously influential in the development of law over the past two centuries. First, both codes were developed during a time of increasing industrialization and expansion of worldwide commerce and trade. Common rules governing contracts and property, as well as individual obligations and rights, were needed to facilitate trade and were crucial in the development of modern industrial society. In addition, imperialism was at its height, fostering cross-national adaptation of laws and legal structures. Further, as new countries formed and older countries sought to modernize in the postcolonial era, and as revolutions and political changes created a need for rules of development, the importation of a full code of laws simplified the process.

Common legal codes also helped to unify new nations, just as they did in postrevolutionary France and postunification Germany, and perhaps will do so in the newly formed Russian republics. The development of indigenous (local) codes, or gradually defining the law through case precedents, as in the case of Common Law, takes many decades. Therefore, unified civil codes provided an umbrella of legal rules, which were adapted to some degree according to local circumstances and local traditions.

Even Iran, which had previously adopted the Civil Law but in 1979 rejected the system in favor of a return to Islamic law, continues to be influenced by the Civil Law in some areas of endeavor, especially with regard to trade and commerce. It is probably no exaggeration to say that the Civil Law is a kind of common denominator for international private law transactions throughout the world today. Thus, the Civil Law will tend to grow in influence as multinational economic cooperation grows and as trade barriers fall in Europe and other parts of the world.

THE COMMON LAW

The **Common Law** is more ancient, more complex, and more difficult than the French or German civil codes. In Anglo-Saxon countries, the Common Law's peculiarities have shaped not only the legal tradition but also a good part of the legal education, criminal procedure, and general approach to law and government. To understand the nature of the Common Law system, we need to look at a few major landmarks in the history of its development.

The King's Court

When William the Conqueror, a French (Norman) nobleman, defeated the English (Saxons) at the Battle of Hastings in 1066 and became king of England, he faced the usual problems of trying to rule a conquered nation. William insisted that French be spoken, but the Saxon language persisted throughout his new kingdom. In general, William found that it was easier to conquer the English than to rule them.

We must remember that this occurred in the eleventh century, some 800 years before Napoleon decided to strengthen his hold on the French people by developing a code of law that they would all have to follow. In William's time, the feudal system was in full sway on the Continent, and the law itself was a peculiar amalgam of Canon Law, feudal customs, and remnants of Roman law that existed throughout Europe. In this era, the civil codes did not have the importance that they would assume in the Enlightenment Europe of Napoleon's time. Therefore, William could not simply call for a new code of laws to usurp the power of the local gentry. He had resources and imagination, however, and he found ways, including taxation and use of the French language, to impose his will on his subjects.

One of the ways that William and his Norman successors consolidated power was to set up courts, known collectively as the King's Court, or Curia Regis. The kings appointed the judges of these courts, and the judges traveled around the countryside, ruling on disputes that had not been settled in the local courts or hearing appeals from the local courts. King Henry II, known as the Father of Common Law, was the most prominent of the twelfth-century judicial pioneers.

Thus, England was the first European country to set up a centralized system of courts available to all free men in the kingdom. This system of courts actually built upon an English tradition of centralized kingly authority that existed before William's time and that contrasted with the prevailing system in Europe, consisting of many competing regional powers (Plucknett, 1940; Van Caenegem, 1973).

Like Solomon, however, the judges of the English courts did not refer to a specific body of laws as a standard for deciding cases. Presumably, they decided crucial political cases in a way that would benefit the king. For conventional cases, however, the judges typically based their decisions on a combination of common sense and local norms and laws.

Although the law itself was not previously defined, the jurisprudence of the King's Court came to be characterized by common procedures, or rules for handling cases. (To this day, procedural matters are crucial to the Common Law.) Over time, a body of law developed that was based on the decisions of the judges of the King's Court. As new cases arose, the judges referred to similar previous cases as authority for their decisions. This established the importance of the precedent as a way of deciding cases. The Latin term **stare decisis** (literally, "it stands decided") is used in Common Law countries to signify the legal force of precedent. Adherence to precedent resulted in the gradual development of rules that were uniform throughout the kingdom. These rules came to be known as the Common Law because they were common to all Englishmen, and thus distinguished from other rules and laws that existed in each local region.

The early kings set up the King's Court as a way to strengthen their power. But over time (after William's and Henry's time to be sure), the force of the rules and precedents that were developed in the Common Law courts was so great that a tradition of **judicial independence** arose. In other words, judges of the Common Law courts saw themselves as bound by the law rather than by the desires of the ruler. Judicial independence is something that we take so much for granted these days, but we forget the long history of political regimes in which absolute rulers made rules, enforced them, and decided cases that arose under them.

Equity Courts

Judicial independence was not really a welcome development to William's successors on the English throne. In addition, the Common Law itself became increasingly cumbersome and rigid in application. Therefore, the practice arose of appealing directly to the king to rule on cases that did not fit well into the Common Law structure. By the fifteenth century, a new set of courts, known as chancery courts, or equity courts, had developed.

As the name implies, equity courts and the law that they administered dealt with efforts to obtain justice, or fairness. The courts did this by developing a set of practices known as equity procedures that helped people bring their cases to court without hazarding the use of the complex Common Law system. Some equity procedures are familiar to us even today. For example, the **writ of mandamus** orders public servants to perform the duties that are part of their jobs. Injunctions are court orders designed to prevent harms that would occur before a case could work its way through the regular court systems.

The United States and England no longer have separate equity courts to handle equity cases; instead, equity cases are now handled by the regular courts. Originally, however, these equity courts were a major innovation, once again making the king more powerful in legal matters. As the equity courts became entrenched, however, they became as rule-bound as the Common Law courts. Further, the judges of the equity courts developed the same inconvenient habit of judicial independence that their Common Law brethren had before them. Thus, English kings again had to set up new courts to do their personal bidding. Star Chamber courts and Courts of High Commission became notorious in the seventeenth century for their ruthless persecution of the kings' enemies (Prall, 1966).

The Modern History of the Common Law

With the decline in the power of the monarchy and the ascendancy of Parliament, the English court system stabilized. Judicial independence was now taken for granted and no longer considered a problem by the English rulers. Even Oliver Cromwell and his Puritan followers, who overthrew the Stuart kings and established a commonwealth in England between 1648 and 1660, feared the possible destabilizing effects of sweeping changes in the law. Cromwell thus made no major effort to supersede the Common Law (Prall, 1966). The English legal system remained a complex system of rules and precedents, interpreted with small shades of meaning and requiring a body of legal experts to deal with it. These legal experts had to serve long apprenticeships to become familiar with the vast number of cases and precedents that would govern their decisions.

The Development of Criminal Procedure. The fact that the Common Law is based on precedent does not mean that this law is not written down in one place. In the eighteenth century, William Blackstone set out to compile all the laws in effect in England up to that time. His monumental work, *Blackstone's Commentaries*, constituted a major step forward in English legal history. Since Blackstone's time, the Common Law has continued to be compiled and brought up to date in various collections.

For most of its existence, the Common Law addressed all matters likely to need settlement in court—not only private concerns such as contracts, property disputes, family questions, and torts against individuals, but also criminal offenses (Holmes, 1923). More important than the actual delineation of criminal offenses was the development of Common Law criminal procedure. Most of the criminal procedure rules that are set forth in the Fourth, Fifth, Sixth, and Eighth Amendments to the U.S. Constitution, as well as the rules about bringing the accused before a judge to question his incarceration (**habeas corpus**), were adapted from Common Law rules and from Parliamentary decrees based on the Common Law. The concern in U.S. courts with detailed criminal procedures, which often seems excessive to people in Civil Law countries, has its origin in the English Common Law criminal procedure. As we will discuss in Chapter 6, the development of criminal procedure in England was a slow process that paralleled the development of the adversarial trial system.

The Definition of Crimes. The definition of crimes themselves, as opposed to the procedure for adjudicating those accused of crimes, has gradually become part of public statutory law rather than case law. For example, when we say that murder is a crime in the state of New York, this is as a result of a law passed by the legislature of that state making murder a crime and prescribing a penalty for the commission of this crime. Of course, murder was also a crime under the Common Law, so it may seem unnecessary to have a statute that outlaws the act. The chief difference is in the penalties attached to various crimes. Thus, when New York passes a law outlawing murder, it has prescribed different penalties at various times in its history, and these penalties are not the same as those that were usually imposed under the Common Law. Therefore, the statutory law is used to both update and codify the case-based results of Common Law.

With the rise of legislative democracy in both England and the United States, the actual rule-making power of the Common Law (through case decisions) was eclipsed by the rule-making power of the legislatures (through codifying laws and penalties). Indeed, in a constitutional system such as that of the United States, the very fact that all laws must be in conformity with state or federal constitutions suggests that a "pure" Common Law, in which judges make the law, no longer exists. Criminal law has been codified for many years, and much lawmaking is concerned with administrative agency regulations and with formerly private regulations such as those dealing with marriage, divorce, and other family concerns.

The Current Status of the Common Law. Does this mean that the Common Law is dying out or dead in the modern world? To answer this question, we need to consider the continued importance of judge-made law in the United States. Constitutional law, in which judges interpret the Constitution based on the precedents of previous interpretations of this document, is a good example. The U.S. Supreme Court, in the 1961 case *Mapp v. Ohio*, interpreted the Constitution's guarantee against unreasonable searches and seizures to mean that evidence obtained by state authorities through an illegal search may not be used at trial. This decision meant that the Exclusionary Rule, formerly required in federal cases, was extended to the states. Subsequent to that decision, the Supreme Court handed down many further interpretations of the dimensions of illegal searches, in each case building on its previous decisions—sometimes extending the scope of police power to search, and other times restricting it (Albanese, 2008). In effect, the judges are continuing to make law built on precedent, in the tradition of the Common Law, even though the source of this law is a fixed statutory or constitutional prescription.

In the Common Law countries, the traditions of the Common Law—its use of precedent, its historically developed procedural forms—continue to be a vital part of the legal process despite the fact that most law has become statutory in modern times. Ironically, the United States, with its need for constant interpretation of constitutional provisions to define the parameters of state and federal relations and of relations between individuals and the state, has become a nation that is more deeply wedded to the Common Law tradition of judge-made law than in England, where Parliament is supreme. U.S. judges have much more discretionary lawmaking power than do English judges.

The Common Law tradition also continues to have a major influence in legal education. In Common Law countries, legal education traditionally occurred through apprenticeship, with the budding lawyer learning large numbers of cases that formed the various precedents necessary for understanding the law. Law schools have largely replaced apprenticeships in the United States, but law school education focuses chiefly on the case law method, thus emphasizing the Common Law tradition and preparing the lawyer to operate within that tradition. In England, trial lawyers are trained at the Inns of Court, essentially continuing the apprenticeship tradition. Civil Law legal education is a less practical, more academic course of study that includes a good deal of philosophy, history, and liberal arts education. Apprenticeships in Civil Law systems follow formal legal education. Case precedents will not be binding on the practicing lawyer and are thus not emphasized in legal education.

Table 3.4 compares and highlights major attributes of the Civil Law and Common Law legal traditions. It can be seen that both now rely heavily on statutory rule making, although case precedents remain an important part of Common Law systems. In addition, the adjudication process in Common Law systems includes public participation as jurors, a feature absent from Civil Law systems.

TABLE 3.4 Major Features of the Civil and Common Law Systems

Civil Law Characteristics	Common Law Characteristics
Law and procedure governed by comprehensive codes of rules to anticipate all situations.	Law and procedure governed by both law and case precedents, which use past cases to guide future decisions.
Legal codes developed through scholarly analysis.	Laws and precedents based on the experience of practitioners from past cases.
Appellate courts apply law according to legal codes with little interpretation.	Appellate courts develop law through their interpretation and decisions.
Adjudication process designed to establish the truth.	Adjudication process designed to culpability only within rules of evidence.
Adjudication process run by lawyers and judges.	Citizens have direct input in their grand jury and trial jury roles.
No presumption of innocence for the accused.	Presumption of innocence for the accused.

THE SOCIALIST LAW

Socialist Law has its origins in socialism, which is a system characterized by the absence of classes and by common ownership of the means of production and livelihood. The political, economic, and social term used to describe socialism is *communism*. Karl Marx (1818–1883) was the major proponent of communist ideology. Marx believed that the current economic system (capitalism) was one that exploited the masses (the proletariat) and supported those who controlled the economic resources (the bourgeoisie). Eventually, Marx predicted, the proletariat would revolt and eliminate the bourgeoisie, and socialism would replace capitalism as the economic system of choice.

Marx addressed the issue of crime when he stated that, after a true communist society was established, the state would "wither away" and there would be no further need of criminal law or sanctions to deal with lawbreakers. In this ideal society, cooperation and concern for community welfare would replace individualism and competitiveness. Property would belong to all, thus eliminating the incentive to rob or steal, and people would not be subject to the pathological urges that make them criminal in conventional societies.

Although Marx's utopian vision has not been realized in any country of the world, communist countries have adhered to one or another version of what is known as Socialist Law (Berman, 1963; David & Brierly, 1978; Glendon, Gordon, & Osakwe, 1985). The former Soviet Union was for decades the most prominent of the Socialist Law nations. By the end of the twentieth century, Cuba was the country most committed to the principles of communism. Other nations that currently retain major aspects of Socialist Law are North Korea, Vietnam, and China. Socialist Law needs to be considered in any study of comparative criminal justice because it has enough distinctive characteristics to warrant separate consideration as a family of law.

The Historical Background of Socialist Law

To understand Socialist Law, we must take a look at legal developments in the former Soviet Union following the Russian Revolution of 1917—a post-revolutionary government dedicated to the destruction of the institutions and laws of the hated old order. As in France, a king and queen (in this case, Czar Nicholas and his wife, Alexandra) were executed to break the bonds with the past and symbolize the destruction of the old ruling class. And as in France, where the revolution, despite its atrocities and excesses, came to represent the triumph of a new ideology of enlightenment and rationalism, the Russian Revolution represented the triumph of a more recent ideology, that of Karl Marx.

It is important to note that Socialist Law is historically grounded in the Civil Law. For centuries, Eastern European countries, including Russia, used recorded codes as a means to rule the populace. Prior to the revolution, Russia's legal system had combined elements of the Civil Law, Canon Law, and traditional Russian customs. Imperial Russian law, however, was chiefly statute-based law that had gone through various phases of codification. The major influence on imperial law was the Germanic law of the Middle Ages, the same Germanic law that had had such an important influence on the two great nineteenth-century codes: the Napoleonic Code and the German Civil Code.

After the revolution, Russia went through a chaotic period in which there was no formal legal structure and revolutionary tribunals dispensed revolutionary law. Vast discretion resided in the judges of these tribunals. However, these judges were not legally trained, since the lawyers and judges of the old regime had been eliminated along with the law. Ultimately, however, with the realization of the need to make the Soviet Union into a viable trading partner and the relaxation of revolutionary fervor during the time of the "New Economic Policy," Russia moved again to develop a code of laws. The result was the "new" Russian Civil Code, which drew from the earlier Russian code, the German Civil Code, the French Civil Code, and the Swiss Civil Code (Glendon, Gordon, & Osakwe, 1985, pp. 230-50).

With the rise to power of Joseph Stalin (1879–1953) in the late 1920s, a new period of communist zeal began. Stalin tried to institute a "pure" communist approach, without great concern for conformity with the law. He soon decided, however, as had William the Conqueror and Napoleon before him, that the law could be used to consolidate and strengthen his power. The Soviet Union entered into a period of "Socialist legalism," rule making that tried to encompass every aspect of the Russian citizen's home and work life. A huge bureaucracy and a highly developed legal system became part of the Soviet state apparatus.

Although the Russian legal system continued to owe much to the civil codes of Western Europe and could easily be identified with them through an examination of rules of procedure, especially criminal procedure, it gradually became such a distinctive system that it is now possible to speak of a Socialist Law family, as distinguished from the Civil Law or the Common Law. With the breakup of the Soviet Union, major changes in the Socialist Law's governmental form and ideology have taken place in Eastern Europe. Many countries such as the former East and West Germany have now adopted the Civil Law system. However, this does not mean the total demise of all remnants of Socialist Law for two key reasons.

First, even the countries that have renounced socialism as their main political ideology will surely retain some principles of the legal system. History tells us that when countries encounter political upheaval and significant change in their legal system, they often find it difficult to totally eschew all aspects of the previous form of law. This is understandable, because basic principles often remain in the collective psyche of the citizens who lived under the previous legal system. In the case of the former Soviet Union, citizens lived under the auspices of Socialist Law for more than 50 years.

Second, Socialist Law will undoubtedly remain as a significant legal and political system because it is still practiced by the most populous country in the world—the People's Republic of China. Although China has adopted some free-market commercial law reforms, it still has many features of the socialist legal system. For this reason, we chose China as a model country to be discussed throughout this book.

Socialism and the People's Republic of China

To understand the formal origins of Socialist Law in China, one must first learn about the history of the country immediately prior to the implementation of socialism. For over 4,000 years, China was ruled by a series of feudal dynasties, which limited any significant attempts to modernize the political, economic, or social structures in the country. The majority of people who lived in the vast regions of China were poor peasant farmers.

The most recent dynasty, the Qing dynasty, was overthrown in 1911. In 1912, the democratic ideals of the Kuomintang (Nationalist party) dominated. However, between 1911 and 1949, the Chinese political situation was chaotic and prone to warlords, corruption, civil war, and invasion by Japan.

It was during this tumultuous time that the ideals of socialism were introduced into Chinese society. Under the direction of Mao Zedong (1893–1976), who was influenced by the ideas of Karl Marx and Vladimir Lenin (1870–1924), the Communist Party in China was formed in 1921. Mao's major contribution was to adapt communist principles to the Chinese political, economic, and social situation. By gaining the support of large numbers of peasants throughout agrarian China and confiscating the land of wealthy farmers, he was able to develop an army and mobilize the masses, thereby furthering the objectives of communism (Terrill, 2003).

The Chinese socialist government, called the People's Republic of China, was officially established in October 1949 when Mao Zedong and his fellow Communists gained full control of the government over the Nationalist party. The Communist government abolished all laws of the Nationalist regime, claiming that these laws represented only the interests of the bourgeoisie, landlord classes, and feudal society (Situ & Liu, 1996).

During the first 30 years of communism under Mao, the government replaced the Nationalist laws with a combination of statutes, rules, and regulations based on the ideals of the ruling party. Large, bureaucratically structured courts were held in disdain, so whenever possible, local lower-level courts and ad hoc tribunals made legal decisions. This rather informal method of settling legal disputes eventually led to the creation of an extensive committee system in China. Committees were set up in neighborhoods, communities, and workplaces to act as systems of surveillance, control, and sanctioning. Also during this era, while more consideration was given to developing a formal legal system, legal decisions in China were made based solely on political needs and ideals.

After Mao's death in 1976, the new leader, Deng Xiaoping (1904–1997), promoted new goals for China that centered on modernization in four key areas: agriculture, industry, defense, and technology. His idea was to develop a special kind of "socialism with Chinese characteristics" (Franz, 1988) that, contrary to Mao, was against isolationism and anti-intellectualism. The People's Republic of China is currently in the process of developing a legal and criminal justice system that will accommodate its needs as a socialist nation, a nation with a long Confucian tradition, and a modern commercial power (Head, 2011). An informal committee system of justice dispensed by relatives, friends, colleagues, or workplace and community leaders remains today in coexistence with a more formal legal system. In the next chapter and throughout this book, we will continue to discuss more about the background and current structure of the legal system in China.

Socialist versus Civil Law

How does Socialist Law differ from a conventional legal system such as exists in other Civil Law countries? Six characteristics of Socialist Law distinguish it from Civil Law:

- The public law/private law distinction
- The importance of economic crimes
- The educational or "social engineering" function of law
- The distinctive role of the procurator
- The distinction between political and non-political justice
- The mitigated independence of the judiciary

The Public Law/Private Law Distinction. Laws regarding private property, inheritance, and personal relations between individuals continue to be important in Socialist Law systems. The ideal of collective ownership of property and of the major means of production by the state, however, has resulted in great importance attached to public law—that is, to statutory laws and regulations of the state. The amounts and kinds of rule making that are involved in centralized, noncompetitive economic production are tremendous, and the socialist state is often choked with bureaucratic regulations because so little of economic life is left to open market competition. To be sure, governmental regulation of the economy through laws controlling trade, production, banking, and other economic matters is familiar in all Western societies today, but socialist and nonsocialist systems continue to place a primary emphasis on public versus private law.

Economic Crimes. In nonsocialist systems, managers and employees are driven to a certain extent by a "bottom line" mentality. Workers who are chronically late for work, who abuse valuable machinery, and who fail to achieve a reasonable level of production usually will lose their jobs, and an enterprise that consistently fails to produce a profit will go out of business. By contrast, in a socialist system where all enterprises are owned by the government and full employment is guaranteed, failure to live up to working standards cannot be handled by dismissal of employees or bankruptcy of organizations. Without these kinds of private punishments the criminal law becomes a means for punishing unacceptable work behavior in socialist systems. Thus, the concept of economic crimes—obstruction of socialist production—is a peculiar aspect of socialist as compared to nonsocialist law.

The Educational Function of the Law. A legal system in which the people have no knowledge of the law would be an absurdity. How can one obey the law if one does not know what it is? But the reality is that most of us do not have much knowledge of the law to which we are subject. We tend to learn those parts of the law that affect us: basic criminal law, traffic law, tax regulations, and simple rules about property and contracts. Entrepreneurs or government administrators learn about the specific laws that affect their enterprises. For the most part, however, we have only a rudimentary knowledge of even the most basic criminal laws of our own states, and we depend on specialized attorneys to interpret the law for us.

In postrevolutionary societies, in which the laws may have changed drastically, there is some urgency about having the citizens learn the new law. The Napoleonic Code was famous for its accessibility. It was relatively short, simple, and direct, without obscure phrasing and indecipherable language. The emperor Justinian, upon promulgating the new code of laws developed in his regime, abolished all previous law and refused to allow commentaries on his new law to be published. In this way, he hoped to negate the insidious influence of the lawyers who previously had been indispensable as mediators between the people and the law.

We might expect, therefore, that the Chinese government after 1949 would have made efforts to familiarize the people with the laws of the new regime. In fact, in post-1949 China, the masses did learn about the ideals of the Communist Party through statements reported to the tightly controlled media and campaigns intended to popularize and implement certain policies. However, formally stated criminal and procedural laws were unclear and tenuous, depending on various shifts in political (Communist) philosophy. In many cases, unwritten and internal rules guided the police, courts, and ruling party in defining crimes and punishments (Lubman, 1983).

The educational or "social engineering" aspects of Socialist Law are another method of familiarizing the people with the new law. One of the basic tenets of communist ideology is that socialism is a transitional stage on the way to a true communist society in which people will no longer be predatory and competitive in nature. Since coercive law is supposed to cease in a true communist society, it is especially important that those who are judged under the present law agree to its reasonableness and justice. In order to achieve this communist society, people need to become reeducated, and one of the prime agents of this reeducation must be the government and the legal system (Berman, 1963).

The Role of the Procurator. The procurator in Civil Law systems is roughly equivalent to the prosecutor in Common Law systems. The **procurator** works on behalf of the government, prosecuting crimes and making sure the proper indictments are

TABLE 3.5 The Duties of the Procurator in the People's Republic of China

1. Investigate and prosecute treason and other criminal cases.
2. Review police cases and determine the appropriateness of arrest and prosecution.
3. Supervise police investigations to determine whether they are in compliance with laws.
4. Conduct public prosecutions of officials.
5. Supervise judicial actions to determine whether they are in compliance with laws.
6. Supervise judgments and court orders in criminal cases to determine whether they are in compliance with laws.
7. Supervise all incarceration facilities to determine whether they are in compliance with laws.

SOURCE: Organic Law for People's Procuracies. People's Republic of China Foreign Broadcast Service. July 1979.

served in the courts. However, in the Socialist Law family, the procurator is far more important than in either the Civil Law or Common Law family.

In the former Soviet Union, the head procurator general was actually one of the most powerful individuals in the government, becoming far more involved in governmental reforms and administrative decision making than most ministers of justice. Local procurators also were generally more powerful than judges in the Soviet system. They served the regime in political cases and generally had final say in decisions to prosecute. Soviet procurators have been described as having nine roles: "criminal investigator, grand jury, criminal prosecutor, judicial ombudsman, executive branch ombudsman, general ombudsman, prison ombudsman, military ombudsman, and propagandist of Soviet law" (Glendon, Gordon, & Osakwe, 1985, pp. 819–820). An **ombudsman** in this sense is an individual who hears complaints and ensures that government agents are performing their functions correctly. As in the former Soviet Union, the procuracy in China is among the most important and powerful positions in the criminal justice system.

Located within a bureaucracy that contains different levels of influence, the office of procurator, according to the Chinese constitution, is "independent and not subject to interference by administrative organs, public organizations, or individuals." In fact, the office is a very complicated one in China because procurators must prosecute offenders, uphold lawfulness of prosecution, obey the law, and check the lawfulness of other security departments and the courts—while also following the leadership of the party (Organic Law, 1979).

Based on the Soviet model, Chinese procurators in the 1950s were also given the responsibility of prosecuting criminal offenders, supervising the entire criminal justice system, and ensuring that all citizens and state personnel carried out the laws and policies of the state. Since being redefined in 1978, the position now can be summarized to include supervisory, investigatory, and prosecutorial functions (Tanner, 1994). Table 3.5 summarizes the duties of the procurator in China.

Political versus Nonpolitical Justice. To speak of "political justice" implies that it is possible to have a kind of justice that departs from a norm of impartiality and engages in some form of partiality that is determined by politics—that is, the influence of those in power. Although we know that political influence often affects the outcomes of legal cases in the United States, the norm or ideal of Western law is "equal justice under law." Therefore, a difficult aspect of Socialist Law is its duality—a distinction between typical cases and those cases in which the state has a particular interest that supersedes the interests of conventional justice.

These latter cases involve what is sometimes called *prerogative law*, under which standard legal procedure is subverted through the intervention of those in power. Prerogative law was actually legitimated in the old Soviet system and was justified by its defenders as necessary to the evolution toward an ideal Communist society. If we read the books of Aleksandr Solzhenitsyn, which describe the terror of life under Stalin, or various accounts by political dissidents in China, we might well find the concept of prerogative justice to mean no more than wanton disregard of matters of guilt or innocence under law. Instead, the overriding principle is the importance of the collective (the many or the state) as opposed to the individual, and it supposes that reasons of state may allow for setting aside normal criminal procedure to neutralize threats or enemies of the state.

The Independence of the Judiciary. Independence of the judiciary means that judges are free to decide cases in accordance with the law and cannot be pressured to rule for any reason other than legality. This principle is highly valued in Western law, although it is honored only in theory in many cases. In the United States, for example, judges in most state court systems are elected and must answer to the voters for their decisions on the bench. Others are appointed by elected officials. One of the reasons the Founding Fathers guaranteed a life term for federal judges (except in rare cases of impeachment) was their hope that these judges could thereby act with total independence and without fear of losing their positions. Again, in reality, a great deal of politics is involved in the appointment and decision making of federal judges; the norm, however, is one of independence.

In the United States, an independent judiciary is tied to the idea of separation of powers, whereby excessive power of government is thwarted by distributing power among different branches. Separation of powers is not considered a desirable governmental arrangement in all socialist countries, however, because it introduces an element of competition and conflict when promoting the public good should be the only goal. In socialist countries, the idea of a benevolent state that rules for the good of its citizens thus replaces the idea of a government that must be curbed because of its tendency to become tyrannical and rule for the good of the rulers instead of the people as a whole. Therefore, even though in theory constitutional rights exist to protect individuals against governmental actions, in practice this ideal is often overshadowed by the primacy of the communist state over individual rights. Similarly, China does not idealize separation of powers or an independent judiciary. In fact, judges in certain courts in China are appointed by a standing committee of that court and can be removed or even replaced by a substitute assistant judge by that same committee.

In practice, this does not mean that judges in all socialist countries are tools of political leaders or that legal judgments in these countries are always arbitrary and determined exclusively by reasons of state. What it does mean is that in cases where the needs of the state conflict with the rights of individuals, the collective always wins.

THE SACRED LAW

The three families of law described thus far in this chapter—Civil Law, Common Law, and Socialist Law—are pervasive in every part of the world today. There is hardly a country, region, or even tribe that has not been brought under the influence of one or the other, at least with respect to certain aspects of social life. A distinguishing characteristic of each of these systems of law is that it is secular in nature. **Secular law** is law that does not pertain to religion or any religious body. None of the three major families of law claims to have the force of a religion behind it, despite the fact that many of the tenets of the laws are derived from religious teachings.

Throughout history, religion and religious texts have always been important sources of influence on the law. The teachings of the early Christian church, including the Canon Law and the Bible, have been incorporated into the Civil Law and Common Law, respectively. The country of India, although deeply infused with English Common Law principles, is rich in religiously based Hindu law, which dates back to about 100 B.C. Much of Hindu law has been influenced by early Hindu doctrine, which stated that adherence to the Vedas, or scriptures, was more important than adherence to the edicts of any king or ruler.

Even today, devout Hindus believe that faithful adherence to correct behavior will help them in a new incarnation. The Confucian legal tradition, also based on morality, continues to influence the Chinese legal system.

In Israel, legal codes are influenced by English Common Law and by Israeli secular laws, but they also include Jewish and non-Jewish religious laws. Israeli religious laws generally apply in personal matters such as marriage, divorce, and alimony. Different religious courts in Israel represent the various religious groups, including Rabbinical, Muslim, Christian, and Druze (Bensinger, 1998). Hebrew law, derived from the Old Testament, is the source of some of modern Israeli laws. As mentioned earlier, the story of Hebrew law is more than 3,000 years old, and it served as a foundation for the later development of the Bible. However, over the centuries there has been a general decline in the overt influence of religion on law. Countries in Europe that were strongly influenced during the Middle Ages by the Canon Law of the Roman Catholic Church later moved away from these influences. In the late eighteenth century, the separation of religion and law became common to many countries, including the United States.

Today, a few countries have retained religious teachings and documents as the dominant if not exclusive source of law. Primarily located in the Middle East, these countries can be classified as being members of the **Sacred Law** legal tradition. The Sacred Law tradition is one that is based on a sacred text or body of religious doctrine. In Sacred Law countries there is no clear separation between the religious and the legal (Friedrichs, 2001). Throughout this book, we refer to Saudi Arabia as the best example of a country rooted in the Sacred Law tradition. Saudi Arabia was chosen because that country uses secular laws closely intertwined with religious laws that have the full force of government behind them. In Saudi Arabia and most other Middle Eastern nations, and in some Asian nations, the legal tradition is not actually called Sacred Law but **Islamic law**. Islamic law is based on the rules of conduct revealed by God with two primary sources: the Shari'a and the Sunnah. The Shari'a (literally, *the way*) is the term used to describe the actual law that is practiced in Saudi Arabia. The Sunnah are the practices, habits, and sayings of Muhammad, the prophet of Islam. For those who believe in Islam, it is important that the law be consistent with Islamic doctrine because the religion is considered a way of life, not just a religious practice.

Islamic law has become increasingly important in recent years, remerging after a period of decline in the nineteenth and early twentieth centuries. Saudi Arabia has been an Islamic state, adhering to Islamic law, since its founding in 1926. In a few Islamic countries, including Iran, Pakistan, and Sudan, it is proclaimed as the basis for all law, including the harsh Islamic criminal law based on retribution. Even in these countries, however, certain concessions are made to modern exigencies of trade, banking (Islamic law does not allow the payment of interest), and industry. Today in Syria, Egypt, Iraq, Lebanon, and Kuwait, Islamic law forms a part of the legal system that most often deals with family law. In two other Islamic countries, Iran and Libya, part of a growing religious fundamentalism necessarily includes a push for greater incorporation of Shari'a into the national law (Freeland, 1997; Coette, 2011). For the remainder of this book, we will use the term *Sacred Law* to describe generally the legal tradition that uses sacred religious text to formulate or dispense law. The term *Islamic law* will be used to reflect any reference to the specific Sacred Law legal tradition of our model country, Saudi Arabia.

Sources of Islamic Law

Islamic law has two primary sources: the Shari'a and the Sunnah (or Sunna). **Shari'a law** may be defined as "the body of rules of conduct revealed by God (Allah) to his Prophet (Muhammad) whereby the people are directed to lead their life in this world" (Nader, 1990, p. 1). Nader lists six key characteristics of the Islamic law:

- It is not given by a ruler but has been revealed by God.

- It has been amplified by leading Muslim jurists such as Abu Hanafi, Shafi, and Malik.
- It remains valid whether recognized by the state or not.
- It originates not in customs and traditions but in divine revelation only.
- It is so comprehensive and all-embracing that it covers every aspect of a legal system—personal law, constitutional law, international law, criminal law, mercantile law, and so on.
- It is not in the nature of "should be" but lays down what the law is.

This list of characteristics requires some amplification. The most important source of Shari'a is the Qur'an, the Muslim holy book. The Qur'an, however, is not in whole or even in part a code of laws. From a total of about 6,000 verses in the Qur'an, only about 80 might be defined as legal rules (Amin, 1985a, p. 9). Therefore, other sources of law are included in Shari'a. Some of these are traditions derived from the statements and actions of the Prophet that were recorded in the Sunnah. The Sunnah (also called the Hadith), the second major source of Islamic law, contains those actions, sayings, and practices of the Prophet that deal with issues not directly addressed in the Qur'an (Moore, 1996). It is important to mention that in addition to the Sunnah and Shari'a there were, and remain, sources of law developed by different schools of Islamic law in the centuries after the death of Muhammad in A.D. 632. These were writings that state the common consent of Islamic jurists and judicial reasoning opinions.

The Prevalence of Shari'a

As you can see, Sacred Law, more specifically Islamic law, is truly distinctive among the families of law that we have considered. It does not represent the bringing together of traditions and customs into either a code law such as the Civil Law or a case law such as the Common Law. David and Brierly claim that Islamic Law is completely original "by its very nature," because it is based on divine revelation and is independent of all other systems that do not derive from that same revelation (1978, p. 429). At the same time, despite its basis in the Qur'an, Islamic law depends on the compilation of cases and traditions from its early centuries. Therefore, it has some of the characteristics of case law: complex rules dependent upon interpretation and local developments.

An important aspect of the history of Islamic law, which had been eclipsed by the laws of countries and of colonial powers in the nineteenth and twentieth centuries, is that it remains in force for devout Muslims within those countries. Because Islamic law is not the established law in many countries and therefore lacks the power of government to enforce its sanctions, it depends on voluntary obedience. Turkey, for example, remains a predominately Muslim nation, even though it has pursued secular modernization aggressively.

India, with a large Islamic minority, presents a unique situation. The desires of the Muslim minority cannot be ignored, and concessions to their beliefs are sometimes incorporated into Indian law. In the famous Shah Bano case, for example, a Muslim citizen of India divorced his elderly wife, Shah Bano, according to Islamic rules, which do not call for alimony in the conventional sense. Shah Bano sued for and was granted economic support according to Indian law. This case caused a furor in the Muslim community, becoming a symbol of Hindu dominance and the repression of Muslims. In the end, the Indian Parliament passed the Muslim Women's Act, which provided for separate divorce regulations when the parties to the suit are Muslims. This law, in effect, acknowledges the power of Shari'a in a nation that otherwise practices separation of church and state (O'Donnell, 1990).

Crime and Punishment under Shari'a

There are four major schools of Islamic law, derived from religious leaders living in different areas and facing different problems in the two centuries following the death of Muhammad. These schools are Hanafi, Hanbali, Maliki, and Shafi'i. The main differences between these schools are in matters of emphasis, whether on tradition, judicial reasoning, or the elaboration of the Qur'an. Different countries tend to follow different schools of Islamic law. Thus, for example, the primary legal tradition in Iraq is that of the Hanafi school, while in Saudi Arabia it is the fundamentalist Hanbali school, named after the great theologian and jurist Ahmad Ibn Hanbal (A.D. 780–855) (Amin, 1985b, p. 12).

In addition to the conventional issues of law, including property, contracts, and inheritance, Shari'a is concerned with many aspects of individual behavior, including dress, food, etiquette, and religious worship. For students of criminal justice, Shari'a presents an interesting contrast to Western systems. Crimes are categorized according to whether they are acts against God or crimes against others and society. Crimes against God (**Hudud crimes**) are very serious and also seen as violation of "natural law": They include theft, robbery, blasphemy, apostasy (voluntary renunciation of Islam or its rules), rebellion, and defamation, as well as drug offenses and sexual crimes such as adultery, sodomy, and fornication (Lippman, McConville, & Yerushalmi, 1988, p. 41).

All other crimes are private wrongs against individuals or against society and are called **tazirat crimes** or Tesar crimes (Souryal & Potts, 1994). Included in those crimes are murder, manslaughter, or assault. If the crime is one that threatens a family's livelihood, then *quesas* (retribution) or *diya* (compensation or fines) may be required. The blood money is given to the victim or the victim's family.

In the case of Hudud crimes, the state must initiate prosecution; in tazirat crimes, the victims or heirs must bring a complaint and serve as prosecutor. In practice, however, the state usually initiates these proceedings. The distinction between Hudud and tazirat crimes is not as great as it seems, therefore, since all criminal cases in Islamic countries are decided in government-run courts, and most punishments are fixed by the courts in accordance with religious or traditional rules (Lippman, McConville, & Yerushalmi, 1988).

It is not only Shari'a law that makes Islamic legal systems different from those of Western countries. Shari'a courts are also different in makeup, procedure, and effect. Sanctions are prescribed in the Qur'an and are often harsh, with the emphasis on corporal and capital punishment. Under Shari'a, imprisonment is the punishment of last resort. Theft is punished by imprisonment or by amputation of hands or feet, depending on the number of times it is committed. Crimes against God, including adultery and acts of homosexuality, are usually punished by death. Thus, the death sentence for apostasy imposed on the Muslim novelist Salman Rushdie (in absentia) by the late Ayatollah Khomeini was peculiar only because Rushdie, as a British citizen, was not subject to Iranian criminal law. As a Muslim, however, he was subject to the Qur'an, and this fact was used as justification for the death sentence.

Another example was the case of a Pakistani man named Ranjah Maseih, who was sentenced in 2003 to life in prison for allegedly tearing down a billboard carrying verses from the Qur'an in Faisalabad, Pakistan. Maseih, a Christian, tore down the billboard during a demonstration following the suicide of Faisalabad's Roman Catholic Bishop John Joseph. (Bishop Joseph shot himself in the head after a judge convicted a Christian of blasphemy.) The convicted Christian was found guilty of defending Salman Rushdie, whose book *The Satanic Verses* infuriated radical Muslims. We discuss more about the Shari'a and punishment in the Sacred and Islamic law country of Saudi Arabia in Chapter 9.

Table 3.6 displays major features of the Socialist Law and Islamic law systems. It can be seen that the ideology of socialism undergirds the Social Law system, while the religious teaching and traditions of Islam underlie its legal system.

Equality and Islamic Justice

Islamic law makes a distinction between men and women in many matters. Although the Qur'an improved the status of women from what it had been previously, there are still aspects of Islamic law that discriminate heavily against women. For example, women do not count as witnesses for certain crimes or may count only half as much as male witnesses (in other words, two women witnesses would be required where only one man was required). Laws relating to ritual religious practices, to finances and property, and to marriage and

TABLE 3.6 Major Features of the Socialist and Sacred and Islamic Law Systems

Socialist Law Characteristics	Sacred/Islamic Law Characteristics
Public law involving state interests supercedes private law concerns of individuals.	Two major sources of Islamic law: Shari'a and Sunnah.
Economic crimes (obstruction of socialist production) are serious violations of law.	Crimes can be acts against God (Hudud crimes) or against other persons (tazirat crimes).
Government and legal system have responsibility for educating public about the justice of the socialist law system.	Shari'a court sanctions are prescribed in the Qur'an.
The procurator has extensive investigation and prosecution authority as well as oversight of judges and prisons.	Four schools of Islamic law alternately emphasize tradition, judicial reasoning, or elaboration of the Qur'an.
Similar legal attributes to Civil Law system but with ideology of socialist economic system.	Few countries are governed by Islamic law, but tradition depends on voluntary obedience. Divine law exists whether or not recognized by the state.

divorce also discriminate against women, although efforts have been made in some countries toward equality of women in some matters (Amin, 1985a, p. 36; Collier, 1994; Hirsch, 1998).

Islamic scholars assert that Islamic law shows great concern for human rights with respect to freedom of religion (only Muslims are required to follow the Muslim law), criminal procedure, and human development (Amin, 1985a, pp. 30–39). According to these scholars, while particular countries, such as post-revolutionary Iran, may treat people arbitrarily and curtail their human rights, this is in not in keeping with Islamic law. Other defenders of Islamic law claim that it can be flexible and adaptable to modern conditions and yet is able to maintain its strong Islamic values despite growing influence from Western influences (Collier, 1994).

Female Circumcision

Female circumcision—or female cutting and mutilation—has existed for some 2,500 years and is practiced in some 40 countries, mainly in Africa. Over 100 million females are affected, and about 2 million are at risk each year (Sussman 1998, p. 197). The principal objective of this practice is to diminish the possibility of female premarital sex and infidelity by removing the clitoris and stitching together the genital lips. At least some of those who immigrate to the United States from countries where this practice is customary want to continue the practice in the United States. A small number of women have fled their native country to avoid genital mutilation and have sought political asylum in the United States on these grounds. In 1996, the U.S. Congress passed into law the Female Genital Mutilation Act, which criminalizes circumcision of females under 18, requires federal health agencies to educate immigrant communities about the harm of genital cutting, and imposes economic sanctions on countries that fail to take steps to prevent such practices (Dugger, 1996; Sussman, 1998). The difficulties of effectively enforcing such a law, which challenges deeply held religious or cultural beliefs, are great. Most Americans are in agreement with this law and regard female genital cutting, or mutilation, as barbaric.

SOURCE: From "Law in Our Lives" by David Friedrichs, 2001.

SUMMARY

International agreements have emerged over the last 50 years that combine the legal traditions of the world to adjudicate international crimes. These legal traditions, or families of law, continue to guide the operation of the police, courts, and corrections within individual countries. Families of law have distinctive characteristics if seen as ideal systems. The Common Law places great emphasis on case precedents and fine distinctions of procedure. The Civil Law combines ancient Roman rules and the laws and customs of medieval Europe with regulations that address modern social and economic problems without the modifications of case law. Socialist Law espouses the idea that the law should be an instrument in the creation of a new socialist society rather than simply a way of settling disputes or dealing with criminal deviance. Sacred Law is used in countries where a sacred text or doctrine is the primary basis for law. Sacred Law is most commonly used in countries that employ Islamic law—where religious revelation is combined with the traditional rules that emanated from the society of faithful Muslims in the early centuries following the death of the Prophet Muhammad.

Comparative Criminal Justice at the Movies

Movies seek to entertain and inform the audience about a story, incident, or person. Many good movies also hit upon important substantive themes relevant to understanding crime and justice in comparative perspective. Read the movie summary below (and watch the movie if you haven't already) and answer the questions to make the subject matter connections to comparative criminal justice.

***Slumdog Millionaire* (2008)**
Danny Boyle, Director

Winner of an Academy Award for Best Picture, this adaptation of a novel by Indian author Vikas Swarup tells the story of Jamal (Dev Patel), a young man from the slums of Mumbai, India, who appears on the Indian version of the television show *Who Wants to be a Millionaire?*, in which the contestant can win up to a million dollars by answering a series of random questions correctly. Contrary to expectations, he does very well on the show, so both the game show host and law enforcement officials are suspicious that he might be cheating.

During an intense interrogation, Jamal relates through flashbacks that he knew the answers because of actual events that happened in his life. These events include the death of his mother and his experiences surviving as an orphan by living from trash heaps with his brother and a young girl, Latika (Freida Pinto). The three later escape from a man who used orphaned children to beg for money. Becoming separated from the young girl, but they go on to make a living, traveling on top of trains, selling goods, picking pockets, and cheating tourists. Jamal and his brother eventually locate Latika a few years later, discovering that she has been taken in by a pimp in order to become a prostitute whose virginity will sell for a high price. After a series of scary situations, Jamal locates the young girl again, finding she is a mistress to a gangster. He professes his love to her and tells he will wait for her, promising to be at the train station every day at 5:00 p.m.

Jamal then tries out for the popular game show *Who Wants to Be a Millionaire?* because he knows Latika will be watching. He makes it to the final question, despite the show's hostile host, who feeds Jamal a wrong answer during a break. Jamal guesses that he has been misled and chooses the right answer. At the end of the show, Jamal has one question left to win the grand prize, but the host calls the police and Jamal is taken into custody, where he is tortured as the police attempt to discover how a simple "slumdog" could possibly know the answers to so many questions.

Questions

1. Although this story is fictional, does Jamal's interrogation involve an issue of public or private law? What is the legal tradition in India?
2. Extracting information from crime suspects through interrogation has been a significant issue in recent years. Do any of the principles from the major legal traditions offer guidance in determining what the limits of such interrogations should be?

None of these kinds of law is practiced in its "pure," or ideal, form in today's world. Countries that practice Common Law are actually closely regulated by statutory law. In countries that practice Civil Law, attorneys are not unmindful of the decisions that higher courts have handed down in previous cases, although they are not bound by them. In countries that formerly or currently practice Socialist Law, the legal system resembles more closely that in the Civil Law countries as communism breaks down as an ideological force. Sacred Law, in the form of Islamic law, is unique among the families of law considered because it is actually expanding in its original form as religious fundamentalism spreads in the Middle East. Even Islamic law, however, must coexist with commercial and other laws required by modernization and industrialization. Indeed, worldwide, increasing transnational business, research, and other enterprises provide the impetus for increasing integration of laws as shown by the European Union and International Criminal Court, discussed later.

The very real tendencies toward integration and amalgamation among legal systems will become more apparent as we consider the criminal process in various countries. Nevertheless, it is a mistake to assume that the heritage of the families of law is breaking down in large part. The fact is that the legal heritage in any country is closely tied to the political and administrative culture of that country, and these cultures continue to be distinctive in many ways.

Critical Thinking Exercise

Critical thinking requires the ability to evaluate viewpoints, facts, and behaviors objectively to assess information and methods of argumentation in order to establish the merit of an action, law, policy, or procedure. Please evaluate this scenario objectively, applying your knowledge of comparative criminal justice to the facts of the case presented, and answer the questions that follow it.

Equal in China?

A regulation in Beijing, China guarantees a victim's right to report domestic violence. It was seen as an indicator of progress in protecting women's rights. The new regulation is part of Beijing's implementation of China's 1992 Law on the Protection of Women's Rights and Interests.

China's first rule on the subject, the Marriage Law, was implemented soon after the People's Republic of China was founded in 1949. That law stipulated that husbands and wives were equal under law, a rule that was expanded in 1954, when the ninety-sixth article of the Constitution stated that women were to enjoy equal rights with men in all aspects of life, including family life.

According to the Marriage Law, divorce was permitted only when mediation (provided by the government) between the husband and wife failed. However, the mediation process could drag on for years. A new Marriage Law in 1980 introduced the option to file for divorce when only one person wanted to end the marriage. According to Chinese government statistics, the province's divorce rate tripled immediately after the new law took effect.

An amendment to the Law on the Protection of Women's Rights and Interests in 2005, was the first to prohibit sexual harassment against women. At a sexual harassment trial in Shaanxi Province in 2007, the judge cited the 2005 law and ruled that the harasser must apologize to the female victim and pay her 15,000 yuan ($2,200) for mental distress. This 2007 ruling was the first to cite the women's rights law. The addition of the phrase "respect for and protection of human rights" to the Constitution was seen as an important step that led to the creation of the new sexual harassment law in China.

Questions

1. Why do you believe it has taken so long for women in China to obtain these legal protections, given the facts above?
2. What characteristics of the Socialist Law system would contribute to this situation?

SOURCE: Li, Li. (2009). "Becoming Equal." *Beijing Review*, vol. 52, 20–21.

DISCUSSION QUESTIONS

1. What are the chief differences between the Common Law and the Civil Law families?
2. Are there common features in the historical developments of the Common Law, Civil Law, and Socialist Law families?
3. Do you believe it is possible to balance the sometimes competing interests between the Islamic legal tradition and the pressures posed by modernization?
4. How do you believe indigenous laws have survived in the United States, given the expansion of legal authority at the federal and state levels in recent years?
5. If you were a political leader in a Socialist Law nation, how would you legislate to educate people about the law? What kind of behavior would be made illegal?

FOR FURTHER READING

De Cruz, P. (2013). *Comparative Law in a Changing World*, 4th ed. London: Routledge-Cavendish.

Glen, H. P. (2010). *Legal Traditions of the World: Sustainable Diversity in Law*, 4th ed. Oxford: Oxford University Press.

Natarajan, M., ed. (2012). *International Crime and Justice*. New York: Cambridge University Press.

Reimann, M., and Zimmermann, R. eds. (2008). *The Oxford Handbook of Comparative Law*. New York: Oxford University Press.

Berman, P. Schiff. (2012). *Global Legal Pluralism: A Jurisprudence of Law Beyond Borders*. New York: Cambridge University Press.

WEB PAGES FOR CHAPTER

For an excellent resource on indigenous and aboriginal law, see http://www.international.gc.ca/indig-autoch/index.aspx?lang=en&view=d.

For more historical background on the Common Law legal tradition, see http://www.scribd.com/doc/35793914/5-differences-between-aCommon-Law-and-Civil-Law-System-detailed-with-reference.

For a comprehensive source on Chinese law, see http://www.chinatoday.com/law/a.htm.

For information on Islamic law provided by LexisNexis, see https://litigation-essentials.lexisnexis.com/webcd/app?action=DocumentDisplay&crawlid=1&srctype=smi&srcid=3B15&doctype=cite&docid=7+J.+Islamic+L.+%26+Culture+27&key=dc7ffded8ee87dc0afe0fb46fccd90bd.

For a source on world nations and their different legal traditions, see the University of Ottawa's JuriGlobe (World Legal Systems Research Group) at http://www.juriglobe.ca/eng/index.php.

4  Six Model Nations

Key Terms and Concepts

Boryokudan
Confucian thought
Cultural Revolution
federalism
Länder
legal pluralism
monarch
National People's Congress (NPC)
organic law
Parliament
Prefect
prefectural police (PP)
prefecture
republican government
shogun
unitary government
welfare state

Chapter 4 Learning Objectives

Discuss the particular historical developments that may have had a major effect on the formation of criminal law and criminal justice administration in each model country.

Analyze contributing factors to the crime rates in each model country.

Identify the distinct approach to criminal justice each model nation exemplifies.

Understand the basic structures of the criminal justice systems in each model country.

Compare the unique crime problems in model countries with crime in the United States.

According to data collected by the Home Office in England, during the 2010–2011 soccer season almost 3,100 English and Wales nationals were arrested at international and domestic soccer games around the globe. Another 3,173 persons were placed under a "football ban," meaning they were not allowed to attend soccer games (Home Office, 12/23/11). In France during October 2011, youths engaged in a series of protests that included strikes and roadblocks; they smashed storefronts, caused hundreds of flights to be cancelled, and left thousands affected by shortages in fuel. The protestors also clashed with riot police in Paris and across the country. This situation was created by the French Senate's move to pass legislation to increase the retirement age to sixty-two years of age (Barchfield, 2010). A branch of police in Saudia Arabia, formally called the mutawa (to be discussed in the next chapter), are called to actively enforce a law that states that women are not allowed to travel without approval of a male guardian or husband. These three examples of crime problems in three of our model countries may be surprising or at least odd to some, especially to Americans, who are often not familiar with the different kinds of crimes and the reaction of the respective criminal justice systems in other parts of the world.

To better place in perspective the problem of crime and the operations of the criminal justice system in any one nation, we need to know something about that country's history, government, and social development. This chapter introduces the six nations that we will examine in depth in the rest of the book. These thumbnail sketches will make it easier to follow the material in subsequent chapters and will help you understand how the respective criminal justice systems have developed.

Our model nations are England, France, Germany, China, Japan, and Saudi Arabia (see Figure 4.1). These nations are designated as "models" not because they provide an ideal that might be copied by other nations but because each exemplifies a distinct approach to criminal justice system and criminal process. The distinctions are based on families of law, governmental arrangements, and historical traditions. For each country, we will provide current background information; a historical sketch of the development of government; and summaries of the current crime situation, criminal law, and criminal justice system.

ENGLAND

Overview

The name England comes from the word *Angeln*, one of the Germanic tribes who settled there during the fifth century. England became a unified state in 927 AD and together with Wales was officially known as the Kingdom of England until 1701, when it united with Scotland to become the Kingdom of Great Britain. Americans know England as a place of old castles, stories of kings and queens, poetry, and literature; for them, the country is one where the police are without guns and the lawyers wear wigs. But the British are responsible for much more, including the Age of Exploration (15th century), which led to the Europeans' discovery of other parts of the world, and the development of the English language and English Common Law. England by any measure has played a significant role in the development of parliamentary democracy and in advancing literature and science. For example, William Shakespeare, Charles Dickens, Jane Austen, and Agatha Christie are among the famous English authors whose work is read across the world. Famous scientists include Isaac Newton and Charles Darwin, and the Industrial Revolution in England led to many significant inventions in the 1800s, including advances in textile manufacturing, metallurgy, mining, and steam power. More recently, the English have developed the jet engine, the electric motor, the first modern computer, and the World Wide Web.

FIGURE 4.1 The Six Model Nations

England is the largest political division within the United Kingdom of Great Britain and Northern Ireland and is the largest entity within the geographic area called Great Britain (England, Scotland, and Wales). England is the historical backbone of the Common Law legal tradition. Scotland, however, continues to operate under a Civil Law tradition mixed with Common Law elements. We will consider only England and Wales rather than all of Great Britain or all of the United Kingdom, as the two form the constitutional successor to the former Kingdom of England. It is important to mention, however, that as of March 2011 the national assembly of Wales has direct lawmaking powers and no longer must consult with England.

England and Wales span 58,350 square miles and include 48 counties and 7 metropolitan counties, including London. England basically operates a capitalist economy, although various forms of socialism have made the country resemble a welfare state. England remains one of the world's great trading powers and financial centers, and boasts one of the four largest economies in Europe. It is also a world leader in the manufacture of heavy machinery, although it has lost much of the smaller industry that formerly was a major source of employment. For more economic and demographic data, see the columns about England and Wales in Table 4.1.

England is a **unitary government**. This means that governmental power is centralized rather than

TABLE 4.1 Selected Demographics Summary

	United States	China	France	Germany	Saudi Arabia	England and Wales	Japan
Area (sq km)	9,826,675	9,596,960	551,500	357,022	2,149,690	71,114	377,915
Capital	Washington, DC	Beijing	Paris	Berlin	Riyadh	London	Tokyo
Population	313,847,465 (11)	1,343,239,923 (11)	65,630,692 (12)	81,305,856 (11)	26,534,504 (12)	56.1 million (12)	127,368,088 (11)
Government							
Type	Federal republic	Communist; party led	Republic	Federal republic	Monarchy	Constitutional	Parliamentary with constitutional monarchy
Divisions	50 states, 1 district	23 provinces, 5 regions, 4 municipalities	22 metro regions, 5 overseas regions	16 states	13 provinces	54 counties, 7 metro counties	47 prefectures
Constitution	Sept. 17, 1787	Dec. 4, 1982	Sept. 28, 1958	May 23, 1949	None	Unwritten	May 3, 1947
Economy							
GDP	$15.29 trillion (11)	$11.44 trillion (11)	$2.246 trillion (11)	$3.139 trillion (11)	$691.5 billion (11)	*$2.418 trillion (11)	$4.497 trillion (11)
Per capita income	$46,400 (09)	$6,500 (09)	$32,800 est. (09)	$34,200 (09)	$20,300 (09)	*$36,600 (11)	$35,600 (11)
Majority Races/Ethnic Groups	White 79.9% Black 12.8 % Hispanic 15.1%	Han Chinese 91.5%	Basques** Celts Germanic	German 91.5%	Arab 90%	White 90%	Japanese 95%
Major Religions	Protestant 51.3% Catholic 24%	Officially atheism Taoism Buddhism	Catholic 85%	Protestant 34% Catholic 34%	Muslim 100%	Christian 72%	Shintoism 83.9% ***Buddhism 71.4
Unemployment Rate	9%	6.50%	9.30%	6%	10.90%	8.10%	4.60%
Language	English		French			English	

*Includes Scotland and N. Ireland.

**The French choose not to identify ethnic groups by traditional forms of race/ethnicity or percentages, but 94% of French are identified as "French."

***Some follow both religions.

SOURCE: CIA World Factbook, 2012.

being divided between states and a central government, as happens in systems of **federalism** such as in the United States and Germany. **Parliament** is the supreme power in England. What makes Parliament so powerful is that parts of the executive, judicial, and legislative branches are contained within it; thus, it can override both executive decisions and Common Law legal decisions made by lower courts. Parliament consists of three parts: the monarch, the House of Lords, and the House of Commons.

A **monarch** is a person who is the sole and absolute ruler of a country, such as a king, queen, or emperor. However, in England, the influence of the monarchy has eroded, and today it serves a ceremonial rather than an executive function. The House of Lords, with 775 unfixed members, is the reviewer of legislation of the House of Commons. It does have some power to reject bills passed by the House of Commons, but its power is limited by various Parliament Acts.

The House of Commons is the major component of Parliament because its 650 fixed elected members discuss and vote on legislation proposed by the executive or by House members. The real leader of the nation is the prime minister, who is the head of the political party that possesses a majority of seats in the House of Commons. The prime minister acts as an advisor to the monarch and chairs of the cabinet. Cabinet ministers are responsible in turn for the administration of various government departments.

Historical Development

From the time of the Norman Conquest of England in 1066 to the end of the 17th century, English history was marked by power struggles between the monarchs and their subjects, both nobles and commoners. For example, William the Conqueror centralized royal power at the expense of the local nobles. In 1215, the nobles retaliated by drafting the Magna Carta, or "great charter," forcing the king to recognize certain of their rights. In the 16th century, the Tudor monarchs, including Henry VIII and Elizabeth I, ruled with increasingly absolute powers. In the 17th century, the first two Stuart kings, James I and Charles I, tried to do likewise but faced an increasingly assertive Parliament and unhappy populace. After a civil war and the execution of Charles I in 1649, England came under the dictatorship of the Puritan leader Oliver Cromwell—hardly an improvement on the monarchy. The restoration of the Stuart monarchy in the latter part of the 17th century was unsuccessful, again because of power struggles between king and Parliament. The Stuart lineage was permanently ended in 1689 when Parliament asked a Dutch ruler, William of Orange, and his wife, the English princess Mary, to take over the English throne.

A condition of the offer of the English throne to William and Mary was that they accept the Bill of Rights passed by Parliament in 1689. This Bill of Rights is another of the "great charters" of British constitutional development. It proclaimed certain important rights related to criminal procedure and freedom of expression. Although they do not have the force or scope that the U.S. Bill of Rights has today, the English Bill of Rights (1689), as well as the Magna Charta (1215), the Petition of Rights (1628), and the Act of Settlement (1701) are of tremendous historical significance in that they all have pioneered a tradition of limited government, with rulers constrained in their actions by a compact with the ruled. Although specific provisions of these great charters have often been superseded by later declarations, laws, and historical developments, they represent major milestones in English constitutional history.

Since the 18th century, Parliament has been the supreme decision-making body in England. Because of the diminished role of the monarch in England, executive functions are performed by the prime minister and the cabinet ministers, who are generally members of Parliament. England has had an independent judiciary, with Parliament also retaining the power to remove judges from office.

Since the rise of the British Empire, many of the legal changes in England have led to the export of English law to the colonies. This export led, in turn, to **legal pluralism**, the mixing of more than one system of law within a particular country or region of a country. Colonies retained many of their customary laws and dispute-settlement procedures while the English-style courts handled major crimes and civil matters. The breakup of the empire has led to new challenges relating to rights and citizenship status of former colonial subjects (Glendon, Gordon, & Osakwe, 1985). Over the past fifty years, the dismantling of the British Empire, which originally stretched over one-fourth of the world, has led to the formation of separate political entities for Wales, Scotland, and most recently (2010) Northern Ireland.

A significant recent development in English jurisprudence has been the formation of the Supreme Court of the United Kingdom. With the Constitutional Reform Act of 2005, the British formed this 12-person court to serve as the court of last resort for all matters under English law, Welsh law, Northern Irish law, and Scottish law (civil law only). The High Court of Judiciary remains the court of last resort for criminal cases in Scotland. The court also has the power to handle devolution disputes—cases in which the three government entities (executive, legislative, and judicial branches) are questioned. Since the formation of the Supreme Court, the United Kingdom now has a more formal legal separation of powers between judicial, legislative, and executive functions similar to that in the United States.

Technically, England does not have a written constitution that can be read, cited, and interpreted. It does, however, as we mentioned earlier, have a strong constitutional tradition that has evolved over centuries. This phenomenon requires some explanation. Written constitutions as we know them today are essentially compacts between people and their governments. These compacts describe the governmental machinery, the rights of the people, and the obligations and powers of the government. Such compacts for the governance of large nation-states did not exist until the late 18th century. They descend from 18th-century Enlightenment thought, which stressed natural rights, reason, and the idea of a "social contract." At that time, constitutions were developed in conjunction with revolutionary movements in the United States and France and reflected attempts to solidify and legitimize new systems that represented radical breaks with the past.

England, perhaps because it did not experience such a radical post-Enlightenment break with the past as France and the United States, has never had a comprehensive compact between government and people. Over the centuries, Parliament, especially its lower house, the House of Commons, was the supreme decision-making agency in Britain. With the formation of the new Supreme Court of the United Kingdom there has been an increased governmental supervision on parliamentary supremacy. But the weight of tradition and a sense of practical limits continue to govern parliamentary exercise of power. The so-called Rights of Englishmen, although not set forth in a single document, are as sacred in England as any established rights in countries with written constitutions. The "unwritten" constitution of the British thus includes the great charters mentioned earlier, plus organic laws, constitutional traditions, and legal procedures, including Common Law and equity procedures.

The **organic laws** are those laws of Parliament that describe the machinery of government. In the 20th century, for example, a series of laws known as Parliament Acts gradually reduced the power of the House of Lords, the hereditary upper house of Parliament. Organic laws also govern the electoral process. A good example of a recent organic law is the Human Rights Act (1998). The Act incorporates the European Convention on Human Rights into English law and allows any violations of this convention to be adjudicated in English courts.

English-constitutional traditions are harder to explain to an outsider. Among other things, they cover relations between the monarch and the rest of the government. The king or queen, for example, always asks the leader of the opposition party to form a new government after a previous government has failed to get a vote of confidence in the House of Commons. Although no law requires this action, no monarch would fail to respect the tradition. Finally, legal procedures, including criminal procedure, evolved within the Common Law as an integral part of the English Constitution. More so than in the United States with its fixed constitutional rights, the rights of the accused in England are subject to revision and have undergone some important changes in recent years.

In sum, English government and the English constitution consist of a plurality of structures, laws, and customs tied to certain basic values about representative government and individual rights. Relationships among parts of this whole are often subtle and complex, and the English criminal justice system reflects these complexities. Containing a peculiar mix of amateur and professional elements, it strives to bring justice closer to the people through lay participation at all stages of the process.

Crime

Crime statistics in England are collected and reported by the Research and Statistics Department of the Home Office. There are primarily two kinds of crime data in England and Wales. The first are police data, which are collected and compiled by local police agencies. The second, believed to be more credible, are the data collected by a national marketing firm's systematic victim study, called the British Crime Survey (BCS). This survey asks around 50,000 people aged 16 and over, living in private households, about the crimes they have experienced in the last year. The survey is comparable to the National Crime Victimization Survey (NCVS) conducted in the United States.

Long-term trends show that BCS crime rose steadily from 1981 through the early 1990s. Then, in 1995, crime began to fall sharply, with a more than 55 percent reduction in total violent crime by the year 2012. As a result, violent crime rates in England now reflect numbers similar to those of 1981. Recent data show a 4.2 percent drop in overall reported crime from 2010–11 to 2011–12. Violent crime dropped 7.2 percent during that period alone (Flatley et. al, 2010; Home Office, 2012). Overall, although the crime rate may be too high for many who live in England and Wales, it is low in comparison to other industrialized countries, especially the United States.

In addition to the common crimes that are listed in the British Crime Survey or police statistics, there are other crime concerns in England of a more international scope. England has continued to witness the effects of the illegal drug trade. Cocaine from Latin America and heroin from Southwest Asia enter there for distribution to the European market, and a cottage industry has developed for the production of various synthetic drugs. Another crime problem related to drug trafficking is money laundering. Because of the large number of financial institutions in England, the country is ripe for this kind of crime. However, it is clear that at least one kind of international crime in England and Wales has abated in recent years—terrorism. The unrest in Northern Ireland that lasted for decades, caused by a conflict between Catholics and Protestants, has slowed considerably since the historic Good Friday Agreement was signed on April 10, 1998. A problem of more of immediate concern for the British is the riots that erupted in August 2011 that were the worst seen there in 30 years. The violence began after the shooting of a man by police in Tottenham and spread to other areas, including London. Some have blamed the riots on frustrations related to economic issues, while the government called it a "criminal spree by opportunistic youths" (Chazan & MacDonald, 2011).

Criminal Law

During the fifth century in England, law developed according to decisions made by judges in individual cases, and the Common Law legal tradition was born. The tradition became stronger after the Norman Conquest in 1066, when judges began to travel around the land ruling on cases as they arose, and these judicial circuit courts survive to the present. However, England and Wales still do not have a unified penal code; rather, the criminal law is a combination of statutes and Common Law practice. Statutes are approved by Parliament, and the Common Law is a body of precedent that has developed over centuries and is written in legal textbooks. The most important offenses, such as murder, are under the Common Law, but their penalties are set by statute. Over time, Parliament has codified other Common Law crimes into statutes.

Since 1967, all crimes in England and Wales are either "arrestable" or "unarrestable" offenses. Arrestable offenses, which include all indictable offenses, are those that a person commits or attempts to commit and that are punishable by a fixed incarceration term—for example, murder, manslaughter, rape, burglary, and assault with intent to rob. All other offenses are nonarrestable, or "summary"; these include drunk and disorderly conduct, loitering, and most traffic offenses. These crimes are generally tried in magistrates' court without a jury. Some summary offenses are more serious in nature, such as carrying a weapon or driving while intoxicated, and thus can be indictable and brought before a higher court; these receive a jury trial.

The Criminal Justice System

England and Wales have a long history of allowing local counties and towns to administer and supervise their own affairs. However, the national government remains very active in the administration of justice, and it retains total control of the judiciary. The Lord Chancellor, who is appointed by the prime minister and is a member of the cabinet and the House of Lords, appoints all judges and supervises the court system of England. See Table 4.2 for a summary of criminal justice system information.

Keeping order in England is a shared responsibility between the national and local government. The police are accountable to the Home Secretary, who is also a member of the cabinet. The Home Secretary sets standards and provides the majority of funding for the police, who are then administered on the local level. Yet local governments retain the right to hire employees and must financially contribute to maintaining the local office (Terrill, 2009). The prison service is also under the control of the Home Secretary; however, most administrative power is given to the wardens, who are in charge of the daily operations of the institutions.

Criminal justice in England is strongly influenced by decisions made in Parliament. Each year, Parliament enacts laws defining more offenses, and every few years it develops legislation, called Criminal Justice Acts, that make changes in the system. For example, the Criminal Justice and Police Act (2001) changed how England trained its police, the 2003 Act introduced sentencing guidelines for judges, and the 2008 Act dealt with immigration issues for those believed to be involved with terrorism.

A further influence on English criminal justice, as well as on Continental justice, has been the gradual "Europeanization" of the separate nations of Europe. England has become part of the European Union (EU) and is thus responsible for developing economic and human rights policies that fit the goals of that organization. Members of the Union must adhere to EU law, which can override English legislation and common law decisions.

Comparisons with the United States

In a review of some key issues concerning the criminal justice systems in England and the United States we can see some striking similarities. England has always been similar to the United States in governmental and cultural traditions, to say nothing of their common language. If we look at English law, we can easily see its strong influence on U.S. law—England and the United States are two of the major Common Law countries in the world today. Relative to the administration of police and municipal government, England and the United States are similar in that they both encourage local administration and funding. Local administration of police, water, and sewage are examples of this administration. Recent crime rates in both countries also seem to be parallel. Although it is clear that the violent crime rate in the United States dwarfs that of Britain, the overall crime in both countries began to dip in the mid to late 1990s. Since that time, the violent crime rate has dropped off in Britain and has continued to drop in the United States. Even though conventional crime has become less of a problem, the media has become obsessed with crime stories in both countries, and as a result the criminal justice systems of both countries have been under scrutiny. The criminal justice systems, or more specifically the elected officials within them, have responded to the scrutiny with a steady stream of legislation by the British Parliament and American Congress to reform criminal justice policies. This trend is sure to continue as "get tough" crime strategies have become commonplace in both countries (Newburn, 2007).

TABLE 4.2 Selected Criminal Justice System Information for Model Countries

Selected Legal Information	United States	China	France	Germany	Saudi Arabia	United Kingdom	Japan
Legal System	Common Law (Unitary)	Socialist and Civil Law (Unitary)	Civil Law (unitary)	Civil Law (federal)	Islamic law (non-constitutional monarchy)	Common Law (unitary constitutional monarchy)	Hybrid; mostly Civil Law (unitary)
Criminal Data Sources	Uniform Crime Reports, self-reports, and victim surveys	China Statistical Yearbook, China Law Yearbook, victim surveys, self-reports	Annuaire statistique de la justice, victim surveys	Criminal Federal Police	Ministry of Justice	British Crime (victim) statistics and police data (Home Office)	Ministry of Justice in White Paper on Crime
Responsibility for Criminal Justice Administration	*Police:* local and state govt. *Corrections:* local and state govt. and Federal Bureau of Prisons *Courts:* county, state, and federal structures	*Police:* Minister of Public Safety *Corrections:* Ministry of Justice *Courts:* Ministry of Justice	*Police:* Minister of Interior and Minister of Defense *Corrections:* Minister of Justice *Courts:* Minister of Justice	*Police, Courts, and* *Corrections:* Länder (states)	*Police:* Ministry of Justice and Director of Public Safety *Corrections:* Bureau of Prisons *Courts:* Minister of Justice	*Police:* Home Secretary *Corrections:* Home Secretary- *Courts:* Lord Chancellor	*Police:* National Police Safety Commission and the National Policy Agency *Corrections and courts:* federal court structure
Crime Issues	Illicit drugs, high violent-crime rates	Illicit drugs, corruption and fraud, human trafficking, civil unrest	Illicit drugs and trafficking, civil unrest, terrorism	Illicit drugs and trafficking, hate crimes	Unknown	Illicit drugs and trafficking, money laundering	Youth crime, organized crime, theft

FRANCE

Overview

The name "France" comes from the latin word *Francia*, which means "country of the Franks." The Franks were a German tribe in the third century that lived along what is now the Rhine River. The pagan Franks, living in the region called Gaul which consisted of large parts of Northern Italy, Switzerland, Germany, France, Belgium and the Netherlands, were governed by the rule of Clovis I. Clovis was the first Germanic conqueror to convert to Catholicism in around 500 AD. As a result, the Franks would turn primarily Catholic and begin a long succession of kings that would affiliate with that Church.

France has been a center of cultural creation for centuries. Many French artists have been among the most renowned of their time, and France is generally recognized in the world for its rich cultural life and traditions. Among the most famous French painters are those that developed new styles of impressionism painting in the 19th century, including Manet, Monet, Renoir, and later Cezanne, Gaugin, and Toulouse-Lautrec. The museums in France are world renowned, especially the Louvre in Paris. Paris is the where the French proudly display their French (gothic) architecture, and it is home to one of the most visited tourist attractions in the world, the Eiffel Tower. The French language is the official language in 29 countries, and it is one of the six official languages of the United Nations. One only needs to visit France, and to order food in English, to learn how important the country feels it is to retain the language as an essential element of preserving their unique and outstanding culture.

The French Republic, with a population of over 65 million, is divided into 22 administrative regions. The French also retain control over 11 regions outside metropolitan France. France boasts one of the four strongest Western European economies, mainly because of its fertile farmland and highly developed industrial sector. In addition to being the leading agricultural producer in Western Europe, France also is a major producer of steel, chemicals, electronics, and nuclear energy. For a summary of more demographic information about France, see Table 4.1.

Like England, France is a unitary state that has always prized a highly centralized form of government in which all major decisions are made through a national bureaucracy situated in the capital city of Paris. Parisians distinguish between Paris and the rest of the country, with the implication that anything that is not Parisian is provincial in the sense of being somewhat backward and lacking in sophistication. France also maintains a strong **republican government** style, in which a president heads the government but the main power remains in the hands of citizens, who vote for representatives who are then responsible to the electorate.

France's 22 administrative regions are further divided into 96 provinces that act as conduits to the central government. Each province is administered by a *prefect* selected by the government to enforce the laws of the nation. During the early 1990s, the government proposed modifying this 200-year-old system of total centralization. Legislation has decentralized authority, giving a broader range of powers to local elected officials. The prefect still retains general power over law and order, but local governments can now hire their own officials, including some local police officers (Terrill, 2009).

France has modified its constitution 15 times since 1789. The constitution of the Fifth Republic, formed in 1958, provides for an independently elected president who is the chief of state. Duties of the president include presiding over the cabinet, which is called the Council of Ministers, and selecting the prime minister, who is the actual head of the government. Like England and the United States, France has a two-house legislature consisting of the National Assembly (lower chamber) and the Senate (upper chamber). Although the constitution calls for an independent judicial system, France does not have an equivalent of the U.S. Supreme Court to consider the constitutionality of cases. Instead, it has a Constitutional Council that gives advisory opinions about legislation that has been passed but has not yet gone into effect.

Historical Development

Over the past 500 years, France has been a major world power with strong influence in Europe and around the world. During the 17th and 18th centuries, France colonized great parts of North America and Southeast Asia. During the 19th and early 20th centuries, France built a large colonial empire that included large portions of Africa and Southeast Asia, as well as many Caribbean and Pacific Islands.

In the centuries prior to the 1789 revolution, France was ruled by a series of Bourbon kings, the most famous of whom was Louis XIV. Under Louis XIV, who ruled from 1643 to 1715, royal power in France became increasingly strong and centralized. His successors, however, were unable to deal with the economic and social change that characterized the 18th century. After borrowing heavily to finance France's wars with England, the monarchy collapsed under the pressure of internal revolutionary forces. King Louis XVI and his wife, Marie Antoinette, were executed in 1792, and the 1790s remained a period of turmoil.

From the standpoint of governmental philosophy, the passage of the Declaration of the Rights of Man and of the Citizen by the French parliament in 1789 was a defining moment in the revolutionary period. The declaration asserted the right to resist oppression, the rights to both liberty and equality, and the need for separation of powers to avoid a tyrannical government. Although not primarily concerned with the administration of justice, 3 of the 17 articles addressed this subject. Most importantly, the declaration asserted the right to a presumption of innocence and to freedom from arbitrary detention.

The republican spirit in France was marred by the excesses of the Reign of Terror that followed the Revolution. This was brought to an end by a renewed absolutism, that of Napoleon Bonaparte, a general in the French army who seized power in 1799. Napoleon's dictatorship brought about major changes in the French government, especially in the administrative and legal structures. In 1804, Napoleon declared himself emperor, and France became an empire. In that same year, the French Civil Code, or Napoleonic Code (described in Chapter 3), went into effect.

After a series of wars that involved most of Western Europe and part of Eastern Europe, Napoleon himself met final defeat in 1815 at the Battle of Waterloo. The rest of the 19th century was characterized by successive attempts at renewed monarchy, republican governments, and even another empire under a nephew of Napoleon. In 1875, following a period of turmoil that included war with Germany and the revolutionary Paris Commune movement in 1871, France again established a republic. This Third Republic lasted until World War II, although the average life of a ruling parliamentary coalition during that time was only six months. Following the postwar downfall of the Vichy government, which had collaborated with the Germans, the Fourth Republic was established. In 1958, the Fourth Republic gave way to the Fifth Republic, a brainchild of the military and political leader Charles de Gaulle (1890–1970). General de Gaulle became prime minister in June 1958, became president later that year, and remained in office until 1969.

Crime

Crime statistics in France have traditionally been derived from the office of the Directory of Justice statistics and are called the *Annuaire statistique de la justice*. These data, describing crimes reported to the police, showed a relatively stable or even slight decrease in crime during the 1990s (Entorf & Spengler, 2002). However, more recent data reported by the French National Monitoring Centre on Crime reflect a significant increase in crime. Recent data show a 24.5 percent increase in crime between 2002 and 2007 as reflected by the number of total indictments brought to French courts, not counting traffic offenses. However, newly developed victimization surveys show only a slight increase in violent crime (1.5 percent) and fraud (3.4 percent), while thefts reported to police dropped 7.3 percent during that same period (Crime in France, 2008). One kind of crime that has shown a steady increase since the early 1980s is simple drug use, more specifically personal use of marijuana. The years 2000 to 2006 saw an increase in arrests from 93,000 to over 142,000. Since 2009 there has been a drop to below 138,000 arrests (National Report, 2010).

Like the English, the French must deal with problems related to drugs, immigration, and terrorism. Like England, France is both a transshipment point for and consumer of South American cocaine and Southwest Asian heroin. With the collapse of its North African colonial empire, France has experienced a large immigration of Arabs from the former colonies of Algeria, Tunisia, and Morocco. Reports of hate crimes and discrimination against these immigrants, racial tension, and cultural conflict have resulted, with attendant problems for law enforcement and judicial operations. With the largest Jewish population in Western Europe, France has also experienced an increase in the number of verbal and physical attacks on Jews.

Terrorism is a concern because France is a crossroads for terrorist activity, from both internal and external sources. As we mentioned in the opening of this chapter, politically motivated acts of violence are a major concern, with many of the problems stemming from labor unions' protests against government cutbacks to services and benefits. Several violent riots have taken place recently, and attacks on police officers and other public officials are not uncommon. Islamic terrorism also remains a concern for the French. With a large Muslim population of over 5 million, rioting by Islamic youths has been a significant problem, especially in housing projects located on the fringes of large cities such as Paris.

France is also a human trafficking destination country for men, women, and children from Eastern Europe, West Africa, and Asia, as well as the Caribbean and Brazil. These persons are subjected to forced prostitution and forced labor and forced domestic servitude. Often their "employers" are diplomats who enjoy diplomatic immunity from prosecution, including those from Saudi Arabia. The Government of France estimates that the majority of the 18,000 women in France's commercial sex trade are likely forced into prostitution (U.S. Department of State, 2010).

Criminal Law

The basic principles of criminal law in France come from the 1789 Declaration of the Rights of Man and of the Citizen. The first penal code was devised in 1810, but it has been revised many times, most recently in 1994. The penal code distinguishes crimes based on their seriousness, from serious felonies, to less serious felonies and misdemeanors (called *delit*), to violations (called *contraventions*). These categories are important because they determine in what court the case will be heard and the kind of punishment that will be implemented.

The French penal code is divided into five books. Book I explains the general provisions in the penal law, including criminal liability and responsibility, lengths of sentences, and kinds of punishments. Book II describes crimes (felonies) and delits (serious misdemeanors) against persons, including crimes against individuals and against human rights. Book III deals with crimes and delits against property. Book IV is devoted to crimes and delits against the nation, the government, and the public order. Book V addresses other crimes and delits not associated with categories included in the other books. The new penal code also distinguishes between completed and attempted acts of crime; addresses recent issues such as corporate crime, alternatives to incarceration, and punishment for serious offenders; and defines new crimes such as ecological terrorism, sexual harassment, crimes against humanity, and genocide (Borricand, 1999).

The Criminal Justice System

Through all the political instability of the past 200 years, French administrative structures have provided an element of continuity that has helped hold the country together. The French bureaucracy has a reputation for being extremely powerful, rule bound, and inaccessible. Within criminal justice, particularly in the court system, France has developed a highly sophisticated (and complicated) system of administrative courts to oversee the legislature and address citizen complaints. In short, the administrative courts supervise the government. The two most influential administrative courts are the Constitutional Counsel Court and Council of State.

The Constitutional Counsel Court (*Conseil Constitutionnel*) reviews legislation proposed by the legislature, prime minister, or president and determines whether it comports with the constitution. The Council of State (*Conseil d'Etat*) is the supreme administrative court. Originally set up to aid the rulers in their contacts with citizens, it has become a leading advocate of citizens' rights in dealing with the government. The Council of State has been especially valuable since the French Constitution makes no provision for challenging the constitutionality of government action, and only in recent years has the Constitutional Council Court extended its mandate to some cases of human rights abuses.

In addition to administrative courts, France has a number of ordinary courts that deal with civil and criminal law cases, the highest of which is the Supreme Court of Appeals (*Cour de Cassation*). A unique feature of the French legal system is the unity of the civil and criminal courts—the same court can hear both criminal and civil cases.

The police in France are generally divided into two bodies: the Police Nationale and the Gendarmerie. Over the last 15 years, smaller cities and towns have been allowed to form their own municipal police, although most still rely on either the Police Nationale or Gendarmerie. Correctional services in France are under the supervision of the Ministry of Justice. It is possible that, in light of the historical and political forces that are present in the country, the criminal justice system in France will change considerably in the next few decades. France historically has had an unstable political environment and has been prone to revolution. Ideological debates over the importance of individual rights versus community interests remain heated. Rising immigration rates and their concomitant problems, along with attempts to decentralize governmental authority, have added to the instability.

Comparisons with the United States

The governments of France and the United States are similar in that they both were developed after a revolution, are republican in style, and are rooted in a written constitution. Although France has moved to enhance the role of local systems of government, these systems remain embedded in a centralized form of government. The United States, through a system of federalism, allows states and local jurisdictions to handle almost all of their own day-to-day functioning. Much of the criminal justice system of France is a highly centralized bureaucracy. Although local police are permitted, most jurisdictions still rely on one of the two national police forces, while courts and corrections remain centralized. Like the United States, France had a stable or declining crime rate for most of the 1990s. But recent French crime statistics reveal an upswing since 2002, especially in violent crime, personal drug use, economic crimes, and inner-city youth crime. Terrorism, a concern in France for decades due to considerable political and economic turmoil, is now a major concern for both countries. And much like the United States and England, increases in various forms of crime have prompted a call for "get tough" and "zero tolerance" measures by French politicians.

GERMANY

Overview

The English word *Germany* derives from the Latin word *Germania*, which is believed to have come into use after it was adopted by Julius Caesar, who used it to describe the people of who lived east of the Rhine River during around 60 BC. The formal name of Germany remains the Federal Republic of Germany, or Bundesrepublik Deutschland. Germany has over 81 million people occupying an area about the size of California. The location and size of Germany are unique in that it is surrounded by nine different countries and is the most densely populated country in Europe. Because it is located at the center of Northern Europe, Germany has a long history of being involved in conflicts and invasions from within and from neighbouring tribes.

Through the centuries, Germans have made major contributions in religion, science, philosophy, literature, and music. For example, Martin Luther challenged the Roman Catholic Church in 1517, leading to the Protestant Reformation. Figures such as Albert Einstein, Johannes Gutenberg, the Brothers Grimm, Bach, Beethoven, and Karl Marx have greatly influenced how the world lives and enjoys life on a daily basis. After a tumultuous 20th century in which it became involved in and lost two world wars, Germany has now joined European and transatlantic partners in championing peace, democracy, and human rights the world over.

By any measure, Germany is one of the richest nations of the world. However, high taxes, high wages, increased immigration, growing unemployment, costs associated with rebuilding the former East Germany, and the recent financial crisis in the European Union, have caused some economic strain in Germany. For a summary of more demographic information on Germany, see Table 4.1. The country is divided into 16 states, called **Länder** (singular Land), and as discussed in Chapter 3, the Civil Law legal tradition is strongly entrenched. Germany is a federal republic in which power is distributed between the federal government and state (Länder) governments. The government contains executive, legislative, and judicial branches, much like the United States. However, the presidency is largely a ceremonial post, and true executive power lies in the hands of the chancellor (the leader of the party that gained the largest number of votes in the most recent elections) and his chosen cabinet. Generally, no party wins a majority of seats, so the cabinet is usually a coalition; that is, it contains both members of the chancellor's party and some members of at least one other party that joins with the chancellor's party to create a majority in the legislature.

Germany has a bicameral (two-house) legislative branch that contains a lower house and principal chamber, known as the *Bundestag*, and an upper house or federal council, called the *Bundesrat*. The federal constitutional court, the *Bundesverfassungsgericht*, stands at the apex of a hierarchy of state and lower federal courts. Half of its judges are elected by the Bundestag and half by the Bundesrat.

Historical Development

The nation of Germany actually did not exist until 1870, when most of the German states in Central Europe were unified in a federation under Emperor William I. Otto von Bismarck, who became chancellor of the new nation, was the architect of German unification. Like Napoleon in France, Bismarck left his imprint on the German administrative apparatus. During Bismarck's term as chancellor, Germany was experiencing a belated industrial revolution and adjusting to centralized governmental power. Bismarck was careful to involve the German nobility in administration at the state level even as he was consolidating policy-making power at the central level. The culture of a strong, elite civil service that was established through these actions survives to this day in Germany. This civil service includes the personnel of all police, judicial, and sanctioning agencies in Germany.

As we learned in Chapter 3, one of the most important changes in German law in modern times was the German Civil Code, developed under Bismarck. This code of laws helped to consolidate and legitimate the new state. Imperial Germany lasted only until 1918, when, following the country's defeat in World War I, a federal republic with a model democratic constitution was established. This republic was known as the Weimar Republic after the city where its constitution was promulgated. The Weimar Republic was short-lived, ending with the ascent to power of Adolf Hitler and his National Socialist, or Nazi, party in 1933. The Nazis abolished federalism and made Germany a centralized, absolutist, and essentially arbitrary and lawless state.

Hitler restored Germany's economic and military strength, but his nationalist themes and aggressive policies, most notably the attempt to eliminate the Jewish population in Europe, led Germany into World War II. The war led to the political and economic destruction of Germany, which surrendered unconditionally in May 1945. At the Yalta Conference in 1945, Germany was split among the "big three" allies of the war: the United States, Britain, and the Soviet Union. Soviet forces assumed control over the eastern half of Germany while the western half came under the supervision of Britain and the United States. The city of Berlin, although it was within the Soviet territory, also was divided up among the three powers. This situation remained until October 1990, when the nation of Germany was reunited after 45 years of postwar division.

The former East Germany was a communist state with a Socialist Law orientation. Since reunification, the nation has operated under the constitution of the former West Germany. This constitution, called the Basic Law, was first promulgated in May 1949. The constitution's framers tried to avoid some of the weaknesses of the earlier constitution that made the Weimar Republic unstable and unable to deal effectively with radical opposition. One of these changes was the establishment of a lawmaking constitutional court, such as exists in the United States, to settle disputes and establish the parameters of power between state and federal governments and between the government and the people.

The Basic Law, which contains 146 articles, describes the composition and functions of the various organs of government, including the system of checks and balances, the distribution of power between the federal government and the Länder, the administration of federal law, government finances, and government administration in emergency conditions. The first 17 articles spell out the rights of Germans. Some of these rights are familiar, such as freedom of religion, freedom of speech and press, and freedom from unreasonable searches and seizures. Other rights, such as the right to "free development of … personality," the provision of special state protection for families and illegitimate children, and the right to choose one's own trade or profession, are different from the rights enumerated in the U.S. Constitution, although they are certainly amenable to interpretation as being implied in the Bill of Rights.

Crime

A perusal of German crime statistics (*Polizeiliche Kriminalstatistik*), which are collected by the Criminal Federal Police (*Bundeskriminalamt*), reflects that in the first few years following reunification, the country experienced a sharp increase in crime. This increase abated, however, and between 1995 and 2004 Germany experienced an overall drop (1.6 percent) in total crimes per 100,000 population. During the same time period, the homicide rate in Germany declined 41.2 percent (Aromaa & Heiskanen, 2008). More recently, between the years 2009 and 2010, overall crime in Germany decreased 2.0 percent, with drug crimes and violent crimes also declining 2.1 percent and 3.5 percent, respectively (Police Crime Statistics, 2010).

As in much of the Western world, drug offenses have become a major problem in Germany, and they account for the significant increase in the incarceration rate since 1991. Drugs are a problem because Germany is a source of chemicals for South American cocaine processors and a transshipment point for and consumer of Southwest Asian heroin and hashish, Latin American cocaine, and European-produced synthetic drugs (CIA, 2012).

The problem of drugs and crime, the extensive immigration from bordering countries, and the related ethnic violence are three of the most important contemporary influences on the criminal justice system in Germany. Immigrants from the former Yugoslavia, Greece, Italy, and Turkey, as well as a new wave of ethnic German immigrants from neighboring countries, have strained the German capacity to assimilate new people. The attendant problems of economic disparity, culture clash, discrimination, and even overt racism are creating cleavages in the formerly homogeneous German society, and these problems carry over into the criminal justice process. Because of economic uncertainty, some right-wing extremist groups have blamed their own hardships on foreigners. Harassment and violence towards foreigners, conducted by a small minority of Germans, has increased in the incidence of hate crimes in Germany.

Since 1990 the number of violent offenses recorded by police as having xenophobic or right-wing connections has risen. In 2008, the police registered nearly 14,000 cases with right-wing or extremist characteristics, including 735 crimes of violence. German human rights advocates have estimated that 136 people have been killed by right-wing violence between 1990 and 2005 (Feltes, 2009).

Criminal Law

In earlier times, German criminal law was a combination of Common Law principles and local indigenous law. In the late 17th century, criminal law became codified in most territories, and in the late 19th century, under Bismarck, a unified criminal code was enacted. This code, called the *Reichsstrafgesetzbuch*, has generally remained in effect despite the many changes that have taken place in Germany over the past 125 years.

German law is a combination of statutes (*Gesetz*), ordinances and administrative rules (*Rechtsverordnung*), and customs (*Gewohnheitsrecht*). Two kinds of statutes comprise the largest portion of German law. The first, called *Bundesgesetz*, are federal statutes enacted by the Bundestag. The second are state (Länder) laws, called *Landesgesetz*, which are enacted by state legislators. Ordinances are issued by the federal government, federal ministers, or state governments. Customs are not considered a formal source of law, but for centuries they provided direction in legal matters because they were habitually practiced and informally acknowledged as having the rule of law.

The criminal codes are carefully integrated bodies of general principles arranged in a highly systematized manner and phrased in abstract language. This enables lawyers and judges to liberally apply the principles of the law to assist them in resolving particular cases. Previous court decisions are used not as sources of law, as in Common Law countries, but as guides by lower court judges, and so they have an influence on legal norms (Herrmann, 1987). The German criminal code distinguishes between felonies and misdemeanors. Felonies (*Schwerverechen*) are punishable by imprisonment of at least one year; misdemeanors (*Vergehen*) are punishable by a fine or a shorter minimum prison term.

Even though Germany is a federal republic that allows individual Länder to attend to their own criminal court matters, almost all criminal and procedural laws are subject to federal legislation. In practice, this means that federal law is applied to the state courts.

The Criminal Justice System

Because Germany is a federalist country, it generally allows individual Länder to handle their own affairs related to policing, corrections, and lower court administration. For example, Article 30 of the federal Basic Law provides legal authority for the Länder over police matters within their own territory. However, this does not mean that the Länder may do whatever they please in the administration of justice; rather, their decisions must be legally within the provisions stated in the federal Basic Law. For example, the (federal) Prison Act of 1976 identifies rehabilitation as a major philosophical principle in German penal law and correctional practice. Even though the individual Länder are allowed to administer their own correctional facilities, they must adhere to the major principles of the Prison Act (Dammer, 1996).

The criminal justice system of Germany reflects the influence of both the Civil Law tradition as it was redefined in imperial Germany and the Common Law tradition as it was applied during the U.S. occupation after World War II. Like the U.S. Supreme Court, the German Federal Constitutional Court has been active in defining the balance of powers between states and the federal government. It also has interpreted the constitutional rights included in the Basic Law. Criminal procedure as practiced in Germany reflects some U.S. influence, but it is still largely a Civil Law process.

Comparisons with the United States

Similar to the United States, Germany has a federal republic system that distributes power between the federal and state governments. As a result, in Germany the Länder can administer police, courts, and corrections as long as policies and procedures are not contrary to the Basic Law. In this way the Basic Law performs like the U.S. Constitution. Contrary to the U.S. practice, Germany is strongly driven by the Civil Law tradition, and all laws are made into codes that are arranged in a highly systematized manner and phased in language that enables lawyers and judges to apply the law. The crime rate in Germany, much like that in the United States, has dropped since the mid-1990s. Crime rates have dropped in Germany related to violence, drugs, and even human trafficking over the past five years. However, drug-related offenses remain a serious problem in both countries. Hate crimes, which have apparently been fueled by immigration and the unification with former East Germany, have risen considerably in recent years and are a major concern to the German government.

CHINA

Overview

China is the world's most populous nation and one of the world's oldest civilizations with thousands of years of continuous history. The word *China* was actually popularized by 13th-century explorer Marco Polo, and the roots of the word are believed to come from Sanskirt and Hindu scriptures. To the Chinese it is called *Zhongguo*, which literally means middle or central kingdom. What is now China was inhabited by the first known erect man, called *homo erectus*, who is believed to have migrated to China from Africa more than 1.2 million years ago. Because of its land size, people, and climate, it is difficult to make general statements about China. China has a population four times that of the United States; it possesses large bursting cities and even bigger expanses of arid hills and desert where one can roam for days without seeing a soul. Although over 60 percent of the population claim Han Chinese as their ethnicity, there are an additional 55 other recognized minority groups (Saich, 2011). In addition, the tremendous changes that the county has seen in recent years related to the economy and politics make it a difficulty country to categorize and understand in any simple fashion. An example of the complexity can be seen by how China has invested in improving its global image thorough increasing the use of electronic media. At the same time, the Chinese have often moved to control the media and even to limit or shut down usage if the information that is being transmitted is critical of the government. One specific example was in October 2010, when author Liu Xiaobo received the Nobel prize for literature but the Chinese government blocked new programs and Internet portals announcing the news. Liu received the news himself while in jail, where he was interned for his writings in 2009, which were viewed by the government at slander and unpatriotic (Weston and Jensen, 2012).

China, the third-largest country in the world after Russia and Canada, is only slightly larger than the United States, with a geographic area of about 3.7 million square miles. Primarily a peasant-based society throughout history, China has made efforts over the last 30 years to modernize in the areas of agriculture, science and technology, and national defense. As of 2011, the population of China was above 1.3 billion, which makes it more populous than Europe, Russia, and the United States combined. For more demographic information on China, see Table 4.1.

China is a unitary, multinational socialist country with 23 provinces (including Taiwan), 5 autonomous regions (including Tibet), and 4 municipalities directly under the authority of the central government (Beijing, Chongquing, Shanghai, and Tianjin). The country is also divided into over 115 autonomous prefectures, 476 cities, 1,894 counties, and 650 districts (Terrill, 2009).

The primary organs of governmental power in China are the presidency, the State Council, and the **National People's Congress (NPC)**. The NPC, theoretically the most powerful, meets annually to review and approve the budget and major new policy directions, laws, and personnel changes. However, in reality, all levels of the Chinese government are subordinate to the Chinese Communist Party (CCP), so the real role of government is to implement party policy. For example, all initiatives proposed by the NPC must be previously endorsed by the CCP's Central Committee.

In the years following the Communist takeover in 1949, the government essentially owned all industry and commercial land holdings. Since 1979, China has sought to convert its economy from a Soviet-type centrally planned economy to a socialist market-based one. What this really means is that China is trying to adapt modern economic practices while retaining the right to oversee policies so they meet Communist ideology. Reforms have included reducing the role of the government in economic policy, promoting household responsibility in agriculture, increasing the power of local officials in industrial plant management, and introducing small-scale enterprise in the service and light manufacturing areas. These reforms worked very well into the 1980s, spurring tremendous growth in agricultural and industrial output. However, problems with inflation have caused public officials to retighten central controls of the economy.

The growth rate of the 1980s has slowed, and unemployment in China has reached over 13 million according to official figures, with a 2011 unemployment rate of 6.5; some even suggest that those numbers only reflect urban areas of employment and that the real number is perhaps twice that high (CIA, 2012; Fang, 1999, p. 35). With the shift from a purely socialist to more eclectic economic system, China has encountered some of the problems associated with such a change, including an overall increase in crime.

Historical Development

The Chinese traditionally have struggled with the formulation of their law and criminal justice system. A succession of dynasties ruled during most of China's 4,000-year-long history, with various systems of bureaucratic controls. The last dynasty, the Qing, reigned from 1644 through the first decade of the 20th century. Some of the more enduring written laws and statutes that surfaced during these times were the Yuxing criminal laws of the Xia dynasty, the Hanlu laws of the Han dynasty, and the Daquing Luli criminal code of the Qing dynasty. In reality, however, the codes of laws developed during dynastic rule were no more than rules implemented to protect the totalitarian governments in place at the time (Terrill, 2009).

Because the concept of equal rights before the law for all persons was absent, disrespect for the law was commonplace, and there was minimal acceptance of any formal codes proposed by the ruling class. What resulted was the adoption of an informal social control system, rooted in Confucian and Taoist thought, that began to take hold in China during the Han dynasty (206 BC–220 AD).

Confucius (551–479 BC) was a philosopher who believed that social order can be achieved through moral and political reforms and that humans are by nature good or capable of goodness. What is essential is that individuals treat one another with kindness and propriety. When individuals act contrary to these virtues, they bring shame to themselves, family, and friends. Thus, the idea of group consciousness or collectivity is the main force motivating people to avoid illegal or immoral activity. In **Confucian thought**, written laws and formal social control may be important, but they are not nearly as important as strong individual moral virtue. As Confucius stated, "The superior man is concerned with virtue; the inferior man is concerned with law" (Confucius, 1989).

Taoist philosophy, which was developed in Asia a century after the introduction of Confucianism, proposed that all forces of nature are connected and that it is necessary for individuals to become "one" with those forces. If a person is in a state of harmony or "oneness" with nature, then conflict will cease to exist. Together, Confucian and Taoist thought have permeated Chinese society, with the goal of getting citizens to be in consonance with those around them, to be in harmony with others and the rules of society. It was believed that the best way to accomplish this was through social persuasion and informal social control. Informal social control mechanisms include family members, neighbors, and fellow workers, as well as local town, city, or countywide boards that point out deviant behavior and provide sanctions. Within the ideals of Confucian and Taoist thought, the Chinese have often rejected legalism and relied on mediation and compromise to settle disputes and conflict. In fact, under Confucianism people were discouraged from using litigation to protect themselves or their rights.

For thousands of years, this informal system of social control dominated in China's vast regions. Between 1911 and 1949, the democratic Kuomintang regime attempted to install a legal system rooted in six basic written laws. However, efforts to formalize the legal system were often subverted by civil unrest, invasions from Japan, and continuing political chaos. The mentality of distrust of formal law also continued into the 20th century, serving as a catalyst for the reconstruction of the law and social order under the Communist Party of the People's Republic of China. From 1949 through 1979, the Chinese government developed a Soviet-style criminal justice system, with overall control in the hands of the Communist Party. Meanwhile, all formal criminal law codes were rejected, and all forms of written codes of law were eliminated. Instead, a series of edicts, rules, and regulations based on the ideals of the ruling party were used to control behavior and punish deviance. These documents were highly politicized, based as they were on the edicts of the CCP. The goal of the Communist law was to destroy economic classes and construct a social order based on the rule of the people rather than the rule of law. The belief was that formal written laws served only those in power and the bureaucracy; the latter was abhorred by Chairman Mao (1893–1976) and the Communist Party.

However, a shift away from total acceptance of unwritten codes and informal social control mechanisms occurred as a result of a series of events that began in 1966. In that year, Mao tried to reform the party, which he saw as becoming "old in thought, culture, customs, and habits." This reform period, called the **Cultural Revolution**, lasted until 1976. Mao and his followers encouraged direct opposition to those in power—most notably, the police and any person who was considered bourgeois—and bands of young supporters called the Red Guard were formed to implement and oversee the reform policies. The goal was to move Chinese society from socialism to a purer form of communism. But the Cultural Revolution was a significant failure. Economic, political, and social institutions were seriously disrupted throughout China. The police, procuracy, and courts were often simply handed over to political activist organizations as tools to harass and arrest those opposed to Mao and his followers. The public order was disrupted, and crime and violence became so prevalent that the army was called in to restore order. By 1976, the year Chairman Mao died, the government was able to declaw supporters of the Cultural Revolution and bring some semblance of order to China.

Under the leadership of Deng Xiaoping (1904–1997), the government sought to promote law as part of an ordered society, in contrast to the chaotic environment of the Cultural Revolution (Lawyer's Committee, 1994, p. 5). Under Deng, the Chinese changed from their previous ideals of the "rule of man" to the principles of the "rule of law." The movement toward a more formal legal system with codified laws was also necessary to Deng's goal of modernizing the economy and increasing contact with the outside world. The current Chinese government, headed by President Hu Jintao and Premier Wen Jiabao, must face many social issues, including rapid modernization and liberalization, severe unemployment, increasing crime, and corruption.

Crime

It is difficult to assess long-term crime rates in China because for the first 30 or more years of Communist rule, crime statistics were rarely available and even less reliable. Since the late 1970s, the Chinese have regularly provided crime data in two forms: the *China Statistical Yearbook* and the *China Law Yearbook*. More recently, the Chinese have developed other kinds of crime data similar to those of the United States, including victimization studies and self-report studies (Liu, 2008).

These data have revealed that over that last 30 years China has experienced at least three crime waves (Ma, 1995; Liu & Messner, 2001; Terrill, 2009). In response to crime increases, the Chinese government initiated different anticrime crackdowns or "Strike Hard" campaigns (called *Yanda*). The most recent of these campaigns took place in June 2012, when the Chinese government arrested over 10,000 persons who allegedly committed Internet crimes such as fraud, spreading pornography, and hacking into personal and government web pages. In addition, over 600 criminal gangs were infiltrated, 62 websites closed, and 30 Internet providers fined (English News, 2012). It is not clear whether these *yanda* campaigns have managed to reduce crime. In fact, some evidence exists that the crime rate actually increased during such reforms (Bakken, 2005; Shenghui & Oberwittler, 2009).

Inspection of long-term crime rates in China reflects an increase in a number of crimes from 1978 to 2003. During that period of time, the homicide rate doubled, rape increased 30 percent, assault 7.5 percent, robbery 4.5 percent, larceny by a factor of 8, and fraud by a factor of 14 (Zhang et al., 2007). After some decline in subsequent years, it has been reported by the Chinese Academy of Social Sciences (CASS) that violent crime and property crimes rose dramatically (15 percent) in 2009 (People's Daily, 2012).

In addition to violent crimes, other major crime concerns for the Chinese are drugs and the growing variety of economic crimes. Drug abuse and drug trafficking in general have increased since the late 1970s, with China a major transshipment point for heroin produced in the Golden Triangle region of Thailand, Laos, and Burma. The Chinese have acknowledged that drug abuse is a serious problem and that the number of addicts in the country has risen significantly (Chang, 2004). Efforts have been made to address the problem as a medical issue through the formation of rehabilitation clinics. With the development of a market economy, economic crimes such as bank, credit card, and check fraud have plagued China. Also, with the rise of privatization and increased economic interactions between the public and private sectors, corruption of public officials has become widespread in China.

Although the growing crime rates in China are a concern, what is even more troubling is that many of the most common crimes, called public order crimes, are not consistently reported. Among the crimes that are handled unofficially or administratively by local police and court officials are theft, assault, gambling, and vandalism. It is clear that if those crimes were reported as they are in most other countries, the Chinese crime figures would be much higher (Liu, 2008).

There has been considerable speculation as to why the crime rate has increased in China. Recently, the CASS claimed that the deteriorating economy has caused people to commit violent crime (People's Daily, 2012). In the past, crime has been explained by the fact that cities have become crowded with people who migrated from rural areas looking for work, meaning a diminished capacity for social control. In some cases, individuals have turned to crime because they are frustrated that they cannot obtain the wealth and prosperity of others around them (Ma, 1995). Many people in China, especially the young, have grown cynical about the politics of the Communist Party while becoming infatuated with capitalism and the idea of individual wealth (Rojek, 1996). As a result of this cynicism, the Chinese have experienced a significant rise in the number of mass demonstrations, protests, and riots. In 2005 alone, over 87,000 demonstrations were recorded, which is a 6-fold increase from 10 years earlier (Zhiqun, 2010). Reports by the CASS state that recent civil unrest is the result of political and economic policies that leave many people without the benefits derived from economic development. The growing gap in living standards between urban and rural residents, unbridled industrial development, and pollution of the environment have exacerbated the situation (AsiaNews.it, 2009).

It appears that the political, economic, and social changes in China have begun to move Chinese society away from the long-standing Confucian ideals that permeated Asian culture for centuries (Sheptycki, 2008). As we progress through the 21st century, it will be interesting to see how China deals with economic and political turmoil and the larger social problems associated with significant change.

Criminal Law

In 1979, the Second Session of the Fifth National People's Congress adopted codes of criminal law and procedure, as well as other laws. The criminal law, which took effect in January 1980, consisted of 192 articles divided into two sections—general (*zongze*) and special (*fenze*) provisions. The general provisions gave the basic principles underlying the application of the criminal law. The specific provisions included chapters addressing eight classes of offenses: (1) counterrevolutionary offenses, (2) offenses endangering public security, (3) offenses against socialist economic order, (4) offenses infringing upon the personal and economic rights of citizens, (5) offenses of encroachment of property, (6) offenses against public order, (7) offenses against marriage and the family, and (8) dereliction of duty and corruption (Lawyers Committee, 1998).

In 1997 the criminal law of the People's Republic of China received a major overhaul. The new law is significantly larger than the old law, with 452 versus 192 articles, and in general is broader in coverage and contains more specific definitions of crimes. An attempt has also been made to unify the criminal law, depoliticize the correctional system, and lessen discretion for officials (Lawyers Committee, 1998). At first glance, it might seem that the Chinese government is "softening" to the idea of increased individual rights for citizens. However, the law still neglects to include provisions for some basic human rights enjoyed by citizens in many other countries, such as freedom of speech and freedom of association. The impact of the new criminal and procedural laws will only be determined over time. And even with the new emphasis on the rule of law in China, the Communist Party remains the major decision-making body in the country, and the government is still unrestrained by the rules of law—unlike the situation in most Civil and Common Law legal systems.

The Criminal Justice System

China's centrally monitored criminal justice system has four components: police, procuratorate, courts, and corrections. Each operates under the guidance of its respective national agency while maintaining offices on numerous levels, including provinces, regions, prefectures, counties, and municipalities.

The Ministry of Public Security is responsible for the police, while the correctional system is under the direct supervision of the Ministry of Justice. The courts are two-tiered (People's Courts and Special People's Courts) and hierarchically organized. The highest court is the Supreme People's Court of China, which oversees both tiers and deals with matters of national importance (Terrill, 2009). The majority of criminal cases are dealt with at the county level under the auspices of the Basic People's Court. The procuratorate, directed by the Supreme People's Procurate, is responsible for supervising criminal justice throughout the country, including investigating and prosecuting crimes and overseeing the courts, police, and correctional facilities (Jiahong & Waltz, 1995).

In theory, the Chinese criminal justice system has a built-in system of checks and balances to curb abuses of power. Arrests by police are approved by the local procurators, and prosecution can be deemed unnecessary by the courts. However, in practice, the courts and procuratorate are typically in collaboration with local political leaders and will generally operate to meet the ideals of the Communist Party.

In addition to the formal system outlined here, China operates an extensive informal system of justice. This informal system supplements the formal system with political, economic, educational, cultural, and judicial methods to help keep social order. Informal justice in China depends on an ancient system devised for different county and municipal agencies to act as social control agents, including neighborhood public security committees, people's mediation committees, and the numerous security departments within businesses, schools, and public agencies (Situ & Liu, 1996). We will discuss more about Chinese informal social control mechanisms in Chapter 9.

Comparisons with the United States

China is a unitary socialist government and thus contrary to the United States, which is categorized as a federalist democratic government. And although China has set up a government bureaucracy with built-in checks and balances much like the United States, all arms of the government are in reality subordinate to the Chinese Communist Party.

One of China's unique features is the way that systems of informal social control permeate the legal culture. These systems, which surfaced from distrustful dynastic rule and were fueled by the core principles of Confucianism and Taoism, have remained despite an effort to modernize the system and strengthen the rule of law.

Understanding crime and crime statistics in China has improved in recent years, although China still chooses to not officially record a number of very common crimes. We do know that contrary to crime in the United States, crime in China has risen considerably of late. Crime statistics show a tripling of crime over the last 30 years. Drug crimes and economic crimes are the most prevalent crime problems. Chinese criminal justice officials have responded with a flurry of Strike Hard campaigns, which are similar to the goals of the "get tough" crime legislation in the United States.

JAPAN

Overview

The country of Japan, in Japanese called *Nippon*, is an archipelago of almost 7,000 islands, with the largest four comprising 97 percent of the land area. The island Honshu includes Tokyo, the largest metropolitan area in the world. We know from archaeological research that people lived in Japan as early as 30,000 BC, and Chinese historical documents dating back to first century AD spoke of the area now called Japan. We also know that the first recorded contact with the West occurred in about 1542, when a Portuguese ship, blown off its course to China, landed in Japan. During the next century, traders from Portugal, the Netherlands, England, and Spain arrived, as did Jesuit, Dominican, and Franciscan missionaries. Because **shoguns**—military rulers who exercised absolute rule in Japan—were fearful about the influence of these interlopers, in around the year 1600 they forced all foreigners to leave and strictly limited contact with the West for over 200 years.

Japan is slightly smaller in area than California but has a population of over 127 million. The country is divided into 47 administrative divisions, called **prefectures**. Japan is one of the most homogeneous countries in the world, with over 99 percent of the people being native Japanese. It is the only non-Western industrial giant in the world. Excellent government–industry cooperation, a strong work ethic, mastery of high technology, and a small defense budget have enabled Japan in the years following World War II to become the second most powerful economy in the world. Its industries are among the world's largest and most technologically advanced. From the 1960s through the 1980s, the country was a model for other capitalist economies. However, beginning in and since the early 1990s, the economy has slowed considerably, and a recession dulled the enthusiasm of investors at home and abroad. To make economic matters worse, on March 11, 2011, a 9.0-magnitude earthquake struck Japan's eastern Sanriku coast, triggering an enormous tidal wave that left 310,000 people homeless, 23,000 dead or missing, and a cluster of unstable nuclear reactors. Estimates of the direct costs of the damage—rebuilding homes and factories—range from $235 billion to $310 billion (CNNMoney, 2011). For a summary of additional demographic information on Japan, see Table 4.1.

The Japanese legal tradition is modeled after the European Civil Law, but it is influenced by the English–American legal traditions. The U.S. occupation of Japan after World War II resulted in a new constitution that mandated three branches of government. Legislative government in Japan is based on a bicameral legislature called the *Diet*, which includes a House of Representatives and a House of Councilors. An executive branch consists of the prime minister, a cabinet that is appointed by the prime minister, and a hereditary emperor. Because the emperorship is primarily a ceremonial position, Japan is technically a constitutional monarchy. The judicial branch is headed by a Supreme Court whose members are appointed by the cabinet. Like France and Britain, Japan is a unitary state; that is, it does not have a federal system of government with division of powers between states and the federal government. Most of the 47 prefectures depend on the central government for financial subsidies.

Historical Development

Japanese legend maintains that Japan was founded in 600 BC by the Emperor Jimmu, a direct descendant of the sun goddess and ancestor of the present ruling imperial family. In about 405 AD, the Japanese court officially adopted the Chinese writing system. Together with the introduction of Buddhism in the sixth century, this event revolutionized Japanese culture and marked the beginning of a long period of Chinese cultural influence. As mentioned earlier, an important peculiarity of Japanese history is the period of isolation from other cultures that started in 1603 and lasted until 1867. During that time, the warlord (shogun) family of the Tokugawas ruled Japan from what is now Tokyo. The emperors, who lived in the holy city of Kyoto, were venerated as deities but had little real power. The Tokugawa shoguns, alarmed by the increasing influence on Japanese society of missionaries and traders from the West, closed the entire country to outsiders during these years. They allowed only a small amount of trade with Dutch merchants in the port of Nagasaki, and missionary efforts to penetrate Japanese society were ruthlessly suppressed. Thus, at a time when other countries were going through a major period of exploration, invention, and international interchanges, Japan was entering a period of introspection and cultural inertia. Prior to this time of isolation from foreign influence, Chinese civilization represented the major external influence on the Japanese. Much of Japanese civilization today, including the writing system, the Buddhist religion, and general social values, is adapted from the Chinese. The Chinese influence was even greater in the years before Western ideas were introduced into Japan. The years of isolation allowed for a strengthening and consolidation of Japanese culture and mores that would keep the culture distinct even after outside ideas began to penetrate the country.

The period during which Japan was opened to Western ideas and trade was called the Meiji Restoration, named after the emperor at that time. Meiji was the winner in a power struggle with the last of the Tokugawa shoguns, and the imperial family ostensibly resumed the leadership of Japan that it had relinquished about a thousand years earlier. In reality, however, a military junta ruled Japan in the 20th century until the end of World War II, with the emperor serving as a father figure and national idol but hardly a strong ruler. Following Japan's defeat of Russia in the Russo-Japanese War of 1904–1905, Japan became increasingly imperialistic and militaristic, hoping to establish Japanese hegemony over all of East and Southeast Asia. Japan's defeat in World War II brought about a major change in Japanese government and society. Japan lost all of its overseas possessions, and the victorious Allies gained full control of the government. Only with the 1972 reversion of the island of Okinawa to Japanese control were the full powers of governing returned to Japan. Since World War II, industrial development has replaced militarism as the chief driving force in the new Japan. Japan's new constitution, called the Showa Constitution, took effect in May 1947. It is modeled after the U.S. Constitution and mandates a parliamentary system similar to Great Britain's. It includes a bill of rights similar to that in the United States and provides for a Supreme Court with the right of judicial review.

Crime

By any standard, crime rates in Japan are remarkably low compared to crime rates in other industrial countries. Crime statistics in Japan are compiled by individual criminal justice agencies and then summarized by the Ministry of Justice into a statistical yearbook called the *White Paper on Crime*. In the decades following the war, the Japanese crime rate dropped considerably to as low as 1,100 per 100,000 in 1975 (Reichel, 1999). After a significant increase from 1974 until 2003, there has been a decline in crime over the last 10 years. The most recent crime data available—for 2009–2010—reflect that the overall reported crimes known to police in Japan dropped 6.9 percent with almost all categories of crime declining, including homicide (–2.5 percent), larceny (–6.6 percent), and cybercrime (–30 percent). The latter was a growing problem in the early years of this century, but it appears that new laws and restrictions on computer use have mitigated the problem. The only crime category that rose was arrests related to use of the drug methamphetamines. Many of the drug arrests of this type have previously been attributed to visitors to Japan. However, even that category—that is, arrests of foreign visitors with drugs—declined in 2009, albeit slightly (National Police Agency, 2010b). Unlike the situation in the United States and Western Europe, the illegal sale and use of other kinds of drugs, such as cocaine and heroin, has not reached serious proportions in Japan.

Organized crime, or **Boryokudan** in Japanese, is known to be a crime problem in Japan and was a main reason for crime increases in recent years. However, the 2010 data reported a 3.2 percent drop in overall offenses committed by the Boryokudan (National Police Agency, 2010b). Organized crime groups are heavily involved in the production and distribution of amphetamines and in a plethora of other illegal activities. Their activities include extensive and violent infighting, many violations of gun laws, gambling, loan-sharking, prostitution, and trafficking in guns and human organs (Bayley, 1996). Recent organized crime concerns center on the growing number of foreign organized gangs, mostly Chinese, that have infiltrated Japanese society (Onishi, 2003).

There are many cultural reasons for Japan's low crime rate, and much has been written on the subject (Bayley, 1996; Komiya, 1999). However, understanding Japanese culture and the effect it has on crime and criminal justice is not an easy task. Japanese culture has many subtleties and contradictory elements that make it difficult for outsiders to understand. The Japanese have traditionally valued harmony, group loyalty, and conformity as opposed to individualism and individual rights. Harmony, conformity, and loyalty are feudal characteristics that contribute in a relatively benign fashion to a cohesive and homogeneous culture void of serious crime problems. Additional factors that may contribute to the low crime rate include a low unemployment rate, lack of urban ghettos, a strong family structure, and strict gun control laws.

Keep in mind, however, that the low crime rate comes with concomitant social costs. One could argue that a darker side of this culture is manifested in the suppression of individuality, subordination of women, and suspicion toward non-Japanese people—even those who have lived in Japan for generations. In addition, Japanese society is changing, just as China is changing, and generalizations based on Asian cultural patterns of even a few decades ago may not be as relevant today (Sheptycki, 2008).

Criminal Law

Attempts to develop a code of laws in Japan can be traced back as far as 604 AD with the Seventeen Maxims of Prince Shotoku, and to the 700s with the Code of Taiho and the Code of Yoro (Wilmore, 1936). Chinese law had the most influence on the Japanese system prior to the closing of Japan in 1603. Much of the subtlety of the Japanese approach to conflict, as well as much of Japanese aversion to formal legal processes, can also be found in Chinese society. The two social orders have much in common, even though the Chinese civilization is more ancient than that of Japan.

But since the 1800s, Japan has developed highly structured legal codes that have been influenced by French, German, Chinese, and U.S. law. At the time of the Meiji Restoration in 1868, Japan adapted the French Penal Code for its criminal justice transactions. In the late 19th century, after the Germans developed their comprehensive civil code, Japan adopted many of the elements of the German code. Even today, the Japanese legal code is predominantly German in character despite the adoption of much of U.S. criminal procedure. Many Japanese legal scholars, especially of the older generation, have spent time studying in Germany.

U.S. law has influenced Japan with respect to constitutional and human rights law. The U.S.-inspired Japanese Constitution, with its listing of constitutional rights and its provision for a Supreme Court to secure these rights, has introduced a new element into Japanese justice, an element that is becoming more influential as time goes on.

The Japanese criminal code actually consists of three integrated codes: (1) the penal code, which defines crimes and punishments; (2) the code of criminal procedure, which sets legal standards for prosecution and sentencing; and (3) prison law, which regulates correctional matters. In many ways, the criminal code articulates a great number of the same basic principles as in the criminal and prison law code that were developed in 1907.

The penal code is divided into two books. The first deals with general provisions such as criminal intent, age of responsibility, and types of sanctions; the second lists the major crimes and the elements of those crimes. Interestingly, the Japanese penal code makes no formal distinction between felonies and misdemeanors, although there is a body of laws that pertain to minor offenses, called the Minor Offense Laws. Instead, crimes are divided into three categories: (1) crimes against the state (such as bribery and crimes against the imperial family); (2) crimes against individuals (such as homicide, assault, bodily injury, rape, indecent assault, kidnapping, theft, fraud, robbery, and embezzlement); and (3) crimes against society (such as indecent behavior in public, arson, and gambling).

The Criminal Justice System

The use of the law or the criminal justice system to settle disputes between individuals in Japan is minimal in comparison to most other countries, especially those with a developed economy and legal structure. In Japan, dispute settlement processes emphasizing compromise, mediation, and consensus are the norm. Further, informal procedures used by police, neighbors, or families are preferred to formal criminal processes for dealing with offenders.

This does not mean, however, that the Japanese lack a formal and organized system of justice. In fact, Japanese criminal justice is largely centralized and in many cases tightly controlled by the national government. The Ministry of Justice generally oversees the correctional system, including the Prison Bureau, which is the primary agency responsible for juvenile and adult correctional facilities. The courts in Japan are hierarchical in nature, with two appellate courts and two trial courts. The Supreme Court is the highest-level appellate court, above the high courts. District courts and summary courts are the trial courts, each with jurisdiction in its own prefecture.

The two national police organizations are the National Police Safety Commission (NPSC) and the National Police Agency (NPA). The NPSC is the administration arm that makes national policy decisions and administers all police affairs, including police education, communications, and criminal statistics. The NPA actually runs the police through the **prefectural police (PP)**, autonomous agencies that carry out police duties within the boundaries of the 47 prefectures.

Ultimately, Japanese law and criminal justice is hybrid, having borrowed from the Chinese, the French, the Germans, and the Americans. The final product, however, is peculiarly Japanese and certainly not analogous to any of the systems of origin. Thus, understanding Japanese justice is a real challenge to the student of comparative justice.

Comparisons with the United States

Japan is unique in that it is a constitutional monarchy with an emperor who has little power and whose position is primarily ceremonial. The prime minister is far more integral to the functioning of the government, with such responsibilities as appointing members of the cabinet. In this way, the prime minster is much like an American president. Possessing a unitary government versus the federalist approach used in the United States, Japan's central government provides direction and financial support to all 47 prefects. One example of the highly regulated unitary approach in Japan is the use of two national police forces to handle the civil order and deviance order police functions.

Much has been written about the comparisons between crime and criminal justice in Japan and the United States (Parker, 2001; Johnson, 2002). Because of their defeat in World War II, the Japanese were forced to adopt a number of

American legal principles, such as a written constitution, a hierarchical court system, and extensive criminal procedure laws. However, even though Japan utilizes many Common Law ideas, they have also borrowed from the Civil Law traditions of France, Germany, and China. As a result. they can be said to be closer to a hybrid tradition rather than a primarily Common or Civil Law legal tradition. Japan has developed an extensive formal criminal justice system that is tightly controlled by the federal government. At the same time, an informal system of dispute resolution, mediation, and consensus building is implemented when conflicts arise between individual citizens and to handle crimes of a nonserious nature.

Even with some increases in crime during the last quarter of the 20th century, the crime rate in Japan pales in comparison to the crime rate in the United States. There are numerous hypotheses as to why Japan has such a low crime rate in comparison to other industrialized and modernized countries. None have been empirically verified, and it is most likely that a combination of factors accounts for this phenomenon. As in the United States, public officials in Japan have recently expressed concern about the rise in drug crimes and overall issues of public safety in light of the events of terrorism around the world. Also similar to the United States, Japanese politicians have adopted "tough" crime policies that clearly reflect their lack of tolerance toward isolated crime incidents reported in the media (Hamai & Ellis, 2006).

SAUDI ARABIA

Overview

Saudi Arabia is mostly uninhabited desert, about one-fifth the size of the United States, with a population of approximately 26.5 million people. Prior to the 1960s, most of the population was nomadic or seminomadic, but due to rapid economic growth and urbanization, most of the population is now settled. The country's economy is based primarily on oil. Saudi Arabia has the second-largest reserves of petroleum in the world, after Venezuela, and ranks as the world's largest exporter of oil, which accounts for a large percentage of government revenues. As a result of the riches produced by oil, Saudi Arabia is has formed a **welfare state** approach; that is, the government plays a key role in the protection and promotion of the economic and social well-being of its citizens.

The culture of Saudi Arabia is derived from Arab tribal traditions and from the Wahhabi form of Islam that evolved in the 18th century. Wahhabi is a fundamentalist interpretation of Islam that places strict limitations on behavior and dress, including no drinking of alcohol. Public expression of opinion about domestic political or social matters is also discouraged. There are no organizations such as political parties or labor unions that may contradict government and religious teachings. Each day, five times a day, Muslims are called to prayer. Friday is the holiest day for Muslims, and celebration of public nonreligious holidays is prohibited except for the 23rd of September, which commemorates the founding of Saudi Arabia as a kingdom.

Thirteen provinces, called *mintaqah* (singular, *minaqat*), make up the country's administrative divisions. Each of the provinces is run by a governor who is under the responsibility of the minister of the interior, but in practice the governors often report directly to the king. Saudi Arabian government is characterized as a nonconstitutional monarchy. The king is the chief of state and head of government, and he rules with the help of a 25-member Council of Ministers, chosen by him. The council serves as an advisory panel, assisting the king in bureaucratic and policy matters. Many high officials in Saudi Arabia, including the highest ones in the police and judiciary, are related to the king.

Saudi Arabia is not a democracy and there is no system of election and representation, so there is no legislative branch. Legislation is enacted by resolution of the Council of Ministers and ratified by royal decree. In 1992, however, the king made some concessions to the westernized elements in his population by providing for a new Consultative Council, appointed by him, to advise the cabinet on laws and decrees. The Consultative Council, or *Shura*, is now a 150-member advisory body with no legislative functions, although it can propose new or amended legislation. On September 25, 2011, King Abdullah announced that women will be able to participate in municipal elections in 2015 and become members of the consultative Shura Council (Human Rights Watch, 2011).

The country plays a leading role in the Organization of Petroleum Exporting Countries (OPEC), which regulates the flow and price of oil in the Middle East and elsewhere. Because of its heavy reliance on oil, Saudi Arabia has been highly affected by the fluctuation in oil prices. In the late 1990s, with the increase in the number of oil fields around the world and the general decrease in the demand for oil, the economy faltered and budgetary problems arose. As a result, the Saudi government has begun efforts to diversify the petroleum economy, mined other natural resources, and encouraged private economic activity, especially in agriculture and manufacturing. The Saudis have also taken advantage of a strong economy to expand education and improve public health. These factors have played a role in creating and sustaining a conservative yet modern Islamic society. For more demographic information on Saudi Arabia, see Table 4.1.

Historical Development

The modern nation of Saudi Arabia dates back only to 1926. However, the territory of present-day Saudi Arabia includes the holy cities of Mecca and Medina, where the Prophet Muhammad lived, and thus has been central to Islam ever since its founding in the seventh century AD. This territory was ruled by Islamic caliphs until the rise of the Ottoman Empire in the thirteenth century. The empire, headquartered in modern Turkey, lasted until the end of World War I, but Islamic law became much attenuated during the nineteenth century, when Ottoman rulers began to integrate European codes into the legal system.

In the period following World War I, the Arabian peninsula, and indeed most of the Middle East, went through a period of turbulence, with the British, the French, and local hereditary rulers vying for power. The kingdom of Saudi Arabia resulted from the conquest of warring factions by Sheikh Abdul Assiz with the support of the British. Since his death in 1953, a succession of Saudi kings has ruled the nation. Prior to the discovery of large oil deposits in 1932 and their major development after World War II, Saudi Arabia was a poor country populated largely by nomadic tribes. Its economy revolved in large part around the pilgrims who traveled to Mecca and Medina, and it spent a good deal of its scarce revenues providing facilities for these pilgrims, restoring the holy places, and protecting them from environmental and human damage.

Oil has been both a blessing and a curse to Saudi Arabia. On the one hand, it has become a rich nation, and its people are extremely prosperous. On the other hand, it has struggled to maintain the degree of Islamic piety that its position in the heart of Islam and its historical legacy demand. The corruption of wealth, the importation of large numbers of foreign workers (not only for the oil fields but also for most hard labor), and the problems attendant upon industrial development have all clashed with Islamic fundamentalism as oil production has come to dominate the economic, social, and even political life of the kingdom. Further, the fields of Saudi Arabia, which produce a large proportion of the world's oil, have become a military target of powerful Middle Eastern rivals.

Because the country is governed according to the Shari'a, there is no separate and formal constitution, although some Saudis consider the Qur'an, the holy book of Islam, to be the constitution. In 1993, a document called the Basic Law of Government (*nizam*) was introduced; it articulates the government's rights and responsibilities. Although not a formal constitution and lacking some of the basic principles of other nations' constitutions, such as the rights of assembly and diverging religious expression, it fulfills many of the same purposes of such a document and some consider it to be a constitution in practice if not in name.

Crime

It is somewhat difficult to summarize the nature and extent of crime in Saudi Arabia. Ali (1985) and

Souryal (1987) identify at least two difficulties in comparing crime statistics for Saudi Arabia with those for other countries. First, crime is often underreported in Saudi crime statistics because the Shari'a promotes informal and nonlegalistic responses to criminal behavior. As a result, fewer cases are handled by the police and courts (Souryal, 1987). Second, there is the problem of determining crime rates over the course of the calendar year. The Arabic lunar calendar is based on the Islamic year, which has only 354 days rather than the Gregorian standard of 364. This slight difference over time makes crime comparisons problematic (Ali, 1985). In addition, much of what goes on in the area of social policy and government in Saudi Arabia is not always released as public information.

Yet, in spite of the obstacles to measuring crime in Saudi Arabia, we can still state with confidence that it is very low in comparison to most countries. Even in comparison to other Islamic countries, Saudi Arabia has a minuscule crime rate.

The most recent crime statistics available for Saudi Arabia reveal a homicide rate of less than 1 (0.71) per 100,000 population. Rape, robbery, and auto theft are also rare occurrences in Saudi Arabia, with rates of 0.14, 5.3, and 76.2 per 100,000, respectively. Even Japan, with its extremely low homicide and robbery rates, ranks higher (Interpol, 2003). The reasons for the low crime rates in Saudi Arabia, as in other countries with low rates, are probably related to a combination of factors. Harsh punishments for drug traffickers, including the death penalty, may help to control the drug problem. At the same time, the low crime rate likely reflects the way the Islamic religion, most notably the Shari'a, permeates every aspect of society. The Shari'a prescription of both prosocial behaviors and strict punishments has helped make Saudi Arabia create a "spiritual and peaceful" society (Souryal & Potts, 1994).

The two issues of concern related to crime in Saudi Arabia are terrorism and human trafficking. Terrorism in Saudi Arabia revolves around religious factionalism. This should come as no surprise in a country where religion and religious orthodoxy are major preoccupations. In recent years, the most serious acts of terrorism in Saudi Arabia have taken two forms. The first are attacks clearly directed at the United States. The second are isolated terrorist attacks aimed at Saudi institutions and governmental offices (U.S. Department of State, 2008a). For the Saudi people, terrorism and extremism have existed as threats dating back for several decades. The most recent problems surfaced in the 1990s when the Saudis moved to freeze the assets and rescind the citizenship of Osama bin Laden. Soon after the bombing of the U.S.S. Cole in Yemen in 2000 and the attacks of September 11, 2001, Saudi Arabia intensified its efforts to fight terrorism. A series of bombings and kidnappings in Saudi Arabia by Al-Qaeda in 2003 resulted in a new and concerted effort to dismantle that terrorist network in Saudi Arabia. Working with international partners, the Saudis have been able increase domestic security and reduce considerably the number of terrorist events in the country (Royal Embassy of Saudi Arabia, 2011). In fact, during 2010 there were no successful attacks in Saudi Arabia and over 100 arrests of suspected terrorists (U.S. Department of State, 2011).

Another crime that is known to occur in Saudi Arabia with some regularity and in violation of international law is human trafficking. Saudi Arabia is a destination country for men and women trafficking. Men and women voluntarily come from numerous countries in Asia and Africa to Saudi Arabia for the purposes of gaining employment as domestic servants or other low-skilled laborers, but what results is involuntary servitude, commercial sexual exploitation, restrictions on movement, withholding of passports, threats, physical or sexual abuse, and nonpayment of wages. The government of Saudi Arabia does not fully comply with the minimum standards for the elimination of trafficking and is not making significant efforts to do so. The government continued, in a limited fashion, to prosecute and convict trafficking offenders under a 2009 anti-trafficking law. The government made modest efforts to improve its response to the vast human trafficking problem in Saudi Arabia by training government officials on victim identification and prevention, and worked to improve victim protection services (U.S. Secretary of State, 2012).

Criminal Law

The Saudi government has not published or disseminated a penal code, code of criminal procedure, or code of judicial procedure, and only a limited number of other laws exist in published form. Any legal decision must be made under the auspices of Islamic law, and all are subject to the approval of government-appointed religious leaders. Recall from Chapter 3 that the Shari'a is the totality of law that results from the Qur'an, the Sunnah, and other traditional sources from the early centuries of the Muslim faith. Of the four major schools of Islamic jurisprudence that developed at that time, the Hanbali school is the most strict in its efforts to return to pure Qur'anic principles. It is to this school that the Wahhabi sect favored by Sheikh Abdul Assiz adhered, and thus Saudi Arabia's law is based on the Hanbali version of Islamic law.

Under the influence of modern development, for which no clear Hanbali precedent exists, Saudi Arabia allows for some variation on the texts. These variations are based first on the precepts of other schools of Islamic jurisprudence and second on the reasoning of contemporary jurists (Amin, 1985b, p. 314). A Judicial Council, including large elements of religious leaders, reconciles conflicts between traditional Islamic law and modern requirements. In addition, the king may supplement Shari'a through decrees when conditions require such extension.

Although Islamic law is the basis for criminal law in Saudi Arabia, commercial transactions are based on laws that were largely put into effect after World War II. In addition, laws regarding civil service, social insurance, mining, labor relations, and various other social and economic issues form part of the whole of Saudi law. A Board of Grievances acts as a supreme administrative court to hear cases against administrative agencies and state officials (Nader, 1990, p. 4).

In each case, the issuance of new codes and royal decrees to meet the challenges of commerce and industry was not undertaken lightly and without concern for reconciliation with Shari'a. When rules for incorporating companies were issued, the Ministry of Commerce and Industry explained in some depth that, although modern development in Saudi Arabia required such rules regarding establishment, dissolution, and conduct of business, these companies were in keeping with the tradition of the Sunnah, in which the Prophet spoke about having partners and allowed companies that existed to continue. Further, according to this directive, "Any such rules or provisions [regarding companies] as were inconsistent with the orthodox Shari'a were excluded, and due regard was given to the various forms of companies established by Muslims in the past" (Amin, 1985b, p. 317). Again, we see the pervasiveness of Shari'a influence in Saudi law.

One of the most difficult aspects of economic development to reconcile with Shari'a is that pertaining to banking. The Qur'an explicitly forbids the charging or paying of interest on money loaned to others. Despite this fact, the Saudis allow traditional banks to exist, and according to some observers, they may avoid the proscription against interest by adding a charge equivalent to interest to financial transactions. However, the Saudis have also developed an Islamic banking system that concentrates on developing aid for the poor through investment (in keeping with the religious duty to devote a portion of one's income to the poor and needy) and providing interest-free loans for various purposes, including the stimulation of agriculture and the building of private homes (Amin, 1985b, pp. 318–319).

Why has Saudi Arabia followed Islamic law ever since its establishment in 1926, while other Muslim territories at that time adopted a hybrid of European and Islamic law? To understand this, we need to look at the father of Abdul Assiz, Muhammed ibn Sa'ud. This earlier Saudi sheikh, who ruled in the nineteenth century, came under the influence of a fundamentalist Islamic sect known as the Wahhabis. The Wahhabis were devoted to a return to pure Islamic principles and the purging of Western influences from Islamic society. One of the reasons King Abdul Assiz was so successful in his campaign to unite the Bedouin tribes of the territory and drive out some of the other claimants to the land was his piety and general nobility of character. He lived modestly and adhered strictly to religious practices and principles.

Thus, Islam was at the foundation of the modern Saudi state. Since Saudi Arabia does not have representative government but is ruled by royal decrees of the king and his advisors, the religious hegemony in government is not likely to change without a major upheaval. In any case, the piety of the rulers reflects the strong faith of much of the population (Al-Farsy, 1986).

The Criminal Justice System

Islamic law as laid out in the Shari'a is the basis for all criminal justice functions in Saudi Arabia. The Ministry of Justice presides over the Shari'a-based judicial system. The system is administered according to the Shari'a through religious courts whose judges are appointed by the king on the recommendation of the Supreme Judicial Council, which is composed of 12 senior jurists. The independence of the judiciary is protected by law. The king acts as the highest court of appeal and has the power to pardon. However, with the reforms during 2007–2009 to reorganize the judicial system, the Saudis have implemented a new judicial arrangement that has abolished some courts and added others, including a new high court much like the U.S. Supreme Court called the High Judiciary Council.

Saudi Arabian police are also highly centralized. Police are under the authority of the director of public safety, who is supervised by the minister of the interior. The minister controls all police forces throughout the kingdom. Local police are commanded by the provincial governors, who answer to the director of public safety. The correctional system in Saudi Arabia is also under the authority of the director of public safety within the office of the Bureau of Prisons (Murty, Roebuck, & Almolhem, 1991).

Comparisons with the United States

The Saudi Arabian law and criminal justice system is unique in many ways and cannot readily be compared to those of England, France, Germany, Japan, China, or the United States. The primary difference is that Saudi Arabia is one of the few countries in the world that emphasizes the Sacred Law legal tradition. In this tradition, there is no clear distinction between religious influence and governmental decision making. This is clearly different from the United States and most other secular legal traditions, where there is a clear separation of church and state in all aspects of the criminal justice system and in government.

Saudi Arabia is a nonconstitutional monarchy. However, many Saudis consider the Shari'a and the relatively new Basic Law as the written constitution. Much like the president's cabinet in the United States, the Saudi Arabian council of ministries selects those that will run the various aspects of the criminal justice system. But unlike in the United States, legal decisions made by judges and other criminal justice officials are closely scrutinized by the government-appointed religious leaders of the country.

There are at least three characteristics of the Saudi criminal justice system that Americans would find peculiar. First, in the Saudi court system we find that the king is the highest court of appeal in the land. He can overturn lower court rulings within the boundaries of Islamic law and distribute pardons. Second, the police in Saudi Arabia are highly centralized and under the complete control of the minister of the interior. Iin the United States, this would be as if the director of the Justice Department advised federal, state, and local police on how to organize and perform the tasks of policing. Third, unlike the United States and most other countries with extensive written codes of criminal and civil laws, Saudi Arabia formally publishes few written laws beyond the Shari'a.

Like the United States, Saudi Arabia is one of the countries in the Middle East that has been greatly affected by terrorism. While Saudi Arabia remains a strong ally of the United States, economic and cultural ties with individuals and groups associated with terrorism have caused both countries to question the safety of Saudi and American interests in the region. Saudi Arabia has taken a number of steps to improve its internal security and support the fight against terrorism.

Even with the many difficulties in assessing crime statistics in Saudi Arabia, by any measure the crime rate is minuscule in comparison to the United States. As in Japan, there appear to be many reasons to explain the difference. Among the most commonly accepted reasons for low crime in Saudi society are harsh punishments, relative homogeneity, economic prosperity, and most notably the way religion permeates all levels of society and culture.

SUMMARY

Out of a total of 196 independent states in the world (including Taiwan, the Vatican, and Kosovo, none of which is a member of the United Nations) six countries may not seem like a very large sample. However, each of the six was chosen for inclusion in this book because it clearly represents one of the different legal traditions present in the world today. We have provided for each of the model countries a demographic and historic overview and a summary of the criminal law, the criminal justice system, and the current concerns related to crime. Also, we have given a summary of how each model country may be compared with the United States.

It is clear that this book does not include a model country within each continent. Africa and Latin America are surely continents that demand further study. While the nations of Latin America are Civil Law nations and base their legal processes on the traditions of that family, there are variations in style and substance that may make these systems

Comparative Criminal Justice at the Movies

Movies seek to entertain and inform the audience about a story, incident, or person. Many good movies also hit upon important substantive themes relevant to understanding crime and justice in comparative perspective. Read the movie summary below (and watch the movie if you haven't already) and answer the questions to make the subject matter connections to comparative criminal justice.

***Crash* (2006)**
Paul Haggis, Director

Winner of an Academy Award for Best Picture, *Crash* is a movie about prejudice based on race, nationality, and ethnicity. Set in Los Angeles, a multicultural city, the story begins with a multiple-car accident. A flashback takes us to the day before the crash, and we see the problems of those involved. An LAPD cop (Matt Dillon) tries to get medical help for his father but has problems with a black health insurance clerk over paying for a second opinion, so he takes out his frustration on a black couple during a traffic stop. A socialite (Sandra Bullock) and district attorney (Brandon Fraser) are carjacked at gunpoint by two black teenagers, and she takes out her anger on a Mexican locksmith changing the door locks to their home. Later, the locksmith is disrespected again by a Persian store owner.

A black detective speaks about the need for people to crash into each other. A Latino woman in the driver's seat of the car says they were hit from behind, and she blames the driver, an Asian woman, making racial jibes.

At a gun shop, an Iranian man and his daughter buy a handgun, but the shop owner gets upset because the Iranians are speaking Farsi. Two young black men leave a restaurant claiming they were victims of racism and poor service. Then they see a white couple walk down the sidewalk displaying fear towards them; the two black men take this as a racial slight and suddenly draw handguns and steal their car. These interlocking stories (and others) unfold throughout the movie, exploring racism and ethnic hatred, with people sometimes rising above it but often succumbing to it. The consequences of these attitudes in producing sometimes random and abusive behaviors illustrates the impact of negative mindsets in creating bad conduct. It is frustrating to see how these attitudes prevent people from seeing the person in front of them for what he or she is, instead of a symbol of something else.

Questions

1. In this chapter, we discussed the backgrounds and legal systems of the six model nations. In each case, the countries pursue justice cases from different traditions, cultures, and legal systems. Why do you believe that people sometimes see their own legal systems as superior to others, when they are all pursuing the same objective?
2. In this film, the characters "crash" into one another, provoking behavior that expresses strong attitudes but is out of context with the current situation, resulting in discriminatory and sometimes violent behavior. Are there ways to promote mutual respect for the beliefs of those of other nationalities, ethnicities, and races?

distinctive. In Africa, we find many examples of legal pluralism, in which local customary laws coexist with those derived from the colonial powers that once ruled. The traditional conflict resolution mechanisms are particularly functional in small villages and rural areas. They are a kind of arbitration process that tends to keep minor cases out of the formal, westernized legal system.

A student of comparative law and justice should take the time to explore other criminal justice systems in addition to those covered in this book. The usefulness of those that are included, as explained previously, is that they exemplify broad kinds of legal processes within different cultural settings. Each is a model system that can be used as a reference for comparison with other systems throughout the world.

Critical Thinking Exercise

Critical thinking requires the ability to evaluate viewpoints, facts, and behaviors objectively to assess information and methods of argumentation in order to establish the merit of an action, law, policy, or procedure. Please evaluate this scenario objectively, applying your knowledge of comparative criminal justice to the facts of the case presented, and answer the questions that follow it.

Oil Industry Faces Trial on Rights Abuses

Royal Dutch Shell appeared in federal court to answer charges of crimes against humanity in connection with the execution of the Nigerian author and activist Ken Saro-Wiwa by Nigeria's former military regime. It was alleged that Shell sought the aid of the former Nigerian regime in silencing Mr. Saro-Wiwa, an outspoken critic, and that Shell paid soldiers who committed human rights abuses in the Niger Delta where its oil operations occurred and a pipeline was to be built.

This case is one of a series of cases involving allegations of misconduct in developing countries by multinational oil companies. The companies have been sued for environmental damage, collusion with oppressive governments, and in aiding human rights abuses. In one case, Chevron faced up to $27 billion in penalties for pollution of the jungle in Ecuador. Exxon Mobil was sued by Indonesian villagers claiming human rights violations by soldiers hired to guard a natural gas plant. These legal problems have occurred at the same time the oil industry is looking for new sources of petroleum.

Shell was the most prominent case of this kind, and it led to major protests against Shell, already under criticism for its environmental record in the Niger Delta. Although civilian rule has returned to Nigeria, violence has escalated, fueled by widespread poverty and corruption. The civil suit against Shell was brought by relatives of Saro-Wiwa and other victims of Nigeria's former military regime, following a U.S. Supreme Court decision that gives foreign victims of human rights abuses access to American courts. Shell has said the allegations are "false and without merit," but oil companies in general have been under growing pressure to follow international and national laws, while operating in countries with poor human rights records, and little effective government oversight.

The case against Shell suit was brought under the Alien Tort Claims Act, a law originally passed in 1789 to fight piracy, but it is increasingly used for lawsuits alleging human rights violations that occurred overseas—in this case the plaintiffs did not trust they could sue Shell in Nigerian courts. The U.S. Supreme Court ruled in 2004 that foreigners could use American courts in limited circumstances, such as cases involving crimes against humanity or torture. While countries themselves cannot be sued, American courts have held that corporations can be sued for their actions in foreign countries.

These suits have brought some results. In 2004, a California oil company agreed to compensate villagers who were used as slave labor in the construction of a pipeline in Burma. In 2008, Chevron was cleared of wrongdoing by a jury when it was accused of involvement in the shooting of Nigerians who occupied an offshore oil barge to protest Chevron's environmental record and hiring practices.

Questions

1. Multinational corporations often do business in developing and post-conflict nations where the rule of law is not always enforced. Under what conditions *should* an American company be held liable for its conduct overseas?
2. What do you believe is the justification under law for allowing alleged crimes occurring outside the United States to be tried in U.S. courts?

SOURCE: The New York Times Jad Mouawad, "Oil Industry Braces for Trial on Rights Abuses," *The New York Times*, May 22, 2009.

DISCUSSION QUESTIONS

1. If the English lack a formal constitution, what do they use as a foundation for determining criminal law and criminal justice procedure?
2. Why have a number of our model countries chosen to respond to increases in crime with "get tough" policies? How would you compare these policies with those implemented by American criminal justice officials in response to the crime of terrorism?
3. Within each of the six model nations, what particular historical developments have had a major effect on their formation of criminal law and criminal justice administration?
4. Compare and contrast the model countries, and identify one distinct approach to criminal justice that each of the model countries exemplifies.
5. Using the demographic data in Table 4.1, hypothesize what data might help to explain the crime rates in the model countries. Then compare your findings with data about the United States. Do you find any significant differences that would account for the high crime rate in the United States?

FOR FURTHER READING

Crawford, A. (Ed.). (2011). *International and Comparative Criminal Justice and Urban Governance, Convergence and Divergence in Global, National and Local Settings*. Cambridge: Cambridge University Press.

Johnson, D. T. (2002). *The Japanese Way of Justice: Prosecuting Crime in Japan*. New York: Oxford University Press.

Liang, B. (2008). *The Changing Chinese Legal System, 1978–Present*. New York: Routledge Press.

Peters, R. (2005). *Crime and Punishment in Islamic Law: Theory and Practice from the Sixteenth to the Twenty-First Century*. New York: Cambridge University Press.

Shaffern, R. (2009). *Law and Justice from Antiquity to Enlightenment*. New York: Rowman & Littlefield Publishers, Inc.

WEB PAGES FOR CHAPTER

The 2011 World Drug Report can be found at http://www.unodc.org/documents/data-and-analysis/WDR2011/World_Drug_Report_2011_ebook.pdf.

The United Nations Interregional Crime and Justice Research Institute's website is http://unicri.it/.

A wide range of statistics can be found at the World Health Organization's website, http://www.who.int/research/en/.

The World Criminal Justice Library Network at Rutgers University is available at http://andromeda.rutgers.edu/~wcjlen/WCJ/index.htm.

Information about legal systems from around the world is available at http://www.nationmaster.com/index.php.

5  Law Enforcement: Functions, Organization, and Current Issues

Key Terms and Concepts

chuzaisho
civil order control
community policing
deviance control
Gendarmerie Nationale (GN)
kidotai
koban
mubahith
mutawa
National Police Agency (NPA)
peace operations
police corruption
Police Nationale (PN)
prefectural police
UNPOL

Chapter 5 Learning Objectives

Explain the two major functions of modern police forces.

Discuss the key elements of effective community policing programs.

Describe the unique features of policing in our model countries.

Understand the key operational issues for police around the world today.

Identify the major examples of international police cooperation.

In the city of Port Said, Egypt, at least 74 soccer fans were killed following a February 2012 soccer game as fans of the local El Masry soccer club attacked supporters of their rival Al Ahly. The post-game riot led to the filing of criminal charges against 75 people, including nine police officers and one top police official who were said to have done nothing to protect the fans (Fahim and El Sheikh, 2012). The police of Oakland, California, used tear gas and flash grenades in January 2012 to quell a demonstration of 1,000 to 2,000 protestors, some of whom threw rocks and flares at the officers and tore down barricades. Over 100 protestors were arrested. In Norway an independent inquest into the mass killings by an anti-Muslim extremist in 2011 resulted in a rebuke of the country's police and intelligence forces. The police reports and inquest showed that the officials could have averted or at least disrupted the planned attack that killed 77 people in Oslo and Utola Island. A number of top police officials have resigned over the incident (Lewis, 2012).

As these three scenarios describe, there is little doubt that the police officer's job today is not an easy one. Police are asked to perform a variety of functions: crime prevention, apprehension of lawbreakers, riot control, community service, protection against internal security threats. Most recently, police have been asked to expand their roles beyond jurisdictional boundaries. While performing these functions, police must be both responsible and responsive. That is, they should be true to the law and at the same time adaptable to the needs of the public they serve.

The term *police* is derived from the Greek word *polis*, which in ancient Greece was used to describe the group responsible for maintaining health, safety, and order in the community. Later, the Romans reconceived the police as an authoritative arm for those in power. Today the terms *police* and *policing* refer to the work of a public, nonmilitary agency that is given the power to enforce the law and secure public order through the use of legitimate force (Mawby, 2011, 2008). In all societies, policing is the most basic function that a government performs to make community life tolerable. At the same time, it can be a problematic function, in that police have both the power and the obligation to respond with force if the occasion requires. This power to use force in the name of the government raises critical questions about police discretion and oversight of police operations by nonpolice institutions. No legitimate government can allow misuse of power by a rogue police organization to continue unchecked.

POLICING IN A DEMOCRACY

The police task is particularly difficult in a democracy, in which the two mandates of responsibility and responsiveness may be contradictory in certain situations. But this task is immeasurably easier in times of prosperity and peace than it is in times of tension, conflict, and civil disorder. In difficult times, the police tend to become the focus of public discontent. The police begin to see themselves as victims, and confrontations with citizens become surrogates for confrontations between government and dissidents.

Recent efforts to implement democratic policing and research about the role of police in democratic societies have revealed at least four key elements that must be present to promote the democratization of the police. First, the police must be willing and able to serve individual citizens and private groups as well as those in political or economic power. This simply means that all citizens, not only the rich or those who support the police, should have total access to police assistance. Second, police must be accountable to the law rather than to the government. Law must not be applied by an arbitrary regime or its supporters but by those who are governed by law and validated by the courts. Third, the police must practice a level of professionalism that includes respecting human rights. Principles of human rights that are expressed in all democratic societies (e.g, freedom of speech and association and freedom from unlawful arrest and detention) should be practiced and supported. Finally, the police should be transparent in all their activities. Police behavior must be observable, reportable, and subject to some outside oversight (Bayley, 2001; Marenin, 2003; Bayley, 2005; OSCE, 2008). Attempts to democratize the police in South Africa have led to the development of 150 indicators of democratic policing, classified under 39 measures that can be used to benchmark police reform (Bruce and Neild, 2005).

In nondemocratic societies, police are expected to be responsive chiefly to the ruling elite. The degree to which they are also law-abiding and responsive to the public depends on the nature of those ruling elite. Examples of this kind of policing can be found in our model countries of the People's Republic of China and, in some respects, Saudi Arabia.

However, it is important to clarify that trying to understand the different kinds of police around the world within the democratic and nondemocratic dichotomy is limiting. Even within these two political spheres there is considerable variation. Because of such variation, it is quite difficult to make generalizations about the models or styles, and especially the quality, of policing around the world. However, what we do know about modern policing may be expressed in at least three generalizations.

First, we know that police agencies around the world are formed and operate within a variety of cultural, historical, and economic factors. Because of these factors, police are a "mirror image of their parent society and often vice versa—that is, a change in one often gets reflected in the other" (Dhillon, 2005, p. 25). For example, with the growth of the democratic ideas brought forth by the Age of Reason and the Enlightenment, policing in England evolved during the 19th century following a model that emphasized the provision of services and operating with the consent of the citizenry within the context of a solid democracy (Dammer, 2010).

With an understanding of how social factors influence the formation and functioning of police, those who study comparative policing have identified a number of models that attempt to explain how policing is conducted around the world. Remember that these models are not clear cut—in some cases countries may operate in more than one model. But they do provide us with a better understanding of how societal conditions influence the formation of the police. The five models that have been identified are as follows:

- *Democratic Anglo-Peelian*—Police are citizen-focused, and service and welfare of the community are as important as crime control and prevention. (e.g., United States, England)
- *Democratic continental*—Police are concerned with legalistic approach that is government- and law-based, are less concerned with pleasing the public, and tend to be more militaristic in dealing with citizens. (e.g., France, Germany, Italy)
- *Developing countries*—Police have few financial resources, are paid poorly, and as a result are prone to corruption. The police may not even be run by the government. (e.g., Somalia, Afghanistan)
- *Authoritarian*—Police are largely a governmental and military force. Citizens are likely to encounter repression, brutality, and torture. Policing may be based on religious law. (e.g., Saudi Arabia, China, and Zimbabwe)
- *Asian*—Police place less emphasis on individual rights and utilize cultural norms to reinforce social order. (e.g., Japan)

Sources: Casey, 2010; Pakes, 2010; Mawby, 2011.

Second, keeping in mind that police in any country are shaped by a variety of factors, we also know that police are organizationally structured in one of three ways: centralized, semi-centralized, or decentralized (UNAFEI, 2003; Reichel, 2013). In centralized police systems, there is a national police force that is centrally commanded and controlled and has unlimited jurisdiction in the country. Semi-centralized police systems place the tasks of policing jointly in the hands of states or provinces, along with some oversight by the central (federal) government. The third type, decentralized policing, places the responsibility of policing solely in the hands of states or provinces. Each country in the world has developed a variation of these three types of systems based on its own particular historical, political, and, in some cases, economic situation. See Table 5.1 for a summary of how these systems fit with our model countries.

Third, we know in general that police perform two major functions or tasks in modern societies: (1) deviance control and (2) civil order control. Both of these functions are necessary to ensure that people feel secure and are able to carry out their everyday business without fear and major disruption. Indeed, failure to perform either one of these functions means that a society is not adhering to the most basic tenet of the social contract that exists between most governments and their citizenry. The lack of such a social contract would surely lead to the vindictive and predatory relations that exist in uncivilized societies or those in a "state of nature."

FUNCTIONS OF POLICE

Deviance Control

Deviance control refers to the police mission and tasks that enforce community values and laws. Police personnel must protect citizens against lawbreakers such as those that steal or assault fellow citizens. In addition, the police seek to discourage alarming or threatening behavior that tends to make people uneasy or insecure. They must also ensure that people can move around freely and exercise their various rights as citizens without fear, harassment, or undue impediments. For example, police are carrying out this mission when they work with troubled juveniles or remove drunks from the streets. This function is profoundly conservative in nature, protecting the community against nonconformists and trying to keep violators of community norms under control. Having direct contact with the community in the form of police-community relations or crime prevention programs may be a part of this function of reinforcing community values and discouraging criminal or other deviant behavior.

Civil Order Control

Civil order control refers to the duty of police to respond to, supervise, or control two or more citizens in any situation that may disrupt the peace and tranquility of a society. This police function may be performed by agencies other than the police or by specialized units within police forces. Civil order control differs from deviance control in that there often is a strong political component to the activities being controlled—actions that disturb the civil order may be extremely threatening to a government. There is always the possibility that police will overreact to or exacerbate the situation. Police may end up being adversaries of the citizens rather than part of the citizenry, and this can be a very uncomfortable role.

It must be emphasized that, when we discuss civil order control, we are not talking about the kind of police forces that are established as personal armies for authoritarian leaders and that have few qualms about ruthless suppression of dissent in their societies. Such forces, although still too common in the world today, cannot be classified as modern police agencies in the sense that we describe others in this book.

Modern police forces generally organize to accomplish the functions of civil order control and deviance control in one of two ways. By far the most common arrangement is to have these functions performed by different divisions within the larger organization. Among our model countries, this is the arrangement favored by Germany, France, China, Japan, and Saudi Arabia. By contrast, in England and the United States, civil order control is not organizationally separated from deviance control but is performed by regular street police. Military units may also be used in extreme cases on an ad hoc basis. Although no democratic country wants to use its military to maintain order internally, the military remains the last resort in a civil order crisis in any country.

TABLE 5.1 Summary of Police Characteristics in Model Countries

	USA	England	France	Germany	China	Saudi Arabia	Japan
Civil Order Functions	Regular street police or military in extreme situations	Regular street police or military in extreme situations	Specialized police in GN and PN called *Republican Security* (PN) and *Gendarmerie Mobile* (GN)	All recruits are trained in civil order policing, called *Bepo*	Ministry of Public Security may turn to the Chinese People's Armed Police, (PAP), which serves as part of the army	Special Forces (Pilgrims) and Festival Police Force, or National Guard or Saudi Army in extreme situations	Specialized police in each prefect called *kidotai,* a quasi-militarized National Guard
Deviance Order Functions	Regular street police in different jurisdictions: local, county, and state	Provincial police forces	PN in Paris and urban areas; GN in towns of less than 10,000	*Schupo* and *Kripo*	Ministry of Public Security	*Mubahith* conduct criminal investigations, domestic security, and counterintel-ligence; *mutawa* are religious/ morals police	Prefectural police
Model	Democratic Anglo-Peelian	Democratic Anglo-Peelian	Democratic continental	Democratic continental	Mixture of Asian and authoritarian	Authoritarian	Asian
Centralized or Decentralized	Decentralized	Decentralized	Centralized	Decentralized	Centralized	Centralized	Centralized
Current Issues of Concern	Drug crimes, violent crimes, gangs	Economic crimes, private policing	Civil disorder, racial tension, drugs	Growing immigration, racial crimes, private security	Economic crimes, corruption, growing crime rates, civil unrest calling for rights	Humans rights issues, equal rights for women, terrorism	*Boryokudan* or organized crime, cybercrimes
Community Policing	Regular police	Regular police through "reassurance policing"	Police de Proximité	Older police especially trained for work in specific neighborhoods	Beat policing—patrolling the community	No formal network of community policing	Community policing posts: *koban* and *chuzaisho*

Countries such as France and Germany that separate the functions organizationally differ among themselves with respect to these arrangements. These differences reflect particular historical developments. Even countries with separate civil order control divisions have had limited success in creating structures that reconcile disparate organizational needs and at the same time are both responsible and responsive. Table 5.1 provides a summary of the methods for performing deviance order and civil order functions in our model countries.

POLICING IN THE MODEL COUNTRIES

In this section we describe some of the historical developments that have helped to form the police in our model countries and examine how the organizational structures perform deviance order and civil order policing. We conclude with a brief description of the issues of current importance for police in our model countries.

England

The modern English police force dates back to 1829, when the Prime Minister Sir Robert Peel urged Parliament to establish the London Metropolitan Police to deal with the unrest, crime, and disorderliness that accompanied urbanization and industrialization in 19th-century London. Because the genesis of the police in England came from democratic ideals and opposition to the form of policing used by the French, the English police have tried to develop the image of being "civilians in uniform": friendly, helpful, and capable. Another way to explain the police reforms put forth by the English is as an effort to gain support of the public by consent rather than by force. Traditionally, they have not carried firearms and in violent confrontations have had only the truncheon as a means of protecting themselves and asserting their power.

The model of "policing by consent" remained a staple of British policing through the twentieth century. Whether the model was totally effective has been debated, but we do know that in general the confrontations between the police and the public, as well as the abuse of power by the police, abated during the 20th century, especially after World War II. We also know that the recorded crime rates following World War II were, by any standard, very low.

For almost 185 years the police in England and Wales have traditionally been an organization that has national standards but is highly decentralized, with each city or town making rules and providing funds for its own police operations and controlling the hiring, firing, and compensation of police personnel. However, there has been some discussion in England and Wales that the police appear to become more centralized; for example, they have begun to use strategies such as such as training and community policing that come from the Government (Jones and van Sluis, 2009). At present, there are 44 total police forces, including 41 provincial police forces in England and Wales. The provincial police, also called territorial police forces, are funded by local districts and regions (50 percent) and by the central government (50 percent). The chief constable is the main administrator for each of the 41 provincial forces. In the local districts, policing is delivered through the formation of basic command units (BCUs). The BCUs make it easier to deliver the various forms of community policing that are so vital to the service role of the British police and the need to solicit citizen cooperation for crime prevention.

In addition to the provincial police, the remaining three forces are the British Transport police and two police forces in greater London: the Metropolitan Police Force (with 31,500 officers) and the London City Police (900 officers). To assist the regular police in the area of London are two other kinds of law enforcement. The first, the Metropolitan Special Constabulary (MSC), was created over 175 years ago. The 2,500 members of the MSC operate in Greater London, and although they are not paid, they have the full powers of an officer (constable). Also, in 2002 the British began to deploy police community support officers

(PCSOs). The force now numbers 13,000 uniformed officers who work along with regular officers in neighborhood policing areas; however, they are not as well trained, receive lower pay, have less equipment, and have less legal power than officers. PCSOs generally "perform routine duties, assisting and supporting Police Officers, gathering intelligence, carrying out security patrols and, through their presence alone, reassuring the public. Where possible, they also attend to matters not requiring police powers" (Metropolitan Police, 2009). The PCSOs cost 25 percent less than regular officers, and they operate throughout London and adjoining suburbs (Muir, 2003). Finally, the British also deploy special police, such as the Ministry of Defence Police and the Port of London Authority Police, that have specific jurisdictional responsibilities. Many have heard the famous English police term *Scotland Yard*. Scotland Yard is actually the location for the Metropolitan Police Force of London; it serves as a national repository for crime statistics, information on criminal activity, missing persons reports, fingerprints, and juvenile delinquent data. As of March 2010, there were almost 144,000 police officers in England and Wales, not counting the transit police (c. 3,000) and special police mentioned above (Dhani, 2010).

The training of police in England has been revamped since the Criminal Justice and Police Act of 2001, which called for the formation of a new training authority called Centrex, and the subsequent development of the National Policing Improvement Agency in 2007 (Terrill, 2009). All trainees start out as constables and must participate in a 14-week course during which recruits learn theoretical and practical information on a variety of topics, followed by a 10-week field experience under the supervision of an experienced constable. After that 24-week period, the new constable remains on probation for the first two years of service while gaining additional classroom training and supervision. Those who aspire to become police administrators attend the police staff college at Bramshill, the central police leadership training college in Britain. For a comparison summary of police training in our model countries, see Table 5.2.

TABLE 5.2 Police Training Standards in Model Countries

Country	Amount of Training	Type of Training	Qualifications
England	24 weeks of initial training; 2-year probation period; administrators attend Bramshill College	Classroom, field, and physical fitness training	Unavailable
China	6 months	Unavailable	High school or college, at least 25 years old
Germany	Varies—generally 2–3 years	Physical fitness, classroom, and field training	Varies—generally midlevel education
Japan	1 year for prefectural police	Classroom, field, and physical fitness training	National qualifying exam, high school
France	For National Police, 1 year	Classroom, field, and physical fitness training	Written and physical test, 19 years old
Saudi Arabia	3 months for lower officers, 3 years at security college for higher officers	For higher officers, extensive academic training	Literacy
United States	2–40 weeks, with an average of 10	Physical fitness and classroom training	High school; in some jurisdictions, some college

SOURCES: UNCJS, 1999, pp. 333–334; Terrill, 2009; Alobied, 1989, pp. 80–84.

The English police, as presently organized, carry out both the deviance and the civil order control functions of police. There is no separate agency or even a well-defined way to deal with civil order control problems in England. On occasion England has used the military to back up its police civil control efforts. The role of the police in riot control was severely tested in early August 2011 when several London boroughs and numerous other English cities and towns experienced a wave of rioting, looting, and arson. Over 3,000 people were arrested, 5 persons died, and dozens were injured; the property damages soared above 120 million U.S. dollars. In London, the Metropolitan Police called on the *Public Order Operational Command Unit* to handle the rioting. In the months following the riots, a study conducted by the London School of Economics that included interviews with over 600 persons found that opportunism, perceived social injustices, and anger and frustration at the way their communities were policed were among the most common reasons cited for the unrest (Lewis and Newburn, 2012).

Issues of Concern for the Police in England. In addition to the fallout associated with the 2011 riots, a major recent challenge for the English police and larger government was the responsibility of providing the security for the Olympics and Paralympics held in London in the summer of 2012. Consider the volume and cost of security needed to handle over two months of sports and events in over a thousand venues. To handle this monumental task, over 12,500 police were assisted by 18,000 military personnel, and over 10,000 private security persons that were hired, trained, and supervised by the private security firm G4S. By some accounts, the largest peacetime security effort in the history of England will cost the equivalent of almost 1 billion U.S. dollars. Despite some concerns about the costs associated with securing the Games, it appears that the efforts of all involved were rewarded with no serious security incidents (Info4 Security, 2012).

Recent social, economic, and technological changes in England have created new crime problems and have called for new and improved methods of policing, including some calls for reform by both the police and the government (Barton and Barton, 2011). The police in England have tried to adapt to social changes through the adoption of a plethora of community policing strategies. Crimes such as illegal immigration, human trafficking, drug trafficking, and computer fraud, called "mobile crimes," have inspired a call for a police force that is more flexible, technologically savvy, and able to cross jurisdictional borders (Kirby, 2011). Some of the common tools used for law enforcement that have evolved since the 1990s include more sophisticated computer technology to identify and catch criminals, better use of DNA testing, and the extensive use of closed circuit television (Johnson, 1999, p. A8; Joyce, 2011). The British have also moved to address national and international crime issues through the formation of new national police organizations such as the National Crime Squad, the National Criminal Investigation Service, the National Security Service (more commonly known as the MI5), and the Serious Organized Crime Agency. These agencies have played an important role in enhancing the communication between law enforcement agencies in England and other law enforcement agencies of the European Community (e.g., Europol and Interpol) (Dammer, 2010).

France

Policing in France has a long history, dating back to at least the year 580 C.E., when night watch systems were common. In 1306 King Phillip le Bel formed the first criminal investigation unit, and around that time the first mounted military police, called the *maréchaussée*, were formed. Between 1697 and 1699, Louis XIV asserted his authority as king over policing, and the *maréchaussée* became the formal law enforcement arm of the country. In, 1789 Napoleon gave them their military flavor and in 1791 they formally became the Gendarmerie. In 1903 they were established as a local military force (Dupont, 2008). The **Gendarmerie Nationale (GN)** forms one leg of the highly centralized national police structure; the second, created in 1966 and previously called the Sûreté Nationale, is the **Police Nationale (PN)**.

In contrast to England, where the stated philosophy is policing by consent, many feel that the French police see themselves more as acting on behalf of the state i.e., the country. It therefore appears that the police have little concern for the rights of the average citizen. In the first few years of the 21st century, a conservative political faction moved to address the growing crime issue and increasing civil unrest in France. Whether this conservative trend in dealing with criminals will continue is unknown now that Nicholas Sarkozy has been replaced in the presidency with Socialist Francois Hollande.

The organization of the French police is an unusual one. Even though the police in France are coordinated by the government and thus regarded as centralized, at the same time the country has two separate police organizations. As mentioned, the two French police organizations are the Police Nationale and the Gendarmerie Nationale. The PN operates within the Ministry of the Interior, whereas the GN operates within the Ministry of Defense. The leadership of both is centralized in Paris. Both have conventional deviance control responsibilities, although in different places, with the PN responsible for Paris and other urban areas and the GN responsible for small towns and rural areas with fewer than 10,000 inhabitants.

The GN oversees ten geographical regions with two main administrative divisions. At a total strength of over 105,000 officers, it performs all basic police tasks for nearly half of the French people. Curiously, working for the GN, the police arm of the military, carries greater prestige than working for the PN under the Interior Ministry. GN training is slightly different: the officers live in barracks, and their training places greater emphasis on the military aspects of police work. For this reason, members of the GN see it as a more disciplined law enforcement agency that is superior to the PN (Terrill, 2009). In addition, a number of specialized units within the GN provide assistance in areas such as security of public officials, maritime and overseas support, airport security and transport, and training.

The PN is the larger police force, with over 150,000 personnel divided into nine departments. Recent legislation has allowed local governments to hire their own police officials and officers. These police forces, called the Police Municipale, carry out duties (specified by the mayors and town councils) related to crime prevention, public order, security, and public safety. The 18,000 officers in the Police Municipale remain under the supervision and jurisdiction of the minister of the interior.

Recruitment and training for the PN and GN are handled separately by each organization. The PN requires police recruits to take written and physical agility tests. If selected, the recruit attends an eight-month training period at one of the eight regional National Police Schools, followed by a four-month in-the-field training period. The recruit is then assigned to a town, city, or local Security Company. Longer periods of training and additional schooling are required for those interested in becoming police inspectors or administrators (Terrill, 2009). When it comes to civil order control, the GN and the PN each have specialized forces that perform this task. In the PN, the Republican Security Companies assume responsibility. In the GN, the Gendarmerie Mobile are assigned to civil disorder and other large-scale problems that involve the possibility of violence. Both of these specialized civil order control branches operate independently of the conventional police work of patrol and criminal investigations.

Issues of Concern for French Police. Civil order control is a major problem for the French police, probably more so than in any of our model countries. The French have a long history of taking to the streets to express their unhappiness about social and political issues. In 1789 the French masses stormed the Bastille and sparked the French Revolution. In addition to simple demonstrations, politically motivated acts of violence are a major concern for citizens, with many of the problems stemming from labor unions protesting government cutbacks of services and benefits. Several violent riots have taken place recently, and attacks on police officers and other public officials are not uncommon. The most damaging of these occurred in 2005 when three weeks of nightly rampages in the suburbs of Paris and several other cities left extensive damage including 10,000 burned cars and 300 damaged buildings. Police arrested more than 6,000 people during the riots, which left 220 police injured (Stinson, 2006). More recently, in the northern French city of Amiens, clashes between youths and police in August 2012 resulted in cars and buildings burned and 17 police officers injured by rocks, fireworks, and gunshot. The police were forced to use tear gas and rubber bullets to quell the riot (Erlanger, 2012).

In addition to the major issues of concern related to civil order control, the French police also have to deal with the issues of drugs, terrorism, and immigration. With the collapse of its North African colonial empire, France has experienced a large immigration of Arabs from its former colonies of Algeria, Tunisia, and Morocco. Racial tension and cultural conflict have resulted, with attendant problems for law enforcement and judicial operations. With the largest Jewish population in Western Europe, France has also experienced an increase in the number of verbal and physical attacks on Jews. And with its central location and efficient fine transportation system, France is also a crossroads for terrorist activity and drug activity from both internal and external sources.

Germany

The first organized police force in Germany dates back to the early 19th century, when some of the German kingdoms adopted a force similar to the one developed by Napoleon in France (Feltes, 2004). During the reign of Otto von Bismarck in the 1870s, Germany became a more centralized government, and the culture of a strong civil service system that developed that survives to this day. The police were an important part of that elite system. German police strength grew from 200,000 to 1.5 million between 1933 and 1945, the years when Germany was under the domination of Hitler and the National Socialist party.

Immediately after the war the German police were placed under the supervision of the military regional governments of the Allies. With the new German constitution of 1949 and the formation of 11 *Länder* (states) in West Germany, each state gained the power to establish its own police force. Under the authority of the Soviet government, the German Democratic Republic (GDR, or East Germany) established a single central police force. The police of the GDR were dissolved after reunification in 1990, and many of the former People's Police (Volkspolizei) of the GDR were subsumed into the police forces of the new states, with the exception of any police member who had close ties to the secret police (*Stasi*) of the GDR.

Today the police of Germany are part of a decentralized executive force. The police laws of the 16 states deal with preventing crime, preserving public security and order, and warding off impending danger. The German constitution (Article 20:3) allows each *Länder* to have its own police law and force. Each *Länder* controls its force from that state's Interior Ministry rather than decentralizing the police to municipalities or other units of local government. Thus, the German system occupies a middle level of decentralization between the highly centralized French system and the highly decentralized and fragmented U.S. system.

Within each state are several kinds of police. The Schutzpolizei (or Schupo) are the equivalent of municipal police; they are the first to arrive at the scene of most crimes and handle all general aspects of law enforcement and simple investigations. The Kriminalpolizei (Kripo) are plainclothes police who handle serious crime investigations and situations that require developing a case against a suspect. The German federal government also has some police agencies at its disposal. The Federal Border Police (Bundesgrenzschutz, or BGS) are organized along military lines but are under the supervision of the Ministry of the Interior, not the Ministry of Defense. Their major functions include border control, sea patrol, and airport and railroad security; they also may assist in major civil disturbances beyond the scope of the *Länder* police. Included within the BGS is a special task force, called Grenzschutzgruppe 9 (GSG 9), that handles terrorist incidents.

An individual who aspires to a career of policing usually joins the German police at the young age of 16 or 17, straight out of vocational secondary school. The first two and a half to three years are spent living in barracks and undergoing basic training. A large part of this training focuses on riot control; the rest involves conventional school subjects, the law, and law enforcement (Zimmerman and Schwindt, 2003). After one year in the training schools, the young officers may be used for civil order control work either in their own states or, if the need arises, in other states of the Federal Republic. While in training or being use as police for civil order control, they are called the Bereitschaftspolizei (Bepo).

After the years of basic training and civil order control work, the Bepo officers spend about six months in general law enforcement training prior to beginning street patrol work. With few exceptions, recruits must go through the street patrol experience for at least a few years. After that time, some of them will undergo several more years of training to become either criminal investigators or middle-management supervisors.

Candidates for the highest management positions (the top 3 percent of recruits) go through another two years of training, with one year at the German Police University in Münster, where they meet and work with top management candidates from other *Länder*. Since 2008 they have been able receive a master's degree in public administration and management. Plans are in progress to offer a Ph.D. for police administrators. Since 2007 the German Police University has offered a degree in police science, and since 2003 a second university (in Ruhr-Bochum) has offered a degree in criminology and police science (Feltes, 2009).

Issues of Concern for German Police. The major problem for the German police over the last 20 years has been related to the large numbers of immigrants entering the country. Since the fall of the Berlin Wall, the number of foreigners who registered in Germany went from 4.2 million in 1987 to 7.4 million in 1997 (Ewald and Feltes, 2003). In 2008 the number declined to 7.2 million; however, these numbers do not reflect the emigrants from Russia, Poland, Romania, and other former Eastern Bloc countries who claimed German ancestry and are thus counted as German citizens, nor do they include the significant number of Turks with immigrant parents. After an initial rise in crime immediately after the unification, overall crime has stabilized in Germany and has actually declined since 2004.

A related problem that arose during the 1990s was hate crimes. The influx of foreigners inspired hostile reactions from some Germans, primarily young, working-class youths, who felt that those from other countries were a threat to their lifestyle and future. The German Intelligence Agency (Verfassungsschutz) has reported that a total of 25,000 right-wing extremists are in Germany, including almost 6,000 neo-Nazis. After 1990 the number of violent offenses recorded by police as having xenophobic or right-wing connections rose. In 2008 the police registered nearly 14,000 cases with right-wing or extremist characteristics, including 735 crimes of violence. German human rights advocates estimate that 136 people have been killed by right-wing violence between 1990 and 2005. In 2010, almost 16,000 crimes were classified as right-wing motivated, compared to almost 19,000 in 2009; these crimes included 762 acts of violence in 2010, compared to 891 in 2009 (Feltes, 2009; Fischer, 2009).

China

The history of the police in China is a long one, with records going back to the Shun monarchy in 2255 B.C., when the geographic area now known as China was not a united kingdom but a loose configuration of tribes in which local officials were designated to handle disputes and maintain order. For most of the next 2,000 years and during long periods of dynastic rule, policing in China remained a grassroots affair that was handled by local officials or, in special situations, by the military of the emperor who were called in to handle civil disorder (Wong, 2009). During the Zhou dynasty in the years 1100–771 B.C., the first Ministry of Justice and professional policing institution were formed to help local officials address security and social order (Bayley, 1985). The Qin dynasty (221–207 B.C.) was important because during this time policing became more formalized and bureaucratic, with a central administration and uniform laws

(Wong, 2009). But even with the beginnings of a bureaucratic and governmentally supported formal police force, China has always been a country where social control is first addressed in the family, then in the community, and then by state officials. This societal trait has continued through the overthrow of the dynastic period in China in 1911 by the Kuomintang (Nationalist Party) and through the tumultuous times that followed.

After gaining power in 1949, the Communist Party handed over policing to three groups: (1) public security forces, which provided basic police services; (2) militia groups, which monitored the border regions; and (3) the People's Liberation Army (PLA), which was the military wing of the Communist Party (Terrill, 2009). In the 1950s, as the Communist Party became more entrenched, formal mechanisms for law enforcement were developed based on the principles outlined in the first constitution of the People's Republic of China in 1954. Basically, the Chinese government formulated a Soviet-style criminal justice system, with overall control in the hands of the Communist Party. From the mid-1950s until 1966, there was little crime or civil disorder in China. But the Cultural Revolution of 1966 changed all that.

Along with Mao's attempt to reform the Communist Party came attacks on police officials and police stations and seizures of courts by the followers of Mao and the Red Guard. Local police were placed under the control of local Communist Party officials. Eventually, Mao had to call on the PLA to restore some semblance of order. This period of lawlessness and disorder continued until the late 1970s, when Deng Xiaoping reestablished the rule of law and restored the police as the main enforcers of law. This return of law and order to the police was reinforced by the Police Law of 1995, which replaced the previous law of 1957. The new law outlined the organizational structure, authority, and duties of police in China and defined the modern roles of police, including maintaining social order, safeguarding state security, protecting personal safety, protecting personal freedom and property, and guarding against and punishing law violators (Yisheng, 1999).

Some feel that the focus of the police in China has changed in the last decade. Although the local aspect of policing remains important and the neighborhood stations remain strong, police have now begun to concentrate more on crime fighting and order maintenance, and less on dealing with political dissent and the provision of social services. And as the police have become more centralized, professional, and accountable, they have also made an effort to recruit without politics as criteria and to follow the new emphasis on the rule of law that was put forth in the 1995 Law on People's Police of the People's Republic of China (Wong, 2010; 2002).

The Chinese police are centrally monitored by the Ministry of Public Security. The ministry formulates policies and regulations, coordinates police work and operations among the 22 provinces, and provides technological and specialized assistance to local police (Du, 1997). The Chinese police are divided into five main components: public security police, state security police, prison police, judicial procuratorates police, and judicial people's courts police. Although this organization may seem straightforward, what confuses our understanding of the Chinese police is the myriad of levels under which they operate. Although the five police agencies are directly answerable to the Ministry of Public Security, they are also under the authority of the individual provinces, 450 prefects, almost 2,000 county security bureaus, and thousands of local police stations (Guo et al., 1999). Thus, whereas in theory the police fall under the leadership of the Ministry of Public Security, in practice the day-to-day administration is governed by a corresponding agency. In many cases, local levels of government can determine their own policing priorities and appoint and promote their own officers (Xiancui, 1998).

The public security police (*gongan*; literally "public peace") provide not only basic uniformed patrol but also 12 other specialized functions, including supervision of probationers and parolees, criminal investigations, fire control, border patrol, and monitoring of all modes of transportation (Cao and Hou, 2001; Wang, 1996). They make up almost 90 percent of all the police in China. On the local levels, the public security police are represented by neighborhood stations called Paichu Su, which were possibly the forerunner of the Japanese *koban* system (Wong, 2010). State security police, established in 1983, are responsible for preventing and investigating espionage, sabotage, and conspiracies. Prison police supervise convicted offenders in prisons. The judicial procuratorates police escort suspects in cases investigated by the procurators (similar to prosecutors). Finally, the judicial police in the people's courts maintain security and order in the various courts and may also carry out death sentences.

Most Chinese police graduate from one of the 300-plus police universities, colleges, or police academies located in the individual provinces, all of which are coordinated by the Ministry of Public Security. Recruits with special skills may be hired without this training, but all must be at least 25 years of age and have a strong physique. Training lasts for an average of six months but will vary depending on officers' future positions and specialization. Potential officers are trained directly by the Ministry of Public Security at one of the three major police universities, whereas nonofficers are trained by their respective governmental offices: province, county, prefect, or municipality (Guo et al., 1999; Wong, 2009).

When there is a civil order dispute in China, the Ministry of Public Security generally calls upon the main public security police in that jurisdiction. However, since the Law on the People's Armed Police Force (PAPF) was passed in August 2009, the more than 660,000 troops of the Chinese People's Armed Police (PAP) are now responsible for dealing with riots, fire emergencies, large disruptions, serious violent crimes, border defense, terrorist attacks, and other emergencies (Wines, 2009). Technically, the PAP serves as part of the army, with dual responsibilities to the Central Military Commission and the Ministry of Public Security.

Issues of Concern for Chinese Police. Over the past 30 years, the Chinese have implemented significant reforms in many social and economic areas. With a free-market economy and an increase in individual wealth have come the social ills of crime. More specifically, the increase in drug use and trafficking and economic crimes such as corruption have been a major cause of concern. As a result, police have been called to crack down on crime through the implementation of various "get tough" (*Yanda*) policies. Citizens have also responded with calls for increased civil rights and democratic participation, often resulting in violence. The most infamous incident occurred in 1989 in Tiananmen Square, Beijing, when over 800 people died in a hail of gunfire from the Red Army as part of a mass demonstration in favor of democracy and freedom. Despite the international furor that followed, Chinese officials defend their actions to this day, stating that they were necessary to maintain public order.

Since the early 1990s, the number of what the Chinese call "mass incidents" has increased dramatically to as many as 127,000 in 2008—348 a day. The government has responded by arresting many individuals for counterrevolutionary crimes (Wedeman, 2009). National surveys in the late 1990s suggested that the public viewed the police in a positive way and had confidence in their abilities (Ma, 1997). However, according to other sources, public attitudes toward the police have shifted since the Cultural Revolution. The Chinese people now seem to view police with more distrust and to see them as bullies or tyrants. The number of complaints against police has increased considerably, and physical confrontations with citizens have become more frequent (Cao, 1995). One example of this distrust is the story of a 28-year-old man who was convicted of killing six police officers in 2008. Yang Jia entered a Shanghai police station and then stabbed and killed the officers, as revenge, he claimed, for having been beaten for stealing a bicycle in October 2007. To the surprise of many, during his two trials a great number of supporters gathered outside the courthouse, wore t-shirts with his image, and called him a hero because he stood up to the police and government injustice (Barboza, 2008).

Recently, at least in public announcements, the Chinese government has begun to recognize the rule of law over the rule of those in political power. But this change is happening too slowly for many Chinese, especially young citizens, who are calling for more individual freedoms. This combination of challenges—economic growth, growing crime, and the call for more citizen rights—will undoubtedly be of great concern for the Chinese government and especially the police in the coming decades.

Japan

Prior to the Meiji Restoration of the late 19th century, Japanese village and community culture monitored the behavior of citizens very closely—not only to keep them from committing crimes but also to keep them from "laziness, neglect of business, quarreling, scandal mongering, etc." (Clifford, 1976, p. 75). After the Meiji Restoration, and with the gradual development of Japan as a militaristic society in the early decades of the 20th century, formal police forces carried on this tradition. For the past 50 years, the Japanese have tried to adapt the American model of democratic policing to Japanese culture. In the years immediately following World War II, the U.S. occupation forces in Japan tried to institute community-controlled police based on the U.S. model. This effort was unsuccessful, and Japan returned to a centralized police organization.

Today, a six-person civilian National Public Safety Commission oversees the **National Police Agency (NPA)** with respect to most aspects of police organization and administration, including training, equipment, recruitment, communications, and criminal statistics. The NPA consists of seven regional bureaus and a force of approximately 1,900 officers, 900 imperial guards, and 4,900 civilians (NPA, 2011). The NPA handles all matters related to national security. It provides training, research, crime investigation, communications, and public safety, as well as support and supervision of the nation's **prefectural police** forces. There are 47 prefectural police forces with approximately 284,000 officers. Each force is autonomous in that it is able to develop policies and procedures based on the needs of the prefect. At the same time, however, they are financially assisted by the national treasury, and all senior officers are employed by the NPA. The metropolitan areas of Tokyo and Hokkaido have their own prefecture force of 42,000 police, called the Metropolitan Police Force of Tokyo.

Prefectures are divided into several local police stations (over 1,200), which in turn are further divided into police substations called **koban** or **chuzaisho**. These tiny police posts, located in all neighborhoods, constitute the heart of the Japanese police operation (Parker, 2001; Reichel, 2013).

The *koban* is a police post located in an urban neighborhood; in large cities, one finds a *koban* every few blocks. There are approximately 6,500 *koban*—many are storefront offices or tiny buildings resembling sentry stations. The officers in the *koban* account for over 20 percent of the total police strength in Japan.

Koban for the most part function as a "community safety center" for the local community. The main duties of *koban* officers include giving directions, securing the scene of accidents, and visiting homes and businesses to learn more about issues of concern to the community (Hirota, 1997). With the changes in family work patterns, increased social mobility, and lessening social cohesion in Japan, it is possible that the *koban* officer may soon find it difficult to achieve the levels of community communication necessary to make the system work effectively. Reforms such as the Koban Liason Councils have been established to enhance community communication, the essential ingredient for the *koban*'s success (Pakes, 2010).

The *chuzaisho* is the rural equivalent of the urban *koban*. There are over 7,500 *chuzaisho*, although their numbers have declined in recent years as Japan has become more urbanized. The rural police officer is known as *chusai-san*. He (almost all are men) lives with his family in a small house provided by the government that also serves as an office for conducting police business. The *chusai-san* spends his time patrolling his district (usually on motorcycle), visiting the residents, or conducting business out of his office in the *chuzaisho*. His duties include visiting each household twice per year, handling emergencies, and attending local functions. All duties are ways to integrate the officer into community life and keep him informed about matters that might aid him in his task of crime prevention and control. In some ways, the *chusai-san* resembles a local sheriff in a rural community in the United States.

To become a police officer in Japan, one must graduate from high school and pass a series of exams and interviews. After this process, the recruit must attend the NPA Training School. If the recruit is a high school graduate, the training lasts one year; if he or she is a college graduate, it lasts six months. The training combines academic and legal courses with martial arts. After completing school training, the recruit receives one year of field experience and then returns to school for six months for further training. As in other countries, officers who advance to higher ranks within the agency are required to undergo additional training to develop their leadership and administrative abilities. The training program for officers is regulated by the NPA.

Civil order control in Japan is handled through a separate division in each prefecture. The division is militarized in the sense that officers live in barracks, receive training in crowd control, and use military formations during civil order crises. There are around 10,000 of these officers, called **kidotai**. Young officers are used for this division and generally serve for three years before returning to conventional street police work.

Issues of Concern for Japanese Police. Since World War II, the Japanese have generally grown to be proud of their police. They believe that the peculiar Japanese police culture is one of the main contributing factors to the low crime rate in Japan. In addition, they believe that the close relationship between the police and the public contributes to social harmony and good neighborhood relations. Among the duties of Japanese police are to act as counselors to troubled individuals in the neighborhood, provide marriage and divorce counseling, offer money management tips, give advice to parents with rebellious children, and help with problems of alcohol addiction. These activities all are part of the police officer's routine (Ueno, 1986).

However, in the 1990s there was been some controversy about the treatment of citizens by the Japanese police. More specifically, the debate is whether the police in Japan are in fact honest guardians respected by the community or if they spend an inordinate amount of time intimidating suspects and being involved in corruption (Mawby, 2008). Since that time, efforts have been made by the Japanese government to provide reforms and curb such abuses, and it appears that confidence in Japanese police has been restored (Kanayama, 2012).

As mentioned in Chapter 4, in addition to the handling of the March 2011 earthquake in eastern Japan, the police in Japan are often occupied with the activity of organized crime (*boryokudan*). The recent concern, is that in addition to their traditional racketeering and violence, they have infiltrated the construction, finance, and industrial waste disposal industries and engaged in securities trading while concealing their organizations. The government and the police have responded by passing the Act on Prevention of Unjust Conducts by Organized Crime Group Members, which calls for the variety of methods to mitigate the influence of the *boryokudan*. Another issue of concern remains the growth of white collar and cybercrimes. In 2010 the National Police Agency reported almost 7,000 arrests for cybercrimes, a new high for the country (NPA, 2011). To address the issue, the National Police Agency has developed a special center for cybercrime and cyberterrorism that will provide technical assistance to the prefectural police and work with international and national agencies to combat technological crimes (Terrill, 2009). In this way, the Japanese police will remain among the most highly technologically trained police in the world.

Saudi Arabia

The Saudi Arabian police, a highly centralized force, are responsible for the maintenance of peace and order throughout the country. Prior to the late 1920s, policing in Saudi Arabia was primarily a tribal affair. A sheik, appointed to supervise a certain region, would have the authority to handle matters related to public safety. He would hire and financially support the local police as well as provide himself with additional security. This power was granted to the sheiks by the different kings that ruled the region between invasions and occupations by the Ottoman Empire (Dammer, 2010). The sheiks even had the power to punish offenders of the civil law. In 1927, however, under the first king of the modern Saudi Arabia, Abdul-Aziz, the country was consolidated and the first recognized police force was established.

The minister of the interior, who is appointed by the king, is responsible for the administration of all police matters. A director is appointed the head of the Saudi police and is then a high-ranked official in the Ministry of the Interior. The director hires most of the managers and officers of the 14 provinces (emirates) and local police forces. The police department is divided into three kinds of police: the regular police, the *mubahith*, and the *mutawa*. The regular police force is actually called the Department of Public Safety, and it handles most of the daily (deviance order control) functions in the country. The **mubahith**, or secret police, conduct criminal investigations and handle matters pertaining to domestic security and counterintelligence.

The "morals force" or "religious police" are known as the **mutawa** (or *mutaween*). This police force ensures that Saudi citizens live up to the rules of behavior derived from the Qur'an. Also called Saudi Arabia's Commission for Promotion of Virtue and Prevention of Vice, it has a membership of around 20,000 men, usually bearded men who wear traditional Arabic white robes (*kamees*). They are not armed and not trained as law enforcement personnel. Their roles are many, including maintaining strict separation of the sexes in Saudi public life, pressuring women to wear the traditional long black robes and face coverings, and stopping women from driving cars in certain locations. The *mutawa* also ensure that businesses are closed during prayer hours, cover up advertising that depicts attractive women, and regulate alcohol use. Because the *mutawa* are sometimes left to their own interpretation of right and wrong, there are numerous reports of the mistreatment and harassment of Saudi citizens, especially women, and foreign workers. Information about the impact of the *mutawa* is difficult to obtain but *Human Rights Watch* has reported that in 2005 the *mutawa* arrested over 400,000 persons for "religious violations" (Setrakian and Abu Khatwa, 2008).

When it comes to training, the Saudi police make a strong distinction between commissioned officers and rank-and-file police. The commissioned officers receive three years of training at King Fahd Security College and are promoted through the ranks from second lieutenant to general. The director of public safety, who heads the Saudi police, usually is a relative of the king (as are many heads of executive agencies in Saudi Arabia). Rank-and-file police personnel must be literate and spend three months in training. They are not eligible to become commissioned officers, however (Alobied, 1989).

Saudi Arabia has a separate "special forces" division to handle civil order control functions. One use of these special forces, called the Pilgrims and Festivals Police Force, is used to control the large throngs that gather during the annual pilgrimage (*hajj*) to the cities of Mecca and Medina. As the guardian of the holy cities, Saudi Arabia must maintain order, sanitary conditions, and food distribution channels among the approximately 2 million Muslims from around the world who go on the pilgrimage each year. In past years, the pilgrimage has been marred by high crowd concentrations and riots, resulting in many deaths and serious foreign relations problems among Saudi Arabia, Iran, and Pakistan. When civil order situations go beyond the control of the special police, the National Guard and Saudi Army are called in (Ross, 1996).

Issues of Concern for Saudi Police. A major challenge for Saudi Arabian police is how to balance the need for maintaining civil order within an Islamic system of justice while staying within the bounds of international human rights standards. Many international organizations (e.g., Amnesty International and Human Rights Watch) have publicly excoriated the Saudis for numerous incidents in which it was believed that the police crossed the line towards more abusive methods of policing. On one level this can be viewed as merely a public relations problem that has little or no impact on the daily practices of the police. However, the issue can become increasingly problematic if Saudi citizens begin to call for more rights and protections, or if the international community exerts pressure on the police—through political and economic sanctions—to bring human rights policies and practices more in line with other countries.

Another significant concern for the Saudi police is the constant threat of terrorism. This is an internal problem for the Saudis: They are highly susceptible to terrorist activity because of the numerous oil fields and the concomitant infrastructure changes they have made from oil production wealth. In addition, current and former citizens of Saudi Arabia associated with terrorism, including Osama bin Laden, have created complications for the Saudi government as other countries have questioned the safety of their interests in the region. Saudi Arabia has taken a number of steps to improve its internal security and support the fight against terrorism.

KEY OPERATIONAL ISSUES FOR POLICE AROUND THE GLOBE

Within the various models and structures we have mentioned, police in different countries go about their business in different ways. This is understandable because countries, or at least those within the different legal traditions, possess unique characteristics that help them form police operations and culture. At the same time, there appear to be some key issues that are of concern to a majority of police agencies everywhere in the world. In the rest of this chapter, we will examine some of the key operational issues that many police around the world are being called on to address. These issues are community policing, diversity, privatization, and police corruption.

Community Policing

A examination of policing from around the globe reveals that community policing is among the most commonly adopted police operational strategies in the world today (Wisler and Onwudiwe, 2009). Representatives from countries around the world have indicated that community policing is a core operational strategy. Interestingly, we even see evidence of community policing in the authoritarian and developing countries (Casey, 2010). **Community policing**—in the United States also called community-based, community-oriented, or problem-oriented policing—is an umbrella term describing programs that represent collaborative efforts between the police and the public to identify crime problems and then find solutions.

Numerous factors have contributed to the growth of community policing (Segrave and Ratcliff, 2004; Murray, 2005). At least two are important to mention here. The first is the ever-present hostility between police and many segments of the public, as evidenced in violent civil order clashes between police and citizens throughout the globe. The second is the fact that the ever-increasing world crime rates, such as those that characterized the United States in the 1970s and 1980s, seem to be impervious to conventional deviance and civil order control activities. Although the implementation of community policing varies greatly across the globe, we can find in the literature four key elements of community policing:

- *Community-based crime prevention*—Police and public work together to solve the root causes of crime and thereby prevent its long-term spread.
- *Reorientation of patrol activities to emphasize non-emergency servicing*—Police are called daily to reorient their activities to improve the daily quality of life and solve problems for citizens in the community.
- *Accountability to the public*—Police are asked to be available and to listen to the needs of citizens and address those needs when necessary.
- *Decentralization of command*—Decentralization calls for having the police working in the neighborhoods and communities where crime may occur, not only in the station house or anonymously driving around town (Skolnick and Bayley, 1988; Skogan, 2006).

There are literally thousands of ways that community policing actually happens in the world today. In short, there is no consensual model of community policing (Wisler and Onwudiwe, 2009). For evidence, just type the phrase *community policing* into any search engine on the Internet and you will find out how many kinds of programs have been articulated.

In the United States, various forms of community policing began during the 1970s, although they flourished as an operational strategy in the 1990s. And as in other countries, most community policing programs in the United States occur at the local (town or city) level. Over the last 15 years, a number of community policing–related programs in the United States have gained national and international notoriety. Among them are order-maintenance policing, or more dramatically named, zero-tolerance policing. In short, zero-tolerance policing is the strict enforcement of laws against minor offenses as a means of preventing more serious crimes (Wilson and Kelling, 1982). Another is the various forms of information-based strategies called proactive (or intelligence-based) policing. In this strategy the goal is to learn more about crime and criminals so as to prevent or intercept crimes in progress. Police use different methods to collect intelligence, including interviews, observation or surveillance, informants, and computer technology. Proactive policing strategies have been adopted by many state and federal criminal justice agencies, especially in fighting organized crime, cybercrime, and terrorism.

Probably the most famous example of the use of computer technology to analyze crime data and assess the extent of crime was the use of CompStat in the New York City Police Department during the 1990s. Compstat (computer comparison statistics) enables police to identify trouble spots and target the appropriate resources to fight crime strategically. It is an extension of the previous uses of geographic information systems (GIS) crime mapping, a technique that involves the charting of crime patterns within a geographic area.

Community policing strategies such as those mentioned here are not without their critics. One objection is that, for a variety of reasons, programs such as community policing may work in one country or jurisdiction but not in another (Bayley, 1996). Another is that, despite its wide acceptance as a policy strategy throughout the world, the true impact and effectiveness of community policing is difficult to determine (Skogan, 2006). Finally, it has been argued that certain forms of community policing, more specifically proactive policing, can be intrusive on citizens because law enforcement officials are actively seeking information about crime and criminals rather than waiting until crime has been committed (Pakes, 2010). Nevertheless, it is quite certain that community policing will remain a key operational strategy for the police for years to come. Here we briefly explain the application of community policing in our model countries.

- *England*—Arguably the first to implement community policing (in the early 1800s), the British community policing system has undergone many changes in recent years. The new emphasis is reassurance policing, which calls for a focus on addressing "signal crimes and disorders" that increase fear of crime and eventually have an "adverse effect on people's sense of security and cause them to alter their beliefs or behavior" (Joyce, 2006, p. 136; Kalunta-Crumpton, 2010).
- *France*—In 1997 the French adopted the policy of *police de proximité* as an official slogan of the National Police. This policy, the French equivalent of community policing, emphasizes improved relations between the police, the public, and governmental agencies. It is hoped this policy will reduce crime and fear of crime among citizens (Zauberman and Levy, 2003). These policies have become the springboard for community policing–type programs in areas such as senior citizen assistance, victim support, community services for offenders, drug prevention efforts, and juvenile delinquency programs. At the same time, the French police have begun patrolling high-crime areas on foot or on motorcycles (Terrill, 2009).
- *Germany*—Throughout Germany the *Kontachbereichsbeamter* (KoB) or contact officer police are older, specially trained officers who have been assigned to a beat or patrol area. They perform what are traditionally the major functions of community police officers. However, there is not just one type of a community policing program in Germany. Each of the 16 German *Länder* has its own police organization, so the kinds of programs can vary considerably depending on the region (Feltes, 2004).

- *China*—Although some question whether community policing can be accomplished in a totalitarian state (Jiao, 1995, p. 69), a more optimistic view is that unique forms of community policing are practiced in China. Clearly, community policing in China has evolved greatly over just the 30 thirty years, from the "mass line" strategies of 1949–1980, to the "strike hard" (*Yanda*) campaigns (1980–2000), to the most recent (since 2002) strategy, called "Building Little Safe and Civilized Communities" (BLSCC). Under BLSCC the Chinese adopt many of the traditional community policing strategies from around the world, including crime prevention through environmental design, developing positive relationships with local communities, holding police accountable for crime increases, and increasing police presence in high crime areas (Zhong, 2009; Wong, 2010).
- *Japan*—With its decreasing crime rates over most of the last 50 years, Japan has provided a model for effective community policing. The model proposed by the Japanese, in the form of the *koban* and *chuzaisho*, was discussed earlier in this chapter. The idea of the *koban* as a small local police station—one that provides direct access to the police for community members and calls for police to address local crime issues—has grown and been adopted in some form in many countries.
- *Saudi Arabia*—The Saudi Arabian police, because of their strong affiliation with Islamic traditions, do not engage in the traditional forms of community policing. Instead, community policing is said to take place in a variety of ways, such as religious education in mosques that teaches about the destructive impact of crime and the harshness of punishment (Jiang et al. 2011). Also, informal committees led by the mayor, or *Umda*, work to solve small problems and prevent crime by having police or average citizens approach anyone suspected of criminal activity and by frequently reporting crime and criminals to local authorities (Humaidan and Sheraya, 2009).

Diversity

In any legitimate society, especially one that espouses democratic values, the police are asked to treat all people with respect and in a fair and professional manner. In fact, community policing programs have often surfaced because the police have historically been in conflict with different groups of citizens—most notably ethnic minorities. With the changing events of the latter half of the 20th century, such as the fall of the Soviet Union, opening of borders, globalization of the economy, regional conflicts, and political unrest, there has been a widespread migration of large numbers of persons from one place to another. The police are asked to deal with the concomitant problems associated with these population shifts. When the police are called in to maintain public order and public safety, they often encounter ethnic and cultural groups acting contrary to the norms of their society. In this way, they are in a difficult situation because they are being asked to enforce the law but at the same being asked to question, arrest, or even incarcerate those that most often feel they are being discriminated against. How they handle these situations reflects their competence and their commitment to legitimate justice, and can even determine the future peace and tranquility within a society (Erez, Finckenauer, and Ibarra, 2003).

When it comes to addressing the issue of police and diverse populations, two issues generally arise. The first is improving how the police interact with diverse populations. This can be accomplished in many ways, but three are paramount. First, police must be trained to be more culturally sensitive to those they serve. This may include a variety of training techniques, such as instruction about cultural differences, communication issues, and important laws. At the same time, the training must be relevant to the day-to-day concerns that police have about how to perform their jobs safely. Second, countries with such problems must enact and enforce legislation that protects minorities and addresses discrimination. Some countries have fully embraced such measures while others lag behind. Finally, sincere efforts must be made to develop strategies to improve police relations with ethnic communities. Examples include community advisory boards, joint citizen–police task forces, and frequent personal contact among all parties involved.

The second main issue, and maybe a key solution, is the diversification of the police force itself. It has often been stated that the police should reflect the diversity of the population that it polices. Making this happen and determining whether such endeavors are successful are not quite so easily achieved (van Ewijk, 2011). Education levels, legal barriers such as citizenship, and even the level of interest on the part of minority groups may often serve as hindrances (Casey, 2010).

A number of our model countries have begun to address the issue of police and diversity. For example, in England chief constables must now develop their own programs for recruiting, monitoring, and retaining minority officers (Holdaway, 1990), and Muslim police officers in London are allowed to wear turbans instead of "bobby" helmets in the hope that it will encourage all minority groups to believe that the Metropolitan Police is an equal opportunity employer (Associated Press, 2003). As of March 2010, there were 6,660 minority ethnic police officers in England and Wales, accounting for 4.6 percent of all officers, compared with 4.4 percent in March 2009 and up from 2.2 in 2000 (Home Office, 2010). Many of the European nations, including Germany, which has experienced an influx of Turkish immigrants, have also begun to realize that is it imperative that they address diversity within the ranks of the police (van Ewijk, 2011). Japan has recently made it a goal to increase the number of female police officers to make up at least 10 percent of the force, up from the current 6.8 percent (Westlake, 2012).

Privatization

Private police can be defined as any independent or proprietary commercial organization that provides protective services to employers on a contractual basis (Schmallager, 2007). There are many forms of private policing. The most common are uniformed guards used to protect businesses and residences, to deliver money, or to protect private citizens. Less obvious are security firms that patrol government agencies, try to prevent and detect white collar and Internet crimes, and sell security equipment to private citizens and public entities. There is also a recent increase in the number of international security firms such as Blackwater, DynCorp, and Wackenhut that even engage in quasi-military and peacekeeping roles around the world (Casey, 2010).

Whatever the form private police take, it is clear that they are one of the fastest-growing components of policing. Just within the European Union there are over 1 million people working in the security industry in comparison to the 1.5 million regular police officers (Button, 2007). There are many reasons for the increase in private policing in recent years, including citizens who are more fearful of crime than they used to be, the decrease in governmental budgets for public policing while the number of places and opportunities for crime grows, and the growth and improved marketing strategies of security-related businesses (Casey, 2010, p. 121). There are many concerns about the influx of private police into the law enforcement arena. The most pressing problem is the lack of regulation in almost every country (Van Steden and Sarre, 2007). Other problems include quality issues, a lack of the same legal accountability as public law enforcement, and an inability to coordinate with public security agencies (Casey, 2010, p. 123). In at least three of our model countries, the explosion of private policing is a major issue. Private security companies are used extensively in England, and it is estimated that there are now more private security officers than sworn police officers—around 300,000 (Jones and Newburn, 2002; Southgate, 1995). The British government has passed legislation to improve the quality and accountability of private security forces (Joyce, 2006). As we mentioned earlier, over 10,000 private security personnel were hired to handle security at the 2012 Olympic and Paralympic Games.

In Germany some 3,000 security agencies employ more than 150,000 people. Their main tasks are securing private buildings and property, transporting money, and providing security services at mass events such as soccer games or concerts. Most private security guards are not armed, but neither are they trained very well. The German law demands only a few weeks of training. More and more, the public police are cooperating with private police, for instance in train stations or during mass events. The results of the World Football Championship in 2006, in which 20,000 private security personnel were involved, showed that the cooperation can be successful. More and more cities outsource security tasks to private companies, mainly in connection with the protection of buildings (Dammer, 2010). In China, with the growth in the number of private businesses and with a large number of public companies becoming privatized, the number of security agencies has increased significantly (Zhong and Grabosky, 2009).

Police Corruption

Later in this book, in Chapter 11, we will discuss the issue of corruption more broadly as it relates to international organized crime. But for the purposes of this chapter, we would be remiss if we did not mention that police corruption as a major issue of concern for citizens and police authorities all over world (Bracey, 1995; Ivkovic, 2005). Transparency International has reported that police in 86 countries were judged the fourth most corrupt public institution after political parties, public officials generally, and parliaments and legislature (Transparency International, 2010).

No geographical region in the world is untouched by this monumental problem. Consider the African country of Nigeria, where police corruption is said to be deeply ingrained in the culture of the police (Aremu et al., 2009; Human Rights Watch, 2010). Corruption is also significant in Kenya, where the average citizen is said to be forced to bribe police 4.5 times per month (Baker and Scheye, 2007). In India, a major government study reported that 87 percent of the citizens who interact with the police believe they are corrupt (CMS, 2005). In September 2011 in Mexico, a state police officer was arrested in connection with the drug cartel casino fire that killed 52 people in the northern industrial town of Monterrey. Police corruption in Mexico is a major issue because it remains one of the biggest obstacles the country faces in its fight against the drug cartels (CNN World, 2011a). In Russia, problems associated with police misconduct have remained despite the birth of democratic processes in that country following the implosion of the Soviet Union (*The Economist*, 2010).

However, police corruption is not only a problem in developing countries or those in transition. In England during the summer of 2011, a number of public officials, including the London police chief and an editor of a major newspaper, resigned, and a dozen persons were arrested, including a police officer, after a phone-hacking scandal led to a major police corruption probe. The story created months of intrigue and was exacerbated by the sudden death of a reporter who originally broke the story (CNN World, 2011b; Lawless, 2012). By no means is the U.S. inoculated from this worldwide problem. Since the formation of the first public police agencies in the U.S., there have been numerous examples of police corruption. In the last decade or so, the large urban police departments of New Orleans, Los Angeles, and New York have experienced major corruption scandals.

There have been numerous attempts to understand and clearly define **police corruption**, each with its own emphasis and inclusivity. For our purposes, we turn to the definition provided by John Kleinig (1996), who states that police officers act corruptly when, "in exercising or failing to exercise their authority, they act with the primary intention of furthering private or departmental/divisional advantage" (pg. 166). In recent decades we have come to learn much about the various forms of police corruption from a number of international scholars and government reports (see Goldstein, 1975; Mollen Commission, 1994; Newburn, 2009; Punch, 2009).

In Table 5.3, we list from a variety of sources some of the more common forms of police corruption. This list is by no means an exhaustive one. In fact, one recent report on the subject has identified 35 different examples of police corruption around the world. This report, written by international police scholars David Bayley and Robert Perito, was based on the analysis of 32 different commissions that have studied police behavior in 58 English-speaking countries since the late 19th century. We suggest the reader take the time to access this informative report because in addition to providing a review of past commissions, it clearly explains how police corruption is formed, cultivated, and how it can be mitigated (Bayley and Perito, 2011).

TABLE 5.3 Common Forms of Police Corruption

Name of Corruption	Description	Common Examples
Corruption of authority	Police officers receiving free goods or services	Free drinks, meals, and other gratuities
Kickbacks	Receiving payment from referring people to other businesses	Cash or gratuities from contractors, automobile service stations, bar owners
Opportunistic theft	Theft from arrestees and crime victims	Keeping alcohol from underage drinkers, taking jewelry/money from corpses
Shakedowns	Accepting bribes for not pursuing a criminal violation	Not giving tickets to speeders
Protection of illegal activity: being "on the take"	Accepting payment from the operators of illegal establishments to protect them from law enforcement and keep them in operation	Obtaining cash or gratuities from brothels, casinos, or drug dealers
Fixing	Undermining criminal prosecutions for bribe or personal favor	Withholding evidence or failing to appear at judicial hearings
Direct criminal activity	Criminal acts committed by law enforcement officers themselves	Burglary, physical abuse of partner, driving while intoxicated
Internal payoffs	Providing prerogatives and perquisites of law enforcement organizations	Hourly shifts and holidays, being bought and sold, overtime abuse
Ticket fixing	Cancelling traffic tickets as a favor	Helping friends, family and other officers "beat tickets" from other police officers
Hazing	Police hazing within law enforcement	Hazing new police recruits

SOURCES: Newburn, 1999; Carter, 1990; Sayed and Bruce, 1998; Punch, 1985; Roebuck and Barker, 1974.

INTERNATIONAL POLICE COOPERATION

The movement of criminals across national borders to commit crime and avoid detection or arrest is certainly not a new phenomenon. However, with the growth in transnational crime of all types, including the increasing threat of terrorism, there has been no time in history when law enforcement cooperation between nations has been so necessary. Fortunately, it appears that the global law enforcement community has heard the recent call for such international collaboration. As time has passed since the earliest collaborative efforts in the mid-1800s, at least two factors, in addition to the growth of international crime, have helped foster the overall growth of international police cooperation. First, the police have been able to gain a significant level of autonomy from the political areas in which they operate. Second, the longevity of certain international police organizations (such as Interpol) has provided credibility to the endeavor and served to motivate police from around the world to join in the cooperative effort (Deflem and McDonough, 2010).

The goals of international police cooperation vary, of course, depending on the jurisdictions involved and their individual needs. However, we can say in general that the goals of such efforts are at least the following activities:

- Share intelligence on criminal activities that assists with the investigation and apprehension of criminal suspects in one or more jurisdictions.
- Create new training and education opportunities, including bilateral exchange of personnel and ideas.
- Provide technical assistance that will help under-resourced police agencies.
- Allow for officers to work in other countries to address crime issues of mutual concern.

- Build professional relationships for future collaboration. (Casey, 2010, p. 105)

As mentioned in Chapter 2, the International Police Association (Interpol), in operation since 1946, has worked with local and national police agencies to share information among its members regarding a range of international policing and crime issues, including names, fingerprints, DNA profiles on international criminals, and information concerning stolen property such as passports and works of art. Lately the organization prioritizes crimes involving terrorism, drugs, organized crime, financial crimes, and human trafficking (Barberet, 2009). Because of the success of Interpol, other kinds of cooperative efforts by police have begun to surface.

In 1997 the United Nations formed what is now called the United Nations Office on Drugs and Crime (UNODC). The 21 field offices and 500 employees of the UNODC serve in three areas: providing technical support to countries that wish to fight illegal drugs, crime, and terrorism; conducting and disseminating research about these issues; and assisting countries that wish to develop and ratify legislation and treaties regarding drugs, crime, and terrorism (UNODC, 2012).

However, the region of the world that seems to have fully embraced the idea of international police cooperation is Europe. In 1992 the EU created Europol—the European Law Enforcement Organization. Like Interpol, Europol acts as an information clearinghouse, and it also lacks the executive powers of search and seizure and arrest. Europol's mission is to make a significant contribution to the law enforcement agencies within the EU so as to better deal with the problems of organized crime, terrorism, unlawful trafficking, immigrant smuggling, environmental crimes, money laundering, and counterfeiting of the euro (Occhipinti, 2003; Casey, 2010; Europol, 2012). Unlike Interpol, Europol is a deliberate legal construction of the European Union and has legislative, executive, and judicial authority. Unlike Interpol, Europol has a mandate for deploying civilian police in peacekeeping situations under the aegis of the European Security and Defense Policy (ESDP). There have been a total of 25 interventions promulgated by the ESDP since its formation in 1999. Currently the policy provides peacekeepers in 14 geographic regions throughout Europe, Africa, and Asia. In addition, the EU has recently formed the European Gendarmerie Force (EGF) for deployment in territories within the continent. The EGF, developed in 2006, now includes six states of the European Union. EGF forces, modelled after the French, Spanish and Italian police forces, provide military police presence and crisis management when called upon in the European region.

Two recent developments that have advanced international law enforcement cooperation in Europe are the Lisbon Treaty of 2009 and the Stockholm Programme of 2010. The Lisbon Treaty was created to provide a new legal framework for cooperation between European member states in the prevention, detection, and prosecution of crime. More specifically, the treaty will provide a streamlined process for decision making relative to when and to what extent law enforcement can intervene in the affairs of a member state. The Stockholm Programme urges member states, agencies, authorities, and EU institutions to coordinate activities to ensure the security of European citizens by successfully suppressing organized crime, terrorism, drug trafficking, corruption, human trafficking, people smuggling, sexual exploitation of children, illegal trafficking of arms, computer crime, cross-border crime, and other transnational threats to the security of citizens (The Stockholm Programme, 2010).

Other regional law enforcement collaborations outside the European continent have also developed in recent years. Organizations that are linked with Interpol are Africa's police chiefs' organizations (PCCOs) and the Southeastern Asian Nations Chiefs of Police (ASEANAPOL); each was formed to foster cooperation between member countries so as to develop agreements to fight drug crimes and terrorism and promote extradition (McDonald, 2005). More broadly, the World Customs Organization, originally called the Customs Cooperation Council, was reorganized and renamed in 1994 and has since worked to combat transnational crime issues such as drug smuggling, money laundering, and theft of art and cultural objects. The Financial Action Task Force (FATF), an international body of 36 countries established in 1989, has the goal of promoting effective implementation of legal, regulatory, and operational measures for combating money laundering, terrorist financing, and other related threats to the integrity of the international financial system (Reichel, 2013).

In addition to the police collaborations that primarily share information and assist in the apprehension of suspects, a number of police agencies have been asked to extend beyond boundaries and assist in military operations in conflict zones around the globe. The term used to describe the range of military, police, and civilian interventions that seek to restore order and create a sustainable society after a period of war is **peace operations** (Casey, 2010, p. 177). Although some of these police operations, such as the EU's European Gendarmerie Force, are regionally supported, the most visible and long-standing are the international police collaborations created and sustained by the United Nations.

Peace operations have been in existence at least since the formation of the United Nations. Since 1948 there have been some 67 UN-sponsored peace operations involving collaboration among the military, civilians, and the police (Haberfeld et al., 2008; United Nations Peacekeeping, 2012). The main organization that currently carries out these operations is the United Nations Police (**UNPOL**, formerly CIVPOL), which was first implemented as a civilian police initiative in 1960 to assist in peacekeeping efforts in the Congo (Terrill, 2000). The organization has since become an integral component of what has traditionally been the function of military peacekeeping operations. As of August 2012, more than 97,000 police from over 120 countries are deployed in 17 different jurisdictions on 4 continents. UNPOL supports the reformation, restructuring, and rebuilding of domestic police and other law enforcement agencies through training and advising. It also provides financial assistance to law enforcement, and in some instances is directly responsible for all law enforcement functions, including the maintenance of law and order. UNPOL officers are, among other things, entrusted with powers to arrest, detain, and search (United Nations Peacekeeping, 2012).

The United States has also been very active in promoting and supporting international police cooperation. One agency that works to share information with international agencies is the U.S. National Central Bureau (USNCB). The USNCB, operating within the guidelines prescribed by the Department of Justice and in conjunction with the Department of Homeland Security, serves to facilitate international law enforcement cooperation as the United States representative with Interpol, on behalf of the Attorney General. In addition to the sharing of information through USNCB, there are more than 1,600 American law enforcement personnel working overseas. Among the agencies represented are the Drug Enforcement Agency (DEA), the U.S. Immigration Service, Customs Service, Coast Guard, Federal Bureau of Investigation (FBI), Internal Revenue Service, Secret Service, and Bureau of Alcohol and Tobacco (Albanese, 2005).

International police cooperation faces many challenges. The most obvious are language barriers, the disparity in resources (e.g., money, data, and technology), the lack of knowledge about the culture or system of another country, and the behavior of peacekeepers who while in the course of duty may see themselves as being "above the law." In addition, the international pacts, agreements, and treaties that are meant to support cooperation can sometimes limit the ability of law enforcement to conduct investigations and extradite criminals (Kearney et al., 2011; McDonald, 2011). But even more detrimental, and maybe more common, is corruption of police and public officials. As stated by Ebbie (1999), "when those who make the laws and those who enforce the law are shamelessly corrupt, then the entire society is corrupted" Pg. 2. When corruption is present in police agencies, it serves as a breeding ground for organized crime and a host of other international crimes such as drug and human trafficking, environmental crime, and human rights violations. And when this occurs, the willingness of citizens and other police agencies to cooperate falters. We will discuss corruption and organized crime in more depth later in this book, but for now we can surely say that it is a major hindrance to effective international police cooperation.

Nevertheless, despite the limitations of and challenges for cooperation across the globe, police have quickly learned that by working together and sharing information and ideas, they can better solve the problems related to crime and justice. Because of the success of cooperative efforts in law enforcement, other aspects of criminal justice system have developed similar efforts.

SUMMARY

The ideal police force is one that prevents crime, keeps order, respects the rights and dignity of citizens, is friendly and courteous, respects the laws, and does not abuse its power through corruption. Throughout the world there have been increasing efforts to improve police practice through the implementation of democratic policing. The peculiarities of police work, however, including the need to keep public order in times of civil tension and the large amount of discretion exercised by individual officers on the street, sometimes may interfere with police operations. Furthermore, the organizational climate and structure are strongly influenced by historical developments and political realities in particular systems.

In the descriptions in this chapter, we have seen manifestations of this historical and political influence time and time again. In England, with its tradition of decentralization and resistance to government power, the police culture has emphasized local control and the idea of "police as citizens." In France, with its tradition of centralization and bureaucratization, the entire police organization is directed from two ministries in Paris. Germany's police operations are highly influenced by twin fears: fear of the kind of public disorder that signaled the end of the Weimar Republic and fear of the excesses that characterized police in the Nazi years. In the People's Republic of China, police have always been

Comparative Criminal Justice at the Movies

Movies seek to entertain and inform the audience about a story, incident, or person. Many good movies also hit upon important substantive themes relevant to understanding crime and justice in comparative perspective. Read the movie summary below (and watch the movie if you haven't already) and answer the questions below to make the subject matter connections to comparative criminal justice.

Rendition (2007)
Gavin Hood, Director

A terrorist bombing kills an American envoy in a foreign country, and the investigation leads to, Anwar (Omar Metwally), an Egyptian chemical engineer who has been living in the United States for a long time and is married to an American. He is apprehended when he is on his way home. The United States transports him to the country where the bombing took place for interrogation involving torture. The practice is known as "extraordinary rendition." An American CIA operative observes the interrogation and is undecided about stopping it. In the meantime, the man's wife Isabella (Reese Witherspoon) tries desperately to find him despite being pregnant, but she is able to obtain no information.

CIA analyst Douglas Freeman (Jake Gyllenhaal) is briefing his chief in a square in North Africa when a suicide attack kills his boss and 18 other people. The target was an interrogator and torturer, Abasi, but he is unharmed. For lack of more experienced staff, Freeman is assigned the task of observing the interrogation of the Egyptian Anwar After Freeman briefly questions and tortures Anwar himself, he is convinced of his innocence. However, his boss insists that the detention continue, justifying such treatments as necessary to save thousands from becoming victims of terrorism. Eventually Anwar confesses to have advised on how to make more powerful bombs, and to have been promised $40,000 in return.

Freeman believes it is a false confession, which is confirmed when he does an Internet search for the names Anwar gives and finds out they are the names of the Egyptian football team from the year Anwar left Egypt. He also expresses doubt as to whether Anwar would be willing to put his life, family, and job in danger for $40,000 when he earns $200,000 in his job. Without the consent of his superiors, Freeman orders Anwar's release and lets him escape through a clandestine trip by ship to Spain. Anwar returns to the United States and is reunited with his family. Freeman then leaks the details of Anwar's detention to the press.

Questions

1. What is the objection to the practice of extraordinary rendition?
2. Should the interrogation rules and practices for terrorism suspects be any different than those for traditional crime suspects? Why or why not?

Critical Thinking Exercise

Critical thinking requires the ability to evaluate viewpoints, facts, and behaviors objectively to assess information and methods of argumentation in order to establish the merit of an action, law, policy, or procedure. Please evaluate this scenario objectively, applying your knowledge of comparative criminal justice to the facts of the case presented, and answer the questions that follow it.

Police Policy of Pay-for-Sex Services Is Challenged

Police in Hong Kong have been challenged over their policy of allowing undercover officers to pay for sex services during anti-vice operations. The approach is banned as unethical by many police forces around the world, and is even illegal in some countries. Officers, most of them working in Mong Kok, routinely make repeated visits to prostitutes—and use public funds to receive massages and masturbation—in the course of operations targeting vice establishments and illegal massage parlors.

Police say the practice, which is widespread and dates back to 1993, is necessary to provide sufficient evidence for prosecutions. The force insists operations are closely monitored by senior officers and stress that policemen are not allowed to receive oral sex or engage in full intercourse.

However, Zi Teng—a welfare group representing prostitutes—claims officers are abusing the policy for their own enjoyment. It alleges that one policeman visited the same prostitute every two weeks for a two-year period before arresting her. "It was ridiculous.... The sex worker considered him an old client," said a Zi Teng representative.

University of Hong Kong academic Simon Young has contacted forces worldwide and found that in Canada and Australia officers are strictly barred from any sexual contact, while in some U.S. states the practice would be illegal. Police and Security Bureau officials will be asked at a meeting with legislators and Zi Teng to justify the controversial tactic.

Mr. Young, deputy director of the university's Centre for Comparative and Public Law, described the practice as "almost like corruption" and argued it was bringing the force into disrepute. "The approach that other police agencies around the world take really demonstrates that you can't just have a little sexual contact—there has to be no sexual contact whatsoever," he said. "There have to be certain professional standards."

Legislator Fernando Cheung Chiu-hung said the policy "undermines the image of the Hong Kong police" and that he would seek to raise it at a security panel if police refused to drop the policy. "Our police should be upholding moral principles," he said. "I don't see why there has to be any sexual contact when an undercover operation takes place."

A police spokeswoman defended the policy and said officers gave operational priority to cases where women or the young were exploited, or where triad gangs were involved. Officers had to pose as customers and "a certain degree of bodily contact is required," she said, adding, "when the evidence is sufficient to satisfy the objective of the operation, the undercover agent should consider stopping the service without waiting for it to be completed."

Asked if any police officers had been disciplined in the past 14 years for receiving sex services beyond those permitted, a spokeswoman replied: "No police officer has so far ever been defaulted for breaching the guidelines."

Questions

1. On what grounds do you believe the Hong Kong Police strategy in dealing with prostitution to be acceptable or unacceptable?
2. To what extent should police tactics be influenced by police operations in other jurisdictions?
3. It is to be expected that police procedures and tactics will vary, but are there (or should there be) baselines for acceptable police conduct and procedures that should transcend national boundaries?

SOURCE: Simon Perry, *South China Morning Post* (June 3, 2007), p. 3.

under the close scrutiny of the Communist Party and are now facing the challenges of economic change and growth. In the postwar years, the Japanese police have become a relatively benign but sometimes intrusive force for service and crime prevention. Saudi Arabia, a small country with few crime problems, has no aspirations to develop democratic policing. Each of our model countries has police issues that currently test its structure and mission, such as civil unrest, organized crime, and cybercrime. Police around the world in general must take heed of four operational issues: community policing, diversity, privatization, and police corruption. As we continue in the 21st century, we can also expect that the police will not only work more closely with citizens but also will cooperate with other police agencies in the international fight against crime.

DISCUSSION QUESTIONS

1. Which of the six model nations do you believe has the most effective police force? Why?
2. How does the United States deal with problems related to civil order control? How do these methods compare and contrast with those of our model countries?
3. How might the *koban* system contribute to a low crime rate in Japan? Would such a system be adaptable to the United States?
4. Using the Internet, find an example of a community policing program operating in the United States and one in a foreign country. How are they the same? Different?
5. Of the key issues that concern the police around the globe, which one do you think will be most important for policing in the 21st century?

FOR FURTHER READING

Bowling, B., and J. Sheptycki (2011). *Global Policing*. London: Sage Publications.

Casey, J. (2010). *Policing the World: The Practice of International and Transnational Policing*. Durham, NC: Carolina Academic Press.

Grabosky, P. (Ed.) (2009). *Community Policing and Peacekeeping*. Boca Raton, FL: CRC Press.

Kethineni, S. (Ed.) (2010). *Comparative and International Policing, Justice, and Transnational Crime*. Durham, NC: Carolina Academic Press.

Wong, K. C. (2012). *Police Reform in China: A Chinese Perspective*. Boca Raton, FL: CRC Press.

WEB PAGES FOR CHAPTER

For a wide range of information about community policing, see http://www.policing.com.

For the web page for the United Nations Police, see http://www.un.org/en/peacekeeping/issues/police.shtml.

To view images of Japanese *kobans*, Google Japanese Kobans or see https://www.google.com/search?q=japanese+koban+system&hl=en&client=firefox-a&hs=gif&sa=N&rls=org.mozilla:en-US:official&prmd=imvns&tbm=isch&tbo=u&source=univ&ei=BsAxUOixG4fm0QGtsIHAAg&ved=0CFsQsAQ&biw=1280&bih=909

For a description of police in over 60 countries, including organizational charts, see http://polis.osce.org/countries/.

See http://www.uncjin.org/Standards/Conduct/conduct.html for the United Nations Code of Conduct for Law Enforcement Officials and other UN documents.

6  Criminal Procedure

Key Terms and Concepts

abstract constitutional review
adversarial system
assessors
courts of assize
dossier
European Convention of Human Rights
garde à vue
inquisitorial system
internationalized courts
judicial review
juge d'instruction
justice of the peace
plea bargaining
popular system
saiban-in
Schöffen
supranational courts

Chapter 6 Learning Objectives

Explore the major differences in criminal procedure among the various families of law.

Analyze the differences between adversarial systems and inquisitorial systems.

Explain the different types of constitutional review.

Describe how convergence has become the norm in criminal procedure in the legal systems around the world.

Identify the general forms of supranational court that deal with issues of human rights and international crime and criminals.

In 2010, an organization called the Trans-Border Institute in California reported that the criminal justice system in Mexico had recently introduced a series of constitutional and legislative changes to its criminal justice system. The changes included changes to criminal procedure law calling for new oral, adversarial procedures in the courts and a greater emphasis on due process rights for defendants, including the presumption of innocence and adequate legal defense (Trans-Boarder Institute, 2010).

Recognizing that legal aid is an essential element of a fair, humane, and efficient criminal justice system, the United Nations in April 2012 passed a resolution forming the United Nations Principles and Guidelines on Access to Legal Aid in Criminal Justice Systems. This resolution includes 18 guidelines calling for improvements in criminal procedure law particularly related to right to counsel. Drawing from international standards, the guidelines "invite" member nations to address legal aid for defendants at all levels of the criminal justice process from arrest to sentencing, special legal aid measures for women and children, and nationwide legal aid systems and oversight (UN Economic and Social Council, 2012).

These two legal developments, both of which address the issue of legal defense, are examples of how criminal procedure rights are now finding a place of importance all over the world. They also reflect how certain ways of handling legal issues are being internationally accepted regardless of historical and cultural differences in how countries approach justice. Another term used to describe this sharing of procedure is *convergence*—a concept we will explore in more depth later in this chapter.

But for now let us explore why you should concern yourself with criminal procedural rights. Consider if you were accused of a serious crime in your country or even while abroad. Removed from home, family, and friends, you might be subject to humiliating, confusing, and painful treatment. Spending time in a jail or prison cell can have its particular horrors. Worst of all, when accused you are fundamentally helpless to act, with the whole power of a coercive, armed, authoritative government aligned against you. If you are innocent of the crimes charged you may be especially vulnerable because you then are a threat to the superior power of the state.

To mitigate this kind of situation in which individuals have been treated unjustly by the government, most legal systems have developed criminal procedure rules designed to redress to some extent the awesome imbalance of power between the accused and the state. In effect, the authorities are supposed to "play by the rules" rather than assert naked power when dealing with an accused person.

Protecting the rights of accused persons is not the only reason that governments have rules of criminal procedure. Rules are necessary to guide the many people engaged in the criminal justice process, to contribute a certain predictability to the process, and to legitimize the government's effort to maintain a criminal justice system. In the highly bureaucratized society of today, detailed rules are a familiar way to frame legal processes and reduce the discretionary power of law enforcement officials.

Many criminal procedure rules are familiar to Americans because they are listed in the Constitution, especially in certain provisions of the Bill of Rights. Mindful of past excesses against accused people, especially political and religious dissenters, the Founding Fathers sought to ensure that the fledgling national government of the United States would not arbitrarily arrest, imprison, or kill those accused of crimes without giving them a chance to prove their innocence.Most of the American rights of the accused actually existed in England prior to the establishment of the American republic, and many had already been incorporated into state constitutions. The criminal procedure rules found in the Constitution include the right of habeas corpus, according to which the state must inform accused persons of the charges against them and justify their imprisonment. The rules also include the right to be free from illegal searches and seizures, the right to an attorney at trial and at various pretrial stages, the right not to be tried twice for the same crime, the right to trial by jury, the right not to testify against oneself, and the right to reasonable bail. Many of these rights have been incorporated into laws in other countries and into international documents such as the United Nations Covenant on Civil and Political Rights or the European Convention of Human Rights.

In this chapter we examine the three major systems of legal procedure that historically and currently influence how defendants are treated in our model countries and throughout the world. These three systems are the adversarial, inquisitorial, and popular (mixed) systems of criminal procedure. We will also address how these systems apply to criminal procedure rules in our model countries and in international courts of law. Finally, we will discuss how governments decide on the legality of criminal procedure laws and the behavior of agents in the criminal justice system.

THE ADVERSARIAL SYSTEM

The **adversarial system** is a set of legal procedures used in Common Law countries to determine the truth during adjudication whereby the prosecution and defense counsel compete against each other while the judge ensures fairness and adherence to the rules. In the adversarial system, it is assumed that the truth will arise from the free and open competition over who has the correct facts (Reichel, 2013). The adversarial system, inspired by the Enlightenment period, was developed in the late 16th and 17th centuries when a series of treason trials in England led to calls for changes in the way the accused could defend themselves against the Crown. Allowance of defense counsel was actually the first step away from private vengeance and toward a trial system that would eventually come to be lawyer-dominated ("lawyerization") versus the prior lawyer-free system (Langbein, 2003; Volger, 2005). In European legal parlance, the adversarial system is also referred to as the *accusatorial system*.

The adversarial system is often compared to a game or contest in which both sides are trying to win and a neutral umpire decides two things: (1) whether they are playing by the rules and (2) which side wins. Often, the judge acts as umpire for both of these aspects of the contest. In some cases, the judge's chief responsibility is to make decisions that ensure a fair contest, while a jury declares the actual winner.

The analogy to a game is appropriate when describing an adversary system. Not only is the accused not obligated to cooperate with the government in a case, but the government may fail to disclose crucial elements of its case against the accused. This does not mean that the government has the right to ignore or suppress evidence that would help the other side in the case—only the accused has that right. But it does mean that the prosecutor, who represents the government, is expected to devote his or her efforts to proving guilt rather than potential innocence once an individual has been indicted and is moving toward trial. In the adversarial system, most of the procedural advantages are on the side of the accused. The right to an attorney, the right to remain silent, the right to be free of unwarranted searches and arrests, the right to compel witnesses to appear for the defense, the right to confront one's accuser, the right to appeal—these and other rules of criminal process help keep the prosecutor from automatically winning a case. These rules have been developed over centuries as a response to abuses of citizens by monarchs and governments in dealing with their citizens, and these rules recognize that arbitrary government action remains a real possibility.

Critics of the adversarial system are concerned that correct criminal procedure has become so extreme that predatory criminals who learn to manipulate the rules of the system are likely to win the game despite their obvious guilt. This problem has led to two major criticisms of the adversarial system. The first is called the *combat effect*. The combat effect allows for truth-impairing procedures to suppress and distort the truth, with the goal being to "win" the courtroom struggle. The second is the related problem of the *wealth effect*, which is the enormous advantage held by those who can afford to hire skilled attorneys and pay for investigators (Langbein, 2003).

However, critics of the adversarial system often do not take into consideration mitigating factors that counteract excessive manipulation of criminal procedure. In the first place, a vast majority of cases that occur in many Common Law countries such as the United States, Canada, India (since 2005), and England and Wales are settled through guilty pleas rather than through court trials. Students of criminal justice in the United States are well aware of the importance of **plea bargaining** and sentence bargaining in the settlement of criminal cases. In these cases, the accused agrees to plead guilty in return for various concessions, such as a lesser charge or a reduced sentence.

Another way to understand the adversarial system is to compare it to its philosophical opposite—the nonadversarial or inquisitorial system. Advocates of the adversarial systems of justice believe that the competition between the two parties is the best process for obtaining truth. Advocates of the inquisitorial system believe that judicial control of the investigative process is the best way to uncover the truth. These fundamentally different beliefs create the differences in the roles of witnesses, attorneys, and judges found in the Common and Civil Law systems (Spader, 1999, p. 119; Hodgson, 2005, p. 26).

THE INQUISITORIAL SYSTEM

The **inquisitorial system** has been a main model of criminal procedure for over 700 years and, although it is most commonly associated with Civil Law systems, it also has touched every legal system in the world. Without it, criminal justice professionals would be unable to conduct any serious criminal investigations.

One myth that has been propagated about the inquisitorial system as a major contrast between Common Law and Civil Law criminal procedure is that in the former the accused is innocent until proven guilty whereas in the latter the accused is guilty until proven innocent. This is indeed not necessarily true, since both kinds of procedure are theoretically based on a presumption of innocence. Nevertheless, the extensive pretrial investigation that characterizes Civil Law systems gives rise to the feeling that defendants who actually are brought to trial are most likely to be guilty.

Criminal procedure in Civil Law countries is characterized as inquisitorial, as opposed to adversarial, in nature. This characterization evokes unfortunate images of the Inquisition, that notorious and cruel institution that persecuted alleged heretics during the 16th and subsequent centuries in Spain and other Catholic countries, extorting confessions through brutal tortures and executing its victims, often by burning. In fact, however, confessions resulting from torture were the norm in both England and continental Europe for secular as well as religious crimes until the right to remain silent became the distinguishing characteristic of the adversarial system of procedure.

What is closer to historical fact is that the inquisitorial system was actually developed to protect defendants against being wrongly convicted. It was believed that to protect defendants from being wrongly convicted it was necessary to condemn the guilty only if he confessed or if there was the evidence of two eyewitnesses. The result was the development of a complex body of laws that created an impediment to justice. The system adjusted and tried to circumvent the laws by allowing defendants to be tortured as encouragement to confess, and the reputation of the inquisitorial system as one of torture began to grow (Delmas-Marty and Spencer, 2002, p. 9; Ambose, 2003). Therefore, in modern Civil Law systems, the inquisitorial system refers not to any legacy of the Inquisition but to the extensive pretrial investigation and interrogations that are designed to ensure that no innocent person is brought to trial. The inquisitorial process can best be described as an official inquiry, in contrast to the contest or dispute that characterizes the adversarial process (Damaska, 1986).

The trial in the inquisitorial system is less like a competition and more like a continuing investigation. As stated eloquently by Reichel (2013):

> The parties in the (inquisitorial) case must provide all relevant evidence to the court. The judges, not the attorneys for the plaintiff or the defendant then call and actively examine witnesses. In this way the inquisitorial system assumes that the truth can be—in fact, must be—discovered in an investigative procedure. (p. 130)

Like the adversarial system, the inquisitorial system is not without its critics. The main issues with the system arise from the extreme power of the judge at both the investigative and the trial levels. Because of the extensive pretrial investigation, which the judge closely oversees, the inquisitorial system is often criticized for delays in the system, including very long pretrial detention for suspects. Another issue is that during the trial the judge must also balance previous knowledge gained through the investigation that he or she guided with the need to maintain impartiality. Without impartiality, the trial becomes merely a review and affirmation of the pretrial investigation. This problem is exacerbated by the fact that the judge in the inquisitorial system must actively guide the trial proceedings by protecting the interests of the prosecution and the defense (Van Kessel, 2002).

THE POPULAR (MIXED) SYSTEM

The third form of administering criminal procedure in the world is the **popular system**, or mixed system, of justice. It is called "popular" because it is a system that calls for the popular participation of citizens who are not necessarily criminal justice professionals. Popular justice is the oldest of the procedural systems of justice, practiced long before the formation of modern societies, and it probably has its roots in the magical as well as group resolutions of community disputes (Vogler, 2005, p. 197). Vigilante groups, such as those that proliferated in the western United States in the 19th century and the south in the early 20th century, are infamous examples of this kind of unsanctioned justice. In most countries, popular justice has evolved to a fully acceptable system that has been integrated into the adversarial and inquisitorial systems. The best example of popular systems is the Anglo-American jury trial system; other, lesser-known examples include the *gacca* courts in Rwanda, the mass line in China, and the South African township courts (Vogler, 2005). The most recent advent of the popular system is the newly formed mixed jury system instituted in Japan (BBC News, 2009).

Currently, the popular or mixed system is a variation of criminal procedure that is used primarily in Civil Law countries but is also found in Socialist and Common Law legal systems. It is a method of adjudication in which one or more lay judges help the professional judge come to a decision. Lay judges are typical citizens, not professional legal personnel. They are usually elected (on the local level) or chosen by the government agency responsible for monitoring the courts. The lay judges either work as volunteers a certain number of days each year or serve a term prescribed by law. Their numbers vary depending on the seriousness of the case, the court level, and the laws of the country; they range from at least two to six.

In effect, the lay judges replace the full jury, providing the balance between the state, which acts against the accused, and the peers of the accused in considering the interests of justice and the community at large. It is possible in many systems for the lay judges to overrule the professional judge. However, in practice, lay judges often defer to the professional judge's knowledge and rarely muster a majority that overrides the professional judge's vote. Their main function seems to be a restraining one, to keep the judge from acting in an arbitrary or unreasonable manner.

The popular (mixed) system in Civil Law countries developed in the 19th century when some European countries attempted to imitate the Anglo-American criminal jury system. Such changes reflects the importance that Civil Law countries place on nonprofessional participation in the court process (Spader, 1999, p. 122).

Examples are present throughout the globe. In addition to Japan, Germany uses lay judges, called **Schöffen**, extensively in courts of appeal for cases of limited jurisdiction (minor offenses) and for first-level cases of general criminal jurisdiction (criminal offenses). Some countries employ all-lay tribunals. In this form, the courts usually have one person who is legally trained to work with and provide advice to laypersons in matters that are considered less serious or during administrative or arbitration hearings. China also employs lay judges, called *lay assessors*, in its people's courts to serve as adjudicators in serious criminal cases of first instance. Lay assessors in China must be 23 years of age and eligible to vote; they are either elected or temporarily invited to sit on the court. The United States and England also use a derivation of this method in their lower courts. Many small towns in both countries utilize a person called a **justice of the peace**, who carries out many legal functions, including adjudicating traffic violations, some misdemeanors, small civil claims, and some domestic matters. In England, in the lower magistrates' court, at least two lay judges must hear all summary (minor) offenses.

COMMON LAW CRIMINAL PROCEDURE

Although there is some variation from country to country, the core practices of criminal procedure in Common Law countries are very similar. Among the most common and important procedures are those related to the pretrial investigation and the rights to counsel, to remain silent, to bail, and to a trial by jury. Table 6.1 provides a comparison list of these criminal procedures for the United States and our other model countries. In the following section, we discuss these criminal procedures, using England as the primary example and, when applicable, the United States as a comparison country. But first we must refer to a larger procedural movement that seems to be occurring at least in Common Law countries.

That movement is called the "international human rights revolution" that we mentioned briefly in Chapter 3. From Canada to Hong Kong, from New Zealand to Northern Ireland, Common Law and mixed legal systems (e.g., South Africa) around the world have taken seriously the call to reform how they protect and prosecute criminals and support victims from a variety of sources. The models for such reforms have come from the adoption of new and improved criminal evidence and procedural law based on human rights–inspired innovation (Roberts and Hunter, 2012). Individual countries, including the United States, have provided the impetus for this movement along with international documents that have produced criminal procedure documents such at the *International Covenant on Civil and Political Rights*, the *European Convention on Human Rights*, and more recently the various courts on an international level that we will introduce later in this chapter. The human rights movement has developed, ironically, from some of the same factors that have caused the rise in transnational crime such as the opening of the borders and the various modes of technology that allow us to know what is happening on the other side of the world in seconds.

Criminal procedure in England has undergone some significant changes over the last 25 years. The changes in the 1980s were the result of measures brought about to address the issue of the interrogation and detention related to terrorist actions that were prevalent in Northern Ireland during that time period. More recent changes are the result of England's entrance into the European Union and their promise to meet the procedural laws of the **European Convention of Human Rights**. The European Convention, like the U.S. Constitution, consists of a series of articles that address basis rights and freedoms evident in democratic countries. Because of England's participation in the European Union, England is obliged to follow the Convention.

The Right to Counsel

The 1586 trial of Mary Stuart, Queen of Scots, clearly illustrates why denying the assistance of

TABLE 6.1 Essential Criminal Procedures for Model Countries and United States

	United States	England	France	Germany	China	Saudi Arabia	Japan
Investigation	Police send crime information to federal, state, or local prosecutor	Police or, in rare cases, individuals send charges to Crown Prosecution Service	Minor crimes and misdemeanors handled by police and prosecutor; felonies handled by the procurator and the *juge d' instruction*	Police investigate and give information to local judge or *Shöffen*	Public Safety Office or procurator or local court can initiate investigation, then give case to procurator	Private citizen or investigator can initiate then hand over prosecutable case to *quadi* (judge)	Police transfer cases to prosecutor for investigation; prosecutor can dismiss case before trial
Right to Counsel	Allowed at point where suspect is taken into custody	Legal advice is provided for all held suspects	Defendant required to have counsel at pre-investigation stage; can choose, or appointed if indigent	Allowed during detention or pretrial investigation	Allowed from the day case is transferred to procurator; indigent offenders provided with council (not guaranteed)	Allowed during investigation and trial stages; public defender appointed if needed; right to defend oneself or appoint counsel	Right to counsel; counsel provided to those who cannot afford it at point where suspect is taken into custody
Right to Remain Silent	Accused can remain silent throughout all steps of process	Can refuse to speak, but silence can be held against suspect	Accused can remain silent throughout all steps of process but expected to answer questions during trial	Accused can remain silent throughout all steps of process	Accused can remain silent, but silence is treated as admission of guilt	No right to remain silent; however, accused does not have to tell the truth	Accused can remain silent, but judicial system relies on confession
Right to Trial by Jury	Right to trial by jury in all felony cases	Right to trial by jury in indictable offenses	Right to trial by jury of nine or by judge and two lay assessors	No trial by jury; trial is by panel of judges	No trial by jury; trial is by panel of judges	No trial by jury	Lay assessors with professional judges for important cases
Right to Bail	Bail allowable but can be refused by judge	Bail allowable but can be refused by judge	Bail allowable at any time, but can be refused by examining magistrate	Bail allowable at any time, but can be refused by examining magistrate	Bail, at discretion of police, is allowable but not a right	Bail is granted for less serious crimes	Bail allowed for some offenses, but can be denied by judge at request of procurator
Kind of Procedural System	Adversarial and popular (justice of peace)	Adversarial and popular (magistrates)	Inquisitorial and popular (lay judges in assize courts)	Inquisitorial and popular (*Shöffen*)	Inquisitorial and popular (people's courts)	Inquisitorial	Inquisitorial and popular (new lay jurors as of 2009)

counsel in a criminal case can lead to dire consequences for any defendant coming before a court of law. Queen Mary was charged with treason for allegedly conspiring to assassinate Queen Elizabeth I. Mary asked for the assistance of counsel, stating that "the laws and statutes of England are to me most unknown; I am destitute of counsellors … and no man dareth step forth to be my advocate." Her requests were denied, and Mary was convicted and executed by decapitation.

Events of this kind led to the Right to Counsel Clause, which served as a defense against the English practice of denying the assistance of an attorney in serious criminal cases and requiring defendants to appear before the court and defend themselves in their own words. Although some defendants were allowed counsel if they could afford it, not until the passage of the Prisoners' Counsel Act (1836) did felony defendants have the formal right of being represented by counsel in English courts. It was believed that the presence of defense counsel would only interfere with the arrival at the truth. Ironically, this rationale is closely aligned with the inquisitorial system of justice.

In the United States, the framers of the U.S. Constitution thought it essential that right to counsel be included as a basic right for all citizens in a democracy where the burden is on the prosecution to establish guilt of the defendant. For 150 years the right to counsel was interpreted to mean that a defendant had the *right* to retain a private attorney. That meant that an indigent defendant did not have the right to counsel. This changed in 1930s after the U.S. Supreme Court began to reverse this interpretation in *Powell v. Alabama* (1932), and was later refined more clearly in a flurry of cases in the 1960s, including the cases of *Gideon v. Wainwright* (1963), *Escobedo v. Illinois* (1964), and *Miranda v. Arizona* (1966).

The difference in the right to an attorney during the pretrial process illustrates how English criminal procedure is not as highly developed as American procedure. In England, with the passing of the 1999 Access to Justice Legislation, legal advice and representation are provided for all persons held for questioning (Joyce, 2006). In the United States, the 1966 Miranda ruling of the Supreme Court requires that a person being taken into custody be informed of his or her right to remain silent and to have an attorney.

To obtain some perspective on the access of legal counsel around the world, we provide in Table 6.2 the most recent results from a study conducted by the World Justice Project (WJP). The WJP studied 66 countries on a variety of factors related to how they apply the rule of law. For our purposes we extract one category, Access to Civil Justice, because it includes, among nine other variables, the access to and affordability of legal advice and representation. Our table includes all of the model countries included in the Project and a number of other selected countries. Take time to visit the WJP website to compare other legal issues between countries at http://worldjusticeproject.org/sites/default/files/wjproli2011_0.pdf.

The Right to Remain Silent

The right to remain silent provides the foundation for the adversarial system of criminal process found in Common Law countries. Although its roots go back to the early years of the Common Law, the

TABLE 6.2 Access to Civil Justice Comparison: Selected Countries

Country	Global Ranking
Norway	1/66
Germany	2/66
Japan	7/66
United Kingdom	10/66
France	14/66
Canada	16/66
United States	21/66
South Africa	23/66
China	44/66
Pakistan	66/66

SOURCE: Agrast, M., Botero, J., Ponce, A., (2011) *WJP Rule of Law Index 2011.* Washington, D.C.: The World Justice Project. Our Model countries in Italics.

right to protection against self-incrimination achieved its real definition during the period of religious conflict in the 16th and 17th centuries. At that time, those accused of crimes were required to take an oath to tell the truth without having been informed of the charges against them or of the identity of those who had accused them. Religious dissenters called on to take the oath faced a serious problem. If they acknowledged their religion, they were subject to state sanctions. If they denied their religion, they were going against their conscience and, in their view, risking eternal punishment.

Some dissenters chose to deal with this dilemma by refusing to take the oath and refusing to testify, claiming that the authorities had no right to require individuals to testify against themselves. Unfortunately, many of them suffered severe punishments as a result of their refusal to take the oath. One of the most famous of these dissenters, the Puritan John Lilburne, defied both King Charles I and Oliver Cromwell and became a popular hero although he was tortured and spent a large part of his life in prison or in exile.

Gradually, over many years and through the courage of many brave dissenters who incurred the wrath of the authorities by their intransigence, the custom of refusing to testify at all became common and was finally legitimized by Parliament in the latter 17th century. This hard-won right was especially precious to the American colonists, since so many of them were the progeny of religious dissenters, such as Quakers and Puritans, who had made a new home in the American wilderness (Levy, 1969).

Since passage of the Criminal Justice and Public Order Act in 1994, the status of the right to silence in England has been altered. Previously, the accused could not be required to incriminate him- or herself, and silence could not be taken to imply guilt. With the passage of the act, however, it is now possible to infer guilt from silence, so there is pressure on the accused to waive the right to silence when being questioned by police (Philips, Cox, and Pease, 1999; Delmas-Marty and Spencer, 2002, p. 25). To view the complete list of 2012 criminal procedure laws in England and Wales, see the website http://www.justice.gov.uk/courts/procedure-rules/criminal.

The right to remain silent remains at the heart of Common Law criminal procedure. The Fifth Amendment to the U.S. Constitution puts it this way: "No person … shall be compelled in any criminal case to be a witness against himself." Thus, the state must prove its case without the help of the accused if the accused chooses not to give that help. At its most basic level, the right to remain silent is designed to protect individuals against forced confessions obtained through torture, threats, or other undue pressures. It also means, however, that the accused can remain silent throughout the pretrial or trial phase of his or her criminal proceedings. In other words, the state must prove that an individual is guilty without the help of that individual.

The Right to Trial by Jury

Although the right to remain silent is the most basic element of the adversarial system, trial by jury is the most venerable of the Common Law procedures and is sometimes seen as the major English contribution to systems of justice worldwide. The origins of this right to be judged by a jury of one's peers (*judicium parium*) goes back at least to the concessions made by King John I to his nobles in the Magna Carta of 1215.

Trial by jury today is used less than previously in Common Law systems. On an aggregate basis, it is estimated that over 90 percent of criminal cases are settled through plea bargains in the United States, even though all felony cases are allowed to be tried by a jury. In England, 58 percent of defendants in Crown court cases plead guilty and 88 percent of those in magistrates' courts accept such a plea (Terrill, 2009). People accused of indictable offenses in England have the right to trial by jury in Crown courts, while summary offenses are heard in magistrates' courts without a jury. In reality, trial by jury remains only a small part of the English criminal justice system (Delmas-Marty and Spencer, 2002, p. 171).

In Common Law jurisprudence, a prosecutor has the obligation not to accept a guilty plea if there is no evidence to support it. However, once a guilty plea is accepted and made before a judge, no further trial is held. Most cases in other Common Law countries are also settled through guilty pleas, despite the claims of legal system personnel that no plea bargaining exists.

The Right to Bail

The right to bail is an interesting aspect of Common Law procedure. When the English Parliament in 1689 called upon the Dutch prince and princess, William and Mary of Orange, to assume the throne of England, it made the offer contingent upon their acceptance of a bill of rights that included, among others, the idea that "excessive bail ought not to be required, nor excessive fines imposed, nor cruel and unusual punishments inflicted" (Laing et al., 1950, p. 14). These words, which were echoed a hundred years later in the Eighth Amendment to the U.S. Constitution, exemplify the importance of bail to the concept of fair criminal procedure in Common Law history.

As stated in the Bail Act of 1974, bail in England is allowed for anyone who is not a fugitive from the law, who is accused of a crime that would not require imprisonment, and whose prior record or history of absconding are not an issue. In 1994, under the Criminal Justice and Public Order Act, the police were empowered to set bail and provide conditions of bail prior to the first appearance of the accused in court. Similarly, judges in the United States will deny bail if the suspect is a flight risk, has a prior record, or has committed a serious current offense.The possibility that bail could be discriminatory toward the poor has been cited as a potentially serious problem for Common Law systems. In Civil Law systems, the criteria for arrest are more stringent than in Common Law systems, but arrestees may be released "when the risk of release is worth taking … ; when the risk cannot be taken, release will not be ordered" (Mueller and LePoole-Griffiths, 1969, p. 24). In all systems, there is concern about the number of individuals who are detained "on remand" pending a trial. As we shall see, however, this is a greater problem in Civil Law systems because of the long periods of pretrial investigation.

CIVIL LAW CRIMINAL PROCEDURE

Civil Law is the most common of all the legal traditions, but there are numerous variations of criminal procedure practiced within that tradition throughout the world. Here, we will use France as our model nation because French criminal procedure presents us with a characteristic Civil Law process.

Criminal law procedure in France, much like that in England, has been under close scrutiny in recent years and has undergone some partial changes. Interestingly, some of the changes have been repealed either prior to coming into force or immediately thereafter because they were thought to excessively increase the rights of criminal defendants and also to contribute to the increase in crime in France (Elliott, 2001; Delmas-Marty and Spencer, 2002, p. 220).For more about the rights of defendants in criminal proceedings in France see the following (in English) web page https://e-justice.europa.eu/content_rights_of_defendants_in_criminal_proceedings_-169-en.do.

The Investigation

As mentioned in Chapter 4, the French divide criminal offenses into three categories: (1) crimes (felonies), (2) delits (serious misdemeanors), and (3) contraventions (minor crimes). This division is important to remember because the category of the offense affects the kind of investigation and the level of involvement by police and the courts. Minor crimes and misdemeanors are handled by police investigators and prosecuting attorneys. Felonies, however, are handled through the extensive process of pretrial investigation (called instruction) that characterizes Civil Law systems. In this section, we trace the process for the more serious felony category.

After a crime has been committed and a preliminary investigation has been undertaken, a suspect can be brought in for questioning called the **garde à vue**. This process was modified in 2011 after the Constitutional Council in France ruled it partially unconstitutional. The current process now states that any person can be held "who is suspected of having committed or attempted to commit a crime or offence punishable by imprisonment for one or more plausible reasons." Offenses punishable only by fines will no longer justify *garde à vue*, and only under special circumstances can a suspect be detained longer than 24 hours (International Law Office, 2011). After the *garde à vue*, the suspect must be released unless the judicial police officer (a member of the criminal investigation branch of the French police) believes there is enough evidence against him or her.

Once it is determined that the evidence is sufficient, the suspect is arrested and formally charged for the offense and then is bound over to judicial authorities. At this stage, the judicial police, the procurator, and the *juge d'instruction* proceed with the investigation. The **juge d'instruction** is the examining magistrate who is responsible for a complete and impartial investigation of the facts.

The pretrial investigation in France involves the calling of witnesses on both sides, extensive gathering of facts and testimony, and careful questioning of the accused prior to a final decision to bring the case to trial. Judicial philosophy in France demands that the accused be part of this process from the outset. In other words, suspects are not investigated by a prosecutor and then faced with charges to which they have not had an opportunity to reply in depth, as in the adversarial system.

In France, as in many Civil Law systems, this pretrial investigation is conducted *in camera* (in secret) by the *juge d'instruction*, with the help of police investigators and the procurator. The reason for secrecy in these proceedings is to protect the accused from adverse publicity prior to the determination that the government has a strong case for prosecution.

In some ways, the investigation is analogous to grand jury hearings in the United States, which are conducted in secret and in which evidence is weighed to decide whether the accused should be indicted. Grand jury hearings are usually short, however, dominated by the prosecutor, and designed to make sure that the prosecution will not be frivolous or willful. Thus, they are really quite different from the careful and lengthy pretrial investigation that occurs in France. After the investigation, the *juge d'instruction* forwards his or her findings to the Indicting Chamber of the Court of Appeals and then, if warranted, to the **courts of assize**, which are the courts of original jurisdiction in criminal matters.

It is in the courts of assize where the dossier becomes important. The **dossier** is actually a complete record of the pretrial proceedings, and it informs the judges, the defense attorney, and others about the testimony of key witnesses and the evidence to be presented. The judge who reads the dossier ahead of time knows fairly well what is going to happen during the trial. The accused, who has participated at each stage of the development of the dossier, also knows what is likely to happen at trial.

The purpose of the inquisitorial proceedings is to protect the accused against unwarranted accusations and trials. However, the potential for abuse in lengthy, secret pretrial proceedings is obvious. In effect, the accused may spend long periods of time in detention, often without possibility of bail, while these proceedings are going on. The power of individual magistrates to work in secret and to keep people incarcerated for long periods of time has come under increasing fire in France. In 2000 the French added a new "liberty and detention" (*juge des libertés et de la detention*) judge to help determine whether a suspect should be released prior to trail. A major change in the role of the *juge d'instruction* was proposed in 2009 by then French President Sarkozy when he suggested that the role of the judge be turned over to the procurator (Terrill, 2009). This caused much consternation in France, and the matter is still not decided. It is now necessary in serious cases for the examining magistrate to present the charges to a Chamber of Instruction, which is now a permanent feature of the Courts of Appeal. Each of these reforms was designed to create greater oversight of magistrates' work and greater shared responsibility for arrest decisions.

The role of the investigation judge in France is not common among other Civil Law countries, especially in continental Europe. In fact the French have received much criticism from the European community about the length of pretrial investigations and the possible abuse of the office of the *juge d'instruction*.

The Right to Bail

The accused or the defense counsel can apply for bail at any time during the case, and the examining magistrate decides whether bail will be granted. The magistrate can order the suspect to pay a cash security. This serves two purposes: (1) to ensure that the suspect will appear in court and (2) to pay fines or damages if he or she is found guilty. The problem with bail in France is that it is so infrequently granted that most suspects spend a considerable amount of time in pretrial detention.

The Right to Counsel

Since 1897, French law has required that an attorney (advocat) represent the accused during the process of detention or pretrial investigation, with a modification in 1994 that now restricts access to an attorney if suspects are involved in terrorist activity. If the suspect cannot afford one, then one is appointed. The *juge d'instruction* may not ask questions of the accused unless this attorney is present, and the accused may not refuse assistance of counsel. Prior to June 2011, the suspect was allowed to see a lawyer for 30 minutes from the start of the detention, but under recent amendments to the law that have come into force, the lawyer may be present during the entire *garde à vue*, including during interrogation of the suspect. The right to counsel is even more stringent in Germany. As of January 2010, any suspect who is in pretrial custody must be provided with counsel. For a 2011 detailed list of German criminal procedure laws (in English) see the web page http://www.gesetze-im-internet.de/englisch_stpo/index.html.

The mandatory representation by an attorney in Civil Law countries is actually contrary to the spirit of pretrial investigations in the inquisitorial process. Originally, the preliminary investigation was to be an informal process that would prevent the need for further system intervention. It could be argued that mandatory counsel has only served to lengthen and add unnecessary formality to the process, especially in France. This contrary situation is another example, however, of how Common Law and Civil Law criminal procedure have merged and are in reality often more similar than different.

The Right to Remain Silent

In addition to requiring the presence of an attorney, French law requires that the accused be informed of his or her right to remain silent during the pretrial proceedings. Since reforms made in 2000, the police must also inform suspects that they are free either to talk or to remain silent. Defendants also have the right to withdraw any pretrial confession. This right, so integral to the adversarial system, represents another modification of the inquisitorial procedure. However, it does not have the stature that the similar right has in Common Law countries, and the presumption on the part of all parties is that the accused will cooperate in the investigation by answering questions and raising points that might help in the defense. If the accused chooses to make a statement later at the trial, he or she is not under oath, as in Common Law procedure, and is not subject to cross-examination.

Any confession in the pretrial or trial process is treated as part of the evidence included in the dossier. This is a major difference from many Common Law countries, especially in the United States, where plea bargaining is the norm. In fact, in most of Europe even if the defendant admits guilt the court is expected to examine the evidence against him. Although this would appear to create a backlog of uncontested cases, different mechanisms have been developed in Civil Law countries to ensure the swift processing of cases. For example, since 2004 in France there has been a procedure of plea bargaining (called the *ordonnance penale)* whereby the defendant will appear in court following a prior admission of guilt that may only be made with the assistance of a lawyer. The presiding judge reviews the genuineness of the facts and their legal classification before registering the declaration of guilt made by the defendant and the penalty suggested by the prosecutor (*procureur*). The judge cannot alter the suggested sentence but must accept or reject it. The procedure is only available in respect of cases with a maximum sentence of five years imprisonment. The French equivalent of plea bargaining.

The Germans have created a process called *Strafbefehlsverfahren* in which the prosecutor gives to the suspect a proposed penalty—a kind of negotiated settlement—which is imposed unless the defendant objects. Plea bargaining in this form is common practice in 20 to 30 percent of German criminal cases and in 2011 was incorporated into the German Code of Criminal Procedure. (Dubber, 1997, p. 550; Turner, 2011).

Right to Trial by Jury

Unlike most other Civil Law countries, including Germany, France has not abandoned trial by jury. The French jury concept was borrowed from Common Law systems and has been used in felony trials in the Courts of Assize since the 19th century. However, the jury trial is modified to allow for greater interchange between the judge and the nine jury members. In this way it is like most Civil Law systems because it allows for considerable engagement by lay assessors.

The trial judge in France (called the *president*) is less of a referee than in adversary systems and more of a participant with a responsibility to discover the truth. At the court of assize level, in addition to the president judge, there are two **assessors**, professional judges selected from other courts to sit in on the trial. Judges question witnesses and defendants, call for further investigation if necessary, and ask to see additional witnesses. Jurors can also question witnesses and the accused if they ask permission from the president. While judges have many of these powers in Common Law systems, the tradition in these systems is for the judge to be disengaged and impartial, rather than proactive and involved as in Civil Law systems. One should remember that use of jury trials is unusual in Civil Law countries. What is more likely is the model used in Germany, in which all adjudication is handled by a judge or a panel of judges, consisting of professional judges or a combination of professional and lay judges.

The major variation on the French procedure that is not found in other Civil Law countries is the extensive use of an examining magistrate, or *juge d'instruction*. A second difference between French criminal procedure and other Civil Law countries is the use of jury trials. As mentioned earlier, the French use jury trials in the courts of assize. By contrast, Germany has no jury trials.

SOCIALIST CRIMINAL PROCEDURE

Criminal procedure in most Socialist Law countries is similar to, and derived from, criminal procedures in Civil Law systems. Thus, criminal procedures in these countries have generally reflected the Civil Law and inquisitorial systems in that state procurators investigate crimes, thorough pretrial inquiries are the norm, and judges take an active role in the trial process. However, there are many differences in the way criminal procedure is practiced in Civil Law and Socialist Law systems. To understand these differences in context, we turn to our model country of the People's Republic of China.

Chinese legal culture, like that of Japan, traditionally has been heavily influenced by Confucian philosophy, stressing informal means of settling disputes and valuing social harmony above individual justice. For years, therefore, China had little or no concern for individual rights, which would have limited the rights of the group or the power of the state (Baker, 1982). Given this philosophy, China operated without a code of criminal procedure for the first 30 years following the Communist takeover. However, the political upheaval of the Cultural Revolution forced the Chinese government to implement changes.

During the Cultural Revolution, the legal system was in shambles and the Ministry of Justice was abolished. Many people, including Communist Party officials, were arbitrarily harassed, punished, and even executed. To control the excesses—and also make the legal adjustments necessary to accommodate a new economic vision—the National People's Congress (NPC) adopted its first Criminal Procedure Law (CPL) in 1979. The CPL, developed over two decades, contained 164 articles covering all stages of the criminal process, from initial detention through investigation, prosecution, trial, appeal, and execution of sentence.

During the 1980s and early 1990s, it became increasingly clear to the Chinese that the 1979 CPL was an ineffective law. Despite three *yanda* campaigns and compromises in the 1979 CPL that lead to reductions in procedural rights, crime continued to increase. The economic reforms and opening to the outside world created new kinds of crimes and complex legal needs that were not addressed in the current criminal laws and criminal procedures. At the same time, international criticism of the Chinese relative to their human rights policies began to mount, especially after the events at Tiananmen Square in 1989. In 1996, the NPC addressed the issue by developing a new Criminal Procedure Law of the People's Republic of China (revised CPL). The law became effective in 1997. The 225 articles in the document contain amendments and additions to the 1979 CPL (Trevaskes, 2007).

In March 2012 the Chinese revised their Procedural Law to reflect what we described earlier as the "human rights revolution." More specifically, the legislature revised the CPL to include the phrase "respecting and protecting human rights" in its first chapter on basic principles as well as other modifications to follow in areas related to the right to remain silent and to legal aid (Judicial News, 2012a, 2012b). These changes do reflect a new move for the Chinese toward the acceptance of international treaties and the "human rights revolution" that we described earlier. In this section, we will examine some of the major elements of the criminal procedure laws in China as they relate to the major procedural elements in the Common and Civil Law traditions. But one should keep in mind three things. First, it is debatable whether the rules listed in the CPL have in fact been implemented throughout the criminal justice system and are available for all Chinese citizens. Second, keep in mind that the criminal procedures in countries that employ the Socialist Law tradition, such as China, North Korea, and Cuba, may vary considerably due to changing economic and political realities. And finally, we do not yet know how the 2012 changes in the CPL will impact the Chinese citizenry and their government's approach to the rule of law.

Pretrial Investigation

Once a crime is committed or alleged, it is reported to the public service agency (police), the procurator, or the court. After a brief preliminary investigation, if it is determined that the matter warrants further state involvement, the case is filed and an investigation conducted by the police or the procurator. If the police investigate, they submit an opinion as to whether to prosecute or to exempt from prosecution.

They then transfer the case to the procurator, who reviews it and decides whether to prosecute. In the revised CPL, victims can ask the procurator to file the case if the police neglect to do so, or they can choose to privately prosecute if the procurator refuses to accept the case (Articles 83 and 88). In the latter situation, the victims, legal representatives, or close relatives have the right to prosecute directly in the people's courts.

The Right to Bail

Bail is more restricted in China than in most other countries. The revised 1996 CPL provides that a detained suspect can apply for and receive bail, but he or she is not entitled to this right. The police maintain complete discretion over whether to approve the application for counsel, and compulsory measures can be placed on defendants who await trial out of custody. The CPL does state that indigent suspects in criminal cases are to be provided with legal aid (Lawyers Committee, 1996, p. 33; Terrill, 2009).

The issue of bail is a very important one to explore in China because it is related to pretrial detention—an area in which China has gained a considerable amount of unwanted attention in the international community. The 1979 CPL authorized five forms of pretrial detention, each of which has come under fire as illegal or improperly implemented. However, the main problem over the years has not been with those five, but with a form of detention unauthorized and unstated in the CPL called "taking in for shelter and investigation." Shelter and investigation was originally developed in the 1960s as a policy to round up migrants and return them to rural areas. However, over the years, the police have greatly expanded its use to detain other kinds of criminals and those suspected of political subversion. Reportedly, persons have been detained under this policy without formal arrest or procurator approval for months and even years. The most infamous example of people detained under this policy was the arrest and detainment of over 2,000 citizens for their involvement in the 1989 Tiananmen Square demonstration. More recently, the April 22, 2012, escape of blind legal rights defender Chen Guangcheng from 19 months of unlawful detention in Shandong province, and his subsequent temporary relocation to the United States, highlighted the alleged abuse of the legal system to persecute those seeking redress for human rights abuses. During his detention, Chen and his family—including his wife, Yuan Weijing, and his elderly mother—were targeted with physical violence by local government officials and security forces and denied their constitutionally guaranteed rights of freedom of movement, expression, and association (Human Rights Watch, 2012).

The 1996 CPL addressed all five forms of pretrial detention and also led indirectly to changes in the use of shelter and investigation. In short, there have been some positive advances in curtailing abuse in the area of pretrial detention in China. However, the changes in the revised CPL leave some gaping holes, and in practice they apparently fail to meet various international standards (Lawyers Committee, 1996).

The Right to Counsel

The modified 1996 CPL stated that all defendants have the right to defend themselves or to appoint someone to defend them, and that for indigent criminal offenders, "economic difficulties" are grounds for the "optional appointment of a defender" (Article 34). Another important modification is the time at which counsel is allowed to enter the case. The current law states that the defendant is allowed counsel from the day when the case is transferred to the procurator for a decision to prosecute (Article 22).

Although these changes seem significant, they have some serious limitations. One problem is that the terms "economic difficulties" and "optional appointment of counsel" lack clarity, and implementation can be left to the discretion of those with the power to permit and provide free counsel. Further, counsel at the investigation stage is limited and can be blocked if it is determined that the case may involve "state secrets." As a result, many Chinese may be unable to exercise this important right.

Unfortunately, the limitations stated within Article 34 that pertain to the right to counsel cause it to fall short of the UN Basic Principles on the Role of Lawyers, adopted in 1990 (Lawyers Committee, 1996, pp. 41–43). The UN document clearly states that all persons are entitled to a lawyer of their choice to protect them at all stages of criminal proceedings.

The Right to Remain Silent

Article 35 in the Chinese CPL reads that the defender shall present, according to the facts and law, materials and opinions proving the innocence of the criminal suspect or defendant, as well as any need for a mitigated punishment or exemption from criminal responsibility. Article 93 states that when interrogating a criminal suspect, the investigators shall first ask the criminal suspect whether or not he has committed any criminal act, and let him state the circumstances of his guilt or explain his innocence; then they may ask him questions. The criminal suspect *shall* answer the investigators' questions truthfully, but he shall have the right to refuse to answer any questions that are irrelevant to the case [emphasis added]. These two articles make it clear that in China it is extremely important that criminal defendants provide and protect their own rights and interests. Further, it would appear that to remain silent during criminal proceedings in China would not be the best way to secure freedom and in fact could lead to a longer period of incarceration or in some cases the penalty of death. At the same time, the CPL also states that it is a prosecutable offense not to give evidence where one has knowledge about the circumstances of the case (Article 38). So then there is some responsibility on the part of the defense lawyer and even the prosecutor to assist in the verification of evidence.

We should keep in mind, however, that the May 2012 changes in the CPL do include amendments relative to the right to remain silent and right to legal counsel. Time will tell us more about when and how these changes will be implemented.

The Chinese Trial and Judicial Fairness

At the standard Chinese trial, the procurator represents the interests of the state and the defendant or legal counsel represents the interests of the defendant. Most cases of first instance are heard in public unless the case involves state secrets or private disputes. Because jury trial does not exist, a panel of judges, whose number is determined by the court level, comes to a verdict. Judicial decisions are determined by majority rule. There is no separate sentencing phase to a proceeding; sentences are handed down immediately after the verdict. The judge or judges have access to material about the defendant's previous criminal history and his or her life situation.

In the trial, more emphasis is placed on the confession of the defendant than on the testimony of witnesses. Witnesses usually do not even have to appear before the court and thus are unavailable for challenge from the defense. Instead, witnesses can submit written testimony prior to the trial. This issue has been addressed but not changed in the revised CPL (Articles 42–47). The judge can take an active role in questioning and guiding the trial, the prosecutor and the defendants or their legal representative can present material and debate on their own behalf, and the decision is made by a panel of judges. In a review of the steps of the typical Chinese trial, we can see a number of similarities to other Civil Law countries. A full list of the trial steps in the typical Chinese trial is given in Table 6.3. Take some time to peruse these steps and compare them with what you know about trials in the United States.

According to the revised law (Article 150) and subsequent interpretations by the Supreme People's Court, the trial judge(s) can only conduct a procedural review prior to the trial. As a result, the investigative duties of the judge now apply during rather than before the trial. The goal here is to eliminate a major problem with Chinese criminal procedure prior to 1997—the determination of guilt before the trial even begins. A common phrase used to explain this process was "decision first, trial later."

According to the revised CPL (Articles 149 and 162), trial judges and the collegial panel now have the authority to determine the verdict and sentence based on majority rule except in difficult or important cases, which are decided by the Judicial Committee. This amendment was created to promote an essential system of checks and balances. However, we must remember that the members of the Judicial Committee are appointed by the NPC and nominated by the president of the court, who is usually a member of the Communist Party. As a result, the independence of the court system is in question because ultimately any sensitive political decision will be controlled by the party (Liu and Situ, 1999).

The criminal procedure elements discussed here are just a few of the key issues and changes that have been promulgated by the revised CPL of 1997. Even with the improvements in the CPL, critics argue that the Chinese are far from meeting international standards when it comes to

TABLE 6.3 Steps in a Typical Chinese Trial

1. The procurator reads the bill of prosecution in court.
2. The defendant replies to bill of prosecution.
3. The victim can make a statement about the charges in the bill of prosecution.
4. The procurator can question the defendant.
5. With the permission of the presiding judge, the victim, as well as the plaintiff and defender in an incidental civil action, can question the defendant.
6. Judges can question the defendant.
7. With the permission of the presiding judge, witnesses and then expert witnesses are questioned by the procurator, parties, defendants, or defense counsel. The presiding judge may halt the line of questioning if he or she deems it irrelevant to the case. The parties and defendant have the right to request that new witnesses be summoned to the session, that new material evidence be collected, that a new expert evaluation be conducted, or that another inquest be held. The collegial panel rules on the merits of each request. If the request is granted and the hearing postponed, the procurator is granted one month to complete the supplementary investigation.
8. Judges can question witnesses and expert witnesses.
9. Procurators and defendants present material evidence in the court.
10. The statements of witnesses who are not present in court are read. If the court has any questions about the evidence presented, it can adjourn in order to verify the evidence.
11. The procurator, victims, defendant, or defense counsel present their opinions, which are heard by the judges. They all can debate the quality of the evidence and facts in the case.
12. After the presiding judge has declared the debate concluded, the defendant has a right to present a final statement.
13. The presiding judge announces an adjournment, and the collegial panel begins its deliberations. Potential decisions include these:
    a. If the facts are clear, the evidence adequate, and the defendant guilty by law, the court should pronounce a verdict of guilty.
    b. If the defendant is found not guilty by law, the court should pronounce a verdict of not guilty.
    c. If the evidence is insufficient, the defendant cannot be found guilty. The court would pronounce a verdict of not guilty on the grounds that there was a lack of evidence or that the charges were not substantiated.
14. Judgments are pronounced publicly in court. The judgment indicates the time limit for appealing the decision and the appellate court to which the appeal should be directed.

SOURCE: Adapted from Terrill, 2009.

the actual implementation of procedural law (Lu and Miethe, 2002). For a full English version of the criminal procedure laws in China, see the web link http://en.chinacourt.org/public/detail.php?id=2693.

Distinctive Aspects of Socialist Law Procedure

What is it that distinguishes Socialist Law criminal procedure from Common and Civil Law procedure? In Common Law and most Civil Law systems, the tendency is to be protective of individual rights. In Socialist Law systems, by contrast, the major emphasis is on the public's interest. This is clearly reflected in Article 1 of the 1996 Chinese CPL, which states:

> *The Criminal Procedure Law of the People's Republic of China is formulated in accordance with the constitution of the People's Republic of China in order to correctly carry out the criminal law to punish crimes, protect the people,*

> *safeguard the state security, ensure the public safety, and maintain the social order of socialism.*

In other words, the collective is more important than any one individual, and individual rights are tempered by the need to further the cause of communism. As a result of this philosophy, the concept of separation of powers, with an independent judiciary, is subordinate to the ideal of the sovereignty of the state. Guarantees regarding rights of the accused are always subject to the needs of the state. Further, as we discussed earlier, in socialist China there are much broader pretrial detention possibilities, defendants have limited rights to counsel, and procurators enjoy extensive discretion. Even so, with the 2012 revisions to the CPL there will soon be, at least in theory, some significant changes in how defendants are treated in China.

Finally, another major difference is that in Common Law and traditional Civil Law systems all kinds of crimes are dealt with in the same procedural fashion. By contrast, in China, cases seem to be handled differently depending on whether they are political or criminal cases. Political cases, which are often the only ones publicized in the West, appear to lack many procedural standards, giving the impression that the accused have few rights and that the criminal justice system in China is highly political. Even though this may be true, conventional criminals, those who commit violent and property crimes, typically are processed according to rules that are largely similar to those used in Western Civil Law–type systems.

SACRED (ISLAMIC) CRIMINAL PROCEDURE

As we discussed earlier in this book, there are some countries that base their legal tradition on some form of sacred text or principles and are referred to as Sacred Law countries. Most of these Sacred Law legal traditions are located in the Middle East, where some deference is made to Islamic law. We choose to focus here on the Islamic legal tradition, more specifically that of Saudi Arabia, because that tradition and that country provide us with the best method of understanding criminal procedure within the Sacred Law legal tradition.

Islamic law is most visible in Iran, Saudi Arabia, Sudan, Pakistan, and Afghanistan. Of those countries, only two (Saudi Arabia and Sudan) can actually say that their criminal justice systems are built on Islamic law, while a few others (Iran, Pakistan, and Afghanistan) try to retain vestiges of Islamic law despite the social and political forces that are forcing the convergence with other forms of law.

The question of rights of the accused in Islamic law has been debated by both Islamic and non-Islamic scholars. Saudi Arabia's reaction to international criticism and to documents such as the UN Universal Declaration of Human Rights is to argue that the universal principles of the Qur'an protect humans better than international treaties and conventions. The prevalent opinion amongst contemporary Muslim lawyers is that "traditional Islamic law affords human rights protections to criminally accused comparable to those recognized in modern international law" (Amin, 1985a, p. 35).

Organizations such as Humans Rights Watch would disagree. They have regularly provided yearly reports stating that Saudi Arabia has violated a number of international standards relative to criminal procedure, including the use of arbitrary arrest, the use of detention without trial, a secretive criminal justice system, and a number of violations relative to cruel punishment. Abuses have been exacerbated by the Saudi antiterrorism policies and some blamed on al-Qaida sympathizers. Women also continue to face severe discrimination, although there is some evidence that women are gaining some political rights in Saudi Arabia. More specifically, women will be able to vote in municipal elections in 2015 (Anderson and Togelius, 2011; Human Rights Watch, 2012b).

There are really three sources of procedural laws in Saudi Arabia: those implied in the Islamic (Shari'a) law, those implied in the 1993 Basic Law, and those more clearly stated in the 2001 enacted Law of Criminal Procedure.

The Islamic or Shari'a law is, in theory, used as a form of criminal procedure before the Shari'a courts. Technically, the Shari'a does not provide a detailed list of procedures for the courts to follow but instead offers general principles as stated in the Qur'an. Such phrases as "God commands … if you judge between people, to do so with justice" (4:58) and "in your devotion to God … bear witness impartially; do not let hatred of others lead you away from justice" (5:8) are examples of how procedure is in theory applied from the Qur'an. The Islamic (Shari'a) law also sets penalties and provides guidance for developing proof of the commission of crimes (Belal, 1993; Crystal, 2001). How the details of criminal procedure are actually implemented in practice is left to the particular jurisdictions and their court systems. As long as the decisions by criminal justice officials are informed by Qur'anic principles and the Islamic (Shari'a) law, it is felt by many traditionalists that there is no need to have a detailed list of procedures to protect criminal suspects.

The second source of procedural protections for suspects is the 1993 Basic Law. As we discussed in Chapter 4, this law with its 53 articles serves as an informal constitution and spells out the government's rights and responsibilities. It is grounded in the idea that the government of Saudi Arabia is "based on the premise of justice, consultation, and equality in accordance with the Islamic Shari'a" (Article 8). The Basic Law provides some broad parameters for criminal procedure, such as Article 26, which declares that the government should "protect human rights in accordance with the Shari'a," and Article 36, which states that "no one shall be arrested, imprisoned, or have their actions restricted except in cases specified by statutes."

To fill the holes in the Shari'a and the Basic Law, in 2001 the Saudi government enacted the first formal Law of Criminal Procedure (LCP). This law, originally described in a document called the Protection of Human Rights in Criminal Procedure and in the Organization of the Judicial System, contains 225 articles, laying out the process for the initiation of criminal action; rules of collecting and preserving evidence; conditions of arrest and pretrial detention, including bail; and the jurisdiction of courts and their proceedings (Ansary, 2008; Royal Embassy of Saudi Arabia, 2012). It also includes a judicial code of law that regulates procedures for the licensing and appointment of lawyers, and their rights and duties. These laws gave Saudi citizens and residents a clearer definition of their rights in detention and at trial and laid out the procedures the investigators and courts must follow. For a detailed view of criminal procedure law in Saudi Arabia, see the web page http://www.wipo.int/wipolex/en/text.jsp?file_id=214810.

We will now describe how Sacred (Islamic) criminal procedure addresses some of the same key procedural issues as our Common, Civil, and Socialist Law countries.

Investigation

Similar to the processes in many Common Law and Civil Law countries, there are two common ways to initiate a criminal investigation in Saudi Arabia. As stated in Chapter 1, in the Law of Criminal Procedure a victim or his heirs may initiate criminal action to a competent court. The *quadi* (judge) will then use his judgment whether to formally prosecute the matter. The second is for any one of a range of government agencies to conduct a criminal investigation with the assistance of the investigator. If the investigator deems the evidence against the accused to be sufficient, he will refer the matter to the respective court and *quadi*, who issues a summons for arrest if the suspect is not already detained.

The Right to Bail

Islamic jurists have argued at length about the kinds of guarantees that should be allowed for persons accused and then detained for crimes. Although preventive detention is recognized by Islamic jurists as legitimate if circumstances call for it, at the same time judges generally respect the right of an individual to be free (Awad, 1982, pp. 102–103). This is essentially the same standard that is applied in Civil Law nations. In short, there is a bail system in Saudi Arabia, but it is generally only applied for those accused of less serious crimes. A number of articles in the Law of Criminal Procedure, especially in Chapters 8 and 9, deal with length of detention prior to formal accusation or trial. For example, if a suspect is detained, notification of the reasons for detention should be prompt: "Whoever is arrested or detained shall be promptly notified of the reasons for his arrest or detention, and shall be entitled to communicate with any persons of his choice to inform him (of his arrest or detention), provided that such communication is under the supervision of the criminal investigation officer" (Article 116). In practice however, and as documented in many instances by international organizations, procedural laws related to bail and pretrial detention are often violated in Saudi Arabia (Human Rights Watch, 2012b; 2008).

The Right to Counsel

The right to counsel may be the best example of the difference between what is theoretically possible and what really occurs in the Saudi criminal justice system. Historically, the accused was expected to take charge of his own legal defense. But with the passing of the new Criminal Procedure Law, this was supposedly modified. According to Chapter 1, Article 4, "Any accused person shall have the right to seek the assistance of a lawyer or a representative to defend him during the investigation and trial stages." However, it appears that not everyone involved in the Saudi system enjoys the benefit of right to counsel. Two stories anecdotally support this position:

> On January 9th, 2009, Saudi Arabia's Supreme Court ordered a retrial of Mohammed Kohail, a Canadian who had been sentenced to death over the accidental death of a Syrian man in a schoolyard brawl. The judge of the Jeddah court that condemned Kohail to death had prevented his lawyer from appearing to defend his client during proceedings and had not allowed the defense to present evidence at trial.
>
> On November 9th, 2009, a courtin Medina sentenced Ali Sibat, a Lebanese Shi'a, to death for sorcery, based on Sibat's prior work in Lebanon as a fortuneteller on a satellite TV station. Sibat had no lawyer. (Human Rights Watch, 2010)

In these two cases, it appears to international observers that foreigners are at a particular disadvantage in Saudi courts. They often have no means to secure legal counsel and are themselves often ignorant of the substance of charges against them and lack knowledge about the arguments and procedures taking place inside the courtroom.

However, despite the many negative stories about the fate of suspects who unsuccessfully seek counsel in Saudi Arabia, there is some good news to speak of. In early 2010 the legislative *Shura* council in Saudi Arabia approved the establishment of a public defender program. The program calls for court-appointed lawyers at the state's expense to be made available to any criminal defendant who cannot afford one (Human Rights Watch, 2010).

The Right to Remain Silent

The Saudi Law of Criminal Procedure does not provide a person with the right to be silent, and it has been documented that suspects who do not participate actively in their investigation and trial may be subject to poor treatment and torture (Human Rights Watch, 2008).

Interestingly, when testifying, the accused does not have to tell the truth. Further, if an accused has confessed, he or she may retract the confession at any time, and it cannot then be used as evidence in a court. These procedures approximate those used in Civil Law nations. Here again, however, the true situation is not always clear, since confessions obtained by force or by deceit may be used (Awad, 1982, pp. 106–107).

The Right to Trial by Jury

No lay assessors are used in trial proceedings in Saudi Arabia. The Law of Criminal Procedure in Saudi Arabia does call for trials to be open to the public. However, this is often the exception rather than the rule in Saudi justice. The *quadi* has no need to justify exclusion of outsiders—they may be excluded if it is deemed necessary to determine the truth, to protect the privacy of the parties, or for the sake of morals (Moore, 1987; Terrill, 2009). This is in obvious contrast to Common Law and Civil Law systems, in which it is common for the trials to be public.

In summary, while the Saudi system does include many protections for those accused of crime in a variety of legal documents, it does not emphasize this aspect of the justice process to the extent found in most Common Law or Civil Law legal systems. In light of the constant criticism from the international community about abuses within the criminal justice system, Saudi Arabia is apparently making some efforts to improve, at least on the surface, its treatment of alleged criminal offenders.

JAPAN: THE HYBRID SITUATION

As we explained in Chapters 3 and 4, the Japanese system of criminal justice is distinct in that it has been so largely influenced by the Civil Law, Common Law, and Chinese Confucian traditions but at the same time has retained a distinctly Japanese flavor. This flavor reflects a Japanese society that is characterized by strong adherence to patterns of deference, group norms, and group loyalties, as opposed to individualism and legalism. These norms are reinforced in the justice process through extensive use of discretion that diverts cases from the process, development of informal methods of settling disputes, and pressure on individuals to avoid the formal justice system in dealing with their problems. Therefore, describing the formal rights of the accused in Japan does not convey the total picture regarding these rights. For example, even though the right to remain silent is present in Japan, confessions are essential to system functioning and correctional rehabilitation. As a result, there is a wide range of tools for obtaining confessions in Japan for both police and prosecutors (Foote, 2002). Bail can be requested by the accused, by his or her counsel, or by the relatives of the accused. But the judge may seek the opinion of the procurator before approving bail. Also, a variety of categories of suspects are excluded from bail (Terrill, 2009, p. 354). These examples of the difference between theory and practice do not negate the fact that the formal law as stated in the Code of Criminal Procedure still guides most of the Japanese criminal process.

> The Japanese Constitution of 1946 contains important provisions regarding criminal procedure. Articles 31 through 40 give the impression that Japanese citizens have all the constitutional rights of the accused that exist in the United States. Indeed, the language of several of these articles is very similar to that found in the U.S. Constitution. The differences indicate in some cases the different procedural practices that existed in Japan prior to the war and in other cases the progression of thought that has occurred in the more than two centuries since the U.S. Constitution was written.

Article 37 of the Japanese Constitution covers much of the same ground as the Sixth Amendment to the U.S. Constitution but includes the proviso that counsel will be provided for those who cannot provide it for themselves. In the United States, this right to counsel for the indigent exists only through interpretation. It was not incorporated into the meaning of the Sixth Amendment until 1963, in the case of *Gideon v. Wainwright* (372 U.S. 335). Article 37 reads:

> *In all criminal cases the accused shall enjoy the right to a speedy and public trial by an impartial tribunal.*
>
> *He shall be permitted full opportunity to examine all witnesses, and he shall have the right of compulsory process for obtaining witnesses on his behalf at public expense.*
> *At all times the accused shall have the assistance of competent counsel who shall,*

> *if the accused is unable to secure the same by his own efforts, be assigned to his use by the State.*

Another point worth noticing in the language of Article 37 is that it makes reference to an "impartial tribunal" rather than an "impartial jury." This difference reflects the fact that trial by jury was abandoned in Japan in 1943. However, this is not the end of the story when it comes to trial by jury in Japan. In 2001, a report by the Criminal Justice Reform Council created a stir by recommending that Japanese justice look to increase citizen involvement. The result in 2009 was the formation of a new "mixed" system in Japan that was to include lay assessors in the criminal trial process by May 2009. These lay assessors, called **saiban-in**, assist the professional judges in serious cases in which there is considerable public interest. The judges and the *saiban-in* make up a panel and hear witnesses, examine evidence, and eventually decide whether a suspect is guilty. A three-year review of the new lay-judge system has received positive reviews, and it now is being considered for inclusion into civil trials in Japan (Wilson, 2012).

Aside from having no full jury, trials in Japan are very similar to those in the United States. They are open to the public, and after the judge provides the defendant with his or her rights, the procurator and the defense present their cases. After the trial is concluded, both parties (procurator and defense) have the right to appeal to a higher court. The vast majority of trials in Japan end up with a guilty plea by the defendant.

Plea bargaining does exist in Japan even though defendants in Japan can technically neither plead guilt nor waive their right to trial. Plea bargaining happens in the following way and is likely to happen even prior to any formal trial. First the prosecutor and the suspect or his attorney discuss the options. If the suspect accepts the "deal" made by the prosecutor, he will then confess. Finally, the prosecutor does as promised. Plea bargaining in Japan is unlike that in America in several ways. First, there are far fewer plea bargaining cases in Japan. Second, plea bargaining is more consensual in Japan. Japanese prosecutors are also far less likely to try to significantly increase the punishment if the offender goes to trial. Finally, the attitude of the offender in Japan is more likely to be remorseful than in the United States (Johnson, 2002, p. 246).

Vestiges of inquisitorial procedure remain despite the elaborate American-style procedural rights found in the Japanese constitution and in the 1948 Code of Criminal Procedure. The judge continues to be actively involved in questioning during the trial stage, and the prosecutor continues to conduct a detailed pretrial investigation of the case. The Japanese prosecutor, however, has considerably more discretionary powers to dismiss cases than his continental European counterparts. This power, similar to the power of the American prosecutor, actually allows for affirmation of the Japanese norm of avoidance of formal judicial processes. To mitigate the discretionary power of the prosecutor however, the Japanese made another significant change to their criminal procedure system in 2009 when they adopted a new grand jury system called the *Kensatsu Shinsakai*, or Prosecutorial Review Commission (PRC). Like the *saiban-in* system, the PRC allows for more citizen participation in the system through the formal criminal prosecution of a suspect when a prosecutor previously decides not to indict (Hiroshi, 2011). To see a full version of the Japanese Criminal Procedure Law, last revised in 2006, see the following web page: http://www.wipo.int/wipolex/en/text.jsp?file_id=214810.

Japan's ability to borrow from the different legal traditions of the world while retaining its own social mores appears to have resulted in a very successful criminal justice system. But it is possible that Japanese criminal procedure, and the Japanese criminal justice system in general, will undergo some changes within the next decade. Some research has shown that the concern for individual rights is beginning to find greater acceptance in Japan (Upham, 1987). In addition, there is a movement afoot to restore the jury system in Japan. Some scholars and lawyers feel that adding a jury will better protect the assumption of innocence, improve human rights, and "inject some of the community's common sense into the court and thereby bolster the legitimacy of verdicts" (Shinomiya, 2003).

CONSTITUTIONAL AND SYSTEM REVIEW

> "Laws of justice which Hammurabi, the wise king, established … That the strong might not injure the weak, in order to protect the widows and orphans …, in order to declare justice in the land, to settle all disputes,and heal all injuries."

This quote from the Hammurabi (Babylonian) Law Code of 1772 BC illustrates that the movement to protect the rule of law and those under the hand of legitimate governments is not a new phenomenon. For at least 4,000 years, the importance of the rule of law and justice for the less empowered has been the norm and not the exception around the world. Unfortunately, however, not all countries and certainly not all public criminal justice officials subscribe to this ideal. So what happens, then, if there is some question as to whether a country's criminal process laws or the behaviors of those in the criminal justice system are valid?

Countries use a variety of methods to deal with this question. For example, in the United States the power to make such decisions falls on the Supreme Court. In general, however, we can conclude that there are four methods used in the world today: (1) judicial review, (2) no review, (3) nonjudicial review, and (4) judicial review with legislative approval. In this section we describe the four ways and briefly describe how the model countries handle this issue of constitutional and system review. For a summary of the constitutional review procedures in our model countries, see Table 6.4.

TABLE 6.4 Constitutional Review Procedures in Model Countries

Country	Forms of Constitutional Review	Constitutional Review Institutions or Arrangements
England	Judicial review	Supreme Court of the United Kingdom has judicial review powers and serves as highest court of appeals.
France	Abstract review	The Constitutional Council, not a court, reviews on request the constitutionality of legislation.
Germany	Judicial review	The Federal Constitutional Court has review powers for constitutional issues and review of division of powers.
Japan	Judicial review	The Supreme Court has judicial review powers.
Saudi Arabia	Judicial review	High Court will handle appeals on procedure from lower courts.
China	Nonjudicial review	The National People's Congress and Standing Committee performs judicial review of Supreme People's Court.

Arrangements for Constitutional Review

The first method used by governments to decide the constitutionality of procedural laws and the legitimacy of actors in the system is through the use of judicial review. **Judicial review** is the power of a court to review actions and legal decisions made by those in the criminal justice system. Judicial review truly can be described as an American institution that, because of its success, has been adapted by many other nations of the world. Much of the push toward adoption of judicial review came after World War II, as many emergent nations broke away from the colonial powers that had controlled their governments and looked to set up systems of their own. In countries that were preoccupied with governmental reforms, the U.S. institutions provided a particularly attractive model. Judicial review is the most commonly accepted form of review in the world today, with over 40 percent of political systems using this method.

In our model countries, Germany and Japan have been using their own form of judicial review for 60 years. England and Saudi Arabia have also recently moved toward judicial review with the formation of new high-level "supreme"-type courts.

No Review

The most obvious alternative to conventional judicial review is no constitutional review. Historically, many systems based on written constitutions, such as the series of French constitutions from 1792 to 1958 and the constitution of Germany's Weimar Republic, have not provided for constitutional review. Another historical example is the former Soviet Union.

How do countries without provision for constitutional review address possible problems with criminal process and behavior of those in the system? In effect, it is not a large problem because a certain respect for basic constitutional arrangements exists in most democratic governments, even those without a written constitution or one that specifically mentions judicial review. For example, in Australia judicial review has become a de facto reality, although it is not provided for in the constitution. This is, of course, also the case in the United States.

In nondemocratic regimes, the matter is moot, since there is little concern for constitutionality in any case. An example of a nondemocratic country without constitutional review is China. Actually, the Chinese have developed formal mechanisms to serve the functions of judicial review. At the apex of that system is the Supreme People's Court. This court is responsible for administration of justice by lower courts, and it handles major criminal cases of national importance and cases on appeal from lower-court levels. In reality, however, the Supreme People's Court does not have the power to conduct any serious form of judicial review of constitutional issues or inappropriate behavior of those in the system. This responsibility is solely the bailiwick of the National People's Congress (NPC) and its Standing Committee. The NPC was discussed in earlier in Chapter 4. It elects and oversees all major officials in the government, approves the budget, develops economic and social development, makes laws, and amends and enforces the constitution. However, because of the short time the NPC is in session—only two weeks—the Standing Committee of the NPC handles the full-time governmental responsibilities.

The Standing Committee consists of about 150 full-time members, including the leading government officials and influential members of the Chinese Communist Party. The NPC and Standing Committee can annul any law or court decision if they find them to contravene the constitution, legal statutes, or administrative rules and regulations. Although this may seem rather benign, the fact is that all members of the Standing Committee are subordinate to the Chinese Communist Party and all initiatives proposed by the NPC and Standing Committee must have been previously endorsed by the party. The real role of the NPC and Standing Committee is to implement party policy. In summary, then, we can say that the Chinese practice most resembles a nonjudicial form of constitutional review.

Nonjudicial Review

Another alternative to judicial review is the establishment of a nonjudicial constitutional review agency to resolve issues of constitutionality. France adopted this alternative in its 1958 Constitution, which provides for a nine-member Constitutional Council. The French system is known as **abstract constitutional review** because the council decides on issues of constitutionality without hearing actual cases that have arisen under specific laws. Abstract review essentially means that the council gives advisory opinions rather than judgments in cases. Since it is not a court, it seems logical that the council would be engaged in abstract review. Abstract review may also be practiced by a court that also hears concrete cases, as is the case in Germany.

Judicial Review with Legislative Approval

Another form of judicial review is to have constitutional decisions by a supreme court subject to approval by a legislative body. This arrangement exists in India, where constitutional amendments may be passed with the approval of two-thirds of both houses of parliament. Thus, an unpopular or unacceptable decision of the Indian Supreme Court regarding the constitutionality of legislation may be nullified with relative ease (McWhinney, 1965; Cappelletti, 1971).

In theory, it would be possible to set up other arrangements for constitutional review. For example, subcommittees of parliaments, committees of elder statesmen, representatives of the various branches of government sitting as a constitutional committee—all are possible agencies for constitutional review. These bodies can practice merely abstract review, or it might be possible to let them do case-based review with respect only to the constitutional issues in particular cases. The fact is, however, that such agencies do not exist.

THE CONVERGENCE OF SYSTEMS

Each country develops its own code of criminal procedure at least partially as a result of its own history, and we would have to scrutinize them all to identify all the differences among them. The classification into adversarial and inquisitorial systems, however, seems to be increasingly a matter of style and history rather than one of major differences in procedure. Civil Law countries, even those in Latin America that have in the past held tightly to the principles of inquisitorial justice, have adopted many of the rules of procedure that protect the accused from arbitrary action by the state (Vogler, 2005, p. 173). Many Civil Law countries have also begun to show an increasing prominence of attorneys during trials, the concomitant diminishing of judicial authority, a shift in emphasis from the pretrial to the trial phase, and the reduced reliance on the accused as a source of testimony (Van Kessel, 2002). Common Law countries have modified the excesses of the adversarial system by allowing for pretrial investigations, by allowing judges to participate more actively in trials, and by making various arrangements for avoiding trial through the use of plea bargains and various forms of mediation.

Convergence can also be seen in Sacred and Socialist legal systems. In Saudi Arabia, Islamic law reflects the inquisitorial system through strong cooperation between the judge (*quadi*) and the investigator. In addition, the defense attorney is less adversarial than in Common Law trials. At the same time, Islamic law includes provisions for the right to confront accusers and even to remain silent for the presumption of innocence. And it can be argued that Chinese may actually have moved from a strict inquisitorial to a semi-adversarial mode by changing the role of judges to a less authoritative role, allowing questioning and cross-examination to be handled more by the prosecution and the defense, and allowing suspects more access to lawyers earlier in the process (Liu and Situ, 2001; Trevaskes, 2007).

There are many reasons cited for the increased convergence in the area of criminal procedure, including the growing influence of international law and supranational courts (Hodgson, 2005). In fact, those courts are currently the best and clearest examples of the convergence of criminal procedure in the world today (Ambos, 2003). Other frequently cited reasons for convergence include the failure of domestic systems of justice in democratic countries; the increasing openness to global perspectives; and the many cultural, economic, and political changes throughout the world (Van Kessel, 2002). The end result of convergence seems to be a certain homogenization of criminal procedure among the legal traditions. This process was predicted by legal scholar John Merryman over 25 years ago when he wrote of the blending of the inquisitorial and adversarial systems:

> *In a sense, it can be said that the evolution of criminal procedure in the last two centuries in the civil law world has been away from the extremes and abuses of the inquisitorial system, and that the evolution in the common law world during the same period has been away from the abuses and excesses of the accusatorial system. The two systems, in other words, are*

> *converging from different directions toward roughly equivalent mixed systems of criminal procedure. (1985, p. 134)*

BEYOND CONSTITUTIONAL REVIEW: SUPRANATIONAL COURTS

What happens when a citizen within a particular country has exhausted all the legal means of redress but still feels that his or her rights have been violated by the criminal justice system? And how do we address the issue of international or transnational criminality that occurs within or across borders? Special criminal courts and courts of human rights have been developed to address such situations. Because these courts and their decisions cross national boundaries and supposedly have a higher legal standing than decisions of courts in individual countries, they are often referred to as international or **supranational courts**. With the explosion in worldwide communications, the globalization of the economy, and the increase in international problems related to crime and justice, supranational courts are developing at a rapid pace. There are three general forms of supranational courts. The first are international courts that have been commonly known and accepted as internationally as legitimate. These include the International Court of Justice and the International Criminal Court. The second are supranational courts that are ad hoc tribunals that been developed for a specific purpose, have a narrowly defined jurisdiction, and are meant to be temporary. Examples of these are the International Criminal Tribunals for Yugoslavia and Rwanda.. The third and final type of supranational criminal courts is **internationalized courts**. Internationalized courts, also called mixed tribunals or hybrid courts, operate with the support of the United Nations to prosecute those responsible for crimes against humanity, war crimes, and violations of domestic law. These courts are generally are located in places where the crimes occur, and they utilize law and judges from the international and domestic jurisdictions. There are a number of these courts active around the world today, including the Special Court for Sierra Leone and the Special Tribunal for Lebanon. We will discuss supranational courts in more detail in Chapter 7. But first we conclude this chapter with a brief discussion about criminal procedure in three specific courts. The International Criminal Court (ICC), the International Criminal Tribunal for Yugoslavia (ICTY) and the Special Tribunal for Lebanon (STL), are examples in each of the three forms of supranational courts. In Table 6.5 we provide a list of key criminal procedure rules that are used in the three courts as well as web pages that you can look up more closely compare the three courts.

The ICC was brought into force through a multilateral international treaty in 2002 with the power to investigate and prosecute serious violations of international human rights law (Hopfel and Angermaier, 2005). The Rules of Criminal Procedure and Evidence were passed in 2002 as part of the Rome Statute to serve as the official rules for ICC judges and lawyers to follow during the prosecution of offenders. The rules were formed from a variety of sources, including the United Nations Covenant on Civil and Political Rights, procedures followed in criminal tribunals of the ICC during the 1990s, and ideas from countries with Common Law and Civil Law procedures. The procedural rules do have aspects of both the adversarial and inquisitorial systems of justice, although some argue that too much emphasis is placed on the latter system (Volger, 2005, p. 282; Walker, 2004). Although many of the criminal procedure rules of the ICC are similar to other supranational courts such as the tribunals, the rules differ in at least three ways. First, a party calling a witness in the ICC may not meet with this witness prior to his or her appearance in the court. This practice called witness proofing is common, but ICC felt it best to protect witnesses and avoid witness

TABLE 6.5 Key Steps of Criminal Procedure for the ICC, the ICTY, and the STL

Investigation

1. Prosecutor must determine whether "there is a reasonable basis to proceed with an investigation." (ICC)
2. If the prosecutor intends to initiate an investigation he or she must first submit to the pretrial chamber a request for authorization of an investigation and any supporting material collected. (ICC)
3. The pretrial chamber shall authorize the investigation if it considers that there is a *reasonable basis* to proceed and that the case appears to fall within the jurisdiction of the Court. (ICC)
4. The prosecutor may summon and question suspects, victims, and witnesses and record their statements, collect evidence, and conduct on-site investigations. (ICTY, STL)
5. The prosecutor undertakes such other matters as may appear necessary for completing the investigation and for the preparation and conduct of the prosecution at the trial and will provide for the safety of potential witnesses and informants. (ICTY, STL)
6. The prosecutor may seek assistance from any State authority concerned or from any relevant international body, including the International Criminal Police Organization (Interpol). (ICTY, STL)

Right to Counsel

1. Office of Public Counsel for the defense provides legal representation and protects the rights of the suspect during the initial stages of an investigation (ICC).
2. All suspects or accused persons are guaranteed free choice of counsel under the Rome Statute. Counsel must be provided without payment if the person does not have sufficient means to pay for it. (ICC)
3. Suspect has the right to be questioned in the presence of counsel unless the person has voluntarily waived his or her right to counsel. (ICTY, STL)
4. Counsel shall be assigned to suspects or accused who lack the means to remunerate such counsel. (ICTY, STL)
5. Defendant has the right to be assisted by counsel of the suspect's choice or to be assigned legal assistance without payment if the suspect does not have sufficient means to pay for it. (ICTY, STL)

Right to Trial (No trial by jury of peers)

1. The trial chamber (professional judges) determines the innocence or guilt of the accused. (ICC)
2. Trial must be held in public hearings, unless special circumstances require that certain proceedings be in closed session. (ICC, ICTY, STL)

Right to Remain Silent

1. Suspect has right to remain silent, without such silence being a consideration in the determination of guilt or innocence. (ICC, ICTY, STL)
2. Suspect shall not be compelled to incriminate himself or herself or to confess guilt. (ICC, ICTY)
3. Suspect has the right to remain silent, and to be cautioned that any statement the suspect makes shall be recorded and may be used in evidence (ICC, ICTY, STL).

Right to Bail

Suspect shall not be subjected to arbitrary arrest or detention, and shall not be deprived of his or her liberty except on such grounds and in accordance with such procedures as are established in the Rome Statute. (ICC)

SOURCES: Rules of Criminal Procedure for ICC at http://www.icc-cpi.int/Menus/ICC/Legal+Texts+and+Tools/Official+Journal/Rules+of+Procedure+and+Evidence.htm; Rules of Criminal Procedure for ICTY at http://www.icty.org/sid/136; Rules of Criminal Procedure for Special Tribunal for Lebanon at http://www.stl-tsl.org/en/documents/rules-of-procedure-and-evidence/rules-of-procedure-and-evidence

contamination. Second, victims in the ICC are viewed as full participants in the trial, not merely as witnesses. Finally, the Rome Statute that formed the ICC calls for victim reparations (Nerlich, 2011). In each of these it is clear that those that developed the procedures for the ICC were very intent on protecting the rights of victims.

The criminal procedure rules for the International Criminal Tribunal for Yugoslavia (ICTY) were formed in 1994 but since that date they have seen 46 amendments; the most recent came in August 2012 when the court decided on a new rule for the nondisclosure of witness identities for protection reasons (UN-ICTY, 2012). The Special Tribunal for Lebanon (STL) is an example of a recently formed internationalized court. It was inaugurated on March 1, 2009, for the purpose of prosecuting and holding those persons responsible for the February 2005 attack that killed 23 people, including the former prime minister of Lebanon. The procedure rules have been amended four times since their adoption in 2009; the most recent changes were made in February 2012 to seven rules of the court, including major changes in victims' rights and participation (STL, 2012). A perusal of the procedure laws of the ICC, ICTY, and STL, as well as other supranational courts, supports the position we stated earlier that there has been a convergence of criminal justice systems in recent decades.

SUMMARY

We have seen how all law systems have gradually developed a series of procedures designed to make certain that accused persons are not treated unfairly or arbitrarily by the government that has jeopardized their well-being by accusing them of breaking its laws. We have also seen how, over time, there has been a large degree of convergence among various families of law with respect to the rights of the accused. This convergence has been influenced by the evolution of the concept of human rights that occurred chiefly in the 20th century and has led to the development of international law and international courts.

By considering the different traditions in our model countries, we have been able to develop some sense of the way that criminal procedure controversies are handled in other modern systems of justice. Civil Law criminal procedure is still largely defined by statute. The inquisitorial process is concerned not with procedural intricacies but with truth-finding in a fair and expeditious manner. In the Common Law, however, the guarantees of protection for the accused historically have been integral to the whole concept of adversarial procedure. Socialist procedure is in many ways similar to Civil Law procedure. Although Socialist Law theory emphasizes the collective good rather than judicial independence or defendants' rights, the law of criminal procedure is designed to provide predictability and fairness in the criminal justice process, at least in nonpolitical cases. Sacred (Islamic) Law criminal procedure has historically relied on the criterion of fairness and justice to secure these rights, although recent changes in procedure have begun to make the system more formalized. It continues to have fewer guarantees regarding the rights of the accused than either the Civil Law or the Common Law. Popular (mixed) systems of justice are available in all legal traditions except in the Sacred Law tradition, where *quadi* justice dominates.

When actors in the system inadequately protect the accused, special mechanisms are available in all systems to force officials to maintain conformity with this higher law. These mechanisms may be relatively simple, consisting largely of higher courts that have the mandate to adhere to the higher law in actual cases, or they may be complex, requiring involvement by other structures of government or other judicial officials. Recently, international bodies called supranational courts have been formed to seek justice beyond borders. There are three categories of supranational courts: international, tribunals, and internationalized courts.

Comparative Criminal Justice at the Movies

Movies seek to entertain and inform the audience about a story, incident, or person. Many good movies also hit upon important substantive themes relevant to understanding crime and justice in comparative perspective. Read the movie summary below (and watch the movie if you haven't already) and answer the questions below to make the subject matter connections to comparative criminal justice.

Lord of War **(2005)**
Andres Niccol, Director

Based loosely on the life of Victor Bout, an infamous international arms dealer, *Lord of War* is told in flashback, showing how an automatic round moves from its manufacture until getting fired from an AK-47 and travelling through the head of a child soldier during a war in Africa. Yuri Orlov (Nicolas Cage) describes through the film how he became an international arms dealer.

Yuri and his family came to United States from Ukraine when he was a boy, his family pretending to be Jewish to escape the Soviet Union. Uri began his career in arms sales, partnering with his brother Vitaly (Jared Leto), after he saw a Ukrainian mob boss kill two would-be assassins.

Yuri gets his first break selling M-16s after the 1982 Lebanon War and becomes "an equal-opportunity merchant of death," selling guns to all sides in any conflict. He develops multiple identities (complete with ID cards) and stores all his records and paperwork in a metal security container. Yuri tells of his first encounter with Jack Valentine (Ethan Hawke), an incorruptible Interpol agent. The incident took place when Yuri was on the ship *Kristol*, smuggling a shipment of weapons. When he learned that Valentine is after him, he repainted the boat and changed its name to *Kono*, thereby eluding capture.

Yuri pursues Ava Fontaine (Bridget Moynahan), a model, and books a photo shoot and the entire hotel so that they have the location to themselves. They later marry and have a son named Nikolai, who takes his first steps on the same day the Soviet Union dissolves.

Yuri rushes to Ukraine after watching Gorbachev's Christmas Day 1991 resignation speech on television. He contacts his uncle, Dmitri, a general of the former Soviet Army, and begins buying Dmitri's tanks and AK-47s to expand his inventory, explaining that the AK-47 is the most reliable assault rifle in the world. Yuri moves on to selling arms to the West African dictator of Liberia, André Baptiste (Eamonn Walker), who pays in blood diamonds. Valentine learns that Yuri will be making a cargo run to Sierra Leone and has fighter planes intercept the plane in flight. Yuri makes an emergency landing on a dirt road, and gives away all the guns to local villagers before Valentine can arrive and detain him. Valentine handcuffs and detains Yuri for 24 hours before being forced to release him.

Valentine keeps Yuri under surveillance, and one day he reveals to his wife, Ava, that Yuri is a major weapons dealer. Ava pleads with Yuri to stop, and he does, instead choosing to exploit the resources of third world nations. However, he dislikes the business, complaining that the profit margins are low and there is too much competition compared to illegal arms. Yuri reenters the arms market when Baptiste approaches him again. Yuri decides to bring along Vitaly, who witnesses a group of villagers beating a mother and child to death and tells Yuri that the entire village will be massacred if the arms deal goes through. He pleads with Yuri to stop the transaction, but Yuri says it's not their conflict. Vitaly then takes a grenade and blows up the truck with half the guns inside. A guard watching the transaction shoots Vitaly to death.

Ava ultimately finds Yuri's hidden security container, which is definitive proof of Yuri's arms dealing. She takes their son and leaves him. When Yuri calls his parents, his mother says, "Both my sons are dead." Valentine detains Yuri and tells him that he has a long jail sentence ahead of him. However, Yuri tells Valentine that he will walk free as a "necessary evil," because the people he supplies are often fighting enemies of the United States. Yuri predicts that a high-ranking officer will come, congratulate Valentine, and then order him to free Yuri. A high-ranking officer does indeed come, and Yuri is released and returns to selling arms.

Questions

1. What aspects of arms trafficking make it perhaps the most serious of all transnational crimes?
2. Victor Bout, the person on whom this movie was based, was ultimately caught in 2008 in a sting operation in Thailand set up by the U.S. Drug Enforcement Administration. As of 2010, Thailand has denied the requests of the United States to extradite Bout to the United States for trial. Can you offer reasons for this denial?

Critical Thinking Exercise

Critical thinking requires the ability to evaluate viewpoints, facts, and behaviors objectively to assess information and methods of argumentation in order to establish the merit of an action, law, policy, or procedure. Please evaluate this scenario objectively, applying your knowledge of comparative criminal justice to the facts of the case presented, and answer the questions that follow it.

Suspects Shot "Casing Videos"
Two men were charged with shooting "casing videos" of the U.S. Capitol Building and other potential terrorist targets. Sadequee, age 19, was ordered held without bail instead of being permitted to stay with his mother living in Georgia. The other suspect, Ahmed, was a 21-year-old student at Georgia Tech. They were accused of meeting with other targets of an FBI probe during a trip to Canada in 2005. The men are alleged to have discussed attacks against oil refineries and military bases. After returning from Canada, the men went to Washington, D.C., allegedly for the purpose of making a series of "casing videos" of potential terrorist targets, including the Capitol, the World Bank, a Masonic Temple, and a fuel depot. The defendants are not charged with terrorism because there is no direct evidence of terrorism involvement.

Questions

Tourists from all over the world come to the United States and take millions of photos and videos of U.S. monuments and buildings that could conceivably be targets of terrorists.

1. What criteria should be used to distinguish innocent videotaping of U.S. buildings by U.S. and foreign tourists from potential "casing videos" for a potential terrorist attack?
2. Do you think this case would be handled differently in Common Law, Civil Law, Socialist Law, or Sacred (Islamic) Law countries?
3. Are there legal or constitutional principles that would help to insure that a proper balance is struck between the government's interests in apprehending potential criminals, while at the same time not catching innocent people in the same net?

SOURCE: Tom Hays, "Prosecutors: Suspects Shot 'Casing Videos,'" *ABC News*, August 16, 2006.

DISCUSSION QUESTIONS

1. Explain major tenets of the adversarial, inquisitorial, and popular (mixed) systems.
2. What are the major differences between Common and Civil Law criminal procedure?
3. If you were on trial for a felony, in which of the model countries would you most like to be tried? In which would you least like to be tried? Why?
4. What are the different methods of constitutional review? Which do you believe is best, and why?
5. How are criminal procedure laws utilized in the ICC, ICTY, and STL similar? How are they different? Use Table 6.5 to assist you in this comparison.

FOR FURTHER READING

Jackson, J., M. Langer, and P. Tillers (Eds.). (2008). *Crime, Procedure and Evidence in a Comparative and International Context.* Oxford, UK: Hart Publishing.

Kamali, M. H. (2008). *Shari'a Law: An Introduction.* Oxford, UK: Oneworld Press.

Langbein, J. H. (2003). *The Origins of the Adversary Trial.* New York, NY: Oxford University Press.

Muhlhahn, K. (2009). *Criminal Justice in China: A History.* Cambridge, MA: Harvard University Press.

Van der Wolf, W., and C. Tolan (Eds.). (2012). *Defense in International Proceedings: Issues in International Criminal Law.* Portland, Oregon, USA: International Courts Association.

WEB PAGES FOR CHAPTER

For the Rules of Procedure and Evidence for the International Criminal Tribunal for Yugoslavia (ICTY), see http://www.icty.org/sid/136.

To find a tabular presentation of forms of constitutional review around the world, see www.concourts.net/tab/.

A web page for the 2012 Rules of the ECHR that includes a short video outlining the rights of all those in the European Union is available at http://www.echr.coe.int/ECHR/EN/Header/Basic+Texts/The+Convention+and+additional+protocols/The+European+Convention+on+Human+Rights/.

For the Rules of Procedure and Evidence for the International Criminal Court (ICC), see http://www.icc-cpi.int/Menus/ICC/Legal+Texts+and+Tools/Official+Journal/Rules+of+Procedure+and+Evidence.htm.

To see the United Nations Rule of Law webpage, see http://www.unrol.org/.

7 

The Courts and Legal Professionals

Key Terms and Concepts

adjudicators

advocates

court

courts of general jurisdiction

courts of last resort

courts of limited jurisdiction

European Court of Human Rights (ECtHR)

indigenous courts

intermediate appeal

International Court of Justice (ICJ)

International Criminal Court (ICC)

International Criminal Tribunal for Rwanda (ICTR)

International Criminal Tribunal for Yugoslavia (ICTY)

internationalized courts

judicial impartiality

judicial independence

jus cogens

legal advisors

legal scholars

Rome Statute

tribunals

Chapter 7 Learning Objectives

Describe the roles of the four categories of legal professionals in developed societies.

Explore the differences between bureaucratically and politically oriented organizations.

Compare similarities and differences that occur in court structures and legal professions in our model nations.

Describe the major forms of supranational courts available in the world today.

Explain the advantages and challenges of supranational courts.

In a Haitian court, defense lawyers clashed loudly with a judge, shouting objections as he rang a small bell to try and regain order. After a heated exchange, the defense lawyers tore off their robes and left the court. The judge suspended the trail for the day but told the accused that if their lawyers did not return the following morning that they would remain in jail waiting for the trial to continue for the next six months. The defense lawyers returned the next morning (Bogdanich and Sontag, 2011).

The trial of Gu Kailai, wife of a Communist Party official in China accused of murdering a British businessman, began and ended in single day, August 19, 2012, with the final verdict to be delivered later by the Intermediate People's Court at an unannounced date—a standard practice in a Chinese court case (Page, 2012).

In February 2011, the United Nations Security Council decided unanimously to refer a possible criminal situation in Libya to the International Criminal Court (ICC) prosecutor. On March 3, 2011, the ICC prosecutor announced his decision to open an investigation in the situation in Libya, and in June 2011 the Pre-Trial Chamber I of the ICC issued three warrants of arrest respectively for Muammar Mohammed Abu Minyar Gaddafi, Saif Al-Islam Gaddafi, and Abdullah Al-Senussi for crimes against humanity (murder and persecution) allegedly committed across Libya. In November 2011, Pre-Trial Chamber I formally terminated the case against Muammar Gaddafi due to his death. The two other suspects remain at large (ICC, 2012).

Courts and courtrooms such as these provide a seemingly endless source of material for both fiction and nonfiction for writers, news reporters, and media producers from around the world. There are many reasons for our fascination with courts and court room drama. The element of suspense is certainly an ingredient: Will the accused be acquitted or convicted? Does the trial appear to be conducted in a "fair" manner? What will surface from witness testimony? Accounts of intrigue, violence, inequity, and lawlessness are of intense interest to those who follow courtroom sagas.

More important than the drama, however, a public trial tends to affirm the community values that the government seeks to protect and promote through the criminal process. As such, it provides vicarious satisfaction that justice is being done, that those who choose to reject these values do not go unpunished. The community is strengthened through this public repudiation of deviance, even if the accused is exonerated. In the end, then, the court system provides us with a sense of security and a feeling that justice is highly valued in society. As these three scenarios recount, the mechanisms of justice in courts around the world are quite diverse. And if they were presented to a lawyer or law student in the United States, they might seem quite peculiar.

In this chapter, we consider the subject of courts in general, the legal professionals who work in courts around the world, the organization of courts in our model systems, and a growing idea called supranational courts. Although we will concentrate on criminal courts, we must remember that courts also handle noncriminal (civil) disputes between individuals or between the government and individuals.

THE CONCEPT OF A COURT

What are courts, and what functions do they serve in a society? What is their role within the political framework of a nation?

A simple definition of a **court** is that it is an agency with power to settle disputes in a society. The word *court* is derived from the Latin term *cohortus*, later shortened to *cohort* or *court*, meaning "being together in the same garden," such as being in the garden of a medieval castle or courtyard (Adler, Mueller, and Laufer, 2009). One of the parties in a court case, the plaintiff, presents the facts of the case and explains how these facts are related to some body of law or principles that are considered binding in the society. The other side, the defendant, disputes these facts and tries to show that the person or issue before the court is not within the jurisdiction of the proscribed law. The crucial word in this definition is "power." The judicial power in a court, whether it be a judge, a panel of judges, or a lay jury, is there to examine the truth and to determine whether the law applies in the case and whether any damage has been done to the plaintiff.

Some voluntary agencies also mediate disputes and may on occasion be called courts, but a court by our definition is an agency of government that has the coercive power of government behind it. The function of courts is to settle, authoritatively and according to predefined legal norms, the many disputes that arise in a society. In complex modern societies, disputes may be between two parties in a civil suit, or they may be between the state and a party accused of a criminal violation. Some countries have separate courts to handle civil and criminal matters and some handle both in the same courts. In societies where communal ties may be strong enough to enable disputes to be settled in informal ways, **indigenous courts** have been formed. Indigenous courts emphasize consensus and mediation with the goal of formalizing justice for persons who are culturally and or geographically removed from the mainstream of society. They serve to make court processes more culturally relevant for indigenous persons and to allow local leaders and citizens to become involved in the justice process and build strong communities.

Although indigenous methods of meting out justice have surely existed in various forms since the formation of communal living, there has been a recent trend in some countries to revitalize this form of court and justice process. One example of a revived traditional justice system is in Rwanda, where *gacaca* courts (rhymes with cha-cha) were reintroduced to deal with the over 120,000 Hum leaders and supporters who are incarcerated for their part in the 1994 massacres in the Rwandan civil war. *Gacaca* courts have tried to bring those suspected of genocide during the massacres to the villages where they allegedly committed the crime. The over 8,000 *gacaca* courts consist of local judges who pass sentences, with forgiveness emphasized, and reduced sentences for those who confess (Gacaca Courts, 2010)

Another example is the case of Australia, which convened the first indigenous urban court in 1999 in Port Adelaide, South Australia, and has since established others in other Australian regions. The processes of the courts vary considerably, but they are similar in the following ways: The offender must be an indigenous person and have entered a guilty plea, the offense must have occurred in an area covered by the courts jurisdiction, and the charge is generally one that was heard in a lower-level court of first instance (Marchetti and Daly, 2004).

Indigenous courts are present in the United States on Native American reservations and in some remote areas. For example, in Alaska most of the population is located in cities, but there are countless remote villages throughout the state that consist largely of native Alaskans. Because of lack of resources to support a formal criminal justice system, many of these villages establish local ordinances and rules and handle undesirable behavior in their own informal manner. The rules and punishments are determined primarily by custom and meted out by village councils or village chiefs. When a matter is of a serious criminal nature, or if the perpetrator does not voluntarily submit to the rules of the jurisdiction, the case is handed over to local and state law enforcement (National Tribal Resource Center, 2010). The formulation of indigenous courts has been partially motivated by the increased sensitivity towards diversity in societies and also by the failure of traditional courts to address the problem of crime and the limits of the justice system.

In the second half of the twentieth century, the role of the courts was expanded beyond national boundaries. After World War II, the Nuremberg trials were held to try Nazi war criminals and to define how international tribunals would handle atrocities of war. More recently, the United Nations has revived the idea of courts with the power to adjudicate international crimes by countries and individuals. These courts have expanded the role of courts in our individual societies to the larger global context. Later in this chapter, we will discuss in more detail the background, purpose, and current status of these supranational courts.

Whatever the reality of court operations in a society, most people can agree that a court should have two basic characteristics to function properly: (1) judicial independence and (2) judicial impartiality.

Judicial independence is a principle that holds that courts and judges are bound to the law and should make decisions without being under the influence, direct or indirect, of other governmental or political agents. In countries that have a democratic government structure, judicial independence is essential for maintaining individual rights for all citizens. In authoritarian states, the independence of the judiciary is often nonexistent. Judges on the side of those in power are there simply to enforce the law of the ruling party or leader in power. For example, we have mentioned in previous chapters how China has eschewed judicial independence under the rationale that it is "better for the society" that all legal decisions be in sync with Socialist ideals. To some extent, Islamic countries such as Saudi Arabia have adopted the same approach to fit their religious values.

Pure judicial independence, to be sure, is an ideal that hardly exists, as innumerable studies of courts, including the U.S. Supreme Court, have shown. But blatant political influence on court operations can usually be recognized, and we say that courts that choose, or are forced, to carry out governmental wishes have become "politicized." Likewise, a court may operate in a politicized manner in particular trials, and we usually call these "political trials." There are many shades of ambiguity surrounding the concept of judicial independence. Nevertheless, it remains a basic ideal in most court structures.

The reality is that adjudicators do not live in a vacuum and are themselves shaped by the circumstances of their society, as well as by their upbringing and training. But the ideal of fairness and independence in accordance with a rule of law is a strong socializing influence and a societal norm that should provide a framework for the work of adjudicators.

Judicial impartiality may be tied to judicial independence in some cases, but it is a broader concept that calls for judicial authorities to treat parties in court as equals. "Equality before the law" is a cherished precept of modern justice systems. A judge who distinguished among plaintiffs by race, creed, or social class would not be practicing judicial impartiality. Of course, judicial impartiality, like judicial independence, is an ideal that often is honored only in the breach. Thus, although these two concepts are important in studying and evaluating the operations of courts, we cannot claim that they must be present for a court to exist.

ACTORS IN THE LEGAL PROFESSION

There are generally four categories of legal professionals in developed societies: adjudicators, advocates, legal advisors, and legal scholars (Ehrmann, 1976, p. 56). Adjudicators are those individuals who decide the outcome of legal disputes; more commonly, these legal professionals are called judges. Advocates represent either the defendant or the prosecution in legal matters before the court. Legal advisors provide legal advice to advocates and citizens outside the court. Legal scholars study the law and discuss it in legal commentaries and professional journals. Advocates, legal advisors, and legal scholars are more generally called "lawyers," which is a comprehensive term used to describe anyone who gives legal advice, manages legal affairs, and pleads cases in court. In this section, we discuss each of these legal professionals in some detail. It should be said here however, that there is often not a clear distinction between the categories of the legal profession. It is not uncommon for lawyers in different societies to fit into more than one of these categories.

Adjudicators

Many countries rely on professional judges who are trained and paid to be adjudicators of legal matters. In other countries, as in the popular (mixed) system discussed in Chapter 6, lay judges, jurors, or a combination of lay and professional judges handle the adjudicatory functions of the courts. More formally defined, **adjudicators** are professional judges or magistrates, "full- and part-time officials authorized to hear civil, criminal and other cases, including in appeal courts, and make dispositions in a court of law. Lay judges and magistrates are persons who perform the same functions as professional judges or magistrates but are not considered as career members of the judiciary" (Aromaa et al., 2003).

There are three primary methods, and their various permeations, for how judges are employed. The most common method, especially in the Common Law tradition, is by appointment. After gaining experience as a lawyer, the prospective judge is selected by an individual within the executive branch of the government or by a special committee. In England and Wales, judicial appointment above the magistrate level has been the result of a process that comes from the Judicial Appointments Commission since 2006.

The second method of judge selection is by career choice path, whereby individuals decide on their own to become judges either during or immediately after their legal training. Exams and extensive apprenticeships follow the decision to become a judge. This kind of career choice system is found in many Civil Law countries and some Islamic Law countries, such as Saudi Arabia. It may seem odd, especially to Americans, for legal actors to decide so early in their careers to become judges before gaining any real legal experience. The need for legal experience may be necessary in the Common Law legal tradition, which necessitates that judges be more knowledgeable so as to better handle the many legal subtleties of the tradition. But in the Civil and Islamic legal cultures, the interpretation of law is limited because of the nature of the law itself. Judges are asked not to make law or even to interpret law, but only to apply the law.

Finally, a less common method of judge selection involves citizen elections. Although this method has been criticized as highly political, it has been adopted by a number of local jurisdictions, counties, and even some states in the United States. Some states have adopted a combination method called the Missouri Plan, which requires judicial candidates to be selected by a committee and then, after some time in office, to face the electorate. For a summary of the methods of judge selection in our model countries, see the box on next page.

Advocates

Advocates are expected to be partisan, and a lack of zeal in pursuing the interests of their client is a serious violation of the norms of this category of legal actor. This is so even in Socialist systems, in which the interests of the state are considered paramount and may influence the degree of advocacy that can be exercised. **Advocates** are legal representatives, usually lawyers, who present the evidence and the arguments that allow adjudicators to make their decisions. Advocates work for the state (prosecution) or the criminally accused (defense). As we have mentioned many times before, advocates working on behalf of the government are called prosecutors or procurators, although their roles vary considerably from country to country (see Ambos, 2000).

Efforts have been made on the international level to ensure the quality of legal assistance throughout the world by standardizing the duties and responsibilities of lawyers and others providing legal assistance. To assist nations around the world with the proper development of lawyers, the United Nations has developed the *UN principles on the role of lawyers*. The Principles address issues such as qualifications and training, duties and responsibilities, and disciplining lawyers.

Like adjudicators, advocates are subject to economic, social, and political pressures that affect their

Methods of Judge Selection in Our Model Countries and the United States

- England: Appointed in magistrates' courts, local committees are responsible for appointments; since 2006, in other courts the Judicial Appointments Commission appoints judges.
- Germany and France: Self-selected candidates undergo an extensive apprenticeship period and then face rigorous civil service examinations.
- China: Elected and appointed. The heads of the courts, called presidents, are elected by the corresponding people's congresses while all other judges are appointed by the corresponding standing committee of the particular court.
- Japan: Self-selected and then promoted by merit. After passing a national-level judicial examination, candidates train for two years at the Legal Research and Training Institute and then move up through the ranks based on merit.
- Saudi Arabia: Self-selected. Candidates must first qualify for this position and then go through a period of apprenticeship before being allowed to decide cases.
- United States: Usually elected on local and county levels, appointed on state and federal level. A combination method plan (Missouri Plan) is available in some states.

work. In two of our model countries, Saudi Arabia and China, advocates for both the prosecution and the defense are under considerable pressure to conform to forces beyond the courtroom. In Saudi Arabia, advocates must be schooled in classic Islamic Law because there is no distinction between religious and secular offenses. In China, lawyers must be approved by the Ministry of Justice and are expected to protect the rights of their clients while also promoting the interests of the state.

Advisors

Legal advisors, akin to paralegals in the United States, are the many legally trained individuals who work outside the courtroom to advise and instruct individuals who have legal problems or needs, both civil and criminal. They handle a large proportion of the paperwork that is necessary for the functioning of large bureaucratic societies: wills, contracts, tax analysis, real estate transactions, and analysis of business regulations. Legal advisors are also the first point of contact in criminal cases. They do investigations and advise clients prior to the start of formal adjudication processes. The position of advisors is often viewed as less prestigious than that of advocates because they do not handle cases in the public arena. However, this is only a matter of perception. In reality, legal advisors handle many of the same legal tasks as advocates and usually possess the same qualifications and training, except that they lack courtroom expertise.

Legal Scholars

In every society, **legal scholars** have played an important role in shaping the law and clarifying its meaning. Legal scholars often work behind the scenes doing the arduous legal research, writing of opinions, and legislation that are necessary for all nations. Their role has been much more prominent in Civil and Islamic Law than in Common Law systems. For example, in a Civil Law country such as Germany, a law professor may consult with legislators and write commentaries on the law. In Saudi Arabia a scholar may be asked to provide judicial reasoning opinions concerning the Shari'a or Hadith. For Americans the distinction between adjudicators, advocates, advisors, and scholars might seem unclear because we often do not distinguish clearly between these categories. For example, a single attorney usually handles all aspects of a case. And judges may have previously held positions as an advocate and law scholar. But again it is important to remember that the categories posed here are functional ones rather than classifications of particular individuals.

CAREER PATHS OF LEGAL PROFESSIONALS

Our discussion of the kinds of legal professional around the world today would be incomplete if we did not briefly discuss the career paths of these individuals. More specifically, we answer the question "how do judges and the different kinds of legal counsel around the world become legal professionals?" One way to understand the career paths of legal actors is to use the distinction between persons employed through bureaucratically based systems and politically based systems (Weber, 1985).

Bureaucratically Oriented Systems

The bureaucratically based systems are found in the countries that have rational systems of law—that is, Civil Law systems. Such an organization has the general characteristics of a rational bureaucracy: (1) It is hierarchical in nature, (2) entry into the organization is based on merit alone, and (3) employees of the organization are highly trained for specific tasks.

Among our model systems, Germany, France, and Japan display the greatest degree of bureaucratic organization of the personnel of the justice system. In each of these countries, students interested in the law follow university programs that emphasize both a general liberal education and specific training in the code law. Upon graduation, many law school students go on to careers in business, public administration, or other nonlegal fields. Those who continue in the legal profession, however, must choose among training to be a judge, an attorney for the state, or an attorney in private practice. This training determines the kind of career that the individual will follow, unless he or she goes into legal scholarship and university teaching. Rigorous examinations and years of apprenticeship are necessary to become fully accredited in the particular branch of legal process that the individual chooses. Both prosecutors and judges have civil service status—that is, they are tenured and rise through the ranks gradually, with some possibility of more rapid advancement for particularly talented individuals.

Exceptions occur chiefly at the highest levels of judicial appointment, such as the Supreme Court in Japan and the Federal Constitutional Court in Germany. In these policy-making courts, the legislature chooses a mixture of career judges, political figures, and legal scholars to serve for fixed terms. While civil service status assures that judges in Civil Law systems are chosen on the basis of merit rather than ideology or politics, a judge's advancement to higher-court adjudication is usually controlled by those in political power. As a result, despite efforts to mitigate this political influence, the system in Civil Law countries tends to reward conservatism and conformity rather than individualism and willingness to risk unpopularity in the cause of equal justice (Ehrmann, 1976, p. 78).

Law school education in bureaucratic systems does not actually prepare students to practice law in any practical sense. Rather, they are prepared through years of apprenticeship to be either practicing lawyers or state officials such as judges and prosecutors. Over the course of centuries, legal education in the Civil Law countries has developed along rather academic lines, with an emphasis on philosophy, political science, and legal history. These educational systems, in which case precedents do not have the force of law, naturally do not emphasize case law as American law schools do.

Politically Oriented Systems

Politically based systems are based on nonrational factors such as appointment by political leaders and election by the people. Individuals in this system generally cannot divorce themselves from the people they serve. Although trained in the law, they are not usually highly prepared for the specific tasks they must undertake.

Of our model countries, England and China, and to a lesser degree Saudi Arabia, might be classified as legal systems that are politically oriented in organization. The United States, as we mentioned earlier, also displays a clear political organization structure. English judges are chosen from among barristers, who are practicing lawyers rather than civil servants trained to be judges. The lord chancellor, a cabinet member who is somewhat analogous to the attorney general of the United States, makes judicial appointments, generally from among the most prestigious barristers, the queen's counsel (QC). The law lords, who sit in the House of Lords and act as the court of final appeal, are also appointed rather than achieving their position through a merit system.

In China, the head judges of the various people's courts are called *presidents*. The presidents are elected by the people's congresses of the respective court levels. For example, the president of the Supreme People's Court is elected by the National People's Congress, while the presidents of the local people's courts are elected by the people's congresses on the local level. All remaining judges are appointed by standing committees at the particular court levels. Politics greatly affects the judge selection process in China because the National People's Congress and the standing committees consist primarily of influential members of the Communist party.

Prosecutors, who are politically chosen in the United States, fall into different categories in both England and China. Although there have been some changes in recent years, English prosecutors have not traditionally specialized even in prosecuting cases. Instead, they are chosen for particular cases from among the ranks of the barristers. Thus, it is quite possible for an individual to be a prosecutor one day and a defense attorney the next.

Prosecutors in China, called *procurators,* are under the direct supervision of the office of the procuratorate. At the federal level, procurators are all appointed (and removed) by the Standing Committee of the National People's Congress. At the provincial, regional, and municipal levels, the chief procurators are elected or removed by the respective people's congresses, and the deputy procurators are selected by the standing committees of the respective level of government.

When we come to Saudi Arabia, our distinction between bureaucratic and political organization breaks down. However, since judges are part of the religious establishment and are chosen from a committee that is approved by that establishment or from the ranks of the royal family, this system tilts toward the political. Advocates and advisors in this system, however, follow the Civil Law model imported from France.

In sum, the distinction between bureaucratic and political arrangements is not always clear-cut. Nevertheless, a dominant style or orientation exists in each of our model systems, and awareness of this style helps us analyze and understand the details of the various systems as we examine them. This dominant style is related to the particular family of law to which a country adheres, with the rational, code-based systems having a rational bureaucratic hierarchy of legal professionals working for the state, and the empirical, case-based systems having a more mixed, even pluralistic culture of the legal profession. As we consider legal training, judicial recruitment, and career paths of prosecutors and defense attorneys in the model systems, these classifications of bureaucratic and political will provide a useful framework for the analysis.

THE COURTS AND LEGAL PROFESSIONS IN OUR MODEL COUNTRIES

There are many ways to study courts and their role in a society. We can look at litigiousness, or the tendency to take cases to court, in various societies, which can tell us a great deal about the levels of consensus or complexity in a society. We can also look at patterns of decision making by judges, as has been done in great detail by scholars of the U.S. Supreme Court. In this chapter we will look at the arrangement and organization of courts within our model countries. To assist in understanding of the various levels of courts around the world, it is helpful to categorize them *generally* into at least four court types or levels. We place the word *generally* in italics to emphasize the point that although these court types apply in many cases around the world, there is also considerable variation in the way courts are organized. This is particularly true in countries where one court may handle criminal and civil cases whereas in another country there are separate courts for such matters. Another example of this variety and complexity is the United States, where there are separate courts systems for the states and the federal government.

The first general types of courts are **courts of limited jurisdiction**. These courts handle minor criminal cases and may also conduct preliminary hearings for cases that will be handled at the next level of courts—courts of general jurisdiction. **Courts of general jurisdiction** are the major trial courts that have jurisdiction over any cases involving criminal law and sometimes civil law. Courts of first or **intermediate appeal** handle appeals from the lower courts. **Courts of last resort** are those that are authorized by law to hear the final appeal on legal matters. These courts are often labeled called supreme courts or high courts. For a table that summarizes the courts in our model countries, see Table 7.1.

COURTS AND THE LEGAL PROFESSION IN ENGLAND

England has established two levels of trial courts for criminal cases: magistrates' courts for minor crimes and crown courts for serious crimes. Magistrates' courts are courts of limited jurisdiction. They handle minor criminal cases and also conduct preliminary hearings in major criminal cases, with the magistrates deciding whether to bind the case over to the crown court. Thus, they serve in lieu of the grand juries or other devices for pretrial hearings that exist in the United States. In addition to trials for petty crimes and preliminary hearings, certain magistrates' courts are designated to handle some minor civil cases and juvenile cases involving defendants under 18 years of age. Over 96 percent of English criminal trials are conducted in the 500 magistrates' courts (Terrill, 2013, p. 45).

There are two types of magistrates: stipendiary magistrates, who are attorneys by trade and are paid by the state for their work, and lay magistrates, who are appointed to serve as volunteer judges. Stipendiary magistrates, also called district judges, usually sit alone, whereas lay magistrates usually sit or groups of two or three and decide large numbers of cases in the course of an ordinary court session. Lay magistrates, also called *justices of the peace,* vastly outnumber stipendiary ones (30,000 to 130), although the numbers of the latter are increasing. Lay magistrates receive a minimal amount of training (about one week in aggregate). Appointment as a lay magistrate is an honor often bestowed on those who belong to the majority political party in a region. Many of them are women, a natural phenomenon since professional men usually do not have the time to devote to this volunteer service. Lay magistrates may serve until age seventy, and they are obligated to sit in court at least twenty-one days each year.

For minor civil cases, the court of first jurisdiction is the county court. If the matter is appealed, it is brought to the High Court of Justice, which is the first level of appeal for the county court but which acts primarily as a court of original jurisdiction for serious civil cases and some criminal cases. The High Court of Justice is divided into three branches: (1) the Queen's Bench Division, which handles the majority of civil and criminal matters of original and appellate jurisdiction, (2) the Chancery Division, which is responsible for matters involving property, trusts, and wills, and (3) the Family Division, which deals with matrimony and guardian issues.

The trial courts, or courts of general jurisdiction for serious crimes in England, are known as crown courts. Cases in crown courts are decided by juries. This is in contrast to the various civil trial courts, such as the county courts and the High Court of Justice, in which jury trial is all but obsolete. Juries have been in existence for over 800 years in England. But despite their historical significance, they are used very infrequently—less than one or two percent of all criminal trials in England result in trials. Low incidents of serious crime, extensive use of plea, and the fact that most cases are tried at the magistrates' court level keep the number of trial in crown courts to a minimum (Pakes, 2004).

The High Court is both a court of original jurisdiction and a court of appeal for both criminal and civil matters. It consists of about eighty judges,

TABLE 7.1 Court Levels in Model Countries and in the United States

	United States	England	France	Germany	China	Saudi Arabia	Japan
Courts of Last Resort	U.S. Supreme Court and (some) state Supreme Courts	Supreme Court of the United Kingdom (formerly House of Lords)	Court of Cassation	*Bundesgerichtshof and Bundesverfassungsgericht:* constitutional questions only	Supreme People's Court	Supreme Judicial Council	Supreme Court (handles criminal and civil appeals and constitutional questions)
Courts of Intermediate Appeal	U.S. Appellate Division of Supreme Court and state Superior Courts of Appeals	Court of Appeals and High Courts (appeals for criminal and civil cases)	Courts of Appeal (Cours *d'appel)*	*Oberlandesgerichte*	Higher people's courts	Courts of Appeal	High Courts; criminal and civil
Courts of General Jurisdiction	U.S. District Courts; state superior, district, or county courts	Crown Courts (criminal cases); High Courts (civil cases)	Assize Courts (Cours *d'Assise)*	*Landgericht*	Intermediate people's courts	High Courts (formerly Kubra Courts)	District Courts (major cases); criminal and civil
Courts of Limited Jurisdiction	Federal Magistrate Courts; County Magistrate or District Courts or Municipal Courts	Magistrates Court (criminal cases); County Courts (civil cases)	*Tribunaux d'instance:* police and correctional	*Amtsgerichte*	Basic (also called primary) people's courts	First Degree Courts	Summary Courts (minor courts); criminal and civil

who are usually assigned cases based on their own expertise. Cases of original jurisdiction are handled by one judge, and appeals cases by two or three judges.

The Court of Appeals, the intermediate appellate court for England, handles both civil and criminal matters. The judges are selected from the High Court of Justice and the House of Lords and are assigned in groups of four or five to review cases. A unique feature of the Court of Appeals is that the judges can actually add time to the sentence (up to three months) if they feel the appeal made by the convicted was frivolous.

Until 2009 the House of Lords (Parliament) served as the court of last resort for England. Since October 2009, however, this role is now held by the newly created Supreme Court of the United Kingdom. The House of Lords remains one of the three chambers of the English Parliament. The new Supreme Court's main role is to hear appeals from courts in the United Kingdom's three legal systems: England and Wales, Northern Ireland, and Scotland (although the latter has its own final court of appeals for criminal matters). The twelve-person Supreme Court also has jurisdiction to determine disputes among the three governments or legislatures, concentrate on cases, and hear appeals on arguable points of law of general public importance (The Supreme Court, 2012).

Until recently, the function of prosecution was in the hands of police, and larger police agencies had prosecution divisions as part of their organizational structure. In minor cases, police officers were the only prosecution representatives in court. For crown court cases, the police appointed barristers to conduct the cases in court. In 1985 Parliament passed a law setting up the Crown Prosecution Service, taking responsibility for prosecution away from the police and placing it in the hands of crown prosecutors. In doing so, Parliament hoped to assure independence and uniformity in the prosecution of cases, to enhance the quality of prosecutions with the public in mind, and to improve court efficiency (Terrill, 2013).

The clear distinction between prosecution and defense as professions that exists in Civil Law and Socialist Law countries, and even in the United States, does not occur in England. Barristers conduct trials in major cases and are experts in courtroom advocacy; which side they are on is less important than their specialized training to perform in public. Solicitors do not have the "right of audience" before the court. They have all the preliminary contacts with the client, gather the evidence in the case, and share their findings with the barrister assigned to the case about their findings and experiences with the client. However, solicitors are forbidden to participate in crown court cases—that is, the more serious cases. They routinely appear in the lower criminal and civil courts.

"Taking silk" (being allowed to wear a silk gown and a more elaborate wig) is the popular term for appointment to the coveted status of QC, or queen's counsel. The QC is a group of preeminent barristers who serve as counsel to the British Crown. Junior (QC) barristers are those that have been practicing law for less than fifteen years who must apply to the Lord Chancellor to become a QC.

Solicitors and barristers receive slightly different legal training. For a career as a solicitor, one option is to complete a three-year university law degree, then serve for two-and-one-half years in an apprenticeship with a solicitor. Another route is to attend a college of law for one year and then serve a four-year apprenticeship. Barristers must receive a three-year law degree from a university, then must join one of the four ancient Inns of the Court: Middle Temple, Inner Temple, Gray's Inn, and Lincoln's Inn. These clubs are where each barrister serves a one-year pupilage under the supervision of a junior barrister. There they gain knowledge about the complex case law not covered in law school (Terrill, 2013). There are around 116,000 solicitors in England and Wales and only 15,000 barristers. For a comparison box of education and legal training in our model countries and the United States see Box on next page.

The role of Lord Chancellor has changed significantly in recent years. Until 2006, the Lord Chancellor was the head of the judiciary of England and Wales and also charged with making all judicial appointments to the courts. This changed with the passage of the Constitutional Reform Act (2005).

Legal Education and Training for Lawyers in Our Model Countries and the United States

- England: Solicitors—three-year university law degree, then serve an apprenticeship with a solicitor for two-and-one-half years, or attend college of law for one year and then serve a four-year apprenticeship. Barristers—three-year law degree from a university, membership in one of the Inns of the Court, one-year pupilage (apprenticeship) under the supervision of a junior barrister
- France—Baccalaureate (undergraduate) degree, three-year law degree, one year for Master of Law, three-year apprenticeship, and must pass national exam.
- Germany—Abitur (undergraduate) degree, three-and-a-half-year education, apprenticeship, national exam.
- China—Entrance exam, four-year undergraduate program, three-year graduate law education, two additional years of legal work (practicum), national bar exam, and approval by the Ministry of Justice.
- Japan—Undergraduate degree including two years in legal studies, national bar exam, then 18-month apprentice training.
- Saudi Arabia—Five-year secondary education at religious school then attendance at a Shari'a institute.
- United States—Undergraduate college degree and three-year law degree.

Since then, the Lord Chief Justice is the presiding judge of the criminal division of the Court of Appeal and thus President of the Courts of England and Wales and the head of the judiciary; he is responsible for judicial appointments. More specifically, the duties of the President include a) representing the views of the judiciary of England and Wales to Parliament, to the Lord Chancellor, and to Ministers of the Crown generally; (b) maintaining appropriate arrangements for the welfare, training, and guidance of the judiciary of England and Wales within the resources made available by the Lord Chancellor; and (c) maintaining appropriate arrangements for the deployment of the judiciary of England and Wales (Terrill, 2013).

The Constitutional Reform Act (2005) was significant for other reasons than changing the role of the Lord Chief Justice and Lord Chancellor. The Act was responsible for the creation of the aforementioned Supreme Court that opened for business in 2009. It also clearly stated for the first time in 900 years that judges were allowed independence from governmental influence and set up an ombudsman mechanism to supervise judicial conduct. But most important for our purposes here, it formed the Judicial Appointments Commission. This Commission is composed of fifteen commissioners who are appointed by the monarch on the recommendation of the Lord Chancellor. The Commission includes a layperson chair, five members of the judiciary, two lawyers (one barrister and one solicitor), five laypersons, one lay magistrate, and one tribunal member (such as a member of the Immigration Appeal Tribunal). Among the general goals of the Commission are to continue to select people to the judiciary based on merit and to encourage a wider and more diverse pool of well-qualified candidates to apply. Each year the Commission provides data as to the number of applicants and selection recommendations for judicial appointments in England and Wales (JAC, 2010; The Supreme Court, 2010).

COURTS AND THE LEGAL PROFESSION IN FRANCE

The court structure in France is relatively complicated when compared to that of the English. Continental Europe is the realm of the bureaucratized system of courts and state attorneys. The rather formal and rational nature of the Civil Law, compared to the case- and tradition-bound Common Law, is reflected in the court structure, with its prominent administrative courts (themselves part of the government bureaucracy) and its other specialized courts. In general, French courts have lesser concern with procedural detail than England or the United States. At the same time, French courts are accessible and fairly inexpensive for defendants in criminal trials and for parties in civil suits. (For an English explanation of the complex French courts, see http://www.justice.gouv.fr/art_pix/2plaquette_justiceenfrance_angl.pdf.)

Criminal cases in France move up a hierarchy of courts much as they do in Common Law countries. The major difference is that there are three levels of trial courts that hear cases according to the seriousness of the crimes involved. The courts of limited jurisdiction are the nearly five hundred minor courts called *tribunaux d'instance*. There are two kinds of these courts, the first being the police courts (Tribunaux de Police), which handle more than half the criminal cases that arise. Minor misdemeanors and violations (contraventions) are heard by these police courts. The maximum sentence in police court is two months in jail, and the maximum fine is approximately $1,000. Judges in police courts are generally younger and less experienced and are just starting up the hierarchy of judicial positions. Matters in these courts are often dealt with outside the courtroom, and when a trial does occur, it is usually very brief (Frase, 1988).

The other minor court is the correctional courts (Tribunaux Correctionnel) in which more serious misdemeanors (delits) are tried. Generally, three or more judges hear the cases in these courts, and the verdict is by majority vote. However, since 1995 a single judge can hear certain types of delits such as traffic offenses, use of soft drugs, and some financial crimes (Terrill, 2013). The accused has the right to appeal the judgment and demand a new trial in a higher court, the assize court.

In addition to hearing appeals from lower courts, the almost two hundred assize courts (*cours d'assise*) have original jurisdiction in major felony cases. In appeals from lower courts, three judges handle the case. In cases where it is a court of original jurisdiction, the court employs three professional and nine lay judges. Unlike the English judge and jury system, in which the jury decides matters of fact and the judge decides matters of law, the French tribunal considers both matters as a group. Further, decision is by a plurality of eight votes rather than by the unanimous or (in some jurisdictions) near-unanimous vote required in the U.S. system for conviction in major criminal cases. Decisions on the sentence, which are made at the same time, are by majority vote. Both verdict and sentence are announced after the deliberations of the tribunal. This court also handles cases involving serious crimes committed by juvenile offenders.

The French courtroom presents a different aspect from the English one. As a legacy of the revolutionary tradition, there are fewer signs of pomp or status. The professional and lay judges seem almost huddled together in the front of the courtroom, which is not raised as prominently as the bench in English courts. However, prosecutors and defense attorneys do wear black gowns with starched white collars when appearing in court.

The case file, or dossier, is available to all the judges prior to the trial. Nevertheless, in cases before the assize courts, the "principle of orality" requires that all evidence be brought out in open court. In the correctional and police courts, it is not necessary to go through each step of the case and each piece of evidence at the actual trial, as is the case in England and the United States. Although spectators may not get the complete recounting of all the facts and circumstances of the case, the judges have all the information at hand (Ingraham, 1987, pp. 86–87; Delmas-Marty and Spencer, 2002, pp. 260, 513).

For civil and criminal cases that are decided at a level lower than that of the assize courts, appeals go to one of the twenty-seven judicial districts and the thirty-three courts of appeal (Cours d'Appel). These courts hear appeals from the lower civil and criminal courts and from a plethora of special courts, including the commercial court and the juvenile court. Three to five judges rule on cases and decide on points of law and of fact (Abraham, 1986; Delmas-Marty and Spencer, 2002, p. 271). Disputes over points of law can be appealed to the next court level.

The highest level of appeal is the Court of Cassation (Cour de Cassation), which hears appeals from the assize courts and the courts of appeal. The Court of Cassation sits in five chambers with fifteen judges in each, although only seven need be present to hear a case. Criminal cases are heard in only one of these chambers. In criminal cases, as opposed to civil cases, the Court of Cassation must hear appeals. Therefore, it does not have the authority to turn down cases, as the U.S. Supreme Court does in most instances through its power to grant or deny a writ of certiorari.

In March 2010 a major reform in the French courts occurred with the reform of the Constitutional Council, which prior to that time did not hear cases but only decided on the constitutionality of laws at the request of high government officials. Now individuals can call on judges in lower courts to rule on constitutional issues and allow the Council itself to rule on specific legislative matters, especially as they relate to individual liberties. This change is significant for the Court of Cassation because it is no longer the default organ for interpreting the constitutionality of certain kinds of legislation (Hunter-Henin, 2011).

The legal professions in both France and Germany fall into the category of bureaucratic systems, and both fall within the Civil Law family. Because there are many similarities between the legal professions of the two countries, it is convenient to group them together. We will discuss the legal professions in France and Germany in tandem after our discussion of German courts.

COURTS AND THE LEGAL PROFESSION IN GERMANY

German trial courts are similar in style and tradition to the French courts. Procedure is based on the inquisitorial model, including extensive pretrial investigation with which the accused is expected to cooperate. As in France, however, procedural safeguards based on the adversarial model, such as the right to an attorney at the trial and pretrial stages of the criminal process, dilute the inquisitorial nature of the process.

The judicial system in Germany consists of three types of courts: (1) ordinary courts, which handle criminal and most civil cases; (2) specialized courts, which hear cases related to administrative issues; and (3) constitutional courts, which deal with judicial review and constitutional interpretation.

At the ordinary level, there are four tiers of courts. The *Amtsgerichte*, which by our earlier classification are courts of limited jurisdiction, hear minor criminal and civil cases at the local level. Many of these more than seven thousand courts are staffed by a single judge, but in some criminal cases, lay judges provide assistance. A large percentage of cases in Germany—for example, minor crimes such as routine traffic offenses—are disposed of through summary procedures and fines at the police and prosecutorial levels. The prosecutor also has the power to handle criminal cases through summary procedures, in which a disposition is offered to a defendant and the case proceeds no further if the disposition is accepted. An accused may always assert the right to trial rather than accepting the summary actions of either police or prosecutor.

Above the *Amtsgerichte* level are courts of general jurisdiction called the *Landgerichte*, which are the more than a hundred regional courts trying major criminal and civil cases and hearing appeals from the amtsgerichte courts. At the top level of the state (Länder) court system are the twenty-four *Oberlandesgerichte*, which primarily hear points of law raised in appeals in the lower courts, thus are courts of intermediate appeal, and hold original jurisdiction in cases of treason and anticonstitutional activity. The fourth ordinary court, called the *Bundesgerichtshof*, or Federal Court of Justice, handles final appeals (thus a court of last resort) in all cases from the lower courts except those involving constitutional interpretation.

The Germans are known for their many specialized courts that deal with five areas: social security, labor, tax law, administrative law, and patent law. These courts are organized on the local, Länder, and federal levels, and within their own subject area. With regard to the constitutional courts, any judge in Germany who believes that a constitutional question is involved in a case may refer that question to the *Bundesverfassungsgericht*, the Federal Constitutional Court. However, individual appellants who believe that their constitutional rights have been violated generally may not appeal to the Federal Constitutional Court until they have exhausted all other avenues of petition and appeal. The Federal Constitutional Court consists of sixteen judges and does not actually decide the outcome of cases; rather, it rules on the constitutional question involved and then returns the case to the lower court for final disposition.

As mentioned, lay judges in Germany serve in courts of limited jurisdiction and in higher-level courts with general criminal jurisdiction (crimes involving potential sentences of three or more years in prison). In the lower criminal courts, we find two lay judges and one professional judge. In the courts in which more serious crimes are tried, there are three professional judges but only two lay judges. The verdict in a trial is by majority vote, so the lay judges theoretically can have an important voice in deciding guilt or innocence. In reality, however, the professional judges dominate both the questioning of the accused and witnesses and the deliberations about the verdict. Since there is no separate jury, the judge does not instruct a jury formally in matters of law, but instead informs the lay judges about the law as part of the general deliberations leading to a verdict. Appeals in criminal cases are heard by professional judges and are restricted to matters of law (Delmas-Marty, 2002, p. 306).

As in England, legal education in France and Germany is both a product of the legal culture and a major influence on the development of the legal profession. In both countries, legal education in its earliest stages consists of a basic university education that encompasses general liberal arts courses and some courses in the law.

In Germany, with its federal structure, basic regulations for legal education are set by the central government with rigorous federal examination requirements have dictated a fairly uniform system. Upon receiving the academic secondary school degree (known as the *baccalaureate* in France and the *abitur* in Germany), students in both countries are eligible to enter the law school at one of the state universities. Both countries continue to have unacceptably large numbers of law students in the various universities (Glendon, Gordon, and Osakwe, 1985, ch. 3). These students do not all go on to become legal professionals, however. In fact, a law school education in these countries also provides the basic liberal education for students who do not wish to go to professional schools of medicine, science, or various technologies.

With respect to duration of studies, the law student in France may graduate in three years with a general degree, known as the *license*. Those who plan to enter the legal profession generally go on to a fourth year, leading to the degree of magister, or master of law. Students must pass national examinations in order to obtain these degrees.

Germany also has a unified bar with a national examination, or *staatsexamen*, that follows three and a half years of university education. German experiments with a more "practical" legal education (often inspired by the case-based education that American students receive) have been limited by the national requirements regarding length and content of study.

University education is followed by an intensive apprenticeship and further training in both France and Germany. In Germany, the decision to specialize is deferred, and the apprenticeship, known as the *referendar* period, rotates students among different specialties. In the end, however, students in both countries must take rigorous examinations to qualify for the civil service positions of judge or prosecutor or the advocacy positions in the law—known as *advocats* in France and *Rechtsanwälte* in Germany (Salas and Alvarez, 2002). Once embarked on a specialty, the student has little opportunity to change career paths. The only major exception to this rule is that in France prosecutors may switch to the judiciary, and vice versa (David, 1972).

There are a number of differences between the courts and the legal professions in Germany and the United States. First, during the trial in Germany, expert witnesses are called and paid for by the state. Second, it is possible for the prosecution to appeal acquittals in criminal cases. However, the law does not allow an increase in severity of sentence if the appeal is successful. Third, all cases in Germany are tried in the state courts and may move through various levels of state jurisdiction before being brought to a federal court of final appeal. Fourth, the five federal supreme courts in Germany are technically the final courts of appeal. The Federal Constitutional Court has the last word in interpreting the constitution, but it remands cases to the lower courts for disposition based on its opinions. Fifth, there are a large number of specialized courts in Germany, for hearing trials and appeals related to social security, labor, tax law, administrative law, and conventional civil and criminal law. Also, with about one-third the population of the United States, it has more than twice as many judges overall. Sixth and finally, due to the bureaucratic method of judge selection, judges in Germany (and France) are much younger than those in United States.

COURTS AND THE LEGAL PROFESSION IN CHINA

The structure of the formal court system in China, first developed in 1949 after the establishment of the People's Republic of China, is outlined in the Constitution and Organic Law of the People's Courts. Chinese courts are highly centralized and organized along four levels: (1) basic (also called primary) people's courts, (2) intermediate people's courts, (3) higher people's courts, and (4) the Supreme People's Court. Except for the Supreme People's Court, each of these courts operates in different geographic territories that include provinces, autonomous regions, municipalities, prefectures, cities, counties, and city districts (Guo et al., 1999).

The lowest level court of limited jurisdiction in the formal Chinese court system is the basic people's court, which is found in each county and municipal area. These courts, around three thousand in number, handle most criminal, civil, and economic matters of first instance unless the matter is a special case. Factors that can make a case "special" include severity and provincial or national importance. Another important purpose of the basic people's courts is to coordinate the people's mediation committees.

People's mediation committees (PMCs), also called grassroots committees, are one of the three informal social control mechanisms implemented throughout China and the only one under the control of the formal court system. The other two—public security committees and security departments of commercial enterprises and institutions—are supervised by the police branch and serve as crime prevention measures. PMCs are found in the workplace, schools, rural areas, and city neighborhoods (Zhang et al., 1996). There are over one million of these committees throughout China.

The PMCs have a two-thousand-year history in China, going back to the early days of Confucianism. The general idea behind the PMC is that harsh punishment does not necessarily control behavior and that moral education is the most prudent method of correcting behavior. A PMC has five to seven members who use the force of public opinion and education to persuade those involved in minor disputes and misdemeanors to resolve their problems without formal court intervention. Therefore, only the most serious crimes are dealt with by the formal court system, with less serious criminal behaviors and civil matters generally disposed of locally through people's mediation (Situ and Liu, 1996, p. 135; Liang, 2008).

The parties involved must agree beforehand to mediation. During mediation, the parties discuss the offense, relevant laws, and the public interest in the matter, and then reach an agreement. The agreement has the force of law and, if violated, could result in further legal action (Ai, 1989). From the 1970s to the early 2000s, the number of cases going to the PMCs decreased nearly 50% (Liang, 2008, p. 183).

More recently, judicial mediation has been revived in China. The revival has occurred as a result of a combination of political and juridical forces. China's courts have been struggling to keep up with the increasing number of cases before them and the growing demand for access to justice. Much of this demand can be traced to the economic and civil law cases resulting from a changing economy that allows for a freer market and more private ownership of businesses (Peerenboom, 2010). Also, the revival of judicial mediation is a reaction of the Chinese government to the growing influence of the adversarial, Western-style legal process. As a result, the judicial mediation has been called upon again as a part of a broader policy to promote mediation as a mainstream dispute-resolution mechanism (Wayne and Xiong, 2011).

Two other formal courts have special legal jurisdiction equal to the basic people's courts. The first are people's tribunals, which handle the duties of the basic people's courts both in rural areas and in large urban districts like Beijing. The decisions of these more than eighteen thousand tribunals are equal in weight to those of the basic people's courts, and any appeal goes directly to the next level, the intermediate people's courts. The second group of formal courts, called the special people's courts, are also equal in the court hierarchy to the basic people's courts: these courts handle military, railway, and maritime matters.

The intermediate people's courts are the courts of general jurisdiction in China; they handle serious criminal, civil, and, economic cases of first instance at the municipal and prefectural levels. They also deal with serious cases that might be transferred from basic people's courts, including murder, rape, robbery, bombing, arson, and grand larceny, as well as special cases related to counterrevolution or involving the death penalty or life imprisonment and cases involving foreigners. These almost four hundred courts also handle appeals from the basic people's courts, and protests from procurators from the lower courts about the decision of a case.

The next level in the formal Chinese court system is the higher people's courts. These thirty courts handle criminal, civil, and economic matters of first instance that may affect the entire province, autonomous region, or municipality, and matters of second instance (appeal) from the intermediate courts. Like the intermediate courts, they also handle first-instance crimes transferred from lower courts and cases protested by the procurator.

The highest court is the Supreme People's Court of China, which deals with matters of national importance. Most of the cases that come before this court are appeals from the next lower level, the higher people's courts. It is divided into seven permanent divisions: two criminal divisions and a single division each for administrative issues, civil matters, communications and transport, complaints and petitions, and economic matters (Terrill, 2013). The criminal courts mostly handle appeals of serious felony crimes, including death penalty cases. The Supreme People's Court also provides explanations and advice to lower courts, interprets laws, and supervises the administration of the military courts.

Every court at every level must consist of a president, two or more vice presidents, one chief judge, and several deputy judges and assistant judges. The president is elected by the people's congress at the corresponding level, while other members are appointed by the standing committees of those congresses. Every court must also set up a judicial committee, whose members are selected by the National People's Congress, to deal with the most difficult or most important cases (Davidson and Wang, 1996).

However, the actual trying of cases in the basic people's, intermediate people's, and higher people's courts is done either by one judge if it is a minor criminal matter or by a collegial bench. The collegial bench is composed of one to three judges and two to four people's assessors depending on the case and court level. The people's assessors are citizens who must be elected, at least 23 years of age, and eligible to vote (Situ and Liu, 1996, p. 129).

Although people's assessors are an important component of trials and involve the public in judicial proceedings, and although technically they may represent a majority when it comes to a verdict, they are not likely to disagree with professional judges on matters of either fact or law. In this way, lay assessors are similar to lay judges in Germany, who follow the leadership of the professional judge in almost all cases. The professional judges are chosen for individual trials by the president or vice president of the respective court.

If we compare the court system of the People's Republic of China with our other model countries, we see a number of both similarities and differences. All of our model countries, including China, have a hierarchical court structure with certain jurisdictional limits; that is, they only handle cases within their own bailiwick. The different levels also handle appeals from the lower levels. Another similarity is the use of laypeople as adjudicators. In China, the collegial panel consists of professional and lay assessors. Lay judges are also used in Germany, and laypeople serve as jurors in serious crimes in England and the United States.

Differences also are clearly evident. Unlike in Common Law countries, Chinese judges are unable to make law. As a result, they often handle cases very flexibly and in accordance with the needs of the government (Leng, 1982). Another significant difference is the extensive informal system in China that prevents cases from moving level by level through the formal court system. The PMCs handle over four million minor civil and criminal matters every year (Liang, 2008).

The Chinese courts are also averse to the implementation of many procedural rights that are available in other countries. The presumption of innocence, the exclusionary rule, protections against self-incrimination, the right to trial by jury, and protection against being tried twice for the same offense (double jeopardy) are absent in Chinese criminal justice (Situ and Liu, 1996). Finally, there are clearly serious questions relative to the issue of judicial independence in China (Zhang, 2002). Verdicts in important legal cases are reviewed by the president of the court, and the most difficult cases are dealt with by the judicial committee. This may at first seem to constitute an extensive method of checks and balances. After review, however, one finds that the president and members of the judicial committee are, in effect, political appointments selected by the National People's Congress, which means that the principle of judicial independence essentially is absent in China.

Since the formation of the People's Republic in 1949, the legal profession in China has undergone a number of considerable changes. After the Communist Chinese came to power, the number of lawyers dwindled to below three thousand, and their influence was reduced considerably. This situation turned from bad to worse in the political turmoil of the late 1950s. The Anti-Rightist Campaign attacked lawyers with considerable vigor, claiming that, by defending criminals and protecting the economic interests of clients, lawyers were in direct conflict with Socialist ideology. Many lawyers were labeled capitalists and rightists and were often persecuted, law offices were closed, and the Ministry of Justice was disbanded (Lawyers Committee, 1998b, p. 15). The Cultural Revolution of 1966–76 resumed the attack on the legal profession, basically abolishing the legal profession and halting the training of new lawyers (Leng and Chiu, 1985).

Following the Cultural Revolution, the Ministry of Justice was reestablished, and all law departments and schools were reopened. With Deng Xiaoping's broad reforms came massive amounts of legislation and the need for qualified lawyers. In 1982 there were only 5,500 lawyers in China, but by the early 1990s the number had grown to 50,000 and by 2007 had risen dramatically again to approximately 130,000 (Situ and Liu, 1996; Clark, 2008). More good news is the growing number of law schools and law students in China. Recent studies show that the number of law schools has increased from 300 in the 1990s to 560 with almost 450,000 law students by the mid-2000s (Lancaster and Xiangshun, 2007; McMorrow, 2010). Although a drastic increase from only ten years earlier, the numbers of lawyers in China remains small in number considering the size of the population, the legal needs of citizens, and the fact that half of the lawyers work part-time as law teachers or legal researchers.

Two pieces of legislation have been paramount in the development of the legal profession in China over the past thirty years. The first, the Provisional Regulations of the PRC on Lawyers, was passed by the National People's Congress in 1980. This law outlined the purpose, rights, activities, and qualifications of lawyers in China and called for an increase in the expansion of the legal profession while calling for lawyers to "serve the cause of socialism" (Lawyers Committee, 1998b, p. 17). The second was the Lawyers Law, which in 1996 was unanimously passed by the Standing Committee of the National People's Congress to address issues such as low pay and protection from governmental influence (Lu and Miethe, 2002).

The Lawyers Law appears to be a serious attempt to improve the quality of legal representation and rule of law. However, it is generally believed that, because of the strong political influence of Communist party, the Lawyers Law lacks some of the essential elements stated in the Basic Principles on the Role of Lawyers as outlined by the United Nations. In comparison with the Basic Principles, the Lawyers Law fails to address lawyers' freedom of expression, due process concerns, and the duty to uphold human rights as recognized in international law (Lawyers Committee, 1998b, p. 46).

The term *lawyer* in China actually refers to a professional who is a legal representative or attorney-at-law and excludes judges, law teachers, and legal scholars. Law teachers and scholars devote most of their time to teaching and research and sometimes dabble in part-time law or legislative drafting. The role of defense counsel in China is very different from that in most other countries (Mc Morrow, 2010). Individuals can represent themselves or allow another to represent them. The legal representative can be a lawyer, someone from an organization the defendant belongs to, or even a relative or friend. Chinese defense attorneys are "encouraged" to help the court render a just verdict. Although the job of the defense counsel is supposedly to prove that the defendant is innocent, the reality in China is that the defense counsel in most cases can only act to help mitigate the severity of the sentence. Until recently, defense attorneys in China were not allowed to meet with defendants until the trial, defense counsel had restricted access to information about the case prior to the trial, and in some cases trials began without defense counsel's having been notified about the case (Chenguang and Xianchu, 1997). There still is some question as to whether Chinese defense lawyers are able to meet with clients, see court transcripts such as confessions, and avoid personal intimidation and detention (Rosenthal, 2000).

Judges in China at most levels are poorly educated and lack any formal legal training. Until recently, many judges were selected from among former military officers. However, efforts have also been made to improve judicial qualifications and standards with passage of the Judges Law, which set new standards for judges (Zhang, 2002). To improve the quality of judges at the lower-court levels, China has established a National University of Judges, and the Supreme People's Court has formed a special training center for senior judges.

Legal training for advocates in China is tightly regulated by the Ministry of Justice and the Ministry of Education. In recent years, law has become an important field of study in China, with the subject being studied in high schools and in numerous kinds of training courses. To pursue a formal career in law as a lawyer, court administrator, procurator, or law enforcement officer, one must first take a national exam to enter either a university law department or legal institute. While in the four-year university program, students take courses in Chinese legal history, political science, foreign languages, and various kinds of law. In the legal institutes, the training is more practical in nature, with courses in investigation, forensics, and criminology (Terrill, 2009). To complete their legal training and become lawyers, students must complete three years of graduate law education and two additional years of legal work, pass a national bar exam, and be approved by the Ministry of Justice.

COURTS AND THE LEGAL PROFESSION IN JAPAN

Japanese court structures, like those of other modern countries, form a hierarchy that begins with the lower courts, known as summary courts, which have limited jurisdiction but do handle minor criminal and civil cases. Procedures in these courts are usually very brief with very few formal trials (Research and Training Institute, 1996). If the defendant agrees, the judge, who is not necessarily a trained lawyer, can decide the case based on the evidence in the case file and on the prosecutor's sentence recommendation. Neither side appears before the judge. If the prosecutor or the defense is unhappy with the ruling, they can ask for a formal trial (Castberg, 1990). If the criminal case before one of the 438 summary courts would result in a prison term of more than three years, or if the civil case would result in a fine of more than 1.4 million yen, then the case would be handled by the district courts level.

The fifty district courts, one each in every prefecture and three in Hokkaido, are courts of general jurisdiction that handle civil and criminal cases and matters that have been appealed from the summary courts by the prosecution or the defense. At the same level as district courts are the family courts, which handle most domestic and juvenile cases.

A single judge presides over most district court cases. In important criminal cases, a three-judge court may be convened. Three judges are always necessary when the sentence would result in imprisonment of more than a year or a death sentence or when civil cases are heard on appeal from the summary courts. Most cases at this level are handled quickly because many defendants confess to the charges brought before the court. When the defendant does contest the charges, a formal trial ensues.

The high courts in Japan are courts of immediate appeal. They generally handle cases that are appealed from the district or family courts, but they also deal with appeals that come directly from summary courts and with cases of initial jurisdiction when a person is charged with insurrection or sedition. Each of the eight high courts has a president and a group of judges, from which a panel of three are chosen to hear an appeal. Although high court cases normally have three judges, in extraordinary cases there may be five. After individual cases are decided, a written majority opinion is provided. If the decision is appealed, it is brought before the Supreme Court.

The Supreme Court is the highest court in Japan and is the final court of appeal in civil and criminal cases. In addition, the Supreme Court, according to the Japanese Constitution (Article 81), determines "the constitutionality of any law, order, regulation, or official act." It is also responsible for nominating judges to the lower courts, determining judicial procedures and training, and supervising the judicial system. Interestingly, the judges on the Supreme Court in Japan are somewhat older and serve less time on the bench than in many other countries. This is due to the fact that, except in extreme cases, the judges are not appointed until at least sixty-four years of age and they are required to retire at age seventy (Repeta, 2011).

In the rare cases dealing with constitutional questions, all fifteen members of the bench preside; eight justices must agree for a law to be declared unconstitutional. For all other cases, the court divides into panels of five justices. Unlike in the high court, both opinions of the court are provided, and the justices can express their personal views on the case (Terrill, 2013).

The Supreme Court of Japan has not developed as the potent political force that the U.S. Supreme Court or even the German Supreme Court have during their histories. This may reflect the fact that Japan has not traditionally been a nation in which the assertion of individual rights and recourse to litigation have been culturally accepted. An important function of the Japanese Supreme Court is general oversight of court administration throughout the country. The U.S. Supreme Court exercises this function for the federal system, and the state supreme courts exercise it for their systems, usually through a separate administrative office.

Judges in Japan have a bureaucratic career trajectory similar to the French model. Judges are chosen upon finishing study at the Legal Research and Training Institute—that is, at a relatively young age—and are reappointed to successive ten-year terms throughout their careers. Since they start at the lowest level and their chances for elevation to higher courts depend on their winning the approval of their superiors, they tend to be conservative and cautious in their approach, rarely handing down unpopular or controversial opinions (Feeley, 2002).

One of the most interesting features of the Japanese legal profession is that, relative to the population, there are very few lawyers. In 2007 there were 24,302 attorneys in Japan. In comparison, the United States produces almost three times as many lawyers each year. These figures comparing lawyers in the United States and Japan are somewhat misleading however, in that they do not count the people in Japan called *quasi-lawyers* who are performing the functions that in the United States would be performed by lawyers such as doing legal research; drawing up legal papers; advising on tax problems; and dealing with inheritances, divorces, and commercial contracts.

The stark contrast between the numbers of lawyers in the two nations is usually explained by the fact that the Japanese people are not as litigious as Americans. According to this analysis, the ideals of harmony and conciliation are so strong in Japan that few people will embark on the inherently conflictual process of formal adjudication. The dearth of lawyers ensures that citizens will find informal ways to settle conflicts rather than taking these conflicts to court. The result is the increased use of mediation in which legal disputes between parties are resolved informally with a mediator rather than through formal court involvement. One common form of mediation is to solve minor disputes between two parties through mediation with police officers and lawyers acting as judges. Another is the use of summary courts that handle minor civil matters and are staffed by untrained lawyers and court clerks.

Finally, since 1949 the Japanese have implemented Civil Liberties Bureaus. The bureaus were formed to hear complaints and provide remedies for individuals whose civil liberties had been infringed. Civil Liberties Bureau personnel are volunteer unpaid commissioners who are nominated by their localities and confirmed by the Ministry of Justice. There are over 11,000 volunteer commissioners, operating in every town and neighborhood. It had roughly the same mission as the Civil Rights Section of the U.S. Department of Justice and undoubtedly was a brainchild of post–World War II reconstructionists in Japan.

It is hoped that changes in the training of lawyers will reduce the dearth of Japanese lawyers. In 2002, the Japanese Diet (Parliament) passed a series of laws and standards, as suggested by the Judicial Reform Council, to increase the number of lawyers and make legal services more accessible to the public. The new laws and standards called for new law schools, new training procedures, increased diversity, and a new bar exam. Unfortunately, the results of this effort were not very successful. Specifically, one of the goals of the 2002 legislation was to increase the rate of those passing the bar exam from 40–50% to 80%. What happened was the opposite: The rate of passage dropped to 24% by 2011 (Nottage and Green, 2011). Results like these have an impact on the number of attorneys available to defend and prosecute criminals and to address the civil cases that arise in Japan.

Only public procurators (prosecutors) are allowed to initiate the prosecution of criminal cases and to direct enforcement of criminal sanctions. Prosecutors in Japan have two major roles: (1) to investigate and collect evidence in the case and (2) to provide information to the judge about the suspect to assist in sentencing. One unique feature of criminal procedure in Japan is the ability to suspend prosecution even when the prosecutor can prove the offender committed a crime. According to the Japanese Criminal Procedure Code (Article 248), if the prosecutor feels the crime or criminal represents or reflects some special situation, he or she can choose to suspend the matter. Among the special situations that can trigger a suspended sentence are the age of the offender, an expression of remorse, the possibility of rehabilitation, and a desire to avoid the stigma attached to being formally processed through the criminal justice system.

Defense attorneys, called private advocates, are provided for all those accused of a crime in Japan. If the accused is indigent, a lawyer is appointed from a list of attorneys from one of the two local branches of the Japanese Bar Association. Although only indigent offenders are eligible for court-appointed counsel, because the court does not often check the financial status of clients there have been some abuses of the system. To address the growing number of persons seeking court-appointed counsel, the Japanese have devised a system called duty lawyers. Duty lawyers meet with the arrested or detained defendant in a court case once free of charge. Defendants who want to retain the lawyer must then apply for legal aid for pretrial defense. This appears to have improved the abuse of the appointed-lawyer problem for the immediate future, although this system still relies on the volunteerism of local attorneys, who often feel that they are insufficiently compensated for such work (Murayama, 2002, pp. 46–48). Because of the high confession rate (over 90 percent) and low crime rate in Japan, there is little business for private advocates, and they must often do other kinds of legal work to make a living (Castberg, 1990; Foote, 2002).

The Japanese judicial process has historically allowed for little opportunity for the citizen involvement in court decisions, either through juries or lay judges. Japan did have a short-lived experiment with juries between 1928 and 1943, during which time a defendant in a felony case could request a jury trial. Because of the course of Japanese history and the cultural realities at that time, the use of juries was not well accepted. However, there has been a recent change to this practice, or lack thereof, and it is sure to change the way Japanese citizens view the criminal justice system for years to come.

In 2009 the Japanese instituted a mixed jury system called *saiban-in seido* (Ohtsubo, 2006). The system calls for the use of lay assessors for serious cases in which there is considerable public interest. The *saiban-in* has been designed with three purposes in mind: (1) to get citizens involved so as to improve understanding and support for the system of justice, (2) to reduce the time it takes to take a case to trial, and (3) to make the criminal justice system more understandable for citizens through increased participation. Lay assessors will be selected from a pool of candidates and asked to serve for one year along with others on a panel consisting of four to six *saiban-in seido* and one to three professional judges (Terrill, 2013).

In the period immediately following its inception, the *saiban-in* received considerable criticism from judges, lawyers, and citizens. But it appears that, three years into implementation, the *saiban-in* system has been accepted as an effective method of judicial decision making. Among the positive results that have been observed are an increased number of cases solved, a more transparent trial process, increased levels of citizen participation, and the full support of higher court levels in Japan. In fact, there has been talk in Japan about the possibility of expanding the *saiban-in* system to the civil court system (Wilson, 2012).

Comparison of the legal profession in Japan with that in our other model countries again shows some basic similarities and differences. It is very difficult to become a lawyer in Japan, and there are very few lawyers there. Essentially, advocates and public professionals have higher status than advisors, although Japan does not have the colorful differences that one finds in England.

Despite efforts by the postwar American occupation authorities to create a more political third branch of government in the sense that such a branch exists in the United States, Japan has largely reverted to the bureaucratic Civil Law model, with career judges and prosecutors chosen according to merit and rising through the ranks of a hierarchical organization (Feeley, 2002).

COURTS AND THE LEGAL PROFESSION IN SAUDI ARABIA

There have been some significant changes earmarked for the Saudi Arabian judicial system because of a royal decree signed by King Abdullah called the Judiciary Law of 2007. The intention of the new law is to shape the Saudi judicial system so that it can meet higher judicial standards and respond to the changing social and economic needs of Saudi society. As a result of the Judiciary

Law, the Saudis have a new judicial arrangement with three primary court levels: the high courts, courts of appeal, and first-degree courts. The new judicial system will assume jurisdiction over most of the civil, commercial, and criminal disputes previously decided by various administrative committees. In most cases, however, the minister of justice, appointed by the king, presides over the judicial system.

The first-degree courts, which are similar to courts of general jurisdiction, are located throughout the country and will divide their caseloads among Labor, Commercial, Criminal, Personal Status, and General Circuits. Each of these is further divided into specialized courts. For example, the General Courts will handle traffic cases, the Personal Courts will handle divorce and the Criminal Court will consist of the following specialized circuits: *qisas* (retaliatory punishment) cases, *hudud* cases (prescribed punishment), ta'zir (discretionary punishment) cases, and juvenile cases. The criminal court will be composed of a three-judge panel. Cases in other courts will be heard by one judge (Terrill, 2013).

The next level serve as intermediate appeals courts, and they are called *courts of appeals*. These courts can overturn decisions by lower courts and take over for the former courts of cassation; they will be established in all thirteen provinces. Each court will function through specialized circuits comprised of three three-judge panels, except for the criminal circuit, which reviews judgments involving certain major crimes, including those which bear the death sentence. It will be composed of five judge panels. Courts of appeals will consist of the following circuits: labor, commercial, criminal, personal status, and civil. Each circuit will be composed of a president appointed by the chief of the appellate court and judges holding the rank of appellate judge. The courts of appeals will hear appealable decisions from lower courts. They will render their judgment after hearing the litigants' arguments in accordance with the Law of Procedure before Shari'a courts and the Law of Criminal Procedure.

Finally, a new court called the High Court will replace the Supreme Judicial Council as the highest authority in the judicial system. The High Court will review rulings issued or upheld by the courts of appeals, including those relating to cases punishable by death and certain other major crimes. The High Court will also review judgments and decisions issued or supported by the courts of appeals on matters not previously addressed (Ansary, 2010). The King of Saudi Arabia can give a pardon or serve as a final appeal to determine whether a verdict was in consonance with the Shari'a (Moore, 1996).

Prior to the implementation of the Judiciary Law, the Supreme Judicial Council served as the highest court of appeal in Saudi Arabia. It will now perform several administrative roles, including supervision of the Shari'a courts and all members of the judiciary. It will also ensure that judges in Saudi Arabia are allowed judicial independence.

In 2008 a special criminal court was formed in Riyadh to deal with terrorism cases. The court is directed toward those accused of joining Al-Qaeda or threatening national security. Charges can involve implementing a terrorist act, such as armed attacks; the manufacture and processing of explosives; car bombings; and hiding known terrorists, in addition to collecting information about people and places, recruiting members, training recruits, fundraising for a movement, illicit arms trading, and facilitating members of a terrorist cell (Terrill, 2013).

Despite the significant changes in the Shari'a court structure, Saudi Arabia has retained an independent administrative judicial commission that responds directly to the King called the Board of Grievances. The Board of Grievances, much like the French Council of State, hears cases involving government rulings and actions including relations of foreign businessmen to the Saudi government. The board has three levels of judicial administrative courts, each with appellate jurisdiction over a lower court or administrative commission.

Not surprisingly, judges in Saudi Arabia require significant training and study in the Islamic law. In addition to meeting several general requirements, aspiring advocates and judges are required to attend religions preparatory schools for five years prior to attending the Shari'a institutes or colleges. After graduation, future judges must attend a Judicial

Academy and an Institute of Public Administration at which they will learn their craft, including two months of training in the commercial, labor, and criminal procedure laws and other relevant regulations. In addition to the judges' educational legal training, Saudi Arabia assigns newly appointed judges to a court for a two-year probation period so that they can become acquainted with its working procedures. During the probation period, the judges are given simple cases and settlements that are referred to them by the court's presiding judge, who reviews and approves the judgment before it is handed down.

Saudi lawyers who practice in court must be male Muslims, a requirement that not only reinforces elite status for this group but also highlights the importance of the religious tradition that infuses national life. According to Islamic tradition, it is not necessary to have a trained advocate in criminal trials. In the Shari'a courts, in fact, the accused are expected to defend themselves, calling on legal counsel, relatives, friends, fellow employees, and others to advise them. Counsel by nonlawyers formerly was so prevalent, amounting to the practice of law without a license, that a Saudi law now regulates the number of cases allowed to be handled by lay counsel (Amin, 1985b, p. 325). Licensed attorneys may also be the advocates of choice. The Ministry of Justice issues licenses for those who wish to practice before Shari'a courts. The Ministry of Commerce issues licenses for practice before the administrative and commercial courts and for general work as a solicitor (Nader, 1990, p. 14). Thus, the dichotomy between these two types of courts is reinforced at the earliest stages of a lawyer's career. Foreign lawyers may act as advisors but not as advocates in Saudi courts.

Court procedures in Saudi Arabia's Shari'a courts are quite informal by Western standards, perhaps because of the long tradition of *quadi* justice, in which the *quadi*, an agent of the caliph, heard and decided cases on an individual basis. As mentioned previously, *quadi* is still the term used to describe Islamic judges who decide cases in the Shari'a courts based on the facts according to their own wisdom and the principles of the religious law. Courtrooms in Saudi Arabia may simply be small rooms in a government building, and proceedings may be held in secret if the judge determines that the interests of morality demand it. Journalists are not permitted in court, and spectators are rarely present.

SUPRANATIONAL COURTS

As we mentioned briefly in Chapter 6, there are now judicial mechanisms that direct judges' decisions across international borders and supposedly have a higher legal standing than decisions of courts in individual countries. The trend to form these judicial mechanisms, called supranational courts, is part of a larger trend to promote global human rights and global justice. The main goals of supranational courts are two in number. First, supranational courts serve to help provide individual citizens who have exhausted all their legal means of redress but still feel that they have been wronged by the justice system in a particular country. Second, supranational courts serve to hold those responsible for international law violations to a higher standard than are present in domestic courts. Relative to the latter goal, we have learned throughout history that allowing serious criminals to escape accountability for their acts can have a negative and long-term impact on a country and often leads to future turmoil. The remainder of this chapter will discuss the historical background, current status, and jurisdictional range of supranational courts. It is important to mention that our discussion here includes only supranational courts that address matters related to criminal justice. There are other supranational courts that deal with a variety of noncriminal justice matters, such as the International Tribunal for the Law of the Sea located in Hamburg, Germany, and the Permanent Court of Arbitration in The Hague.

The Background of Supranational Courts

The idea of developing courts to handle legal matters across boundaries and/or for violations of international standards is not a novel one. For centuries, serious violations of international law (i.e., war crimes) were prosecuted in the national criminal courts where the violations occurred, and this method continued well into the twentieth century. An actual prosecution for violations across boundaries, instituted by two or more states, was believed to occur first in 1474, when Peter von Hagenbach was tried by twenty-eight judges of the allied states of the Holy Roman Empire. He was prosecuted and beheaded for "violations of the laws of God and man" because he allowed troops to commit war atrocities during the Swiss-Burgundian War of 1474 (Bassiouni, 1991; McCormack, 1997; Schabas, 2007). It is believed that modern history of international judicial arbitration dates back to the Jay Treaty of 1794, when the United States and Great Britain agreed to settle a number of unresolved issues that were present after the American Revolution. The nineteenth century brought at least two attempts to prosecute individuals for acts of military aggression: first an unsuccessful prosecution for Napoléon early in the eighteenth century, and later trials for "crimes against humanity" in Crete following the Cadia massacres in 1898.

The first multinational criminal court was convened after World War I and signing of the Versailles Treaty of 1919, which called for a special international tribunal to prosecute Germany's Kaiser Wilhelm II. However, the trial never occurred because Wilhelm fled to the Netherlands for sanctuary. Also at that time, an unsuccessful attempt was made by the League of Nations to establish an international tribunal to deal with war crimes. Instead, more than three thousand war crimes tribunals were conducted by the French and Belgians. International **tribunals** are generally temporary bodies that are organized to judge persons for their behavior during a specific time for a specific event. They have usually been formed as military courts to adjudicate atrocities committed during times of war or civil unrest.

Surely the most famous international tribunals of the twentieth century were the Nuremberg and Tokyo war tribunals formed following World War II. With the drafting of the Nuremburg Charter, an international military tribunal was formed to bring to trial and punishment the major war criminals of the Axis powers. The Nuremburg tribunal had jurisdiction or authority to adjudicate crimes against the peace, crimes against humanity, and war crimes. The tribunal lasted from November 1945 until September 1946 and ended with the conviction of twenty-two defendants, twelve of whom were sentenced to death by hanging. See the following web page for a graphic layout of the Nuremburg Trial http://law2.umkc.edu/faculty/projects/ftrials/nuremberg/nuremberg.htm.

In Tokyo, the international military tribunal for the Far East was held from April 1946 through November 1948. The tribunal, following the model of the Nuremberg tribunal, eventually convicted twenty-eight defendants, and seven were sentenced to death. Some 5,700 other Japanese were charged with lesser crimes such as prisoner abuse. A lesser-known fact is that following World War II, China also held 13 tribunals of its own, resulting in 504 convictions and 149 executions of Japanese nationals.

The Nuremberg and Tokyo tribunals, although not the first or only war crimes trials, were very important because they established the basis of contemporary international law (Pakes, 2010; Browne-Marshall, 2011). More specifically, the Geneva Convention of 1949 was codified using much of the customary law on which the Nuremberg Trials were based, and it now serves as the legal foundation for many of our current supranational courts and cases.

Supranational Courts Today

The longest-running and most permanent supranational court is the **International Court of Justice (ICJ)**. Located at the Peace Palace in The Hague, Netherlands, the ICJ serves the United Nations in the capacity of adjudicating disputes among member countries. The ICJ was established under the original Charter of the United Nations in 1945 and held its first session in April 1946. The ICJ was actually the successor to a judicial body called the Permanent Court of International Justice, which was established by the League of Nations in 1922. As the principal judicial body of the

United Nations, the ICJ has fifteen judges, with no more than one from any one country, all of whom are elected by the General Assembly and Security Council of the United Nations. In some instances, the ICJ can be divided up into smaller chambers of three or more judges to handle the volume of cases.

Also known as the *World Court*, the ICJ has a dual role: (1) to settle, in accordance with international law, legal disputes submitted to it by the 192 member states and neutral parties (Nauru and Switzerland) and (2) to give advisory opinions on legal questions referred to it by international organizations. The decisions of the court are binding—no appeal is available, and all decisions are decided in accordance with international treaties, international conventions, international custom, general principles of law, and, in a few cases, prior judicial decisions and teachings (ICJ, 2012).

Although the ICJ does not often directly address *criminal* matters, it does make decisions that influence criminal proceedings around the world. For example, in April 2012 the ICJ began a complex case to determine which country has the right to try Hissene Habre, the former president of Chad, who has been indicted in two nations in connection with political killings, torture, and other brutalities. Senegal and Belgium have both charged Habre, but Senegal has stalled legal action and refused to try him or extradite him to Belgium. Since 1946, the ICJ has addressed 152 cases in a number of areas such as maritime issues, use of force, international treaties, environment issues, and territorial frontiers.

Another example of a supranational court that deals with international criminal justice in an indirect fashion is the **European Court of Human Rights (ECtHR)**. The ECtHR allows individuals, groups of individuals, or nongovernmental organizations to bring complaints against a European state to a judicial body after they have been denied relief in their national courts. Issues it addresses include the death penalty, police misconduct, and terrorism. For example, in 2010 the Court upheld a complaint against British antiterrorism law that allowed police to stop and search people without firm grounds for suspicion. The mission of the ECtHR in general is to interpret and uphold the European Convention on Human Rights and Fundamental Freedoms, a treaty that was prepared by the Council of Europe in 1950.

In almost 50 years, the ECtHR has delivered more than 10,000 judgments. There has been a tremendous increase in the number of cases brought to the ECtHR in recent years, with an average of 50,000 cases brought annually to the Court. This has led to a serious backlog of over 120,000 cases as of 2011. However, with the inclusion of Russia in 2012, 46 member states have ratified reform procedures that will soon enable the ECtHR to deal with the backlog and increasing number of cases. The ECtHR should not be confused with the European Court of Justice (ECJ), which is the highest court of the European Union (EU). The ECJ rules on questions of EU laws and also acts as arbiter between the EU's institutions to determine whether they are acting within their prescribed powers.

Although some global regions like Europe have made attempts to develop methods to address past or current abuses of human rights, these and other problems of global crime and justice have often become too complicated for regional courts to handle. This can happen, for example, when justice should be meted out to an individual or individuals responsible for illegal acts that are in violation of international standards or treaties especially related to criminal law. In response, the international community has developed three additional forms of supranational courts that deal directly with criminal matters in violation of international law. Each has a judicial body with a higher legal standing than decisions of courts in individual countries. The first are ad hoc tribunals, the second is a permanent international criminal court, and the third are recently formed **internationalized courts**.

The two supranational tribunals dealing with international criminal law violations are ad hoc tribunals, meaning they have been developed for a specific purpose, have a narrowly defined jurisdiction, and are meant to be temporary. The first, established in 1992 by the UN Security Council, using the powers vested in it in Chapter VII of the United National Charter, is the **International**

Criminal Tribunal for Yugoslavia (ICTY). The ICTY was formed to deal with the atrocities committed during the conflicts in Croatia (1991–1995), Bosnia and Herzegovina (1992–1995), Kosovo (1998–1999), and the Former Yugoslav Republic of Macedonia (2001). Since it was created in 1993, the ICTY, located in The Hague, Netherlands, has indicted or served arrest warrants on 161 suspects and sentenced 64 convicted criminals. Most of those convicted have been soldiers, guards, midlevel military officers and a few commanders. The ICTY did attempt to prosecute Slobodan Milosevic, the former president of Yugoslavia, for his crimes in the region, but he died of a heart attack in his cell in The Hague before his trial was completed. There are 35 ongoing proceedings before the ICTY, and all are requested to be completed by the end of 2014.

During legal proceedings, those accused and being tried before the court are held in the ICTY's Detention Unit. However, the Unit is not a penitentiary for the long-term incarceration of criminals. After conviction and sentencing, all criminals are transferred to a prison outside the Netherlands. Seventeen nation states have signed an agreement stating that they will enforce the sentences of the ICTY and take into long-term custody those found guilty by the Tribunal (UNICTY, 2012).

The second supranational tribunal was formed in November 1994 by the UN Security Council and is called the **International Criminal Tribunal for Rwanda (ICTR)**. The ICTR was established for the prosecution of persons responsible for genocide and other serious violations of international humanitarian law committed in the territory of Rwanda between January 1994 and December 1994. Located in Arusha, United Republic of Tanzania, the ICTR also deals the prosecution of Rwandan citizens responsible for genocide and other such violations of international law during the same period. Since issuing its first indictment in 1995, the ICTR has completed a total of 69 cases with 59 convictions (17 of those pending appeals) and 10 acquittals. Among those convicted include Jean Kambanda, the prime minister of the Rwandan government during the genocide, who was the first head of a government to be indicted and subsequently convicted for genocide. If convicted by the ICTR, the sentence is carried out in Rwanda or in a number of states that have agreed to incarcerate persons convicted by the Tribunal, including the governments of Mali, the Republic of Benin, Swaziland, Italy, Sweden, and France (UNICTR, 2012).

Although the war tribunals in Yugoslavia and Rwanda may be direct descendants of the trials in Nuremberg and Tokyo, they differ in a number of significant ways. For one, the ICTY and ICTR have been developed with the full support of the international community under the direction of the United Nations. With full support of the United Nations comes acknowledgment by the international community of the legitimacy of the actions taken by the tribunals and acceptance of the results. The problem however, is that without full occupation and total victory, it is quite difficult to capture and prosecute all those involved. Some procedural differences are also present. Within the rules of the current war tribunals, it is not possible to prosecute individuals in absentia. Also, there was no appeal process in Nuremberg, whereas those convicted by the ICTY and the ICTR can appeal their cases to special chambers within the tribunals. Further, the charter for the current war tribunals allows for concurrent jurisdiction in other countries. This means that other nations that agree to follow the procedures outlined by the tribunals can assist in prosecuting and trying the persons responsible for serious violations of international humanitarian law. The ICTY and ICTR are funded by regular contributions from UN member states. Additional funds are in the form of donations from international agencies and donors, but all contributions must comply with the United Nations policies on donations.

International Criminal Court

Over sixty years ago, the United Nations first recognized the need to establish an international criminal court to prosecute crimes such as genocide. Finally, in July 1998, at a UN diplomatic conference in Rome, delegations from 160 countries passed the first-ever permanent treaty, the **Rome Statute**, that would establish the **International Criminal Court (ICC)**. The Rome Statute is an international treaty binding only on those states that formally express their consent to be bound by its provisions. These states then become parties to the statute, and anyone from those states who then commits any of the crimes under the statute after this date are liable for prosecution by the Court. The crimes are the most serious crimes of concern to the international community as a whole, namely, the crimes of genocide, war crimes, crimes against humanity, and the crimes of aggression. The Rome Statute entered into force on July 1, 2002, once 60 states became parties. In July 2012, Guatemala brought the number of states party to the statute to 121. Held at The Hague, the ICC is an independent institution. The Court is *not* part of the United Nations, but it maintains a cooperative relationship with the UN. Like the aforementioned tribunals, the ICC's expenses are funded primarily by state parties, but it also receives voluntary contributions from numerous sources.

Judges for the ICC may impose a prison sentence, fines, or forfeiture of proceeds from crimes committed. The Court cannot impose a death sentence, and the maximum prison sentence allowed is 30 years, although life imprisonment is an option. Like the ad hoc tribunals, those convicted by the ICC serve their sentences in a state designated from the list of states that agree to accept convicted persons. As of May 2012, the ICC is involved in sixteen individual cases in seven different legal matters (ICC, 2012).

The development of a permanent ICC seems to be a good idea. Among the reasons that have been presented by UN human rights expert Lyal Sunga in support of such a court are the following:

- Crimes under international law that go unchecked hinder international peace, fuel instability, and can lead to long-term armed hostilities and war.
- International criminal law cannot be effective unless it is enforced systematically and on a regular basis.
- International instability should not be able to dictate that international law is relative.
- Individuals who commit crimes in violation of international law should always be punished, and this principle should take precedence over other factors such as politics, administrative convenience, or historical accident.
- Ad hoc tribunals such as the ICTR and the ICTY are created retrospectively and with some discretion, leaving open the question as to whether criminals will always be prosecuted and punished.
- Creation of a permanent court would symbolize the international community's determination to enforce international law universally. (Sunga, 1997, pp. 329–331)

However, the ideal of a permanent ICC has raised some opposition. Among the arguments against the ICC is the sticking point of the role and powers of the prosecutor. Some feel that the UN Security Council should have the final say with regard to who is prosecuted. Others feel that giving the countries in the Security Council the right to veto will eliminate cases that would otherwise be brought to prosecution. Another major limitation is that the court is limited to exercising jurisdiction only if the state or territory is a party to the Rome Statute, and it relies heavily on the cooperation of states to fulfill its functions (Hopfel and Angermaier, 2005; Pakes, 2010).

The United States is among a group of countries (others include China, Israel, Iran, Russia, Syria, and Pakistan) that have not ratified the treaty. Although the Clinton administration signed the treaty in late 2000, the Bush administration immediately "unsigned" the treaty after taking office in early 2001—a move unprecedented in over 200 years. Soon thereafter, in 2002 the U.S. Congress passed the American Service Members Protections Act, which prohibits American cooperation with the ICC and authorizes the president to use military force against the court if it attempts to prosecute an American citizen.

The main concern of those against the ICC is the fear that a country as powerful as the United

States, with military might present throughout the world, would be vulnerable to prosecutions. As a result, it is possible for high-ranking officials from the secretary of defense to soldiers in the field to be accused of crimes. Detractors of this position state that the U.S. position is really reluctance on the part of the United States to be held accountable for gross human rights violations or to the standard established for the rest of the world (Elsea, 2006).

The Obama administration has taken a different direction on whether to support the Rome Statue and the ICC from the previous administration. Although there has been no movement to sign the statue or join the ICC, the administration has said it will work with the ICC on prosecution on certain matters. More specifically, the formal position of the U.S. State Department on the International Criminal Court as stated in May 2010 is as follows:

> From Nuremberg to Yugoslavia to Liberia, the United States has seen that the end of impunity and the promotion of justice are not just moral imperatives; they are stabilizing forces in international affairs. The United States is thus working to strengthen national justice systems and is maintaining our support for ad hoc international tribunals and hybrid courts. Those who intentionally target innocent civilians must be held accountable, and we will continue to support institutions and prosecutions that advance this important interest. Although the United States is not at present a party to the Rome Statute of the International Criminal Court, and will always protect U.S. personnel, we are engaging with State Parties to the Rome Statute on issues of concern and are supporting the ICC's prosecution of those cases that advance U.S. interests and values, consistent with the requirements of U.S. law.
>
> Although the United States is not a party to the ICC's Statute, the Obama administration has been prepared to support the Court's prosecutions and provide assistance in response to specific requests from the ICC prosecutor and other court officials, consistent with U.S. law, when it is in U.S. national interest to do so (U.S. Department of State, 2012).

The final type of supranational courts is the **internationalized courts**. Internationalized courts, also called mixed tribunals or hybrid courts, operate with the support of the United Nations to prosecute those responsible for crimes against humanity, war crimes, and violations of domestic law. These courts are similar to each other in that they generally are located in places where the crimes occur and they utilize law and judges from the international and domestic jurisdictions. At the same time, these courts are each distinctive and face their own challenges, including government influence of domestic judges and security issues (Fichtelberg, 2008, pp. 52–54).

There are a number of these courts currently active around the world. All serve to address conflicts that occurr in their respective countries. At least three are currently in operation: the Extraordinary Chambers in the Courts of Cambodia (ECCC), the Special Court for Sierra Leone, and the Special Tribunal for Lebanon. The ECCC is a domestic court supported with international staff, established in accordance with Cambodian law. Under the terms of an agreement between the United Nations and the Royal Government of Cambodia, the ECCC has brought to trial senior leaders of Khmer Rouge regime and those who were most responsible for the crimes and serious violations of Cambodian penal law, international humanitarian law and custom, and international conventions recognized by Cambodia that were committed during the period from 1975 to 1979 (ECCC, 2012). In early 2012, the ECCC found Kaing Guek Eav guilty of numerous crimes against humanity and grave breaches of the Geneva Convention of 1949 for his involvement in the torture and killing of over 16,000 people in the Phnom Penh region. He was sentenced to 35 years in prison.

Also currently in operation with the support of the United Nations is the Special Court for Sierra Leone. This court, held in the Netherlands for security reasons, has been formed to hold legally responsible the perpetrators of serious violations of international humanitarian and Sierra Leonean law committed in that country since 1996. On April 26, 2012, the judges for the Special Court for Sierra Leone convicted former Liberian President Charles Taylor of eleven counts of war crimes and crimes against humanity for his role in the eleven-year civil war in Sierra Leone that ended in 2002 and left more than 50,000 dead. The Taylor trial is significant because he is the first head of a state to be brought to judgment by an international tribunal since WWII. He will be sentenced in May 2012 (Special Court for Sierra Leone, 2012).

Finally, the Special Tribunal for Lebanon (STL) was established in 2005 with support of the United Nations, but it is an independent judicial organization, not a UN court. The STL began work in March 2009 in The Hague, its main purpose being to hold trials for those accused of a deadly attack that killed 23 people in Lebanon in February 2005 including Prime Minister Rafiq Hariri. The STL has handed down no convictions as of April 2012 (STL, 2012). See the box below for a list of supranational courts (with their dates of establishment) that have dealt with criminal matters over the last 60 years.

The Legal Jurisdiction of Supranational Courts

Where does international humanitarian law come from, and what gives the supranational courts the power to decide the fate of individuals around the world? The answer has three parts. First, the United Nations, as the only international body of power in the world and with support of its member states and the Security Council, provides the initial legal jurisdiction. Without the approval of the UN, there would be no ICJ, no ICC, and no criminal tribunals. Second, as we mentioned briefly with regard to the ICJ, various international courts gain legal legitimacy and power through the application of international laws that have been developed over time in the form of conventions and treaties. Examples of such laws are the Geneva Conventions of August 1949 and, most recently, the Rome Statute of 2002.

The final source of legal power and legitimacy for the supranational courts is the general legal principle of **jus cogens**, whereby fundamental norms are recognized on the international level as having status superior to other norms. What this means in practical terms is that, if one country believes it is "in the right," this belief may be acceptable within its own borders. However, if the international community condemns the behavior of that country as illegal, the latter supersedes the former in a court of law. The principle of jus cogens likely evolved from a similar Roman concept of jus gentium—a term that describes the law practiced by Roman jurists and later medieval jurists, who stated that basic principles of right reason are applicable to all human relationships across borders. Later, Dutch jurist Hugo Grotius (1583–1645) used this principle

Supranational Courts and Dates of Establishment

- 1945 and 1946 Nuremberg and Tokyo International Military Tribunals
- 1993 UN International Criminal Tribunal for the former Yugoslavia (ICTY)
- 1994 UN International Criminal Tribunal For Rwanda (ICTR)
- 1999 Hybrid Courts in Kosovo
- 2000 East Timor and Indonesia*
- 2002 Special Court for Sierra Leone (SCSL)
- 2002 International Criminal Court (ICC)
- 2005 War Crimes Section, State Court, Bosnia and Herzegovina
- 2006 Extraordinary Chambers in the Courts of Cambodia (ECCC)
- 2007 Special Tribunal for Lebanon (STL)

**Special Panels for Serious Crimes; Serious Crimes Investigation Team and the Indonesian ad hoc Tribunal for East Timor.*

as legal authority to develop rules for international law (Mueller, 1997).

Challenges Facing Supranational Courts

Although the concept of supranational courts has become generally accepted around the world, they do face considerable challenges. Among the key issues of concern are cost effectiveness, logistics of implementation, and political influences. It is estimated that from 1993, when the first wave of the current supranational courts were formed (beginning with the ICTY), to 2015, when most of them are proposed to close, the international community will have spent nearly $6.3 billion (Ford, 2011). As a result, many have questioned whether the effectiveness as measured by the scant number of convictions is worth the incurred cost. Another major issue is the problem of implementing the process of justice from arrest through incarceration. Supranational courts do not have their own police force able to gather suspected criminals and bring them to the respective courts for prosecution. In the few cases that have been prosecuted, the courts have generally depended on suspects to turn themselves; in only a few instances were they able to execute arrest warrants with the full cooperation of member states. Relatedly, if a conviction is obtained, the courts must find member states willing to incur the costs and security risks associated with long-term incarceration.

Probably the biggest obstacle for supranational courts, however, is their inability to gain full political support of key member states. Can supranational courts really gain influence and respect around the world stage if major powers do not support them? For example, among the UN member nations that do not support the ICC are the United States, China, and Russia. Individual countries have various reasons for their decision to support supranational courts, but probably the most common is the fear of giving up state sovereignty. Many countries, especially those who have a long history of having unbridled global power, are concerned about answering to any international body. It is clear that supranational courts have gained legitimacy over the last twenty years, but these and other hurdles will need to be addressed if they wish to grow in acceptance and achieve sustained success.

SUMMARY

As we consider the issue of courts and the legal profession, we can see that there are many similarities and differences alike in our model countries. In each system, courts of limited jurisdiction, often staffed by laypeople, dispense justice in minor matters. Serious cases are heard in trial courts of general jurisdiction. In all countries we looked at, the possibility of error at the lower level is handled through the institution of intermediate courts of appeal. A high court of final appeal is at the top of each judicial hierarchy. Courts in all these systems lay claim to impartiality and independence in making decisions, and an opportunity for both sides to be heard is guaranteed in the proceedings.

It is the differences among systems, however, that show the relation among culture, tradition, and legal process. In England, the successful struggle to curtail the powers of the monarchs is reflected in the strong emphasis on procedure and on lay participation through the jury. The continental Civil Law systems of France and Germany, with their specialization of courts and their civil servant judicial personnel, reflect the rational bureaucratic approach to administration that infuses other aspects of their state apparatus. The judicial system of the People's Republic of China takes a highly centralized form, with both informal and formal mechanisms that assist in educating the citizenry about the Socialist society. In Japan, Western-style judicial process coexists with a premodern emphasis on harmony, consensus, and nonconflictual relationships. In the Islamic society of Saudi Arabia, deep religiosity and devotion to

Qur'anic principles dominate the criminal law process and much of family law.

Legally trained professionals hold positions of high status and relatively high income in each system that we have examined, as they do in all modern nations. Looking back at the various systems of justice, however, we find important points of difference that allow us to make some broad generalizations about legal actors in different families of law. These generalizations deal with legal education and training, as well as with the four functional categories of legal actors: adjudicators, advocates, advisors, and scholars.

The international community has developed supranational courts that deal directly with criminal matters in violation of international law. Each has a judicial body with a higher legal standing than decisions of courts in individual countries. The first are the permanent courts supported by the United Nations and the EU including the ICJ, ECtHR, and ICC. The next are ad hoc tribunals such as the ICTY and ICTR. Finally, there are the recently formed internationalized courts that have arisen to deal with the ravages of civil wars in Sierra Leone, East Timor, Kosovo, and Cambodia. Supranational courts gain their support from the United Nations, international laws and treaties, and the legal principle of jus cogens. Although supranational courts have gained many supporters, they must address significant challenges, including cost effectiveness, logistics, and politics.

Comparative Criminal Justice at the Movies

Movies seek to entertain and inform the audience about a story, incident, or person. Many good movies also hit upon important substantive themes relevant to understanding crime and justice in comparative perspective. Read the movie summary below (and watch the movie if you haven't already) and answer the questions below to make the subject matter connections to comparative criminal justice.

Last King of Scotland (2006)
Kevin MacDonald, Director

The movie depicts Ugandan President Idi Amin (Forest Whitaker) and recounts his reign of violence and terror through the eyes of a fictional character, Nick Garrigan (James McAvoy), a young doctor from Scotland who travels to Uganda hoping to help people. Nick is hopeful about the charismatic new president Amin, as was the rest of the world at the time. After an automobile accident, Nick is called in to treat the president's wounds, and Amin is impressed by Nick and charms him into becoming his personal physician.

Nick enjoys his new life of privilege but does not grasp the reality of the situation. Amin is charismatic but also moody, extremely violent, and paranoid about hidden supporters of the previous regime in Uganda. At one point, Amin decides to expel all Asians from his country, regardless of how many years they have lived there. Nick tries to talk him out of it. Amin later becomes furious that international newspapers have labeled him a madman and a cannibal for this decision. Amin screams, "These are all lies!" and threatens to throw all foreign journalists out of Uganda. Nick protests that he tried to talk Amin out of it, but Amin replies, "Ah, but you did not persuade me!"

When he finally realizes the atrocities Amin is inflicting upon his people and that the president is killing those around him whom he falsely labels conspirators or traitors, Nick tries to make a frantic escape before it's too late. Idi Amin is said to have killed more than 100,000 people in his country during his reign from 1971 to 1979. Forest Whitaker won the Academy Award for Best Actor for his portrayal of Amin.

Questions

1. A country with a dictator usually suffers from the moods and excesses of its leader. What does an independent judicial system provide in a country to prevent the excesses seen in Uganda?
2. In real life, Idi Amin was ultimately overthrown as a result of his own ambitions to expand his empire. He fled to Libya and then to Saudi Arabia where he died in 2003. Make an argument for what you believe would be a more just outcome, and why do you believe it did not occur at the time?

Critical Thinking Exercise

Critical thinking requires the ability to evaluate viewpoints, facts, and behaviors objectively to assess information and methods of argumentation in order to establish the merit of an action, law, policy or procedure. Please evaluate this scenario objectively, applying your knowledge of comparative criminal justice to the facts of the case presented, and answer the questions that follow it.

Questions about South Korea's Constitutional Court

When South Korea's three-decade authoritarian regime collapsed in 1987, the victorious political forces rushed to transform their country into a liberal constitutional democracy. The Constitution was quickly revised, and a new institution was created: the Korean Constitutional Court, a tribunal composed of judges with the power to overturn legislative enactments and executive orders if they were found to be inconsistent with the highest law in the country, the Constitution.

The Korean Constitutional Court is outside of the hierarchical system of the ordinary courts, which consists of the Korean Supreme Court and the lower courts. The Korean Supreme Court hears appeals from judgments by the appellate courts. In contrast, the Korean Constitutional Court exclusively exercises constitutional review of statutes. Ordinary courts are barred from so doing, though they may refer constitutional questions to the Constitutional Court.

The rationales for granting a special court the exclusive power of judicial review are twofold. First, the arrangement strengthens the independence of the ordinary courts by taking the constitutional review of statutes away from them so that they can be free from political influence by lawmakers. Second, the special court's efficiency and expediency secure effective protection of both human rights and the Constitution because the power of judicial review is concentrated with an independent court and exercised under a unitary procedure.

Unexpectedly, since its creation in 1988, the Constitutional Court has successfully introduced into the political system a new dimension of constitutional review and has substantially helped the democratic transition in South Korea. Nevertheless, the Constitutional Court has often aroused resentment and opposition from powerful political elements in society. It has frequently had to say no to the legislature, the executive branch, and powerful private entities in its decisions. A very large proportion of the high-profile cases brought to the Constitutional Court have involved intense political controversies, which grew out of power struggles between opposing political forces.

The dominant characterization of a court as a legal institution leads to the general belief in judicial objectivity and neutrality, derived from the doctrine of separation of powers, and which makes it wrong for judges to let their individual preferences influence judicial deliberations. But there is an opposing perspective that in the course of settling disputes in accordance with existing law, courts often have no choice but to make new rules. It is this policymaking function, much more than dispute resolution, that places the judiciary at the center of controversy.

Questions

1. Traditional theories of judicial review hold that neutral or principled grounds are the only legitimate bases for judicial decisions and reject political motives in judicial decision making. Do you believe this is true? Do you see principled versus political motives in important U.S. Supreme Court constitutional decisions that overturn laws passed by legislatures (such as restrictions on gun ownership or loosening of restrictions on marijuana use)?
2. Interestingly, those behind high-profile cases brought to the court are often those in pursuit of political agendas. In Korea, they defer to the Korean Constitutional Court when a political deadlock is reached (and they were unwilling or unable to settle contentious public disputes in the legislature). Politicians may invite judicial intervention deliberately to avoid public criticism of their incapability of action and to divert responsibility to the Court. Do you think this is true in the United States? If so, can you provide a specific example?
3. Judicial review is a double-edged sword. It can be exercised courageously, but prudently, to defend the rights of those politically and economically disadvantaged or to hold the line against abuses of power. On the other hand, judicial review can easily become a formidable instrument for legitimating the interests of existing political and economic elites. Can you provide examples of cases where the U.S. Supreme Court, like the court in Korea, attempted to walk the line between government power and the rights of individuals without that power?

SOURCE: Cha Dong-wook, "The Constitutional Court: Political or Legal?," Korea Herald (February 1, 2008).

DISCUSSION QUESTIONS

1. What is the difference between judicial independence and judicial impartiality? Which is more important, in your opinion?
2. To what extent are laypeople (that is, those not legally trained) used in the court systems of our model countries? What are the advantages and disadvantages of such a system?
3. Debate in class the advantages and challenges of supranational courts and/or whether the United States should support the International Criminal Court.
4. In your class, in small-group discussions, rank the court systems from 1 (worst) to 6 (best) in terms of what you think it would be like to be involved in them as a defendant, and discuss why. Then compare your results with the other groups.
5. Go to the United Nations document "Basic Principles on the Role of Lawyers" at http://www1.umn.edu/humanrts/instree/i3bprl.htm and determine whether any of the model nations would have a compliance problem with the principles. What principles would be most problematic? For what countries?

FOR FURTHER READING

Bell, J. (2003). "Legal Education." In P. Crane and M. Tushnet, eds., *The Oxford Handbook of Legal Studies* (pp. 901–919). New York: Oxford University Press.

Podgor, E., and R. Clark (2009). *International Criminal Law: Cases and Material*, 3rd ed. Newark: LexisNexis.

Ryngaert, C., ed.. (2009). *The Effectiveness of International Criminal Justice*. Mortsel, Belgium: Intersentia Press.

Schabas, W. A. (2007). *An Introduction to the International Criminal Court*, 3rd ed. Cambridge: Cambridge University Press,.

Trevaskes, S. (2007). *Courts and Criminal Justice in Contemporary China*. New York: Lexington Books.

WEB PAGES FOR CHAPTER

To view an interesting 50-minute film of the Nuremburg Trials, see the YouTube site http://www.youtube.com/watch?v=FPXc8JjtidM

For more about the ICC, including live video from proceedings, see http://www.icc-cpi.int/

To review each of the 161 indictments brought before the ICTY, see http://www.icty.org/sections/TheCases/KeyFigures

For information about the U.S. State Department's Office of Global Criminal Justice International Criminal Tribunals, see http://www.state.gov/j/gcj/c52591.htm

For the full text of the United Nations document "Basic Principles on the Role of Lawyers," see http://www1.umn.edu/humanrts/instree/i3bprl.htm

8

After Conviction: The Sentencing Process

Key Terms and Concepts

community service

control of freedom

day fine

deterrence

diyya

electronic monitoring

exile

fine

flow design

forfeiture

house arrest

incapacitation

jail

noncustodial sanctions

penal populism

prison

probation

rehabilitation

remand prison

restitution

restoration

restorative justice

retribution

stock design

warnings

Chapter 8 Learning Objectives

Discuss the purposes of the five different criminal sanctions that are used to rationalize punishment.

Identify the different forms of criminal sanctions that are predominant around the world today.

Explore the reasons for the extreme nature of criminal punishments in Islamic countries.

Describe the major weaknesses in international prison data available in the world today.

Explain the general trend in the use of the death penalty on the international level.

Consider the following:

- A man convicted of murder in New Zealand has been given a lighter sentence after his mother apologized to the victim's family. The family forgave him after a traditional Samoan apology in which someone who has done wrong presents him- or herself, covered in fine mats, to the victim's family. As the man was in prison, he was unable to complete the ceremony, so his mother stepped in to take his place. The remorse shown and his mother's actions were factors in the judge's agreeing to sentence him to life imprisonment with a minimum non-parole period of ten years, the lightest sentence he could have received in the circumstances (Robinson, 2012)
- Colombia's Constitutional Court has approved the government's proposal to decriminalize the possession of small amounts of cocaine and marijuana for personal use. Anyone caught with less than 20 grams of marijuana or one gram of cocaine may receive physical or psychological treatment depending on their state of consumption, but may not be prosecuted or detained. The move is part of a growing trend in Latin America (Nadleman, 2012).
- A judge in Saudi Arabia has asked doctors in the country whether they can damage a man's spinal cord as an "eye for an eye" punishment after he was convicted of paralyzing a fellow countryman in a cleaver attack. The punishment can be waived if the victim chooses to accept *diyya*, or "blood money," in reparation (Foxnews.com, 2010).

In these examples of sentencing practices in four different regions of the world, we see how different countries sentence criminal offenders. Such differences in sentencing practices can tell us a great deal about what individual societies feel about justice, crime, and criminal offenders. The decisions made about crime and criminals are sometimes influenced by an individual crime incident or troubling crime trends. For example, in the 1990s a "three strikes" policy was developed in California after the murder of two young females by former inmates on parole. In contrast, some countries, such as those in Scandinavia, have low rates of violent crime and a high tolerance toward offenders, and are more likely to support rehabilitation-based sanctions. In this chapter, we will look at the varieties of sentencing policies that are used around the world and the extent to which they are utilized. In the next chapter, we will concentrate more on the issues and problems surrounding imprisonment, especially in our model countries.

THE PURPOSES OF CRIMINAL SANCTIONS

What does a society hope to gain from punishing wrongdoers? The classic answer is that one or more of the following should be accomplished:

- **Retribution**—The offender should "pay back" society for the harm he or she has done.
- **Rehabilitation**—The offender should be transformed into a law-abiding person through programs of medical, psychological, economic, or educational improvement.
- **Deterrence**—The offender, or other possible offenders, through various methods , such as certainty of punishment or length or severity of punishment, should come to the conclusion that crime is not worth the risk of the resulting punishment.
- **Incapacitation**—The offender, usually through prison or exile, should be denied the opportunity to commit further crimes.

- **Restoration**—The community, victim, and offender are involved in the sentencing process with the aim of restoring the victim and the community to its previous state.

In practice, motives for imposing criminal punishment on offenders are usually mixed. At different times and places, however, one or the other of these purposes has been stressed (Clear, Cole, & Reisig, 2011). For centuries, deterrence and retribution were emphasized. During the nineteenth century, the "classical school" of criminologists saw simple retribution, applied equitably, as the major goal of sentencing in much of Europe. In the United States, where rehabilitation as a philosophy of punishment held sway for much of the twentieth century, there was an abrupt swing in sentencing theory and practice during the 1970s toward a more classic retributive approach. During the 1990s, the United States promoted incapacitation, as evidenced by the prison-building boom and longer sentences for drug and violent crimes. In Europe, the philosophy of rehabilitation developed in earnest in the later twentieth century, but an increase in crime has inspired some nations to call for more of a retributive philosophy. An exception is the Scandinavian countries, where "neoclassicism," as it is called there, developed parallel to the classical movement in the United States.

A recent trend in sentencing in a number of countries, which is in some ways one of the oldest sentencing methods, is **restorative justice**. Restorative justice is a revitalized paradigm that calls for participation by the offender, victim, and community in the sentencing process and allows the offender to atone for the offense and be restored to community life. Proponents of restorative justice believe that for the community, victim, and offender to be restored, the offender must understand the harm caused by the offense, accept responsibility for it, and repair the harm done. To accomplish this, it is imperative that all parties (offender, victim, and community) become involved in the criminal justice process (Pranis, 1993; Van Ness & Strong, 2010).

The idea of restoration has its roots in Judeo-Christian religious thought, dating back to ancient Middle Eastern civilization. Religious traditions taught that those who offended against their neighbors could atone for their offenses and be restored to community life if they made reparation for their misdeeds and promised to never repeat them. In fact, penitence, expiation, and forgiveness are central concepts of Judeo-Christian morality. Precolonial African societies adopted restorative forms of punishment aimed at resolving consequences to victims rather than punishing criminals. Indigenous populations in North America, New Zealand, and Australia have used variations of this idea for quite some time, and more recently numerous nations from every continent have adopted programs with a restorative intent. The decade has seen multinational bodies such as the United Nations and the European Union endorse restorative justice. (For a timeline of significant worldwide advances concerning restorative justice, see Van Ness and Strong, 2010, pp. 33–35.) For example, the United Nations Economic and Social Council adopted the "Basic Principles on the Use of Restorative Justice Programmes in Criminal Matters" with the goal of encouraging member states to implement restorative justice in juvenile justice.

Some non-Western countries seem to have their own ideas about the goals of punishment. In China, it is important that criminal offenders be persuaded to reform not for themselves but for the good of their family, village, and especially society. To promote public security throughout the country, China utilizes what are termed "administrative penalties" for a variety of crimes such as disturbing social order, endangering public safety, infringing on the rights of others, and encroaching upon public or private property. Administrative penalties and more serious sanctions state the formal purpose as one of rehabilitation or returning the citizen to become a better-functioning member of Chinese society.

In countries that practice Islamic justice, punishment is justified by deterrence, retribution, rehabilitation, and protection of the community by incapacitating the offender (Al-Sagheer, 1994; Peters, 2005, p. 30). However, actual implementation of these practices in Islamic states varies considerably depending on a number of factors, including the influence of Islamic law within the state apparatus and historical developments in specific countries. While some have practiced Islamic law for decades and even centuries, others, such as a region in Northern Nigeria, that began implementing the Shari'a only in the last 12 years. For a summary description of the kinds of punishment purposes implemented in our each of our model countries and the United States, see Table 8.1.

The five purposes of criminal sanctions, as mentioned above, all have to do with what happens to wrongdoers and with their capacity to be changed or to do further damage. From a more global perspective, however, we discover that penal sanctions have had less acknowledged and less legitimate functions in many societies at different times in history. One of these has been the economic function of providing cheap labor that the society could not afford or could not otherwise entice its citizens to do. For decades, transportation to penal colonies and sentencing to galleys, Siberian prison camps, and road gangs all had a lot to do with economic development, as well as with penal sanctions (Rusche & Kirchheimer, 1939; Committee on Foreign Affairs, 1984, p. 2).

More recently, the same issue has arisen with respect to the fruits of Chinese prison labor. Prisoners in China are subject to institutions called *laogai* believed to promote "thought reform through labor." In the laogai, inmates are required to work at prison farms and factories to support the economic system in China. Even more disturbing, however, are the allegations that over 1,000 Chinese prisoners have been executed and then had their organs harvested for financial gain (Wu, 1995). In today's world, it is an infraction of international standards (see the International Labor Organization of the United Nations) to provide prison labor for economic development.

Another economic function that criminal sanctions may serve is that of social control, providing the kind of working class necessary for an organized, industrial society (Melossi & Pavarini, 1981). In his classic book about the historical foundation of prisons, David Garland explains how during the beginning of capitalist development, the United States used prisons as a storage facility for surplus laborers and as a school to spread capitalist values (Garland, 1990). The factories of Massachusetts and plantations of South Carolina in the late eighteenth and early nineteenth centuries are early examples of this concept (Hindus, 1980).

Finally, an illegitimate but much-practiced use of criminal sanctions that is also condemned in international law is punishment of a regime's political enemies. The twentieth century saw a number of examples of this abuse of criminal sanctions in countries such as Russia, China, and South Africa. Some have laid criticism for such violations on the United States for their ongoing internment of hundreds of al-Qaida supporters captured since the

TABLE 8.1 Purposes of Criminal Sanctions in Our Model Countries and in the United States

Model Country	Retribution	Rehabilitation	Deterrence	Incapacitation	Restoration
England and Wales		X		X	X*
Japan	X	X			X
France		X		X	X
Germany		X		X	X*
China	X	X			X*
Saudi Arabia	X	X	X		
USA	X	X	X	X	X*

*Used primarily with juvenile offenders or as a supplement to rehabilitation

events of 9/11 and the subsequent occupation of Iraq and Afghanistan. Often, it is difficult to draw the line between political persecution and simple diligence in carrying out the criminal law. For example, was it political repression or basic law enforcement to imprison antiwar demonstrators who, in defiance of the law, publicly burned their draft cards during the Vietnam War?

Political uses of the criminal law may also be tied to religious persecution, especially where a state-sponsored religion believes itself to be threatened by independent religious groups. Although religious fervor is not as likely to lead to criminal sanctions in today's secular nations as it was in earlier times, the example of countries such as Saudi Arabia, Iran, Pakistan, and now Nigeria, which apply Islamic law to promote religious tenets, shows that this practice continues. Any investigation into the purpose of criminal sanctions clearly reflects that it is an increasingly complex subject, one that does not allow for simple explanations. In most systems, a mixture of social, economic, and political factors is at work and needs to be analyzed to understand the criminal justice process.

SENTENCING PRACTICES

Despite the call for increasing punishments and the abuses that continue for some of those who are incarcerated, sentencing practices have generally become more humane over the centuries. We have only to compare the fate of would-be assassins or assassins of rulers in seventeenth-century France, the nineteenth-century United States, and the twentieth-century United States to illustrate this. After a crazed Frenchman made an unsuccessful attempt to murder King Louis XV, he was hanged, was cut down while still alive, had his intestines pulled out and roasted before him, and was then draw and quartered. When Charles Guiteau assassinated President James Garfield in 1881, he was hanged despite the fact that he suffered from delusions and displayed other symptoms of mental illness. On the other hand, when Lynette "Squeaky" Fromme, a follower of the notorious killer and cult leader Charles Manson, attempted to kill President Gerald Ford, she received a life term in a California penitentiary with the possibility of parole after 15 years. John Hinckley, the delusional young man who attempted to kill President Ronald Reagan in 1980, was placed in a mental facility and in 2003 was granted home visitation privileges.

In recent years many countries, especially those in Europe, have actually made an effort to reduce sentencing severity for a number of crimes (Ashworth, 2000; Tonry, 2007). For example, in Germany, prison sentences of less than six months have been virtually eliminated in favor of community sanctions. In Finland, policy makers have been successful in forming penal policies more like those of other Scandinavian countries such as Norway, Sweden, and Denmark rather than those of their eastern neighbors Russia and the Baltic republics (Lappi-Sceppala, 2006). There has also been a worldwide reduction in the number of countries that utilize the most severe penalty, capital punishment. We will discuss this global trend in more detail later in this chapter.

The treatment of offenders after arrest or sentencing has also been an important issue of interest in the international community in recent decades. Charters of human rights, including the UN Universal Declaration of Human Rights, the UN Standard Rules for the Treatment of Prisoners, and the European Convention on Human Rights, are among the international treaties and laws used to outlaw the use of torture and inhumane treatment of prisoners. Although the phrasing in such documents is vague, subject to different interpretations, and often ignored, we can safely say that the harshness of criminal punishment, and often its practice, has become more lenient throughout much of the world over time. We will discuss these international standards further in the next chapter when we broach the issue of prisoner treatment.

It is difficult to clearly determine whether any one kind of criminal sanction is more or less prevalent in the world today. One reason for this is the dearth of international data about the types and extent of punishments implemented in the world today. Countries are very wary of reporting such data for fear of being criticized for excessive punishments of criminals. But if we review the results of the past United Nations Criminal Justice Surveys (UNCJS), we can see some general patterns. The surveys indicate that the majority of adults were punished in the community through methods related to some control in freedom and through fines, warnings, community service, and probation. Over one-third of countries still relied heavily on deprivation of freedom. The following is a list of definitions that briefly describe some of the most common forms of punishments used in the world today.

- *Corporal punishment*—any sentence in which a person's body is subjected to physical pain, such as flogging, mutilation, electric shock, or branding.
- *Life imprisonment*—any sentence in which a person is deprived of liberty in an institution of any kind for the duration of his or her natural life.
- *Deprivation of liberty*—a variety of forms of detention, including combined or split sentences, jail, and any period of incarceration short of life imprisonment.
- *Control in freedom*—includes probation, electronic monitoring, any conditional sentence with supervision requirements, and other forms of controlled liberty that have special requirements.
- *Warnings*—also called admonitions; suspended sentences, conditional sentences and dismissals, formal and informal warnings with findings of guilt, and conditional discharges.
- *Fines*—all sentences that involve paying a sum of money.

Source: Weitekamp, 2003, p. 150.

This is not to imply that there is no variation among individual countries when it comes to sentencing. In some countries (such as Slovenia, Japan, Germany, Finland, Austria, and Egypt), warnings, fines, and noncustodial sanctions account for up to 70 percent of total sentences; in others (such as Colombia, Singapore, and Moldova), more than 50 percent of sentences are custodial. At the same time, some countries show no preference for any one kind of punishment (Zvekic, 1997).

As we examine various sentencing practices, we can place them in four basic categories: (1) corporal punishment, (2) noncustodial sanctions, (3) imprisonment, and (4) the death penalty. In the following sections, we will explore these practices in more detail.

CORPORAL PUNISHMENT

Corporal punishments such as flogging, branding, dunking, and maiming have a long global history. The methods of corporal punishment most commonly used today are flogging and in rare cases amputation. Although these methods have gradually disappeared as official, court-imposed sanctions in most countries, especially in Western nations, this does not mean that corporal punishment is in disuse. From a variety of sources, we know that around 60 countries employ some form of the sanction and that such punishments are carried out even in a number of enlightened societies. Further, cross-national research on the use of such sanctions has shown that countries where economic disparity is greatest are more likely to employ corporal punishment as a possible sanction against criminal offenders (Gould and Pate, 2011).

Overall, such punishments are not sanctioned in most countries. Human rights instruments or conventions do not specifically prohibit or prevent corporal punishments as a sentence, although many countries exclude such penalties because they feel that they are included as part of the general definition of inhumane or degrading punishment (Kurki, 2001).

One major exception to the gradual disuse of corporal punishment sanctions is found in Islamic countries, where measures of punishment that seem extreme to most Americans can, and sometimes do, take place (Metz, 1993; Peters, 2005).

Since the Qur'an describes not only forbidden acts but also the penalties for engaging in these acts, societies that are faithful to Islamic law have little choice but to carry out these penalties. The force of such punishments is mitigated, however, by the fact that the standards of proof are so high that many of them are infrequently carried out. This is so especially in cases involving sexual misconduct, a most serious crime in Islamic law. People who are guilty of adultery are supposed to be stoned to death. But there must have been a valid confession or four witnesses to the crime. Further, the only witnesses who can be used, according to most interpretations, are male Muslims. Needless to say, convictions for adultery are extremely rare even in countries that follow Shari'a criminal law. It is not uncommon for a year to pass without an execution for adultery.

A Westerner who is appalled by the severity of punishments prescribed under Islamic law might also consider the following rationales for such punishments:

> The Hudud penalties are designed to avoid unreasonable limitations on individual freedom to the extent that they are "bodily penalties." They are executed in limited duration and cause momentarily severe physical pain to the criminal and remain unforgettable to him so that in most cases, he will refrain from future criminal conduct. These penalties contrast with prison sentences which the criminal becomes accustomed to, having experienced them for long periods of time. Thus, imprisonment soon loses its deterrent effect and prisoners lose their sense of responsibility. Often after being released, they return to prison to serve a longer sentence. Thus execution of the "bodily penalty" allows the criminal to resume his work immediately thereafter; he is also not prevented from supporting himself and his children. Similarly, Islam teaches that to undergo the Hudud punishment is in itself an act of penance and remission after which the offender resumes his normal life as a good citizen….
>
> In Islamic society, the reliance on Hudud penalties brings about peace, stability, and security. When these were abandoned in favor of foreign theories of penology, Islamic societies experienced increased crime rates. (Mansour, 1982, pp. 201–202)

An interesting point about sanctions under Islamic law is that imprisonment is considered a proper sanction only for recidivists, people who have not changed as a result of the more direct corporal punishments. Thus, a person who has been convicted of theft for the third or fourth time is sentenced to prison. With the first conviction, one hand is amputated by an authorized doctor; with the second conviction, the other hand is amputated; with the third conviction, however, the penalty may be either amputation of a foot or "imprisonment until repentance" (Lippman, McConville, & Yerushalmi, 1988, p. 42; Ghassemi, 2010). One might well ask, "Which is preferable? Twenty years in the state penitentiary or the loss of a hand or foot?"

Another extreme use of corporal punishment has been used in the country of Malaysia. Amnesty International (2010) has documented that around 10,000 persons per year are caned in that country. The cases of Malaysia and Islamic countries aside, a general repugnance for visible violence has made the application of corporal punishment not useful as a criminal sanction in modern Western society.

NONCUSTODIAL SANCTIONS

The search for noncustodial sanctions is as old as the practice of imprisonment itself. **Noncustodial sanctions**, also called alternatives to incarceration, are legal sanctions handed out to offenders that do not require time served in a correctional facility. The call for such alternatives became increasingly intense in the latter part of the nineteenth century, when European criminologists, assessing almost a century of experience with prison as the favored mode of punishment, voiced widespread disillusionment with the practice. Declaring that prison did little to change or rehabilitate offenders, these criminologists directed their attacks mainly at short-term imprisonment of nondangerous offenders. At that time, short-term sentences were by far the punishment of choice for convicted offenders. Franz von Liszt, a leading German criminologist, summed up these sentiments in 1885: "The short prison sentence in its present form is worthless, indeed harmful. It does not deter, it does not improve, it contaminates" (Kalmthout & Tak, 1988, p. 3). Alternatives, including fines and special systems of juvenile justice, were the answer to the dysfunctional aspects of short-term imprisonment, according to von Liszt and other European reformers.

In more modern times, the search for alternatives has both humanitarian and utilitarian motives. From a humanitarian standpoint, minimization of short-term imprisonment of nondangerous offenders increases the possibility of rehabilitation through work programs, counseling, and restitution plans, whereas imprisonment breeds further crime and alienation from conventional society. From a utilitarian standpoint, alternatives alleviate the financial and other problems involved in dealing with an ever-growing prison population, especially in England and the United States.

The call for alternatives to incarceration is heard in much of the industrialized world, especially in Europe. Germany, for example, imposes fines as the sole sanction on two-thirds of all property offenders, and in England the number is almost half. Community service is commonly used for property offenses in many countries in the European Union such as England, Sweden, the Netherlands, France, and Austria. As recently as 2011, courts in Ireland imposed more community-based penalties than prison sentences, with the number of community court orders increasing by 40 percent. The increase followed legislation introduced in October 2011 calling for judges considering a sentence of 12 months or less to first examine the appropriateness of community service (Lally, 2012).

The United Nations has often promulgated resolutions calling for alternatives to incarceration such as the Vienna Declaration and the Tokyo Rules, which was the most detailed international document to promote the use of community-based alternative sanctions. What are the alternatives? Because each country approaches the issue differently, it would require a book of considerable length to document the many options available today. To keep our discussion within the limits of this chapter, we will focus on the most commonly used alternatives within two general categories: (1) monetary payments and (2) community supervision.

It is important to mention here that our discussion of alternatives to incarceration will only include measures that are implemented subsequent to adjudication. Noncustodial sanctions prior to adjudication, such as pretrial detention, bail, release on recognizance, diversion programs, and related issues (such as promoting decriminalization and dealing with social conditions that help create crime), will not be addressed here.

Monetary Sanctions

Fines. The **fine** is a penalty imposed on a convicted offender by a court or, in some countries, by another arm of the criminal justice system, requiring that he or she pay a specified sum of money. Fines have been around for centuries and are among the most common noncustodial sanctions in the world (O'Malley). They are used in as many as 97 percent of cases in Japan and in more than 85 percent of cases in most of Western Europe; the percentages are much lower in countries in transition and in the developing world (Zvekic, 1997; Albrecht, 2001; Terrill, 2013).

Fines are not popular in the United States as punishment for felonies or serious misdemeanors, despite their extensive use for minor crimes. This is probably because judges have not found them to be very effective as a deterrent to crime or because of the difficulty in collecting the fines. Because judges are not required to assess fines rather than incarceration for many kinds of offenses, including cases of repeat offenders (as in Germany), and because they have little knowledge about or faith in offenders' ability to pay, they tend to use other options. Nevertheless, fines are often imposed in addition to other sanctions. In any case, many judges perceive conventional fines, which are legislatively determined by the nature of the crime rather than by a combination of this factor and the offender's ability to pay, as discriminatory against the poor.

Fines can serve many benefits for the criminal justice system and for society in general. Government coffers benefit from fines, especially given that fines are inexpensive to administer by the court system. Fines also can lower the numbers of persons in jails and prisons and thus save taxpayers money. Consider the example of the practical use of fines in the United States when the major investment banking firm Citigroup was fined over $100 million in connection with the collapse of Enron and also agreed to pay $2 billion to settle Enron investors' claims (Friedrichs, 2010).

In addition to providing economic benefits, fines can serve the correctional purposes of rehabilitation. When offenders are required to pay fines, they can learn to be more financially responsible and can also remain in the community to work and interact with family and friends.

There are two ways that fines can be determined. One is the fixed-sum rate system. In this system, specific offenses are allocated a certain "value," and offenders are fined according to the offenses they commit. This method appears easy to administer and rather equitable. However, not all offenders are able to pay the fines assessed for their crimes. Typically, offenders with more economic resources are able to pay the fines, whereas poorer offenders find themselves in violation of the court order, which can lead to further legal difficulties. A second fine-setting method is called the day fine.

Day Fines. In response to the concern that fines exact a heavier toll on the poor than on the wealthy, Scandinavian countries developed the **day fine** (also called the structured fine), a criminal penalty that is based on the amount of money an offender earns in a day's work. Day fines thus take into account the differing economic circumstances of offenders who have committed the same crime. In Germany day fines have been used as a replacement for short- term imprisonment even for some relatively serious offenses like burglary. Some of the countries that have made use of day fines outside Europe are the United States, New Zealand, Australia, Mexico, Canada, Macau (China), Cuba, Costa Rica, and Bolivia. Finland, which pioneered this penal reform in 1921, uses only day fines. The amount of the fine is calculated in a two-stage process. First, the number of units of punishment is determined according to the seriousness of the offense and such factors as the offender's prior record. Second, the monetary value of each unit of punishment is established in light of the offender's financial circumstances. Thus, the total penalty—the degree of punishment—should place an equivalent economic burden on offenders of differing means who are convicted of similar offenses. For example, a person making $36,500 a year and sentenced to 10 units of punishment would pay $3,650; a person making $3,650 and receiving the same penalty would pay $365.

Day fines have at least two advantages. First, they provide a balance between the crime committed and the offender's ability to pay for the crime. Offenders are required literally to "pay for their crimes" but not beyond what is possible for them financially. This reduces discrimination of sentencing and increases the likelihood of payment. Second, the day fine provides courts and correctional officials with another alternative to incarceration, one that is more punitive than probation supervision but less harsh than jail or prison. Day fines are generally not used for minor misdemeanors, because the basic intent is to make them true alternatives to incarceration.

Until recently, day fines were not as widely used in the United States as in Europe. As the need for alternatives to incarceration becomes ever greater because of prison crowding, however, the use of day fines is increasing. Day fines often are promoted as a way to improve the use of fines as sanctions in the United States. The concept is being used in the federal system and in several different states, including Arizona, Connecticut, Iowa, New

York, and Washington (Clear, Cole, & Reisig, 2011).

However, fines and day fines are not a panacea, and they have been criticized both in countries that have refused to adopt them and in the countries where they are most used. Some claim that fines tend to overpenalize the poor, who still find their living standard appreciably lowered when they have to pay a fine. Day fines tend to be mechanically applied, and they leave little discretion to the sentencing judge. Also, the actual financial circumstances of offenders often are hard to determine, and certain categories of offenders, such as students, housewives, and the unemployed, are not amenable to any fine system.

Confiscation and Forfeiture. The increase in law enforcement measures to combat international drug trafficking and organized crime has resulted in a revised form of economic sentences called confiscation and forfeiture. Confiscation and **forfeiture** is the governmental seizure of property derived from or used in criminal activity. In the United States confiscation and forfeiture takes both civil and criminal forms. Under civil law, property used in criminal activity (e.g., equipment to manufacture illegal drugs, automobiles, or boats) can be seized without a finding of guilt. Under criminal law, forfeiture is imposed as a consequence of conviction and requires that the offender relinquish various assets related to the crime. Similar confiscation and forfeiture laws and conventions have been passed in a number of countries throughout the world due to the cooperation of the United Nations and regional organizations such as the Council of Europe (Albrecht, 2001, p. 318).

Restitution and Community Service. When an offender is required or volunteers to participate in community service or to pay money to make reparation for harm resulting from a criminal offense, then **restitution** is being made. With restitution, payment is made by the offender and is received by the victim, his or her representative, or a public fund for victims of crime.

The idea of paying crime victims for losses, damage, or injuries is an ancient idea that actually predates formal criminal justice systems. Both the Old Testament of the Bible and the 4,000-year-old Code of Hammurabi state that the offender must repay crime victims "in kind or extent." In ancient times, Babylonian, Greek, Roman, and Jewish law all contained provisions for compensation to be paid by offenders. Our current conceptions about restitution have developed over many centuries. In prehistoric times, people acted on their own to punish others for transgressions against them. But as people began living in large tribes, blood feuds between different groups surfaced, and vigilante groups developed for the purpose of administering punishment. To resolve violent feuds between tribes, the crime victims or their families were given compensation for the crimes committed against them. Over time, the family's role in the compensation process diminished, and by the thirteenth century the state (or reigning monarch) had become the offended party in criminal offenses. With this development, the state assumed responsibility for punishing offenders and collecting fines. As time passed, victims became less and less involved in the punishment process. In eighteenth-century England, the concept of restitution resurfaced when philosopher Jeremy Bentham argued that payment of monetary fines was essential to his idea that the punishment should equal the crime.

One form of restitution used in Islamic countries is called **diyya**, which is paid directly to the victim or his or her family as compensation for five different *quesas* (retribution) crimes. Because *diyya* is technically a collective responsibility, the offender's family or the government may be asked to pay. Many other rules regulate the payment of *diyya,* including those related to the offense, religious affiliation, the sex of the victim, and the financial status of the families involved (Jousten & Zvekic, 1994, p. 16; Souryal, 2004).

In **community service**, an offender is asked to personally "pay back" the community by performing a set number of hours of unpaid work for a not-for-profit agency. Community service mixes two historical traditions: (1) ordering offenders to make reparation for crimes and (2) requiring unpaid labor as punishment. Community service as part of restitution can be traced back to ancient times. The sanction also was used in the Middle Ages in Germany, when it was handed out in lieu of other punishments; tasks included building city walls and cleaning canals. In the early seventeenth century, offenders in England were persuaded to join the Royal Navy in lieu of more formal punishment. In some cases, they were transferred to English colonies to work as servants for free settlers (McDonald, 1992, p. 184). Reformers in nineteenth-century France mounted a crusade for the use of community service to replace detention for those who had defaulted on fines. Community service as a substitute for paying a fine was codified as early as 1889 in Italy, in 1902 in Norway, in Germany in 1924, in Portugal in 1929, and in Switzerland in 1942 (Kalmthout & Tak, 1988, p. 14). By the late 1990s, community service programs were accepted correctional practice in the England, Canada, Australia, New Zealand, Netherlands, Finland, Germany, and the United States (Tonry & Frase, 2001). In some cases, such as in the United States and the United Kingdom, community service has been used as both as an alternative to incarceration and as a supplement to probation in minor matters related to traffic, DWI, and juvenile justice.

Community Supervision

Probation. With **probation**, a criminal sanction given in lieu of imprisonment, the offender is given the chance to remain within the community and demonstrate a willingness to abide by its laws. Probation usually is accompanied by a suspended sentence and includes some form of supervision in the community. Probation sentences may also require the offender to pay restitution to the victim or provide free services to the community to compensate for the crime. Further, the probationer may be ordered to attend treatment programs to deal with problems that led to criminal involvement. On the international level, probation is generally referred to as **control of freedom**.

In this country, probation began with the innovative work of John Augustus, a Boston boot maker who was the first person to stand bail for defendants under authority of the Boston Police Court. Augustus probably borrowed the idea of probation from the British, who in the 1820s combined the Common Law surety and recognizance systems by releasing young offenders into the hands of employers (UNAFEI, 1997, p. 119).

Of all the forms of supervising offenders in the community, probation is the most common. This form of noncustodial sanction is practiced in some form in almost all criminal justice systems in the world, although specific practices may vary considerably. In some jurisdictions, offenders are kept under close supervision to ensure that the conditions of probation are followed and the individuals are properly reintegrated into the community. In others, offenders have very limited contact with their probation officers and receive little or no community support. Variation also exists in terms of who supervises the probationers (volunteers or professionals) and whether a violation of probation conditions automatically leads to revocation and incarceration (Jousten & Zvekic, 1994).

Probation is generally administered by a probation officer employed by the local judiciary. In some cases, probation departments are part of the executive branch of government, run by state or federal organizations. In China, probation is sometimes supervised by the police or by one of the many community units. In Indonesia, it is implemented by the office of the prosecutor (UNAFEI, 1997, p. 232). In a few countries in Europe, private companies have been brought in by government to supervise and run probation agencies (van Kalmthout & Durnescu, 2008).

In many regions of the world, the use of probation is increasing; in others, its use is declining. According to results in the tenth UNCJS, probation use has increased in a number of countries in recent years. The countries with among the highest rates of probation are the United States, Canada, and England. Table 8.2 gives data on the use of probation in these three countries and Japan, which is the

TABLE 8.2 Annual Probation Totals and Rate per 100,000 Population, 2000 and 2006

	2000 Rate Per 100,000	2006 Rate Per 100,000	2000 Persons on Probation, Adult and Juvenile	2006 Persons on Probation, Adult and Juvenile
Canada	435.64[a]	358.44	132,869[b]	116,769
England and Wales	260.01[a]	257.12	137,000[b]	146,532
Japan	42.85	33.29	54,416	42,593
Germany	N/A	210.80	N/A	174,207
USA	1,836	1,399	3,839,532	4,237,000

[a]1999 rate
[b]Adults only
SOURCE: Seventh and Tenth UNCJS.

only other model country included in the tenth UNCJS.

Probation is not only a sanction devised by governments but also a general framework for a series of programs that can be developed to fit the needs of offenders and their communities. As a result, very few aspects of probation are the same around the world. A review of international probation procedures would reveal a diverse set of programs that reflect local cultural norms and political aims and provide a variety of sentencing options (Hamai et al., 1995).

House Arrest. With **house arrest**, offenders are sentenced to terms of incarceration, but they serve those terms in their own homes. Some offenders might, after a time, be allowed to venture out to go to work or to run errands. Others might be allowed to maintain their employment for the entire duration of their sentence. Whatever the details, the concept has as its basic thrust the use of the offender's residence as the place of punishment.

The use of house arrest (also called home confinement, home detention, or home probation) is hardly a novel form of punishment. Throughout history, people have been confined to their homes for violating the laws of the land. These include Galileo, who was confined to his home for making scientific statements contrary to the teachings of the Roman Catholic Church, and, more recently, Lech Walesa in Poland and Winnie Mandela in South Africa. There are at least three kinds of house arrest, which can be best understood in terms of levels of restrictiveness. The lowest level involves a simple curfew, when an offender is required to be home after a certain hour. The next level is when an offender is allowed to be away from home during certain hours of the day for work, school, religious reasons, or counseling sessions; this is often called *home confinement.* The third and most punitive form of house arrest requires the person to be home at all times, unless a special situation arises such as medical or legal appointments.

Electronic Monitoring. One of the largest growing approaches to noncustodial supervision is the use of **electronic monitoring** (EM) to expand the surveillance capacity of supervision. The original goals of EM were to reduce crime, promote a therapeutic relationship with clients, and provide a humane alternative to incarceration (Schwitzgebel, 1969). The more common use of EM in the United States dates back to 1983, when a New Mexico judge, inspired by the *Spiderman* comic strip, placed a probation violator on EM for one month. Other states soon adopted the idea, and by 2005 an estimated 125,000 persons were being monitored in all 50 states and the federal government (Stacey, 2006). Recently, the use of global positioning systems (GPS), which use satellite tracking devices to monitor offenders while living in the community, has expanded the use of probation in the United States and is sure to catch on internationally.

EM ordinarily is combined with house arrest and is used to enforce its restrictions. However, EM has been utilized in many other ways in corrections. EM has been used for intensive probation supervision (IPS) programs, work furlough–home detention programs, temporary detention of juveniles, gang supervision, narcotic surveillance, traditional home detention, and the supervision of parolees and pretrial defendants. EM is now used in Canada, Taiwan, Singapore, Australia, New Zealand, Denmark, Finland, Sweden, the Netherlands, Germany, Belgium, Portugal, Italy, Argentina, Israel, England, France, Switzerland, and Scotland (Albrecht, 2001; Paterson, 2007).

Exile. Another time-honored sanction that has assumed various forms throughout recorded history is **exile**. Most of us are familiar with the tales of the Old West in which outlaws were ridden out of town and threatened with being shot on sight if they appeared again. In small tribal communities, banishment frequently was equivalent to a death sentence. Without a sustaining community, subject to attack by enemy peoples and wildlife of various kinds, and at the mercy of the elements, the offender often did not survive exile for very long. Exile to prison colonies was a widespread practice until the end of the nineteenth century. England had discontinued transportation in the middle of the nineteenth century.

Exile is rarely used today except in some indigenous cultures in remote areas of the world. When it is implemented, it is usually internal and accompanied by another alternative to incarceration. Such is the case in Italy, where offenders may be sent to a town far from where they committed their crimes but must remain under the supervision of the local police.

Andrei Sakharov, the Nobel Prize winner in physics, was no doubt the best known of the internal exiles in the former Soviet Union. After he became disillusioned with the Soviet regime and was vocally critical of its human rights abuses, Sakharov was convicted of undermining the state and sentenced to exile. Sakharov could not practice his vocation in exile or engage in the kind of political activity that had put him under so much suspicion. In effect, the Soviets removed him from the center of action, thinking (albeit wrongly, since Sakharov generated a lot of concern and publicity even in exile) that he would no longer be able to engage in activities embarrassing to the regime.

Warnings. In many countries, especially in Europe, warnings are used in a large number of cases. These **warnings** (also called admonishments) are provided at the adjudication stage by the judge and usually are accompanied by the threat of incarceration if criminal behavior does not desist. In the United States, warnings are used extensively in the juvenile justice system.

Other Punishments. In addition to the more common sentences mentioned here, there are some other forms of less frequently employed sentencing options available around the globe. Some are imposed in connection with crime commission but are not often viewed as criminal penalties, such as loss of driver's license, cancellation of professional licenses, mandatory notification of release and registration of sex offenders, loss of voting rights or citizenship, reduction of social service benefits, and loss of employment (Kurki, 2001).

IMPRISONMENT

Imprisonment is today the severest punishment inflicted in most societies. It is also the most problematic of punishments, in that so little other than short-term incapacitation appears to be achieved through its use. It is used almost universally, but there are major differences among criminal justice systems in duration of prison sentences and in prison conditions and programs. Here, we briefly examine the extent of the use of prison as a sentence around the world. In the next chapter, we will consider prison policies more broadly and issues related to incarceration in our model countries.

It is important to note that we use the term *prison* exclusively to describe any facility used to incarcerate criminal offenders. Technically, at least in the United States, there is a difference between prisons and jails. **Prisons** are used almost exclusively for serious offenders who receive sentences of more than one year; **jails** are facilities that house less serious offenders who are generally sentenced to less than one year or who are awaiting trial or transfer to another institution. We use the term *prison* in these chapters because it is more representative of the terminology used throughout the world. In many countries, due to lack of financial resources, untried prisoners are not separated from those already convicted. When a country separates inmates, it typically uses the term **remand prison** to describe the facility used to house unconvicted inmates.

International Prison Data

To understand the extent of the use of incarceration around the world today, we turn to data provided by the ninth edition of the *World Prison Population List*. The *World Prison Population List,* prepared by Roy Walmsley, an English researcher and consultant to the United Nations, provides the number of prisoners in 218 independent countries and territories as of May 2011 (Walmsley, 2011). The list reflects the differences in the levels of imprisonment across the world and provides the information necessary to estimate the world prison population. Derived from a variety of sources, the list specifically includes the number of those incarcerated in remand (jail) or prison, the estimated national population, the rate of inmates per 100,000 population, and the date of data compilation. The list does have some limitations, including missing data, some variability in the dates, and limited information about special categories of offenders such as remand, juvenile, and mentally ill offenders. There is also some question as to what constitutes a prisoner from country to country (Walmsley, 2011). Even with its limitations, the list is the best comprehensive source of international prison data compiled to date. A second and regularly updated source called the *World Prison Brief*, prepared at the International Centre for Prison Studies (ICPS), provides a list of individual prison population rates for 222 countries rated from highest to lowest as of May 2012. We will utilize the *World Prison Brief* in the next chapter to discuss prisons in our model countries and issues related to prison crowding.

A review of the *World Prison Population List* indicates that as of 2011 there were over 10.1 million people in correctional institutions throughout the world as either pretrial (remand) or convicted and sentenced criminals, with the world prison population rate estimated at 146 per 100,000, a slight drop from 2009, when it was 150 per 100,000. The countries with the highest total number of inmates were in the United States (2.29 million), followed by China (1.65 million sentenced prisoners) and Russia (around 800,000). The highest prison population rate was in the United States (743 per 100,000 people) followed by the Rwanda (595 per 100,000) and Russia (568 per 100,000 people) For comparison, more than one half of the countries and territories around the world have rates below 150 per 100,000 (Walmsley, 2011). Walmsley and the ICPS data provide an excellent source of information for comparisons among countries at one period of time, in what is called **stock design**. But as we have come to learn more about comparative data, we now know that incarceration rates in a stock design are very limited in their scope. One suggestion for improvement would be to study the number of prison admissions over time, in what is called **flow design** (Lynch, 1988). This would allow us to separate the tendency to incarcerate and the length of time served. With this in mind, we address the issue of how international prison rates have changed over time.

If we look simply at the numbers provided by stock design, we can surmise that there has been an increase in prison populations in many parts of the world in recent years. More specifically, there has been an increase in the prison population in 78 percent of the world's countries, with a total increase of over 1.3 million inmates since previous *World Prison Population Lists* were compiled in 2010, 2008, 2003, and 1999. If we wish to further support the position of prison population growth over time, we can compare our current world prison population rate of 146 per 100,000 with data from the first UNCJS. Those data reveal that the rate in developing countries in 1972 was around 40 per 100,000 and the rate in developed countries was around 85 per 100,000 (Newman, 1999, p. 97). In addition to the total number of inmates incarcerated, two issues of concern for those who study international imprisonment rates are the increasing number of women and the rising number of minority groups that are incarcerated worldwide.

Women and Incarceration. The second *World Female Imprisonment List*, also published by Roy Walmsley, revealed that as of January 2012 more than 625,000 women and girls are in prison around the world and that the female prison population has grown 16% since 2006 (Walmsley, 2012). The rise in imprisonment for females is believed to be directly related to the international fight against drugs. This has been the case for years in the United States, but more recently the same has been true in other countries. For example, over 31,000 women across Europe and Central Asia are imprisoned for drug offenses, representing 28 percent of all women in prisons in these regions, according to a new report by Harm Reduction International (Iakobishvili, 2012).

Minorities and Incarceration. A second issue of concern relative to imprisonment around the world is the significant number of minorities incarcerated in the world today. It is probably safe to state that as of December 2010 the United States is the world leader in this category, with over 60% of its prison population being Black or Hispanic (BJS, 2012). This is troubling in light of the fact that Blacks and Hispanics make up only 13 and 16 percent of the U.S. population, respectively. However, the United States is not alone in the incarceration of disproportional number of minorities. Within our model countries alone, England and Wales, France, and Germany all have experienced an increase in minority incarcerations in recent years. In addition, many countries have a high percentage (at least 30 percent) of incarcerated foreigners, including Gambia, Qatar, Switzerland, United Arab Emirates, Austria, Belgium and Italy (Reichel, 2013). The reason for such a high number of minority inmates is complicated and quite controversial. Some argue that institutional and in some cases societal racism is the reason, while others argue that certain communities commit more serious crimes. Others claim people go to prison because of a combination of social and economic factors that lead to incarceration (see Walker, Spohn, & DeLone, 2007; Clear, Cole, & Reisig, 2011).

Prisons and Politics. There are many theories as to why prison populations have soared recently throughout the world. The most common is that the increase in prison populations is directly related to the increase in the crime rate. However, there is little data to support this assertion. In fact, many researchers have presented evidence that there is little or no relationship between incarceration rates and crime rates (Young & Brown, 1993; Newman, 1999, p. 91; Tonry & Frase, 2001, p. 10; Brodeur, 2007).

Looking back at the last 35 years, we find that politics has had a major role in the punishment trends in many regions of the globe, especially in Western democratic countries. One trend has been to increase the use of punishment for certain crimes and to increase the lengths of punishments for criminal offenders. Although overall crime rates and crime seriousness may have had some role to play in the development of harsher sentencing structures, it is now clear that conscious policy decisions made by public officials are the major reason for increased punishments (Kuhn, 1994; Tonry & Frase, 2001). More specifically, the increases in the prison populations in England, the Netherlands, and especially the United States have occurred because of the will of politicians to be "tough on crime" (Tonry, 2007b; Kury & Shea, 2011).

Much of the call for increasing the severity of the sentences has been fueled by **penal populism**. This is a term given to criminal justice policies that are designed to appeal to the public appetite for punitiveness with little concern for program effectiveness or the clear understanding of community views. Those who practice penal populism, individuals called penal populists, may exploit the misinformed opinion of the public in the pursuit of electoral advantage. Penal populism is in contrast to penal policies that are grounded in justice and draw on a body of sentencing research (Roberts et al., 2003, pp. 7–8; Pratt, 2007). The United States is especially vulnerable to penal populism because of the emphasis on the individual politician rather than on the party he or she is supporting, the role and power of the American media, and a history of politicians receiving pressure from single-issue groups (Roberts et al., 2003, p. 73).

A number of sentencing strategies and larger criminal justice policies have developed internationally as a result of penal populism and the will to "get tough" on crime and criminals. They include *mandatory sentencing* laws that eliminate any judicial discretion in sentencing, *sentencing guidelines* that provide strict limits on discretion, and the *transfer of juveniles* who commit serious crimes to the adult criminal justice system. *Three-strikes* laws that call for a lifetime sentence after the conviction for a third serious offense, *truth-in-sentencing* laws that restrict parole release, and the self-explanatory sentence of *life without parole* are examples of specific strategies formulated by legislators in the United States to promote this kind of sentencing agenda.

It should be noted that not all researchers agree that rising incarceration rates are caused by penal populism, or that incarceration rates are in fact rising everywhere as some data reflect. A diverging opinion by comparative penologist Michael Tonry states that further explication of the data reveals that in fact incarceration rates in many countries, especially those in Europe, have actually declined in recent years and that penal populism is not in fact a global problem but one that is located primarily in two countries, the United States and England (Tonry, 2007b).

Limits of International Prison Data

As with international crime data, there are a number of pitfalls to comparing international prison data. As we noted in Chapter 2, one of the weaknesses of international crime data is that many countries fail to report or underreport their crime data. The same can be said for international prison data. Despite the best attempts by private researchers and international organizations to collect this data, many countries simply fail to respond truthfully or competently to inquiries about prison populations.

Prison data also suffer from a form of nonstandardization when it comes to definitions. The definitional problems involve what counts as a prison and who counts as a prisoner. Some countries include all correctional facilities in the statistics, whereas others exclude certain types of institutions such as remand facilities (jails), special work camps, and juvenile facilities. When counting inmates, some countries may not feel it necessary to include inmates who have yet to be tried. Others may exclude certain groups of inmates because they are mentally ill. For example, in the Netherlands, those convicted of murder or rape are sent to special mental hospitals run by health authorities (Stern, 1998).

Another larger methodological problem with incarceration figures is that they do not account for sentence length. Rates of incarceration are naturally tied to sentence length, since longer sentences tend to increase the rate at any one time (Young & Brown, 1993; Kuhn, 1996). The United States, for example, with longer sentences than other countries, will tend to have a higher rate of imprisonment.

Many researchers have presented possible ways to improve methods of collection and presentation of international prison data. As we have already mentioned, one option is the use of stock designs and flow designs to measure the number of prison admissions over time. Other options include the ideas that the incarceration rate should be determined by dividing the number of persons sentenced to prison by the number convicted during that same year, that we should compare the prison population to the number of prosecutions in the country, and that we should also take into account changes in criminal procedure (Rahim, 1986; Buck & Pease, 1993; Tonry, 2007b). Each of these methods may bring us closer to a more precise understanding of international incarceration rates.

International prison data serve as a reminder once again that even simple comparisons among countries with respect to some facet of the criminal justice process need to be scrutinized very closely. As with the even more problematic comparative crime rates, careful evaluations of multiple indicators of the extent of the phenomenon are preferable to unidimensional comparisons.

THE DEATH PENALTY

The penalty of death has been a sentencing option since the beginning of civilization. In biblical times, criminals were stoned to death and their bodies hung up as an act of deterrence. Ancient Athenian society restricted the use of the death penalty and actually humanized the process by allowing the condemned to drink poison. The Romans used many forms of execution, including burning, stoning, strangulation, drawing and quartering, crucifixion, and, famously, throwing the criminal to the lions. In medieval times, executions were conducted through the use of ordeals, in the belief that God would protect the innocent from extreme physical harm while permitting the guilty to succumb (Johnson, 1988). Hanging, shooting, electrocution, and lethal injection remain the major forms of execution throughout the world, although some countries (primarily Islamic nations) still resort to more ancient methods such as stoning and crucifixion.

Other regions of the world, including China, ancient India, Western Europe, and North America, all adopted the penalty of death hundreds if not thousands of years ago. The movement to abolish the death penalty began in the late 1700s, when European criminologists Cesare Beccaria (1748–1794) and Jeremy Bentham (1748–1832) first tried to persuade the English Parliament to abolish the death penalty for certain crimes (Simon & Blaskovich, 2002).

According to the human rights organization Amnesty International, 676 persons were officially reported executed in 20 countries in 2011. This number is an increase from 2010, when 527 were documented. The actual number of executions throughout the world is sure to be higher because data are very difficult to determine. Some countries do not publish these figures, and others do not give accurate figures. In fact, the 676 known executions do not include the numbers from China, which refused to reveal how many were executed there in 2011. Amnesty International claims that China is probably the country with the highest number of executions in any given year and that evidence from previous years and a number of current sources indicates that the figure remains in the thousands. Other countries that remain in the top five in known executions are Iran (360+), Iraq (68+), Saudi Arabia (82+), and the United States (43), and Yemen (41+) (Amnesty International, 2012).

China has claimed that the number of executions has gone down since 2007, when it became mandatory for a high court to review death penalty cases. And in February 2012 the National People's Congress passed a law that removed the death penalty as punishment for 13 crimes. At the same time, however, the Chinese added a number of new crimes and expanded the scope of other crimes to include the death penalty (Amnesty International, 2012b). International death penalty scholar Roger Hood has recently completed a key study about the death penalty in China that provides hope for abolitionists. He found that "despite secrecy around the country's death penalty, no one can doubt that a movement towards restriction and eventual abolition has got under way." He attributes the shift in attitudes on the death penalty to the emerging international narrative that suggests capital punishment should be treated not as "a weapon of national criminal justice policy," but as "a fundamental violation of universal human rights: not only the right to life but the right to be free from excessive, repressive and tortuous punishments—including the risk that an innocent or undeserving person may be executed" (Hood, 2009). In the coming years, human rights activists will surely keep a close eye on China, seeing that they are apparently the world leader in the execution of criminals.

The trend, however, is toward the worldwide abolition of the death penalty. As of March 2012, 97 countries have abolished the death penalty for all crimes, 8 have abolished it for ordinary crimes—the exception being war crimes—and 36 exercise de facto abolition, meaning they no longer implement the death penalty in practice although it still exists in the law. This means that by the end of 2012, 141 nations in the world had outlawed the death penalty by law or in practice while 57 retained its use. The most recent country to abolish was Latvia in 2012. To better understand the move toward abolition, consider that in 2004 the numbers were 118 and 78 respectively (DPIC, 2012).

Abolition of the death penalty has also become an important issue for international bodies. One of the most important developments in recent years has been the adoption of international treaties related to the use and abolition of the death penalty. The most recent of these is the Treaty of Lisbon, which was passed into law on December 1, 2009, calling for all members of the European Union to prohibit extradition to a country where capital punishment might be imposed. The supranational criminal tribunals established by the United Nations for the former Yugoslavia, Rwanda, Sierra Leone, and Lebanon all exclude the death penalty; and the International Criminal Court may not impose the death penalty (Hill, 2010). For a list of international treaties on the death penalty and the number of countries that have ratified or signed them, see http://www.amnesty.org/en/death-penalty/ratification-of-international-treaties.

The general view of the United Nations relative to the topic of capital punishment is quite clear. In December 2007 and 2008, the United Nations General Assembly adopted resolutions calling for a moratorium on the use of the death penalty. Since then, other regional bodies or civil society coalitions adopted resolutions and declarations advocating for a moratorium on executions as a step toward global abolition of the death penalty. In December 2009 the top United Nations human rights official called for the universal abolition of the death penalty, citing a host of reasons ranging from the fundamental right to life to the possibility of judicial errors. UN High Commissioner for Human Rights Navi Pillay said,

> I am opposed to the death penalty in all cases.... I hold this position for a number of reasons: these include the fundamental nature of the right to life; the unacceptable risk of executing innocent people by mistake; the absence of proof that the death penalty serves as a deterrent; and what is, to my mind, the inappropriately vengeful character of the sentence. (United Nations News Center, 2009)

Criminologists Franklin Zimring and Gordon Hawkins have asserted that the declining use of executions in some countries is part of a "long-term evolutionary process—the development process of civilization." Statutory abolition, they tell us, was preceded in each case by long periods in which no one was executed in normal times; in other words, de facto abolition preceded de jure abolition (1986, p. 8).

Research conducted on behalf of the United Nations has supported the position that countries are justified in the abolition of the death penalty. More specifically, the research consistently failed to find convincing evidence that the death penalty deters crime more effectively than other punishments and found that there is no apparent relationship between the increase in crime rates and the reduction in the use of the death penalty. For example, in Canada the homicide rate per 100,000 population was 3.09 in 1975. In 2002, 26 years following the abolition of capital punishment in Canada, the homicide rate was 1.85 per 100,000 population (Hood, 2002). However, recent research in the United States has reached a slightly different conclusion. In short, the research on the deterrent effects of the death penalty has failed to reach a consensus. Some identify a strong deterrent effect, whereas others claim that any results in that direction are due to methodological anomalies (see Apel and Nagin, 2011).

It is important to make clear that, although the international trend is to abolish the death penalty, international courts have not specifically ruled that the death penalty is inhumane or degrading punishment. Also, abolition has not been accepted as customary international law, which means it is binding on all states regardless of whether the treaties have been ratified (Hodgkinson & Rutherford, 1996). At the same time, certain restrictions on the application of the death penalty have attained the status of customary law, such as those stated in the UN resolution Safeguards Guaranteeing Protection of the Rights of Those Facing the Death Penalty. Among the international standards that have become customary international law related to capital punishment are the following:

- Capital punishment may be imposed only for the most serious crimes.
- Capital punishment may not be applied retroactively.
- Capital punishment may not be imposed on juvenile offenders under 18 years old when they committed their crime.
- Capital punishment may not be imposed on mentally incompetent or insane persons.
- Capital punishment may not be imposed on pregnant women or new mothers.

Sources: Kurki, 2001; Amnesty International, 2012c.

One may well ask, in the face of these facts, why the United States and Japan, two of the most powerful modern nations in the world, continue to execute offenders. Various opinions exist concerning this phenomenon. Japan entered the company of democratic nations late in its history, and thus it may not yet have achieved the maturity in its criminal process that abolition would signify. The United States, on the other hand, has a history of violence, as reflected in the widespread possession and use of firearms, lynchings, and brutality in the case of the institution of slavery. Thus, there is greater tolerance for violence, including execution of convicted murderers, and executions serve a ritualistic function that responds to the cultural reality in the country. But it appears that even these two world powers may be softening in the application of the death penalty.

The number of those receiving the death penalty in Japan has fluctuated in recent years. From July 2011 through March 2012 there were no executions in Japan, the first time a year or more had passed without an execution for 19 years. This respite and possible move towards abolition was short-lived, however, and in 2012 three murderers were executed. The chance for total abolition is surely affected by the fact that 85 percent of the citizens of Japan favor the penalty (Parry, 2009; McCurry, 2012).

It appears that the United States has not totally ignored the international trend away from the death penalty. As of January 1, 2012, the United States has executed 1,277 persons since the death penalty was reinstated in 1977. Despite continuing to carry out executions, however, the United States is showing some signs of turning against the death penalty. The total of executions in the USA dropped to 43 executions during 2011, a 56 percent drop since 1999, and the number of inmates sentenced to death fell below 100 for the first time since 1977. Even in Texas the number of executions dropped to 13, a drop of 46 percent in only two years (DPIC, 2012). In 2005, the Supreme Court in *Roper v. Simmons* struck down the death penalty for juveniles, and in January 2011 Illinois became the sixteenth state to end the death penalty when the state governor signed a new law. Also in 2011, Oregon called for a moratorium on the death penalty. There are at least three reasons for the United States' turn toward abolition.

First, the United States has received some pressure from the international community to reconsider its stance on the death penalty. This pressure takes the form of being formally accused of human rights violations or having limits placed on trade and international business operations. Also of serious concern is the possible impact that continued support for the death penalty would have on the fight against transnational crime, including terrorism. European countries such as Germany and France, and even neighbors Canada and Mexico, have begun to refuse to extradite criminals who have escaped to their countries as long as the penalty of death is a possibility in the United States (Dieter, 2003).

Second, the move toward abolition of the death penalty in the United States may also be spurred by recent news of offenders who have had their convictions overturned or sentences commuted because of inequities in the system or legal mistakes found in the investigation or trial. Between 2000 and 2011, there was an average of five such exonerations per year in the United States. In each case, inmates were released from death row based on legal evidence of their innocence (DPIC, 2012).

Finally, it appears that the American public's attitudes toward the death penalty have also begun to change. In 2011 the National Gallup Poll reflected that 61 percent of Americans supported the death penalty—down from a high of 80 percent in 1994. And the same poll showed that if those questioned are provided with the option of life without parole instead of the death penalty, the number of those who support the death penalty sentence drops to 46 percent (Gallup, 2012). It is also important to mention that Americans are not alone in their general support for the death penalty. The World Millennium Study conducted by Gallup reflects that the majority of people living in the world today (52%) support the penalty of death (Unnever, 2010). Interestingly, however, statutory abolition has occurred in many countries *despite* public opinion in favor of continuing the death penalty. Only time will tell whether the pressures that bear on the American leaders will be enough to create any serious movement toward abolition.

SUMMARY

There is no doubt that many nations have come a long way from the cruel practices that constituted sanctions in earlier centuries. Ideas about human rights, including rights of the convicted, although certainly not honored universally, have achieved a kind of legitimacy through the efforts of international organizations and gradually developing international standards.

Criminal sanctions have moved over the past 200 years from primary reliance on corporal punishment and transportation, to heavy reliance on conventional imprisonment, to the development of alternative sanctions. The most common of these alternative sanctions include probation, fines, day fines, restitution, and community service. The reliance on incarceration has increased over the last 20 years. Corporal punishment and the death penalty remain as sentencing alternatives around the world. In countries that adhere to Islamic law, corporal punishments are preferred to imprisonment, and indeed in these societies imprisonment is a last resort for truly intractable offenders. Although the death penalty has virtually been abolished in Western Europe and Latin America, it is still practiced in many parts of the world, albeit usually on a very limited scale. In the United States, the use of the death penalty has remained a viable sentencing alternative although there is some evidence of its reduced use and reduced support in recent years.

The philosophy of sentencing also has undergone changes in the past 200 years. In the nineteenth century, the classical school of criminologists spearheaded the move toward rational sentencing linked to the severity of the crime. In the early twentieth century, under the influence of progressive reformers and with the United States in the lead, the philosophy of sentencing became increasingly rehabilitative. Over the past 30 years, however, there has been a backlash against the rehabilitative philosophy, again with the United States in the lead. The philosophy of sentencing and sentencing practice are important indicators of the mood of a country and its stage of development. Sometimes this mood is set, however, by those who are likely to benefit politically from a punitive punishment philosophy. The most troublesome aspect of corrections in many countries, however, remains the administration of actual imprisonment as a form of punishment. We will consider this topic in the next chapter.

Comparative Criminal Justice at the Movies

Movies seek to entertain and inform the audience about a story, incident, or person. Many good movies also hit upon important substantive themes relevant to understanding crime and justice in comparative perspective. Read the movie summary below (and watch the movie if you haven't already) and answer the questions below to make the subject matter connections to comparative criminal justice.

Traffic (2001)
Steven Soderbergh, Director

Traffic considers America's war on drugs using three interconnected story lines. The first plot involves a police officer in Mexico, Javier Rodriguez (Benicio Del Toro), who attempts to disrupt a cocaine shipment in the desert with a corrupt partner, Manolo Sanchez (Jacob Vargas). Working in this highly corrupt environment, Rodriguez is himself investigated by a suspect Mexican general who happens to be the U.S. drug enforcement liaison between Mexico and the United States.

A second story line occurs in Ohio and Washington, D.C., where a newly appointed conservative federal drug czar, Ohio judge Robert Wakefield (Michael Douglas), has his antidrug fervor dampened when he discovers that his 16-year-old daughter is a habitual drug user, a situation his wife has tried to keep secret.

A third plot line tells the story of Carlos Alaya (Steven Bauer), a drug kingpin in San Diego who is caught in a DEA sting operation by agents Montel Gordon (Don Cheadle) and Ray Castro (Luis Guzman), leaving behind his pregnant and clueless wife, Helena (Catharine Zeta-Jones). Carlos's shady lawyer, Arnie Metzger (Dennis Quaid), encourages Helena to carry on the "family business," which she does with tragic results.

Each of these stories plays out and overlaps with one other, and *Traffic* shows the complexity, frustration, and consequences of the war on drugs without taking a position on the issue. The Michael Douglas character expresses the frustration when he says "It's hard fighting a war on drugs when the enemy is ourselves."

Based on the 1980s British television miniseries *Traffik*, the film was nominated for five Academy Awards, including Best Picture. It won for Best Director, Best Supporting Actor (Benicio Del Toro), Best Editing, and Best Screenplay.

Questions

1. It can be said that the current "war on drugs" has forced organized crime groups to become more sophisticated, as they did during Prohibition, in order to avoid apprehension and keep making money. If better law enforcement produces fewer, but more highly developed, drug networks, what would you propose as a solution to this problem?
2. *Traffic* shows the interplay among supply, demand, traffickers, and law enforcement in dealing with illicit drugs. Explain which of these four factors you believe requires the most attention in dealing with illegal drugs more effectively.

Critical Thinking Exercise

Critical thinking requires the ability to evaluate viewpoints, facts, and behaviors objectively to assess information and methods of argumentation in order to establish the merit of an action, law, policy, or procedure. Please evaluate this scenario objectively, applying your knowledge of comparative criminal justice to the facts of the case presented, and answer the questions that follow it.

A Possible Move from the Adversarial to the Inquisitorial Legal System?
A provincial Deputy Police Commissioner, Nick Kaldas, has questioned the future of Australia's adversarial legal system, claiming that modern criminal trials are often too complex for juries to understand. Addressing the International Criminal Law Congress in Sydney, Mr. Kaldas admitted there were discussions in law enforcement circles about the effectiveness of the jury

system, particularly in complicated cases such as long-running terrorism trials.

"There's an enormous amount of material for a normal person to try and absorb, analyze in their minds, and understand what that means for the prosecution," Mr. Kaldas said. "It's that sort of matter at the moment which we think juries may well struggle with, and it's something for us to think about." The provincial director of public prosecutions, Nicholas Cowdery, confirmed he had been involved in similar conversations.

"I've had some discussions about moving towards some aspects of the inquisitorial system too, in the context of the International Association of Prosecutors," Mr. Cowdery said. "I'm sure these discussions are being held all over the place very often."

Although Kaldas and Cowdery stressed that the conversations they had been privy to had all been strictly informal, Sydney barrister James Fliece, who attended the morning session, described the deputy commissioner's comments as disturbing and said, "Trial by jury is an integral part of the Australian criminal justice system. What they're talking about is a major change to our system of justice."

"What's more, it is based on the false premise that a jury is incapable of understanding and deciding these issues. In fact, juries have been demonstrating for years that they have innate understanding of most issues and an innate sense of justice."

But these aren't the only high-profile figures to have recently raised the possibility of making changes to the legal system. Crown prosecutor Christopher Maxwell—who has worked in both the British and the continental systems—recently expressed his preference for the inquisitorial model, under which a judge inquires about the case during the hearing with the help of the advocates for the parties, while the attorneys-general of two Australian provinces have indicated that the jury system might need reform and one has set up a working group to examine a number of issues, including potential improvements to the jury system.

Questions

1. What do you believe is behind the views expressed in this article by police and prosecutors about the abilities of juries in an adversarial system?
2. What are the major differences in court procedure between the adversarial and inquisitorial legal systems?
3. What would replace the decisions of juries in an inquisitorial legal system?
4. What do you think of the criticism expressed in the article of the existing adversarial system in Australia?

SOURCE: Mathew Clayfield, "Trials Too Difficult for Juries," The Australian, October 10, 2008, p. 6.

DISCUSSION QUESTIONS

1. Which purpose of criminal sanctioning seems to be predominant in the world today? Which purpose do you believe is most effective?
2. Explain whether you believe alternative sanctions are a viable solution to incarceration for criminal offenders. What might be some challenges to their implementation in the international community?
3. How would you summarize the data that describe the recent trends in the use of imprisonment in the world today?
4. Why do the United States and Japan continue to use the death penalty when most industrial nations have outlawed it? What might be the reasons for change in death penalty policies in these two world powers?
5. What are the political advantages of supporting crime policies that call for the increased use of incarceration?

FOR FURTHER READING

Garland, D. (2001). *The Culture of Control: Crime and Order in Contemporary Society*. Chicago: University of Chicago Press.

Gavrielides, T. (2007). *Restorative Justice Theory and Practice: Addressing the Discrepancy*. Helsinki: Academic Bookstore.

Hood, R., and C. Hoyle (2008). *The Death Penalty: A Worldwide Perspective*. Oxford: Oxford University Press.

Peters, R. (2005). *Crime and Punishment in Islamic Law: Theory and Practice from the Sixteenth to the Twenty-first Century*. New York: Cambridge University Press.

Tonry, M. (Ed.). (2007). *Crime, Punishment, and Politics in Comparative Perspective*, vol. 36. Chicago: University of Chicago Press.

WEB PAGES FOR CHAPTER

For a website about corporal punishment throughout the world, in history and the present day, see http://www.corpun.com.

To learn more about the implementation of restorative justice around the world, see http://www.restorativejustice.org.

To view up-to-date international information about the death penalty, see http://www.deathpenaltyinfo.org/home.

To read a 2012 report about human rights and punishment around the world, see the Amnesty International website at http://www.amnestyusa.org/sites/default/files/air12-report-english.pdf.

9  After Conviction: The Problem of Prison

Key Terms and Concepts

administrative detention
conjugal visiting
crime control model
Geneva Convention
independent monitoring board
parole
private prison
progressive movement
public surveillance
reeducation through labor (*laojiao*)
reform through labor (*laogai*)

Chapter 9 Learning Objectives

Describe unique correctional practices and current incarceration rates in each of the model countries.

Analyze the effects of prison crowding.

Explore suggested solutions to prison crowding.

Summarize the major international documents that encourage legal protections for prison inmates.

Explain how the sentences of supranational criminals are carried out around the world today.

After a full day of manual labor digging ditches in coal mines and breaking rocks, it has been reported that hundreds of Chinese prisoners were forced to play online computer games to build up credits for prison guards who would trade the credits for real money. The process, known as "gold farming," calls for the building up credits and value through the monotonous repetition of basic tasks in games such as *World of Warcraft*. After accruing virtual assets, the gamers are prepared to trade real money for the online credits, which they use to progress in the online games against other players. If Chinese inmates did not reach their online work quota, they would be subjected to the unlimited power of the prison guards, who would use physical punishment to force compliance (Vincent, 2011). Unfortunately, this situation does not appear to be anomaly for the Chinese. For decades, human rights groups and Chinese citizens have accused Chinese correctional officials of violence, intimidation, humiliation, isolation, brainwashing, harassment, and psychological torture.

In this example of the use (or misuse) of incarceration in China, one of the world leaders in the incarceration of criminals, one can see how prison administration and the treatment of offenders is often unique and at times quite troubling to the international community. Variation in the administration of prisons is created by a number of factors including a country's history, economics, politics, and recent trends regarding how certain offenders should be treated and what works in correctional (penal) practice. Such variation makes the study of prisons both interesting and complicated. There is no single way to run a prison, and every country has its own rationale for choosing one system over another. For those that hope to improve their system, the main task is to determine what correctional policy can work, for whom, and in what socioeconomic context.

Unfortunately, prisons today are often viewed as symbols of the failure of the criminal justice system to achieve the changes in human attitudes and behavior that would make their use worthwhile. It may be that depriving people of their freedom is not a good way to teach them to act as proper citizens in countries in which freedom of action and thought are emphasized in governmental and economic ideologies. It may be that no system has really devoted the necessary resources to programs of rehabilitation. Or it may simply be that no programs exist that can change the conditioning patterns that individuals undergo in their earliest years. Despite the lack of evidence that shows prisons work, many governments from all around the world, especially the United States, continue to incarcerate people at an alarming rate. In this chapter, we will discuss some of the important issues related to incarceration. More specifically, we will describe a brief history of prisons; then, after an examination of penology in our model countries, we will discuss some of the common problems that face penal systems around the globe, including prison crowding and the rights of prisoners.

THE EVOLUTION OF PRISON SYSTEMS

The history of the birth of prisons is unclear and open to debate. We know that in ancient times prison had a different purpose from in modern times. From the late 1500s, prisoners were incarcerated for relatively short periods of time while they awaited draconian physical punishments or execution. History tells us that in 621 B.C. a Greek magistrate and politician named Draco (hence the term *draconian*) was known for his law setting that included the extensive use of the death sentence and other harsh punishments such as starvation, poisoning, death by exposure, and banishment. But notably absent in the historical records is the frequent use of long-term incarceration (DeLisi & Conis, 2010).

We also know about a large spring-water cistern that was constructed in Rome around the same time as Draco but later (in 64 B.C.) was used as a vast primitive prison and called Mamertine Prison. But again, only high-profile political and military prisoners were kept there, and only until they could be paraded in public prior to some gruesome death. Roman law at the time did not recognize imprisonment itself as punishment. During the reign of Constantine I (306–337 A.D.), it is believed that the Christian Church began the custom of providing sanctuary for penitence rather than physical punishments and death and that eventually led to a form of imprisonment and the formation of monasteries.

In the Middle Ages, prisons remained largely for minor offenses and for those in debt, but the purpose of some prisons became expanded to include longer incarceration terms as punishment rather than awaiting punishment. Prisons came to be viewed as an alternative to and an improvement on physical punishments and the inhumane treatment incurred while incarcerated. Some early prisons and their methods were greatly influenced by religious groups. For example, the medieval Roman Catholic Church expanded on the use of the monastic cell as a place for punishment for criminal offenders. In 1593 the Protestants of Amsterdam built a house of correction for women, and one for men in 1603. It is believed that the Dutch were the first Europeans to segregate serious criminals from vagrants and minor criminals, and Dutch courts were believed to be the first to regularly substitute imprisonment for corporal punishments. The term used to describe this sentence was *penal bondage,* which included all forms of incarceration (Spierenburg, 1995).

In England, secular houses of correction, called Bridewells, were instituted by King Edward VI in 1553 and later served as models for similar institutions in Holland, France, Germany, and Italy. These institutions were often used to house prostitutes, vagrants, debtors, and other minor criminals. Inmates were subject to stern discipline and set to work with the goal of making a "habit of industry more conducive to an honest livelihood" (Fox, 1952; Hirsh, 1992). The early European prisons were rarely called prisons but instead went by the terms *dungeon, tower,* or *gaol*—the latter of which eventually evolved into the word *jail.* The ancient and medieval prisons, then, primarily served to temporarily house those awaiting trial, minor offenders, and those awaiting harsh physical punishments. Later, they were places where criminal offenders could be held more humanely, for longer periods of time, and with the hope that they would be reformed into better citizens.

The American Experience with Incarceration

The beginning of the modern prison is also up for debate, although we do know that Alexis de Tocqueville, Charles Dickens, and even Karl Marx spent time in the United States in the second quarter of the nineteenth century with the purpose of studying the American system of penitentiaries, which had achieved international fame as a major reform of the criminal justice process. Various American reformers hoped that a regime of solitude (the Pennsylvania system) or of silent, controlled work (the Auburn system) would provide a humane way to bring about a change of disposition and lifestyle in convicted criminals. The American prison system developed in response to the arbitrary, often cruel corporal punishments that were inflicted on offenders in previous eras in the hope that they would deter others from crime.

The American experiment rapidly became the focus of reform discussions in other countries. In France and England, prison systems began to take the place of transportation of offenders to remote prison colonies. The criminal law was reformed to provide sentences to prison instead of the prevailing corporal punishments and the excessive use of the death penalty for relatively minor crimes. By the middle of the nineteenth century, prison became the normative punishment rather than the exception. Unfortunately, by the early twentieth century it was obvious that prisons were not fulfilling their promise and in fact were generally as cruel and inhumane as any previous method of punishment.

One of the hallmarks of the American **progressive movement** of the early twentieth century was the interest in a new approach to corrections: rehabilitation of the individual offender by specialists in corrections. A whole panoply of new or renewed proposals for change, including probation, parole, therapeutic prison regimes, and separate juvenile justice mechanisms became the dominant ideological, if not practical, reform proposals of the movement. However, the rehabilitation movement was short lived.

Faced with high crime rates and high recidivism rates, since the early 1970s criminal justice officials throughout the world and especially in the United States have turned to a **crime control model** of corrections. The crime control model, also called the "new penology," assumes that criminal behavior can be controlled by more incarceration and other forms of strict supervision in the community (Shahidullah, 2014). As a result of the crime control model in the last half of the twentieth century, we have seen the decline of correctional rehabilitation and a punitive ethos that has led to dealing more strictly with drug offenders, violent offenders, and career criminals. Mandatory sentences, longer sentences, intensive supervision of probationers, and detention without bail have increased jail and prison populations to record levels in the United States and around the world.

In summary, it appears that the early penitentiary movement, subsequent reforms, and "get tough" strategies have not lived up to the expectations of the reformers who conceived them. Indeed, the only two goals of sentencing that prisons seem to achieve are the ones that admit to failure: retribution and incapacitation. The more optimistic goals of rehabilitation, deterrence, and more recently restoration have not been fully realized even in the most progressive, humane, and costly prison systems in the United States or elsewhere. As measured by recidivism figures, there is little indication that we know how to change people by putting them in prison and subjecting them to various programs of reform.

PENAL POLICY IN THE MODEL NATIONS

There are many cross-national similarities in penal policy among modern nations. Each nation nevertheless also has its distinctive approaches to this matter. Often, these distinctive approaches are historically or culturally based, and we need to look at the factors that resulted in today's organization and practices. An examination of penal policy in our model nations will illustrate some of these similarities and differences.

England and Wales

The English correctional system has experienced major reforms and reorganizations over the past 200 years. Transportation to penal colonies was largely abandoned by the middle of the nineteenth century, overreliance on the death penalty was mitigated, and prison administration was transferred from localities to the central government. Prison became the major recourse for dealing with convicted offenders. Between 1842 and 1848, 54 fortress-type prisons were built, containing a total of 11,000 cells (Fox, 1952, p. 38). Some of these prisons continue to hold prisoners to this day.

The latter part of the nineteenth century saw many of the same arguments about deterrence, rehabilitation, sentence length, and prison regime that are familiar to us today. English prisons, however, were notorious for their rigid regimes and harsh conditions, with prisoners forced to do hard labor and essentially go without amenities. Only later were they permitted a more "comfortable" existence, with a mattress, a few books, and some correspondence with the outside world. According to one author, "For death itself the [British] system had substituted a living death" (Fox, 1952, p. 51).

The twentieth century saw movements of concern, efforts to reform, new ideas, and new failures.

Influenced by the progressive movement in the United States, some reformers called for less reliance on prison as a way of punishing offenders. The early twentieth century also saw increased concern for juveniles, through the development of both separate court processes and the Borstal training system, which soon became famous as a way of dealing with youthful offenders. During the 1970s a series of prison riots began that continued into the 1990s. The Woolf Report, published in 1991, reported that overcrowding, poor food, limited programs, and ineffective grievance procedures were cited as the reasons for the uprisings and that more security, control, and justice needed to be installed into the prison system. According to some, it appears that security and control have been realized but the third element—justice—has been neglected (Cavadino & Dignan, 2007).

The current prison population in England and Wales, including remand inmates, has increased from over 66,000 in 2001 to almost 87,000 in December 2012. Not only do England and Wales have the highest number of inmates in Western and Northern Europe, their prison population rate increased from 127 per 100,000 population in 2001 to 154 per 100,000 in 2012 (ICPS, 2012). The reader can refer to Table 9.1 to find the prison statistics for model countries and the United States.

To address the considerable increase in the prison population, the English government began a series of prison expansion projects, including adding over two dozen new facilities since the 1980s and modernizing some nineteenth-century facilities. The expansion was fueled by the "Prison Works" slogan adopted by Home Secretary Michael Howard and addressed three main issues: (1) the rise in the use of custodial sanctions by courts, (2) the increase in the length of sentences, and (3) the increase in the time served by those in remand prisons (Ryan & Sim, 1998; Roberts et al., 2003). To address the costs of this endeavor, the British have turned to the privatization of prisons and prison services. In short, privatization is the use of private companies to provide services or facilities rather than relying totally on public agencies and their employees to administer programs or deliver services. England has decided to utilize the services of several private prisons, although some argue that they add to the correctional problems rather than help the situation (Cavadino & Dignan, 2007). We will discuss private prisons in greater depth later in this chapter.

TABLE 9.1 Prison Statistics for Model Countries and the United States

Country	PP	PR	OR	% Female	% PT	# Facilities
England and Wales	86,708	154	108.9%	4.7	13.2	134
France	67,373	102	117.4%	3.4	25.2	191
Germany	67,671	83	86.6%	5.7	16.5	186
China	1,640,000	121	n/a	5.1	n/a	700*
Japan	69,876	55	83.3%	7.6	11	188
Saudi Arabia	49,000	173	n/a	5.7	58.7**	116
USA	2,266,832	730	106%	8.7	21.5	4,575

*Number estimated does not include 320 reeducation centers
**2002 data
KEY: *PP:* Total prison population
PR: Prison rate; number of inmates per 100,000 population
OR: Occupancy rate
% Female: Percent of inmates that are female
% PT: Percent of inmates that are pretrial or remand
 # Facilities: Number of correctional institutions
SOURCE: ICPS (2012). Accessed October 2, 2012, from http://www.prisonstudies.org/info/worldbrief/.

The 134 prisons in England and Wales are of five basic types: (1) remand centers; (2) local prisons for offenders awaiting trial or sentencing or serving very short sentences (similar to county jails in the United States); (3) closed and open training institutions that hold the majority of British inmates, who generally are sentenced to between eighteen months and four years, or long-term prisons that house inmates serving more than four years; (4) highly secure prisons, formerly called dispersal prisons, that handle high-security and dangerous inmates; and (5) closed and open institutions that incarcerate only young offenders. Prison rehabilitation programs are available in the training and long-term institutions, but because of crowding, not all programs are available to all inmates.

There have been considerable changes in the administration of the prison service in recent years. For decades the prisons were centrally administered under the office of the Home Secretary, who is equivalent to an interior minister in other European countries. However, in 1993 the Prison Service was formed as a civil service agency to decentralize the administration of corrections and improve its efficiency. The chief executive officer of the Prison Service is appointed by the minister of justice, who since 2007 is also the lord chancellor. In 2004, the National Offender Management Service (NOMS) was created. The NOMS serves as an agency that coordinates in 10 geographic regions the services of both the prison system and the probation service so inmates who are leaving prison are supervised and provided with the best release plan possible (Joyce, 2006).

Despite these changes, there are still considerable challenges for the English correctional system. The familiar combination of increasing crime, hardening of attitude, crowding of prisons, deterioration of conditions and relationships within prison, and desperate temporary measures to decrease the prison population characterizes the English system today. The crisis is exacerbated by the racial tensions that have followed the influx of immigrants from Britain's former colonies. This influx has created an urban underclass that suffers from severe political, social, and economic disadvantages in English society and is disproportionately represented in the English prisons. The United Kingdom has been the defendant in a number of cases that have been brought to the European Court of Human Rights (ECtHR).

In response, considerable efforts are made in England and Wales to address the protection of human rights of inmates. Three institutions—a prisons inspectorate with right of entry to all prisons at any time, a prisons and probation ombudsman, and local independent monitoring boards—all are set up to provide checks and balances to the prison system and enhance inmates' rights (Owers, 2006). **Independent monitoring boards**, until 2003 called the boards of visitors or visiting committees, represent a way to bring outsiders into the prisons to help with problems of administration and discipline. The nearly 2,000 volunteers, an average of 15 members for each board, act as an independent watchdog on the prisons, meeting with inmates and staff to safeguard the well-being and rights of all prisoners. Their origins are in nineteenth-century committees set up by judges to inspect the local prisons.

The government of England and Wales has also made an effort in recent years to develop and implement noncustodial sanctions. For example, the number of those on probation supervision of some kind ballooned from 51,000 in 1990 to over 141,000 in 2009. Since 2001 probation in England has been under the supervision of a new agency called the National Prison Service. The noncustodial options in England include warnings or admonitions, probation, restitution, community service, fines, curfews, suspended sentences, and an idea called the combination order, which includes aspects of probation and community service (HEUNI, 1999, p. 139; Terrill, 2013). Those on probation may also be placed in a probation hostel. This facility is designed to provide probationers with a residence while they are working, paying off restitution, or needing to acquire skills to become productive members of the community. One nongovernmental agency in England and Wales that is deeply involved in the promotion of hostels is the National Association for the Care and Resettlement of Offenders (NACRO). The agency fully supports the use of volunteers in the supervision and placement of offenders, increases in diversion programs, and the reduction of mandatory sentences. In the United States, the community-based corrections center or halfway house serves the same purpose.

France

In the generally dismal worldwide history of treatment of criminal and political offenders, France occupies a place that is at least as undistinguished as England's and, on the record, somewhat worse. Large numbers of real or imagined enemies of the regime were incarcerated without trial in France during the sixteenth and seventeenth centuries through the infamous *lettres de cachet,* which were simply orders of the king that a person be imprisoned indefinitely. Transportation to work colonies and the use of prisoners to man the oars on French naval ships were equivalent to death sentences in most cases, since few prisoners survived the appalling conditions in these places for more than a few years. Imprisonment as a sanction was used chiefly for debtors and for women and juveniles, who were not sent to the galleys. As in England, the prison as we know it was preceded by workhouses that incarcerated not only criminal offenders but also the destitute, who had no other means of survival.

As in England, a great wave of reform sentiment accompanied the Enlightenment of the late eighteenth century, and in the nineteenth century a series of controversial changes made large-scale imprisonment the major sentencing mode. In the twentieth century, the same effort was made to emphasize rehabilitation and to introduce certain concomitant sentencing possibilities, such as suspended sentences, that characterized first the American and then the English correctional systems. Probation and parole, however, which played an important role in American corrections throughout the twentieth century, were not used in France until after World War II. In addition, France persisted in the use of transportation of prisoners long after this practice had been phased out in England. In fact, the closing of the final prison colony in Guyana did not occur until 1946 (Wright, 1983).

In the postwar years, France moved from an emphasis on prison reform to a generally harsher philosophy of punishment. The large increase in the crime rate during the 1970s contributed to a repressive mood on the part of the public and the government. The socialist government that came into power in the 1980s tried through a number of reforms to soften punishments, but public reactions to murders and terrorist bombings soon took precedence over reform sentiments. During the 1990s there was a slight increase in the number of violent crimes in France, and the public clamored for more punishment. The government responded with tougher policies in the form of longer sentences, which is thought to be the most significant factor in the increase in the incarceration rate (Roche, 2007). To mitigate the problems associated with a growing prison population, in 2011 then-president Nicolas Sarkosy called for the building of 20,000 additional prison beds. Since his ouster in April in early 2012, the issue has been largely dismissed.

The numbers clearly reflect the increase in prison as a sentencing option in France. In 2001 there were 44,618 inmates in French prisons with a rate of 75 per 100,000 population. By July 2012 the numbers had risen to 67,373 and 102 per 100,000 population (ICPS, 2012). See Table 9.1 to find the prison statistics for France and our other model countries. The 191 French correctional institutions are one of three general types: jails, prisons, and special institutions. Jails, as in most countries, are for pretrial inmates and those serving very short sentences. The prisons are either detention centers, penitentiary centers, or high-security facilities. Special institutions are for those inmates who have physical handicaps, those with psychological disorders below the level of insanity, females, juveniles, and the aged (Terrill, 2013).

Two distinguishing features of the French penal system are the proportion of pretrial detainees and the office of corrections judge. With respect to pretrial detainees, figures show that almost 25 percent of French inmates are remand (unconvicted) or serving less than a one-year sentence. Although Civil Law nations typically have long pretrial detention while the case is being thoroughly examined, France has acquired a reputation of excessiveness in this area. Some detainees are kept in jail for several years while their cases are being investigated by the examining magistrates. The good news is these numbers are down over 10 percent from five years prior (ICPS, 2012). Reasons for the drop include the increased use of pretrial diversion programs and rules stating that a maximum of one year of pretrial detention is allowed in less serious cases (those that would result in a sentence of less than five years).

The French have also tried to deal with the problem of increasing incarceration rates through the office of *juges de l'application des peines* (corrections judges). These judges are appointed by the government to perform several functions, including determining the length of time that a particular prisoner remains in prison and whether the prisoner should be released on parole. Most interesting, however, is the function of overseeing prison conditions and prison disciplinary procedures. The corrections judges have the responsibility of visiting the prison or prisons in their jurisdictions at least once a month; hearing individual inmate complaints; and keeping informed about prison programs, physical plants, and general conditions. Although this program has met with a good deal of opposition, especially from prison administrators, and can hardly be considered an unqualified success, it represents an effort to make the dark world of French prisons somewhat more open to outside scrutiny and thereby more accountable to the government and the public. In this sense, the office of corrections judges performs some of the same functions that the boards of visitors have served in England for almost a century. At the same time, these officials have a major influence on the actual sentences served by particular inmates.

The French have lagged behind the rest of Europe in developing and implementing a range of alternatives to incarceration. Recently, however, efforts have been made to increase their usage. There are primarily four noncustodial sanctions in France: fines, suspended sentences, community service, and probation. The French have also used pardons and amnesties more than most to reduce high incarceration rates, resulting in reduced prison populations for short periods of time (Levy, 2007).

Germany

Germany, with its federal system of government, administers prisons at the level of the states, or *Länder.* With the exception of the period of National Socialism, when all German institutions, including corrections institutions, were centralized, each German state has run its own prison system since the creation of the German Empire in 1871. Within the German *Länder*, prison administration falls under the jurisdiction of the Ministry of Justice, with varying kinds of administrative and regional subdivisions.

During the latter eighteenth century, over 60 workhouses incarcerated petty criminals, vagrants, and poor people in the German states (Melossi & Pavarini, 1981, p. 49), but these states soon took part in the early nineteenth-century movement to develop large-scale prisons as the major form of criminal corrections. The infrastructure for the prison system of today was established in the German states prior to the 1871 unification.

For over a century, Germany operated under the post-unification penal code of 1871, which itself was based on the Prussian Code of 1851. The Prussian Code was heavily influenced by the repressive French Code of 1810 and the Bavarian Code of 1813. These various codes enshrined the classic philosophy of punishment under law that was prevalent in the nineteenth century. Although there were many amendments to the 1871 code, a complete overhaul did not occur until the Prison Act of 1976.

The Prison Act of 1976, formally called the Code on the Execution of Prison Sentences, sets forth all of the principles and methods to be practiced in German correctional facilities. The code proclaims the correctional system goal of rehabilitation and reintegration into society for offenders. At the same time, the code includes provisions for safeguarding certain rights accorded to prisoners, including visiting rights, home leave of up to 21 days per year, medical care, and productive paid work. The law sets the pay for prison labor at 9 percent of average outside wages, an increase from 5 percent in the 1990s (Bindzus, 2004). To be sure, these rights were tempered by the discretionary power of prison administrators to grant or deny them in accordance with particular circumstances, including availability of funds to pay for prison labor. Nevertheless, the law represents a major comprehensive statement of purpose and a major effort to codify the regulations for the German penal system (Feest, 1982; Dammer, 1996).

As of 2012 there were 186 correctional institutions in Germany, but less than 10 of these institutions have a capacity of over 500 prisoners, making Germany quite progressive in terms of prison size. Interestingly, Germany has actually decreased its prison population and incarceration rates over the last 25 years. In 1992 the Germans incarcerated 57,448 inmates at a rate of 71 per 100,000 persons. These numbers increased to high levels of 81,166 and 98 per 100,000 in 2004. But since 2004 the numbers have dropped. As of January 2012, over 67,600 offenders were incarcerated with rate of 83 per 100,000 persons (ICPS, 2012).

Most prisons within Germany have various levels of security integrated within the institution. When offenders enter prison, they begin at a high level of security. As they serve their sentences and show progress toward rehabilitation, they can move to a lower security level. Special units within the prisons are used to discipline inmates who repeatedly break the rules or are at risk of hurting themselves or others. Several maximum-security institutions in Germany incarcerate escape-risk inmates, terrorists, and those who have proven to be unmanageable in other institutions. A new feature of German corrections is that each prison has formed a special unit for sex offenders staffed by extra psychologists (Bindzus, 2004).

German prisons are known for their extensive use of rehabilitation programs. In a study of five German prisons, it was determined that at least three features strongly support the rehabilitative philosophy: (1) unique environmental conditions, (2) extensive work and training opportunities, and (3) community integration programs (Dammer, 1996).

Of the unique environmental conditions in German prisons, the physical location and structural design are most obvious. German prisons are almost always located within cities or in nearby suburban communities. Because of a scarcity of unutilized land, the Germans cannot afford to use valuable agricultural land for correctional institutions. Having prisons in cities and nearby towns also makes it easier for families to visit and for inmates to utilize the community for home leave, work, and educational opportunities. Although some large monolithic structures remain, many prisons in Germany look less like secure correctional institutions and more like factories or hospitals. The belief is that keeping the physical appearance more like that of a factory and creating more "normal" living conditions will foster rehabilitation.

German prisons also often provide inmates with extensive work and training opportunities to prevent idleness, reduce institutional costs, and help inmates improve themselves so they can become better citizens upon release. A large percentage of the inmates in German prisons engage in some work or rehabilitation program.

A third common rehabilitative practice is the frequent use of three community reintegration programs: home leave, conjugal visiting, and half-open release. Home leave is one of the rights included in the 1976 Prison Act that has been increasingly implemented. These leaves are given at the discretion of the authorities in specific prisons, with most of the leaves from low-custody as opposed to high-custody institutions.

With the **conjugal visiting** program, inmates can receive private visits from their spouses and children for four hours every two months. They obtain this privilege after being incarcerated for two to three months and lose it only if they violate a serious prison rule or are involved with drugs. Another program that promotes rehabilitation and reintegration is the *Freiganger*, a half-open work release program. In this program, inmates who have served at least one-half of their sentence can earn the privilege to leave the institution during the day for school or work and then return to the institution in the evening. The *Freiganger* program is guided by the belief that gradual release will assist in the inmates' successful reintegration into the community. Many state correctional systems in the United States implement programs, called work release programs, that are similar to the half-open German programs.

We have seen how the British prison system, with its boards of visitors, and the French system, with its corrections judges, have dealt with some aspects of inmate grievances. Germany has also addressed this matter, albeit in a somewhat different manner. The Prison Act of 1976 provides for inmate access to courts for any violations of prisoners' rights spelled out in the act. Special court panels are constituted to consider inmate grievances, and appeal to the state high courts is possible. This procedure, which involves litigation, is thus more formal than either the French or the English procedures and has resulted in an increase in court claims involving prisoners' rights.

If we compare the use of noncustodial sanctions in England, France, and Germany, we can see that Germany is clearly the leader in the use of such sanctions. Over the past 30 years, Germany has tried to follow a policy of reduced use of imprisonment. In addition to extensive measures to prevent the use of pretrial detention, Germany has implemented community service, fines, day fines, offender-victim mediation, and educational programs for juveniles (HEUNI, 1999; Dunkel, 2004).

China

China in the post-1949 communist era has developed a correctional system that retains remnants of both the Confucian and legalist perspectives. The basic principle of Confucian thought—bringing out the good nature of people and creating change through imposing moral education—has meshed with the communists' need to reeducate the people in socialist values. The ancient legalist view promoting the use of strict punishments to punish wrongdoing and prevent crime is also within the philosophical framework of the communist regime, which believes that punishment and reform go hand in hand.

Over the past 65 years, the government of the People's Republic of China has developed a correctional system that retains, in essence, these two historical perspectives. Informal social control mechanisms such as the people's mediation committees (see Chapter 7) support both Confucian and socialist ideologies in families, neighborhoods, rural areas, work units, and schools. The punishment aspect of the legalist perspective has been fused with the concept of reform and implemented through formal social control mechanisms that Westerners may call prisons or correctional facilities. Technically, the Chinese do not use the terms *corrections* or *correctional facilities* (Liang & Wilson, 2008), but we use the term loosely here for those who are familiar with similar types of institutions in the United States. The seven kinds of formal social control mechanisms in China are (1) jails, (2) reeducation-through-labor camps, (3) reform-through-labor camps, (4) prisons, (5) detention centers, (6) drug detoxification centers, and (7) schools of discipline and education for young adults and juveniles (Shaw, 2010). Detention centers, jails, and drug detoxification centers, like jails in the United States, house offenders awaiting sentencing and those serving less than a two-year sentence. Education and manual labor are commonplace in these institutions.

Reeducation through labor (also called rehabilitation through labor and, in Chinese, *laojiao*) is both a policy and the name of the kind of correctional facility that incarcerates those who have administrative detention status. **Administrative detention** is a form of punishment in the People's Republic of China that allows authorities to impose fines and incarcerate people without the benefit of a trial and formal adjudication as criminals. It is technically a noncriminal sanction that can be applied to both youths and adults, and it can include incarceration for up to four years. This policy has provided the legal support for the incarceration of hundreds, and maybe thousands, of persons for their involvement in the Tiananmen Square incident in 1989 (Lawyers Committee, 1994). The kinds of crimes that would warrant incarceration in one of these institutions include disturbing the public order, carrying a weapon, breaking and entering, theft, traffic offenses, prostitution, gambling, distributing pornography, and some drug violations (Yong, 2002). Recently, prominent lawyers in China have called on the government to reform the *laojiao* system because of reports of citizens being sentenced to forced labor without first undergoing a trial (Yinan, 2012).

Reform through labor is also both a policy and the name of the kind of correctional facility for offenders who have been tried and convicted of a criminal offense, in most cases a serious one requiring between one and ten years of incarceration. Nonfelony adult and serious criminals who are not seen as dangerous are placed in these institutions. These camps, called *laogai,* are most famous for their forced labor policies and their extreme attempts at thought reform (Wu, 1992). They are based on the military practice model, and the inmates participate in agricultural or industrial production, construction, or service work (Shaw, 1998). Our vignette at the beginning of this chapter is one example of the exploitation that has been reported in Chinese prisons.

Prisons in China generally house the more dangerous inmates, including those with a sentence of more than 10 years, a life sentence, or a sentence of death. These inmates require total separation from society and are usually confined to their cells, perform only simple labor, and receive heavy doses of thought reform. There are also schools of discipline and education designed for juveniles. Work-study schools provide the discipline needed for youths who have caused trouble in schools and committed minor criminal offenses such as theft, gambling, or fighting (Bracey, 1988). The juvenile schools of education, akin to American reformatories, are for serious juvenile offenders between the ages of 14 and 18, who participate in intensive work and moral education programs (Shaw, 2010).

Labor is an important element of the Chinese correctional system through all the forms of incarceration. Although labor is not formally recognized to be as important as reform and rehabilitation, it constitutes the main activity in many of the prisons, camps, and other facilities. Its primary purpose is to augment the education and reform process: Correctional labor teaches work skills, helps inmates pass the time, and also provides financial assistance to the institutions (Shaw, 1998, p. 192). For years, China's leaders have boasted that prison labor is vital to the country's economic growth. They claim that using inmates to staff prison factories that do light assembly work and even to work in coal and asbestos mines contributes funds to the Chinese treasury that can be reinvested in the economy. Chinese officials have estimated that 350,000 inmates are in some form of prison labor program (Judicial News, 2010c), although the numbers reported from human rights groups are much higher. The financial success of these Chinese *laogai* has even been challenged in an extensive study by James Seymour, who argues that prison businesses make "no significant contribution" to the Chinese economy. He claims that an unmotivated work force that is often skilled at sabotage has negated the positive benefits of inmate labor (Seymour & Anderson, 1998).

Among the most controversial of the educational and reform methods used in Chinese correctional facilities are programs that promote thought reform. Thought reform includes having inmates confess to their wrongdoing, attack their criminal identity, and construct a new self-image that fits with the beliefs of the socialist agenda. Other tactics used to encourage thought reform include the study of socialist doctrine and the constant recitation of important texts.

The incarceration figures for China are difficult to determine because China often fails to report such data and does not allow outside scrutiny of its correctional system. The large number of work camps located throughout the vast regions of China and the frequent transfer of inmates between the camps contribute to the counting problems. Although some sources claim China has almost 1,500 correctional facilities, official reports claim to have only 700 correctional facilities (Shaw, 2010; ICPS, 2012). The official number of correctional inmates in China is around 1.64 million. If we use the conservative number of facilities provided by the Chinese government, the numbers of inmates and correctional facilities do not match—the United States, with around 600,000 more inmates, has less than 5,000 correctional facilities. We also know that the incarceration rate in China has increased from 101 per 100,000 population in 1995 to 121 per 100,000 population in 2012 for sentenced inmates (ICPS, 2012). The number of acknowledged inmates also does not account for at least 800,000 in administrative detention and around 100,000 in pretrial detention centers (ICPS, 2012). For example, in 2009 Human Rights Watch reported on interviews with dozens of Chinese citizens who claim they were detained in "black jails" or "black houses." These facilities, run by provincial law enforcement officials, are believed to be used primarily to detain citizens who come to large cities to complain about governmental policies, such as those displacing them from their homes or local corruption (CNN, 2010).

As a supplement to the extensive informal and formal social control mechanisms, the People's Republic of China also provides various forms of noncustodial sanctions. Probation, called **public surveillance**, can be imposed from three months to two years and requires that the offender report regularly to the local public security agency. Suspended sentences can be handed out to nondangerous offenders with a sentence of less than three years. Fines and two lesser-used sanctions are restricting offenders' right to vote and confiscating offenders' property (Terrill, 2013).

The Chinese have made some effort to improve, at least in appearance, their record on human rights for inmates. In 2009 the government launched the National Human Rights Action Plan (2009–2010). Included in the plan is a pledge to "improve the legislation concerning prison management and take effective measures to ensure detainees' rights and humanitarian treatment." A second initiative calling for a new prison management system that would direct prisons in China on the main task of providing jobs for the rehabilitation of offenders was also put forth in 2009 (Wang, 2010). It is not clear at this time whether these or other plans meant to improve the situation for Chinese prisoners have been implemented, nor do we know about their efficacy.

Japan

A visitor to Kawagoe Youth Prison near Tokyo reacts first to the beautiful landscaping in the Japanese style, with carefully placed shrubs and trees not only in the large prison yard inside the walls but also in the small courtyard behind the interview rooms where prisoners are tested, classified, and assigned to work and education programs. Additional facilities include a drill ground, where prisoners exercise in military formations under the direction of guards for at least one hour a day.

Some of the over 1,000 inmates are enrolled in vocational courses including hairdressing, welding, woodwork, gardening, construction, and carpentry. The remainder work in large, hangar-like facilities, each containing a different industry. The industries include auto repair and manufacture of garden ornaments and tatami mats. A correctional official foreman in each industry salutes, clicks his heels, and reports on the productivity of his group in clipped military speech. The prisoners work in the industries 44 hours each week, including four hours on Saturday.

After 5:00 p.m., inmates are confined to their cells, where they also receive their meals. The six-man cells are neat but rather bare, with futons and tatami mats for bedding stacked in one corner and a television set in the center. There are a few one-man cells, smaller but also furnished with a futon and mat stacked in the corner and a small television receiver, for prisoners who present discipline problems and cannot adjust to the group life of the other cells.

Kawagoe Prison illustrates several facets of Japanese prison life and penal philosophy. There is a strong emphasis on work, with prison administrations contracting to manufacture products or provide services. Prisoners receive some pay for this work, although much of the money earned is used to offset prison maintenance costs. Prison life is also strongly regimented, with little freedom of movement or individual programming once an inmate has been assigned to a particular regime. Prisoners have few rights as such, and Japan does not provide the kind of treatment staff that most European and American prisons have. Correctional staff are trained, however, to emphasize resocialization into the community as one aspect of the prison regime.

Japanese prisons are administered centrally by a division of the Ministry of Justice called the Correction Bureau. The system is divided into eight regions, with broad decision-making powers existing at the regional level. The prisons themselves are differentiated according to age, sex (7 percent of Japanese prisoners are women), pretrial or post-conviction status, and type of prison regime. The Correction Bureau operates 188 correctional facilities, which are divided into adult prisons, detention centers, medical prisons, medical branch prisons, and juvenile prisons. The imprisonment rate in Japan is quite low compared to other countries. The population of Japanese prisons as of January 1, 2011, was 69,876 with a rate of 55 per 100,000 population. These numbers represent a drop from 2008, when over 80,000 were incarcerated at a rate of 63 per 100,000 were recorded (ICPS, 2012). See Table 9.1 for a more detailed view of the incarceration figures for Japan.

For the less serious crimes, the Japanese courts are most likely to administer fines, which account for 97 percent of all sanctions for crimes. As a result of these sentencing practices, fewer offenders are incarcerated and still fewer receive other traditional noncustodial sanctions such as probation. When someone is placed on probation in Japan, he or she is likely to have contact with one of the nearly 50,000 volunteer probation officers (VPOs) who assist the full-time officers in community supervision. Nearly two-thirds of all defendants sentenced to prison are granted a suspended sentence. When an offender does actually receive an incarceration sentence, it is often quite short, especially in comparison to sentences in the American criminal justice system. Of those imprisoned in 2004, for example, 14.9 percent were sentenced to less than one year, and another 72 percent received a term of no more than three years (Terrill, 2009, p. 364).

Inmates in Japanese prisons reportedly are afforded individualized treatment that allows them to become rehabilitated and reintegrated into the community. As in the Chinese system, offenders progress through a system that allows them more privileges and freedoms as they successfully serve their sentence. Success is measured by prisoners' ability to work well in the prison factory or maintenance job, get along with others, abide by prison rules, and otherwise be actively involved in rehabilitation programs. Because of the industrial arrangements in most prisons, the system actually operates without cost to the Japanese government. One example of a unique rehabilitative program that is practiced in many Japanese correctional facilities is *naikan*, a method of therapy in which individuals use introspection to understand the impact of their behavior on others and that of others on themselves.

However, it should not be implied that all is well with the Japanese prison system. There are at least three key issues of concern. First are the unflattering reports about the treatment of offenders in Japanese prisons. Human rights groups have in the past accused Japanese prisons of being overly repressive and restrictive in regime. In particular, they voiced concerns about the "cruel, inhuman and degrading treatment through the use of handcuffs and other instruments of restraint, and the imposition of severe penalties for minor infractions of complex prison rules" (Amnesty International, 1998). To address matters of prisoner treatment, the Japanese passed the Act on Penal Detention Facilities and Treatment of Inmates and Detainees in 2005. Among the changes in the Act is a call for authorization to appoint citizens to a visiting committee for each correctional institution. Each committee will be charged with the task of making recommendations to prison administrators. It is hoped that these committees can provide the supervision necessary to improve the treatment of inmates in the Japanese prison system.

Second is the growing number of inmates who are member of gangs or organized crime groups. It is estimated that more that 25 percent of Japanese inmates are involved in these security threat groups.

Finally, as in many prisons around the world, an increasing number of inmates are coming into prison with drug abuse and mental health issues (Nomura, 2009; Terrill, 2012). This problem is sure to tax the strict regime methods of the Japanese prison system. Because of the strong emphasis on conformity in Japanese life, prisons are a symptom of failure, and being a prisoner is a particular disgrace for both the inmates and their families. The Japanese believe that the tough methods used in prisons are necessary costs for a safer society (Kristof, 1995). These methods are believed to break down a prisoner's resistance and force him to acknowledge guilt and remorse. The goal is to integrate the inmate back into society, an obedient and peaceful citizen once more. What an American might view as abuse the Japanese see as rehabilitation. The Japanese also believe that such harsh treatment is necessary to control prison violence and protect inmates. The extremely low levels of prison violence, especially in comparison to the high U.S. rates, provide support for their position. Thus, there is little public involvement in prison conditions, and the correctional process remains an operation that receives little scrutiny.

Saudi Arabia

Prison is not the conventional sentencing recourse in Saudi Arabia that it is in our other model countries, primarily because of the tendency to use other methods, such as the corporal punishments outlined in Chapter 8. Nevertheless, prisons, managed under the Interior Ministry, do exist to house those awaiting trial and also those intractable offenders who are not deterred by the corporal punishments. A supreme council for prisons, chaired by a representative from the Interior Ministry, has been established to conduct studies relevant to improving prisons. This same council has been commissioned to consider the development of alternatives to incarceration, because noncustodial sanctions are almost nonexistent in Saudi Arabia. Terms of imprisonment are sometimes reduced and pardons provided during the religious holiday of Ramadan (United Nations, 1999).

As of October 2011, the prison population was reported by the National Prison Administration of Saudi Arabia to be 49,000 with a rate of 173 per 100,000 population, in 116 correctional institutions including 12 reformatories. This is an increase from 2002, when 28,617 inmates and a rate of 132 per 100,000 were reported (ICPS, 2012). It is very difficult to assess the kind and quality of the correctional facilities in Saudi Arabia because of the lack of available information.

Saudi correctional theory implies that written rules to regulate the prison system are unnecessary because the rights of prisoners are guaranteed according to Islamic law (Shari'a) (United Nations, 1999, p. 7). The Shari'a forms the basis for all Islamic codes and regulates all principles of the justice system, including corrections. In fact, "justice" is the fundamental principle that governs all actions in Islamic law, whether by the police, courts, or correctional system. Westerners sometimes are aghast at the way "justice" is meted out by the Saudis, claiming it is unduly harsh. But the perception of Muslims is different. As explained by Saudi expert Frank Vogel, "What the Saudis might consider obedience to God's direct command, the Westerner often calls arbitrary, capricious, and cruel" (Daniszewski, 1997).

Efforts to persuade the Saudis to comply with various international treaties that outline protections for inmates have been unsuccessful. For example, the Saudis have rejected the 1987 Convention for the Prevention of Torture or Inhumane or Degrading Treatment because it contains articles that would forbid countries to deport or extradite individuals where there is risk of torture. The Saudi rejection of such conventions would imply that they condone such methods.

Based on individual accounts reported to organizations, we can determine that, by Western standards and those outlined in international prisoners' rights conventions, the imprisonment conditions in Saudi Arabia are quite harsh. The use of arbitrary arrest and incarceration, torture, and corporal and capital punishment have been said to be common in both political and criminal cases in Saudi Arabia. Human Rights Watch recently reported that in

2011 prisoners and detainees in several prisons described inhumane conditions (Human Rights Watch, 2012). Until international organizations and private researchers are allowed to visit and conduct studies in Saudi Arabia on a regular basis, much of what we hear about corrections in Saudi Arabia will remain negative and anecdotal (Human Rights Watch, 2008).

PRISON CROWDING

Overcrowding in prisons exists in rich and poor countries, and in Common and Civil Law jurisdictions alike. Consider that in the one month of July 2012 stories about prison crowding surfaced in no less than 11 countries, including Australia, Columbia, Iran, Uganda, and the United States (ICPS News Digest, 2012). It is clear that prison crowding is the single most pressing problem faced by prison systems across the world today. In this section we discuss the extent of, reasons for, effects of, and solutions to this worldwide problem.

Reasons for Crowded Prisons

It is difficult to clearly understand the reasons for crowded prisons throughout the world because the problem is complicated by a combination of historical, political, and economic factors. As we discussed in Chapter 8, much of the rise in the incarceration rates of countries may be directly tied to sentencing decisions made by policy makers. Relatedly, earlier in this chapter we discussed how the crime control model has helped to exacerbate the rise in the prison population. However, there are certainly other reasons for prison crowding, because some countries that have not changed their laws and policies still have experienced the problem. Although this does not appear to be the case in most Western nations, one reason may simply be that the increase in prison resources has not kept pace with the population or crime rate. It is also possible that in some poorer countries, such as Pakistan, Malaysia, and Kenya, a lack of correctional resources is a major reason for prison crowding, along with a slow and inefficient criminal justice system and lack of alternatives to incarceration (UNAFEI, 2001). Another possibility may be that the criminal justice system in any country may have gained in competence or reduced corruption, leading to more arrests and more convictions. Or maybe there has been a single incident or kind of crime that has led to the incarceration of a large number of offenders such as increased organized crime activity or mass violence. Two examples of this are the jump in arrests and incarcerations in Germany immediately following their reunification and the more drastic case of Rwanda, where over 100,000 Hum leaders and supporters were incarcerated for their part in the 1994 massacres in the Rwandan civil war. Whatever the reasons, it is clear that the problem of prison crowding has a definite impact on corrections internationally.

Prison Crowding Data

In Chapter 8 we discussed the problems associated with using stock designs to determine incarceration numbers and incarceration rates. The same problems exist with such a methodology if we wish to measure the extent of prison crowding. Nevertheless, we continue to use them because they still represent the most easily understandable and most accessible data about the topic. The most common way to measure prison crowding is to use the occupancy rate. This is accomplished by comparing the number of prison beds with the number of prison inmates on a given day. If the number of inmates exceeds the number of beds, then we can conclude that the occupancy rate is beyond 100 percent. In Table 9.2 we list the countries with the most inmates in the world and their respective incarceration rates. In Table 9.3 we list the countries with the highest occupancy rates. The reader can refer to Table 9.1, Prison Statistics for Model Countries and the United States, to find the same data for our model countries.

Some observations can be made from a perusal of the incarceration numbers. First, as we have mentioned earlier on a number of occasions, the United States is clearly the world leader in

TABLE 9.2 Top Ten Countries by Number of Incarcerated Persons and Rate of Incarceration

Country	Total	Rate*
1. United States of America	2,266,832	730
2. China	1,640,000	121
3. Russian Federation	722,200	505
4. Brazil	514,582	260
5. India	368,998	30
6. Iran	234,678	333
7. Mexico	237,580	206
8. Thailand	234,678	337
9. South Africa	157,375	310
10. Ukraine	153,318	338

*Rate is per 100,000 persons. Rates listed are not ranked.
SOURCE: ICPS (2012). Retrieved October 2, 2012. from http://www.prisonstudies.org/info/worldbrief/.

TABLE 9.3 Top Ten Countries by Occupancy Rates

Country	Occupancy Rate
1. Haiti	335.7%
2. Benin	307.1%
3. Philippines	~300%
4. Iran	294.1
5. Burundi	258.7%
6. Sudan	255.3%
7. French Polynesia	254.5%
8. El Salvador	253.57%
9. Mozambique	245%
10. Bangladesh	237.2%
11. Uganda	223.0%

SOURCE: ICPS, 2012. Accessed October 2, 2012, from http://www.prisonstudies.org/info/worldbrief/.

incarceration. To keep pace with the increase from 200,000 inmates in 1970 to slightly under 2.3 million in 2011, the United States built more prisons than any country in history. Yet, even with the massive building of prisons in the United States to relieve crowding, some court decisions still had to force prison administrators to deal with poor conditions related to crowding.

However, as we move deeper into the second decade of this century, it appears that even in the United States prison building and incarceration have slowed. For the first time in almost 40 years, the United States has seen a drop in the total number of persons incarcerated. Prison construction has been halted in almost all jurisdictions. And in some states correctional facilities have actually been closed. It appears that economic issues and a drop in violent crime to 1970s levels are the major reasons for these developments. For those who advocate a reduction in the reliance on incarceration and the promotion of alternatives to incarceration, now is a good time to unite, plan, and move their agenda forward.

One also notices that the rates of incarceration for our European countries are relatively low and well below the average rate of the world, which has been estimated at 146 per 100,000 persons (Walmsley, 2011). The exception, and the leader in incarceration in Europe, is England. Interestingly, England is the county most like the United State relative to its crime policy.

A third observation about the incarceration numbers is that all of the countries on the occupancy list, and most of incarceration number and rates list, are poor or under-resourced nations. The exception, of course, is the United States. One might surmise that the reason for this obvious fact is that persons in these countries (not counting the United States) have few opportunities for legal employment and many lack the hope that they can survive without engaging in a life of crime. Or it might be that after committing a crime the system is unable to provide any alternatives to incarceration or any forms of rehabilitation due to cost factors.

Finally, it should be mentioned that key data are missing from the imprisonment totals mentioned here. China may be the *real* world leader in incarceration, but because of incomplete and questionable data we are unable to accurately assess or judge its imprisonment status. And some incarceration numbers from Saudi Arabia are even more difficult to acquire than those from China, so we are also dubious about the total numbers of those incarcerated and the occupancy rate in that country.

Effects of Prison Crowding

As we illustrated in the beginning of this section, there are many stories that can be told about the impact of prison crowding in the world today. In general, prison crowding can limit the ability of correctional officials to do their work and clearly increases the potential for violence. For example, consider the cases of two prison riots in Central America in 2012.

Twenty-five people were killed and dozens wounded during a riot at Yare prison in Venezuela when two groups of prisoners waged a gun battle inside the prison while hundreds of relatives were visiting (Caribbean 360, 2012). Two prisoners were killed and six others injured when a gang-related fight broke out in La Reforma, Costa Rica's largest prison. The Justice Minister has been warning for many months that violence in the prisons would increase because of overcrowding due to a lack of money to build more prisons and hire more guards and support staff (Inside Costa Rica, 2012). These two examples of prison unrest are not the exception but the norm in many prison systems around the world.

Equally problematic on the international level are the instances where mental and physical health is endangered by prison crowding. For example, during the first six months of 2012 the number of prisoners committing suicide in Portuguese prisons quadrupled in comparison with the same period in 2011, according to data from the General Prison Services Board. Since 2008, 75 people have died in prison in New Zealand, where the suicide rate is 11 times higher than in the general population (ICPS News Digest, 2012). Communicable diseases such as HIV/AIDS, tuberculosis, hepatitis, and sexually transmitted infections have contributed to a high rate of inmate deaths and post-release mortality. To address this problem, a conference of prison health care officials gathered in 2009 and developed the Madrid Recommendation to emphasize that health protection in prisons is an essential part of public health in Europe today (World Health Organization, 2011).

The United States is not exempt from this problem. In 2004 it was estimated that over 23,000 inmates in the U.S. prison system were infected with HIV or AIDS (Clear, Cole, & Reisig, 2009).

Solutions to Prison Crowding

Responses to prison crowding have varied among countries. The Scandinavian countries and the Netherlands, which have earned a reputation for enlightened penal philosophy, are particularly noteworthy (Lappi-Seppala, 2009). Even in Denmark, which suffered from a large increase in crime between 1960 and 1980, authorities responded by instituting a program of decriminalization, abolishing indeterminate sentences, and expanding the probation system. Japan has been able to avoid the problem of prison crowding because it has created a system that prevents the situation from arising. More specifically, Japan has made frequent use of noncustodial sanctions, adequate use of bail, effective use of parole, and required prosecutors to handle cases in an expedient manner (UNAFEI, 2001, p. 375). Other countries have made laws that mandate release of prisoners when the prisons become crowded. This practice has also been adopted in the United States in jurisdictions where judges have ordered emergency release of inmates in crowded jails and prisons. Yet others have judiciously reviewed their sentencing laws and moved toward reducing the kinds and lengths of prison sentences for certain crimes (Tonry, 2007b).

Another common strategy is the use of amnesty and/or pardons to shorten sentences to counteract the large increase in crime and convictions. Thailand recently released 25,000 prisoners to commemorate the recent birthdays of the Queen and Crown Prince. In India 750 prisoners held in Tihar Prison were granted remission on their sentence of up to 45 days as part of the country's sixty-sixth Independence Day celebrations (ICPS News

Digest, 2012). Similarly, Sweden and France have responded to their prison population problems with large-scale amnesty or pardons programs as well as determined efforts to cut down on sentencing and increase community-based sanctions (Levy, 2009).

In many countries, the answer to the problem of prison crowding has more often than not been simply to build more prisons. This practice has been criticized by a number of well-respected academics and social reformers who claim that it is illogical to think that prison can be offered as its own remedy (Foucault, 1979; Tonry, 2001; Clear, 2007).

Building prisons to reduce the crowding problem has been called the construction strategy (Blumstein, 1995). This policy is the result of a generally more conservative and hard-line attitude toward crime and criminals. Prison building has been a growth industry in many countries, especially the United States, but even the prison explosion cannot keep up with the burgeoning prison populations. Antiquated fortress prisons built in the nineteenth century continue to be used in Russia, Mexico, England, Germany, and the United States, to name just a few. In some cases, as in Lancaster, old castles in England have been converted to prisons in order to deal with the crush of prisoners. And in 1996 England even purchased a large ship from the United States and turned it into a low-security prison (Stern, 1998, p. 280).

One way in which the construction strategy has been advanced in the United States and, more recently, in other countries has been through the development of **private prisons**—correctional institutions operated by private firms on behalf of governments. Although various aspects of prison administration have been privatized since their inception, such as food services or medical care, the first entirely private prison is believed to be in the United States. The first such institution was opened in Pennsylvania in 1975, and by the end of 2007 there were over 150 private prisons holding over 125,000 inmates in the United States, Puerto Rico, and the District of Columbia (Clear, Cole, & Reisig, 2009). The private prison business worldwide is dominated by the European company Sodexo and two American companies, the Wackenhut Corporation and the Corrections Corporation of America (CCA). These corporations have formed alliances with businesses throughout the world, and private prisons are operating in Poland, Belize, France, New Zealand, Australia, South Africa, Canada, and England and Wales (Stern, 1998, p. 297; Roth, 2006).

Some supporters feel that private prisons can save money for some correctional systems, while others dispute this claim (Pratt & Maahs, 1999). Other criticisms of private prisons include poor wages and conditions for employees, inadequate services for inmates, and the ethical arguments that claim the government should not delegate basic social functions to private money-making corporations (Reisig & Pratt, 2000; Nathan, 2004). Interestingly, in 2004 the Israeli legislature passed a law permitting the establishment of private prisons, but in 2009 the Israeli Supreme Court ruled them to be unconstitutional (Zarchin, 2009).

In addition to the construction approach, Alfred Blumstein (1995) proposed three other ways to address the crowding crisis: the null strategy, the intermediate sanctions strategy, and the prison population reduction strategy. Although Blumstein presents these in a North American context, they can be applied across boundaries; in fact, a number of countries have already implemented them in various forms, as in Scandinavia.

Proponents of the null strategy say that nothing should be done, that prisons should be allowed to become increasingly congested. The hope is that criminals will be deterred by living in such conditions or that a change in the demographics of the crime cohort will resolve prison crowding. Although this may be the cheapest and most politically acceptable approach in the short run, in the long run it may not solve the crowding problems and may lead to some of the problems mentioned previously, such as riots, disease, and general system failure.

Proponents of the intermediate sanctions strategy call for the development of punishments short of incarceration. Probation, which allows the offender to remain outside of prison, and **parole**, whereby offenders are released to community supervision after a period of incarceration, are especially important mechanisms for decreasing prison populations. Other intermediate punishments, as we discussed in Chapter 8, include fines and day fines, community service, restitution, home confinement, and electronic monitoring. They continue to play a role in reducing the prison population, even in a crime-control, post-progressive, and (as the Europeans call it) neoclassical period of disillusionment with rehabilitation efforts.

Finally, proponents of the population reduction strategy call for a two-step process of changing sentencing practices and developing more methods for letting inmates out of prison. With regard to the former, called "front-door strategies," those who determine sentences (legislators) must write laws that limit the use of imprisonment. The importance of this strategy was explained in Chapter 8 when we discussed the recent directions that some countries have taken to "get tough" on crime. With regard to the latter, "back-door" strategies such as parole, work release, and good time must be implemented to get offenders out of prison before the end of their terms in order to free space for newcomers (Blumstein, 1995). Different countries have adopted a variety of strategies to address prison crowding. A mixture of approaches that best suits the needs of a particular correctional system is probably the optimal solution to the problem.

RIGHTS OF PRISONERS

- A report issued by a group of Egyptian human rights organizations revealed that prisoners are subjected to 'inhumane' tests following visits by their family members. The report said inmates at Tora prison are forced to drink water with soap, which causes severe vomiting and diarrhea, so that the prison administration can make sure their stomachs do not contain any prohibited items.
- A federal court judge says Canada's prison system is breaking the law by failing to deal with prisoner grievances in a timely manner, saying the backlog is contributing to growing tensions and violence within the system.
- A report released by the public defender's office in country of Georgia following the inspection of the N8 prison in Gldani found that many prisoners had been awaiting transfer to other prisons for a long time and without being provided with a firm timetable for their transfer. Prisoners are only allowed 15–20 minutes exercise per day, the prison shop lacks healthy products such as fruit and vegetables, and prisoners are only allowed brief phone privileges twice per month (ICPS News Digest, 2012).

In each of these stories, we see examples of violations of international and in some cases national laws that prohibit torture and ill treatment of persons in custody. Legal challenges to prison conditions and prisoner treatment have become common only in the past 30 or so years, although they did occur earlier. These challenges were especially prominent in the United States, where civil litigation regarding prison conditions, especially prison crowding, has become a major consideration in corrections administration. The legal basis for challenges to prison conditions in the United States comes from the Eighth Amendment of the U.S. Constitution, which states that "excessive bail shall not be required, nor excessive fines imposed, nor cruel and unusual punishments inflicted."

In the international community, legal challenges relative to a number of human rights issues arise from a number of covenants and conventions. The foundation for these documents is rooted in the UN Universal Declaration of Human Rights, which states that "no one shall be subjected to torture, or cruel, inhuman or degrading treatment or punishment" (Article 5). The declaration, originally proposed in 1948 by the United Nations and subsequently ratified by a large number of nations, was the result of the desire to combat the massive violations of human rights that occurred in World War II (Margaryan, 2010). Since then, other international organizations have produced documents that support Article 5, such as the European Convention on Human Rights, the African Charter on Human and People's Rights, and the Inter-American Convention on Human Rights.

In 1955 the United Nations developed what has become the most well known of prison guidelines, the Standard Minimum Rules for the Treatment of Prisoners. The rules include 95 standards that address a plethora of prisoner issues, including prison living conditions, amenities and programs, methods of discipline, and the treatment of those who are unconvicted. In 1953 the European Convention on Human Rights was developed by the newly formed Council of Europe (1949), which in 1987 revised its own set of prison rules, a more detailed set than the UN standards (Stern, 1998). A recent development in the formation of inmate rights was the 2010 approval by the United Nations of the Bangkok Rules. More formally called the United Nations Rules for the Treatment of Women Prisoners and Non-custodial Measures for Women Offenders, the Bangkok Rules are new in the sense that they are the first specific UN standards for the treatment of women offenders. The UN Standard Minimum Rules for the Treatment of Prisoners did not draw sufficient attention to women's particular needs. For a more inclusive list of international treaties that deal with these issues see the box below.

Prisoner rights litigation and international agreements regarding human rights do not guarantee that prison conditions will be safe and humane. In fact, according to the United Nations and Human Rights Watch, a number of countries have been unable to meet the minimal standards outlined by the United Nations, and few if any prison systems observe all their prescriptions (United Nations, 1996; Human Rights Watch, 1999).

However, it is clear that the creation of enforceable international standards concerning sentencing and the imposition of punishment is inevitable in the next century (Tonry, 2001). The United Nations has worked toward that end with the development of a treaty called the Optional Protocol to the Convention against Torture and Other Cruel, Inhuman or Degrading Treatment or Punishment (OPCAT). OPCAT was adopted by the General Assembly on December 18, 2002 and has been in force since June 22, 2006. As of January 2010, 146 nations are parties to the treaty and another 10 countries have signed but not ratified it. The treaty provides for the establishment of "a system of regular visits undertaken by independent international and national bodies to places where people are deprived of their liberty, in order to prevent torture and other cruel, inhuman or degrading treatment or punishment" to be overseen by a Subcommittee on Prevention of Torture and Other Cruel, Inhuman or Degrading Treatment or Punishment. The UN subcommittee would make detailed recommendations to state authorities regarding necessary improvements to their detention facilities, and the authorities would be expected to implement these recommendations.

International Treaties Related to the Treatment of Offenders and Those in Custody

- United Nations Standard Minimum Rules for Non-custodial Measures (The Tokyo Rules)
- UN Standard Minimum Rules for the Treatment of Prisoners
- Basic Principles for the Treatment of Prisoners
- Convention against Torture and Other Cruel, Inhuman or Degrading Treatment or Punishment
- Optional Protocol to the Convention against Torture and Other Cruel, Inhuman or Degrading Treatment or Punishment
- International Covenant on Civil and Political Rights
- The Second Optional Protocol to the International Covenant on Civil and Political Rights (aiming at the abolition of the death penalty)
- United Nations Standard Minimum Rules for the Administration of Juvenile Justice (The Beijing Rules)
- Rules for the Specific Treatment of Women Offenders (The Bangkok Rules)

INCARCERATION OF SUPRANATIONAL CRIMINALS

As we discussed in previous chapters, supranational courts have been formed to deal with those accused of crimes such as genocide and other crimes against humanity. As these courts begin to pass verdicts and sentences, the international community must decide how and where to place the criminals. The International Criminal Tribunal for Rwanda (ICTR) has built within the Arusha prison in Tanzania a United Nations Detention Facility (UNDF) that has 56 cells. Other African countries, including Mali and Benin, currently incarcerate 32 inmates in addition to the thousands that have already been tried, convicted, and incarcerated in Rwanda for the atrocities committed during its civil war in 1994.

Another example is the International Criminal Tribunal for the former Yugoslavia (ICTY), which has indicted 161 persons since beginning operation in the 1990s. As of April 2011, 17 nation-states have signed an agreement stating they would be willing to incarcerate those convicted in the ICTY trials. Until being transferred to one of the 17 permanent facilities, the ICTY's Detention Unit (DU) is the temporary remand center (jail) and is located within a Dutch prison complex in The Hague. As of 2011, 48 convicted criminals are incarcerated in European countries for a variety of crimes against humanity. The most famous of the ICTY criminals, Slobodan Milosevic, died of natural causes in detention in March 2006 prior to sentencing. For the list and location of the ICTY criminals currently incarcerated in European prisons, see http://www.icty.org/sid/10276.

In October 2005 the Federal Minister of Justice of Austria and the President of the International Criminal Court (ICC) signed an important agreement that will affect the penal systems in a number of countries for years to come. That agreement was the first between any country and the ICC that will allow the enforcement of ICC sentences handed down by the Court. Austria is now able to incarcerate persons who will be convicted by the ICC in The Hague. Such developments are important because they help fulfill the requirements of the Rome statute (Article 103), which states that sentences handed down by the judges "shall be served in a State designated by the Court from a list of States which have indicated to the Court their willingness to accept sentenced persons." Other countries that agree to the incarceration of international crimes will be required to meet international standards such as those proposed by the UN Standard Minimum Rules for the Treatment of Prisoners. The incarceration of criminals who are tried and convicted in supranational courts will be an interesting topic for those who study comparative penology in future years.

TREATMENT OF OFFENDERS IN THE CUSTODY OF THE UNITED STATES

The treatment of criminal offenders in the United States has been a major issue in correctional management for the last 40 years. Prior to that, the basic judicial policy was one of noninterference with the internal administration of prisons. However, in the case of *Cooper v. Pate* (1964) the federal courts ruled that prisoners could sue state officials over prison conditions, poor treatment, or the denial of basic rights. After *Cooper v. Pate,* the number of suits brought by state inmates in federal courts alone rose from 218 in 1966 to 41,952 in 1996 (Clear & Cole, 2003, p. 98). Although the U.S. Constitution may be the primary legal force behind the treatment of offenders, there are others. Statutes passed by legislatures at all levels of government, case law created by judges in certain cases, and regulations formed by federal, state, and local agencies also support the legal rights of people under correctional supervision.

In addition to domestic laws, a number of international documents prescribe the legal obligations of any U.S. official, military personnel, or representative of the U.S. that prohibits torture and other ill-treatment of any person in custody in all circumstances. Those documents include the international humanitarian law and **Geneva Convention** (also called "the laws of war"), the relevant treaties listed in the box on page 232, and special domestic laws developed to incorporate international prohibitions against torture and mistreatment. Among the special domestic laws recently created are the Uniform Code of Military Justice, the War Crimes Act of 1996, the Military Extradition Act of 2000, and a federal anti-torture measure enacted in 1994 that provides for prosecution of anyone in the United States for actions committed outside the country (Human Rights Watch, 2004).

This issue of the treatment of those in custody by American officials was brought to the international stage in 2004 when it was found that detainees held by the United States in Iraq and Afghanistan were subjected to numerous abuses. In July 2004, U.S. Army investigators announced 94 cases of confirmed or alleged prisoner abuse in Iraq and Afghanistan (Kelly, 2004). More telling was a 53-page report written by Army Major General Antonio Taguba, completed in February 2003, that concluded that there were "institutional failures of the Army prison system." Specifically, Taguba found that between October and December of 2003 there were numerous instances of "sadistic, blatant, and wanton criminal abuses" at Abu Ghraib prison in Iraq. Evidence to support the allegations included, according to Taguba, "detailed witness statements and the discovery of extremely graphic photographic evidence." Some of the wrongdoing included:

> Breaking chemical lights and pouring the phosphoric liquid on detainees; pouring cold water on naked detainees; beating detainees with a broom handle and a chair; threatening male detainees with rape; allowing a military police guard to stitch the wound of a detainee who was injured after being slammed against the wall in his cell; sodomizing a detainee with a chemical light and perhaps a broom stick; and using military working dogs to frighten and intimidate detainees with threats of attack, and in one instance actually biting a detainee. (Hersh, 2004)

As of September 2012, the United States still holds 167 detainees in the Guantanamo Bay Naval Base. Over the course of the last 11 years almost 800 persons have been incarcerated there and 9 have died while in custody, including Adnan Farhan Abdul Latif, a Yemeni national who had been held in the base since January 2002 and died in September 2012 (Amnesty International, 2012).

In addition to this highly controversial issue of custody and treatment of those abroad, American prisons on the federal and state levels have been criticized by Human Rights Watch for issues raised by the spread of ultramodern "super-maximum" security prisons and for the issue of custodial sexual abuse related to woman inmates. It should be mentioned, however, that by most measures the United States correctional system is considered among the world's leaders in innovation and in setting and meeting standards to support the fair and just treatment of those in custody. Very few countries, except perhaps one or two Scandinavian countries, can boast of better overall prison conditions than those in the United States.

Not coincidentally, countries that are generally more amenable to human rights considerations are the ones that have been at the forefront of protecting prisoners' rights, while those countries that chronically violate the human rights of their citizens typically also pay little attention to prisoners' rights. Nevertheless, the very fact that this issue has become prominent in terms of litigable rights, rather than conventional reform efforts, has led to greater attention to prison conditions and the problems of individual prisoners.

SUMMARY

In the United States and throughout the world, there have been many changes in correctional systems. Advances have occurred in many countries in the form of improved prison conditions, adherence to international standards, and increases in the number of different kinds of rehabilitation programs available. Because meeting the goals of rehabilitation has been elusive, however, some countries have become discouraged with the rehabilitation approach. The result is an increase in the number of prisoners who are dealt with purely through incapacitation.

A review of the correctional practices of the model countries reveals a number of similarities. Most systems make some effort to separate serious convicted criminals from the unconvicted and lesser criminals. Most correctional systems have developed some form of classification system that segregates inmates according to time to be served or seriousness of the offense. All of our model correctional systems, even China and Saudi Arabia, propose some kinds of rehabilitation programs to assist offenders in their reform and reintegration efforts. The quality and kinds of these programs vary greatly, however.

One of the major problems facing many correctional systems throughout the world is prison crowding. Almost all of our model countries, with perhaps the exception of Japan and Saudi Arabia, suffer from the effects of this malady. The crime control and "get-tough" attitude toward crime has caused many countries to build more prisons as a solution to the problem. Of the many issues that arise as a result of prison crowding, one of concern to many in the international community is its effect on inmates' rights. A significant number of documents and international covenants have tried with varying degrees of success to standardize the treatment of offenders. An issue of growing importance is determining what to do with those incarcerated for violations of international law.

While prison conditions and prison crowding remain a concern, there has been some movement toward the increased use of alternatives to prison, especially probation and fines, in dealing with convicted offenders. Perhaps in the twenty-first century we will see the development of an "ideal" solution to the prison crisis—some panacea that will turn an intractable and antisocial offender into a law-abiding citizen.

Comparative Criminal Justice at the Movies

Movies seek to entertain and inform the audience about a story, incident, or person. Many good movies also hit upon important substantive themes relevant to understanding crime and justice in comparative perspective. Read the movie summary below (and watch the movie if you haven't already) and answer the questions below to make the subject matter connections to comparative criminal justice.

Return to Paradise (1998)
Joseph Ruben, Director

Vince Vaughan, Joaquin Phoenix, and David Conrad are three friends on a five-week vacation in Malaysia and use and possess drugs for recreational use while there. Two of the friends return to the United States, and they all go their separate ways.

Two years later a young lawyer (Anne Heche) tracks down the two friends in the United States, informing them that the third (Joaquin) has been jailed for the last two years in Malaysia and faces a possible death sentence there for drug possession. Apparently, a few days after they left Malaysia from their vacation, police raided their camp and found large quantities of hashish. Phoenix was still residing there, so he was held responsible. He is now scheduled to be put to death in eight days, and the only way the charges can be reduced is if the two friends come back to "paradise" and take their share of the responsibility. If they do,

continued on following page

continued from previous page

they both will spend three years in prison. If only one does, he will spend six years behind bars.

The film centers on the agonizing decisions of Vaughan and Conrad in deciding whether they should go back to Malaysia in the hope of saving their friend. *Return to Paradise* poses one of the ultimate ethical dilemmas: Should you sacrifice your freedom for a friend when you have at least partial responsibility for his predicament?

In a subplot, a journalist (Jada Pinkett) gets wind of the story of the pending execution in Malaysia and wants to write a story about it, but she is begged by the lawyer not to write about it because Malaysia is very sensitive about American criticism of Malaysian justice and a critical story might endanger the agreement to reduce Joaquin Phoenix's death sentence. The journalist must make the decision either to sit on the story because it might affect the outcome of the case, or to print it because it is an important story.

Questions

1. Why do you believe Malaysia is sensitive about American criticism of Malaysian justice? Could other countries be critical of aspects of American justice? What is the best way to avoid such finger pointing?
2. Would you return to face six years in prison to spare a friend's life in a similar situation? What would be your rationale?

Critical Thinking Exercise

Critical thinking requires the ability to evaluate viewpoints, facts, and behaviors objectively to assess information and methods of argumentation in order to establish the merit of an action, law, policy, or procedure. Please evaluate this scenario objectively, applying your knowledge of comparative criminal justice to the facts of the case presented, and answer the questions that follow it.

The Global Shift against the Death Penalty

The Universal Declaration of Human Rights (UDHR) was adopted by the newly formed United Nations in 1948, soon after World War II when the nations of the world wanted to prevent tragic incidents like the Holocaust from occurring again. The United Nations was established as a mechanism to channel global human rights and citizen protection efforts, and for the first time in history, the UDHR spelled out basic civil, political, economic, social, and cultural rights that all human beings should enjoy, regardless of the country in which they live. Of course, there were intense discussions preceding the adoption of the 1948 Declaration about the divide between nations that favored the death penalty and those that opposed it. The death penalty was not included among the violations of human rights listed in the final text of the Declaration. But since 1948, opposition to capital punishment has grown significantly.

This opposition culminated in 2007 when the United Nations General Assembly approved a nonbinding global moratorium on the death penalty with the support of 104 nations, a resolution which had failed repeatedly in prior years. The debate about the death penalty has gone on over the course of western civilization. In ancient Greece, Plato favored the death penalty for intentional murder as an issues of proportionality between crime and punishment. But support waned during the Enlightenment in the 18th century, when reason and science were seen as a better way to reform society than tradition and faith. Thinkers during this period, such as Italian philosopher Cesare Beccaria stated, "it seems to me absurd that the laws, which are an expression of the public will which detest and punish homicide, should themselves commit it, and that to deter citizens from murder, they order a public one."

Contemporary supporters of capital punishment view it from a moral standpoint as a "just" punishment, and a deterrent to protect society. Opponents argue that the evidence does not show that the death penalty deters crime, that it has resulted in many irreversible executions when suspects have been wrongfully convicted, and that it violates the most important of all human rights: the right to life.

These are reasons in the modern world why the use of the death penalty deserves renewed attention. Three important factors are relevant: the effect of the death penalty on the war on terror; the new role of transnational justice; and the strength of transnational civil society. Recent experience suggests that the death penalty is not a remedy against terrorism, because extremists are quite willing to die for their beliefs. This creates martyrs, rather than punished offenders. Second, the UN criminal tribunals on the former Yugoslavia and Rwanda, and the International Criminal Court, do not allow for the death penalty in their statutes, so that that individuals guilty of the highest form of crime in these tribunals—crimes against humanity—are not punishable with the death penalty, but those who have committed common murders can be sentenced to death in some countries. Third, the opposition to the death penalty raised by citizens around the world has resulted in legislative action in many countries in recent years. Amnesty International finds that more than two-thirds of all nations have now abolished the death penalty in law or in practice. And more than 45 countries abolished the death penalty for all crimes since 1990.

The 2007 UN resolution only asks retentionist states to suspend the application of capital punishment. The moratorium asks for a "pause for reflection" which opens a window of opportunity for a broader and civilized debate about the death penalty. It's a debate that should ask the question of what should be counted as basic civil, political, economic, social, and cultural rights that all human beings should enjoy, regardless of the country in which they live.

Questions

1. There is a clear world trend away from capital punishment. What do you see as the most important reasons for this trend?
2. Should the United States be influenced by this world trend in establishing its own national punishment policy? Why or why not?
3. How do you explain the fact that the United States is one of the few nations in the world that actively employs the death penalty, and that the other nations are largely those with which the United States shares very little in common (i.e., few are U.S. allies or developed countries)?

SOURCE: Massimo D' Alema, Italy's deputy prime minister and minister of foreign affairs, "The Global Shift against the Death Penalty," *Christian Science Monitor*, December 26, 2007, p. 9.

DISCUSSION QUESTIONS

1. Based on what you learned about the different rationales for punishment in Chapters 8 and 9, which of our model countries seem to genuinely believe in rehabilitation? Incapacitation? Retribution?
2. What factors do you believe contribute to high occupancy rates? Why does the United States have a much higher incarceration rate than most other countries?
3. Refer to the web page with the UN Standard Minimum Rules for the Treatment of Offenders at http://www2.ohchr.org/english/law/treatmentprisoners.htm and discuss the degree to which they are implemented in our model countries. Which standards do you believe are most difficult to achieve? Why?
4. Explain what strategies for reducing prison crowding you believe to be most effective.
5. In light of some countries' abuses in the use of incarceration and violations of prisoners' rights, what can be done to influence a country to change its policies? What might be the limits to the enforcement of such policies?

FOR FURTHER READING

Allen, R., and V. Stern. (Eds.). (2007). *Justice Reinvestment — A New Approach to Crime and Justice.* London: International Centre for Prison Studies.

Cavadino, M., and J. Dignan (2006). *Penal Systems: A Comparative Approach.* London: Sage.

Pratt, J. (2007). *Penal Populism.* London: Routledge.

Roth, M. (2006). *Prisons and Prisons Systems: A Global Encyclopedia.* Westport, CT: Greenwood Press.

Simon, R., and C. De Waal (2009). *Prisons the World Over.* Plymouth, UK: Lexington Books.

WEB PAGES FOR CHAPTER

For excellent international prison reform resources, see Penal Reform International at www.penalreform.org.

The Laogai Research Foundation provides information about China's labor camps and can be found at http://www.laogai.org.

For the U.S. Department of State web page that provides the 2011 Country Reports on Human Rights, see http://www.state.gov/j/drl/rls/hrrpt/.

For the UN Minimum Standards for the Treatment of Offenders, see http://www2.ohchr.org/english/law/treatmentprisoners.htm.

For the most recent (2012) Annual Report produced by Amnesty International see http://www.amnesty.org/en/annual-report/2012.

10  Terrorism

Key Terms and Concepts

agents of biological origin (ABOs)
Al-Qaida
asymmetrical warfare
Department of Homeland Security
domestic terrorism
Good Friday Accord
international terrorism
jihad
new terrorism
Osama bin Laden
Patriot Act
religious terrorism
revolutionary terrorism
state-sponsored terrorism
terrorism
weapons of mass destruction (WMDs)

Chapter 10 Learning Objectives

Outline the key historical events in the development of terrorism

Clarify the reasons behind the complexity of defining terrorism

Explain the different goals of those involved in terrorist activity

Describe the prevalence of domestic and international terrorism in the world today

Explore the responses to terrorists and terrorism on the national and international levels.

At 11:35 p.m. on the evening of May 1, 2011, President Barack Obama uttered these words: "Tonight, I can report to the American people and to the world that the United States has conducted an operation that killed Osama bin Laden, the leader of Al-Qaida, and a terrorist who's responsible for the murder of thousands of innocent men, women, and children." With this late-night announcement came the details of the event that had occurred hours earlier when the President gave the order for a team of U.S. Navy SEAL Team Six to fly into Abbottabad, a Pakistani suburb 75 miles from Islamabad, the country's capital. According to official accounts, after a brief firefight the SEALS had shot and killed the leader of al-Qaeda and four others, including one of bin Laden's sons, in the presence of one of his wives. The Americans took possession of bin Laden's body, moved it briefly to Afghanistan for identification, and then buried it at sea within 24 hours, in accordance with Muslim practice.

It is unclear at this time what impact the death of bin Laden will have on the operations of his terrorist organization, called *al-Qaeda*, or on the broader issue of terrorism in the United States and around the world. Unfortunately, it appears from news reports that terrorism has only become more prevalent and complicated over the past decade. And for many, living with and fighting against terrorism is not a new or recent phenomenon. For example, what can be called "modern" terrorism has been a part of daily life in the Middle East for decades.

But whether terrorism strikes in the Middle East, Asia, Europe, or North America, we cannot underestimate its impact. Most painful and obvious are the tremendous loss of life and astronomical economic costs associated with terrorism. Just consider the costs of 9/11. Almost 3,000 persons were killed or missing. Lower Manhattan lost nearly 30 percent of its office space. The physical assets lost and cost of rescue and cleanup totalled over $27 billion. Wall Street shut down for a week, then opened and lost 15 percent, or $1.2 trillion in financial investments (9/11 Commission Report, 2004).

The cost of the "war on terror" and concomitant law enforcement efforts has been immeasurable and has probably directly or indirectly affected the livelihood of every person on the planet. Consider that following 9/11 the U.S. government immediately allocated $4.8 billion to protect the aviation industry and then formed at least two large federal agencies, the Transportation Security Administration and the Department of Homeland Security. Only three years after 9/11, conservative estimates placed the cost of combating and preventing terrorism in America, including the military interventions in Iraq and Afghanistan, at $500 billion, or 20 percent of the U.S. federal budget (Zalman, 2010). Also consider the increased transaction costs and inefficiencies imposed on the economy by terrorism, and the fact that increased spending on security necessarily diverts labor and capital resources away from productive private sector activities and toward necessary, but less productive, antiterrorist activity (Joint Economic Committee, 2002).

If the economic numbers are not unfathomable enough, imagine trying to measure the psychological effects of terrorist events. Behind every bomb that kills innocent victims are hundreds, and in some cases thousands, of stories about people injured and loved ones lost forever. Anger and animosity have developed against certain ethnic and religious groups. Countries that were once allies have expressed distrust and scorn for each other, stating that each has not done enough to recognize and prevent such events. On the individual level, fear has become a palpable emotion that has changed the way people live their daily lives.

What we do know is that the main concepts explaining terrorism have changed little over time. Because of advanced technology and globalization, there are merely new players and new advances to spread this worldly scourge. And it has become painfully clear that no matter how they are explained and what form they take, acts of terrorism kill and injure innocent people, often at random and often in large numbers, and this makes terrorism a particularly agonizing problem.

In this chapter, we will focus on terrorism as a problem for the criminal justice system. We will discuss the background, definition, prevalence, and purposes of terrorism. We will proceed with some ways that countries from around the world have responded to terrorism and conclude with terrorism issues that may surface in the years to come.

THE HISTORICAL BACKGROUND OF TERRORISM

Terrorism has an ancient lineage and has traditionally been a tool of groups trying to terrorize a population or overthrow a regime either through military means or in a more clandestine fashion. Ancient history tells us that the Assyrians organized a military in the ninth to the seventh centuries B.C. to conquer large populations and terrify its enemies (Law, 2009). In the first century A.D., terror was used by the Roman Empire through the brutal suppression of Spartacus's followers after the Servile War of 73–71 and later by the Romans in conquered territories (Martin, 2003). Terror and assassination were also used by the Jewish Zealots, who opposed Roman rule in Palestine, in the first century A.D. The Zealots were crushed by the Romans, and the Jews were banished from Palestine, beginning the long period of Jewish life in forced exile, or diaspora (Schlagheck, 1988; Fagin, 2006).

In seventh-century India, a group called the Thugs was formed; their goal was for their victims "to experience terror and to express it visibly for the pleasure of Kali, the Hindu goddess of terror and destruction" (Rapoport, 1984). The Thugs lasted for over seven centuries and killed millions of people using their typical method of execution—hanging (Barghothi, 1996). A third group, active during the eleventh through thirteenth centuries, was the Assassins, who were supporters of Hasan ibn al-Sabbah (d. 1124) and Islam in the Persian Gulf area; they used the dagger and the reward of martyrdom to promote their terrorist objectives (Barghothi, 1996). Interestingly, the word *assassins* is allegedly derived from the word *Hashassins* because of the drug hashish, which some believe to have been consumed by the followers of al-Sabbah prior to committing acts of violence. Another term to describe the early assassins was *fedayeen*, which is still a term used by modern Middle Eastern revolutionaries who believe that their sacrifice will guarantee them entry into paradise.

The English term *terrorism*, which originally comes from the term *regime de la terreur*, was first coined by philosopher Edmund Burke during the French Revolution and the Jacobean Reign of Terror of 1793–1794 (White, 2009). A century later, a group of Russian terrorists called the Narodnaya Volya used similar tactics in an effort to overthrow the czar, eventually assassinating him by using a bomb in March 1881 (Hoffman, 2006). What is important to remember is that each of these historical terrorist groups was at least partly successful, and this success undoubtedly influenced the development of modern terrorist organizations.

One interesting view on the beginning of the most recent period of terrorism has been proposed by terrorism scholar Jonathan White (2005), who argues that, beginning right after World War II, terrorism has passed through three transitions or phases. The first phase, lasting from around 1948 to 1960, centered on anticolonial revolts by groups and even small countries. The rebels no longer wished to be ruled by those with overwhelming economic and military resources, and they used asymmetrical warfare to defeat those in power. **Asymmetrical warfare** is a method of warfare used by one side in a conflict or war when it believes that it lacks the military power of the other and so must use strategy or tactics that differ from conventional, or symmetrical, warfare. Over the years, asymmetrical warfare has been used interchangeably with terms such as *guerilla warfare, terrorism, counterterrorism*, and more recently *insurgency* and *counterinsurgency*. Asymmetrical warfare was shown to be successful by two national revolutionary groups during the 1940s: the Japanese and the Jewish Zionists. The Japanese used their brand of asymmetrical warfare to defeat European colonial powers in key battles early in World War II. Two Jewish terrorist groups, the Irgun Zvai Leumi and the Stern Gang, were both successful in the 1940s at convincing the British to withdraw from Palestine. Both of these revolutionary groups showed the world that terrorism or asymmetrical warfare can be effective.

After 1960 ideological terrorism came into vogue. Those espousing this form of terrorism had as their goal the overthrow or disruption of economic and social symbols of Western democracies. During this time, terrorist groups began to go global because they felt their cause was more than just national. Anti-Vietnam groups in the United States and abroad, as well as nationalist groups in Ireland, Spain, Latin America, and the Middle East, were representative of this group. But the strength and growth of democracy, including the transition of the former Soviet Union, led to the demise of these efforts by the late 1980s. What resulted, however, was a variant form of ideological terrorism that we continue to deal with today—religious terrorism (White, 2005, p. 70).

Religious terrorism is the third and most current phase of terrorism as proposed by White (2005). He explains that religious terrorism has "transmogrified" over the last 30 years from a regional problem located primarily in the Palestine region to a range of methods responsible for international death and destruction. The group largely responsible for this transformation is Al-Qaida. Following the success of the *mujihadeen* fighters in Afghanistan, and with the financial support of wealthy Muslims such as Osama bin Laden, Al-Qaida was formed to take asymmetrical warfare across borders.

As we enter the post-9/11 era there are many experts who feel we are entering a new era in terrorism formed by what is called "**new terrorism**." *New terrorism* is defined as terrorist activity committed by individuals or groups who may or may not be formally connected to a loose, cell-based organizational structure, with religious motivations, using asymmetrical tactics to achieve ideological goals often linked to promoting Islamic ideology (Hoffman, 2006; Emerson, 2011). Al-Qaida, which will be discussed in more detail later in this chapter, is an example of this kind of loosely and indirectly linked network. In fact, most current groups or individuals involved in terrorist acts have no direct link or connections with Al-Qaida group, but because of their shared sense of purpose particularly against the West, they are willing to carry out attacks in solidarity with the larger Al-Qaida network. Looking more closely, we see that there are a number of ways in which the new terrorism of today is different from the pre-9/11 style terrorism. Russell Howard and Margaret Nencheck note at least eight identifiable differences:

1. The new terrorists are more difficult to detect.
2. The new terrorists are more violent.
3. The new terrorists are more transnational, less concerned with local politics.
4. The new terrorists are better financed than their predecessors.
5. The new terrorists are better trained.
6. The new terrorists' hierarchical structures are less likely to be infiltrated.
7. The new terrorists have more access to weapons of mass destruction.
8. The new terrorists are less likely to be "defeated." (Howard and Nencheck, 2011)

In the United States, the individuals or small groups that are involved in this *new terrorism* are referred to as "homegrown, jihadist-inspired" terrorists. They are American citizens, legal permanent residents, or radicalized longer-term visitors who carry out or plan violent terrorist activity on United States soil. From May 2009 through October 2011, there were 32 arrests made regarding this type of terrorist incident in the United States. This number is a considerable increase from the 21 total incidents of this type from 9/11 through 2009 (Bjelopera, 2011). Two successful terrorist attacks by homegrown jihadists took place in 2009: a shooting in Fort Hood, Texas, by a U.S. Army major named Nidal Hasan, and another shooting at a U.S. Army-Navy Career Center in Little Rock, Arkansas, by Abdulhakim Muhammed.

Terrorism in the United States Prior to 9/11

Although the face of terrorism in the United States has changed in recent years, it is important to keep in mind that terrorism in the United States did not begin with the events of 9/11. In fact, it has been argued that the United States has a long history of terrorism-related activities since its formation. It would not be surprising if the British viewed the events of the mid-1770s and the violent means used by colonists to overthrow their government as terrorism. Likewise, who could fault Native Americans in the nineteenth century for feeling terrorized when they witnessed large portions of their population displaced or slaughtered by miners, settlers, and later the U.S. military? The term *terrorism* could also be used to describe the violent actions that arose from both sides during the labor movement that began with the mythical Molly Maguires in Eastern Pennsylvania during the late 1860s and later led to the Haymarket riot in Chicago in 1886. Into the twentieth century, we know of terrorizing acts by groups such as the Ku Klux Klan that were opposed to the newly won rights of slaves and by anarchists, who in 1919 tried to use bombs to assassinate key American capitalists such as John D. Rockefeller and J. P. Morgan. In fact, a bomb attack on Morgan's Wall Street bank in New York City in 1920 was the most destructive terrorist attack on U.S. soil until the bombs exploded at the World Trade Center in 1993 and in Oklahoma City in 1995 (Law, 2009).

During the 1960s, during the time of the Vietnam War, many radical leftist organizations are said to have carried out terrorist acts because of their opposition to the government and the war. More recently, ecoterrorist groups such as the Earth Liberation Front (ELF) and animal welfare groups such as the Animal Liberation Front (ALF) have carried out hundreds of less violent but highly destructive acts in support of their cause. Although some have called for these acts to be classified as criminal offenses, the federal government and the FBI have investigated these groups and have counted any arrests as terrorists crimes solved or prevented. On the other side of the political spectrum are rightist domestic groups that due to their violent past could also be considered terrorist groups. Among these are the Aryan Nation, the National Alliance, Public Enemy Number 1, and the Oklahoma Constitutional Militia (Freilich et al., 2009).

Of course, the events of 9/11 have brought a reality to terrorism that was previously unimaginable to the American people. That event, the political response with air strikes on bin Laden's camps in October 2001, and the subsequent invasion of Iraq and Afghanistan signalled a global "war on terrorism" that has surely reformulated the way future generations view terrorism and has maybe led to many of the changes in new terrorism that we described earlier.

DEFINING TERRORISM

Over the years, literally hundreds of definitions have been proposed and much has been written on the subject of defining terrorism. Some have argued that each single definition is best (Laqueur, 1999), while others advocate having a consensus definition that uses the key elements of a number of definitions by numerous scholars (Schmid & Longman, 2005). Consider that on September 28, 2001, only a few miles away from the still-smoldering ruins of the World Trade Center, delegates from the United Nations Security Council adopted a U.S.-sponsored resolution obliging UN member states to deny funds, support, and safe haven to terrorists groups and to exchange intelligence to fight them. Only one week later, however, after five days of debate, further draft resolutions of the UN General Assembly were shelved because of disagreement among the 189 members. The biggest area of disagreement was over the question of who is a terrorist. We can agree about the severity of terrorism, but we cannot agree on what terrorism is.

Why is it so difficult to reach a consensus on the definition? The central problem involves the larger ideological argument about whether the acts committed are "criminal" or are in the interest of promoting the "greater good." It has been often stated that one man's terrorist is another man's freedom fighter. Terrorists themselves may not view their activities as illegal or immoral, and they may not believe themselves to be criminals. In fact, they may look upon themselves as martyrs. At the same time, those in power may label any individual or political movement acting against them as terrorist related.

Defining terrorism is further clouded by a change in status for those who are involved with terrorism. In the 1980s, President Reagan called the African National Congress a terrorist group, but the group subsequently was applauded for the sacrifices it made in the fight to eliminate apartheid in South Africa under the direction of Nelson Mandela. Menachem Begin, former Israeli prime minister, was well known as a leader of the previously mentioned terrorist group called Irgun Zvai Leumi. He later shared a Nobel Peace Prize with Anwar Sadat. In that same part of the world, Yasir Arafat, long excoriated as a terrorist, became the leader of the moderate element of the Palestine Liberation Organization that supported and signed the Oslo Peace Accords in 1993.

Finally, terrorism is difficult to define because the meaning of the term, like that of crime, can change and even expand over time because it is a socially derived term (Hoffman, 1999; White, 2005). During the French Revolution, terrorism had a positive connotation because it was associated with democracy. In the nineteenth century, some Russians were proud to call themselves terrorists because it meant they were connected to the overthrow and assassination of the czar and his followers. After World War II, *terrorism* came to be used in a more pejorative way to describe behavior by groups or individuals to support a cause or destabilize governments or occupying forces (Miller & File, 2001). Since the events of 2001, there appears to be a movement to expand the use and definition of the terms *terrorism* and *terrorist*, at least in the United States. Consider these examples:

- In 2002, Americans were made acutely aware of a new form of terrorism when John Allen Mohammad and his accomplice, Lee Boyd Malvo, went on a rampage of sniper shootings mostly around the Washington, D.C. area.
- In 2004, U.S. Secretary of Education Rod Paige referred to the National Education Association, the national teachers' union, as a "terrorist organization" because of the "obstructionist scare tactics" that it used in its fight over the nation's education laws (Associated Press, 2004a).
- In 2006, a Bronx construction worker was tried under New York State's antiterrorism law for his involvement in violent street gangs in New York City.

In the future, will criminal behavior by hate groups, street gangs, or even labor unions be called terrorism because they "terrorize" groups of persons or neighborhoods? How about military forces that invade and strike fear into the hearts of the enemy? If we simply view any act that creates terror as terrorism, then the potential actions to be included are limitless. These examples illustrate how defining terrorism and deciding who is a terrorist is often an elusive process and is highly sensitive to a number of factors.

Despite the challenges to the adoption of an internationally agreed-upon definition of terrorism, it is important to subscribe to at least one formal definition. Without a definition it is impossible to make laws that can prevent such acts or allow law enforcement officials to catch and prosecute those responsible for terrorism. In the United States, terrorism has been defined by numerous criminal justice agencies such as the U.S. State Department, the Department of Defense, the FBI, the CIA, the NSA, and the DEA (Law, 2009). But for our purposes of understanding terrorism today, we will use the following definition related to terrorism, which was adopted in 2005 by the National Counterterrorism Center (NCTC) and is contained in Title 22 of the U.S. Federal Code Section 2656f (d)(2):

> **Terrorism**: the premeditated, politically motivated violence perpetrated against noncombatant targets by subnational groups or clandestine agents.

Although some may consider this definition to be too broad and others may find it not encompassing enough, it does provide us with a starting point from which to begin to understand and study terrorism around the world today.

From this point we can proceed to a better understanding about the different types of terrorism, including two general types: domestic and international.

Domestic terrorism involves persons or groups committing a terrorist act or acts in their own country, having some domestic agenda as the goal. One famous example in the United States would be the 1995 bombing of the Federal Building in Oklahoma City by Timothy McVeigh and his associates, who attacked in large part as an act of war against the federal government. McVeigh also chose April 19 as a symbolic date for the attack because it was the anniversary of the Battle of Concord and of the Waco, Texas, fire at the Branch Davidian cult site (Martin, 2003). An example of domestic terrorism in a country other than the United States would be the July 2011 sequential terrorist attacks in Norway. Both attacks were committed by 32-year-old Norwegian gunman and right-wing extremist Anders Behring Breivik, who first set off a car bomb adjacent to a government building in Oslo that killed eight people and later in the day opened fire at a summer camp, killing 69 people and injuring 110.

International terrorism involves citizens or territory of more than one country and has an impact that goes beyond a domestic agenda. International terrorism may involve an act of violence or destruction within the United States, such as the events of 9/11. A recent example of an act considered international terrorism on U.S. soil was the 2009 Christmas Day attempted bombing of a Detroit-bound passenger airplane by a 23-year-old Nigerian named Umar Farouk Abdulmutallab.

Alternately, international terrorism may occur in a location far away from the country that it intends to harm. Two serious examples occurred in Nairobi, Kenya, where 291 persons were killed in 1998 when bombs devastated the U.S. embassy, and in Aden, Yemen, in 2000 when a small boat laden with explosives blew up alongside the USS *Cole*, killing 17 U.S. sailors. The numbers of reported incidents of domestic and international terrorism will be discussed in more detail later in this chapter.

THE GOALS OF TERRORISM

What is it that terrorists are trying to achieve? Again, it is not easy to explain the goals of terrorism. In some cases, there are multiple purposes; in others, the goals are not clearly understood even by those involved. In any case, it is important to have some grasp of why people choose to become involved in terrorist activity throughout the globe.

One goal of terrorists is to force a government to respond to their violence in a harsh manner, in the hope that such repression will lead to discontent among the people and ultimately to revolution. In this case, terrorism may be used to destabilize colonial governments and occupation forces. Such terrorism is directed at a specific goal that is easy to articulate and understand, such as overthrow of the current political regime or change in a specific policy. This kind of terrorism, often referred to as **revolutionary terrorism**, may result from the absence of democratic opportunities and ways to petition those in power in a legitimate fashion. Revolutionary terrorism in its purposes is similar to the anticolonial and ideological terrorism activities that were described earlier in this chapter. The longest-lasting examples of this kind of terrorism have involved the twentieth-century efforts of various groups in Palestine to unseat the Israelis in the Middle East, and the Irish Republican Army's attempt to free Northern Ireland from British rule—a movement that remained active until the late 1990s. A more recent example of revolutionary terrorist activity occurred in March 2010, when suicide bombers with Muslim and Chechnyan ties killed 38 people in Moscow.

Terrorism is also practiced by governments against their own citizens when they wish to protect their own political or economic interests. For example, they may use their power to harass, arrest, torture, or kill alleged enemies of the state. Governments may also implement covert actions against other countries for political, economic, or military reasons. These activities by governments against their own citizens or other countries are called **state-sponsored terrorism**. Examples of this form of terrorism during the twentieth century include Stalin's brutal repression in the former Soviet Union, the wholesale killing of Cambodians by the Khmer Rouge, state-sanctioned killing and torture of citizens in several South and Central American countries, and the more recent genocidal activities in Rwanda and Yugoslavia. These are just a few chilling reminders that governments are frequently guilty of violence designed to terrorize their own citizens.

Another frequently stated goal of terrorist groups is to promote a certain religious system or protect a set of beliefs within a religion. Religion is at the very core of these groups' political, social, and revolutionary agendas. This kind of terrorism, called **religious terrorism**, was mentioned earlier as the most common and powerful form of terrorism in our current era (White, 2005). Examples of this kind of terrorism may include violent Christian anti-abortionists in the United States; Hindu extremists in India; and the use of **jihad**, or holy war, by Islamic fundamentalists who wish to protect their religion from "creeping secularism and cultural imperialism posed by Western countries such as the United States" (Martin, 2003).

The growth and popularity of religious terrorism have certainly been fueled by the transnational reach of **Al-Qaida**. The relative success of Al-Qaida as a religious terrorist organization is thought to be due to early realization by its founders that they must convince its members that they are in a battle with evil, that the use of violence to win that battle is totally justified, and further that to become a martyr for that cause is the highest form of sacrifice and will lead to an eternal reward. Leaders of Al-Qaida, most notably Osama bin Laden and Ayman al-Zawahiri, decentralized the power of the organization, gave it training and financial support, and sent the religious fanatics to fight evil not just nationally or regionally but around the world. The CIA has stated that Al-Qaida operates in 68 countries worldwide (Schmalleger, 2009, p. 649). After the death of bin Laden in May 2011, al-Zawahiri became the leader of Al-Qaida, and he remains at large with a $25 million bounty. For a more detailed description of Al-Qaida, see the box on the next page.

Whatever the many goals of terrorism are, probably the most important goal of any single terrorist activity is to generate publicity on a worldwide scale: "Terrorism is not simply what terrorists do, but the effect they create by their actions" (Jenkins, 1978, p. 119). Terrorists want their actions to be publicized to get their message before a larger audience. Because of the horrifying nature of terrorist acts, the media usually oblige and give them extensive coverage. This heightens the sense that we live in an insecure world and might be the victim of random violence at any time. Extensive publicity also enables terrorists to focus attention on the reasons for their actions, which is very important if they wish to initiate any change, gain a reaction from those in power, and even generate some sympathy for their plight. And, given the improvements in technology and world communications, it is not uncommon for videotaped segments of in-progress terrorist activity to be instantaneously broadcast

Al-Qaida: The "Base" of Transnational Terrorism

Al-Qaida, literally meaning "the base," is made up of Sunni Islamic extremists who were originally formed as a group of Arab nationals to fight the Russians during the war in Afghanistan. Since 1989, the group has quickly developed into probably the most feared international terrorist organization in the world thanks to the financial support and leadership of **Osama bin Laden**. The primary goal of bin Laden and his supporters was to liberate Palestine, with secondary goals of removing the Saudi ruling family from power and driving Western military forces and their corrupt, Western-oriented governments from predominantly Muslim countries.

We now know that bin Laden built up his Al-Qaida terrorist network into a worldwide force much like a large corporation. In addition to the money inherited from his father, bin Laden and Al-Qaida received contributions from a variety of sources in the Middle East, including wealthy businessmen who make protection payments to prevent terrorist attacks. Islamic charities throughout the world contributed large sums when their legitimate organizations were infiltrated by Al-Qaida members. Fake business firms were created to hide the flow of money that eventually landed in many Middle Eastern banks. The banks then transferred money to Al-Qaida operatives throughout the world. It is believed that Al-Qaida was responsible for providing financial support to those who carried out the 9/11 attacks.

Because of the international span of the Al-Qaida network, law enforcement officials have found it difficult to find, investigate, and apprehend the terrorists. The situation is exacerbated by the diffuse structure of Al-Qaida. After being trained in camps throughout the globe, terrorists return home or relocate in different countries to establish cells—small groups of like-minded terrorists—and operate as "sleeper agents" who blend into society while planning terror strikes. The cells are allowed to act without any close connections to Al-Qaida; this makes them especially dangerous and hard to detect. Bin Laden and Al-Qaida are believed to have supported and trained thousands of terrorist fighters in Afghanistan, Tajikistan, Bosnia and Herzegovina, Chechnya, Somalia, Sudan, Yemen, the Philippines, Egypt, Libya, Pakistan, and Eritrea. Literally hundreds, maybe thousands, of international terrorist incidents have been at least tangentially linked to Al-Qaida operatives over the past 20 years. The group has been designated as a terrorist organization by the United Nations and by at least 15 countries. Al-Qaida has become a "symbol of Islamic resistance to Western powers and Western culture with an influence that has stretched far beyond its core membership in Afghanistan and Iraq" (Fichtelberg, 2008, p. 167).

In December 2011 Ambassador Daniel Benjamin, coordinator of the U.S. Office of the Bureau of Counterterrorism, stated that the death of bin Laden was a significant event given that he had been the commander, strategist, and emotional leader of Al-Qaida for 22 years. Also in 2011, at least four other key Al-Qaida leaders were killed, including the person moved to second-in-command after bin Laden's death, Atiya Abdul Rahman, a highly capable operational commander who was killed in Pakistan. As a result of the recent loss of key leadership it is thought that the international power of Al-Qaida has been diminished.

across the world (White, 2009). Live telecasts of planes diving into the sides of the World Trade Center and the subsequent collapse of the Twin Towers will surely leave unforgettable images in the memories of millions of Americans for decades.

Even more unsettling is terrorism that appears to have no clear or immediate goal or that gains publicity through acts that will not further a goal in any evident way. General dissatisfaction with German society seems to inspire most of the serious acts of terrorism by Nazi skinheads in recent years. Terrorism in France over the years has been a major problem, but it does not have a clear goal other than to vent frustration and create insecurities within the population. A more recent example of this apparently mindless terrorist activity was when American citizen Thomas Janis was murdered by Revolutionary Armed Forces of Colombia (FARC) terrorists in February 2003 in Colombia. Mr. Janis was the pilot of a plane that crashed in the jungle. He and a Colombian service member were wounded in the crash; the terrorists shot them when they were discovered. Three U.S. citizen passengers on the plane—Keith Stansell, Marc D. Gonsalves, and Thomas R. Howes—were kidnapped and remained hostages of FARC until they were rescued in 2008. Such incidents are particularly difficult to understand because they run counter even to the general goal of advertising a cause, the goal that is usually so important in terrorist action.

THE PREVALENCE OF TERRORISM

Although one would think that with the dramatic increase in both the amount of terrorism-related literature and public interest in the matter that information about terrorism activity would be readily available and easy to comprehend. Unfortunately, this is not the case. In fact, it can be argued that in some ways access to such data has actually diminished over the past five or so years. Just as with other kinds of general crime information, the accuracy and availability of terrorism data suffers from at least three problems. First, the definition of what terrorism is and what constitutes a terrorist act have not been universally agreed upon. This creates differences in reporting across law enforcement agencies and jurisdictions. Second, the ability to collect valid crime data varies greatly from agency to agency. Some countries—and the criminal justice organizations within those countries—have far more resources than others when it comes to crime data collection methods, access to and expertise in statistical packages, data storage systems, and so forth. Finally, and not least important, politics can often affect the free and accurate flow of terrorism-related information. Understandably, elected government officials are reluctant to have the success or failure of their decisions based on the rise or fall of crime statistics. Americans need only to study the recent story of the U.S. State Department and terrorism data to understand this point.

In 1982, the U.S. government began publishing an annual report called *Patterns of Global Terrorism*. The report provided helpful transnational terrorism information by year, by region, and about individual terrorist groups. But in 2004 the numbers cited in the report more than tripled from around 200 incidents to over 650 incidents (Glasser, 2005). This was at the same time that the Bush Administration was claiming that worldwide terrorism was dropping over the previous two years. A sea of criticism surfaced, and the results were as follows: (1) the name of the report was changed to *Country Reports on Terrorism*, (2) statistical data and chronology of terrorist attacks were dropped, and (3) a new agency called the National Counterterrorism Center (NCTC) was formed to collect and report terrorism activity (LaFree et al., 2006). Since 2005 the NCTC has utilized the Worldwide Incidents Tracking System (WITS) as the source for its database on terror attacks and to publish its *Country Reports on Terrorism* and the *NCTC Report on Terrorism*. The U.S. government and the NCTC have refrained from returning to reporting global patterns of terrorism because it does not believe that a simple comparison of the total number of attacks from year to year provides a meaningful measure, although they do provide the number of incidents in Iraq and Afghanistan since 2007 (NCTC, 2009; U.S. Dept. of State, 2012). Interestingly, neither the *Country Reports on Terrorism* nor the *NCTC Report on Terrorism* mentions any data that reflect totals for international terrorist attacks on U.S. soil for 2010 or 2011.

Another valuable resource for terrorism incidents around the world is the Global Terrorism Database (GTD). The GTD includes domestic and international terrorist incidents from 1970 through 2010 and now includes more than 98,000 cases. The results of the GTD are distributed by the National Consortium for the Study of Terrorism and Responses to Terrorism (START), a research agency within the University of Maryland. Other data about terrorist incidents can be obtained through the RAND Corporation, the Memorial Institute for the Prevention of Terrorism (MIPT), and the International Terrorism: Attributes of Terrorist Events (ITERATE) database at Duke University.

The available data offer three insights. First, relatively few terrorist incidents occur in the United States. In 1982, terrorist acts in the United States reached a high of 51; in 1994, the number dropped to zero—no terrorist acts were committed. More recent figures indicate that since 1995 no more than five acts of terrorism occurred in any one year in the United States, and in several years (1996, 1998, 2000, 2002, 2007, 2009, 2010) there were zero successful attacks/incidents (U.S. Dept. of State, 2004; NCTC Terrorism Reports, 2005–2011). Keeping these figures in mind, it is easy to see that the number of individuals killed by international or domestic terrorist activity in the United States in any year (excluding 9/11) is minuscule when compared to homicides in general, accidents, or other causes of death.

A larger concern for law enforcement and government officials in the United States is the number of attempted terrorist acts, especially by homegrown terrorists, that have occurred in recent years. Since September 11, 2001, at least 50 incidents of prevented terrorist activity on U.S. soil have been recorded (McNeill, 2010; Bjelopera, 2011). These prevented acts include the previously mentioned attempt at bombing a Detroit-bound airline on Christmas Day in 2009 and the May 1, 2010, attempted Times Square car-bombing incident.

Second, as we mentioned earlier, the number of domestic terrorist incidents in the United States greatly outnumbers international incidents. Studies indicate that domestic attacks outnumber international attacks in the United States 7 to 1 (LaFree et al., 2006). We know that of the recorded terrorist acts that were attempted between 2001 and 2011, almost all of them were by U.S. citizens, legal permanent residents, or radicalized longer-term visitors who gained citizenship.

Finally, we are well aware that by any measure the number of international terrorism incidents that have occurred outside the United States has risen astronomically over the last decade. Between 2003 and 2004, the U.S. State Department recorded an increase of worldwide terrorist incidents from 208 to 655. Remember, in 2004 the U.S. government cancelled the *Patterns of Global Terrorism* reports, but the new NCTC/WITS recording system fared no better. In 2005, the number skyrocketed to 7,193, and that number does not include any incidents that can be counted as terrorist activity in Iraq or Afghanistan. However, it should be mentioned again that the numbers listed here are surely not exact and should be interpreted within the limits of understanding any crime data. In some cases, they may severely underestimate the number of terrorism incidents and in other cases they are sure to exaggerate. Take, for example, the case of Israel, which claims that between 2000 and 2004 there were 22,406 "terror attacks" on Israeli targets alone (Israeli Defense Force, 2004).

The good news is that there has been some decrease in the number of worldwide terrorist incidents from the peak of nearly 14,500 in 2007. Although over 10,000 terrorist attacks occurred in 2011, affecting nearly 45,000 victims in 70 countries and resulting in over 12,500 deaths, the total number of worldwide attacks in 2011 dropped by almost 12 percent from 2010 and nearly 29 percent from 2007. And these numbers do include terrorist activity in Iraq, Afghanistan, and Pakistan, which account for almost two-thirds of the attacks worldwide (NCTC, 2011).

FOREIGN TERRORIST GROUPS

Literally hundreds of terrorist groups have surfaced over the course of the past century. Some 50 groups have been designated as terrorist organizations by the U.S. State Department and the Office of the Coordinator for Counterterrorism as of September 2012. See http://www.state.gov/j/ct/rls/other/des/123085.htm for a list of the designated terrorist groups. Three legal conditions must be present to receive the designation of being a terrorist group. First, the group must be a foreign organization. Second, the group must engage in terrorist activities as defined by Title 22 of the U.S. Federal Code, or must retain the capability or intent to engage in terrorism. Third, the organization's terrorist activity or terrorism must threaten the security of U.S. nationals or the national security (national defense, foreign relations,

TABLE 10.1 Key Terrorist Groups around the Globe

South America	Africa	Europe	Asia	Middle East
Colombia: Revolutionary Armed Forces of Colombia (FARC), National Liberation Army (ELN), United Self-Defense Forces (AUC)	*Algeria, Somalia, and Kenya:* Al-Qaida operatives	*Spain:* Basque Fatherland and Liberty (ETA), Al-Qaida operatives *Northern Ireland:* Real IRA *France:* ETA, Corsican Separatists, Al-Qaida operatives *Turkey:* Kurdistan Workers' Party (PKK) *Russia:* Chechen separatists	*Uzbekistan:* Al-Qaida operatives *Pakistan:* Jashkar E-Jhangvi, Jaish-E-Mohammad, Lashikar E-Taiba *Sri Lanka:* Liberation Tigers of Tamil Eelam *Philippines:* Abu Sayyaf, Al-Qaida operatives including Jermaah Islamiyah, Moro Islamic Liberation Front, New People's Army	*Israel, West Bank, Gaza Strip:* Hamas Palestine Islamic Jihad, al-Aqsa Martyrs' Brigades (AAMB) *Lebanon:* Hezbollah, Al-Qaida operatives including Asbat al-Ansar (AAA) *Iraq:* Tawhid W'Al Jihad and Al-Qaida Iraq (AQI)

SOURCES: U.S. Department of State (2011), *Country Reports on Terrorism*, available at http://www.state.gov/j/ct/rls/crt/index.htm. Laqueur, W. (2004). "World of Terror." *National Geographic*. November 2004. pp. 72–74.

or economic interests) of the United States (U.S. Dept. of State, 2012b).

There are very few areas of the world today that have not been greatly affected by terrorism. However, it is clear that some areas are more affected than others. In Table 10.1, we list different regions of the world and some of the more active terrorist groups that have been actively operating over the last five years. For more details about the level of terrorist activity within specific countries, including our model countries but not the United States, see the *Country Reports on Terrorism Report* for 2011 provided by the U.S. State Department at http://www.state.gov/j/ct/rls/crt/index.htm.

RESPONSES TO INTERNATIONAL TERRORISM

Organized responses to international terrorism are not simple matters of crime detection, apprehension, and punishment. The complexity of dealing with crime and criminals across borders, the range of motivations for terrorist activity, and the large number of terrorists and terrorist groups create many problems for criminal justice and government officials. So, what can be done to stem the tide of international terrorism? Foreign policy interventions, international cooperation strategies, military and police operations, legislation, and adjudication all play a prominent role.

Foreign Policy

In some cases, the best way to deal with protracted struggles between two parties that are both engaging in and contributing to terrorism is to utilize foreign policy. Foreign policy in its most simple terms is the use of political and economic pressure, negotiation, and compromise rather than violence to solve conflicts between nations or groups. Unfortunately, these efforts often have been for naught and sometimes have actually exacerbated the bad feelings between the parties involved. The last century has seen two serious attempts of employing foreign policy to mitigate terrorism and improve relations between combatants, with varying success.

The first has been the over 60-year conflict in the Middle East between the Israelis and the Arabs. Since 1948 the two groups have engaged in a number of armed conflicts, with the Israelis gaining the upper hand because of their economic, military, and political strength. In response to the Israeli stranglehold on the region, Muslims have developed a number of terrorist groups beginning with the parent organization, the Palestinian Liberation Organization (PLO), and continuing with Hezbollah and Hamas. Unfortunately, numerous foreign policy efforts by various parties in the Middle East and the United States have been unsuccessful in solving that long-standing conflict.

Another more successful example of foreign policy is the resolution of the situation in Northern Ireland. The "troubles" between England and Ireland are centuries old, with the central issue in the twentieth century being the partition of Ireland into a northern area, which was largely Protestant, and the remainder, which remained Catholic. This partition led to a protracted conflict between the English government and the Irish Republican Army (IRA), and later a plethora of splinter groups including the Provisional Irish Republican Army (PIRA) of Northern Ireland, the Continuity Irish Republican Army (CIRA), the Irish National Liberation Army (INLA), and, more recently, the Real IRA (RIRA).

The violence continued into the early 1990s, with the IRA, PIRA, and RIRA perpetuating violence as the primary means of trying to dislodge the British troops from Ulster and unite this area with the Republic of Ireland through the use of violence. Through bombings in England and attacks on British soldiers in England and Northern Ireland, they hoped to wear down British resistance to unification.

However, a breakthrough in the violence happened in September 1994 through February 1996, when a ceasefire was observed by the IRA and a truce declared by Great Britain and the Republic of Ireland. In April 1998 feuding Catholic and Protestant parties signed the Belfast Agreement or the **Good Friday Accord**, which was a historic agreement outlining a power-sharing arrangement to share multiparty administration of Northern Ireland. In 2007, after some important conditions of the agreement were finally met by both parties, a power sharing to govern Northern Ireland was finally realized.

Another foreign policy option utilized by the Unites States is to designate countries as state sponsors of terrorism. The purpose of this designation is to promote international cooperation in condemning state-sponsored terrorism and to bring maximum pressure against those involved. A range of bilateral and multilateral sanctions is needed to discourage states from supporting terrorism. More specifically, countries are placed on this list if they assist terrorists by providing sanctuary, arms, training, logistical or financial support, or diplomatic immunity to groups or individuals. As of July 2012, four countries have been designated by the United States as state sponsors of terrorism: Cuba, Iran, Sudan, and Syria.

Dealing with terrorism within the confines of foreign policy may remain the first option, but other responses may be more viable.

International Cooperation Strategies

In the aftermath of terrorist bombings in Madrid in 2004 and London in 2005, the Council of Europe swiftly agreed to condemn the attacks, strengthen the European commitment to fighting terrorism, and propose new counterterrorism measures (DeFlem, 2006). A similar situation occurred after September 11, 2001, when numerous multinational organizations, including the United Nations, the European Union, the Organization of American States, and the Organization of African Unity, issued declarations of support and pledged assistance to the United States. These are only two examples of what most countries around the world now realize—that international cooperation is essential in the fight against terrorism.

Often, due to the efforts of the United Nations, treaties provide the general framework for this cooperation. Fourteen multilateral UN treaties, called conventions, related to combating terrorism have been formed since 1963 (United Nations, 2012). Not all states have ratified each of these legal instruments, and others have not implemented them. One of the most important came in 1999, when a UN working group finalized an international convention aimed at cutting off all legal and illegal sources of funding for terrorism. The convention came into force with the ratification of the legislative bodies of 22 countries.

In addition to these treaties, other instruments may be relevant to particular circumstances, such as bilateral extradition treaties and UN Security Council and General Assembly resolutions related to a variety of international terrorism issues. Between 1972 and March 2010, there have been 63 such terrorism-related resolutions, and 11 since September 11, 2001. In addition to the multilateral UN-based treaties, a number of regional instruments have been formed by countries in Asia, Africa, South America, the Middle East, and Europe, although only in the latter region do such efforts seem to work effectively (Taulbee, 2009).

But none of the international collaborations mentioned here may prove to be more important than the one created by the United Nations General Assembly when in 2006 they adopted the United Nations Global Counter-Terrorism Strategy. In September 2008, all 192 member states of the United Nations confirmed their commitment to the strategy, and its adoption marks the first time that all member states have agreed to a common strategic and operational approach to fight terrorism. The strategy, with the force of the Counter-Terrorism Implementation Task Force (CTITF), hopes to accomplish the following four "pillars": (1) address the conditions conducive to the spread of terrorism, (2) develop ways to prevent and combat terrorism, (3) work to provide assistance to the international community to counter terrorism, and (4) defend human rights while combating terrorism (UN, 2009).

Probably the best example of the effectiveness of international cooperation is the situation of the European Union and terrorism. Over the years, extensive information sharing and cooperation have greatly aided criminal justice officials in the global fight against terrorism. There are numerous examples of this cooperation, but consider the results of the midair bombing of Pan Am Flight 103 over Lockerbie, Scotland, in 1988. The flight originated in Frankfurt, stopped in London, and exploded over Scotland while on its way to the United States. An international investigation ensued, including countries in the Middle East who were believed to be involved. Then followed the extradition of the perpetrators to the Netherlands, where they were tried by a panel of Scottish judges and later transferred to a prison in Scotland to serve life sentences. Prior to the formation of the European Union, and surely during the days of the Cold War, such cooperation between criminal justice officials would have been virtually impossible.

Military and Police Detection and Apprehension Strategies

Following terrorist attacks, an outraged public usually expects the government to take strong measures to prevent further incidents. Detection and apprehension strategies are at the heart of antiterrorist activity because in general the use of military agencies to deal with internal terrorist acts is unacceptable in democratic governments. International incidents are another matter, since police departments do not have jurisdiction to operate across borders or to engage in the kind of intelligence operations that are crucial to preventing terrorist acts or tracking down terrorists. The large number of international terrorist operations in today's world of easy transport and communications poses a particularly difficult problem of response. Still, over the years, military agencies, civilian police forces, and intelligence agencies have developed an increasingly sophisticated apparatus of response to terrorism. Many countries have passed laws allowing for extraordinary antiterrorist measures by government authorities. The kinds of laws and measures used are a function of the level of terrorist threat and the history of terrorism in the particular country.

For example, because it is the constant target of terrorist attacks near its borders and even within its cities, Israel represents an extreme case of having a planned response to terrorism. Israeli authorities have a firm policy of refusing to negotiate or give in to terrorist demands. This policy is often honored only in the breach, especially when Israeli soldiers have been captured, but it remains a pillar of Israeli response. Military incursions against known or suspected terrorist bases are a common Israeli response to terrorist incidents. Antiterrorism squads, which themselves practice a form of terrorist assassination, have formed part of the Israeli response, as in the assassination of a PLO vice chairman in Egypt in 1991, and the killing of Hamas leaders over the course of the last five years. Israel has even practiced counter-kidnapping, as in the abduction of Muslim clergyman Sheik Obeid. Israel has also probably developed the most security-conscious airline system in the world today. Having lived with terror for decades, over 20 years ago Israel developed an impenetrable flight security system; the country has not experienced a single hijacking since 1968.

Many countries plagued by terrorist acts employ special units in both their police and their military to deal with terrorism. They may pass special laws that allow for martial law, curfews, and abrogation of certain criminal procedure guarantees such as habeas corpus. This kind of legislation poses serious questions about abuse of civil rights, especially when governments use the military to quell domestic matters; military force is supposed to be used as a last resort or in severe emergencies.

In international cases, by contrast, the military and military intelligence units are more likely to be deeply involved. This was the choice made by the United States when after September 11, 2001, the United States, in coalition with a number of other nations and an Afghan organization called the Northern Alliance, utilized air and cruise missile attacks on established terrorist bases in Afghanistan in October 2001. Special Operations forces were also sent in to reduce the capabilities of terrorists to function. At the same time, humanitarian aid programs were sent for Afghans who left for Pakistan and those who remained. Local government structures and economic alternatives to the opium trade were proposed to peaceful Afghans. By the end of 2003, there was no evidence of an active Afghan terrorist network, although it appears that in recent years there has been a resurgence of terrorist activity in that country in the form of smaller, loosely connected Al-Qaida networks.

In addition to the military units such as the Delta Force and the SEAL Team Six, the United States also has at its disposal two primarily civilian units: the FBI's Hostage Rescue Team (HRT) and the CIA's Special Activities Staff (SAS). The HRT team is an elite counterterrorism unit that handles terrorist or hostage situations inside the borders of the United States. The SAS is an elite group whose members are drawn from the ranks of the best of the military, the Delta Force, the SEAL Team Six, and the CIA itself. As we mentioned in the beginning of this chapter, a SEAL Team Six unit was responsible for killing Osama bin Laden in May 2011. The SAS carries out a number of delicate operations as directed by the president of the United States. Because of the secrecy of its missions, the SAS is probably the least known of the units operating on behalf of the United States.

Legislation

Over the past 10 years, most countries around the world have enacted new laws to combat terrorism, punish terrorists, and respond to terrorist attacks. This is especially true of individual states and the federal government in America. Understandably, New York passed what has been called the toughest and most comprehensive package of antiterrorism laws in the nation, establishing six laws for persons who commit terrorist acts, make terrorist threats, solicit or provide material support for terrorist acts, or hinder the prosecution of terrorists. On the federal level, two significant laws were passed following September 11, 2001. The first was the **Patriot Act**, and the second, the Homeland Security Act.

The U.S. Patriot Act was passed six weeks after September 11, 2001, with the goal of broadening law enforcement agencies' authority to conduct surveillance on U.S. citizens and residents. Supporters of the Act claim that it has been an effective tool in the fight against terrorism. However, many have been highly critical of the Patriot Act. Civil libertarians have been very critical of the Patriot Act, believing that the balance between liberty and power has tipped too far in the direction of the government. In February 2005 and 2006, the Patriot Act was reauthorized and now includes some new measures, but according to critics it still falls short in the area of protecting civil liberties. On May 26, 2011, President Obama used an autopen to sign a four-year extension of three key provisions in the Act while he was in France.

The National Strategy for Homeland Security Act and the Homeland Security Act were passed in late 2002 with the purpose of establishing the **Department of Homeland Security** (DHS). The DHS is a federal agency that combines and reorganizes dozens of federal agencies, with just under 230,000 employees and a budget of over $59 billion for FY 2013, making it the second-largest U.S. cabinet department after the Department of Defense. The mission of the Department of Homeland Security is to "ensure a homeland that is safe, secure, and resilient against terrorism and other hazards where American interests, aspirations, and way of life can thrive" (U.S. Department of Homeland Security, 2012).

Adjudication

- During the September 6, 2012, hearing for his involvement in the November 2009 Fort Hood shooting, Nidal Hasan twice offered to plead guilty, but U.S. Army rules prohibit the judge from accepting a guilty plea in a death penalty case.
- The trial of a man accused of trying to blow up a commercial airliner above Detroit with a bomb sewed into his underwear ended just a day after it had begun on October 11, 2011, when Umar Farouk Abdulmutallab said he would plead guilty to all of the federal counts against him.
- In December 2008, a German court in Dusseldorf convicted Youssef Muhammad el-Hajdib of multiple counts of attempted murder for his failed attempt to bomb two trains (Kulish, 2008).
- During 2007, a number of young British Muslims of Pakistani decent were convicted of conspiring to plant bombs in public places in the United Kingdom (Long & Cullen, 2008).

These are just some examples of another method used to respond to terrorism—the implementation of formal adjudication. When innocent people are killed by terrorists, emotions run high, and a certain spirit of mob vengeance can develop. Even governments dedicated to the rule of law have difficulty dealing objectively and lawfully with suspected terrorists. Within this hostile environment, they must form some method to maintain the essential elements of their justice system while appearing to be "tough" on terrorism and terrorists. The United States, for example, has chosen to develop special courts for terrorism suspects such as those captured by U.S. forces in Afghanistan and Iraq.

Unfortunately, terrorist excesses can become an excuse for suspension of rights or even the development of a repressive paramilitary regime. Human rights organizations have found that justice system abuses in the name of terrorism prevention have become too common throughout the world. For example, in Australia the government has used the rhetoric of counterterrorism to justify its hard-line policies on refugee and asylum issues and has sought extended powers of detention for its security agency. Chinese officials have stepped up their campaign against Uighur separatists in Xinjiang province by invoking the war on terror, blurring the distinction between peaceful activists and those with genuine connections to international terrorist organizations. Russia has continued to justify its actions in Chechnya as a tightly focused counterterrorism operation, despite the fact that it has produced vast civilian casualties, including extrajudicial executions and forced disappearances. The measures adopted by the U.S. government after the September 11, 2001, attacks have also offended some because they appear to violate fundamental provisions of international human rights and humanitarian law.

Terrorist leaders may believe that such developments will lead to further support for their own revolutionary causes, but this is seldom the case. In extreme cases, a country may slide into dictatorship and lose whatever traditions of democracy it once may have had. And there is no guarantee that adjudication will result in the desired impact. In an independent study of federal terrorism prosecutions in the United States since September 11, 2001, it was determined that of the 64,000 referred for criminal charges, fewer than one-third were formally charged, only 879 were convicted, and only 5 received a correctional sentence of more than 20 years. In fact, the median sentence given for those convicted was 14 days (Associated Press, 2003). Another study of prosecutions showed that from 2001 to 2006, of the 417 people charged with some terrorism-related matter, the majority faced immigration or other related charges and only three were convicted of actual terrorism (Criminal Justice News, 2006).

As we have seen, international terrorism is not simply a problem of crime and punishment. The growth of religious terrorist groups such as Al-Qaida has complicated this equation. However, we must not lose sight of the fact that terrorist actions are crimes. In dealing with individual terrorists, then, we need to view them as criminals who have committed acts of murder, assault, arson, robbery, and the like rather than as pawns in an international power struggle. Otherwise, the system of crime and punishment in any country, as well as the rule of law, may be seriously diminished.

THE FUTURE OF TERRORISM

In our increasingly technological world, a relatively small number of terrorists potentially can wreak havoc out of all proportion to their numbers. A number of possibilities loom as means of committing domestic and international terrorism for the twenty-first century. Of greatest concern for most are the potential uses of **weapons of mass destruction (WMDs)**. WMDs are nuclear, chemical, or biological weapons that by their nature can cause mass casualties and extensive property damage. The possibility that a terrorist or terrorist group may obtain a nuclear device increases all the time, as knowledge about their manufacture becomes more available. This would be a far cry from the bomb-carrying anarchist terrorists of the early twentieth century. The poisoning of water and food supplies through chemical alterations, and the use of biological agents or agents of biological origin, may be used to attack large population centers. **Agents of biological origin (ABOs)** generally fall into one of four categories: bacteria, viruses, plagues, or toxins (White, 2009). One example of the use of ABOs was the sarin nerve gas attack in the Tokyo subway system in March 1995; another was the anthrax-laced letter sent to Senator Patrick Leahy at his office in 2001. Other new and more sophisticated technological methods can also be converted into weapons by terrorists who have a high degree of scientific knowledge. Electromagnetic pulse technologies can disable electronic components such as microchips or computers with a burst of energy from a generator. New kinds of plastics can easily be converted into weapons that are undetectable by metal detectors. And some chemicals based on liquid metal embrittlement technology weaken metals when applied and could conceivably be applied to vehicles and aircraft (Martin, 2003). With advances in the technology related to communications, terrorists will also find it easier to work across boundaries, and it is more likely that their message can be heard around the globe within minutes of, if not during, terrorist activity.

However, the terrorist threat that probably looms largest in the twenty-first century is cyberterrorism. Potential acts of computer terrorism range from viruses that infect individual computers and spread to unexpected users, to complex attacks infiltrating defense systems, cutting water and power supplies, and disrupting transportation systems. In Estonia in 2007 and in Georgia in 2008, large scale denial-of-service attacks left the countries vulnerable to a number of massive access problems. Large international gatherings such as Olympic games or World Cup soccer tournaments produce opportunities for this form of terrorism. The possibilities for terrorist mischief in this area seem as endless as the uses of computers themselves.

In addition to the methods themselves, we can project about who will be those most likely to commit terrorism in the future and where hotbeds of terrorism will most likely develop. One serious challenge for law enforcement officials will be the many small pockets or cells of terrorists that have spread around the globe. These groups, such as those of Al-Qaida, are loosely organized, are not tied to any larger terrorist organization, and may have their own agendas that are difficult to predict and interpret. Another challenge is the growth and collaboration of criminal enterprises such as the Russian Mafia, Triads, and Mexican and Colombian drug gangs. For example, we now know that the terrorists behind the Madrid, Spain, train bombings in 2004 and other deadly bombings in Bombay, India, were also linked to drug trafficking organizations. These groups have begun to link political and religious extremism with their propensity for transnational crime, and the results have been highly profitable and extremely violent (Martin, 2003; Kaplan, 2005). With the globalization of the economy, the ease of travel, and improved communications, terrorism will likely continue to grow beyond the historically troubled regions of the past such as Northern Ireland and the Middle East. Regions of the world with growing populations, ethnic clashes, governmental instability, and large-scale economic problems are ripe areas for terrorism. These include the Balkans in Europe, Northern Africa, and parts of Latin America and South Asia. Whatever the method, kind of group, or location, it is likely that terrorism will continue to be a worldwide problem for generations to come.

SUMMARY

The threat of terrorism and the impact of terrorist activity have changed the way people view the world and the way they act on a daily basis. Terrorism is not a new phenomenon, and the general goals have changed little over the past century, but the form and frequency of terrorist activity certainly have been transformed. There appears to have been a concurrent increase in the number of terrorist groups that have surfaced, although they vary considerably in their size and effectiveness. Among the options for dealing with the problem are foreign policy, international cooperation, legislation, and adjudication. Although the quantity and quality of counterterrorism measures seem to have had some impact on the incidence of terrorism and the apprehension of terrorists, the problem still remains because of the new and improved methods of spreading terror. Understandably, the United States has been at the forefront of terrorism prevention, detection, and apprehension. Laws have been created, agencies formed, and policies developed that have changed the course of daily life for many Americans and affected a considerable portion of the globe. Although impossible to predict with any precision, we can project who will engage in future terrorism and what methods will be used to continue to combat this worldwide scourge.

Comparative Criminal Justice at the Movies

Movies seek to entertain and inform the audience about a story, incident, or person. Many good movies also hit upon important substantive themes relevant to understanding crime and justice in comparative perspective. Read the movie summary below (and watch the movie if you haven't already) and answer the questions below to make the subject matter connections to comparative criminal justice.

***Syriana* (2005)**
Stephen Gaghan, Director

Syriana is a thriller involving power, corruption, and terrorism in the oil industry. The film tells four parallel stories, which intertwine over the course of the movie.

First, an experienced CIA agent, Bob Barnes (George Clooney), is disgraced following an unsuccessful mission dealing missiles in Lebanon, where he is kidnapped. Once he is released, he returns to the United States and is involved in a secret plot against a Persian Gulf prince, Nasir Al-Subaai (Alexander Siddig). Second, attorney Bennett Holiday (Jeffrey Wright) is investigated by the U.S. government regarding the merger of two American oil companies. The investigation does not appear to be making progress, however, in understanding the true situation that exists. Third, energy analyst and oil stockbroker Bryan Woodman (Matt Damon) allies himself with Prince Nasir, offering him advice on how to improve his country with oil revenues once he becomes emir. This is complicated by the fact that the oil companies do not want Nasir to become emir, because the prince wants the U.S. military bases out of his country. Nasir also wants to make peace with other countries in the Persian Gulf and not waste money on unnecessary items such as expensive warplanes. Fourth, a Pakistani immigrant worker is fired by the oil company, resulting in his recruitment as a suicide bomber.

These interrelated stories illustrate how there is a world shortage of oil, despite its apparent abundance, which is resulting in corruption, moral compromise, and violence. The movie does not take a clear position on these stories other than to tell them. Yet it makes it obvious that the entire picture of oil production, control, and its consequences is not fully understood by any of the parties involved: oil company executives, federal investigators, Middle Eastern princes, CIA spies, or oil stock-market traders. *Syriana* earned two Academy Awards: George Clooney for Best Supporting Actor and Stephen Gaghan for Best Original Screenplay.

Questions

1. How might you explain the presence of terrorism in both poor countries and countries possessing wealth?
2. Are there strategies that might be pursued toward reducing the corruption, violence, and terrorism associated with oil-producing nations?

Critical Thinking Exercise

Critical thinking requires the ability to evaluate viewpoints, facts, and behaviors objectively to assess information and methods of argumentation in order to establish the merit of an action, law, policy, or procedure. Please evaluate this scenario objectively, applying your knowledge of comparative criminal justice to the facts of the case presented, and answer the questions that follow it.

Fighting Terrorism through Anti-Drug Investigations?
The two units that prosecute federal terrorism and international narcotics cases in New York have been merged. The Terrorism and National Security Unit and the International Narcotics Trafficking Unit were merged "to more aggressively combat the threat America faces from the growing nexus between narcotics and terrorism." Extremist Islamic groups are believed to be involved in the drug trade in order to finance their illicit activities with the decline of state-sponsored terrorism and the need for terrorist groups to finance their own activities. Subsequent cases have confirmed this suspicion.

In one case, suspects overseas conspired to provide hundreds of kilograms of heroin to men they believed

continued on following page

continued from previous page

were associated with Hezbollah, but who were actually working as DEA (Drug Enforcement Administration) informants. In another case, defendants agreed to sell both kilogram-quantities of heroin and automatic weapons to a DEA confidential informant in Kandahar. The DEA informant represented that the heroin was going to be sent to the United States for resale, and that the heroin proceeds and the weapons would ultimately be given to the Taliban.

The need for terrorist groups to turn to drug trafficking and kidnapping is due in part to increased pressure on other means of financial support, such as Islamic charities and private donors. By merging the terrorism and narcotics units, two investigative units are combined that possess similar skills in working abroad in hostile environments, using classified information in their operations, and the ability to build complex cases against sophisticated targets, which are difficult to identify and prosecute.

A new federal law gives drug agents the authority to pursue narcotics trafficking and crimes of terrorism crimes committed anywhere in the world, if they can establish a link between the drug offense and a terrorist act or group. Terrorist groups operate in an underworld where it is difficult to determine the source of its money to supports its operations. "Terrorists and insurgents are increasingly turning to crime to generate funding and acquire logistical support," according to the U.S. Assistant Attorney General. The proceeds from these crimes subsidize terror group training, travel, weapons, and actual operations.

In another case, Mannor Arbabsiar, a naturalized U.S. citizen holding both Iranian and U.S. passports, admitted to conspiring with officials in the Iranian military, to assassinate the Saudi Arabian Ambassador while the Ambassador was in the United States. Arbabsiar acknowledged that he traveled to Mexico on several occasions to arrange the assassination of the Ambassador. With his co-conspirators, he unwittingly hired a DEA confidential source who claimed to be a representative of a drug cartel. Arbabsiar agreed to pay $1.5 million to the DEA informant and discussed a plan to murder the Ambassador at a restaurant in Washington, D.C., illustrating the overlap of drug trafficking activity to help support terrorist objectives.

Past cases show that it is unusual for senior leaders of terrorist groups to be involved in the actual trafficking of drugs, much in the same way that leaders of organized crime and drug trafficking groups work to distance themselves from hand-to-hand transactions in an effort to insulate themselves from detection and prosecution. Therefore, a combined focus on drug and terrorism cases might reveal possible overlapping connections earlier in an investigation.

Questions

1. What specific arguments can be made that combining terrorism and drug investigation units together will be more effective against terrorism?
2. What contrary arguments can be made that this approach may narrow the investigative effort against terrorism, resulting in more missed cases?

SOURCES: William K. Rashbaum, "United States Attorney Plans Drug-Terrorism Unit," *The New York Times* (January 18, 2010), p. 16; U.S. Attorney for the Southern District of New York. *United States v. Henareh, Et Al., and Taza Gul Alizai.* U.S. Department of Justice. (July 26, 2011); *Statement of Assistant Attorney General Lanny A. Breuer Before the Senate Judiciary Subcommittee on Crime and Terrorism.* Washington, D.C. U.S. Department of Justice (November 1, 2011); Drug Enforcement Administration. *Man Pleads Guilty in New York to Conspiring with Iranian Military Officials to Assassinate Saudi Arabian Ambassador to the United States.* Headquarters News. (October 17, 2012).

DISCUSSION QUESTIONS

1. Use the chapter and the Internet to find out the major reasons for terrorism in the Middle East. What is the relationship between the Middle East and Al-Qaida?
2. Why has "homegrown" religious terrorism emerged as the most serious and common form of terrorism in the United States today?
3. Explain the possible reasons why the data on terrorist activity reflects such a significant change in the last 10 years.
4. What terrorist group do you believe is the greatest threat to the world today? To the United States?
5. Speculate as to what you feel will be the biggest terrorism threat of the immediate future. Why?

FOR FURTHER READING

Deflem, M. (2010). *The Policing of Terrorism: Organizational and Global Perspectives*. New York: Routledge.

Howard, R., and B. Hoffman (Eds.). (2012). *Terrorism and Counterterrorism: Understanding the New Security Environment*. New York: McGraw Hill.

Law, R. (2009). *Terrorism: A History*. Malden, MA: Polity Press.

Martin, G. (Ed.) (2011). *The Sage Encyclopedia of Terrorism*, 2nd ed. Thousand Oaks, CA: Sage Publications.

White, J. (2009). *Terrorism and Homeland Security*. Belmont, CA: Wadsworth Cengage Learning.

WEB PAGES FOR CHAPTER

To learn about the Department of Homeland Security and the full National Security strategy, see http://www.whitehouse.gov/issues/homeland security/.

For information on the U.S. Department of State Bureau of Counterterrorism and access to the *Country Reports on Terrorism*, see http://www.state.gov/j/ct/index.htm.

For the 2011 NCTC Report on Terrorism that provides country reports on terrorist activity, see http://www.nctc.gov/docs/2011_NCTC_Annual_Report_Final.pdf.

For United Nations Terrorism Conventions concerning terrorism, see http://www.un.org/terrorism/instruments.shtml.

The website for the Combating Terrorism Center (CTC) at West Point is available at www.ctc.usma.edu/.

11  Transnational Organized Crime

Key Terms and Concepts

advance fee fraud
Cali cartel
corruption
Cosa Nostra
child soldiering
cybercrime
ethnicity trap
hawala
identity theft
organized crime
Russian Mafiya
trafficking in human beings
Triads
UN Convention against Corruption
UN Convention against Transnational Organized Crime
Yakuza

Chapter 11 Learning Objectives

Define organized crime.

Discuss the types of organized crimes and their contemporary forms.

Explain variations in organized criminal activity in different parts of the world.

Compare different government responses to organized criminal activity and their effectiveness.

Recognize the central role of corruption in facilitating organized criminal activity.

Understand the important of transnational organized crime in the modern world.

Brighton Beach in Brooklyn is where the Russian-speaking population in New York City is centered. Many of its residents were born in Russia and lived under a communist system in which the laws were often circumvented or ignored. The neighborhood has one of the highest health care fraud rates in the United States.

In one case, a New York City scheme was discovered involving 10 doctors, 9 separate clinics, and 105 different corporations all engaging in a health care fraud ring designed to steal money from insurance companies by making false claims. The nine clinics provided unnecessary medical treatments, including physical therapy, acupuncture, pain management, psychological services, x-rays, and MRIs. New York State's no-fault-insurance law permits drivers and passengers of vehicles to receive benefits of up to $50,000 per person for injuries they suffer in accidents, regardless of fault. The scheme involved faked accidents, false injuries, false claims, and false reports, all disguised to make them look authentic to insurance companies.

The ring was the largest single no-fault insurance fraud case in U.S. history, and its members were charged with conspiring to steal $279 million, most of it from private insurance companies.

A total of 36 people were arrested on charges including racketeering, conspiracy, health care fraud, mail fraud, and money laundering. According to the indictment, the ring sought reimbursement for so many excessive and unnecessary medical treatments that it had to set up three separate billing processing companies just to handle the paperwork (Rashbaum, Moynihan, & Stelloh, 2012).

This case is an example of organized crime, involving several different offenses. It shows how organized crime is always centered on the provision of illicit goods and services and/or the infiltration of legitimate business or government.

Mario Puzo's best-selling novel *The Godfather* and the films that were based on it evoked the image of organized crime held by Americans and many others around the world. A close-knit Italian family and its associates, headed by a respected patriarch, engages in extortion, the procurement of illicit goods, and violence. Gang warfare erupts in which potential usurpers and others are killed. The victims of this violence are part of the organized crime underworld. Journalistic accounts of organized crime activities, and even autobiographies and biographies of major figures such as Joe Bonanno, John Gotti, and Sammy Gravano, have reinforced this image.

Organized crime is not that simple, though. It is a complex phenomenon that is found in many countries and among diverse national and social groups. There may be ongoing organizations in one country and loose networks in others. The Italian mafia organizations in Italy with their American counterparts are one example. The term "mafia" is synonymous with **Cosa Nostra**, referring to groups of organized crime "families" in the United States in a number of larger cities. The members of these groups are of Italian descent and often are unrelated to each other; hence, the term "family" is not descriptive, but this language was introduced into the lexicon in 1963 through the testimony of criminal informant Joseph Valachi (Albanese, 2011a). The Chinese secret societies that trade in heroin and extortion and have established affiliates in cities around the world are another. Loosely connected and non-ethnic networks dominate in many other parts of the world, producing, importing, and exporting drugs, stolen property, and other goods and services.

In this chapter, we will look at the phenomenon of organized crime as a major problem in the administration of justice worldwide. After a general introduction to the concept, the chapter describes the scope of this problem. We will also examine the changing nature of both organized crime and in the types of groups that engage in it. It will be shown how newer organized crime networks are organized and operate differently today, given the challenges they face in the illicit marketplace.

WHAT IS ORGANIZED CRIME?

It is often stated in the research literature that an acceptable definition for organized crime is hard to come by. However, an analysis of the different definitions used by authors over the years arrived at a consensus definition: "**organized crime** is a continuing criminal enterprise that rationally works to profit from illicit activities that are often in great public demand. Its continuing existence is maintained through the use of force, threats, monopoly control, and/or the corruption of public officials" (Albanese, 2011a, p. 4). What distinguishes organized crime from most other forms of criminal behavior is that it emanates from a continuing enterprise; its crimes are rationally planned; it requires force, threats, monopoly control, or corruption to insulate itself from prosecution; and it often caters to public demand for illicit goods and services. There is less consensus that organized crime has exclusive membership, has ideological objectives, is specialized in its criminal activity, or operates under a code of secrecy. However, to fully understand organized crime in the 21st century, we must keep in mind that it has also become a sophisticated international venture as well, involving connections among individuals and groups across borders.

Defining organized crime requires an understanding of its scope. Too often we hear of incidents that have the "earmarks" of organized crime, or that "suggest" organized criminal involvement, but this adds to the conceptual confusion. Organized crime involves two types of activity: provision of illicit goods and services and/or infiltration of legitimate business. Examples of the provision of illicit goods and services are illegal gambling, loansharking, prostitution, illegal narcotics, and stolen property. The infiltration of legitimate business involves exploiting a legal business in order to make illegal profits. These two broad types of organized crime are summarized in Table 11.1.

The provision of illicit goods and services involves consensual activities between the organized criminal group and the customer, and there is no inherent violence in the activity, although it produces economic harm to the larger society. On the other hand, the infiltration of legitimate business is inherently nonconsensual, because organized crime elements force themselves on a legal business to illegally extort funds. Virtually all organized criminal activity can be placed in one of these two categories.

Table 11.1 also illustrates how the manifestations of these basic forms of organized crime have changed in recent years. There has been an evolution from fencing stolen televisions and stereos to theft of intellectual property, such as software codes and pirated copies of movies. There has been an evolution from traditional prostitution to **trafficking in human beings**, in which victims are moved using fraud or

TABLE 11.1 Typology of Organized Criminal Activities

Type of Activity	Traditional Nature of Activity	Examples of More Contemporary Forms	Harm
Provision of illicit goods and services	Gambling, lending money, sex, narcotics, stolen property	■ Theft of intellectual property ■ Illicit arms trafficking ■ Money laundering ■ Trafficking in persons	■ Consensual activities ■ No inherent violence in the activity itself ■ Economic harm
Infiltration of legitimate business or government	Coercive use of legal businesses or government agencies (from the inside or from the outside) for purposes of exploitation	■ Business and consumer fraud ■ Extortion by computer ■ Corruption using intimidation	■ Usually nonconsensual activities ■ Threats, violence, extortion ■ Economic harm

coercion to make them forced laborers or sexual slaves (see more on this crime later in this chapter). In analogous fashion, simple business scams have moved toward more sophisticated (and harder to detect) insurance and bankruptcy fraud schemes. Police in the Washington, D.C., area have worked undercover to document the growing complexity of organized crime operations. Organized crime elements tell criminals what types of property to steal in order to ensure that the most marketable products are taken. The D.C. undercover operation found that laptop computers, digital cameras, camcorders, and credit cards were targeted. Fences then bought the stolen merchandise from the criminals and shipped much of it overseas, both maximizing its value and minimizing chances of discovery (Wilber, 2004). The wide-ranging nature of these stolen property rings is demonstrated by the fact that the fronts for these illicit enterprises included a newsstand, a gas station, an auto body shop, a pizza shop, and a Chinese restaurant. Other examples of the transnational nature of organized crime are cases in Germany where police discovered groups in different locations detaining 35 illegal Chinese immigrants. The Chinese smuggling ring was alleged to move people into Western Europe via Russia, Ukraine, and the Czech Republic. In another case, suspects from Algeria and Egypt were arrested for smuggling people from North Africa into Germany (Associated Press, 2004b; Zhang, 2008).

The methods by which organized criminal groups engage in their activities have limitless variations. Alan Block (1983) distinguishes between "enterprise syndicates" and "power syndicates." Enterprise syndicates provide goods and services, while power syndicates seek control and wealth through extortion or "protection" and other types of crime that provide no real services. Enterprise syndicates, as their name suggests, have parallels to corporations, with specialist employees and capital investment. Power syndicates, especially as they existed in the past in Italy and the United States, were involved in social control and thus paralleled government efforts to rule through intimidation and fear of sanctions. Large-scale organized criminals today, however, find that the big profits are in providing illegal commodities, and pure power syndicates are fewer.

The use of violence in organized crime occurs either as part of an extortion scheme or else to enforce "agreements" with customers of illicit goods and services. Because agreements to provide illegal products cannot be enforced in court, organized crime groups must enforce agreements with threats and sometimes with actual violence. The use or threat of violence has several objectives. It intimidates outsiders, strikes terror into the hearts of would-be informers, discourages competition, and settles disputes. Therefore, threats and violence enforce contracts and serve symbolic functions in discouraging undesirable behaviors, similar to the use of force by legal governments.

Ethnicity is often used to explain organized crime, but organized crime is committed by a wide variety of individuals from many different ethnic groups that sometimes work together. This use of ethnicity to explain organized crime is called the **ethnicity trap** because ethnicity does not help to explain the development or continuance of organized criminal groups or networks. Therefore, the depiction of organized crime "today" by the U.S. President's Commission on Organized Crime is particularly misleading. It described 11 different groups including La Cosa Nostra (Italian), outlaw motorcycle gangs, prison gangs, Triads and Tongs (Chinese), Vietnamese gangs, Yakuza (Japanese), Marielitos (Cuban), Colombian cocaine rings, Irish organized crime, Mafiya (Russian), and Canadian organized crime. Such a confusing array alternately uses national origin, type of crime, place of origin (prison), and means of transportation (motorcycles). Does this mean there is no organized crime in Western Europe, Africa, elsewhere in Asia, or by nationals in other countries not mentioned? A growing body of evidence indicates that forms of organized crime exist in all cultures and that organized crime activity is commonly interethnic (Albanese, Das, & Verma, 2003; McIllwain, 1999, 2004). For example, a United Nations survey found 40 different organized criminal groups in 16 countries, but only one-third were ethnically based (2000).

Organized criminal groups, like their activities, can be placed into two categories: social/cultural groups that exist apart from criminal activity and

TABLE 11.2 Typology of Organized Crime Groups

Type of Group or Network	Nature of Activity	Examples
Ethnic or culturally based groups that associate in both criminal and non-criminal social activity	Group performs social functions apart from just criminal activity. Group defines relationships among members, inspires loyalty, and has an ongoing structure.	Mafia groups in Italy and the USA, Yakuza in Japan.
Groups or networks that emerge to exploit a specific criminal opportunity	Group acts as a network in which members come together because of access, connections, or expertise needed to carry out a particular criminal scheme, but there is no ongoing group structure.	Smaller networks involved in specific enterprises, such as human trafficking, counterfeiting, or fraud, as seen in recent cases emanating from Eastern Europe, Asia, and Africa.

those that form around specific criminal opportunities. The characteristics of these types are summarized in Table 11.2.

Mafia (Italy and USA) and Yakuza groups (Japan) are good examples of organized crime of the "pre-existing" type. They each have ongoing hierarchical structures from "bosses" to "soldiers," and they also socialize as a group and engage in neighborhood life together apart from crime. Their criminal activities are often long-standing due to their influence in a local area, and their reputation is enhanced by their longevity and insulation from prosecution even though individual members may be imprisoned from time to time. On the other hand, the **Russian Mafiya** and related Ukrainian networks have been found to operate in Brooklyn, New York, where partners are taken on when needed to carry out a criminal activity, but there is no hierarchy that exists independent of the criminal scheme. Therefore, Russian and Ukrainian organized crime, as well as organized crime in South Africa, is more entrepreneurial and has less structure than "traditional" groups such as the mafia or the **Yakuza** in Japan, which are more hierarchical in nature. The generic term for organized criminal groups in Japan is "boryokudan," which means "violent ones." But the criminals call themselves "yakuza," which refers to the worst possible hand in a popular Japanese card game. Yakuza commonly have ornate tattoos and dress distinctively. Unlike organized crime groups in the United States, gangs in Japan are usually open about their Yakuza affiliation, so membership in Yakuza groups is much larger than that of the American mafia, which attempts to remain invisible. There are at least seven major Yakuza gangs in Japan, and they engage primarily in extortion (McIllwain, 1999; Shaw, 1999; Finckenauer & Waring, 2000; Varese, 2001).

The United Nations survey of 16 countries found the structure and organization of organized criminal groups to exist with gradual distinctions at five different levels:

- Rigid hierarchy—single boss with strong internal discipline within several divisions.
- Devolved hierarchy—regional structures, each with its own hierarchy and degree of autonomy.
- Hierarchical conglomerate—a loose or umbrella association of otherwise separate organized crime groups.
- Core criminal group—a horizontal structure of core individuals who describe themselves as working for the same organization.
- Organized criminal network—individuals engage in criminal activity in shifting alliances; rather than being affiliated with a particular criminal group, they associate with various groups according to skills they possess to carry out the illicit activity.

These group structures are listed from the most organized to the least structured. It was found that group members were usually unrelated but were drawn from similar social background (United Nations, 2000). Most significant was the finding that two-thirds of the groups identified were active in three or more countries, illustrating the significance of transnational organized crime. For example, in a study based on interviews with 90 people involved in organizing and transporting Chinese nationals to the United States (in New York, Los Angeles, and China), researchers found that "these smuggling rings are made up of decentralized associations of criminals of diverse backgrounds, and the relationships among core members mostly horizontal." The groups were found to be small, ad hoc, with a limited hierarchy and limited group cohesiveness, although the smuggling activity itself was highly organized. No connection was found between these smuggling groups ("Snakeheads") and traditional Chinese criminal groups (such as the **Triads**) (Zhang & Chin, 2002; Zhang, 2008).

THE SCOPE OF THE ORGANIZED CRIME PROBLEM WORLDWIDE

Organized crime was originally a local or regional phenomenon. It has become an international problem for several reasons. The most significant is the globalization of the world economy, due in part to the fall of the Soviet Union, the switch to a free-market economy in China, and emerging democracies around the world. These events have been accompanied by a worldwide surge in economic independence. Concomitant with these economic changes has been an opening of the borders to trade and travel, and growing ease of communication via the Internet, e-mail, and mobile telephone communications. It has been observed that the rise of transnational organized crime is "an unfortunate by-product of globalization, through which technological advances and lower barriers to trade have created seamless electronic environment and empowered new classes of actors which bypass nation-states. Like legitimate business, transnational criminal enterprises are embracing globalization by adopting new communications and transportation technologies which allow them to pursue global markets" (Center for Strategic and International Studies, 2001).

These global changes have had the effect of "shrinking" the world, making possible the shift from local, neighborhood enterprises to national and international schemes. The distance between product and consumer has become smaller as illicit money, drugs, stolen property, and even human beings can move quickly from source to destination. Reflecting the shift in the nature of organized crime in recent years, the "smuggling of migrants and the trafficking of human beings for prostitution and slave labour are two of the fastest growing global problems," according to the United Nations (2003a).

The true scope of organized crime is difficult to determine. We can only speculate as to how many billions of dollars are accumulated by criminal enterprises, how much government revenue is lost to tax-free trade in illicit products and services, how much damage is done to the environment, and how many lives are lost or ruined in the process. It is a fact that arrests for drug offenses have increased dramatically over the last two decades in many countries around the globe, but arrest statistics are dependent on police enforcement priorities, so it is difficult to determine the extent to which these crimes have changed versus law enforcement priorities. In addition, no systematic data are gathered on other crimes such as arms trafficking, intellectual property theft, money laundering, and other difficult-to-detect forms of organized criminal conduct (Bassiouni & Vetere, 1998; Meslo, Dobovsek, & Kesetovic, 2009). Despite the lack of organized crime statistics, a growing body of research studies has documented its existence in many regions of the world, involving a variety of different crimes. For example, the Bank of New York case was distinguished by nearly 400 correspondent accounts of uncertain ownership in Eastern Europe for which each fund transfer made money for the bank, ultimately totaling $1 billion per year. The result was an alliance between a legitimate business and criminal interests (Block, 2004). Cases of systematic theft of works of art in Italy have been documented, as has smuggling of all sorts of goods through Georgia and other developing nations, often finding their way into developed countries (Galletti, 2004; Kukhianidze, 2004; Massy, 2008). The scope of organized crime is immense, and systematic study of its extent is required to better understand its true nature.

HUMAN TRAFFICKING

Trafficking in persons is a special concern in transnational organized crime for three reasons. First, the late 20th and early 21st centuries have witnessed many nations emerging from conflict and civil war, creating large numbers of displaced, unemployed, and oppressed persons looking for some way to support themselves and their families. This has resulted in a large pool of desperate and very poor people who are willing to take risks and who can be exploited by unscrupulous criminals. Second, the United States enacted the Trafficking Victims Protection Act in 2000, recognizing the emergence of human trafficking as a distinct and serious offense, and the United Nations enacted a global agreement to prevent, prosecute, and protect victims in its Protocol to Prevent, Suppress and Punish Trafficking in Persons, Especially Women and Children (which supplements the United Nations Convention against Transnational Organized Crime). The UN Human Trafficking Protocol has since been ratified by three-fourths of the world's nations, attesting to the global concern about human trafficking. Third, it can be argued that human trafficking is one of the most serious of all organized crimes because the victims of human trafficking can be victimized over and over again, as opposed to other crimes such as trafficking in drugs or stolen property.

As noted earlier in the chapter, trafficking in human beings involves moving victims, using fraud or coercion to make them forced laborers or sexual slaves. It usually occurs as a three-step process in which victims are recruited, transported, and then exploited. Recruitment often occurs in a developing, postconflict country, although some trafficking victims have been found among runaway youths in the United States (Winter, 2012). Potential victims are recruited by a promise to move them to a better location with an opportunity to make money (usually in some form of legal labor: farm work, nannies, house cleaners, or dancers at clubs). Once the victims are moved, the agreed-upon fee (often between $10,000–$30,000) is suddenly increased, so the smuggling victims now become trafficking victims who are not free to leave until they work to pay off the debt. To make matters worse, the promise of legitimate employment turns out to be a lie, and the victims are forced to work as prostitutes or drug couriers to pay off the debt. Victims are prevented from escaping through close monitoring and threats by their captors, who exploit them at their destination (often a developed country with customers willing to pay for illegal services). Table 11.3 illustrates how trafficking victims are controlled by restricting their movements and through harmful living and working conditions.

TABLE 11.3 Methods of Controlling Human Trafficking Victims

1. Restriction of movement:
- a. Confiscating passports, visas, and/or identification documents
- b. Constantly accompanying the victim, insisting on answering questions on behalf of the victim, and/or translating all conversations
- c. Isolating the victim by not disclosing his or her location or address
- d. Requiring the victim to live and work in the same location

2. Harmful living conditions:
- a. Restricting access to food and appropriate clothing
- b. Forbidding access to appropriate medical care
- c. Not allowing time off or sufficient time to sleep

3. Harmful working conditions:
- a. In exchange for work opportunity, charging a large fee that is difficult or impossible to pay off
- b. Requiring unusually long work hours with few or no breaks
- c. Restricting the number of days off
- d. Providing little to no pay or irregular pay

SOURCE: U.S. Department of State, 2012.

Another type of human trafficking is **child soldiering**, which involves the unlawful recruitment or use of children as combatants or other forms of labor (using force, fraud, or coercion) by armed forces. Perpetrators include government armed forces, paramilitary organizations, or rebel groups. Many children are forcibly abducted to be used as combatants. Others are unlawfully made to work as cooks, servants, messengers, or spies. Young girls have been forced to marry or have sex with male combatants (Eichstaedt, 2009; Dallaire, 2011).

The Child Soldiers Prevention Act (CSPA) of 2008 was signed into law in the United States, and the 2012 CSPA list includes governments in the following countries who have been identified as using child soldiers: Burma, Libya, Congo, South Sudan, Sudan, and Yemen. A number of international agreements limit the age at which young persons can fight in wars and conflict (generally age 18). Underage children are used in armed conflicts because they can be controlled and manipulated more easily than adults. Their small size has also been exploited to use them as scouts, decoys, couriers, and spies. Children also require less food and no payment, which are major problems in most conflict areas (International Labor Organization, 2003; Gates & Reich, 2010).

Effective response to human trafficking has been hampered by a lack of training and resources to address the problem at local, national, or international levels (Dandurand, 2012). The United States evaluates the world trafficking situation annually, as mandated by its Trafficking in Persons Act (TVPA). Countries are ranked into three tiers based on observations made by the U.S. State Department.

Tier 1—Indicates that a government has acknowledged the existence of human trafficking, has made efforts to address the problem, and meets the TVPA's minimum standards.

Tier 2—Countries whose governments do not fully comply with the TVPA's minimum standards but are making significant efforts to bring themselves into compliance with those standards.

TABLE 11.4 Global Prosecutions and Convictions for Human Trafficking

Year	Prosecutions	Convictions
2006	5,808	3,160
2008	5,212	2,983
2010	6,017	3,619
2011	7,909	3,969

SOURCE: U.S. Department of State, 2012.

Tier 3—Countries whose governments do not fully comply with the TVPA's minimum standards and are not making significant efforts to do so.

Countries in tier 3 can suffer sanctions that include the withholding of nonhumanitarian foreign assistance. In 2012, the identified tier 3 countries included Algeria, Central African Republic, Congo, Cuba, Equitorial Guinea, Iran, Kuwait, North Korea, Libya, Madagascar, Papua New Guinea, Saudi Arabia, Sudan, Syria, Yemen, and Zimbabwe.

The European Union passed a new comprehensive antitrafficking directive in 2011 on preventing and combating trafficking in human beings and protecting its victims. The directive defines human trafficking and sets standards for member country responses to trafficking, similar to the TVPA in the United States (Care, 2011). Together with regional and United Nations efforts, these initiatives place pressure on both developed and developing countries to take specific action against human trafficking at both the supply and demand ends of the exploitation.

The results of these efforts have been slow but encouraging. For example, global prosecutions of suspects in human trafficking cases are now tracked, and the trend is moving upward (see Table 11.4).

Table 11.4 indicates that prosecutions have risen 36 percent and convictions are up 26 percent over the last five years. This has been the result of increasing global attention, new national laws, and international pressure to devote more resources to the problem. An evaluation of human trafficking prosecutions found that important factors in limiting the number of prosecutions include lack of awareness among practitioners and the broader community, reliance on reactive (rather than proactive) victim identification strategies, unmet victim needs, negative attitudes towards human trafficking victims, lack of awareness and experience with human trafficking laws, lack of institutional resources and infrastructure, and low prioritization of human trafficking prosecutions (Farrell et al., 2012). Therefore, greater attention to these deficiencies should result in more prosecutions.

Government prosecution efforts have been supplemented by efforts to insure the rights of trafficking victims. For example, the nongovernmental organization End Human Trafficking Now and UN.GIFT (the UN Global Initiative to Fight Human Trafficking) partnered with Microsoft Corporation to create an online curriculum for business managers and employees to identify the risk of human trafficking in their product supply chain and explore ways they can reduce that risk (U.S. Department of State, 2012). Additional victim support is needed (and is being provided in some places) to protect victims from trafficker retaliation and provide basic living necessities, housing, medical care, legal assistance, language training, job training, and family reunification. Human trafficking has captured the world's attention, but concrete efforts to improve the situation require more resources and international pressure.

CYBERCRIME

The misuse of computers and the Internet to carry out criminal activity is called **cybercrime**. Cybercrime refers to a method rather than a particular criminal offense, because many different kinds of offenses can be carried out by misusing computers and the Internet. Fraud is the most common example (e.g., lottery scams, bank account, identity theft), but cybercrime can also include threats, extortion, stolen property transfers, violation of international trading bans, and related kinds of schemes. All these criminal schemes have in common the intent to commit a crime, primarily by deception or coercion using computers and the Internet.

The objective of most cybercrimes is illicit financial gain. A Global Economic Crime Survey is conducted annually, soliciting responses from nearly 4,000 businesspeople from 78 countries. Because businesses are most often the targets of cybercrime (due to their accumulation of assets and profits), their victimization experiences are instructive. In 2011, for example, 56 percent of frauds committed against companies were from people on the inside, versus 40 percent external to the company. A quarter of these frauds were committed by computer. Both companies and individuals are concerned about cybercrime because of its threat to their reputation, the theft of personal identifiable information, theft of data or one's intellectual property (e.g., licensed software or music or trademarked property), and service disruption to businesses.

Table 11.5 illustrates that there are dramatic variations in the extent of fraud among countries, from two-thirds of all businesses in Kenya to only 6 percent in Japan. Of course, there are many reasons for these variations, usually involving the creation or reduction in criminal opportunities through punitive laws, effective law enforcement, and the extent to which private companies take seriously their own security through investment in secure business processes, payment schemes, and regular audits.

Another indicator of the extent of cybercrime is provided by the Internet Crime Complaint Center (ICCC), which logs complaints from victims about crimes committed using the Internet, and it provides services to both victims of online crimes and to law enforcement. The ICCC receives more than 300,000 complaints per year with a dollar loss of nearly $500 million. Table 11.6 summarizes the top five most common crimes reported to the ICCC. **Identity theft** and **advance fee fraud** have often occurred transnationally using e-mail contacts with prospective victims.

The scope of cybercrime displays a dramatic range. For example, a husband-and-wife team from Latvia, ages 22 and 23, created a phony advertising agency and claimed that they represented a hotel chain that wanted to purchase online advertising space on a newspaper website. Those who clicked on the website were then infected with a malicious

TABLE 11.5 Global Fraud Levels

High Levels of Fraud	Percentage of Respondents Reporting Victimization
Kenya	66
South Africa	60
United Kingdom	51
New Zealand	50
Spain	47
Australia	47
Argentina	46
France	46
United States	45
Malaysia	44
Mexico	40
Low Levels of Fraud	
Japan	6
Indonesia	16
Slovenia	17
Greece	17
Italy	17
Netherlands	17
Switzerland	18
Turkey	20
Slovakia	21
Sweden	22
India	24
Romania	24

SOURCE: Global Economic Crime Survey, 2011.

software program that caused users' computers to "freeze up" and then generate a series of pop-up warnings in an attempt to trick users into purchasing purported "antivirus" software, which was, in fact, fake. Users' computers "unfroze" if the users paid the defendants for the fake antivirus software, but the malicious software remained hidden on their computers. Users who failed to purchase the fake antivirus software discovered that all information, data, and files stored on the computer became inaccessible. The United States has pursued their extradition from Latvia, and they face up to 20–30 years in prison under U.S. law (International Search, 2012).

TABLE 11.6 Top Five Crimes Reported to the Internet Fraud Complaint Center

Crime Type	Definition
FBI-Related Scams	Scams in which a criminal poses as the FBI to defraud victims.
Identity Theft	Unauthorized use of a victim's personal identifying information to commit fraud or other crimes.
Advance Fee Fraud	Criminals convince victims to pay a fee to receive something of value but do not deliver anything of value to them.
Non-Auction/ Non-Delivery of Merchandise	Purchaser does not receive items purchased.
Overpayment Fraud	An incident in which the complainant receives an invalid monetary instrument with instructions to deposit it in a bank account and send excess funds or a percentage of the deposited money back to the sender.

SOURCE: Internet Fraud Complaint Center, *2011 Internet Crime Report* (2012).

Another example is provided by romance scams. In 2011 alone, the ICCC received more than 5,600 complaints of romance scams, in which individuals searching for companionship or romance online were targeted. The victims believed they were "dating" an honest person, but the online contact was a criminal with a rehearsed script that scammers have used repeatedly and successfully. Offenders search chat rooms, dating sites, and social networking sites looking for victims, using poetry, flowers, and other gifts to reel in victims while declaring their love. Stories of severe life tragedies, family deaths, and personal hardships are used to keep their victims concerned and responsive. Invariably, victims are asked to send money to help overcome a claimed financial hardship. The scope of this kind of cybercrime is huge, resulting in an annual reported loss of more than $50 million (Internet Fraud Complaint Center, 2012).

The Council of Europe's Convention on Cybercrime entered into force in 2004, and it is the only binding international instrument on this issue. It provides guidelines for any country looking to develop comprehensive national legislation against cybercrime. The Convention also offers a framework for international cooperation among countries. As of this writing, only 35 parties (countries) have ratified the convention, so there is a long way to go. Concern about cybercrime has lagged behind concern about human trafficking, but with the growth of serious international incidents like those cited above, cybercrime prevention and control is certain to gain center stage as a transnational crime.

ORGANIZED CRIME IN SELECTED WORLD REGIONS

Several world regions have attempted to assess transnational organized crime more accurately in order to better understand its size, scope, and harm produced. With a better understanding of organized crime, more effective control strategies can be designed.

Europe

Europe is a continent in transition as the European Union (EU) has expanded from 15 to 27 countries. It now includes many emerging democracies that were formerly part of the Soviet Union. Longstanding traditions of smuggling and underground economies have combined with the new ease of travel, expanded communication, and a common currency to create a serious organized crime problem. According to Europol, "the impact and influence of organized crime within the European Union has been growing over the last 15 years" (Europol, 2003, p. 5; Europol, 2011).

Specific regions, major organized criminal activities, types of organized criminal groups involved, and non-European connections are summarized in Table 11.7. This summary is drawn from an organized crime threat assessment conducted by Europol.

Table 11.7 illustrates how Europol has organized the 27 countries of the European Union into five groups, or "hubs," based on their proximity to major destination markets, geographic location, history of organized crime problems, and migration processes. These five geographic hubs manifest different kinds of organized crime problems based on their proximity to the supply for certain kinds of drugs, developing countries with residents anxious to emigrate, and producers of illicit goods seeking developed nations with the purchasing power to buy them. It is useful to read Table 11.7 while looking at a map of the European continent in order to appreciate the role that geography plays in trafficking flows and the development of organized criminal groups to exploit them.

Many non-European groups operate in Europe because it is a highly developed continent and therefore has both high demand and money to patronize illegal goods and services. Here again, the situation is similar to that in the United States, where non-U.S. organized crime largely caters to indigenous U.S. demand.

It is important to note that most groups do not specialize; they operate in a range of illicit activities as opportunity, supply, and demand warrant. Also, most groups work with other groups in connecting illegal products with consumers. Therefore, single nationalities are a poor explanation of organized crime activities. It is more accurate to say that organized criminal groups "network" as needed to advance particular illegal schemes, and these networks often change or dissolve as opportunities for crime shift in response to changes in the market and law enforcement efforts.

Asia

Organized crime is less well documented in most other world regions compared to Europe. An often overlooked region in Central Asia, home of the "Stans"—Kazakhstan, Tajikistan, Turkmenistan, Uzbekistan, and Kyrgyzstan (which changed its name in 1999 to the Kyrgyz Republic). Little is

TABLE 11.7 European Organized Criminal Activity, Groups, and Non-European Connections

Five Criminal Hubs in EU	Major OC Activities	Non-European Union Connections	Types of OC Groups Involved
Northwest (Netherlands, Belgium, United Kingdom, Ireland)	Drug distribution: heroin, cocaine, cannabis, synthetic drugs	Middle East (money laundering) and Pakistan (heroin processing)	Drugs arrive via the southwest hub (and Morocco), with cocaine, cannabis, and heroin reaching the Netherlands through Turkey and the Balkans. Synthetic drugs are produced by local and African, East European, Turkish, Pakistani, Vietnamese, Chinese, and Colombian groups, which are often comprised of second-generation members residing in the EU. Drugs are re-trafficked to North America, Israel, Australia, the Middle East, and Asia.
Southwest (Iberian peninsula: Portugal, Spain, Andorra)	Cocaine, cannabis, trafficking in human beings, and illegal immigration	West and Northwest Africa (suppliers of illicit drugs and immigration)	West Africa has a geographically significant position in the chain between South America, the source of cocaine, and the EU, a major destination market. There is also a human smuggling route passing through Libya and Algeria to Spain, Malta, and Italy. Libya and Tripoli form the supply route for illegal immigration and trafficking of human beings across the Mediterranean.
Northeast (Sweden, Finland, Denmark, Estonia, Latvia, Lithuania)	Human trafficking, illegal immigration, drugs (synthetic precursors, heroin), cigarettes, counterfeit goods	Eastern Europe (Russia, Ukraine, Belarus) supply and transit just outside EU borders	Cannabis products originate from Morocco and transit via Spain. Lithuanian groups traffic a variety of illicit commodities from the East toward the West in concert with groups in Russia, Belarus, Estonia, Latvia, and Poland.
Southern (Italy)	Trafficking of cocaine and cannabis products, illegal immigration, smuggling of counterfeit goods, counterfeit cigarettes, and production of counterfeit Euros.	All main Italian OC groups are active in drug trafficking, and they generally cooperate with Albanian, Colombian, Turkish, and African criminals.	Mafia-type groups based in Italy use systematic violence and intimidation as well as influence over local societies and economies. These groups cooperate with multiple criminal groups outside Italy.
Southeast (Greece, Romania, Bulgaria, Hungary)	Illegal immigration, synthetic drugs, counterfeit Euros and payment card fraud, cocaine trafficking	Albanian groups are in the cocaine distribution chain, but West Africa is also a transit zone. Romania is a gateway for immigration into the EU, while Bulgaria, Ukraine, Moldova, Albania, and Turkey have involvement with synthetic drugs, counterfeit Euros, and payment card fraud.	Cocaine enters the EU through Turkey or the Balkans. Ukraine is a transit point for heroin into the EU. Heroin is trafficked through Turkey by Turkish groups, often cooperating with Bulgarian groups, via the Balkans. The Southeast criminal hub is a key entry point for both counterfeit and genuine smuggled cigarettes. These cigarettes originate from the Ukraine, Moldova, the Balkans, and the Far East.

SOURCE: Compiled from Europol, 2009, 2011.

TABLE 11.8 Organized Crime in Central Asia

Countries	Nature of Organized Crime Activity
Kazakhstan Krygyz Republic Tajikistan Turkmenistan	Drug trafficking—a natural route due to Central Asia's geographical proximity to major heroin centers in Afghanistan and southeast Asia.
	Human trafficking—transit country for South Asian victims moved into Europe and the United Arab Emirates.
	Arms smuggling—due to weak regulation of import and export of firearms and explosives.
	Corruption—of state officials by organized criminal groups.
	Money laundering—using the oil industry, other fraud, and weak banking and financial controls at borders.

SOURCE: Compiled from Redo (2004).

known about these countries, so Table 11.8 summarizes existing knowledge about organized crime in this region.

The countries of Central Asia are developing countries with a combined size about half that of the United States. It is a resource-rich region with plentiful water and oil, but these resources have not been fully developed. Corrupt governments, long-standing ethnic divides, and a geographic location between major drug-producing regions place Central Asia at high risk for organized crime problems. Table 11.8 makes it clear that the smuggling of people and goods is a major part of organized criminal activity in Central Asia. For an idea of the scope of the problem, consider these cases from the region:

- A Kazakh businessman illegally sold a $1.5 million military plane to the Congo for $35,000.
- In a corruption probe, the minister of the interior disguised himself as a truck driver and transported melons from the Kyrgyz Republic to Kazakhstan. During his route, 36 police officials requested cash bribes (or the equivalent in melons).
- A study by the IOM estimated that approximately 4,000 Kyrgyz women are transported to the United Arab Emirates each year as sex workers.
- More than 1,000 Tajik border troops were scrutinized for corruption and drug smuggling, resulting in 25 percent of them being fired or reassigned (Redo, 2004).

These cases illustrate how entrenched organized crime becomes difficult to overcome, because widespread corruption serves to maintain its power and influence. An assessment by the United Nations Office on Drugs and Crime found that 25 percent of the 380 tons of heroin manufactured in Afghanistan is trafficked north through Central Asia and into Russia. In 2010, 35 to 40 tons of raw opium were trafficked through northern Afghanistan toward Central Asian markets (UNODC, 2012).

An assessment of organized crime in eight Asian countries and administrative regions in the eastern part of the continent included Cambodia, China, Hong Kong, Japan, Macau, the Philippines, Taiwan, and Thailand. Researchers interviewed 139 subjects familiar with organized crime, including 61 Asian law enforcement officials, 30 U.S. officials (e.g., Federal Bureau of Investigation legal attachés, Drug Enforcement Administration representatives, immigration and customs officials, resident legal advisors for a U.S. embassy and consulate, and secret service personnel), 27 professors/researchers, 13 nongovernmental organization (NGO) workers, 6 persons engaged in commercial sex acts (i.e., prostitutes, exotic dancers, and other employees) or owners of sex establishments (such as brothels, sex clubs, and massage parlors), and 2 reporters. The Asian respondents saw kidnapping and human trafficking as the principal forms of transnational crime involving China and the United States. Officials in Taiwan stated that fake IDs are used to gain Taiwanese passports for travel to the United States by Chinese who are being smuggled. But these offenses are not seen as high-priority problems in Asia. On the other hand, human trafficking and smuggling were indeed high-priority issues for most of the U.S. authorities interviewed.

Human trafficking was a problem with wide differences in perspective between Asian and U.S.

authorities. The Asian authorities saw the transnational movement of people as mostly smuggling, with people wanting to leave China and paying smugglers to transport them. Because there is little or no coercion in most of these cases, Asian authorities do not see them as serious issues. Asian experts interviewed saw that human trafficking was indeed "organized" but believed that it was not a form of organized crime because the operations were very small in size. None of the three most prominent organized criminal groups in Hong Kong (the San Yee On, the Wo Shing Wo, and the 14K) were seen as involved in human smuggling or human trafficking. Police authorities in Taiwan said there was no evidence that human smugglers engaged in other transnational organized crime activities or were involved with well-established organized criminal groups (Finckenauer & Chin, 2007).

Other World Regions

The situation appears similar in other regions, involving a variety of groups, activities, and nations. Organized crime is believed is to be responsible for $8 billion in "dirty money" that flows through South Africa's borders each year. A study found organized crime in South Africa to involve "a loose and highly interchangeable association of people," which includes corrupt government officials and businesses (Africa News, 2003). In Central Africa, the current instability is connected to trafficking in minerals and other forms of contraband. Some of the offenders are members of illegal armed groups and corrupt elements in the military who are operating as criminal groups profiting from the unstable situation. Their largest source of money is the minerals trade, with the illicit trade in gold from the Congo alone worth an estimated $120 million. This is 10 times the value of the country's legal gold exports and twice the value of coffee, its largest agricultural export. Other sources of illegal income include trafficking in cannabis, illicit timber, and elephant ivory (UNODC, 2011).

In a North American case, U.S. and Canadian drug agents arrested more than 120 persons in the United States and 50 more in Canada in an international drug conspiracy case. It was alleged that Wong Ze Wai, a Chinese national, controlled Ecstasy manufacturing, importation, and distribution operations from Toronto. His organization imported large quantities of Ecstasy in powder form and then pressed it into pills in Canada, so-called "drug candy," that was then shipped to the United States. Le Thi Phuong Mai, a Vietnamese national, was alleged to have coordinated money laundering from Ottawa that was designed to take cash from the street and nightclub sales in the United States to hide its illicit origins. The indictment alleged that the enterprise extended across North America, from Canada to distribution points in at least 16 U.S. cities. Operation Candy Box resulted in the seizure of more than 500,000 Ecstasy pills and more than $6 million in U.S. currency. It was alleged that the laundering wing of this organization was able to move $5 million in cash a month (Federated News Service, 2004).

In another case, a Mexican woman was sentenced to 10 years in prison for running a family-based operation for more than a decade in which uneducated women and girls from impoverished areas of Mexico were deceived and coerced in a scheme to force them to prostitute themselves in brothels in the New York City area. The operator and her family made hundreds of thousands of dollars in profits, but the victims received almost nothing (U.S. Department of Justice, 2009).

In New Zealand, traffickers were caught trying to smuggle 20 pounds of crystal methamphetamine into the country by mixing the illegal drug into the liquid part of lava lamps. The lamps were arriving in New Zealand from China, and a Chinese student was arrested in the case (Associate Press, 2004c). These cases, occurring on different continents, illustrate the creative, changing, and serious nature of transnational crime and those who engage in it.

CORRUPTION

Corruption and organized crime are inextricably linked. They rely on each other to maintain their power, influence, and profitability. **Corruption** is defined as abuse of a position of power for illegitimate private gain. It is defined under law in various ways, including conflict of interest, embezzlement, bribery, political corruption, nepotism, or extortion.

Many factors contribute to corruption. They include a weak government that is poorly managed and cannot enforce its own rules, weak accountability in government agencies, low pay of civil servants, corruption in the criminal justice system (especially police and judiciary), and the influence of organized crime. In order to combat corruption, the United Nations began a global program in 1999 that attempts to reduce corruption through four initiatives:

1. Providing technical assistance to member states in strengthening their legal and institutional anticorruption framework
2. Supporting and servicing international groups of Chief Justices on strengthening judicial integrity
3. Developing and disseminating anticorruption policies and tools
4. Enhancing interagency anticorruption coordination (United Nations Office on Drugs and Crime, 2003b)

These anticorruption efforts are crucial because of continued instances of serious, entrenched corruption around the world, which threatens the legitimacy of governments and in some cases puts organized crime in a position of regional or even national power and influence. Consider these cases:

- In Taiwan, 4,000 people were indicted on corruption charges in a period of 2.5 years, while in Beijing the heads of a state-owned securities firm, a state tax bureau, and a police chief were executed in Chinese corruption, bribery, and embezzlement scandals (Agence France Presse, 2002, 2003; Associated Press, 2003).
- In the United States, data show that convictions for official corruption remain constant, with approximately 600 federal convictions every year (TRAC Reports, 2011).
- Mohamed Suharto of Indonesia, allegedly one of world's most corrupt leaders, is said to have embezzled $35 billion in a country whose gross domestic product is less than $700 per capita (Transparency International, 2004).
- The United Nations Development Programme reports that 57 percent of Jamaicans believe their entire justice system is corrupt (UNDP, 2012).

Efforts to measure the extent of corruption have increased in recent years. The Corruption Perceptions Index (CPI) produced by Transparency International examines the perceptions of businesspersons and analysts both inside and outside of 180 countries worldwide. Transparency International draws on 13 different polls and surveys from 10 independent institutions to compose its annual index of corruption, on which it ranks all 180 countries. The CPI has been referred to as an indicator of "high-level corruption" because it assesses a country's institutional and governance framework for controlling corruption and the degree of success it has had. On the other hand, a great deal of corruption is found at the local level, which led the International Crime Victims Survey (ICVS) to include the question below in its survey of private citizens:

> *In some countries there is a problem of corruption among government or public officials. During (the past year), did any government officials, for instance a customs officer, a police officer, a judge, or an inspector in your company ask you or expect you to pay a bribe for his or her services?*

In the 30 countries included in the ICVS, only 2 percent of respondents reported any incident of corruption, and most countries reported rates under 0.5 percent.

The results of the CPI and ICVS are summarized in Table 11.9. Interestingly, these two separate indicators of corruption have been shown to correlate highly with each other, so their results are generally quite similar. For example, the relatively high corruption prevalence rates reported for Greece, Poland, Estonia, and Hungary reflect comparably higher corruption perceptions on the CPI index.

The relationship between organized crime and corruption has been empirically documented in research studies as well. In an important multinational

TABLE 11.9 Measuring Corruption

Corruption Comparisons	High-Level Corruption (in business and government)	Lower-Level Bribe-Taking (gov't official soliciting bribes from citizens)
Source	Transparency International Corruption Perceptions Index	International Crime Victims Survey
Number of countries included in survey	180 countries	30 countries
Countries with lowest corruption	New Zealand, Denmark, Finland, Sweden, Singapore, Norway, Netherlands, Australia, Switzerland, Canada	Northern Ireland, Finland, England and Wales, Sweden, Netherlands, Japan, Iceland, Spain, Ireland (tie)
Countries with highest corruption	Somalia, North Korea, Myanmar, Afghanistan, Uzbekistan, Turkmenistan, Sudan, Iraq, Haiti, Venezuela	Greece, Mexico, Bulgaria, Hungary, Poland, Estonia, France

SOURCE: Compiled from Transparency International (2011) and van Dijk, van Kesteren, and Smit (2007).

study, researchers used indicators compiled by the International Crime Victims Survey to develop an index of corruption that records the frequency with which citizens were asked for bribes by public officials. An index of organized crime was also used, incorporating the World Economic Forum's survey of businesses to provide an estimate of businesses victimized by organized crime. The results showed that lack of "independence and integrity of the judiciary was the most important predictor of the extent of organized crime," followed by lack of effective police. Organized crime was also more prevalent in less affluent countries. Interestingly, the correlates of corruption were quite similar. High levels of corruption were correlated with low judicial independence, low level of the human development index (socioeconomic factors), low independence of civil servants, and weak public democratic institutions. The authors concluded that "levels of organized crime and of corruption in the public sector are determined first and foremost by the quality of core public state institutions, such as the police, prosecution and the courts. That relationship seems to hold for countries at all levels of development." The results also point to "the vicious circle of poverty exploited and compounded by organized crime and grand corruption. In extreme cases, dysfunctional state agencies are 'captured' by organized crime" (Buscaglia & van Dijk, 2003, p. 31; van Dijk, 2007).

This study is important in examining a large number of countries on several different variables that demonstrate empirically the connection between corruption and organized crime. A related study conducted a comparative analysis of perceptions of organized crime in 59 countries. The study found that when the state fails to perform key state functions, or when a poor economy exists (i.e., high unemployment, low standards of living, reliance on underground markets), the growth of criminal syndicates is stimulated to supply goods, services, and jobs. The study also found that black-market activity was a key correlate of predatory organized crime (Sung, 2004).

Controlling corruption has clear implications for controlling organized crime. The **United Nations Convention against Corruption** entered into force in 2005, and as of this writing, 160 nations have now ratified it, representing more than three-fourths of the world's nations. The Corruption Convention has provisions that focus on prevention, criminalization, international cooperation, and asset recovery. Prevention measures include binding safeguards to promote transparency in government procurement, recruitment of personnel based on merit, and efforts to raise public awareness. The Convention requires countries to establish offenses to cover a wide range of acts of corruption, including trading in influence and the concealment and "laundering" of the proceeds of corruption. Countries are bound by the Convention to render specific forms of mutual legal assistance in gathering and transferring evidence for use in court and to extradite offenders. Countries are also required to undertake measures that will support the tracing, freezing, seizure, and confiscation of the proceeds of corruption. In the case of embezzlement of public funds, confiscated property must be returned to the state requesting it or to compensate the victims. The implementation of the Corruption Convention in the coming years will help to level the playing field around the world by making more uniform the efforts to control it and thereby making it more difficult for organized crime to maintain its influence in government affairs.

RESPONSES TO ORGANIZED CRIME

Effective responses to organized crime are difficult, but efforts are under way in many places. For example, Slovak police raided the birthday party of an alleged Mafia boss in a hotel in southwestern Slovakia and discovered 141 people connected with the Slovak and Hungarian underworld. The police action was a part of a new offensive strategy by the Slovak police. "We won't tolerate any demonstration of the power of underworld, because it raises fear and nuisance among citizens," said the police force vice president. The birthday party was visited not only by mafia members but also by businessmen. Their goal is "preventing demonstrative manifestations of arrogance, power, unity, financial power and supremacy of organized crime groups over ordinary citizens" (BBC Worldwide Monitoring, 2003a). This approach to organized crime control begins with the government taking a firm anticorruption stand.

Another example of strengthening the credibility of law enforcement may be seen in Ukraine, where the head of the organized crime department in Kiev was dismissed for poor performance. According to the interior minister, the department's performance deteriorated. "I am outraged when they report to me that the Kiev organized crime department's big achievement is the detention of a group of four people who were selling counterfeit videos," said the minister. The heads of 10 regional directorates for fighting organized crime were dismissed for poor performance. In addition, 132 senior officers were demoted and disciplinary measurers were taken against another 1,436 officers in organized crime divisions. The minister claimed that the directorate needs to stop launching criminal procedures into petty crimes and focus instead on more serious crimes, such as illegal migration, accepting bribes among high officials, kidnapping, and human trafficking (BBC Worldwide Monitoring, 2003b). A report analyzing the record of Nigeria's Economic and Financial Crimes Commission, the country's most important anticorruption agency, found that since its establishment in 2002, the agency has arraigned 30 nationally prominent political figures on corruption charges, including 15 former state governors. However, most cases made little progress in the courts, and not a single politician is serving prison time for any of these alleged crimes (Human Rights Watch, 2011).

Another important response to organized crime is to better organize the law enforcement effort to detect these activities. Canada opened an integrated operational center of the Combined Forces Special Enforcement Unit/Integrated National Security Enforcement teams (CFSEU/INSET). The facility permits investigators from 11 different agencies at the federal, provincial, and municipal levels to work together on major criminal extremist and organized crime investigations. The Toronto facility includes a state-of-the-art Special Operations Centre that will improve the ability of agencies to share intelligence and to coordinate major operations. CFSEU has a mandate to uncover, investigate, prosecute, and disrupt criminal organizations (New, 2003). The Serious Organised Crime Agency (SOCA) was established in the United Kingdom in 2005 with stated priorities to develop intelligence and investigate serious drugs and organized immigration crime and human smuggling. In addition, SOCA focuses on frauds, high-tech crime, counterfeiting, the use of firearms and serious robbery, and recovering the proceeds of crime.

Transnational organized crime can only be challenged effectively when governments cooperate against it. Such multilateral cooperation is increasingly important as organized crimes become more sophisticated. Consider the U.S. indictment that described a sophisticated heroin trafficking enterprise that linked conspirators in Pakistan, Thailand, Canada, California, and the Washington, D.C., area. The indictment alleged that heroin was shipped from Pakistan and Thailand into the United States and Canada via London in a crate of soccer balls and other athletic equipment. Payments for the shipments were made through an underground paperless banking system known as **hawala**. In this system, money is deposited in one country with a trusted broker and withdrawn the same day from a broker in another country. The system keeps no records and relies on mutual trust (Gibson, 2003). The need for international cooperation in detecting such schemes is evident. In an unrelated case, testimony from the U.S. Justice Department in Washington, D.C., concluded that the manufacture of optical discs that contain pirated music, movies, software, and video games appears to be most prevalent in Asia and in parts of the former Soviet Union. These discs are distributed around the world, sometimes through Central and South America into the North America, Europe, Australia, and consumer countries around the world. The need for international cooperation was highlighted at the hearing: "Because most of these syndicates operate outside the United States, we must rely on foreign government for much of the enforcement efforts in these areas. The importance of international cooperation cannot be overstated" (Congressional Testimony, 2003).

The best example of international cooperation against organized crime is the **United Nations Convention against Transnational Organized Crime**, the first international instrument of its kind. By ratifying the document, nations commit themselves to adopting a series of measures that include criminalizing participation in a criminal group, money-laundering laws, extradition laws, mutual legal assistance, specific victim protection measures, and law enforcement provisions. Since entering into force in 2003, the Convention has been ratified by 168 countries, more than three-fourths of the world's nations. Implementation of the anti–organized crime measures is monitored by the United Nations, which also provides technical assistance to countries in developing these tools against organized crime. The Convention is an important first step toward legally binding agreements among nations to tackle problems of transnational consequence.

It is important to remember that some of the most significant cases in the history of organized crime were made only with international cooperation. The **Cali cartel** in Colombia was one of the largest cocaine-trafficking organizations in history. After the decline of its predecessor, the Medellin cartel, the Cali cartel had a great deal of entrepreneurial success and grew into a multinational cocaine distribution network of immense size. Only when law enforcement agencies began to cooperate and share information was the cartel successfully infiltrated. The Cali case changed drug trafficking organizations in Colombia and elsewhere, shrinking them in size and the altering the measures they now take to insulate themselves from prosecution (Chepesiuk, 2003).

A final important element to defeating organized crime is a public that is intolerant of the phenomenon and its impact on their lives. In Japan, for example, a joint effort launched by government agencies and private citizens aims to go into neighborhoods that have a host of porn shops, sex businesses, and unlicensed street vendors, which are believed to have to pay gangsters in order to operate there, and replace those businesses with legitimate enterprises. (For example, major organized criminal groups are said to have their offices in Tokyo's Shinjuku Ward, a busy entertainment district.) Periodically, regular citizens walk the local streets at night along with members of the Metropolitan Police's Organized Crime Control Bureau. "It's about time somebody got around to doing this!" exclaimed one woman, claiming that shady characters and businesses hurt legitimate businesses and kept their regular customers away. It is hoped that cooperation between government agencies and the local community will one day stanch the flow of money to organized crime. "We've finally all banded together," said a community leader. "We've said, whether our actions are small or big, let's give it our best shot" (Prideaux, 2004; Tabuchi, 2010).

SUMMARY

Organized crime is a wide-ranging phenomenon that is difficult to define and equally difficult to assess in scope. We do know that it is a widespread problem that greatly impacts societies in overt and covert ways. In the past, ethnicity was often used to explain organized crime, but organized crime is committed by a wide variety of individuals from many different ethnic groups. New groups and new forms of organized crime activity are constantly being introduced, and it appears that loose international networks are becoming organized crime enterprises. There is not a region in the

Comparative Criminal Justice at the Movies

Movies seek to entertain and inform the audience about a story, incident, or person. Many good movies also hit upon important substantive themes relevant to understanding crime and justice in comparative perspective. Read the movie summary below (and watch the movie if you haven't already) and answer the questions below to make the subject matter connections to comparative criminal justice.

Blood Diamond (2006)
Edward Zwick, Director

Blood Diamond opens with the capture of fisherman Solomon Vandy (Djimon Hounsou) by the Revolutionary United Front (RUF) rebels in Africa. Solomon is forced to work in the diamond fields as a slave to fund the RUF war, with diamonds being traded for weapons. Solomon's overseer is Captain Poison (David Harewood), who observes Solomon bury a rare 100-karat pink diamond just as they are both captured by government troops.

Danny Archer (Leonardo DiCaprio) is a white mercenary from Zimbabwe who trades guns for diamonds with the RUF. He was earlier imprisoned for smuggling diamonds into Liberia and is looking for a way to repay a South African mercenary, Colonel Coetzee (Arnold Vosloo), for the diamonds he lost when captured. Coetzee works for a South African diamond company. Archer overhears talk about the large pink diamond and offers to help Solomon find his family in exchange for the diamond.

Archer meets an American journalist, Maddy Bowen (Jennifer Connelly), who is covering the war and the illegal diamond trade. He convinces her to help him find Solomon's family—ultimately discovering them in a massive UN refugee camp. Solomon's son is found to have been kidnapped and brainwashed by the RUF into becoming a child soldier, and Archer promises to get Solomon's son back if he can get the diamond.

Archer and Solomon pretend to be part of Bowen's group of journalists and find themselves under attack as they locate both the diamond and Solomon's brainwashed son in the RUF-controlled camp. There is a violent struggle, and Archer kills Colonel Coetzee and is shot himself. Archer and Solomon escape up a mountain being chased by soldiers, and Archer, suffering from his wound, makes a final call to Bowen for help in getting Solomon out of the country, reuniting him with his family, and selling the diamond.

Bowen secretly photographs the diamond's sale to the diamond company executive and publishes a magazine article exposing the trade in "conflict" or "blood" diamonds. The film closes with Solomon speaking to a conference on blood diamonds in Kimberly, South Africa. The conference refers to an actual meeting in 2000 that led to the Kimberly Process Certification Scheme, which aims to certify the origin of diamonds in order to curb the illicit trade in conflict diamonds. *Blood Diamond* was nominated for five Academy Awards, including Best Actor (DiCaprio) and Best Supporting Actor (Hounsou).

Questions

1. *Blood Diamond* shows shifting alliances among the companies seeking diamonds, rebels seeking guns, mercenaries seeking money, and innocent civilians caught in the middle. Explain how this can be considered a transnational criminal enterprise and conspiracy.
2. This movie highlights the power of the media in spotlighting injustices and helping to bring about change. Can you provide other examples where media attention to criminal activity helped to provoke positive changes?

Critical Thinking Exercise

Critical thinking requires the ability to evaluate viewpoints, facts, and behaviors objectively to assess information and methods of argumentation in order to establish the merit of an action, law, policy, or procedure. Please evaluate this scenario objectively, applying your knowledge of comparative criminal justice to the facts of the case presented, and answer the questions that follow it.

International Money Laundering Scheme

Two Bulgarians were sentenced to four years in prison for their roles as money launderers for a transnational criminal group based in Eastern Europe. The suspects also had to pay more than $600,000 in restitution. The scheme involved posting advertisements on eBay and other websites, fraudulently offering expensive cars and boats for sale that they did not actually possess. When victims expressed interest in the merchandise, they were contacted directly via e-mail by a purported seller. The victims were then instructed to wire transfer payments through "eBay Secure Traders" (an entity with no actual affiliation to eBay), a ruse to persuade the victims that they were sending money into a secure escrow account pending delivery and inspection of their purchase.

The victims' funds were actually wired directly into bank accounts in Hungary, Slovakia, the Czech Republic, and Greece that were controlled by the suspects and their coconspirators in Poland and Romania. According to court documents, in less than one year, the criminal conspiracy netted more than $1.2 million from U.S. victims alone.

Questions

1. Can you name the different types of organized crime offenses that took place during this scheme?
2. Why was it so easy to transfer funds across national boundaries? Is there a way to make this more difficult without impeding legitimate business activity?

SOURCE: "Two Foreign Nationals Sentenced for Roles in International Money Laundering Scheme." (2009). *Drug Week*. December 18; U.S. Department of Justice. (2011b). *Foreign National Pleads Guilty*. Office of Public Affairs. April 11.

world that is untouched by organized crime. Major activities of organized crime are evolving from simpler forms (such as extortion and selling stolen property) to more complex forms (such as trafficking in human beings and cybercrime).

Corruption and organized crime are closely connected, each requiring the other to maintain its power and influence. Successful strategies against corruption and organized crime require international police cooperation, research, and international conventions supported by the United Nations. Better organized law enforcement efforts, and greater intolerance of organized crime activity by public officials and the citizens within corrupt jurisdictions are also necessary in the fight against corruption.

DISCUSSION QUESTIONS

1. Should the United States try to control drug production at the source through the use of U.S. troops, agents, and money, or should it concentrate on controlling traffic and consumption within the United States?
2. Invite a federal agent to your class and discuss some ways that organized crime may affect your community or city.
3. What are ways in which products and services can be better protected against exploitation by organized crime?
4. Of all the possible responses to organized crime and drug trafficking, which do you believe is the most effective? Why?

FOR FURTHER READING

Albanese, J. S. (2011). *Organized Crime in Our Times*, 6th ed. Burlington, MA: Elsevier.

Glenny, M. (2009). *McMafia: A Journey through the Global Criminal Underworld*. New York: Vintage.

Redo, S. (2004). *Organized Crime and Its Control in Central Asia*. Huntsville, TX: Office of International Criminal Justice.

Winterdyk, J., B. Perrin, and P. Reichel. (2012). *Human Trafficking: Exploring the International Nature, Concerns, and Complexities*. London: CRC Press.

Zhang, S. X. (2008). *Chinese Human Smuggling Organizations: Families, Social Networks, and Cultural Imperatives*. Palo Alto, CA: Stanford University Press.

WEB PAGES FOR CHAPTER

For CIROC, the Centre for Research and Information on Organized Crime, see http://www.ciroc.org/.

For the International Association for the Study of Organized Crime, see www.iasoc.net.

Yahoo's links to other organized crime pages (of varying degrees of reliability) are listed at http://dir.yahoo.com/Society_and_Culture/Crime/Organized_Crime/.

For the United Nations Office on Drugs and Crime, see http://www.unodc.org/unodc/index.html.

The Terrorism, Transnational Crime and Corruption Center web page is at http://policy-traccc.gmu.edu/.

12  Juvenile Justice in International Perspective

Key Terms and Concepts

Convention on the Rights of the Child

delinquency

due process

Guidelines for the Prevention of Juvenile Delinquency

Minimum Rules for the Administration of Juvenile Justice

parens patriae

Rules for the Protection of Juveniles Deprived of Their Liberty

status offenses

Youth Aid Section

Chapter 12 Learning Objectives

Explain the definition of juvenile justice and its variations.

Discuss the way in which delinquency is measured and adjudicated.

Summarize four primary international agreements that address juveniles and the legal process.

Explain variations in punishment versus rehabilitation as a philosophy in dealing with juvenile law violators.

Compare delinquency prevention approaches in terms of their use and effectiveness.

Examine juvenile justice operations in six model countries.

Discuss the visibility of juvenile justice proceedings, the community context of delinquency, and anticipating trends, and their importance to the future of juvenile justice.

FBI agents arrested Jeffrey Lee Parson, charging him with creating and disseminating a "Blaster Worm" and using it to gain unauthorized remote access to 7,000 computers belonging to others. FBI agents tracked Parsons through a website, a web hosting company, and two other contacts, before finding him under his code name. He was charged with computer crime violations by intentionally causing damage to computers. Parson had just turned 18, although he was engaged in this conduct as a juvenile. He was convicted and sentenced to 18 months in prison (Brenner, 2010).

The problems of juvenile delinquency and doing justice in cases involving young people are global. Most of these problems occur within particular countries, but no country has the avoided the problem of serious juvenile crime. Consider the following cases:

- In Japan, an 11-year-old girl brutally slashed the neck of her classmate and left her to bleed to death in their classroom. Three weeks later, Japanese police took a 13-year-old girl into custody for allegedly pushing a Chinese boy off a building. Two 15-year-olds were arrested over the stabbing of a stranger with a kitchen knife at a festival (Kakuchi, 2004).
- In Australia, children as young as 10 have been linked to violent bashings, home invasions, car theft, and break-ins (Wallace and Jacobsen, 2012). Two teenage girls wearing masks set fire to a nine-year-old girl in Sydney, leaving the victim critically burned. The victim was walking with her step-mother and two younger siblings at the time of the attack. In an unrelated case, rampages by juveniles held at a detention facility resulted in assaults on 10 staff members, two fires, and a walk-out by 12 of its 15 youth workers (Rao, 2004; United Press International, 2004).
- Most adolescents sent to long-term group homes in Los Angeles, after being charged with a serious offense, reported they were still involved with crime or drugs seven years later, according to a survey of more than 400 youths aged 13 to 17 (Rand Corporation, 2009).
- The Danish government proposed to lower the age of criminal responsibility by a year to 14 and called for the use of electronic bracelets on juvenile delinquents to fight rising child crimes. The proposals could see children as young as 12 wearing electronic bracelets on the ankle to monitor their whereabouts (Denmark, 2009).
- In Malaysia, more than half the children who commit a crime are reconvicted within a decade—most on multiple occasions—highlighting a fundamental failing in the juvenile justice system. Over the last two years, the authorities placed nearly 4,000 young people in institutions for offences such as property crimes, violence, breaking court-ordered supervision, drug use, gambling, and dealing in weapons and firearms (Mustaza, 2010; Zhi, 2011).
- In Panama, the president announced her intention to drive through tough new reforms to the penal code to clamp down on juvenile delinquency, modeled closely on efforts in El Salvador, Honduras, and Guatemala, in an effort to counter the threat posed by teenage street gangs (*Latinnews Daily*, 2004).
- In Hong Kong, more than 150 teenagers—some as young as 13—were hauled off by police over a single weekend during a series of raids on popular hang-outs, which focused on entertainment venues known as "upstairs" bars that authorities fear have been targeted by drug dealers and other criminals. It was the latest in a string of police crackdowns on teenage crime (Ngo, 2011).
- In Washington, D.C., juveniles were arrested for violent robberies or carjackings on average at least once

> a day last year. The shift is seen as a troubling indicator that the city's youngest offenders are growing more aggressive and confrontational (Klein, 2011).

The problem of juvenile crime, and the societal and legal response to it, poses difficulties more complicated than those faced in addressing adult criminality. This chapter will delve into eight key issues that are relevant to juveniles around the globe: What Is Delinquency?, Measuring Delinquency, Adjudicating Juveniles, The United Nations and Juvenile Justice, Correcting Juveniles, Delinquency Prevention, Juvenile Justice in Six Model Countries, and The Future of Juvenile Justice.

Important experiences from nations around the world will be highlighted to show the similarities and differences in their approaches to juvenile delinquency. Although no single country has all the answers, innovations do exist in many parts of the world that offer promise.

WHAT IS DELINQUENCY?

Nations around the world have drawn an arbitrary line to distinguish juvenile delinquents from adult criminals in the eyes of the law. If a criminal act is committed by a person under the legal age established by the government, the act is considered **delinquency**. The same illegal act committed by someone who has reached this age threshold is considered to be a crime. Therefore, delinquency is distinguished from crime not by the behaviors engaged in but by the age of the offender.

In the United States, a person becomes an adult in legal terms at age 18. Unlike most other countries, the United States empowers individual states with unique legal authority, so in three U.S. states a person legally becomes an adult at age 16, in seven states the legal age is 17, and in one state the legal age is 19. In most states, however, the age that distinguishes juvenile delinquency from adult crime is age 18.

Around the world, there is similar variation among nations in establishing the threshold age at which an act of juvenile delinquency becomes an adult crime. An analysis of 22 countries found that the age of criminal responsibility ranged from 7 to 21 years of age (Meuwese, 2003). United Nations agreements (discussed below) indicate that age 18 is the most universally accepted age of adult criminal responsibility. In most countries, including the United States, there is a also certain age below which a child cannot be held legally responsible for any law violation. In the United States, that age of minimum responsibility is usually 7 years old, but it ranges from ages 6 to 16 in different countries. The reason for establishing a minimum age is that small children are seen as not being old enough to fully understand the consequences of their actions, and so cannot be adjudicated as either a juvenile delinquent or an adult criminal. Therefore, juvenile delinquency is confined, in general terms, to the law violations of young people between the ages of 7 and 18.

Some nations add a middle category for which there is no criminal liability; often this category includes children from 7 to 12 years of age, but children may still be subject to child welfare interventions. This keeps young juveniles out of the adjudication process but permits governments to intervene in their lives due to misbehavior.

One factor in defining delinquency is the existence of **status offenses**, acts for which only juveniles can be held liable. Status offenses do not involve violations of the criminal law but are undesirable behaviors designed to thwart more serious delinquent behavior. Examples of status offenses include habitual truancy, curfew violations, repeated running away, and failing to respond to the reasonable requests of parents. Noncriminal offenses such as these are especially common in industrialized countries, where younger children are not expected to participate in the workforce. In England, for example, children under age 10 are not held criminally liable, but those between ages 10 and 16 are subject to special juvenile laws that provide for different treatment under law and levels of liability at different ages. Nevertheless, countries like Canada and Germany do not have status offenses.

It is clear that the selection of *any* precise age to distinguish delinquency from crime is arbitrary, yet age limits continue to be used throughout the world. In fact, age is used as an arbitrary demarcation in many ways in society. For example, a person must be 25 to be elected a representative in the U.S. Congress, 30 to be a U.S. Senator, and 35 to be President of the United States. In England no one can be elected a member of Parliament until he or she is 21 years old. There are similar wide variations around the world (and within the United States) in the ages at which people can have consensual sex, marry, join the military, drive an automobile, vote, and otherwise participate fully in civil life. It should be seen that age is merely an administrative convenience that is used as an arbitrary marker for "maturity" in the broadest sense.

An alternative to using age to distinguish delinquents from criminals might be to use the adjudication process solely as a fact-finding hearing to determine whether the suspect did indeed commit the offense alleged. If proof beyond a reasonable doubt could be established in a given case, the offender would then face a disposition hearing at which a judge would impose some kind of punishment, treatment, or both, after an investigation into the offender's background, experiences, needs, and maturity to determine an appropriate disposition (Albanese, 2008). This would be one way to avoid the arbitrary age cutoffs that cause problems in trying to answer difficult questions of the appropriate disposition when young persons commit very serious crimes or very minor offenses.

MEASURING DELINQUENCY

The true extent of delinquency is unknown. Most acts of delinquency are not serious and escape detection, and there is evidence that arrested juveniles are not representative of all juvenile offenders. For example, arrests of juveniles (those under age 18) in the United States have dropped substantially in recent years. Table 12.1 lists the eight most common types of juvenile arrests, followed by three serious crimes of violence. It can be seen that most juveniles are arrested for crimes against property. The percentage of juveniles arrested for arson, motor vehicle theft, vandalism, burglary, and other property crimes is between two to six times greater than juvenile involvement in violent crimes, such as criminal homicide, forcible rape, and aggravated assault.

Most interesting is the fact that juvenile arrests have been dropping for nearly all crimes, as an increasing proportion of those arrested are age 18 and older. All told, juveniles accounted for 21 percent of all arrests in the United States in 1980. This percentage dropped to 13 percent in 2010. As noted above, arrest statistics are an incomplete indicator of criminal activity because most offenders are not caught, and arrests also rely on changes in police actions (such as changing policy focus on juvenile crimes or police department reallocations of resources). In Canada and England and Wales there was a similar significant drop in youth

TABLE 12.1 U.S. Arrests of Persons under Age 18 (percentage of all those arrested)

Offense	1980	2010	Change
Arson	44%	41%	−3%
Motor vehicle theft	43	22	−21%
Vandalism	49	31	−18%
Burglary	45	23	−22%
Larceny	38	22	−16%
Stolen property	30	16	−14%
Liquor laws	33	19	−14%
Robbery	30	24	−6%
Murder	9	9	No change
Rape	15	14	−1%
Aggravated assault	15	11	−4%

SOURCE: Federal Bureau of Investigation, *Crime in the United States—Uniform Crime Report* (U.S. Government Printing Office, 2011).

crime during the 1990s (Bala, Hornick, & Snyder, 2002). However, examining arrest trends within and among countries is not a reliable way to assess trends in juvenile crime.

An alternative way to measure the extent of delinquency is *self-reports*. As mentioned in Chapter 2, self-reports are anonymous interviews or questionnaires administered to juveniles in which they self-report the types and extent of the delinquency they have engaged in, whether or not it was ever detected by authorities.

Self-report studies have existed for 70 years, and their results have been remarkably consistent. Regardless of the sample of juveniles selected, self-reports have found that nearly all juveniles break the law at one time or another but that only a small proportion engage in persistent or serious criminal behavior (Hindelang, Hirschi, & Weis, 1981; Puzzanchera, 2000; Krohn et al., 2010). This finding appears to be universal. Self-reported delinquency studies in England and Wales, the Netherlands, and Spain found that "the problem of youth offending is similar in each country." Juveniles first engage in antisocial or delinquent behavior at ages 11 to13, and it generally decreases as juveniles near adulthood (Barberet et al., 2004).

It can be seen in Table 12.2 that despite some variations among the three countries, property crimes (primarily larceny) and traffic offenses were most common, followed by vandalism, drug use, and violent crimes (mostly assault). Most remarkable is the generally high proportion of juveniles who reported acts of delinquency.

A more extensive analysis of self-report studies across examined data collected in 31 countries. Six country clusters were used: Anglo-Saxon (Canada, Ireland, USA), Northern European (Denmark, Finland, Iceland, Norway, Sweden), Western European (Austria, Belgium, France, Germany, Netherlands, Switzerland), Mediterranean (Cyprus, Italy, Spain, Portugal), Latin American (Aruba, Netherlands Antilles, Suriname, Venezuela), and Eastern and Central European (the post-socialist countries of Armenia, Bosnia-Herzegovina, Czech Republic, Estonia, Hungary, Lithuania, Poland, Russia, and Slovenia). There were wide variations in the findings, but the universality of juvenile delinquency and the low likelihood of apprehension was a common finding (Junger-Tas et al., 2010).

Self-reports reveal a much higher volume of offending than is found in official arrest statistics, because most offenders are never caught. Important differences between arrest statistics and self-report data involve gender, socioeconomic class, and race. Juvenile arrest statistics are dominated by males, poor and working-class juveniles, and minorities, who are disproportionately represented (in the United States, the ratio is 5:1 male to female and lower class to middle class). The ratio revealed by self-reports is much closer; it appears that males, minorities, and those in the lower socioeconomic classes are much more likely to be arrested than females, middle-class juveniles, and whites (Elliott & Ageton, 1980; Bala, Hornick, & Snyder, 2002). The reasons for this discrepancy include police deployment tactics, strength of the family unit, access to legal representation, and other factors that make it more likely for poor minority males to be arrested and more likely for middle-class majority females to avoid arrest.

TABLE 12.2 Lifetime Prevalence Rates Using Self-Reports (percent)

	Property Crimes	Violent Crimes	Vandalism	Traffic Offenses	Drug Use
England and Wales	35.8	19.8	25.6	34.7	29.5
The Netherlands	60.5	23.5	45.3	66.1	21.3
Spain	50.1	33.9	55.2	58.4	24.5

SOURCE: Barberet et al., 2004.

ADJUDICATING JUVENILES

When a juvenile is apprehended for a suspected crime, how *ought* the child be handled? Should the juvenile be handled punitively, or be seen as deserving of treatment or assistance, or simply be given legal counsel to face the charges?

Virtually all countries have some kind of separate juvenile justice system (exceptions include Albania, Liberia, and Burundi). But not all of these countries are vigilant in their separation of the treatment of juvenile and adults in court, jail, or prison.

The differences in the treatment of juveniles versus adults in the adjudication process after arrest largely reflect how juvenile misconduct is viewed in a society. Over the years, juvenile delinquents have been alternatively viewed as young people in need of rehabilitative treatment, persons who need to be protected by law from a sometime arbitrary government, or criminals deserving punishment. The nature of juvenile justice changes depending on which view is most widely accepted at a given time.

Three basic philosophies of juvenile justice are summarized in Table 12.3. The underlying philosophy behind the original recognition of a need for juvenile justice was rehabilitative. It saw delinquency as a symptom of underlying family and supervision problems that required treatment for the welfare of the children. In the United States, this founding philosophy at the turn of the twentieth century was termed ***parens patriae***. The term referred to a medieval doctrine stating that the English Crown was able to intervene in family matters if the parents were unable or unwilling to care for the welfare of a child. The state could therefore act as parent for the child. As such, the emphasis of the justice process was changed from the adjudication of guilt to diagnosis of a condition to be corrected through rehabilitative treatment, not punishment. The evolution of juvenile justice in western Europe is generally similar in its origins (Blatier, 1999; Home Office Prison Service, 2002; Juvenile Justice, 2009). By the mid-twentieth century, there was disillusionment with the rehabilitative philosophy of juvenile justice, stemming from the state's poor record in trying to act as a surrogate parent. In addition, numerous instances of child maltreatment and neglect while children were in state custody led to cynicism about the rehabilitative ideal. The result was a shift toward a system of juvenile justice that ensured a young person's legal rights to make certain that juveniles were dealt with fairly during interactions with criminal justice officials and that their legal rights as citizens were protected. This model, which took hold during the 1950s through the 1970s, focused on ensuring justice for juveniles by closely guarding their **due process** rights under law and thereby ensuring, among other rights, fair and equitable hearing procedures. The welfare of the child was secondary to fair legal treatment in the adjudication process. Finally,

TABLE 12.3 Three Philosophies of Juvenile Justice

Primary Thrust of Adjudication	Underlying Philosophy	Adjudication Outcome
Rehabilitative (Welfare of child)	Serve best interests of *child* by changing juvenile's ability to lead a life that conforms with the law.	Rehabilitative treatment of juvenile.
Due Process (Legal rights)	Serve best interests of *justice* by ensuring a fair and equitable proceeding.	In accord with the rule of law (process more important than outcome).
Punitive (Crime control)	Serve best interests of *public* by making sure that public safety is not put in jeopardy.	Punishment to ensure public safety.

beginning in the 1980s, a third shift occurred during a general rise in the crime rate in the United States and elsewhere (Pfeiffer, 1998; French, 1999; Dambach, 2007). This rise in the overall crime rate (although rates of juvenile delinquency declined in many countries), combined with disillusionment from poor success in rehabilitation efforts, led to the emergence of punishment as the primary objective of juvenile justice. The result was changes in attitude, law, and policy, reflecting the view that the public safety was more important than the welfare of the child. The possibility of crime and victimization came to be seen as more important than any underlying problems a juvenile might have. The outcome was a juvenile justice system that treats juveniles similarly to adults, much in the way it was in the nineteenth century. The difference, of course, is the existence of many more legal protections in the adjudication process, but these protections increasingly treat juveniles and adults alike—resulting in a juvenile justice system that looks more and more like the adult criminal justice system (Bala, Hornick, & Snyder, 2002; Albanese, 2008; Urbina & White, 2009).

Not every country has had the same experience as the United States, but a look at efforts in the United Nations (in next section) shows that the recommendations coming from a consensus of nations around the world suggest that two of the three philosophies of juvenile justice are widely held. For example, rehabilitative goals are evident in those international standards that state that children should be diverted from the formal system of justice wherever appropriate to avoid being labeled as criminals, and custodial sentences should be used as a last resort, for the shortest possible time and limited to exceptional cases. At the same time, there is concern to protect the legal rights of juveniles accused of crimes, as the international standards state that children have the same rights of due process accorded to adults plus additional rights because of their special status as children. There is little evidence that punitive treatment of juveniles is recommended, but some countries, such as the United States, have dealt with this issue by treating juveniles charged with serious crimes as adults under law, thereby removing them from the juvenile justice system entirely. As Malcolm Klein has observed, "[Y]ounger children are being remanded to adult courts, more misdemeanors are being given felony status ... juvenile courts are becoming more adult-like, and the welfare/justice balance is leaning further to the right" (Klein, 2001, p. 275). This circumstance has produced some unforeseen consequences. For example, one study found that juveniles tried in adults courts were punished more severely than young adults with similar backgrounds sentenced in adult courts for the same crimes, suggesting that punitive policies might result in more harm than intended (Kurlychek & Johnson, 2004; Benekos & Merlo, 2008).

Nevertheless, there is some recent evidence of a shift away from extremely severe penalties for juveniles. During the last decade, China, Saudi Arabia, Pakistan, and Yemen have banned the death penalty for juveniles, and very few countries still allow the execution of juvenile offenders (see the critical thinking exercise at the end of this chapter). In an unprecedented move in 2004, Canada, Mexico, and other U.S. allies, along with Nobel Peace Prize winners, former American diplomats, and the country's largest physician's association, asked the U.S. Supreme Court to end the execution of killers who committed their crimes as young teenagers. The Supreme Court ruled in 2005 that the death penalty is unconstitutionally cruel for juveniles, and it prohibited mandatory life terms for juveniles in 2012 (Nettles, 2005; Liptak & Bronner, 2012).

Table 12.4 illustrates some possible modifications to traditional juvenile court adjudication that are not universally practiced but that might improve the quality of juvenile justice. Training of juvenile court judges, use of specialized police units, use of juvenile records, legal representation in court, and parental responsibility are issues that reflect the seriousness with which countries treat juveniles in the adjudication process. In the case of New Zealand, for example, the **Youth Aid Section** is a national police unit of trained officers that diverts more than half of young offenders out of the justice system. Several other countries have special police units

TABLE 12.4 Juvenile Justice Adjudication Initiatives

Juvenile Justice Initiative	Reason	Where Practiced
Specialized training for juvenile court judges	To develop understanding of differences in underlying philosophy, law, adjudication, and disposition alternatives in juvenile cases.	Training is required in England, Wales, New Zealand. Optional or absent in many other countries.
Specially trained police units for juveniles	To make maximum use of diversion and community resources in handling juvenile delinquency.	Australia and New Zealand have specialized youth aid sections in police departments. Ireland also has trained juvenile liaison officers.
Use of juvenile records	To achieve consensus regarding whether or not juvenile court records can be used after the youth reaches adulthood.	Canada, Scotland, New Zealand, and Northern Ireland generally do not permit use of juvenile records; the United States, England and Wales, the Republic of Ireland, and Australia permit their use under certain circumstances.
Legal representation in court	To ensure that arrested youth and their parents are informed of legal rights and options during adjudication.	Many countries provide for at least some kind of legal aid for juveniles facing serious charges. In England and Wales, aid is based on parents' income. In Canada, New Zealand, and the United States, government-paid lawyers are provided for most cases.
Parental responsibility	To inform parents of juveniles that they are required to attend court proceedings in most countries.	Parental attendance is not required in the United States or Canada. In some developed countries, parents can be held civilly liable for damages caused by their children.

to deal with juveniles in the hope of reserving official adjudications for only truly serious offenders (Maxwell & Morris, 2002; Winfree, 2004). Greater uniformity in the legal treatment of juveniles within and among nations suggests greater importance being placed on the value of juveniles as citizens in a society.

THE UNITED NATIONS AND JUVENILE JUSTICE

The United Nations is a voluntary organization that is comprised of nearly all the countries in the world. Its charter states that its mission is, in part, "to reaffirm faith in fundamental human rights, in the dignity and worth of the human person, in the equal rights of men and women and of nations large and small, and to establish conditions under which justice and respect for the obligations arising from treaties and other sources of international law can be maintained, and to promote social progress and better standards of life in larger freedom" (United Nations Charter, 2004). Juvenile justice is clearly part of the UN's mission in its efforts to promote human rights, worth of the human person, equal rights, respect for law, social progress, and better standards of living.

As mentioned earlier in the book, the United Nations attempts to achieve its goals by developing rules, guidelines, standards, principles, and conventions by consensus among member nations. These mechanisms are used to promote the evolution of most desired practices on a worldwide scale in fulfillment of the UN charter. "Conventions" are more significant than "rules," principles," or "guidelines" because they are binding in nature, requiring ratifying nations to abide by their provisions or else face sanctions. In the area of juvenile justice, there have been four major United Nations efforts to develop international standards relating to juvenile delinquency.

- Convention on the Rights of the Child (1990)
- Minimum Rules for the Administration of Juvenile Justice ("Beijing Rules," 1985)
- Rules for the Protection of Juveniles Deprived of Their Liberty (1990)
- Guidelines for the Prevention of Juvenile Delinquency ("Riyadh Rules," 1990)

The **Convention on the Rights of the Child** entered into force in 1990, and it has since been ratified by nearly all UN member countries. No other international agreement relating to justice has su[illegible] support. It defines a child as a perso[illegible]nd established many prot[illegible]n against cruel, inhum[illegible]t. It states that arrest, det[illegible]f a child shall be in co[illegible] every child deprived of [illegible]e the right to prompt ac[illegible]ropriate assistance, and th[illegible]aw violations shall be tr[illegible]ent with the promotion of the child's [illegible] worth. It also states the desirability of promoting the child's reintegration and resumption of a constructive role in society. Furthermore, the Convention states that children are presumed innocent until proven guilty according to law, should have appropriate assistance in the preparation and presentation of his or her defense, and must not be compelled to give testimony or to confess guilt; it also describes related legal protections (United Nations Convention, 1990).

The **Minimum Rules for the Administration of Juvenile Justice** were adopted in 1985 at the United Nations meeting in China (and thus are sometimes called the Beijing Rules). The Beijing Rules are historic in that they constitute the first international legal instrument to detail comprehensive rules for the administration of juvenile justice with a child rights and child development approach. The Beijing Rules predate the binding Convention on the Rights of the Child; they provided earlier guidance for countries on protecting children's rights and observing their needs in separate juvenile justice systems. Many of the Beijing Rules were later incorporated into the Convention on the Rights of the Child. The Beijing Rules encouraged fair and humane treatment of juveniles, emphasizing their well-being and the importance of rehabilitation for young people (United Nations Standard Minimum Rules, 1985).

The **Rules for the Protection of Juveniles Deprived of Their Liberty**, adopted in 1990, are standards for the treatment of persons under age 18 when confined to any institution or facility by the order of a court or similar body. These Rules set forth principles to universally define the circumstances under which children can be deprived of their liberty, emphasizing that deprivation of liberty must be a last resort, for the shortest possible period of time, and limited to exceptional cases. Rules are also included for the training of juvenile justice personnel and the inspection of juvenile facilities (United Nations Rules, 1990).

The **Guidelines for the Prevention of Juvenile Delinquency** (called the Riyadh Guidelines) were also adopted in 1990. They represent a proactive approach to delinquency prevention involving the roles of the family, the school, the community, the media, social policy, legislation, and juvenile justice administration. Prevention should involve "efforts by the entire society to ensure the harmonious development of adolescents." Countries are encouraged to develop community-based interventions to prevent children from coming into conflict with the law, and to use legal systems only as a last resort in addressing juvenile delinquency. The Riyadh Guidelines also call for the decriminalization of status offenses (United Nations Guidelines, 1990).

These four international agreements demonstrate an evolving international consensus regarding

Summary of International Agreements Related to Juvenile Justice

- All children should be respected as fully fledged members of society, with the right to participate in decisions about their own futures, including in official proceedings, without discrimination of any kind.
- Children have the same rights to all aspects of due process as those accorded to adults, as well as specific rights due to their special status as children.
- Children should be diverted from the formal system of justice wherever appropriate and specifically to avoid being labeled as criminals.
- There is a set of minimum standards that should be provided to all juveniles in custody.
- Custodial sentences should be used as a last resort, for the shortest possible time, and limited to exceptional cases.
- A variety of noncustodial sentences should be made available, including care, guidance and supervision orders, counseling, probation, foster care, education, and vocational training programs.
- Capital and corporal punishment of children should be abolished.
- There should be specialized training for personnel involved in the administration of juvenile justice.
- Children have the right to be released from custody unless there are specified reasons why a release should not be granted.
- Children have the right to measures to promote recovery and reintegration for victims of neglect, exploitation, abuse (including torture and ill-treatment), and armed conflict.
- States are obliged to establish a minimum age of criminal responsibility that is not set too low but reflects children's capacity to reason and understand their own actions.
- States should invest in a comprehensive set of welfare provisions to contribute to preventing juvenile crime (International Human Rights, 2004).

the appropriate response to juvenile delinquency. The combined substance of these agreements is summarized in the boxed insert.

New national statutes affecting juvenile justice were passed in a number of countries during the 1990s and early 2000s. Most of these attempted to make national legislation consistent with United Nations agreements, illustrating the influence of international agreements on the policies of individual countries.

CORRECTING JUVENILES: PUNISHMENT VERSUS REHABILITATION

Despite the existence of a growing international consensus and binding international rules, delinquency prevention and juvenile justice often do not draw adequate attention in many countries. Due to other pressing social and economic problems, violent conflict within and between some nations, corruption that hamstrings the effectiveness of government, or a punitive ideology that seeks punishment for all offenders regardless of age or circumstance, there is much to be done to improve juvenile justice around the world. Consider the examples below.

- Incarcerated youth in Rio de Janeiro endure beatings by guards and other concealed abuses that go unpunished because state juvenile detention centers lack independent monitoring. A 50-page report documented routine physical abuse, squalid living conditions, and other forms of inhumane treatment in the youth detention centers in Rio de Janeiro, Brazil (Human Rights Watch, 2005).
- A report by the Prison Reform Trust found that the number of children sentenced to custody in England and Wales more than tripled between 1991 and 2006, and the UK now has

the highest proportion of children in custody in Western Europe. Despite the official policy of only jailing children in exceptional circumstances, many children in jail have not committed serious or violent offences (Verkaik, 2009).

- A U.S. Department of Justice investigation found that New York State uses excessive force on youths in custody; the federal department says it will sue the state if changes are not made. A state-appointed task force said use of force and lack of mental health care are acute problems for the 1,600 children held in New York's juvenile facilities each year. Federal investigators found that youths in four facilities were routinely pinned to the ground and handcuffed for infractions as minor as laughing loudly, sneaking a cookie or refusing to get out of bed. The restraints caused concussions, broken teeth, and broken bones (Moore, 2010).
- A study by the U.S. Bureau of Justice Statistics surveyed more than 9,000 young people in custody and found that 12 percent reported being sexually abused one or more times, mainly by staff members. Particularly alarming, it identified several juvenile facilities where 30 percent or more of the young people reported being raped (Sentenced to Abuse, 2010).

Public and political opinions need to be informed by facts rather than by preconceived notions or prejudice. In the United States, for example, declining rates of juvenile arrests over the last 20 years have resulted in *more* punishment for juveniles, rather than less. Incarceration rates for juveniles have climbed, and less diversion out of the system has occurred; these trends, along with increases in drug arrests and longer average sentences, have combined to greatly increase the number of juveniles in custody. This has led to growing debate over the impact of treating juveniles harshly and sometimes as adults in the justice system (Klein, 2001; Pettus-David & Garland, 2010; Feld, 2010).

Comparatively few countries around the world keep regular data on how many juveniles are placed in some form of custody, deprived of their liberty. One estimate places the number at 1 million juveniles worldwide, but no one knows for sure (Cappelaere, Grandjean, & Naqvi, 2000). It would seem that the failure to keep track of the dispositions of juvenile offenders shows a peculiar lack of interest in their fates, when young offenders offer the most hope for change and will have many years of life on the street once their incarceration has ended.

Table 12.5 presents the percentage of the prison population comprised of juveniles. The figures shown are probably smaller than the actual numbers because of the ways nations count inmates. In the United States, for example, separate government agencies count juveniles in custody and adults in custody. The International Centre for Prison Studies reports that only 0.4 percent of U.S. inmates are under age 18, but this count includes only those juveniles in *adult* jails or prisons. If one looks at juvenile facilities, there approximately 134,000 juveniles, which adds another 6.7 percent to the total incarcerated population in the United States (for a total of 7.1 percent) (Sickmund, 2004; International Centre for Prison Studies, 2012). There are likely similar analogies in other countries, so it is difficult to say with certainty the true extent of juveniles incarcerated around the world.

In Kenya there are an estimated 40,000 street children who are frequently arrested simply because they are homeless, aggravating a major social problem into a criminal justice problem. In Ukraine, 11 closed juvenile facilities operate under a military

TABLE 12.5 Juveniles in Prison

Country	Juveniles in Prison (percent of total prison population)
China	1.4
France	1.2
Germany	3.2
Japan	0.5
England and Wales	1.6
United States	7.1

SOURCE: International Centre for Prison Studies, 2012.

system in which children have to march daily, and the staff is required to dress in military uniforms. On the other hand, Germany provides an example of a sincere effort to "correct" juveniles; there, the juvenile justice system is based on the principles of education and resocialization. Detention is reserved for more serious juvenile offenders, who are medically screened when entering the institution and are provided various educational and vocational training programs (Meuwese, 2003). The best juvenile correctional systems are those that make dedicated efforts to prepare juvenile offenders for a productive life in the community, rather than displaying a single-minded focus on punishment without investing resources to develop the skills needed to support long-term behavior change.

DELINQUENCY PREVENTION APPROACHES

"It is much better to drain the swamp than fight the alligators," says an international report on juvenile confinement. This study of juvenile justice in 22 countries recommended, based on its findings, that no children under age 15 be put in prison, that the conditions of confinement must be improved, that alternatives to imprisonment should be used, and that the focus should be placed on prevention (Meuwese, 2003, p. 135). The United Nations concluded that "clear evidence exists that well-planned crime prevention strategies reduce crime and victimization and are a more humane and cost-effective response than the formal criminal justice system" (United Nations Economic and Social Council, 2002). Despite these endorsements for delinquency prevention, a coordinated approach has been lacking.

The task of delinquency prevention is daunting. As self-reports indicate, virtually all juveniles break the law, but very few go on to become serious or frequent offenders. Distinguishing these groups is not easy, but important clues exist. A comprehensive report on youth violence by the U.S. Surgeon General reviewed existing studies and experience in delinquency prevention. The results are summarized in Table 12.6.

This review of existing knowledge in Table 12.6 reveals that some delinquency prevention programs work, although many do not. The interventions

TABLE 12.6 Summary of Findings on Delinquency Prevention

Major Findings and Conclusions about Delinquency Prevention
1. A number of youth violence intervention and prevention programs have demonstrated that they are effective; assertions that "nothing works" are false.
2. Most highly effective programs combine components that address both individual risks and environmental conditions, particularly building individual skills and competencies, parent effectiveness training, improving the social climate of the school, and changes in type and level of involvement in peer groups.
3. Rigorous evaluation of programs is critical. While hundreds of prevention programs are being used in schools and communities throughout the country, little is known about the effects of most of them.
4. Nearly half of the most thoroughly evaluated strategies for preventing violence have been shown to be ineffective—and a few are known to harm participants.
5. In schools, interventions that target change in the social context appear to be more effective, on average, than those that attempt to change individual attitudes, skills, and risk behaviors.
6. A child's involvement with delinquent peers and gang membership is one of the most powerful predictors of violence, yet few effective interventions have been developed to address these problems.
7. Program effectiveness depends as much on the quality of implementation as on the type of intervention. Many programs are ineffective not because their strategy is misguided but because the quality of implementation is poor.

SOURCE: U.S. Surgeon General, 2001.

that work best address both problems of the individual (the need to build skills and competencies) and conditions in the social environment (parents, schools, peer groups). The interventions that have shown the most effectiveness are also those that are implemented properly by highly motivated individuals. There appears to be no magic associated with a particular type of program; proper implementation is required. Unfortunately, most prevention programs have not kept adequate records to assess their effectiveness, and this lack of information has limited the amount of knowledge there is to draw upon. Some violence prevention programs actually harmed juveniles, so it is important that programs be based on the best available knowledge and experience rather than on ad hoc efforts or passing fads in delinquency treatment. In addition, school programs have been found to work best when they are aimed at changing social circumstances (peer groups, gangs, an anti-education subculture). Finally, associating with delinquent peers and gangs is a powerful predictor of violence, and more work needs to be done to diminish those antisocial influences in the lives of young people.

Three principles must be followed if delinquency prevention is to be more effectively sought: learning from the past, evaluation of existing efforts, and greater imagination in handling juveniles. A large number of studies have been done over the years that point to many strategies that have failed, and a few that had success, in reducing delinquency. It is crucial that the lessons of the past not be ignored if time, money, and resources are to be expended wisely. China, for example, is responding to juvenile delinquency through early interventions, school projects, education, and juvenile reformatories (Chen, 2000; Wong, 2001; Yisheng & Yijun, 2006). The accumulated experiences of localities and nations in knowledge gathering, technical assistance, and training must be documented and the reasons for successes and failures built upon in order to avoid duplication of past failed efforts. A number of promising delinquency prevention efforts have been identified through careful evaluation of programs and their outcomes (see Hodges et al., 2011; Burraston, Cherrington, & Bahr, 2012; Farrington, 2012).

Imagination is also important in thinking beyond the false dichotomy of prison versus freedom for juvenile offenders. In South Africa, for example, a restorative justice model is being used in an effort to resolve and manage conflict in the community in harmony with customs indigenous to the community. The South African approach closely resembles a civil justice model in which responsibility and restitution supersede notions of guilt or punishment. It also helps to divert young offenders from the formal justice system and increase community satisfaction with outcomes (Skelton, 2002; Jensen & Jepsen, 2006).

JUVENILE JUSTICE IN SIX MODEL COUNTRIES

There is much more variation in juvenile justice systems around the world than there is in adult criminal justice systems. Most countries have established separate rules for youthful offenders, but the nature of the rules and the manner in which they are implemented varies greatly. This section will highlight some of the interesting aspects of juvenile justice in our six model countries.

England

England's approach to juvenile justice has many similarities to that of the Untied States. Youths under age 18 in England can be tried in adult courts and can receive an adult sentence in serious cases. In cases where homicide is charged, trial as an adult is mandatory. On the other hand, children under age 10 cannot be prosecuted for any offense, but those between 10 and 13 can be prosecuted for serious offenses. A "young person" is 14 to 17 and is considered responsible under law, and juveniles as young as age 14 can be tried as adults for serious crimes. In 1991, the juvenile court was replaced by a "youth court" where proceedings are not public, although its mandate is quite similar to that of juvenile court.

Youth custody has replaced borstal training in England. Borstal training combined vocational, counseling, and education for repeat juvenile offenders between the ages of 15 and 21. It existed from the early 1900s and resembled a juvenile reformatory or prison more than a school. Over a long period of years, the high recidivism rates of those released reduced confidence in the borstal system. Youth custody makes fewer claims and is designed to confine youths ages 15 to 20. There is less emphasis on education or reform.

In recent years England has expressed great concern over persistent young offenders. The Crime and Disorder Act (1998) permits local governments to established curfews for children even under age 10. The Youth Justice and Criminal Evidence Act (1999) permits first offenders to be referred to a youth offender panel, which agrees on a contract with requirements to alter the juvenile's behavior with typical provisions including mediation, restitution, community service, home curfew, school attendance, drug and alcohol treatment, and avoidance of certain people or places (Gelsthorpe & Kemp, 2002).

Antisocial behavior orders (Asbos) were introduced in England in 1999, also designed to prevent and intervene in persistent misbehavior. The so-called "yob culture" in England is a significant issue for many. In the words of the Prime Minister, "It doesn't always get the headlines but if you've got difficult people living next door or down the street, if you've got groups of young people misbehaving, it makes life absolute hell." Asbos prevent offenders from committing specific acts for at least two years. Only local councils, police, and registered social landlords can apply for them, but individual citizens usually provide the evidence. Examples of Asbos include a ban on a 14-year-old boy from saying the word "grass" until 2010. Another youth was ordered to stop wearing a glove to signify gang membership. Other Asbos were used to stop spitting, congregating in certain areas, or visiting pubs (Grice & Russell, 2004). This reflects an ongoing conflict over the extent to which noncriminal behaviors of juveniles should be targeted, and the comparatively high rates of juvenile incarceration found in England and Wales, as measured against the rest of Europe (Muncie & Goldson, 2006; Graham & Moore, 2008).

France

French juvenile justice began in 1945 when the treatment of juveniles was removed from the adult prison setting. The principles of the French juvenile justice system include individualized treatment and sparing use of removal of juveniles from their home and community environment. Children under age 13 are exempt from court proceedings involving criminal behavior, those between ages 13 and 15 can be held responsible for serious crimes, and those 16 and 17 can be sentenced as adults under certain circumstances. The age of adult criminal responsibility is 18.

The juvenile judge handles cases from beginning to end, and a procurator is responsible for initiating the prosecution process from the outset. The guiding principle is to determine appropriate treatment and reform of juveniles rather than establishing guilt and punishment (Blatier, 1999). Therefore, the court process is less formal than in the case of adults. Interestingly, both the juvenile and his or her parents are required to attend juvenile hearings, emphasizing the importance placed on appropriate parental supervision.

The community service order was developed for both juveniles and adults in France as a rehabilitative form of disposition. It involves unpaid community service work in an effort to integrate the offender's interests with those of the community. France, like other countries, continues to struggle to develop rehabilitative programs that reduce recidivism without costly incarceration, which has not been shown to impact future youth crime. For example, diversion programs might be used to keep juveniles out of the justice process as much as possible. Police youth squads might help police maintain community contacts, keep an eye on problem youths, and offer education programs for juveniles.

Despite efforts to toughen the system in recent years through increased power to prosecutors, France has closed education centers for some juvenile offenders, but they are not fenced facilities and are designed for education, and juveniles are not incarcerated with adults (Wyvekens, 2008).

Germany

Germany is distinguished by its long-standing philosophy that punishment is not an effective way to deal with youth crime. Even though a juvenile becomes an adult in the eyes of the law at age 18, youths as old as age 20 can still be prosecuted as juveniles if it is seen as being in their best interest. Resocialization of youth through social welfare interventions has characterized German juvenile justice for more than a century. As Doob and Tonry have observed, "there appears to have been a widely shared philosophical basis for the German juvenile justice system throughout the twentieth century: less criminal justice intervention is better than more" (2004, p. 12).

Criminal responsibility begins at age 14 in Germany, which is older than in many countries. Germany sees criminal responsibility as occurring only after a child is fully socialized and morally developed. Children under this age can be treated by youth welfare departments, although this is considered a last resort.

Since German reunification and the normalization of border controls between Eastern and Western Europe during the 1990s, there has been an increase in juvenile crime in Germany. The crimes that have increased most include drugs arrests (cannabis and Ecstasy), fraud (fare dodging), assault (mostly against other juveniles), and simple street robberies. Therefore, most juvenile crime increases have been for offenses that "take place in public, in groups, and against other juveniles, and are of low seriousness." Longitudinal research indicates that as many as 70 percent of juvenile offenders are one-time offenders, suggesting rehabilitative rather than punitive interventions (Albrecht, 2004, p. 460; Dunkel, 2008).

In the justice process, victims may be present during trial proceedings, reflecting the growing acknowledgement of victims' rights. Virtually all adolescent offenders are sentenced under the Youth Court Law, even those charged with serious crimes. Contrary to punitive trends around the world, more than 60 percent of all young adults are sentenced as juveniles, reflecting Germany's unique emphasis on rehabilitative approaches to juvenile delinquency. This approach has been threatened in recent years by a number of sensational hate-crime incidents committed by young people (BBC Monitoring International Reports, 2004; Bleich, 2007).

China

China enacted its first comprehensive law to provide systematic protection of minors in 1991, reflecting the principles of the United Nations agreements. In 1999, China enacted its first law focusing on the prevention of juvenile delinquency, which emphasized treatment, education, and protection (Wong, 2004).

China's first specialized panel to hear juvenile cases was established in Shanghai in 1984, and several thousand specialized courts have been established since then around the country. The jurisdiction of these courts includes juveniles ages 14 to 18, and there is no provision for transfer so that a juvenile can be tried as an adult. Juvenile courts in China emphasize "double protections" to balance the protection of the juvenile and that of the community. Excessive leniency would produce no deterrent effect, but punishments that are too severe can harm juveniles. Like juvenile courts elsewhere, those in China are more informal than adult courts and the court acts as a "parent." Many countries have a conundrum in using age as the sole demarcation of criminal responsibility; however, China allows juveniles as young as age 14 to bear adult criminal responsibility if they commit certain serious crimes of violence or drug trafficking. This approach shows how China simultaneously distinguishes criminal responsibility by age, unless certain types of serious crimes are committed.

Nevertheless, China has many nonjudicial approaches for juvenile rehabilitation, such as "bangjiao" (help and education) and work-study schools. Bangjiao is often performed by a group of parents, neighbors, or others close to the juvenile in an effort to provide corrective supervision. Work-study schools began in 1955, and 88 now exist, involving an alternative education program that lasts nine years. They involve a combination of education and employment to achieve rehabilitation through discipline, learning, and work (Zhao, 2001; Chen, 2000; Zhang, 2007).

Japan

All cases involving alleged crimes committed by juveniles ages 14 to 19 are sent to Family Court in Japan. Japan distinguishes three types of juvenile misconduct under law: (1) juvenile offenders are those between 14 and 20 who violate the criminal law, (2) a "lawbreaking child" violates the criminal law while under age 14, and (3) a "pre-offense juvenile" commits a status offense such as running away, loitering, smoking, or another lesser offense.

Similar to many other countries, Japan operates under the philosophy of *parens patriae*, in which the court acts as a surrogate parent when dealing with juveniles. A background investigation of each juvenile is conducted for the court; they involve interviews with the juveniles, parents, teachers, and relevant others. If there is a question of guilt, the probation officer suspends the background investigation and asks the judge to hold a fact-finding hearing. These hearings are not public and, according to law, they are held in a "mild atmosphere with warm consideration." Interestingly, juveniles have a right to counsel, but the counselor need not be a lawyer—a parent, teacher, volunteer, or other competent person can serve as counsel. Another unusual aspect of Japanese family court hearings is that the public prosecutor used to have no right to be present or to appeal family court decisions. This practice was changed in 1998 to allow the prosecutor's presence in cases where the juvenile denies guilt. Nevertheless, the evidence prepared for the judge is submitted by the public prosecutor, so there is significant prosecution input into issues of guilt or innocence (Araki, 2002).

Japan's commitment to rehabilitation is reflected by the presence of nearly 50,000 volunteer probation officers who assist professional officers. There also exist child guidance centers, providing a combination of medical and psychologist assistance. Japan also makes use of alternative home placements in placing juveniles in cases of parental neglect and failure to supervise a juvenile. Japan rarely uses training schools or prisons for juveniles. Juveniles under age 16 cannot be sentenced to prison by law (Yokoyama, 2002; Elrod and Yokoyama, 2006).

Saudi Arabia

Saudi Arabia does not have a separate juvenile justice system, so the age of majority is not defined and is not a controlling factor in the adjudication process. Corporal punishment is viewed as having deterrent value, so it is commonly used. The United Nations Committee on the Rights of the Child has expressed international concern about discrimination against women and non-Muslims in Saudi Arabia, and about the need to end child floggings. Even though Saudi Arabia has ratified a number of international human rights treaties, including the UN agreements, it has been criticized for failing to live up to its responsibilities (Amnesty International, 2000; Nebehay, 2001).

A source of difficulty has been the wide discretion of judges under Saudi Arabian Islamic law. They have been accused of being contemptuous of the modern world, issuing restrictive rulings to preserve Saudi "purity." Therefore, the justice process for juveniles in Saudi Arabia is based on the principle of social rehabilitation of convicted persons, and males under 18 are placed in "surveillance centers" rather than in public prisons. Reform and rehabilitation programs are based on religious instruction, social reorientation, education, training, and work (Gilani, 2006).

It can be seen that in our model countries, and throughout the world, it is widely accepted among nations of the world that youthful offenders should receive mitigated punishment; they should be treated differently in the justice process, and kept separate from adults after sentencing. Nevertheless, there remain exceptions, and there is movement toward more severe punishment of juveniles in many countries.

THE FUTURE OF JUVENILE JUSTICE

Three issues are key to the future of juvenile justice: visibility, community, and anticipating trends. First, the adjudication process for juveniles tends to be less visible than the adult trial system. Juvenile hearings are often closed, and there is often little public interest in their cases after they are adjudicated. Once in custody in some kind of correction facility, abuses are prone to occur when there is little oversight. A generally declining juvenile crime rate in recent years has had the unfortunate consequence of making juvenile justice a low public priority, resulting in less funding, fewer and lower-paid staff, and more overcrowding of juvenile facilities. This situation provides a fertile ground for neglect, maltreatment, and abuse of young people, which the juvenile justice system, ironically, was established to prevent. Adequate oversight of the juvenile justice process is crucial to preventing and intervening in misuses of the government's authority in handling juveniles in custody.

Second, when a juvenile is charged with a serious crime, it is quickly forgotten that juveniles are the products of their families, neighborhoods, extended family, schools, community organizations, town, and wider culture (Klein, 2001). Juveniles are not adults. They are young people who require proper and adequate attention to develop into productive adults. It is important that the future of juvenile justice be guided by the recognition that communities are essential to producing delinquency, and are essential in its prevention and in the reintegration of delinquents in society. As soon as we "throw away the key" on juveniles, we are giving up not only on this generation but on the next one as well (Cohen and Piquero, 2009).

Third, it is important that nations do a better job at anticipating trends that will affect juvenile justice. Many countries are experiencing general declines in birth rates. At the same time, there have been increases in birth rates among indigenous peoples and some racial minority groups. Also, global migration continues at a high rate and disproportionately involves young families and children.

Analyses of current trends can help us to anticipate coming problems before they become serious. Current delinquency trends of concern, such as the use of synthetic drugs, school violence, and overcrowding of juvenile corrections facilities, can be anticipated sooner with more research and analysis of social behavior, economics, and demographic trends so that attention to them can occur before problems become widespread.

SUMMARY

Juvenile crime and juvenile justice pose special problems for justice officials around the globe. The initial factors that must be addressed are the identification of just who are the juvenile offenders and what is the nature and extent of their criminality. Subsequent to apprehension, the system must then decide how to deal with the juvenile offender. One of three philosophical ideals generally directs how juvenile offenders are treated. To assist those in the system who make decisions about delinquent behaviors and offenders, international standards have been devised as guidelines for justice system officials and professionals around the world. Although punishment and rehabilitation have traditionally served as the main strategies for dealing with offenders upon adjudication, there has been a recent trend in many countries toward developing and implementing prevention strategies. Each of our model countries provides some unique system features that are in consonance with the philosophy of the justice system or its historical and political background.

Comparative Criminal Justice at the Movies

Movies seek to entertain and inform the audience about a story, incident, or person. Many good movies also hit upon important substantive themes relevant to understanding crime and justice in comparative perspective. Read the movie summary below (and watch the movie if you haven't already) and answer the questions below to make the subject matter connections to comparative criminal justice.

Midnight Express (1978)
Alan Parker, Director

Based on an actual case, *Midnight Express* tells the dramatic story of a young American tourist who attempts to smuggle two kilos of hashish out of Turkey but is caught at the airport. He is arrested and ultimately sentenced to 30 years in a Turkish prison. Billy Hayes (Brad Davis) suffers the harsh realities of the Turkish prison system of that period, involving violence and brutality. He finds hope when his father (Billy Kellin) arrives from the USA to secure his release. His father's efforts fail, however, and, facing continuing horrible prison conditions, Billy opts to try to break out of jail and ride the "midnight express" (prison slang for an escape to freedom).

The movie shows how Billy's foolish conduct as a young man places him in circumstances over which he has no control. Even the U.S. government is unable to intervene in this case. The Turkish courts use Billy Hayes as an example to others, sentencing him to more than 30 years in prison as a drug trafficker. Hayes ultimately has two opportunities for release: the appeals made by his lawyer, his family, and the American government (which had been unsuccessful); and the "midnight express."

The movie is based on a book of the same name, written by Billy Hayes about this experience. *Midnight Express* was nominated for Best Picture and won two Academy Awards for Best Screenplay (Oliver Stone) and Best Original Music score (Giorgio Moroder).

Questions

1. Is there a valid justification for sentencing a young person with no prior record to 30 years in prison for attempting to smuggle a small amount of hashish?
2. Is there an alternative way to handle occasional cases like this one, in which a young tourist is arrested abroad for illegal conduct, that would serve the ends of justice while not ignoring the laws of the country where the offense occurred?

Critical Thinking Exercise

Critical thinking requires the ability to evaluate viewpoints, facts, and behaviors objectively to assess information and methods of argumentation in order to establish the merit of an action, law, policy, or procedure. Please evaluate this scenario objectively, applying your knowledge of comparative criminal justice to the facts of the case presented, and answer the questions that follow it.

Ending Life without Parole for Juvenile Offenders
by Human Rights Watch (a nongovernmental organization)
Human Rights Watch has joined 25 other organizations in filing an amicus brief before the U.S. Supreme Court in the cases of *Miller v. Alabama* and *Jackson v. Arkansas*. Both involved offenders who were sentenced to life without the possibility of parole for crimes they committed when they were 14 years old. The United States is the only country in the world that sentences youth to life without the possibility of parole for offenses committed before the age of 18. Universally accepted standards, including several treaties to which the United States is a party, condemn such sentencing of youth. We argue that international practice, opinion, and treaty obligations support holding all life-without-parole sentences for juveniles unconstitutional.

Virtually every other country in the world either has never engaged in or has rejected the sentencing of persons convicted of crimes committed when they were under 18 to life without possibility of parole. The few countries in which juveniles were previously reported to be serving life sentences without parole have either changed their laws or explained that juvenile offenders can apply for parole.

Universally accepted standards condemn sentencing juvenile offenders to life without the possibility of parole. All countries except the United States and Somalia are parties to the Convention on the Rights of the Child, which prohibits the sentence. Several treaties that the United States is party to have also been interpreted to prohibit the sentence.

The community of nations rejects sentencing any juvenile offender to die in prison, whatever the offense. Allowing the practice to continue in the United States would be inconsistent with contemporary standards of decency and contrary to the Eighth Amendment. The appropriate remedy is to ensure that persons incarcerated for crimes committed when they were under the age of 18 have a meaningful opportunity to obtain release at the end of a term-of-years sentence or through parole consideration.

Questions

1. Why do you believe that a few countries continue to execute juveniles or sentence then to very long prison terms despite overwhelming world practice disallowing it? Does the nature of the countries involved provide any clues?
2. Under what conditions does the United States allow for the execution or life imprisonment of juveniles? See www.deathpenaltyinfo.org/juveniles-and-death-penalty.

SOURCE: Human Rights Watch, www.hrw.org (2012).

DISCUSSION QUESTIONS

1. Age has historically been used to determine whether someone should be responsible for his or her behavior. Do you think this is the best method? Any other ideas?
2. List and rank relative to their level of usefulness the three main philosophies of dealing with juveniles. Be able to support your position.
3. Why is rehabilitation the main form of treatment of juveniles around the world?
4. If you were asked to determine the extent and kind of delinquent activity in a town or country, what kind of data would you utilize?
5. In your view, what is the best method for the prevention for juvenile delinquency?
6. Describe at least one unique feature of juvenile justice in each of our model countries.

FOR FURTHER READING

Tonry, M., and A. Doob, eds. (2004). *Youth Crime and Youth Justice: Comparative and Cross-National Perspectives*. Chicago University of Chicago Press.

Esbensen, F., and C. L. Maxson, eds. (2012). *Youth Gangs in International Perspective: Results from the Eurogang Program of Research*. New York Springer.

Friday, P. C., and X. Ren, eds. (2006). *Delinquency and Juvenile Justice Systems in the Non-Western World*. Monsey, NY: Criminal Justice Press.

Junger-Tas, J., and S. H. Decker, eds. (2008). *International Handbook of Juvenile Justice*. New York: Springer.

Junger-Tas, J., and F. Dünkel, eds. (2010). *Reforming Juvenile Justice*. New York: Springer.

Sherman, F., and F. Jacobs, eds. (2011) *Juvenile Justice: Advancing Research, Policy, and Practice*. Hoboken, NJ: Wiley.

U.S. Surgeon General. (2001). *Youth Violence: A Report of the Surgeon General*. Washington, D.C.: Department of Health and Human Services.

WEB PAGES FOR CHAPTER

For information on research about a variety of projects related to youth in Germany, see http://www.dji.de./cgi-bin/projekte/output.php?projekt=818.

A site that is dedicated to the protection of children's rights in Europe can be found at http://eurochild.org/.

For a site where one can learn about children and children's issues in African countries, see http://www.crin.org/organisations/viewOrg.asp?ID=1475&name=Children+First+%28South+Africa%29&type=All+Organisations.

For statistics about juvenile crime in the United States and about related sites, see http://www.ojp.usdoj.gov/.

Glossary

abstract review review whereby advisory opinions rather than judgments are rendered because constitutionality is decided without hearing an actual case that has arisen under a particular law

adjudicator individual who decides the outcome of legal disputes; judge

administrative detention form of punishment in the People's Republic of China that allows authorities to impose fines and incarcerate people without benefit of a trial for up to four years

advance fee fraud criminals convince victims to pay a fee to receive something of value but do not deliver anything of value to them

adversarial system procedure used in Common Law countries to determine the truth during adjudication whereby the prosecution and defense compete against each other with a judge ensuring fairness and adherence to the rules

advocat an attorney in France

advocate a legal representative, usually a lawyer, who presents the evidence and the arguments that allow adjudicators to make their decisions

agents of biological origin (ABOs) bacteria, viruses, or toxins used by terrorists to poison water and food supplies

al-Qaida group of Sunni Islamic extremists who were originally formed as a group of Arab nationals to fight the Russians during the war in Afghanistan; currently aligned with bin Laden

assessor in France, a professional judge selected from another court to sit in on trials and assist the president judge

asymmetrical warfare method of warfare used by one side in a conflict or war when it feels that it lacks the military power of the other so it must use strategy or tactics that differ from traditional or symmetric warfare

boryokudan used to describe organized crime groups in Japan

cali cartel a smaller drug trafficking organization that is part of the larger Columbian drug cartel in South America

canon law body of law developed by the Catholic Church that dealt with church and spiritual matters including provisions regulating family life and morals and rules for church governance

child soldiering involves the unlawful recruitment or use of children as combatants or other forms of labor (using force, fraud, or coercion) by armed forces. Perpetrators include government armed forces, paramilitary organizations, or rebel groups. Many children are forcibly abducted to be used as combatants. Others are unlawfully made to work as cooks, servants, messengers, or spies

chuzaisho local police post in villages and rural areas of Japan

civil law all law that is not criminal; the body of rules that regulates behavior between individuals, which does not involve the potential of criminal sanctions (contracts, torts, wills, property, family matters, and commercial law)

civil order control function the duty of the police to respond to, supervise, or control two or more citizens in any situation that can disrupt the peace and tranquility of society

commercial law body of law developed in Europe during the Middle Ages regulating the buying and selling of goods and services between cities and nations

common law body of law developed in the eleventh and twelfth centuries in England based on decisions of the judges of the King's Court, incorporating Canon Law, feudal custom, and Roman Law

community policing umbrella term describing programs that serve as collaborative efforts between the police and the public to identify the problems of crime and then involve the public in finding solutions

community service penalty for criminal actions that requires offenders to personally "pay back" in time and effort, by working for a not-for-profit agency

comparative criminal justice investigating, evaluating, and comparing the criminal justice processes of more than one country, culture, or institution

comparative criminology the study of the causes and correlates of crime in two or more cultures

Confucian thought the belief that social order can be achieved through moral and political reform, because man is by nature good or capable of goodness; the idea of group consciousness or collectivity is the main force behind motivating people to avoid illegal or immoral activity

conjugal visiting program in German prisons that allows an inmate private visits from his or her spouse and children for four hours every two months

control of freedom term used on the international level to refer to probation

Convention on the Rights of the Child United Nations document that establishes a number of key legal protections and rights for those under 18 years of age

corpus juris civilis body of laws resulting from the compilation and codification of the law in force in the Roman world in the sixth century A.D.; also known as the Institutes of Justinian

corruption the abuse of a position of power for illegitimate private gain. It is defined under law in various ways, including conflict of interest, embezzlement, bribery, political corruption, nepotism, and extortion

Cosa Nostra synonymous with the term *mafia* in referring to groups of organized crime "families" of Italian descent that are located in the United States in a number of larger cities

Council of Ministers the cabinet in France and Saudi Arabia, presided over by the President

court an agency with power to settle disputes in a society

court of assize in France, the court of original jurisdiction in criminal matters

court of general jurisdiction a major trial court that has jurisdiction over any cases involving criminal law and sometimes civil law

court of intermediate appeal a court that handles appeals from the lower courts such as courts of limited and general jurisdiction

court of last resort court or courts that are authorized by law to hear the final appeal on legal matters

court of limited jurisdiction court that handles minor criminal cases, and may also conduct preliminary hearings for cases that will be handled at the next level of courts or the courts of general jurisdiction

crime control model corrections model where it is assumed that criminal behavior can be controlled by more incarceration and other forms of strict supervision in the community

criminal justice system It consists of police, courts, and corrections agencies, which act to enforce the law, adjudicate suspects, and deal with convicted offenders

criminal law body of rules that defines crimes, sets punishments, and provides the procedures for adjudication

critical thinking mental activity which permits us to examine the relative strength of evidence, arguments, and alternative courses of conduct

cultural revolution reform period in China under Chairman Mao from 1966 to 1976 with the goal of moving Chinese society from socialism to a purer form of communism

cybercrime The misuse of computers and the Internet to carry out criminal activity. Cybercrime refers to a method, rather than a particular criminal offense, because many different kinds of offenses can be carried out by misusing computers and the Internet

dark figure the amount of unknown crime

day fine criminal penalty based on the amount of income an offender earns in a day's work

delinquency a criminal act committed by a person under the legal age established by the government

Department of Homeland Security (DHS) a U.S. federal agency that combines and reorganizes federal agencies to mobilize and organize the homeland against terrorist attacks

deterrence purpose of criminal sanctions or punishment whereby offenders, through various devices, such as certainty of punishment or length or severity of punishment, should come to the conclusion that crime is not worth the risk of the resulting punishment

developed country country with a high level of development, measured by the factors such as per capital income, gross national produce, and industrialization indicators, plus other indicators such as gross domestic product and industrialization

developing country country with a low level of material and social development, measured by such indicators as income per person, life expectancy, and literacy rates. A majority of the world's nations are developing countries

deviance control function a traditional police mission to reinforce community values and laws, protecting the community against nonconformists and trying to keep violators of community norms under control

Diyya restitution used in Islamic countries, which is paid directly to the victim or his or her family as compensation for five different *Quesas* (retribution) crimes

domestic terrorism the type of terrorism that involves a citizen or group of citizens committing a terrorist act in their own country

dossier in France, a complete record of the pretrial proceedings that informs the judge, the defense attorney, and others about the testimony of key witnesses and the evidence to be presented

due process (for juveniles) a model that focuses on ensuring justice for juveniles by closely guarding their constitutional rights under law during any contact with criminal justice officials

electronic monitoring an approach to noncustodial supervision that uses electronic monitors to expand the surveillance capacity of supervision; ordinarily combined with house arrest

ethnicity trap when ethnicity does not help to explain the development or continuance of organized crime groups or networks, especially insofar as many networks involve individuals of different national and ethnic background

ethnocentrism the view that one's own country or culture does things "right" and all other ways are "wrong" or "foreign"

European Convention on Human Rights an agreement that consists of a series of articles that address basic rights and freedoms evident in democratic countries

European Court of Human Rights a supranational court that allows persons who have been denied relief in their national courts to bring complaints against a government official or jurisdiction

exile form of punishment where a criminal is banished from a society

federalism form of government that allows for the power and responsibility to be divided between the national government and state government

fine penalty imposed on convicted offenders by a court or, in some countries, by another arm of the criminal justice system, requiring that they pay a specified sum of money

flow design measuring the number of persons in prison over a period of time

forfeiture (and confiscation) a criminal sanction used by governments who seize property derived from or used in criminal activity

garde a vue the initial questioning period in the French legal system

gendarmerie nationale (GN) French police organization operating within the Ministry of Defense that is responsible for rural areas and communities in France with populations of less than 10,000 people

Geneva Convention the first codified international humanitarian law treaty of a set of war crimes; more precisely, four separate conventions, with protocol added in 1977

globalization the process whereby the world has become interdependent in terms of events and the actions of people and governments around the world

Good Friday Accord historic agreement signed in April 1998 by feuding Catholic and Protestant parties in Ireland whereby both parties would share multiparty administration of Northern Ireland

Guidelines for the Prevention of Juvenile Delinquency United Nations document that provides a proactive approach to delinquency prevention involving the roles of the family, school, community, the media, social policy, legislation, and juvenile justice administration

habeas corpus court order requiring that a prisoner be brought before a judge to explain by what lawful authority he or she is being detained

hawala an underground paperless banking system in which money is deposited in one country with a trusted broker and withdrawn the same day from a broker in another country; the system keeps no records and relies upon mutual trust

house arrest incarceration sentence that uses the offender's residence as the place of punishment

Hudud crime in Islamic Law, a crime against God that is likely to endanger the social order

hybrid legal tradition a legal tradition that combines different aspects of more than one legal tradition

Identity theft unauthorized use of a victim's personal identifying information to commit fraud or other crimes.

incapacitation a purpose of criminal sanctions or punishment whereby offenders, usually through prison or exile, are kept from committing further crimes

independent monitoring board one of several committees in England that act as an independent watchdog on the prisons, meeting with inmates and staff to safeguard the well-being and rights of all prisoners and to help with the problems of discipline and administration

independent state It refers to people who are politically organized into a sovereign state with a definite territory

indigenous court a type of court emphasizing consensus and mediation that has been developed to formalize the process of justice for indigenous persons who are culturally or geographically removed from the mainstream of society

indigenous law native laws of persons who originate from or live in a particular area

injunction an order of the court designed to prevent harms that would occur before a case works its way through the regular court system

inquisitorial system a procedure used in nonadversarial systems to determine the truth during adjudication; characterized by extensive pretrial investigations and interrogations designed to ensure that no innocent person is brought to trial

International Court of Justice the principal judicial body of the United Nations, located in The Hague, Netherlands, with the dual role of setting, in accordance with international law, legal disputes submitted by the 191 UN member states and neutral parties and giving advisory opinions on legal questions referred by international organizations

international crime crime based on international agreements between countries or on legal precedents developed through history; includes offenses such as genocide, torture, and enslavement of populations

International Crime Victim Surveys (ICVS) the most extensive standardized survey of victims in the world; the primary collection tool used in the ICVS is computer-assisted telephone interviewing, which randomly selects and calls a sample of 800 to 2,000 individuals in each country

International Criminal Court a permanent supranational court with jurisdiction over the most serious crimes of international concern such as genocide, war crimes, crimes against humanity, and aggression; it was ratified by the required 60 states on April 11, 2002

International Criminal Tribunal for Rwanda tribunal established in 1994 by the Security Council of the United Nations after the outbreak of genocide in Rwanda

International Criminal Tribunal for Yugoslavia tribunal established in 1992 by the Security Council of the United Nations to deal with the atrocities committed during the civil war in the former Yugoslavia

international human rights movement occurred after World War II when the nations of the world wanted to prevent incidents like the Holocaust from occurring again. The United Nations was established as a mechanism to channel global human rights and citizen protection efforts, and it adopted of the Universal Declaration of Human Rights (UDHR) in 1948. For the first time in history, the Declaration spelled out basic civil, political, economic, social, and cultural rights that all human beings should enjoy, regardless of the country in which they live.

international terrorism type of terrorism that involves the citizens or territory of more than one country

internationalized court also called a mixed tribunal or hybrid court; operates with the support of the United Nations to prosecute those responsible for crimes against humanity, war crimes, and violations of domestic law

Interpol the International Police Organization, which acts as a clearinghouse for information on offenses and offenders believed to operate across national boundaries

Islamic law legal tradition in Islamic countries based on the rules of conduct revealed by God, with two primary sources: the Shari'a and the Sunnah

jail facility used for less serious offenders who are generally sentenced to less than a one-year sentence or for those awaiting trial or transfer to another institution

jihad a holy war by Islamic fundamentalists who want to protect their religion from "creeping secularism and cultural imperialism posed by Western countries such as the United States"

judicial impartiality a concept whereby judicial authorities treat parties in court as equals

judicial independence a principle holding that judges are bound to the law rather than influenced by the desires of those in power; the freedom of judges to make their decisions without any form of outside pressure

judicial review the power of a court to review actions and legal decisions made by those in the criminal justice system

juge d'instruction in France, the examining magistrate who is responsible for a complete and impartial investigation of the facts

jus cogens term used to explain that fundamental norms are recognized on the international level to have a superior status over other norms

justice of the peace lay judges in small American towns who carry out many legal functions such as traffic violations, some misdemeanors, small civil claims, and some domestic court matters

kidotai civil order police officers in Japan who live in barracks, receive training in crowd control, and use military formations during civil order crises

koban a local police post in urban areas of Japan

Länder term for states in Germany

legal advisor legally trained individual who works outside the courtroom to advise and instruct individuals who have legal problems or needs, both civil and criminal

legal pluralism the mixing of more than one system of law within a country or region of a country

legal scholar individual who studies the law and writes on it in legal commentaries and professional journals

Minimum Rules for the Administration of Juvenile Justice the first international legal instrument to detail comprehensive rules for the administration of juvenile justice with a child rights and child development approach

monarch a person who is the sole and absolute ruler of a country, such as a king, queen, or emperor

mubahith the secret police or special investigative police officers of the General Directorate of Investigation in Saudi Arabia who conduct criminal investigations and handle matters pertaining to domestic security and counterintelligence

mutawa the morals force, or religious police, that assures that Saudi Arabian citizens live up to the rules of behavior derived from the Qur'an

National Crime Victimization Survey (NCVS) crime survey developed in the United States that is now an annual survey covering six crimes: rape, robbery, assault, larceny, burglary, and motor vehicle theft; in order to know who has been the victim of a crime, a representative sample of the population (from 76,000 households including more than 135,000 persons) is selected, and participants are asked questions about their experience with crime in recent months

National People's Congress (NPC) theoretically, the highest organ of power in China; meets annually to review and approve major new policy directions, laws, the budget, and major personnel changes

National Police Agency (NPA) the central police organization in Japan, supervised by the National Public Safety Commission, with eight regional police bureaus and a number of special divisions to handle training, research, crime prevention, public safety functions related to the environment and transportation, and matters of national security and multiple jurisdiction

new terrorism a form of terrorist activity committed by an individual or group that may or may not be connected to a loose, cell-based organizational structure, with religious motivations, using asymmetrical tactics to achieve ideological goals often linked to promoting Islamic ideology

noncustodial sanction a legal sanction handed out to an offender that does not require confinement in a correctional facility

ombudsman an individual in Socialist Law systems who hears complaints and ensures that government agents are performing their functions correctly

organic laws term for those laws of English Parliament that describe the machinery of government and govern the electoral process

organized crime a continuing criminal enterprise that rationally works to profit from illicit activities that are often in great public demand; its continuing existence is maintained through the use of force, threats, monopoly control, and/or the corruption of public officials

Osama bin Laden the terrorist leader believed to have supported and trained thousands of terrorist fighters in numerous countries

parens patriae a medieval English doctrine used as a founding philosophy for the American juvenile court system that declares the state can act as parent on behalf of the child

Parliament governmental structure in England consisting of the monarch, the House of Lords, and the House of Commons

parole the practice of releasing offenders to community supervision after a period of incarceration

Patriot Act a law passed by the U.S. Congress six weeks after September 11, 2001, with the goal of broadening law enforcement agencies' authority to conduct surveillance on U.S. citizens and residents

peace operations term used to describe the range of military, police, and civilian interventions that seek to restore order and create a sustainable society after a period of war

penal populism criminal justice policies designed to appeal to the public appetite for punitiveness with little concern about program effectiveness or the clear understanding of community views

plea bargaining the process whereby the accused agrees to plead guilty in return for various concessions, such as a lesser charge or the promise of a lenient sentence

police corruption when the police, in exercising or failing to exercise their authority, act with the primary intention of furthering private or departmental/divisional advantage

police nationale (PN) the French police organization within the Ministry of the Interior responsible for Paris and other urban areas

popular (mixed) system a system of administering criminal procedure that calls for popular participation of citizens who are not necessarily criminal justice professionals

prefectural police midlevel police agency in Japan organized under the regional police bureaus, with local police stations under them, specialized riot police forces living in barracks, and a national police academy

prefecture administrative division in China and Japan

prison facility used almost exclusively for serious offenders who receive sentences of more than one year

private law law that regulates behavior between individuals within the state; also known as civil law

private prison correctional institution operated by a private firm on behalf of a government

probation the sentence offenders receive when they are convicted of a crime but are allowed to continue to reside in the community under certain conditions

procurator in Civil Law systems, roughly equivalent to the prosecutor in Common Law systems; in Socialist Law systems, the person who prosecutes criminal offenders, supervises the criminal justice system, and ensures that all citizens and state personnel carry out the laws and policies of the state

progressive movement early twentieth-century movement calling for a new approach to corrections; focused on rehabilitation of individual offenders by specialists in corrections, probation, parole, therapeutic prison regimes, and separate juvenile justice mechanisms

public law law that is developed by modern states in their legislatures or through their regulatory process dealing largely with relations between governments and citizens

public surveillance probation in China

quadi Islamic judges who decide cases in the Shari'a courts based on the facts according to their own wisdom and the principles of the religious law

reeducation through labor in China, both a policy and a kind of correctional facility that incarcerates those who have administrative detention status whereby they are imprisoned without benefit of a trial

reform through labor in China, both a policy and a place for offenders who have been tried and convicted of a criminal offense, with emphasis on forced labor and extreme attempts at thought reform

rehabilitation a purpose of criminal sanctions or punishment whereby offenders should be transformed into law-abiding persons through programs of medical, physiological, economic, or educational improvement

religious terrorism terrorism used to promote a certain religious system or protect a set of beliefs within a religion

remand prison facility used to house unconvicted inmates

republican government a form of government in which a president is head of the government but the main power remains in the hands of citizens who vote for representatives, who are then responsible to the electorate

restitution process whereby an offender is required to or volunteers to pay money or otherwise make reparations for harm resulting from a criminal offense

restoration the community, victim, and offender are involved in the sentencing process with the aim of restoring the victim and the community to its previous state.

restorative justice correctional method that calls for participation by the offender, victim, and community in the sentencing process and allows the offender to atone for the offense and be restored to community life

retribution purpose of criminal sanctions or punishment asserting that the offender should "pay back" society for the harm done

revolutionary terrorism form of terrorism that forces a government to respond in a harsh manner in the hopes that such governmental actions will lead to discontent among the people and to revolution

risk of crime the evaluation of the probability that certain crimes will occur and their potential harm

Rome Statute treaty passed in 1998 that established the International Criminal Court (ICC)

Rules for the Protection of Juveniles Deprived of their Liberty United Nations standards for the treatment of persons under age 18 when confined to any institution or facility by the order of a court or similar body

Russian Mafiya organized crime group operating in Russia involved with arms smuggling, prostitution, racketeering, narcotics trafficking, gasoline theft and fraud, car theft, and the illegal export of raw materials from the territories of the Russian Federation

Sacred Law a body of law and legal family that relies on some sacred text as the basic source of law

saiban'in seido the use of lay assessors in Japan in serious cases where there is considerable public interests

Schöffen lay judges in Germany used extensively in courts of appeal for minor offenses and for first-level criminal offenses

secular law law that does not pertain to any religion or religious body

self-report survey research method whereby people are asked to report their own delinquent and criminal acts in an anonymous questionnaire or confidential interview

Shari'a law the rules of conduct revealed by God (Allah) to his Prophet (Muhammad) specifying how the people are to live in this world

shogun military leader who exercised absolute rule in Japan during the years of isolation from other cultures, from 1603 to 1867

Socialist Law a family of law with its origins in socialism, a system characterized by the absence of social classes and common ownership of the means of production and livelihood; the emphasis is on communal values at the expense of the individual

stare decisis literally, "it stands decided"; the principle used in Common Law countries to signify the legal force of precedent

state-sponsored terrorism the form of terrorism practiced by governments against their own citizens or another country in order to protect their own political, economic, or military interests

status offense an act for which only juveniles can be held liable

stock design measuring the number of persons in prisons at any one point in time

supranational court judicial mechanism that directs its decisions across borders and supposedly has a higher legal standing than decisions of courts in individual countries

tazirat crime type of crime in Islamic law that includes crimes against society and against individuals, but not against God

terrorism the premeditated, politically motivated violence perpetuated against noncombatant targets by sub-national groups or clandestine agents, usually intended to influence an audience

trafficking in human beings crime in which victims are moved using fraud or coercion to make them forced laborers or sexual slaves

transnational crime offenses whose inception, commission, and/or direct or indirect effects involve more than one country

triads traditional Chinese criminal group

tribunal generally a temporary body that is organized to judge persons for their behavior during a specific time for a specific event; usually formed as a military court to adjudicate atrocities committed during times of war or civil unrest

Uniform Crime Reports (UCR) crime statistics collected by over 16,000 city, county, and state law enforcement agencies about 29 types of crimes that have been brought to their attention with or without an arrest, and then compiled by the FBI into an annual published report

unitary government governmental organization in which power is centralized

United Nations Convention against Corruption an international convention that addresses issues related to corruption, such as prevention, criminalization, international cooperation, asset recovery, and implementation mechanisms

United Nations Convention against Transnational Organized Crime an international convention that provides nations with legal measures for criminal participation in a criminal group, money-laundering laws, extradition laws, mutual legal assistance, specific victim protection measures, and law enforcement provisions

United Nations Survey of Crime and Trends and Operation of Criminal Justice Systems (CTS) the CTS questionnaire consists of four parts dealing with primarily statistical information about the main components of the criminal justice system (police, prosecution, courts, and prisons) and an annex; the annex was developed for countries in Europe and requests supplementary information on police-recorded crime statistics relating to homicide and thefts of motor vehicles

UNPOL the International Civilian Police Program, formed by the United Nations in 1960 to assist in international peacekeeping operations

warning penalty provided at the adjudication stage by the judge and usually accompanied by the threat of incarceration if the criminal behavior does not desist

weapon of mass destruction (WMD) nuclear, chemical, or biological weapon, which by its nature can cause mass casualties and extensive property damage

welfare state the government plays a key role in the protection and promotion of the economic and social well-being of its citizens

writ of mandamus an order of the court requiring public servants to do the duties that are part of their jobs

Yakuza hierarchical organized crime group in Japan; the generic term for organized crime groups in Japan is *boryokudan*, which means *violent ones*, but the criminals call themselves *yakuza*, which stands for the worst possible hand in a popular Japanese card game. Yakuza commonly have ornate tattoos and dress distinctively

Youth Aid Section a special national police unit of trained officers in New Zealand that works to divert young offenders out of the criminal justice system

Bibliography

Abramson, A. M. (2003). Sustainable relationships and competing values: Restorative justice initiatives and the police—a case study. *Police Practice & Research, 4*, 391–398.

Adler, F. (1983). *Nations not obsessed with crime*. Littleton, CO: Rothman.

Adler, F. (1995). Our American society of criminology, the world, and the state of the art. The American Society of Criminology 1995 Presidential Address. *Criminology, 34*, 1–9.

Adler, F. (1996). A note on teaching "international." *Journal of Criminal Justice Education*, 7(4), 223–225.

Adler, F., Mueller, G., & Laufer, W. (2009). *Criminal justice* (5th ed.). New York: McGraw-Hill.

Agrast, M., Botero, J., & Ponce, A. (2011). *WJP rule of law index 2011*. Washington, DC: The World Justice Project. Retrieved from http://worldjusticeproject.org/sites/default/files/wjproli2011_0.pdf

Ai, Xue. (1989). New "people's mediation committee's organic rules" promulgated in China. *Outlook Weekly, 42*, 10.

Akers, R. L., & Sellers, C. S. (2008). *Criminological theories* (5th ed.). New York, NY: Oxford University Press.

Albanese, J. (2008). *Criminal justice* (4th ed.). Boston, MA: Allyn & Bacon.

Albanese, J., Das, D., & Verma, A. (Eds.). (2003). *Organized crime: World perspectives*. Upper Saddle River, NJ: Prentice Hall.

Albanese, Jay S. (2007). The International Center at the National Institute of Justice: The first 8 years, 1998–2006. In H. Dammer & P. Reichel (Eds.), *Teaching about comparative and international criminal justice* (2nd ed.) (pp. 17–25). Greenbelt, MD: Academy of Criminal Justice Sciences.

Albanese, Jay S. (2011a). *Transnational crime and the 21st Century: Criminal Enterprise, Corruption, and Opportunity*. New York, NY: Oxford University Press.

Albanese, Jay S. (2011b). *Organized crime in our times* (6th ed.). Burlington, MA: Elsevier.

Albanese, Jay S. (2012). *Professional ethics in criminal justice: Being ethical when no one is looking* (3rd ed.). Upper Saddle River, NJ: Prentice Hall.

Albrecht, H. J. (2004). Youth justice in Germany. In M. Tonry & A. Doob (Eds.), *Youth crime and youth justice: Comparative and cross-national perspectives* (p. 460). Chicago, IL: University of Chicago Press.

Ali, B. (1985). Islamic law and crime: The case of Saudi Arabia. *International Journal of Comparative and Applied Criminal Justice, 9*, 45–57.

Alobied, A. (1989). Police functions and organizations in Saudi Arabia. *Police Studies, 10*, 84–88.

Al-Sagheer, M. F. (1994). Diya legislation in Islamic Shari'a and its application in the kingdom of Saudi Arabia. In U. Zvekic (Ed.), *Alternatives to imprisonment in comparative perspective* (pp. 80–94). Chicago, IL: Nelson-Hall.

Ambos, K. (2000). The status, role and accountability of the prosecutor of the International Criminal Court: A comparative overview on the basis of 33 national reports. *European Journal of Crime, Criminal Law and Criminal Justice, 8*(2), 89–118.

Ambos, K. (2011). International criminal procedure: "Adversarial," "inquisitorial" or mixed? *Third International Criminal Law Review, 3*, 1–37.

Amin, S. A. (1985a). *Islamic law in the contemporary world*. Glasgow, KY: Royston.

Amnesty International. (2000). Saudi Arabia: Global campaign to end secrecy, suffering and silence. Retrieved September 1, 2004, from http://web.amnesty.org/library/index/ENGMDE230232000

Amnesty International. (2004). Amnesty International report 2004: Saudi Arabia. Retrieved June 4, 2004, from http://web.amnesty.org/report2004/sau-summary-eng

Amnesty International. (2006). International standards on the death penalty. Retrieved April 20, 2010, from http://www.amnesty.org/en/library/asset/ACT50/001/2006/en/61251e61-d469-11dd-8743-d305bea2b2c7/act500012006en.pdf

Amnesty International. (2009, August 25). Photographic evidence shows the cruelty of caning in Malaysia. Retrieved April 20, 2010, from http://www.amnesty.org/en/news-and-updates/news/photographic-evidence-shows-cruelty-caning-malaysia-20090825

Amnesty International. (2010). Figures on the death penalty. Retrieved April 10, 2010, from http://www.amnesty.org/en/death-penalty/numbers

Amnesty International. (2010, December 6). Malaysia: Torture practiced systematically in widespread caning. Retrieved September 28, 2012, from http://www.amnesty.org/en/news-and-updates/report/malaysia-torture-practiced-systematically-widespread-caning-2010-12-06

Amnesty International. (2012a, March 26). Death sentences and executions 2011. Retrieved September 25, 2012, from http://www.amnestyusa.org/research/reports/death-sentences-and-executions-2011

Amnesty International. (2012b). The state of the world's human rights. Retrieved September 25, 2012, from http://www.amnestyusa.org/sites/default/files/air12-report-english.pdf

Amnesty International. (2012c). Death penalty and human rights standards. Retrieved September 28, 2012, from http://www.amnestyusa.org/our-work/issues/death-penalty/international-death-penalty/death-penalty-and-human-rights-standards

Amnesty International. (2012d, September 12). Amnesty International news. USA: Guantánamo death highlights urgent need to end indefinite detention. Retrieved October 7, 2012, from http://www.amnesty.org/en/news/usa-guant-namo-death-highlights-urgent-need-end-indefinite-detention-2012-09-12

Ancel, M. (1952). Observations on the international comparison of criminal statistics. *International review of criminal policy*, *1*, 41–48.

Anderson, E., & Togelius, L. (2011). Women oppressed in the name of culture and religion, Saudi Arabia and the Convention on the Elimination of All Forms of Discrimination Against Women. (Unpublished bachelor's thesis). Malmo University, Sweden. Retrieved August 22, 2012, from http://dspace.mah.se/handle/2043/11782

Ansary, A. F. (2010). A brief overview of the Saudi Arabian legal system. Retrieved March 1, 2010, from http://www.nyulawglobal.org/globalex/saudi_arabia.htm

Apel, R., & Nagin, D. S. (2011). General deterrence. In M. Tonry (Ed.), *The Oxford handbook of crime and criminal justice* (pp. 85–105). New York, NY: Oxford University Press.

Araki, N. (2002). The administration of juvenile justice in Japan. In M. Feeley & S. Miyazawa (Eds.), *The Japanese adversary system in context* (pp. 220–225). New York, NY: Palgrave MacMillan.

Aremu, A. O., Pakes, F. & Johnston, L. (2009). Locus of control and self-efficacy as means of tackling police corruption in Nigeria. *International Journal of Police Science and Management*, *11*, 97–107.

Aromaa, K., & Heiskanen, M. (2008). Trends of recorded crime. In K. Aromaa & M. Heiskaned (Eds.), *Crime and criminal justice systems in Europe and North America, 1995–2004* (pp. 72–82). Helsinki: HEUNI.

Aromaa, K., Leppa, S., Nevala, S., & Ollus, N. (Eds.). (2003). *Crime and criminal justice systems in Europe and North America 1995–1997*. Publication Series No. 40. Helsinki: HEUNI.

Ashworth, A. (2000). European sentencing traditions: Accepting divergence or aiming for convergence? In M. Pagon (Ed.), *Policing in Central and Eastern Europe* (pp. 219–236). Ljubljana: College of Police Studies.

AsiaNews. (2009, December 22). Academy of Social Sciences: Increase of mass revolts and crime in China. Retrieved July 20, 2012, from http://www.asianews.it/news-en/Academy-of-Social-Sciences:-increase-of-mass-revolts-and-crime-in-China-17184.html

Associated Press. (2003, June 17). Muslim police in London allowed to wear turbans. *Scranton Times*, p. 2.

Associated Press. (2004, February 24). Page calls NEA "Terrorist Organization." *FoxNews.com*. Retrieved April 25, 2010, from http://www.foxnews.com/story/0,2933,112247,00.html

Auld, A. (2002). *Review of the criminal courts of England and Wales*. London: Lord Chancellor's Department.

Awad, A. M. (1982). The rights of the accused under Islamic criminal procedure. In C. Bassiouni (Ed.), *Islamic Criminal Justice System* (pp. 91–107). Dobbs Ferry, NY: Oceana Publications.

Baker, B., & Scheye, E. (2007). Multi-layered justice and security delivery in post-conflict and fragile states. *Conflict, Security and Development*, 7, 503–528.

Baker, B. G. (1982). Chinese law in the eighties: The lawyer and the criminal process. *Albany Law Review*, *46*, 751.

Bakken, B. (2005). Introduction: Crime control, and modernity in China. In B. Bakken (Ed.), *Crime, punishment and policing in China* (pp. 1–29). New York, NY: Rowman & Littlefield.

Bala, N., Hornick, J. P., Snyder, H. N., & Paetsch, J. J. (Eds.). (2002). *Juvenile justice systems: An international comparison of problems and solutions*. Toronto, ON: Thomson.

Barberet, R. (2009). Legacy of INTERPOL crime data to cross-national criminology. *International Journal of Comparative and Applied Criminal Justice*, *33*(2), 192–210.

Barberet, R., Bowling, B., Junger-Tas, J., Rechea-Alberola, C., van Kesteren, J., & Zurawan, A. (2004). *Self-reported juvenile delinquency in England and Wales, the Netherlands, and Spain*. Helsinki: HEUNI.

Barboza, D. (2008, November 27). Police officers' killer, hero to some Chinese, is executed. *The New York Times*, p. A18.

Barchfield, J. (2010, October 20). French protests take violent turn. *The Record* (Hackensack, NJ), p. A15.

Bassiouni, M. C., & E. Vetere. (Eds.). (1998). *Organized crime: A compilation of UN documents 1975–1998*. New York, NY: Transnational.

Bayley, D. H. (1991). *Forces of order: Policing in modern Japan* (2nd ed.). Berkeley, CA: University of California.

Bayley, D. H. (1996a). Lessons in order. In S. Heiner (Ed.), *Criminology: A cross-cultural perspective* (pp. 3–14). St. Paul, MN: West Publishing.

Bayley, D. H. (1996b). Policing: The world stage. *Journal of Criminal Justice Education*, 7, 241–252.

Bayley, D. H. (1998). *What works in policing*. New York, NY: Oxford University Press.

Bayley, D. H. (2001). *Democratizing the police abroad: What to do and how to do it.* Washington, DC: National Institute of Justice.

Bayley, D. H. (2005). *Changing the guard: Developing democratic police abroad*. New York, NY: Oxford University Press.

Bayley, D. H., & Perito, R. (2011). *Police corruption: What past scandals teach about current challenges*. United States Institute of Peace Special Report 294. Retrieved August 17, 2012, from http://www.usip.org/files/resources/SR%20294.pdf

BBC News. (2009, August 3). Japan relaunches trials by jury. Retrieved August 25, 2012, from http://news.bbc.co.uk/2/hi/asia-pacific/8181225.stm

BBC Worldwide Monitoring. (2003, February 25). Dismissals in Ukraine.

BBC Worldwide Monitoring. (2003, January 18). Slovakia changes police tactics toward organized crime.

BBC Worldwide Monitoring. (2004, April 28). Germany registers 263 anti-semitic crimes in 2004 first quarter.

Beirne, P., & Nelken, D. (Eds.). (1997). *Issues in comparative criminology*. Dartmouth, UK: Ashgate.

Belal, A. A. (1993, August). Procedural safeguards in islamic law and islamic criminal justice. Paper presented at the 11th International Congress on Criminology, Budapest, Hungary.

Bellis, M. A., Hughes, K., Wood, S., Wyke, S., & Perkins, C. (2011). National five-year examination of inequalities and trends in emergency hospital admission for violence across England. *Injury Prevention*, *17*, 319–325.

Benekos, P. J., & Merlo, A. V. (2008). *Controversies in juvenile justice and delinquency* (2nd ed.). Cincinnati, OH: Anderson Publishing.

Berman, H. (1963). *Justice in the USSR*. New York, NY: Random House.

———. (1983). *Law and revolution: The formation of the Western legal tradition*. Cambridge, MA: Harvard University Press.

Bjelopera, J. (2011, November 15). American jihadist terrorism: Combating a complex threat. Washington, DC: Congressional Research Service.

Blatier, C. (1999). Juvenile justice in France. *British Journal of Criminology*, *39*(Spring), 240–251.

Bleich, E. (2007). Hate crime policy in Western Europe: Responding to racist violence in Britain, Germany, and France. *American Behavioral Scientist*, *51* (October), 149–165.

Block, A. (1983). *East Side, West Side: Organizing crime in New York, 1930–1950.* New Brunswick, NJ: Transaction Press.

Block, A. (2004). Banking, fraud and stock manipulation: Russian opportunities and dilemmas. In S. Nevala and K. Aromaa (Eds.), *Organised crime, trafficking, drugs.* Helsinki: European Institute for Crime Prevention and Control.

Blumstein, A. (1995). Prisons. In J. Q. Wilson & J. Petersilia (Eds.). *Crime.* San Francisco, CA: ICS Press.

Bogdanich, W., & Sontag, D. (2011, November 1). Raucous trial is a test of Haiti's legal system. *The New York Times*, pp. A1, A12.

Bossard, A. (2003, March). Crime and globalization. *Crime and Justice International*, 38.

Bracey, D. (1988). Like a doctor to a patient, like a prison to a child: Corrections in the People's Republic of China. *The Prison Journal, 68*(1), 24–33.

Bracey, D. (1995). Police corruption. In W. G. Bailey (Ed.), *The encyclopedia of police science.* (pp. 401–410) New York, NY: Garland.

Bradford, T. (1995, May 19). $12 million high-tech heist one of largest ever. *USA Today*, p. A3.

Brandl, S. G., & Stroshine, M. (2011). The relationship between gun and gun buyer characteristics and firearm time-to-crime. *Criminal Justice Policy Review, 22*, 285–300.

Brenner, Susan W. (2010). *Cybercrime: Criminal threats from cyberspace.* Santa Barbara, CA: ABC-CLIO.

Bresler, F. (1993). *Interpol.* Toronto, ON: Penguin Books.

Brodeur, J. P. (2007). Comparative penology in perspective. In M. Tonry (Ed.), *Crime and justice: A review of research, vol. 36* (pp. 49–91). Chicago, IL: University of Chicago Press.

Brown, R. M. (1979). Historical patterns of American violence. In T. Graham & T. Gurr (Eds.), *Violence in America.* (pp. 167–179) Thousand Oaks, CA: Sage Publications.

Browne-Marshall, G. (2011). International tribunals and hybrid courts. In M. Natarajan (Ed.), *International crime and justice* (pp. 350–356). New York, NY: Cambridge University Press.

Bruce, D., & Neild, R. (2005). *The police that we want: A handbook for oversight of police in South Africa.* Johannesburg: Centre for the Study of Violence and Reconciliation in association with the Open Society Foundation for South Africa.

Buck, W., & Pease, K. (1993). Cross-national incarceration comparisons inherently misleading. *Overcrowded Times, 4*(1): 5–6, 17.

Buckwalter, J. (Ed.). (1990). *International perspectives on organized crime.* Chicago, IL: Office of International Criminal Justice.

Burraston, B. O., Cherrington, D. J., Bahr, S. J. (2012). Reducing juvenile recidivism with cognitive training and a cell phone follow-up: An evaluation of the RealVictory Program. *International Journal of Offender Therapy & Comparative Criminology, 56* (February), 61–80.

Burnham, R. W. (1998). *Analysis of the United Nations data set on crime trends and the operations of criminal justice systems: Part I.* Washington, DC: National Institute of Justice, U.S. Department of Justice.

Burnham, R. W. (1999). History of world crime surveys. In G. Newman (Ed.), *Global report on crime and justice* (pp. 190–195). New York, NY: Oxford University Press.

Buscaglia, E., & van Dijk, J. (2003). Controlling organized crime and corruption in the public sector. *Forum on Crime and Society, 3*(December), 3–4.

Cao, G. (1995, December 15). Bringing police in Hunan Province to account: Before and after. *Outlook Weekly* [Beijing], p. 49.

Cappelaere, G., Grandjean, A., & Naqvi, Y. (2002). *Children deprived of liberty: Rights and realities.* Paris: Editions Jeunesse et Droit.

Cappelletti, M., & Cohen, W. (1979). *Comparative constitutional law.* New York, NY: Bobbs-Merrill.

Care. (2011). *EU directive on human trafficking.* Retrieved June 25, 2012, from http://www.care.org.uk/advocacy/human-trafficking/eu-directive-on-human-trafficking

Caribbean 360. (2012, August 22). 25 dead and dozens injured in Venezuela prison riot. Retrieved October 5, 2012, from http://www.caribbean360.com/index.php/news/venezuela_news/608720.html#axzz25bvziRHq

Casey, J. (2010). *Policing the world: The practice of international and transnational policing.* Durham, NC: Carolina Academic Press.

Castberg, A. (1990). *Japanese criminal justice.* New York, NY: Praeger.

Cavadino, M., & Dignan, J. (2007). *The penal system: An introduction* (4th ed.). London: Sage.

Center for Strategic and International Studies. (2001). *Global Organized Crime Project.* Washington, DC: CSIS.

Chazan, G., & MacDonald, A. (2011, August 10). London Sweeps Up as Riots Simmer to North. *The Wall Street Journal,* p. A11.

Chen, H. (2001). *An introduction to the legal system of the PRC* (4th ed.). Cincinnati, OH: Lexis Nexis.

Chen, X. (2000). Educating and correcting juvenile delinquents: The Chinese approaches. *Journal of Correctional Education, 51,* 334–346.

Chenguang, W., & Xianchu, Z. (1997). *Introduction to Chinese law.* Hong Kong: Sweet and Maxwell Asia Press.

Chepesiuk, R. (2003). *The bullet or the bribe: Taking down Colombia's Cali drug cartel.* New York, NY: Praeger.

CIA. (2010). The world factbook. Retrieved January 15, 2010, from https://www.cia.gov/library/publications/the-world-factbook/rankorder/rankorderguide.html

CIA. (2012). The world factbook. Retrieved July 5, 2012, from https://www.cia.gov/library/publications/the-world-factbook/

Clark, G. (2008). An introduction to the legal profession in China in the year 2008. *Suffolk University Law Review, 41,* 833. Retrieved September 6, 2012, from http://papers.ssrn.com/sol3/papers.cfm?abstract_id=1270242

Clear, T. (2007). *Imprisoning communities: How mass incarceration makes disadvantaged neighborhoods worse.* New York: Oxford University Press.

Clear, T. R., & Cole, G. F. (2003). *American corrections* (6th ed.). Belmont, CA: Wadsworth.

Clear, T. R., Cole, G. F., & Reisig, M. (2011). *American corrections* (9th ed.). Belmont, CA: Wadsworth.

Clear, T. R., & Dammer, H. R. (2003). *Managing the offender in the community.* Belmont, CA: Wadsworth.

Clifford, W. (1976). *Crime control in Japan.* Lexington, MA: Lexington Books.

CNN. (2009, November 12). China criticized over alleged "black jails." *CNN World.* Retrieved March 3, 2010, from www.cnn.com/2009/WORLD/asiapcf/11/12/china.prisons.hrw.report/index.html

CNN. (2011, March 23). Japan earthquake could cost 309 billion. Retrieved July 22, 2012, from http://money.cnn.com/2011/03/23/news/international/japan_earthquake_cost/index.htm

CNN World. (2011a, September 2). Police officer arrested in deadly casino fire investigation. Retrieved July 24, 2012, from http://articles.cnn.com/2011-09-02/world/mexico.casino.fire_1_drug-cartel-zetas-casino-fire?_s=PM:WORLD

CNN World. (2011b, July 18). Phone-hacking scandal expands with police probe, whistleblower's death. Retrieved July 30, 2012, from http://articles.cnn.com/2011-07-18/world/uk.phone.hacking_1_andy-coulson-rebekah-brooks-phone-hacking-scandal?_s=PM:WORLD

Cochran, J. (1987). *The variable effects of religiosity on deviant behavior.* (Doctoral dissertation). Ann Arbor, MI: University of Michigan Press.

Coette, L. (2011). *Criminal law reform and transitional justice: Human rights perspectives for Sudan.* Surrey, UK: Ashgate Publishing.

Cohen, L., & Felson, M. (1979). Social change and crime rate trends: A routine activities approach. *American Sociological Review, 44,* 588–608.

Cohen, M. A. & Piquero, A. R. (2009). New evidence on the monetary value of saving a high-risk youth. *Journal of Quantitative Criminology, 25,* 25–49.

Collier, J. F. (1994). Intertwined histories: Islamic law and Western imperialism. *Law and Society Review, 28,* 395–408.

Committee on Foreign Affairs. (1984). *Forced labor in the Soviet Union. Subcommittee on Human Rights and International Organizations, 98th Congress, First Session, Nov. 9, 1983.* Washington DC: U.S. Government Printing Office.

Confucius. (1989). *The analects of Confucius.* (A. Waley, Trans.). New York, NY: Vantage Books.

Congressional Testimony. (2003, March 13). U.S. House of Representatives, Subcommittee on Courts, the Internet, and Intellectual Property, Committee of the House Judiciary Committee. Organized Crime Groups and Intellectual Property.

Cordner. A., Dammer, H. R., & Horvath, F. (2000). A national survey of comparative and international criminal justice courses in universities in the United States. *Journal of Criminal Justice Education, 11*(2), 32–45.

Cornish, D. B., & Clarke, R. V. G. (Eds.). (1986). *The reasoning criminal: Rational choice perspectives on offending.* New York, NY: Springer-Verlag.

Crime in France. (2008). *French National Monitoring Center on Crime: 2008 report.* Paris: Observatoire National de la Délinquance.

Criminal Justice News. (2006). Terror threat in U.S. more modest than feared in 2001. *Criminal Justice News*. New York, NY: John Jay College of Criminal Justice.

Cronin, B. (2002). International law. In B. Cronin (Ed.), *World at risk: A global issues sourcebook* (pp. 386–407). Washington, DC: CQ Press.

Crossette, B. (2002, April 12). War crimes tribunal becomes reality, without U.S. role. *The New York Times*, p. A3.

Daibd, R., & Brierly, J. C. (1978). *Major legal systems in the world today*. New York, NY: Free Press.

Dallaire, R. (2011). *They fight like soldiers, they die like children: The global quest to eradicate the use of child soldiers*. New York, NY: Walker and Company.

Dambach, M. (2007). Shifting paradigms towards a culture of control within juvenile justice in New South Wales, Australia. Paper presented at Berlin, Germany. Law & Society Annual Meeting.

Dammer, H. (1996). Rehabilitation in German prisons. *Journal of Offender Rehabilitation, 24*(1–2): 1–10.

Dammer, H. (2010). Policing in selected countries: Organization and structure. In S. Kethineni (Ed.), *Comparative and international policing, justice, and international crime* (pp. 149–176). Durham, NC: Carolina Academic Press.

Dammer, H., & Reichel, P. (Eds.). (2007). *Teaching comparative/international criminal justice*. Greenbelt, MD: Academy of Criminal Justice Sciences.

Dammer, H., Reichel, P., & He, N. (2005). Comparing crime and justice. In P. Reichel (Ed.), *Handbook of transnational crime and justice* (pp. 20–42). Thousand Oaks, CA: Sage Publications.

Dandurand, Y. (2012). International cooperation. In J. Winterdyk, B. Perrin, & P. Reichel (Eds.), *Human trafficking: Exploring the international nature, concerns, and complexities*. Boca Raton, FL: Taylor and Francis.

Danelski, D. (1971). The Chicago conspiracy trial. In T. Becker (Ed.), *Political trials*. Indianapolis, IN: Bobbs-Merrill.

Daniszewski, J. (1997, January 31). Judging the divine law of Islam. *The Los Angeles Times*, p. A1.

David, R. (1972). *French law: Its structure, sources, and methodology*. Baton Rouge, LA: Louisiana State University Press.

Davidson, R., & Wang, Z. (1996). The court system in the People's Republic of China with a case study of a criminal trial. In O. Ebbe (Ed.), *Comparative and international criminal justice systems* (pp. 139–154). Boston, MA: Butterworth-Heinemann.

Deflem, M. (2006). Europol and the policing of international terrorism: Counterterrorism in a global perspective. *Justice Quarterly, 23*(3), 336–360.

Deflem, M., & McDonough, S. (2010). International law enforcement organizations. In S. Kethineni (Ed.), *Comparative and international policing, justice, and international crime* (pp. 127–148). Durham, NC: Carolina Academic Press.

DeLisi, M., & Conis, P. (2010). *American corrections: Theory, research, policy, and practice*. Burlington MA: Jones & Bartlett.

DeLisi, M., & Conis, P. (2011). *Violent offenders: Theory, research, policy, and practice*. Burlington, MA: Jones & Bartlett.

Delmas-Marty, M., & Spencer, J. R. (Eds.) (2002). *European criminal procedures*. Cambridge, MA: Cambridge University Press.

Denmark. (2009, October 7). Denmark turns on the screws to fight juvenile delinquency. *Agence France Presse*.

Department of Homeland Security. (2010). Strategic Plan. Retrieved May 31, 2010, from http://www.dhs.gov/xabout/strategicplan/

Deutch, K. (1996). Systems theory and comparative analysis. In R. Brown & R. Macridis (Eds.), *Comparative politics* (8th ed.) (pp. 20–32). Belmont, CA: Wadsworth.

Dhani, A. (2011, September). *Police service strength*. (Home Office Statistical Bulletin.) Retrieved August 18, 2012, from http://www.homeoffice.gov.uk/publications/science-research-statistics/research-statistics/police-research/hosb0312/hosb0312?view=Binary

DiNicola, A. (2005). Trafficking in human beings and smuggling of migrants. In P. Reichel (Ed.), *Handbook of transnational crime and justice* (pp. 181–203). Thousand Oaks, CA: Sage Publications.

Doob, A., & Tonry, M. (2004). Varieties of youth justice. In M. Tonry & A. Doob (Eds.), *Youth crime and youth justice: Comparative and cross-national perspectives* (pp. 24–58). Chicago, IL: University of Chicago Press.

DPIC. (2010). Death Penalty Information Center. Retrieved April 26, 2010, from http://www.deathpenaltyinfo.org/documents/FactSheet.pdf

DPIC. (2012). Death Penalty Information Center. Retrieved September 25, 2012, from http://www.deathpenaltyinfo.org/home

Dubber, M. D. (1997). American plea bargains, German law judges, and the crisis of criminal procedure. *Stanford Law Review*, *49*, 547.

Dugger, C. (1996, December 28). Tug of taboos: African genital rite vs. U.S. law. *The New York Times*, p. A1.

Dunkel, F. (2004). Reducing tension and improving rehabilitation by opening prisons: Day leave and prison furloughs in Germany. In F. Dunkel & H. von Hofer (Eds.), *Crime policy in Europe: Good practices and promising examples* (pp. 159–180). Strasbourg: Council of Europe Publishing.

Dunkel, F. (2008). Juvenile justice in Germany: Between welfare and justice. In J. Junger-Tas & S. H. Decker (Eds.), *International Handbook of Juvenile Justice* (pp. 225–262). Dordrecht: Springer.

Dupont, B. (2008). The French police system: Caught between a rock and a hard place—The tension of serving both the state and the public. In M. Haberfeld & I. Cerrah (Eds.), *Comparative policing* (pp. 247–276). Thousand Oaks, CA: Sage Publications.

Durkheim, E. (1947). *The division of labor in society*. Glencoe, IL: Free Press.

Ebbe, O. N. I. (1999). Political-criminal nexus: The Nigerian case. *Trends in Organized Crime*, *4*(3), 29–59.

Ebbe, O. N. I. (Ed.). (2000a). *Comparative and international criminal justice systems: Policing, judiciary, and corrections* (2nd ed.). Boston, MA: Butterworth-Heineman.

Ebbe, O. N. I. (2000b). The judiciary and criminal procedure in Nigeria. In O. Ebbe (Ed.), *Comparative and international criminal justice systems: Policing, judiciary, and corrections* (2nd ed.) (pp. 277–290). Boston, MA: Butterworth-Heineman.

The Economist. (2010, March 18). Cops for hire: Reforming Russia's violent and corrupt police will not be easy. Retrieved August 16, 2012, from http://www.economist.com/node/15731344

Ehrmann, H. (1976). *Comparative legal cultures*. Englewood Cliffs, NJ: Prentice-Hall.

Eichstaedt, P. (2009). *First kill your family: Child soldiers of Uganda and the Lord's Resistance Army*. Chicago, IL: Lawrence Hill Books.

Elliott, C. (2001). *French criminal law*. UK and Portland, OR: Willan Publishing.

Elliott, D. S., & Ageton, S. S. (1980). Reconciling race and class differences in self-reported and official estimates of delinquency. *American Sociological Review*, *45*(February), 95.

Elrod, P., & Yokoyama, M. (2006). Juvenile justice in Japan. In P. Friday & X. Ren (Eds.), *Delinquency and juvenile justice systems in the non-Western world* (pp. 211–228). Monsey, NY: Criminal Justice Press.

Elsea, J. (2006). U.S. policy regarding the International Criminal Court. Retrieved September 11, 2012, from http://www.fas.org/sgp/crs/misc/RL31495.pdf

Emerson, S. (2011). The new terrorism. In G. Martin (Ed.), *The Sage Encyclopedia of Terrorism*. Thousand Oaks, CA: Sage Publications.

English News. (2012). Chinese bust 600 online criminal gangs. Retrieved July 27, 2012, from http://news.xinhuanet.com/english/china/2012-07/26/c_131738868.htm

Entorf, H., & Spengler, H. (2002). *Crime in Europe: Causes and consequences*. Berlin: Springer-Verlag.

Erez, E., Finckenauer, J., & Ibarra, P. R. (2003). Introduction to the special issue on policing a multicultural society. *Journal of Police and Society*, *7* (April), 12–15.

Erlanger, S. (2012, August 14). French leader promises order after youths riot in a northern city. *The New York Times*. Retrieved August 18, 2012, from http://www.nytimes.com/2012/08/15/world/europe/hollande-pledges-order-after-rioting-in-northern-france.html

Europol. (2003). *2003 European Union organised crime report*. Luxembourg: Office for Official Publications of the European Communities.

Europol. (2011). *European Union organized crime threat assessment 2011*. Retrieved June 27, 2012, from https://www.europol.europa.eu/sites/default/files/publications/octa2011.pdf

Europol. (2012). About Europol. Retrieved August 18, 2012, from https://www.europol.europa.eu/content/page/about-europol-17

Ewald, U., & Feltes, T. (2003). Multicultural context, crime and policing in Germany: Challenges after unification. *Police and Society*, 7(April), 165–196.

Fagin, J. (2006). *When terrorism strikes home: Defending the United States*. Boston, MA: Pearson Education.

Fahim, K., & El Sheikh, M. (2012, March 15). 75 charged in deaths at soccer riot in Egypt. *The New York Times*. Retrieved July 30, 2012, from http://www.nytimes.com/2012/03/16/world/middleeast/75-charged-in-deaths-at-soccer-riot-in-egypt.html

Fairchild, E. (1988). *German police*. Springfield, IL: Charles Thomas.

Falsafi, S. (2010). Civil society and democracy in Japan, Iran, Iraq and beyond. *Vanderbilt Journal of Transnational Law, 43*, 357–435.

Fan, C. (Ed.). (1997). *Chinese criminal procedural law*. Beijing: Chinese University Law Publishing House.

Fang, B. (1999, October 4). China, at 50, on a long march to modernity. *U.S. News & World Report*, p. 37.

Farrell, A., McDevitt, J., Pfeffer, R., Fahy, S., Owens, C., Dank, M., et al. (2012). *Identifying challenges to improve the investigation and prosecution of state and local human trafficking cases*. Washington, DC: Urban Institute.

Farrington, D. P. (2012). Should the juvenile justice system be involved in early intervention? *Criminology & Public Policy, 11*(May), 265–273.

Federal Bureau of Investigation. (2010). *National incident-based reporting system* (NIBRS). Retrieved May 7, 2012, from http://www.fbi.gov/about-us/cjis/ucr/frequently-asked-questions/nibrs_faqs

Federal Bureau of Investigation. (2011). *Crime in the United States 2010: Uniform crime report*. Washington, DC: U.S. Government Printing Office.

Feeley, M. M. (2002). The bench, the bar, and the state: Judicial independence in Japan and the United States. In M. M. Feeley & S. Miyazawa (Eds.), *The Japanese Adversary System in Context* (pp. 67–68). New York, NY: Palgrave Macmillan.

Feeley, M. M., & Miyazawa, S. (Eds.). (2002). *The Japanese adversary system in context: Controversies and comparisons*. New York, NY: Palgrave MacMillian.

Feld, B. C. (2010). In defense of waiver and youthfulness as a mitigating factor in sentencing. In N. Frist, J. Freilich, & T. Clear (Eds.), *Contemporary issues in criminal justice policy* (pp. 321–326). Belmont, CA: Wadsworth.

Felson, M. (2010). *Crime and everyday life* (4th ed.). Los Angeles, CA: Sage Publications.

Feltes, T. (2005). Police forces and correctional systems of Germany. In G. Kurian (Ed.), *The world encyclopedia of police forces and correctional systems* (pp. 1073–1078). Detroit, MI: Gale Publishing.

Feltes, T. (2009, July 10). Personal interview with Thomas Feltes, chair of Criminology and Police Science at the Ruhr University-Bochum and former rector of the Fachhochschule for Polizei, Villingen-Schwenningen.

Fields, C. B., & Moore, R. H., Jr. (Eds.). (1996). *Comparative criminal justice: Traditional and nontraditional systems of law and control*. Prospect Heights, IL: Waveland Press.

Finckenauer, J. O. (2000). Meeting the challenge of transnational crime. *National Institute of Justice Journal*, July, 1–7.

Finckenauer, J. O., & Chin, K. (2007). Asian transnational organized crime and its impact on the United States. Washington, DC: National Institute of Justice.

Finckenauer, J. O., & Schrock, J. L. (Eds.). (2004). *The prediction and control of organized crime: The experience of post-Soviet Ukraine*. New Brunswick, NJ: Transaction Publishers.

Finckenauer, J. O., & Waring, E. J. (1998). *Russian Mafia in America: Immigration, culture and crime*. Boston, MA: Northeastern University Press.

Findlay, M. J., & Henham, R. (2012). *Transforming international criminal justice*. London: Routledge.

Fischer, S. (2011, July 1). Verfassungsschutz warnt vor getarnten Neonazis. *Spiegel Online*. Retrieved August 19, 2012, from http://www.spiegel.de/politik/deutschland/jahresbericht-2010-verfassungsschutz-warnt-vor-getarnten-neonazis-a-771647.html

Flatley, J., Kershaw, C., Smith, K., Chaplin, R., & Moon, D. (2010). *Crime in England and Wales 2009/10: Findings from the British Crime Survey and police recorded crime* (3rd ed.). London: Great Britain Home Office, Research and Statistics Department.

Foote, D. (2002). Reflections on Japan's cooperative adversary process. In O. Ebbe (Ed.), *Comparative and*

International Criminal Justice Systems: Policing, Judiciary, and Corrections (2nd ed.) (pp. 29–41). Boston, MA: Butterworth-Heineman.

Ford, S. (2011). How leadership in international criminal law is shifting from the U.S. to Europe and Asia: An analysis of spending on and contributions to international criminal courts. *Saint Louis University Law Journal, 55*, 953.

Foucault, M. (1979). *Discipline and Punish*. Harmondsworth, UK: Penguin Books.

The 419 Coalition. (2003). The Nigerian scam defined. Retrieved October 13, 2004, from http://home.rica.net/alphae/419coal

Fox, L. (1952). *English prisons and borstal systems*. London: Routledge and Kegan Paul.

Foxnews.com. (2010, August 19). Saudi judge asks hospital if it can damage convict's spine as punishment for paralyzing man. Retrieved September 12, 2012, from http://www.foxnews.com/world/2010/08/19/report-saudi-judge-asks-hospital-damage-convicts-spine-paralyzed-man/

Franz, U. (1988). *Deng Xiaoping*. (T. Artin, Trans.). New York, NY: Harcourt Brace Jovanovich.

Frase, R. (1988). Introduction. In G. Lock & R. Frase (Eds.), *The French Code of Criminal Procedure* (pp. 1–40). Littleton, CO: Rothman.

Freeland, R. (1997). Islamic law: An introduction. *New Law Journal*, June 13, 893–896.

Freilich, J., & Chermak, S. (2008). Creation of a database of U.S. extremist criminal activity, 1990–2007: Preliminary indings. College Park, MD: University Maryland.

Freilich, J., Chermak, S., & Caspi, D. (2009). Critical events in the life trajectories of domestic white supremacist groups: A case study analysis of four violent organizations. *Criminology and Public Policy, 8*(3), 497–530.

French, H. W. (1999, October 12). Japan's troubling trend: Rising teenage crime. *The New York Times*, p. A6.

Friday, P., & Ren, X. (Eds.). (2006). *Delinquency and juvenile justice systems in the non-Western world*. Monsey, NY: Criminal Justice Press.

Friday, P. L. C. (1996). The need to integrate comparative and international criminal justice into a traditional curriculum. *Journal of Criminal Justice Education*, 7(2), 227–240.

Friedrichs, D. O. (2001). *Law in our lives: An introduction*. Los Angeles, CA: Roxbury Publishing.

Friedrichs, D. O. (2010). *Trusted criminals: White collar crime in contemporary society* (4th ed.). Belmont, CA: Wadsworth.

Frist, N., Freilich, J. D., & Clear, T. R. (Eds.). (2009). *Contemporary issues in criminal justice policy*. Belmont, CA: Wadsworth.

Gabor, L., Genovesi, A., Larsen, G., Fullerton-Gleason, L., Davis, A., & Olson, L. (2008). A comparison of law enforcement and medical examiner reports in a violent-death surveillance system. *Homicide Studies, 12*, 249–263.

Gabrys, E. (2002). The international dimensions of cyber-crime, part 2: A look at the Council of Europe's cyber-crime convention and the need for an international regime to fight cyber-crime. *Information Systems Security, 11*(5), 24–32.

GACACA Courts. (2010). The National Service of Gacaca Jurisdictions. Retrieved March 25, 2010, from http://www.inkiko-gacaca.gov.rw/En/Generaties.htm

Galletti, S. C. (2004). Mediterranean Sea and the protection of the underwater cultural heritage. In S. Nevala & K. Aromaa (Eds.), *Organised crime, trafficking, drugs* (pp. 31–51). Helsinki: European Institute for Crime Prevention and Control.

Gallup. (2010). Little change in recent years despite international opposition. Retrieved April 10, 2010, from http://www.gallup.com/poll/123638/In-U.S.-Two-Thirds-ContinueSupport-Death-Penalty.aspx

Gallup. (2012). Death penalty. Retrieved September 25, 2012, from http://www.gallup.com/poll/1606/Death-Penalty.aspx

Garland, D. (1990). *Punishment and modern society*. Oxford: Clarendon.

Garland, D. (2001). *The culture of control: Crime and order in contemporary society*. Chicago, IL: University of Chicago Press.

Gates, S., & Reich, S. (Eds.). (2010). *Child soldiers in the age of fractured states*. Pittsburgh, PA: University of Pittsburgh Press.

Gearan, A. (2004, July 19). High court asked to end child executions. *Associated Press Online*.

Gelsthorpe, L., & Kemp, V. (2002). Comparative juvenile justice: England and Wales. In J. Winterdyk

(Ed.), *Juvenile justice systems: International perspectives* (pp. 127–169). Toronto: Canadian Scholar's Press.

Geneva Declaration Secretariat. (2008). The global burden of armed violence. Retrieved July 9, 2010, from www.genervadeclaration.org.

Ghassemi, G. (2009). Criminal punishment in Islamic societies: Empirical study of attitudes to criminal sentencing in Iran. *European Journal on Criminal Policy and Research, 15*(1–2). Retrieved September 28, 2012, from http://www.springerlink.com/content/jh31h4h24v711v91/

Gibson, G. (2003, September 16). Arrests break international heroin ring. *The Baltimore Sun*, p. 1.

Gilani, S. N. (2006). Juvenile justice in Saudi Arabia. In P. Friday & X. Ren (Eds.), *Delinquency and juvenile justice systems in the non-Western world* (pp.145–163). Monsey, NY: Criminal Justice Press.

Glaser, S. (2005, April 27). U.S. figures show sharp global rise in terrorism: State Dept. will not put data in report. *The Washington Post*. Retrieved May 29, 2010, from http://www.washingtonpost.com/wp-dyn/content/article/2005/04/26/AR2005042601623.html

Glen, H. P. (2000). *Legal traditions of the world: Sustainable diversity in law*. Oxford: Oxford University Press.

Glendon, M. A., Gordon, M., & Osakwe, C. (1985). *Comparative legal traditions*. St. Paul, MN: West Publishing.

Glenny, M. (2009). *McMafia: A journey through the global criminal underworld*. New York, NY: Vintage.

Global Economic Crime Survey. (2011). Retrievd June 26, 2012, from http://www.pwc.com/gx/en/economic-crime-survey/index.jhtml

Goldstein, H. (1975). *Police corruption: A perspective on its nature and control*. Washington, DC: Police Foundation.

Graham, J., & Moore, C. (2008). Beyond welfare versus justice: Juvenile justice in England and Wales. In J. Junger-Tas & S. H. Decker (Eds.), *International Handbook on Juvenile Justice* (pp. 25–39). New York, NY: Springer.

Grove, N. (1997). *Atlas of world history*. Washington, DC: National Geographic Society.

Guo, J., Xiang, G., Zongxian, W., Zhangun, X., Xiaohui, P., & Shuangshuang, L. (1999). *World factbook of criminal justice systems: China*. Retrieved from http://www.ojp.usdoj.gov/bjs/pub/ascii/wfbcjchi.txt

Haberfeld, M., & Cerrah, I. (Eds.). (2008). *Comparative policing: The struggle for democratization*. Thousand Oaks, CA: Sage Publications.

Haberfeld, M., McDonald, W., & von Hassell, A. (2008). International cooperation in policing: A partial answer to the query? In M. Haberfeld & I. Cerrah (Eds.), *Comparative policing: The struggle for democratization* (pp. 341–376). Thousand Oaks, CA: Sage Publications.

Hagan, F. (2000). *Research methods in criminal justice and criminology* (5th ed.). Needham Heights, MA: Allyn and Bacon.

Hagan, F. (2007). *Introduction to criminology: Theories, methods, and criminal behavior* (6th ed.). Thousand Oaks, CA: Sage Publications.

Hamai, K., & Ellis, T. (2006). Crime and justice in modern Japan: From re-integrative shaming to popular punitivism. *International Journal of the Society of Law, 34*(3), 157–178.

Hamai, K., Ville, R., Harris, R., Hough, M., & Zvekic, U. (Eds.). (1995). *Probation around the world: A comparative study*. London: Routledge.

Harris, J. F. (1995, October 23). UN anniversary celebration opens with notes of discord: Clinton urges global effort against crime. *The Washington Post*, p. A1.

Head, J. W. (2011). *Great legal traditions: Civil law, common law, and Chinese law in historical and operational perspective*. Durham, NC: Carolina Academic Press.

Herrmann, J. (1987). The Federal Republic of Germany. In G. Cole, S. Frankowski, & M. Gertz (Eds.), *Major criminal justice systems* (pp. 106–133). Thousand Oaks, CA: Sage Publications.

HEUNI, European Institute for Crime Prevention and Control. (2003). *Connecting, coordinating and cooperating: A short introduction to the institutes comprising the United Nations Crime Prevention and Criminal Justice Programme Network*. Helsinki: HEUNI.

Hill, G. (2002). The French prison service steadily improves. *Corrections Compendium, 27*(12), 7–10.

Hill, G. (2010). Capital punishment: An international update. *Corrections Compendium, 35*(3), 31–34.

Hindelang, M., Hirschi, T., & Weis, J. G. (1981). *Measuring crime*. Thousand Oaks, CA: Sage Publications.

Hindus, M. (1980). *Prison and plantation*. Chapel Hill, NC: University of North Carolina Press.

Hiroshi Fukurai, H. (2011). Symposium on comparative jury systems: Japan's quasi-jury and grand jury systems as deliberative agents of social change. *Chicago-Kent Law Review, 86,* 789.

Hirota, T. (1997). A day in the life of a Tokyo police officer. In G. Newman (Ed.), *Global report on crime and justice* (pp. 25–27). New York, NY: Oxford University Press and United Nations.

Hirsch, S. F. (1998). *Pronouncing and persevering: Gender and the discourse of disputing in an African Islamic court.* Chicago, IL: University of Chicago Press.

Hirschi, T., & Gottfredson, M. (1990). *A general theory of crime.* Stanford, CA: Stanford University Press.

Hodges, K., Martin, L. A., Smith, C., & Cooper, S. (2011). Recidivism, costs, and psychosocial outcomes for a post-arrest juvenile diversion program. *Journal of Offender Rehabilitation, 50*(October), 447–465.

Hodgkinson, P., & Rutherford, A. (1996). *Capital punishment: Global issues and perspectives.* Winchester, VA: Waterside Press.

Hodgson, J. (2001). The police, the prosecutor and the juge d'instruction: Judicial supervision in France, theory and practice. *British Journal of Criminology, 41,* 342–361.

Hodgson, J. (2005). *French criminal justice: A comparative account of the investigation and prosecution of crime in France.* Portland, OR: Hart Publishing.

Hoffman, B. (2006). *Inside terrorism.* New York, NY: Columbia University Press.

Holdaway, S. (1990). *Recruiting a multiracial police force.* London: H.M.S.O.

Holmes, O. W. (1923). *The common law.* Boston, MA: Little, Brown.

Home Office. (2011, December 23). Football disorder at record low. Retrieved July 2, 2012, from http://www.homeoffice.gov.uk/media-centre/news/football-arrests-record-low

Home Office. (2012). *Crime in England and Wales 2011/12.* London: Great Britain Home Office, Research and Statistics Department.

Home Office Prison Service. (2002). Prisons: Sources of information on prisoners, history and architecture. London: Home Office.

Homeland Security. (2012). U.S. Department of Homeland Security. Retrieved October 10, 2012, from http://www.dhs.gov/mission

Hood, R. (2002). *The death penalty: A worldwide perspective* (3rd ed). Oxford: Clarendon Press.

Hopfel, F., & Angermaier, C. (2005). Adjudicating international crimes. In P. Reichel (Ed.), *Handbook of transnational crime and justice* (pp. 45–60). Thousand Oaks, CA: Sage Publications.

Howard, G. N., & Pridemore, W. A. (2000). Theory, method, and data in comparative criminology. In R. Kaminski & N. La Vigne (Eds.), *Criminal Justice 2000, Volume 4: Measurement and Analysis of Crime and Justice.* Washington, DC: U.S. Department of Justice, Office of Justice Programs.

Howard, R., & Nencheck, M. (2012). The new terrorism. In R. Howard & B. Hoffman (Eds.), *Terrorism and counterterrorism: Understanding the new security environment.* (pp. 142–164). New York, NY: McGraw Hill.

Humaidan, M., & Sheraya, A. (2009, July). Saudi Arabia: Tendency towards activating the role of 'umda: Umdas neighborhood chiefs in the neighborhoods. *Middle East (Alsharq Al Awsat)* no. 11189. Retrieved July 24, 2012, from http://www.aawsat.com/details.asp?section=43&article=527824&issueno= 11189

Human Rights Watch. (2003a, May 28). Press release by Human Rights Watch. Retrieved July 23, 2004, from http://hrw.org/press/2003/05/saudimemo0503.htm

Human Rights Watch. (2003b). Asian security talks risk giving green light to repression: Human rights abused in name of fighting terrorism. *Human Rights News.* Retrieved August 7, 2004, from http://www.hrw.org/press/2003/06/asean061603.htm

Human Rights Watch. (2004). Human rights abuses against prisoners. Retrieved July 27, 2004, from http://www.hrw.org/prisons/abuses.html

Human Rights Watch. (2005). In the dark: Hidden abuses against detained youths in Rio de Janeiro. Retrieved from http://www.hrw.org/en/news/2005/06/08/dark-hidden-abuses-against-detained-youths-rio-de-janeiro

Human Rights Watch. (2008, March 24). Precarious justice: Arbitrary detention and unfair trials in the deficient criminal justice system of Saudi Arabia. Retrieved April 20, 2010, from http://www.hrw.org/en/reports/2008/03/24/precarious-justice-0

Human Rights Watch. (2009, November 12). An alleyway in hell—China's abusive "black jails." Retrieved April 20, 2010, from http://www.hrw.org/en/reports/2009/11/12/alleyway-hell-0

Human Rights Watch. (2010a, January 14). Saudi Arabia: Criminal justice strengthened: Shura council approves legal aid program. Retrieved March 20, 2010, from http://www.hrw.org/en/news/2010/01/14/saudi-arabia-criminal-justice-strengthened

Human Rights Watch. (2010b, August 17). Everyone's in on the game: Corruption and human rights abuses by the Nigerian police force. Retrieved July 24, 2012, from www.hrw.org/reports/2010/08/17/everyone-s-game-0.

Human Rights Watch. (2011). Corruption on trial? The record of Nigeria's Economic and Financial Crimes Commission. Retrieved June 27, 2012, from http://www.hrw.org/reports/2011/08/25/corruption-trial-0

Human Rights Watch. (2011a, September 26). Saudi Arabia: Women to vote, join shura council. Retrieved July 20, 2012, from http://www.hrw.org/news/2011/09/26/saudi-arabia-women-vote-join-shura-council

Human Rights Watch. (2012a). World report 2012: Saudi Arabia. Retrieved October 1, 2012, from http://www.hrw.org/world-report-2012/world-report-2012-saudi-arabia

Human Rights Watch. (2012b, June 1). China: Legacy of Tiananmen denial erodes rule of law: Impunity for June 1989 massacre impedes needed legal reform. Retrieved August 28, 2012, from http://www.hrw.org/news/2012/06/01/china-legacy-tiananmen-denial-erodes-rule-law

Human Rights Watch. (2012b). World report 2012: Saudi Arabia. Retrieved August 20, 2012, from http://www.hrw.org/world-report-2012/world-report-2012-saudi-arabia

Hunter-Henin, M. (2011). Constitutional developments and human rights in France: One step forward, two steps back. *The International and Comparative Law Quarterly*, *60*(1), 167–188.

Iakobishvili, E. (2012, March). *Cause for alarm: The incarceration of women for drug offences in Europe and Central Asia, and the need for legislative and sentencing reform.* Retrieved September 25, 2012, from http://www.ihra.net/files/2012/03/11/HRI_WomenInPrisonReport.pdf

ICC. (2012). International Criminal Court. Retrieved September 11, 2012, from http://www.icc-cpi.int/Menus/ICC/Situations+and+Cases/

ICJ. (2012). International Court of Justice. Retrieved April 26, 2012, from http://www.icj-cij.org/homepage/index.php

ICPS. (2012a). International Centre for Prison Studies: World prison brief. Retrieved October 10, 2012, from http://www.prisonstudies.org/info/worldbrief/

ICPS. (2012b). International Centre for Prison Studies 10th Edition, July–August 2012. Retrieved October 1, 2012, from http://www.prisonstudies.org/images/news_events/newsdigestjulyaug2012.pdf

ICTY. (2010). International Criminal Tribunal for the former Yugoslavia. Retrieved April 9, 2010, from http://www.icty.org/sid/10095

Ignatius, D. (2000, January 9). Global corruption threatens the 21st century. *Buffalo News*, reprinted in *The Washington Post*, p. H5.

Info4 Security. (2012, August 13). London Olympics security news. Retrieved August 16, 2012, from http://www.info4security.com/section.asp?navcode=976

Ingraham, B. (1987). *The structure of criminal procedures.* Westport, CT: Greenwood Press

Inside Costa Rica. (2012, January 4). Justice minister says he has warned against increased violence in prisons. Retrieved October 1, 2012, from http://www.insidecostarica.com/dailynews/2012/january/04/costarica12010402.htm

International Court of Justice. (1998, March 23). Overview. Retrieved from http://www.un.org/Overview/Organs/icj.html

International Court of Justice. (2010). Criminal Justice. Retrieved April 5, 2011, from http://www.icj-cij.org/

International Human Rights Instruments. (2004). Retrieved August 1, 2004, from www.streetchildren.org.uk

International Labor Organization. (2003). *Wounded children: The use of children in armed conflict in central Africa.* Geneva: International Labor Organization.

International Law Office. (2011, August 1). New legal rules for persons held in garde a vue. Retrieved

August 30, 2012, from http://www.international-lawoffice.com/newsletters/Detail.aspx?g=a806e044-a1e8-4645-ad86-aa14afb1ea01

International Search. (2012, May 11). International search begins for Latvian hacker suspected of cybercrimes in U.S. *Baltic News Service.*

Internet Fraud Complaint Center. (2012). 2011 Internet crime report. Retrieved June 26, 2012, from http://www.ic3.gov/default.aspx

Irving, J. (2011, March 24). Sex trafficking ring leader sentenced to 40 years in prison. *New York Paralegal Blog.*

Israeli Defense Force. (2004). Successful vs. unsuccessful terrorist attacks. Retrieved December 27, 2004, from http://www.1.idf.il/dover/site/mainpage.asp?sl=EN&id=22&docid=16703.

Ivkovic, S. (2005). *Fallen blue knights: Controlling police corruption.* New York, NY: Oxford University Press.

JAC (2010, December 2). Judicial Selection and Recommendations for Appointment Statistics, England and Wales, April 2010 to September 2010. Judicial Appointments Commission. Retrieved September 13, 2012, from http://jac.judiciary.gov.uk/static/documents/JAC_OS_Dec_10_report.pdf

Jackson, J. D., & Summers, S. J. (2012). *The internationalisation of criminal evidence: Beyond the common law and civil law traditions.* New York, NY: Cambridge University Press.

Jacobs, J. (2006). *Mobsters, unions, and Feds: The Mafia and the American labor movement.* New York, NY: New York University Press.

Jenkins, B. (1978). International terrorism: Trends and potentialities. *Journal of International Affairs, 32*(1): 115–124.

Jensen, E. L., & Jepsen, J. (Eds.). (2006). Juvenile law violators, human rights, and the development of new juvenile justice systems. Oxford: Hart Publishing.

Jiahong, H., & Waltz, J. R. (1995). *Criminal prosecution in the People's Republic of China and the United States: A comparative study.* Beijing: China Procuratorial Press.

Jiang, G., Garris, C. P., & Bendania, A. (2011). Community involvement in crime prevention and judicial process: The experience of Saudi Arabia. *British Journal of Community Justice, 8*(3), 49–61.

Johnson, D. (2002). *The Japanese way of justice: Prosecuting crime in Japan.* New York, NY: Oxford University Press.

Johnson, E. H. (1996). Japanese version of community corrections: Volunteer probation officers and hostels. In O. Ebbe (Ed.), *Comparative and international criminal justice systems* (pp. 185–198). Boston, MA: Butterworth-Heinemann.

Johnson, H. A. (1988). *History of criminal justice.* Cincinnati, OH: Anderson Publishing.

Johnson, K. (1999, August 25). Scotland Yard confounded by crisis of confidence. *USA Today*, p. 3.

Joint Economic Committee. (2002). The economic costs of terrorism. United States Congress. Retrieved May 15, 2012, from http://www.house.gov/jec/terrorism/costs.pdf

Jones, T., & Newburn, T. (2002). The transformation of policing? Understanding current trends in policing systems. *British Journal of Criminology, 42*, 129–146.

Jones, T., & van Sluis, A. (2009). National standards, local delivery: Police reform in England and Wales. *German Policy Studies, 5*(2), pp. 117–144.

Jousten, M. (1994). Victimology and Victim Policy in Europe. *The Criminologist, 19*(3), pp. 9–12.

Jousten, M., & Zvekic, U. (1994). Noncustodial sanctions: Comparative overview. In U. Zvekic (Ed.), *Alternatives to imprisonment in comparative perspective* (pp. 1–42). Chicago, IL: Nelson-Hall.

Joyce, P. (2006). *Criminal justice: An introduction to crime and the criminal justice system.* Portland, OR: Willan Publishing.

Joyce, P. (2011). *Policing: Development and contemporary practice.* London: Sage Publications.

Judicial News. (2012a, March 8). Law amendment to balance human rights protection, penalty in criminal procedure: NPC spokesman. Retrieved August 30, 2012, from http://en.chinacourt.org/public/detail.php?id=4668

Judicial News. (2012b, April 12). Senior leader urges all-out efforts to reeducate, reform prisoners for harmony. Retrieved October 1, 2012, from http://en.chinacourt.org/public/detail.php?id=4625

Judicial News. (2012c, May 28). Senior Chinese leader stresses human rights. Retrieved August 28, 2012, from http://en.chinacourt.org/public/detail.php?id=4685

Judiciary of England and Wales. (2012). Judiciary of England and Wales: The Supreme Court. Retrieved September 13, 2012, from http://www.judiciary.gov.uk/about-the-judiciary/introduction-to-justice-system/the-supreme-court

Junger-Tas, J., Marshall, I. H., Enzmann, D., Killias, M., Steketee, M., & Gruszczynska, B. (Eds.). (2010). *Juvenile delinquency in Europe and beyond.* New York, NY: Springer.

Junger-Tas, J., Terlouw, G., & Klien, M. (Eds.). (1994). *Delinquent behavior of young people in the Western world—First results of the International Self-Report Delinquency Study.* Amsterdam, NY: Kluger.

Juvenile Justice. (2009). A basic framework for the implementation of a functional juvenile justice system. *Commonwealth Law Bulletin, 35* (June), 301–313.

Juviler, P. (1976). Revolutionary law and order. New York, NY: Free Press.

Kakucki, S. (2004, July 29). Japan—Rise in violent teen crime worries the nation. *IPS News.*

Kalmthout, A., & Tak, P. (1988). *Sanctions systems in the member states of the Council of Europe—Part I.* Norwell, MA: Kluwer Law and Taxation.

Kalunta-Crumpton, A. (2010). Patterns of community policing in Britain. In D. Wisler & I. Owundiwe (Eds.), *Community policing: International patterns and comparative perspectives* (pp. 149–166). Boca Raton, FL: CRC Press.

Kanayama, T. (2009, February). A decade from police reforms in Japan, has a police for the people been realized? Police Policy Research Center, National Police Agency of Japan. Retrieved August 15, 2012, from http://www.npa.go.jp/english/seisaku/A_DECADE_FROM_POLICE_REFORMS_IN_JAPAN-HAS_A_POLICE_FOR_THE_PEOPLE_BEEN_REALIZED.pdf

Kaplan, D. (2005, December 5). Paying for terror. *U.S. News and World Report,* pp. 41–54.

Karch, D. L., & Logan, J. E. (2008). Data consistency in multiple source documents: Findings from homicide incidents in the National Violent Death Reporting System, 2003–2004. *Homicide Studies, 12,* 264–276.

Kelle, M. (2004, July 23). Army reports allegations of prisoner abuse. *The Tribune* (Scranton, PA), p. A6.

Kerney, J., Botzios, S., & Hadden, T. (2011). Addressing the accountability challenges of international policing in peace support operations. *Crime, Law and Social Change, 55*(2/3): 217–239.

Killias, M., & Aebi, M. E. (2000). Crime trends in Europe from 1990 to 1996: How Europe illustrates the limits of the American experience. *European Journal of Criminal Policy and Research, 8,* 43–63.

King, L. E., & Ray, J. M. (2000). Developing transnational law enforcement cooperation. *Journal of Contemporary Criminal Justice, 16*(4), 386–408.

Kirby, S. (2011). Policing mobile criminality: Implications for police forces in the UK. *Policing, 34*(2), 182–197.

Klein, A. (2011, May 30). Crimes by D.C. teens growing violent. *The Washington Post,* p. 1

Klein, M. W. (2001). Thoughts on juvenile justice systems and research. *European Journal of Criminal Policy and Research, 9*(Autumn), 273–281.

Kleinig, J. (1996) *The ethics of policing.* Cambridge, MA: Cambridge University Press.

Klenowski, P. M. (2009). Peacemaking criminology: Etiology of crime or philosophy of life? *Contemporary Justice Review, 12,* 207–222.

Komiya, N. (1999). A cultural study of the low crime rate in Japan. *British Journal of Criminology, 39*(3), 66–75.

Kommers, D. (1976). *Judicial politics in West Germany.* Thousand Oaks, CA: Sage.

Kristof, N. (1995, March 14). Japanese say no to crime: Tough methods, at a price. *The New York Times,* p. A1.

Krohn, M., Thornberry, T., Gibson, C., & Baldwin, J. (2010). The development and impact of self-report measures of crime and delinquency. *Journal of Quantitative Criminology, 26*(December), 509–525.

Kudish, N. (2008, December 10). Man receives life sentence for an attempt to bomb German commuter trains. *New York Times,* p. A22.

Kuhn, A. (1994). What can we do about prison overcrowding. *European Journal on Criminal Policy and Research, 2*(4), 101–106.

Kuhn, A. (1996). Incarceration rates: Europe versus the United States. *European Journal on Criminal Policy and Research, 4*(3): 46–73.

Kukhianidze, A. (2004). Organized crime and smuggling through Abkhazia and South Ossetia. In S. Nevala & K. Aromaa (Eds.). *Organised crime, trafficking, drugs* (pp. 34–41). Helsinki: European Institute for Crime Prevention and Control.

Kurian, G. (2005). *The world encyclopedia of police forces and correctional systems.* Detroit, MI: Gale Publishing.

Kurki, L. (2001). International standards for sentencing and punishment. In M. Tonry & R. Frase (Eds.), *Sentencing and sanctions in Western countries* (p. 352). New York, NY: Oxford University Press.

Kurlychek, M. C., & Johnson, B. D. (2004). The juvenile penalty: A comparison of juvenile and young adult sentencing outcomes in criminal court. *Criminology, 42*(May), 485–517.

Kury, H., & Shea, E. (2011). *Punitiveness: A global phenomenon?* (Crime and Crime Policy Vol. 8/1). Germany: Bochum.

LaFree, G. L., Dugan, H. F., & Scott, J. (2006). Building a global terrorism database. Final report to the National Institute of Justice. Retrieved from www.ncjrs.gov/pdffiles1/nij/grants/214260.pdf

Lafree, G. S., Yang, M., & Crenshaw, M. (2009). Trajectories of terrorism: Attack patterns of foreign groups that have targeted the United States, 1970–2004. *Criminology & Public Policy, 8*(3), 445–473.

Laing, L., Vernon, M., Eldersveld, S., Meisel, J., & Pollock, J. (Eds.). (1950). *Sourcebook in European governments.* New York, NY: Sloane.

Lally, C. (2012, August 16). Community work penalties up 40% after law change. *Irish Times.* Retrieved from http://www.irishtimes.com/newspaper/ireland/2012/0816/1224322257160.html

Lancaster, R., & Xiangshun, D. (2007). Addressing the emergence of advocacy in the Chinese criminal justice system: A collaboration between a U.S. and a Chinese law school. *Fordham International Law Journal, 30*, 356–66.

Langbein, J. (1977). *Comparative criminal procedure: Germany.* St. Paul, MN: West Publishing.

Langbein, J. (2003). *The origins of the adversary trial.* Oxford: Oxford University Press.

Lappi-Seppala, T. (2007). Penal policy in Scandanavia. In M. Tonry (Ed.), *Crime and justice: A review of research, vol. 36* (pp. 217–296). Chicago, IL: University of Chicago Press.

Laqueur, W. (1999). *The new terrorism: Fanaticism and the arms of mass destruction.* New York, NY: Oxford University Press.

Lauderdale, P. (1997). Indigenous North American jurisprudence. *International Journal of Comparative Sociology, 38*, 131–148.

Law, R. (2009). *Terrorism: A history.* Malden, MA: Polity Press.

Lawless, J. (2012, January 29). London cops arrest five in British police bribery probe. *Scranton Times–Tribune.* Retrieved August 18, 2012, from http://scrantontimestribune.newspaperdirect.com/epaper/viewer.aspx

Lawyers Committee. (1994). *Criminal justice with Chinese characteristics.* New York, NY: Lawyers Committee.

Lawyers Committee. (1996). Opening to reform?: An analysis of China's revised criminal procedure law. New York, NY: Lawyers Committee for Human Rights.

Lawyers Committee. (1998a). Frequently asked questions about the International Criminal Court. New York, NY: Lawyers Committee for Human Rights.

Lawyers Committee. (1998b). Lawyers in China: Obstacles to independence and the defense of rights. New York, NY: Lawyers Committee for Human Rights.

Lawyers Committee. (1998c). *Wrongs and rights: A human rights analysis of China's revised criminal law.* New York, NY: Lawyers Committee.

Lee, M. R. (2001). Population growth, economic inequality, and homicide. *Deviant Behavior: An Interdisciplinary Journal, 22*, 491–516.

Leng, S. (1982). Criminal justice in post-Mao China: Some preliminary observations. *The Journal of Criminal Law and Criminology, 73*, 204–237.

Leng, S., & Chiu, H. (1985). *Criminal justice in post-Mao China.* Albany, NY: SUNY Press.

Levy, L. (1969). *Essays on the making of the Constitution.* New York, NY: Oxford University Press.

Levy, R. (2007). Pardons and Amnesties as Policy Instruments in Contemporary France. In M. Tonry (Ed.), *Crime and justice: A review of research, vol. 36* (pp. 551–590). Chicago, IL: University of Chicago Press.

Lewis, C. (1999). Difficulties in interpreting and recording crime statistics. In G. Newman (Ed.), *Global report on crime and justice* (p. 43). New York, NY: Oxford University Press.

Lewis C. (1999). Police records of crime. In G. Newman (Ed.), *Global report on crime and justice* (p. 55). New

York, NY: Oxford University Press and United Nations.

Lewis, M. (2012, August 13). In Norway, panel lists police faults in massacre. *The New York Times.* Retrieved August 18, 2012, from http://www.nytimes.com/2012/08/14/world/europe/norway-panel-on-massacre-finds-litany-of-government-failures.html

Lewis, P., & Newburn, T. (2012, July 1). Reading the riots: Investigating England's summer of disorder. *The Guardian.* Retrieved August 18, 2012, from http://www.guardian.co.uk/uk/2012/jul/01/introducing-phase-two-reading-riots

Liang, B. (2008). *The changing Chinese legal system, 1978–present: Centralization of power and rationalization of the legal system.* New York, NY: Routledge.

Liptak, A., & Bronner, E. (2012, June 25). Justices bar mandatory life terms for juveniles. *The New York Times,* p. A1.

Liu, J. (2008). Data sources in Chinese crime and criminal justice research. *Crime, Law and Social Change, 50*(3), 131–147.

Liu, J., & Messner, S. (2001). Modernization and crime trends in China's reform era. In J. Liu, L. Zhang, & S. Messner (Eds.), *Crime and social control in changing China* (pp. 151–160). Westport, CT: Greenwood Publishing.

Liu, J., Zhang, L., & Messner, S. (Eds.). (2001). *Crime and social control in a changing China.* Westport, CT: Greenwood Press.

Liu, P., & Situ, Y. (2001). Mixing inquisitorial and adversarial models: Changes in criminal procedure in a changing China. In J. Liu, L. Zhang, & S. Messner (Eds)., *Crime and social control in changing China* (pp. 133–150). Westport, CT: Greenwood Publishing.

Liu, W., & Situ, Y. (1999). Criminal courts in China transition: Inquisitorial procedure to adversarial procedure? *Crime and Justice International, 15*(25), 13–21.

Lock, G. L., & Frase, R. S. (1998). *The French Code of Criminal Procedure.* Littleton, CO: Rothman.

Long, M., & Cullen, S. (2008). United Kingdom: Democratic policing—global change from a comparative perspective. In M. Haberfeld & I. Cerrah (Eds.), *Comparative policing* (pp. 277–302). Thousand Oaks, CA: Sage Publications.

Lu, H., & Miethe, T. D. (2002). Legal representation and criminal processing in China. *British Journal of Criminology, 42,* 267–80.

Lubanga Trial. (2012). *The Lubanga Trial at the International Criminal Court.* Retrieved June 13, 2012, from http://www.lubangatrial.org/

Lubman, S. (1983). Comparative criminal law and enforcement: China. In S. Kadish (Ed.), *Encyclopedia of crime and justice* (pp. 21–29). New York, NY: Free Press.

Lynch, J. (1988). A comparison of prison use in England, Canada, West Germany, and the United States: A limited test of the punitive hypothesis. *Journal of Criminal Law and Criminology, 79,* 180–217.

Lynch, J. P. (1993). A cross-national comparison of the length of custodial sentences for serious crimes. *Justice Quarterly, 10*(4), 121–136.

Lynch, J. P., & Jarvis, J. (2008). Missing data and imputation in the uniform crime reports and the effects on national estimates. *Journal of Contemporary Criminal Justice, 254,* 69–85.

Ma, Y. (1995). Crime in China: Characteristics, causes, and control strategies. *International Journal of Comparative and Applied Criminal Justice, 19*(2), 57–66

Ma, Y. (1997). The Police Law of 1995: Organization, functions, powers, and accountability of the Chinese police. *Policing: An International Journal of Police Strategy and Management, 20,* 113–135.

MacDougall, C. (2012, April 27). Taylor guilty. *The Christian Science Monitor,* p. 3.

Maier-Katkin, D., Mears, D. P., & Bernard, T. J. (2009). Towards a criminology of crimes against humanity. *Theoretical Criminology, 13*(2), 227–255.

Maki, Amos. (2012, January 25). Crimes lurk in Memphis Police Department memo. *The Commercial Appeal,* p. 1.

Mansour, A. (1982). Hudud crimes. In C. Bassiouni (Ed.), *The Islamic criminal justice system* (pp. 195–201). New York, NY: Ocean Publications.

Marchett, I. E., & Daly, K. (2004). *Indigenous courts and justice practices in Australia. Trends and issues in crime and criminal justice.* (Report No. 277). Canberra: Australian Institute of Criminology.

Marenin, O. (Ed.). (1996). *Policing change, changing police: International perspectives.* New York, NY: Garland.

Marenin, O. (2003). *Building a global police studies community*. Paper presented at the conference "Status Check: Police Studies," held at Eastern Kentucky University, Richmond, KY, June 12–14.

Margaryan, S. (2010). International human rights movement. In S. Kethineni (Ed.), *Comparative and international policing, justice, and international crime* (pp. 243–268). Durham, NC: Carolina Academic Press.

Marshall, C., Robinson, T. H., & Kwak, D. (2005). Computer crime in a brave new world. In P. Reichel (Ed.), *Handbook of transnational crime and justice* (pp. 114–138). Thousand Oaks, CA: Sage Publications.

Martin, G. (2003). *Understanding terrorism: Challenges, perspectives, and issues*. Thousand Oaks, Ca: Sage Publications.

Massy, L. (2008). The antiquity art market: Between legality and illegality. *International Journal of Social Economics, 35*, 729–738.

Mawby, R. (2012). *World policing models*. In M. Natarajan (Ed.), *International crime and justice*. New York, NY: Cambridge University Press.

Mawby, R. I. (2008). Models of policing. In T. Newburn (Ed.), *The handbook of policing* (2nd. ed.) (pp. 17–46). Cullompton, UK: Willan Publishing.

Maxwell, G., & Morris, A. (2002). Juvenile crime and justice in New Zealand. In N. Bala (Ed.), *Juvenile justice systems*. Toronto, ON: Thomason Education.

McCormack, T. L. H. (1997). From Sun Tzu to the sixth committee: The evolution of an international law regime. In T. L. H. McCormack & G. J. Simpson (Eds.), *The law of war crimes: National and international approaches* (pp. 31–63). Cambridge, MA: Kluwer.

McCurry, J. (2012, March 29). Japan hangs three prisoners after 18-month stay of executions. *The Guardian*. Retrieved September 25, 2012, from http://www.guardian.co.uk/world/2012/mar/29/japan-hangs-three-prisoners-executions

McDonald, D. C. (1992). Punishing labor: Unpaid community service as a criminal sentence. In J. Byrne, A. Lurigio, & J. Petersilia (Eds.). *Smart sentencing: The emergence of intermediate sanctions*. Thousand Oaks, CA: Sage Publications.

McDonald, W. F. (2012). The longer arm of the law: The growth and limits of international law enforcement and criminal justice cooperation. In M. Natarajan (Ed.), *International crime and justice* (pp. 437–444). New York, NY: Cambridge University Press.

McIllwain, J. S. (1999). Organized crime: A social network approach. *Crime, law, and social change, 32*, 301–323.

McIllwain, J. S. (2004). *Organizing crime in Chinatown: Race and racketeering in New York City, 1890–1910*. New York, NY: McFarland.

McMorrow, J. A. (2010). Professional responsibility in an uncertain profession: Legal ethics in China (October 25). *Akron Law Review, 43*(3), 311–25.

McNeill, J. (2010, May 7). Times Square terror plot: The right formula for stopping terrorism has not changed. Retrieved May 29, 2010, from http://www.heritage.org/Research/Reports/2010/05/Times-Square-Terror-Plot-The-Right-Formula-for-Stopping-Terrorism-Has-Not-Changed

McPhedran, S., Baker, J., & Singh, P. (2011). Firearm homicide in Australia, Canada, and New Zealand: What can we learn from long-term international comparisons? *Journal of Interpersonal Violence, 26*, 348–60.

McWhinney, E. (1965). *Judicial review* (4th ed.). Toronto, ON: University of Toronto Press.

Melossi, D., & Pavarini, M. (1981). *The prison and the factory*. New York, NY: Macmillan.

Merryman, J. H. (1985). *The civil law tradition*. Stanford, CA: Stanford University Press.

Meslo, G., Dobovsek, B., & Kesetovic, Z. (2009). Measuring organized crime in Slovenia. *Problems of Post-Communism, 56*, 58–62.

Metz, H. C. (1993). *Saudi Arabia: A country study* (5th ed.). Washington, DC: Federal Research Division, Library of Congress.

Meuwese, S. (Ed.). (2003). *Kids behind bars*. Amsterdam, NY: Defence for Children International.

Minimum Rules for the Administration of Juvenile Justice United Nations Office on Drugs and Crime. (2010). United Nations Office on Drugs and Crime. Retrieved February 20, 2010, from http://www.unodc.org

Mollen Commission. (1994). *Report of the commission to investigate allegations of police corruption and the anti-corruption procedures of the police department*. New York, NY: Mollen Commission.

Moore, M. T. (2010, February 3). Youth system under pressure. *USA Today*.

Moore, R. (1987). Courts, law, justice, and criminal trials in Saudi Arabia. *International Journal of Comparative and Applied Criminal Justice, 11*(1), 61–67.

Moore, R. (1996). Islamic legal systems: traditional (Saudi Arabia), contemporary (Bahrain), and evolving (Pakistan). In C. Fields & R. Moore (Eds.), *Comparative criminal justice* (pp. 390–410). Prospect Heights, IL: Waveland Press.

Mortimer, J. (1978). *Rumpole of the Bailey*. London: Penguin Books.

Mueller, G. O. W. (1997). Enforcing international criminal justice. In W. McDonald (Ed.), *Crime and law enforcement in the global village* (pp. 139–150). Cincinnati, OH: Anderson Publishing.

Mueller, G. O. W., & Adler, F. (1996). Globalization and criminal justice: A prologue. In C. Fields & R. Moore (Eds.), *Comparative criminal justice* (pp. 3–5). Prospect Heights, IL: Waveland Press.

Mueller, G. O. W., & LePoole-Griffiths, F. (1969). *Comparative criminal procedure*. New York, NY: New York University Press.

Muncie, J., & Goldson, B. (2006). England and Wales: The new correctionalism. In J. Muncie & B. Goldson (Eds.), *Comparative youth justice* (pp. 34–47). London: Sage Publications.

Murayama, M. (2002). The role of defense lawyers in the Japanese criminal process. In M. Feeley & S. Miyazawa (Eds.), *The Japanese Adversary System in Context: Controversies and Comparisons* (pp. 142–166). New York, NY: Palgrave McMillan.

Murray, J. (2005). Policing terrorism: A threat to community policing or just a shift in priorities? *Police Practice and Research, 6*(4), 347–361.

Murty, K. S., Roebuck, J. B., & Almolhem, M. A. (1991). Profile of adult offenders in Damman Central Prison, Saudi Arabia. *International Journal of Comparative and Applied Criminal Justice, 15*(1), 89–97.

Mustaza, M. (2010, August 9). More than half the children who commit a crime are reconvicted within a decade—most on multiple occasions. *New Straits Times* (Malaysia).

Nader, M. M. J. (1990). *Aspects of Saudi Arabian law*. Riyadh: Nader.

Nadleman, E. (2012). Colombia decriminalizes cocaine and marijuana, as Latin American momentum for drug policy reform continues. Retrieved September 12, 2012, from http://www.huffingtonpost.com/ethan-nadelmann/colombia-decriminalizes-c_b_1638395.html

Naim, M. (2006). *Illicit: How smugglers, traffickers, and copycats are hijacking the global economy*. New York, NY: Anchor Books.

Natarajan, M. (2002). International criminal justice education: A note on curricula resources. *Journal of Criminal Justice Education, 13*, 479–498.

Natarajan, M., (Ed.). (2012). *International crime and justice*. Cambridge, MA: Cambridge University Press.

Nathan, S. (2004). Private prisonisation. Retrieved July 26, 2010, from www.penalreform.org/english/frset_map_en.htm.

National Counterterrorism Center. (2012). The National Counterterrorism Center report on terrorism: 2011. Retrieved October 10, 2012, from http://www.nctc.gov/docs/2011_NCTC_Annual_Report_Final.pdf

National Counterterrorism Center Terrorism Reports. (2005–2009). World Incidents Tracking System. Retrieved May 29, 2010, from http://wits-classic.nctc.gov/Reports.do

National Police Agency. (2010a). Japanese statistical yearbook: Chapter 25, justice and peace. Ministry of Internal Affairs and Communications. Retrieved January, 25, 2010, from http://www.stat.go.jp/data/nenkan/pdf/yhyou25.pdf

National Police Agency. (2010b). Crime in Japan (2010). Police Policy Research Center, National Police Academy. Retrieved July 5, 2012, from http://www.npa.go.jp/english/seisaku/Crime_in_Japan_in_2010.pdf

National Police Agency. (2011). National Police Agency of Japan. The white paper on police 2011. Retrieved August 19, 2012, from http://www.npa.go.jp/hakusyo/h23/english/Contents_WHITE_PAPER_on_POLICE2011.htm

National Report. (2010). 2010 national report (2009 data) to EMCDDA: France. REITUX. Retrieved July 28, 2012, from www.ofdt.fr

National Tribal Resource Center. (2010). Home. Retrieved March 29, 2010, from http://www.tribalresourcecenter.org/

Neapolitan, J. L. (1996). Cross-national crime data: Some unaddressed problems. *Journal of Criminal Justice*, *19*(1), 95–112.

Neapolitan, J. L. (1999). A comparative analysis of nations with low and high levels of violent crime. *Journal of Criminal Justice*, *27*(3), 259–274.

Nelken, D. (2010). *Comparative criminal justice: Making sense of difference*. Thousand Oaks, CA: Sage Publications.

Nerlich, V. (2011). The International Criminal Court 2002–2010—A view from the inside. *Criminal Law Forum*, *22*, 199–214.

Nettles, Z. Z. (2005). The United States' elimination of the death penalty for children and international law. *Women Lawyers Journal*, *90*(Spring), 28–33.

Nevala, S., & Aromaa, K. (Eds.). *Organised crime, trafficking, drugs*. Helsinki: European Institute for Crime Prevention and Control.

New Canadian Centre for Law Enforcement. (2003, February 11). New Canadian Centre. *Canadian Newswire*.

Newburn, T. (1999). *Understanding and preventing police corruption: Lessons from the literature*, (Police Research Series, Paper 110). London: Home Office.

Newburn, T. (2007). "Tough on crime": Penal policy in England and Wales. *Crime and Justice*, *36*(1). Retrieved July 2, 2012, from http://www.jstor.org/stable/10.1086/592810

Newman, G. (Ed.). (1999). *Global report on crime and justice*. New York, NY: Oxford University Press and United Nations.

Ngo, Jennifer. (2011, December 19). Scores of teens held in raids of hang-outs. *South China Morning Post*.

Nieuwbeerta, P. (2002). Introduction. In P. Nieuwbeerta (Ed.), *Crime victimization in comparative perspective* (p. 3–5). The Hague: Netherlands: Juridische Uitgevers.

9/11 Commission. (2004). *The 9/11 Commission Report*. New York, NY: Norton.

Nomura, T. (2009). Current situation and future tasks for psychiatric services in Japanese prisons. *Journal of Nippon Medical School*, *76*(4), 182–192.

Nottage, L., & Green, S. (2011). Who defends Japan?: Government lawyers and judicial system reform in Japan. *Asian-Pacific Law & Policy Journal*, *13*(1), 129–173.

Occhipinti, J. D. (2003). *The politics of EU police cooperation: Toward a European FBI?* Boulder, CO: Lynne Reinner Publishers.

O'Donnell, E. (1990). The Shah Bano case (1985) and the Muslim Women Act. (Unpublished master's thesis). North Carolina State University, Raleigh, NC.

Ohtsubo, Y. (2006). On designing a mixed jury system in Japan. In M. Kaplan & A. Martin (Eds.), *Understanding world jury systems* (pp. 199–214). New York, NY: Taylor & Francis.

O'Malley, P. (2011). Monetary sanctions as misguided policy: Politicizing the case for fines. *Criminology & Public Policy*, *10*(3). Retrieved September 25, 2012, from http://onlinelibrary.wiley.com/doi/10.1111/j.1745-9133.2011.00736.x/pdf

Onishi, N. (2003, September 6). Crime rattles Japanese calm, attracting politicians' notice. *The New York Times*, p. A1.

Organization for Security and Co-Operation in Europe. (2008). Guidebook on democratic policing. Retrieved August 18, 2012, from http://www.osce.org/spmu/23804

Owers, A. (2006). The protection of prisoners' rights in England and Wales. *European Journal on Criminal Policy and Research*, *12*(2), 85–91.

Page, J. (2012, August 10). Tried in 1 day, China's Gu Faces Fate. *The Wall Street Journal*, p. A6.

Pagon, M. (2000). *Policing in Central and Eastern Europe: Ethics, integrity, and human rights*. Ljubljana: College of Police Studies.

Pakes, F. (2010). *Comparative criminal justice* (2nd ed.). New York, NY: Willan Publishing.

Parker, L. C., Jr. (2001). *The Japanese police system today: A comparative study*. New York, NY: M. E. Sharpe.

Parry, L. (2009, September 19). Japan's death penalty effectively scrapped with arrival of Keiko Chiba. *The Times*. Retrieved April 20, 2010, from http://www.deathpenaltyinfo.org/international-use-death-penalty-may-sharply-decline-japan

Paterson, C. (2007). Commercial crime control and the electronic monitoring of offenders in England and Wales. *Social Justice*, *34*(3/4), 98–110.

Peak, K. (1991). The comparative systems course in criminal justice: Findings from a national survey. *Journal of Criminal Justice Education*, *2*, 267–272.

Penal Reform International. (1999). Promoting Penal Reform Worldwide. Retrieved from http://www.penalreform.org

People's Daily Online. (2010, March 1). CASS: China's violent crimes rise for the first time in a decade. Retrieved July 29, 2012, from http://english.people.com.cn/90001/90782/90872/6905399.html

Peerenboom, R. (Ed.) (2010). *Judicial independence in China: Lessons for global rule of law promotion*. New York, NY: Cambridge University Press.

Perry, R. L., & Robertson, J. D. (2002). *Comparative analysis of nations: Quantitative approaches*. Cambridge, MA: Westview Press.

Peters, R. (2005). *Crime and punishment in Islamic law: Theory and practice from the sixteenth to the twenty-first century*. New York, NY: Cambridge University Press.

Pettus-Davis, C., & Garland, E. (2009). Ban juvenile transfer to adult court in homicide cases: Brain development and the need for a blended sentence approach. In N. Frist, J. Freilich, & T. Clear (Eds.), *Contemporary Issues in Criminal Justice Policy* (pp. 311–320). Belmont, CA: Wadsworth.

Pfeiffer, C. (1998). *Trends in juvenile violence in European countries*. Washington, DC: National Institute of Justice.

Piquero, A. R., Brezina, T., & Turner, M. G. (2005). Testing Moffitt's account of delinquency abstention. *Journal of Research in Crime & Delinquency, 42* (February), 27–54.

Plucknett, T. (1940). *A concise history of the common law*. London: Butterworth.

Police Crime Statistics. (2008). Federal Republic of Germany. Retrieved January 20, 2010, from http://www.bundeskriminalamt.de/pks/pks2008ev/pcs_2008.pdf

Police Crime Statistics. (2010). Police crime statistics: Germany. Wiesbaden, Germany: BKA. Retrieved July 2, 2012, from http://www.bka.de/nn_194552/EN/Publications/PoliceCrimeStatistics/policeCrimeStatistics__node.html?__nnn=true

Prall, S. (1966). *The agitation for law reform during the Puritan revolution, 1640–1660*. The Hague: Martinus Nijhoff.

Pranis, K. (1993). Restorative justice: Back to the future in criminal justice. Minneapolis, MN: Minnesota Citizens Council.

President's Commission on Organized Crime. (1987). *The impact: Organized crime today*. Washington, DC: U.S. Government Printing Office.

Prideaux, E. (2004, June 13). Cops and citizens bid to blitz street sleaze. *The Japan Times*, p. 3

Prison Brief. (2010). International Centre for Prison Studies, Kings College London. Retrieved April 20, 2010, from http://www.kcl.ac.uk/depsta/law/research/icps/worldbrief/

Punch, M. (1985). *Conduct unbecoming: The social construction of police deviance and control*. London: Tavistock.

Punch, M. (2009). *Police corruption: Deviance, accountability and reform in policing*. Cullompton, UK: Willan Publishing.

Puzzanchera, C. M. (2000). *Self-reported delinquency for 13-year-olds*. Washington, DC: Office of Juvenile Justice and Delinquency Prevention.

Qi, S., & Oberwittler, D. (2009). On the road to the rule of law: Crime, crime control, and public opinion in China. *European Journal on Criminal Policy and Research, 15*(1–2), 137–157.

Rahim, M. A. (1986). *On the issue of international comparison of "prison population" and "use of imprisonment."* (Report no. 1986-41. Statistics Division, Programs Branch.) Ottawa: Ministry of the Solicitor General.

Rand Corporation. (2009, April 10). Study finds most adolescents sent to group homes still involved with drugs/crime 7 years later. *Drug Week*, 3–7.

Rao, S. (2004, July 27). Ministers enter the fray—Visit to scene of prison riots. *The Daily Telegraph* (Sydney, Australia), p. 3.

Rapoport, D. (1984). Fear and trembling: Terrorism in three religious traditions. *American Political Science Review, 78*, 658–677.

Rashbaum, W. K., Moynihan, C., & Stelloh, T. (2012, March 1). A $250 million fraud scheme finds a path to Brighton Beach. *The New York Times*, p. 1.

Redo, S. (2004). *Organized crime and its control in Central Asia*. Huntsville, TX: Office of International Criminal Justice.

Reed, J. S. (1974). *The enduring South*. Chapel Hill, NC: University of North Carolina Press.

Reichel, P. (Ed.). (2005). *Handbook of transnational crime and justice*. Thousand Oaks, CA: Sage Publications.

Reichel, P. (2013). *Comparative criminal justice systems: A topical approach* (6th ed.). Upper Saddle River, NJ: Pearson.

Reiman, J. (2007). *The rich get richer and the poor get prison: Ideology, class, and criminal justice* (8th ed.). Boston, MA: Allyn & Bacon.

Reisig, M., & Pratt, T. (2000, June). The ethics of correctional privatization. *Prison Journal, 80*, 210–222.

Repeta, L. (2011). Reserved seats on Japan's Supreme Court. *Washington University Law Review, 88*(6), 1713–1733.

Reuters. (2012, April 25). Crime business one of the world's top 20 economies: United Nations. *The Huffington Post.* http://www.huffingtonpost.com/2012/04/23/crime-business-united-nations_n_1445742.html

Reyes, Cassandra. (2009). Corrections-based drug treatment programs and crime prevention: An international approach. *Journal of Offender Rehabilitation, 48*, 620–634.

Richard, A. O. (2000). *International trafficking in women to the United States: A contemporary manifestation of slavery and organized crime.* Washington, DC: U.S. Department of State, Center for the Study of Intelligence.

Roberts, J., Stalans, L., Indermaur, D., & Hough, M. (2003). *Penal populism and public opinion.* New York, NY: Oxford University Press.

Roberts, P., & Hunter, J. (2012). Introduction - The human rights revolution in criminal evidence and procedure. In P. Roberts & J. Hunter (Eds.), *Criminal evidence and human rights: Reimaging common law procedural traditions* (pp. 57–70). Portland, OR: Hart Publishing.

Robinson, V. (2012, July 11). Apology cuts sentence in love triangle murder. Retrieved September 20, 2012, from http://www.stuff.co.nz/national/crime/7259970/Apology-cuts-sentence-in-love-triangle-murder

Roche, S. (2007). Criminal justice policy in France: Illusions of severity. In M. Tonry (Ed.), *Crime and justice: An annual review of research, vol. 36* (pp. 471–550). Chicago, IL: University of Chicago Press.

Rojek, D. G. (1996). Changing directions in Chinese society. In C. Fields & R. Moore (Eds.), *Comparative Criminal Justice* (pp. 390–410). Prospect Heights, IL: Waveland Press.

Rosen, L. (1992). Law and indigenous peoples. *Law and Social Inquiry, 17*, 363–371.

Rosenthal, E. (2000, January 6). In China's legal evolution, the lawyers are handcuffed. *The New York Times*, p. A1.

Ross, J. I. (1996). Policing in the Gulf States: The effect of the Gulf conflict. In O. Marenin (Ed.), *Policing change, changing police: International perspectives* (pp. 77–105). New York, NY: Garland.

Royal Embassy of Saudi Arabia. (2011, January). The Kingdom of Saudi Arabia initiatives and actions to combat terrorism. Retrieved July 20, 2012, from http://saudiembassy.net/files/PDF/Reports/Counterterrorism.pdf

Royal Embassy of Saudi Arabia. (2012). About Saudi Arabia: Law of Criminal Procedure 2001. Retrieved September 3, 2012, from http://www.wipo.int/wipolex/en/text.jsp?file_id=214810

Rusche, G., & Kirchheimer, O. (1939). *Punishment and social structure.* New York, NY: Russell and Russell.

Ryan, M., & Sim, J. (1998). Power, punishment and prisons in England and Wales, 1975–1996. In R. Weiss & N. South (Eds.), *Comparing prison systems* (pp. 175–205). Amsterdam, NY: Gordon and Breach.

Sageman, M. (2008). *Leaderless jihad: Terror networks in the twenty-first century.* Philadelphia, PA: University of Pennsylvania Press.

Saich, T. (2011). *Governance and politics in China.* New York, NY: Palgrave Macmillan.

Sartori, G. (1996). Comparing and miscomparing. In B. Brown & R. Macridis (Eds.), *Comparative politics* (8th ed.) (pp. 20–30). Belmont, CA: Wadsworth.

Sayed, T., & Bruce, D. (1998). Police corruption: Towards a working definition. *African Security Review*, 7(1), 3–14.

Schabas, W. A. (2007). *An introduction to the International Criminal Court* (3rd ed.). New York, NY: Cambridge University Press.

Schiff Berman, P. (2012). *Global legal pluralism: A jurisprudence of law beyond borders.* New York, NY: Cambridge University Press.

Schlagheck, D. (1988). *International terrorism.* Lexington, MA: Lexington Books.

Schmid, A., & Jongman, A. (2005). *Political terrorism: A new guide to actors, authors, concepts, data bases, theories, and literature.* Somerset, NJ: Transaction Books.

Schwartz, B. (Ed.). (1956). *The Code Napoleon and the common law world*. Westport, CT: Greenwood Press.

Schwitzgebel, R. K. (1969). Issues in the use of an electronic monitoring system with chronic recidivists. *Law and Society Review*, 7, 597–611.

Sentenced to Abuse. (2010 January 15). *The New York Times*, p. 26.

Setrakian, L., & Abu Khatwa, H. (2008, February 8). Drinking coffee a crime in Saudi Arabia. ABC-News. Retrieved August 15, 2012, from http://abcnews.go.com/International/story?id=4261213#.UDG4YqAn9GY

Seymour, J. D., & Anderson, R. (1998). *New ghosts, old ghosts: Prisons and labor reform camps in China*. Armonk, NY: Sharpe.

Shahidullah, S. (2012). *Comparative criminal justice systems: Global and local perspectives*. Burlington, MA: Jones and Bartlett Learning.

Shaw, M. (1999). The development and control of organized crime in post-apartheid South Africa. In S. Eisenstein & M. Amir (Eds.), *Organized crime: Uncertainties and dilemmas* (p. 114). Chicago, IL: Office of International Criminal Justice.

Shaw, V. N. (1998). Productive labor and thought reform in Chinese corrections: A historical and comparative analysis. *The Prison Journal*, *78*(2), 186–211.

Shaw, V. N. (2010). Corrections and punishment in China: Information and analysis. *Journal of Contemporary Criminal Justice*, *26*(1), 53–71.

Sheptycki, J. (2008). Transnationalisation, orientalism and crime. *Asian Journal of Criminology*, *3*(1), 13–35.

Sheptycki, J., & Goldsmith, A. (Eds.). (2007). *Crafting transnational policing: Policing capacity building and global police reform*. Portland, OR: Hart Publishing.

Sherman, L. W. (2003). Reason for emotion: Reinventing justice with theories, innovations, and research—the American Society of Criminology 2002 Presidential Address. *Criminology*, *41*(1), 1–38.

Sherman, T., & Margolin, J. (2011). *The Jersey sting: A true story of crooked pols, money-laundering rabbis, black market kidneys, and the informant who brought it all down*. New York, NY: St. Martin's Press.

Shinomiya, S. (2002). Adversarial procedure without a jury: Is Japan's system adversarial, inquisitorial, or something else? In M. Feeley & S. Miyazawa (Eds.), *The Japanese adversary system in context* (pp. 114–127). New York, NY: Palgrave MacMillan.

Sickmund, M. (2004). *Juveniles in corrections*. Washington, DC: Office of Juvenile Justice and Delinquency Prevention.

Simon, R., & Blaskovich, D. (2002). *A comparative analysis of capital punishment: Statutes, policies, frequencies, and public attitudes the world over*. New York, NY: Lexington Books.

Situ, Y., & Liu, W. (1996). An overview of the Chinese criminal justice system. In O. Ebbe (Ed.), *Comparative and international criminal justice systems: Policing, judiciary, and corrections* (2nd ed.) (pp. 66–78). Boston, MA: Butterworth-Heineman.

Skelton, A. (2002). Restorative justice as a framework for juvenile justice reform: A South African perspective. *British Journal of Criminology*, *42*(Summer), 496–513.

Skogan, W. G. (2006). *Police and the community in Chicago—A tale of three cities*. New York, NY: Oxford University Press.

Skolnick, J., & Bayley, D. (1986). *The new blue line*. New York, NY: Free Press.

Souryal, S. (1987). The religionization of a society: The continuing application of Shariah law in Saudi Arabia. *Journal for the Scientific Study of Religion*, *26*, 249–265.

Souryal, S., & Potts, D. W. (1994). The penalty of hand amputation for theft in Islamic justice. *Journal of Criminal Justice*, *22*(3), 249–265.

Spader, D. J. (1999). Teaching comparative criminal procedure: Russian dolls, color charts, and cappuccino. *Journal of Criminal Justice Education*, *10*(1). 25–37.

Special Court for Sierra Leone. (2012). Home. Retrieved September 11, 2012, from http://www.sc-sl.org/

Spierenburg, P. (1995). The body and the state: Early modern Europe. In N. Morris & D. Rothman (Eds.), *The Oxford history of the prison* (pp. 49–77). New York, NY: Oxford University Press.

Stacey, T. (2006). Electronic tagging of offenders: A global view. *International Review of Law, Computers and Technology*, *20*(1–2), 117–121.

Stack, S. (1984). Income inequality and property crime: A cross-national analysis of relative deprivation theory. *Criminology*, *22*, 119–257.

Stern, V. (1998). *A sin against the future: Imprisonment in the world*. Boston, MA: Northeastern University Press.

Stinson, J. (2006, October 27). Fear of replay of '05 riots has French on edge. *USA Today*. Retrieved from http://www.usatoday.com/news/world/2006-10-26-france-riot-anniversary_x.htm

STL. (2012). Special Tribunal for Lebanon. Retrieved September 5, 2012, from http://www.stl-tsl.org/en/

STL. (2012, February 8). Special Tribunal for Lebanon: Rules of procedure and evidence. Retrieved August 26, 2012, from http://www.stl-tsl.org/en/documents/rules-of-procedure-and-evidence/rules-of-procedure-and-evidence

The Stockholm Programme. (2010, May 4). An open and secure Europe serving and protecting citizens. *Official Journal, C 115*, 1.

Sung, H. (2004). State failure, economic failure, and predatory organized crime: A comparative analysis. *Journal of Research in Crime & Delinquency, 41*, 111–129.

Sunga, L. S. (1997). *The emerging system of international criminal law*. The Hague: Kluwer Law International.

Sussman, E. (1998). Contending with culture: An analysis of the Female Genital Mutilation Act of 1996. *Cornell International Law Journal, 31*, 194–270.

Sutherland, E., & Cressey, D. (1974). *Criminology*. New York, NY: Lippincott.

Tabucchi, H. (2010, November 19). Japan works to cut ties between Mob and business. *The New York Times*. P. A5.

Tang Ming, Z. (2004). More efforts to secure public order. Retrieved January 16, 2004, from www.1.chinadaily.com.cn/en/doc/2004-01/03/content_295428.htm

Tanner, H. (1994). Crime and punishment in China: 1979–1989. (Doctoral dissertation). Columbia University. Ann Arbor, MI: UMI Dissertation Services.

Terrill, R. (2000). Policing and human rights: International lessons from the 1990s. In G. Mesko (Ed.), *Policing in Central and Eastern Europe: Ethics, integrity, and human rights*. Ljubljana: College of Police and Security Studies.

Terrill, R. (2009). *World criminal justice systems: A survey* (7th ed.). New Providence, NJ: LexisNexis.

Thaman, S. C. (1998). Spain returns to trial by jury. *Hastings International and Comparative Law Review, 21*, 201–225.

Tonry, M. (Ed.). (1993). *Crime and justice: A review of research*, Vol. *17*. Chicago, IL: University of Chicago Press.

Tonry, M. (2001). Punishment policies and patterns in Western countries. In M. Tonry & R. S. Frase (Eds.), *Sentencing and sanctions in Western countries* (pp. 3–28). New York, NY: Oxford University Press.

Tonry, M. (2007). *Crime, Punishment, and Politics in Comparative Perspective*. In M. Tonry (Ed.), *Crime and justice: A Review of Research, vol. 36*. Chicago, IL: University of Chicago Press.

Tonry, M. (2007). Penal policy, political culture, and constitutional obsolescence. In K. Aromaa (Ed.), *Penal policy: Justice reform and social exclusion* (pp. 80–99). Helsinki: European Institute for Crime Prevention and Control.

Tonry, M., & Doob, A. (Eds.). (2004). *Youth crime and youth justice: Comparative and cross-national perspectives*. Chicago, IL: University of Chicago Press.

Tonry, M, & Frase, R. S. (Eds.). (2001). *Sentencing and sanctions in Western countries*. New York, NY: Oxford University Press.

TRAC Reports. (2011). *Official corruption convictions*. Retrieved June 27, 2012, from http://tracfed.syr.edu

Transcrime. (2002). MON-EU-TRAF: A pilot study on three European Union key immigration points for monitoring the trafficking of human beings for the purpose of sexual exploitation across the European Union. (Final Report). Trento, Italy: Author.

Transparency International. (2004). *Global corruption report*. Retrieved August 10, 2004, from http://www.globalcorruptionreport.org/download.htm

Transparency International. (2009). *Corruption perceptions index*. Retrieved from http://www.transparency.org/policy_research/surveys_indices/cpi/2009

Transparency International. (2010). *Global corruption barometer*. Berlin: Transparency International.

Trevaskes, S. (2007). *Courts and criminal justice in contemporary China*. New York, NY: Lexington Books.

Tseloni, A., Mailley, J., Farrell, G., & Tilley, N. (2010). Exploring the international decline in crime rates. *European Journal of Criminology, 7*, 375–394.

Turner, J. (2011). German Bundestag passes plea bargaining law. Retrieved August 25, 2012, from http://www.concurringopinions.com/archives/2009/07/german-bundestag-passes-plea-bargaining-law.html

Ueno, H. (1986). Maintaining police integrity: Japan. *Police Studies, 9*(18), 2–33.

Uludag, S., Colvin, M., Hussey, D., & Eng, A. L. (2009). Democracy, inequality, modernization, and internal variations in personal crime victimization. *International Criminal Law Review, 19*, 265–86.

UNAFEI. (1997). *Annual report for 1996.* Tokyo: United Nations Asian and Far East Institute for the Prevention of Crime and Treatment of Offenders.

UNAFEI. (2003). *Annual report for 2001.* Tokyo: United Nations Asia and Far East Institute for the Prevention of Crime and Treatment of Offenders.

UNDPKO. (2010). United Nations Department of Peacekeeping Operations. Retrieved March 1, 2010, from http://www.un.org/en/peacekeeping/

UNICTR. (2012). International Criminal Tribunal for Rwanda. Retrieved August 7, 2012, from http://www.unictr.org/tabid/114/default.aspx

UNICTY. (2012). International Criminal Tribunal for Yugoslavia. Retrieved September 11, 2012, from http://www.icty.org/sections/TheCases/KeyFigures

United Nations. (1996). *United Nations standards and norms in the field of crime prevention and criminal justice: Use and application of the Standard Minimal Rules for the Treatment of Prisoners.* (New York: United Nations Economic and Social Council. E/CN15/1996/19.)

United Nations. (1997). *Fifth United Nations survey of crime trends and operations of criminal justice systems.* Vienna: Crime Prevention and Criminal Justice Branch.

United Nations. (1999). *Use and application of United Nations Standards and Norms in Crime Prevention and Criminal Justice: Report of the Secretary General.* New York: United Nations Economic and Social Council. E/CN.15/1999/7.

United Nations. (2012). *UN action to counter terrorism.* Retrieved October 10, 2012, from http://www.un.org/terrorism/instruments.shtml

United Nations Center for International Crime Prevention. (2000). Assessing transnational organized crime: Results of a pilot survey of 40 selected organized criminal groups in 16 countries. *Trends in Organized Crime, 6*(Winter), 118.

United Nations Charter. (2004). UN Charter. Retrieved August 1, 2004, from http://www.un.org/aboutun/charter/index.html

United Nations Convention on the Rights of the Child. (1990). Convention on the Rights of the Child. Retrieved August 1, 2010, from http://www.unhchr.ch/html/menu2/6/crc/treaties/crc.htm

United Nations Development Programme. (2012). Human development and the shift to better citizen security. Retrieved June 27, 2012, from http://hdr.undp.org/en/reports/regional/latinamericathe caribbean/name,24269,en.html

United Nations Economic and Social Council. (1996). United Nations standards and norms in the field of crime prevention and criminal justice: Capital punishment and implementations of safeguards guaranteeing the protection of rights of those facing the death penalty. Report of the Secretary-General. United Nations (Document E/CN 15/1996/19).

United Nations Economic and Social Council. (2002). Effective community-based crime prevention. (E/CN.15/2002/4). Retrieved August 6, 2004, from http://www.unodc.org/pdf/crime/commissions/11comm/4e.pdf

United Nations Economic and Social Council. (2012, May). The United Nations principles and guidelines on access to legal aid in criminal justice systems. Retrieved September 1, 2012, from http://daccess-dds-ny.un.org/doc/UNDOC/LTD/V12/528/23/PDF/V1252823.pdf?OpenElement

United Nations Guidelines for the Prevention of Juvenile Delinquency. (1990). Guidelines for the Prevention of Juvenile Delinquency. Retrieved August 1, 2010, from http://www.unhchr.ch/html/menu3/b/h_comp47.htm

UN-International Criminal Tribunal for the former Yugoslavia (ICTY). (2012). Rules of procedure and evidence. Retrieved August 29, 2012, from http://www.icty.org/sid/136

United Nations News Centre. (2009, December 15). At UN human rights chief calls for universal abolition of the death penalty. *UN News Centre.*

United Nations Office on Drugs and Crime. (2003, November). The global programmes. The United Nations rules for the protection of juveniles deprived of their liberty (1990). Retrieved August 1, 2004, from http://www.unhchr.ch/html/menu3/b/h_comp37.htm

United Nations Office on Drugs and Crime. (2011). Organized crime and instability in Central Africa: A threat assessment. Retrieved June 27, 2012, from http://www.unodc.org/documents/data-and-analysis/Studies/Central_Africa_Report_2011_web.pdf

United Nations Office on Drugs and Crime. (2012a). About UNODC. United Nations Office on Drugs and Crime. Retrieved August 15, 2012, from http://www.unodc.org/unodc/index.html?ref=menutop

United Nations Office on Drugs and Crime. (2012b). Opiate flows through northern Afghanistan and Central Asia: A threat assessment. Retrieved June 27, 2012, from http://www.unodc.org/documents/data-and-analysis/Studies/Afghanistan_northern_route_2012_web.pdf

United Nations Peacekeeping. (2012). United Nations Peacekeeping. Retrieved August 15, 2012, from http://www.un.org/en/peacekeeping/

United Nations Standard Minimum Rules for the Administration of Juvenile Justice. (1985). Minimum Rules for the Administration of Juvenile Justice. Retrieved August 1, 2004, from http://www.unhchr.ch/html/menu3/b/h_comp48.htm

Unnever, J. (2012). Global support for the death penalty. *Punishment & Society, 12*(4), 463–484.

Upham, F. (1987). *Law and social change in postwar Japan.* Cambridge, MA: Harvard University Press.

Urbina, M., & White, W. (2009). Waiving juveniles to criminal court: Court officials express their thoughts. *Social Justice, 36*, 122–139.

U.S. Bureau of Justice Statistics. (2010). National Criminal Victimization Survey (NCVS). Retrieved May 7, 2012, from http://bjs.ojp.usdoj.gov/index.cfm?ty=dcdetail&iid=245#Publications_and_products

U.S. Bureau of Justice Statistics. (2012). Corrections. Office of Justice Programs. U.S. Department of Justice. Retrieved September 25, 2012, from http://bjs.ojp.usdoj.gov/index.cfm?ty=tp&tid=1

U.S. Department of Justice. (2003). Criminal Division. Public Integrity Section. Report to Congress on the activities and operations of the Public Integrity Section for 2002. Retrieved from http://www.usdoj.gov/criminal/pin/AR_Final_2002.pdf

U.S. Department of Justice. (2009). Office of Public Affairs. Mexican citizen sentenced to 121 months in prison: Forced young Mexican women into sexual slavery in New York. Washington, DC: Civil Rights Division.

U.S. Department of Justice. (2011a, March 23). Chinese counterfeit perfume importers indicted for allegedly trafficking in counterfeit goods. *U.S. Department of Justice Office of Public Affairs.*

U.S. Department of Justice. (2011b, March 24). Sex trafficking ring leader sentenced to 40 years in prison. *U.S. Department of Justice Office of Public Affairs.*

U.S. Department of Justice. (2011c, April 11). Foreign national pleads guilty for role in international money laundering scheme. *U.S. Department of Justice Office of Public Affairs.*

U.S. Department of Justice. (2012, April 11). North Hollywood, California man sentenced in Los Angeles to 20 years in prison for participating in international child pornography ring. *U.S. Department of Justice Office of Public Affairs.*

U.S. Department of State. (2008a). Country reports on terrorism: Saudi Arabia. Retrieved April 30, 2008, from www.state.gov/s/ct/rls/crt/2007/104112.htm

U.S. Department of State. (2008b). Trafficking in persons report, county reports: Saudi Arabia. Retrieved June 5, 2008, from www.state.gov/g/tip/rls/tiprpt/2006/65990.htm

U.S. Department of State. (2010a). Tracking in persons report. Retrieved July 10, 2012, from http://www.state.gov/j/tip/rls/tiprpt/2010/index.htm

U.S. Department of State. (2010b, January 19). Foreign terrorist organizations. Retrieved May 30, 2010, from http://www.state.gov/s/ct/rls/other/des/123085.htm

U.S. Department of State. (2010c, May). International Criminal Court. Retrieved September 11, 2012, from http://www.state.gov/j/gcj/icc/index.htm

U.S. Department of State. (2011). Country reports on terrorism, 2010. Retrieved July 20, 2012, from http://www.state.gov/documents/organization/170479.pdf

U.S. Department of State. (2012a). Trafficking in persons report 2012. Retrieved June 24, 2012, from http://www.state.gov/documents/organization/192587.pdf

U.S. Department of State. (2012b, July 31). National Counterterrorism Center: Annex of Statistical

Information: Country reports on terrorism 2011. Retrieved October 7, 2012, from http://www.state.gov/j/ct/rls/crt/2011/195555.htm#

U.S. Department of State. (2012c, September 28). Foreign Terrorist Organizations. Retrieved October 7, 2012, from http://www.state.gov/j/ct/rls/other/des/123085.htm

U.S. Government. (2000). *International crime threat assessment.* Washington, DC: Author.

U.S. Secretary of State. (2012). Trafficking in persons report 2012. Retrieved July 20, 2012, from http://www.state.gov/j/tip/rls/tiprpt/2012/index.htm

U.S. State Department. (1997). Patterns of global terrorism: Overview of state-sponsored terrorism. Retrieved from http://www.state.gov.www/global/terrorism/1996report

U.S. Surgeon General. (2001). *Youth violence: A report of the Surgeon General.* Washington, DC: Department of Health and Human Services.

Van Caenegem, R. (1973). *The birth of the English common law.* Cambridge, MA: Cambridge University Press.

Van Dijk, J. (2007). Mafia markers: Assessing organized crime and its impact upon societies. *Trends in Organized Crime, 10,* 39–56.

Van Dijk, J. (2008). *The world of crime.* Los Angeles, CA: Sage Publications.

Van Dijk, J., van Kesteren, J., & Smit, P. (2007). *Criminal victimization in international perspective.* The Hague: Bibliotheek WODC.

Van Ewijk, A. (2012). Diversity within police forces in Europe: A case for the comprehensive view. *Policing, 6*(1), 76–92.

van Kalmthout, K., & Durnescu, I. (2008). Probation in Europe. Utrecht: Wolf Legal Publishers.

Van Kessel, G. (2002). European trends towards styles in criminal procedure and evidence. In M. Feeley & S. Miyazawa (Eds.), *The Japanese adversary system in context* (pp. 225–246). New York, NY: Palgrave MacMillan.

Van Kesteren, J. N., Mayhew, P., & Nieuwbeerta, P. (2000). Criminal victimisation in seventeen industrialised countries: Key findings from the 2000 International Crime Victims Survey. The Hague: Ministry of Justice, WODC.

Van Ness, D., & Strong, K. H. (2010). *Restoring justice: An introduction to restorative justice* (4th ed.). Cincinnati, OH: Lexis Nexis.

Van Steden, R., & Sarre, R. (2007). The growth of privatized policing: Some cross-national data and comparisons. *International Journal of Comparative and Applied Criminal Justice, 31*(1), 51–71.

Varese, F. (2001). *The Russian Mafia: Private protection in a new market economy.* New York, NY: Oxford University Press.

Varese, F. (2012). How mafias take advantage of globalization. *British Journal of Criminology, 52*(March), 235–253.

Verkaik, R. (2009, May 12). Children in jail: Lottery of justice is revealed. *The Independent* (London), p. 2.

Ville, R., Zvekic, U., & Klaus, J. F. (Eds.). (1997). *Promoting probation internationally.* Proceedings of the International Training Workshop on Probation, July, Valletta, Malta. Rome/London: United Nations Interregional Crime and Justice Research Institute.

Vincent, D. (2011, May 25). China used prisoners in lucrative internet gaming work. *The Guardian* (London). Retrieved June 1, 2012, from http://www.guardian.co.uk/world/2011/may/25/china-prisoners-internet-gaming-scam

Vogler, R. (1996). Criminal procedure in France. In J. Hatcher, B. Huber, & R. Volger (Eds.), *Comparative Crminal Procedure* (pp. 14–95). London: British Institute of International and Comparative Law.

Vogler, R. (2005). *A world view of criminal justice.* Aldershot, England: Ashgate Publishing.

Walker, A. J. (2004). When a good idea is poorly implemented: How the International Criminal Court fails to be insulated from international politics and to protect due process duarantees. *West Virginia Law Review, 106*(2), 245–304.

Walker, S., Spohn, C., & DeLone, M. (2011). *The color of justice: Race, ethnicity, and crime in America* (4th ed.). Belmont, CA: Wadsworth.

Wall Street Journal. (2000, February 26). EU police push for cross-board e-eavesdropping. *The Wall Street Journal,* p. 8.

Wallace, N., & Jacobsen, G. (2012, April 28). Children as young as 10 have been linked to violent bashings, home invasions, car theft and break-ins. *Sydney Morning Herald* (Australia) p. 1.

Walmsley, R. (2008). World prison population list (8th ed.). Retrieved April 1, 2010, from http://www.kcl.ac.uk/depsta/law/research/icps/downloads/wppl-8th_41.pdf

Walmsley, R. (2011). World female imprisonment list. Retrieved September 22, 2012, from http://www.prisonstudies.org/images/news_events/wfil2nd edition.pdf

Walmsley, R. (2011). World prison population list (9th ed.). Retrieved September 22, 2012, from http://www.prisonstudies.org/images/news_events/wppl9.pdf

Wang, Z. (1996). The police system in the People's Republic of China. In O. Ebbe (Ed.), *Comparative and international criminal justice systems: Policing, judiciary, and corrections* (2nd ed.) (pp. 81–95). Boston, MA: Butterworth-Heineman.

Wang, Z. (2010). Prison enterprise financial management innovation in the context of China's prison system reform. *International Business Research, 3*(2), 100–105.

Wayne, V., & Xiong, P. (2011). The relationship between mediation and judicial proceedings in China. *Asian Journal of Comparative Law, 6*(1). Retrieved August 28, 2012, from http://works.bepress.com/vicki_waye/3

Weber, M. (1985). *Rechtssoziologie.* Neuwied: Hermann Luchterhand Verlag.

Wedeman, A. (2009). Enemies of the state: Mass incidents and subversion in China. APSA 2009 Toronto meeting paper. Retrieved from http://ssru.co/com/abstrct=1451828

Weiss, R. P., & South, N. (Eds.). (1998). *Comparing prison systems: Toward a comparative and international penology.* Amsterdam, NY: Gordon and Breach.

Weitekamp, E. G. M. (2003). Sanctions. In K. Aromaa, S. Leppa, S. Nevala, & N. Ollus (Eds.), *Crime and criminal justice systems in Europe and North America* (pp. 150–175). Helsinki: European Institute of Crime Prevention and Control.

Westlake, A. (2012, July 25). Japanese police aim to increase ratio of female officers to 10%. Retrieved August 15, 2012, from http://japandailypress.com/japanese-police-aim-to-increase-ratio-of-female-officers-to-10-257328

Westney, E. (1987). *Imitation and innovation.* Cambridge, MA: Harvard University Press.

Weston, T., & Jensen, L. (Eds.) (2012). *China: In and beyond the headlines.* New York, NY: Rowan & Littlefield.

White, J. (2005). Terrorism in transition. In P. Reichel (Ed.), *Handbook of transnational crime and justice* (pp. 65–78). Thousand Oaks, CA: Sage Publications.

White, J. (2009). *Terrorism and homeland security.* Belmont, CA: Wadsworth.

Wilber, D. Q. (2004, August 16). D.C. cracks down as stolen-goods dealers evolve. *The Washington Post,* p. A1.

Williams, F., & McShane, M. (2009). *Criminological theory* (5th ed.). Upper Saddle River, NJ: Prentice Hall.

Wilmore, J. H. (1936). *A panorama of the world's legal systems.* Washington, DC: Washington Law Book.

Wilson, J. Q., & Kelling, G. L. (1982, March). Broken windows. *The Atlantic Monthly,* pp. 29–38.

Wilson, J.Q., & Petersilia, J. (Eds.). (1995). *Crime.* San Francisco, CA: ICS Press.

Wilson, M. J. (2012, May 20). Prime time for Japan to take another step forward in lay participation: Exploring expansion to civil trials. Retrieved September 6, 2012, from http://papers.ssrn.com/sol3/papers.cfm?abstract_id=2063269

Winer, J. M. (1997). International crime in the new geopolitics: A core threat to democracy. In W. McDonald (Ed.), *Crime and law enforcement in the global village* (pp. 41–64). Cincinnati, OH: Anderson Publishing.

Wines, M. (2009, August 27). China approves law governing armed police force. *The New York Times.* Retrieved August 17, 2012, from http://www.nytimes.com/2009/08/28/world/asia/28china.html

Winfree, L. T., Jr. (2004). New Zealand police and restorative justice philosophy. *Crime & Delinquency, 50*(April), 189–213.

Winslow, R. W., & Zhang, S. X. (2008). *Criminology: A global perspective.* Upper Saddle River, NJ: Prentice Hall.

Winter, M. (2012, June 25). FBI: 79 teen prostitutes rescued, 104 alleged pimps arrested. *USA Today,* p. 1.

Winterdyk, J. (2002). *Juvenile justice systems: International perspectives.* Toronto, ON: Canadian Scholar's Press.

Wisler, D., & Onwudiwe, I. D. (2009). *Community policing: International patterns and comparative perspectives.* New York, NY: CRC Press.

Wolfgang, M. (1967). International criminal statistics: A proposal. *Journal of Criminal Law, Criminology, and Police Science, 58,* 65–69.

Wong, D. S. W. (2001). Changes in juvenile justice in China. *Youth & Society, 32,* 492–509.

Wong, D. S. W. (2004). Juvenile protection and delinquency prevention policies in China. *The Australian and New Zealand Journal of Criminology, 37*, 52–66.

Wong, K. C. (2002). Policing the People's Republic of China: The road to reform in the 1990s. *British Journal of Criminology, 42*, 281–316.

Wong, K. C. (2009). *Chinese policing: History and reform*. New York, NY: Peter Lang.

Wong, K. C. (2010). A Chinese theory of community policing. In D. Wisler & I. Owundiwe (Eds.), *Community policing: International patterns and comparative perspectives* (pp. 215–256). New York, NY: CRC Press.

Wong, K. C. (2012). *Police reform in China: A Chinese perspective*. London: Taylor and Francis.

World Health Organization. (2011). The Madrid Recommendation: Health protection in prisons as an essential part of public health. Retrieved October 1, 2012, from http://www.penalreform.org/files/Madrid%20Rec.pdf

Wright, G. (1983). *Between the guillotine and liberty*. New York, NY: Oxford University Press.

Wu, H. (1992). *Laogai—The Chinese gulag*. Boulder, CO: Westview.

Wu, H. (1995, June). A grim organ harvest in China's prisons. *World Press Review*, 22–23.

Wyvekens, A. (2008). The French juvenile justice system. In H. Junger-Tas & S. Decker (Eds.), *International handbook of juvenile justice* (pp. 173–186). New York, NY: Springer.

Yang, J. (2008). China: From prison to freedom. *Journal of Democracy, 19*(2), 88–93.

Yinan, Z. (2012, August 16). Lawyers calling for reform of laojiao system. *China Daily*. Retrieved October 12, 2012, from http://www.chinadaily.com.cn/china/2012-08/16/content_15679394.htm

Yisheng, D., & Yijun, P. (2006). An introduction to the juvenile justice system in China. In P. Friday & X. Ren (Eds.), *Delinquency and juvenile justice systems in the non-Western world* (pp. 191–210). Monsey, NY: Criminal Justice Press.

Yokoyama, M. (2002). Juvenile justice and juvenile crime: An overview of Japan. In J. Winterdyk (Ed.), *Juvenile justice systems: International perspectives* (pp. 321–352). Toronto, ON: Canadian Scholar's Press.

Yost, P. (2012, April 27). ATF: 68,000 guns in Mexico traced to U.S. *The Washington Post*, p. 3

Young, W., & Brown, M. (1993). Cross-national comparisons of imprisonment. In M. Tonry (Ed.), *Crime and justice: A review of research, vol. 17* (pp. 1–49). Chicago, IL: University of Chicago Press.

Zalman, A. (2010). Economic impact of terrorism and the September 11 attacks: Direct economic impact was less than feared, but defense spending rose by 1/3. Retrieved May 15, 2010, from http://terrorism.about.com/od/issuestrends/a/EconomicImpact.htm

Zarchin, T. (2009, November 20). International legal precedent: No private prisons in Israel. *Haaretz*. Retrieved April 25, 2010, from http://www.haaretz.com/print-edition/news/international-legal-precedent-no-private-prisons-in-israel-1.3774

Zauberman, R., & Levy, R. (2003). Police, minorities, and the French republican ideal. *Criminology, 41*(4), 1065–1101.

Zhang, L., & Liu, J. (2007). China's Juvenile Delinquency Prevention Law: The law and philosophy. *International Journal of Offender Therapy & Comparative Criminology, 51*, 541–554.

Zhang, L., Messner, S., & Lu, J. (2007). Criminological research in contemporary China. *Journal of Offender Treatment and Comparative Criminology, 51*(1), 110–122.

Zhang, L., Zhou, D., Messner, S., Liska, A., Krohn, M., Liu, M. J., et al. (1996). Crime prevention in a communitarian society: Bang-jiao and tiao-jie in the People's Republic of China. *Justice Quarterly, 13*(2), 199–222.

Zhang, M. (2002). International civil litigation in China: A practical analysis of the Chinese judicial system. *Boston College International & Comparative Law Review, 59*, 92–105.

Zhang, S. X. (2008). *Chinese human smuggling organizations: Families, social networks, and cultural imperatives*. Palo Alto, CA: Stanford University Press.

Zhang, S. X., & Chin, K. (2002). Entering the dragon: Inside Chinese human smuggling organizations. *Criminology, 40*(November), 737–767.

Zhao, G. (2001). The recent development of juvenile justice in China. In Z. Liu & S. S. Messner. (Eds.), *Crime and social control in a changing China* (pp. 177–188). Westport, CT: Greenwood Press.

Zhi, R. (2011, May 22). Big jump in juvenile crime. *New Straits Times* (Malaysia), p. 5.

Zhiqun, Z. (2010). *Global studies in China* (13th ed.). New York, NY: McGraw Hill.

Zhong, L. (2009). Community policing in China: A new era of Mass Line policing. In Grabosky, P. (Ed.), *Community policing and peacekeeping* (pp.169–186). Boca Raton, FL: CRC Press.

Zhong, L., & Grabosky, P. (2009). The pluralization of policing and the rise of private policing in China. *Crime, Law and Social Change, 52*(5), 433–455.

Zimmerman, J., & Schwindt, F. (2003). The German Polizei. *Law and Order, 51*(3), 36.

Zimring, F. E. (2006). The necessity and value of transnational comparative study: Some preaching from a recent convert. *Criminology & Public Policy, 5*, 615–22.

Zimring, F. E., & Hawkins, G. (1986). *Capital punishment and the American agenda*. New York, NY: Cambridge University Press.

Zvekic, U. (Ed.). (1994). *Alternatives to imprisonment in comparative perspective*. Chicago, IL: Nelson-Hall.

Zvekic, U., & Alvazzi del Frate, A. (1995). *Criminal victimization in the developing world*. Rome: United Nations Interregional Crime and Justice Research Institute.

Index

Note: page numbers with *f* indicate figures; page numbers with *t* indicate tables

G

M

N

O

P

Q

R

S

U

V